MOSBY'S MANUAL OF
EMERGENCY CARE
PRACTICES AND PROCEDURES

MOSBY'S MANUAL OF
EMERGENCY CARE
PRACTICES AND PROCEDURES

SUSAN A. BUDASSI, RN, MSN, MICN, CEN

Clinical Specialist,
Emergency and Ambulatory Services,
St. Joseph Hospital and Health Care Center,
Tacoma, Washington
Clinical Associate Professor,
Graduate Division, School of Nursing,
University of Washington,
Seattle, Washington

JANET M. BARBER, RN, MS, CEN

United States Air Force, N.C.,
USAF School of Health Care Sciences (ATC),
Sheppard Air Force Base, Texas

Second edition

with 415 illustrations

The C. V. Mosby Company

ST. LOUIS • TORONTO • PRINCETON   1984

MOSBY

A TRADITION OF PUBLISHING EXCELLENCE

Editor: Barbara Ellen Norwitz
Assistant editor: Bess Arends
Manuscript editor: Timothy O'Brien
Design: Staff
Production: Carol O'Leary, Teresa Breckwoldt, Margaret B. Bridenbaugh

Second edition

Printed in the United States of America

The C.V. Mosby Company
11830 Westline Industrial Drive, St. Louis, Missouri 63146

Library of Congress Cataloging in Publication Data

Budassi, Susan A., 1948-
  Mosby's manual of emergency care.

  Rev. ed. of: Mosby's manual of emergency care /
Janet M. Barber. 1979.
  Bibliography: p.
  Includes index.
  1. Medical emergencies. 2. Emergency nursing.
I. Barber, Janet Miller. II. Barber, Janet Miller.
Mosby's manual of emergency care. III. Title.
IV. Title: Manual of emergency care. [DNLM: 1. Emer-
gency medical services—Handbooks. WX 215 B234m]
RC86.7.B83   1984   616'.025   83-9354
ISBN 0-8016-0453-2

AC/VH/VH 9 8 7 6 5 4 3   01/A/066

To Sheehy, the brave soul who had the courage
to propose to me and who gave me
the love and understanding it took for me to accept.

Ditto,
Budassi

Preface

Mosby's Manual of Emergency Care: Practices and Procedures is a quick reference for emergency care practitioners, physicians, nurses, emergency medical technicians, and paramedics. The step-by-step approach of presenting material assures that basic concepts are understood. Safe and effective delivery of emergency care in prehospital, emergency department, and intrafacility settings is stressed.

The book is divided into five units. Unit 1, "Basic Principles of Emergency Care," includes the essential skills for communication, data collection, reporting, and recording. Basic and advanced life support, intravenous therapy, and shock are also included.

Unit 2, "Medical Emergencies," includes the most current diagnostic and treatment regimens. The following types of emergencies are covered: cardiac, pulmonary, neurologic, sickle cell crisis, hemophilic, metabolic, toxicologic, environmental, genitourinary, and infectious.

Unit 3, "Trauma Emergencies," represents a change from the previous edition in that it has been separated out from the medical emergencies unit. Included is wound management, care of patients who have sustained trauma to the head, spinal cord, face, eye, ear, nose, throat, chest, abdomen, and limbs. In addition, dental trauma, multiple trauma, and burns have been included.

Unit 4 deals with obstetric, gynecologic, and pediatric emergencies, while Unit 5 deals with psychiatric emergencies.

Unique to this edition is the addition of a quick-reference trauma notebook. New artwork enhances the appearance of the book. Extensive updating of bibliographies assures a comprehensive knowledge base.

Mosby's Manual of Emergency Care: Practices and Procedures presents practical considerations, clinical guidelines, and procedures needed to assure performance excellence for today's emergency care practitioner.

Susan A. Budassi

Acknowledgments

Writing a book such as this is never a solitary effort. My life, both professionally and personally, has been blessed with people who have taught me so much, given me so much, and become so much a part of my life—people like Chuck McElroy, my first mentor in emergency care (why not start with the best?), who taught me emergency medicine theory and so much about kindness and human concern; Jim Fulcher, who taught me that management and clinical skills can be practiced simultaneously without sacrificing excellence; Ron Stewart, that kind, gentle soul, who taught me what it means to be truly dedicated to a cause; John Bibb, who taught me that a sense of humor is essential for survival in emergency care; Barbara Weldon, who taught me that the most important element in the emergency care system is the people; Mark Jergens, who taught me (or maybe we taught each other) the fine art of clinical debate and about dedication; Maybelyn Mabitad Romano, who taught me what clinical excellence in nursing is all about; Paul Auerbach, who taught me about the cure for political migraine headaches; Frank Pratt and Dave Schatz, MDs, and Tom Wohlstadter (soon to be DO), who have made me so proud to have been one of their teachers; the emergency department staffs at Brotman Medical Center (a sentimental favorite), Vail Valley Medical Center, San Francisco General Hospital, and Deaconess Hospital for making my job so easy and so enjoyable because of their enthusiasm to learn and to try new things; and the EMTs and paramedics of Los Angeles County (L.A. City F.D., Beverly Hills F.D., Los Angeles County F.D., and Culver City F.D.), San Francisco, Vail, Spokane, and Tacoma, who give so much more than they realize.

A very sincere and warm thank you to the emergency and administrative staffs at St. Joseph Hospital and Health Care Center for giving me the opportunity to practice and share my own brand of emergency nursing and for allowing me the professional freedom required to grow; to the emergency department staff for welcoming me as a member of their team, for their constant desire for new knowledge, for their enthusiasm and excellent level of patient care, even on the worst of full-moon-Friday nights, and for their willingness to try some of my far-fetched new ideas and my constant room-rearranging; to Ann Chilton, my role model, for having the determination to create a position for me, for allowing me the space to be creative, and for being my colleague and friend.

A very special thank you to Steve Schultz, artist and paramedic extraordinare, for the many beautiful illustrations found throughout this book and for his zany antics at times when they were needed the most.

To the Emergency Department Nurses Association (EDNA) goes a huge thank you for the so many opportunities they have given me to grow professionally through the *Journal of Emergency Nursing,* the *EDNA Standards of Emergency Nursing Practice,* the Scientific Assembly, etc., etc. A very special note of thanks to Torry Sansone and Gail Nichol for their constant support and encouragement.

Writing a book such as this is not only a professional effort, but a personal effort. And personal effort takes the love and support of many friends and family members. There have been many friends in my life. Among the most important people in my life are my Mom, Dad, and brother, Steve, who is also involved in emergency care as the Chief Paramedic of the City and County of San Francisco, and my best friend, Susan August— their love and encouragement has given me so much energy. I would also like to thank my friends, who have been with me through the sad times and the happy times—Kate Hendricks, Mr. and Mrs. O, Al Downing, Tom Tootell, Karen Hoxeng, Gail Pisarcik Lenehan, Peggy Patton, Jesse Mares, Kim and Sue Barbee, Kriss and Ralph Cruikshank, TK, Bess Arends and my "new family," the Sheehys, Mickey, Tom, Robbie, and Marty, the Whites, the Cinq Mars and the Nelsons.

This may seem a bit bizarre, but I have very fond memories and a wealth of gratitude to a very special friend, Cloud, my dog who died this year. He was with me for 6 years, keeping my feet warm during the late night and early morning hours while I wrote this manuscript (and all the others, too). He sat patiently and waited for dinner when I had "one more line to type," and listened eagerly when I read the manuscript pages to him.

And, last but especially not least, an extra special thank you to someone who is making life a lot easier for me and others by offering me a last name that's a lot easier to spell and pronounce, "Sheehy" (Steve Sheehy), my fiancé.

Susan A. Budassi

Contents

BASIC PRINCIPLES OF EMERGENCY CARE

CHAPTER 1 Communicating with patients

An unexpected and unplanned entry into the prehospital care system and a visit to the emergency department are anxiety-producing experiences for almost anyone. The environment and the faces are unfamiliar, and there may be pain or other uncontrollable signs or symptoms. The equipment is foreign, the room is noisy, the words used are from a "foreign language," and the patient may have no idea of the outcome. There may be other patients who are ill or injured or have just died. There is invasion of privacy with very personal questions asked by strangers—people the patient has not met before and to whom he has entrusted his care. His family or friends may not be present or may be restricted to the waiting area. The patient is an alien in this foreign land. He may feel helpless. Truly, a visit to the emergency department may be stress producing to say the least.

Every person involved in the delivery of emergency care should be aware of the psychologic factors surrounding a patient's entry into the emergency care system. The relationship between the emergency care provider and the patient, his family, and friends can make a difference in the patient's level of anxiety and in the overall outcome of the emergency care given. Understanding these factors is the key to the delivery of quality emergency care. The key word is *communication*. By definition, communication is the process of sending and receiving a message, which can be verbal or nonverbal. Communication is the process by which the patient–emergency care provider relationship occurs. The level of competence of health care delivery is based on the level of interpersonal skills possessed and demonstrated by the emergency care provider. The better the interpersonal relationship, the better the therapeutic relationship.

Here are some basic assumptions about therapeutic communication:

All communication is learned.

Communication of some sort is inevitable in any relationship.

There are formal and informal channels of communication in any relationship.

Any behavior is a form of communication about the relationship.

It is impossible *not* to communicate.

The message sent is not necessarily the message received.

Each of us has a unique perception of the world. This uniqueness is reflected in our behavior, language, and actions. Language is a personal attribute that reflects a person's values, beliefs, and life-style. Being aware of this fact may offer a reference point for establishing meaningful contact with the patient and providing beneficial interventions. In emergency care it is important to talk with a patient at his level, so that he can understand what is being said. Effective communication means that the patient must feel that he is also being heard. Time should be taken to listen. Although all people talk and listen a good deal, communication skills are not easy to acquire. Good therapeutic communication takes training, practice, and skill.

SPECIAL ASPECTS OF THERAPEUTIC COMMUNICATION
Empathy vs. sympathy

Empathy is an objective skill that allows the emergency care provider to experience an individual in such a way as to be with that person during his feelings but not to be joined with him. The emergency care provider can show respect and concern for what the patient is experiencing while maintaining a separateness that allows the relationship to be therapeutic. Sympathy is subjective—it is an actual sharing of emotion with the other person. It is important to remain empathetic rather than sympathetic in the emergency care setting so that a level of energy can be maintained. Sympathy can sap the care givers' energy, and energy is necessary to be effective when helping the patient cope with the problem or crisis at hand.

Recognizing feelings

Patients need to know that their feelings are noted and recognized as legitimate by emergency care personnel. Care givers should never belittle or criticize feelings expressed by a patient and his family or friends, as this would inhibit effective therapeutic communication. Care givers can use verbal techniques to convey the attitude that they are willing to help the patient recognize his feelings and try to understand why these feelings are happening. Recognizing emotions can sometimes decrease the patient's fear of the experience to a point at which the level of anxiety becomes manageable. A statement as simple as, "It's all right to be anxious about all that you have been through today" can do much to relieve anxiety. If the care giver can accept the patient's feelings as legitimate and work with him, the care giver will communicate an attitude of acceptance that promotes health and encourages problem solving.

Care givers should be careful not to try to read into the patient's feelings—most of the time feelings cannot be read. The patient's behavior can be observed and inferences can be made about why the behavior is taking place. For example, seeing a patient crying can lead to the interpretation that the patient is upset about something. But it is possible, for example, that the patient is crying because he is relieved to find out that he did not actually have a myocardial infarction. Feelings are sometimes expressed as behaviors. The care giver should attempt to have the patient focus on communicating his feelings verbally. This is preferable to trying to interpret his behavior.

It is important for those working in emergency care to focus on their own feelings and how they affect therapeutic communication with the patient. Emergency care givers should strive toward a climate of mutual trust and respect. This requires patience, knowledge, skill, and caring. Acceptance of a patient is recognition of him without value judgment. It is the commitment to see the person as a unique human being with very individual needs.

Need for therapeutic communication

Therapeutic communication is established before the initial contact with the patient. The first encounter a person has with emergency care personnel will guide his attitude toward the entire emergency care experience. If invasive procedures must be performed immediately because of the urgency of the patient's condition, verbal contact should be used briefly to explain the procedures, gain the patient's confidence, and establish rapport. No therapeutic intervention should ever be performed without at least a brief explanation to the patient. He should know why the intervention is being made and should be made aware of any pain or discomfort the intervention will cause. Even if the patient is nonresponsive, a brief explanation of the therapeutic intervention is necessary.

TECHNIQUES IN COMMUNICATION
Supportive

The supportive technique helps the patient maintain or regain self-control in the face of anxiety. Ways of being supportive include:

Recognizing that the patient is an individual with special needs

Verbalizing support

Being available to listen when the patient needs to talk

Listening carefully (taking the time to listen)

Accepting the patient's feelings as legitimate

Staying with the patient when he has a fear of loneliness or isolation

Commenting about efforts to understand what it must be like for the patient even though the care giver cannot really know

Observing and carefully commenting on behaviors or mannerisms that are clues to the patient's feelings

Touching the patient—his hand, his arm, his shoulder—if it is comfortable for both patient and care giver

Initiating actions that visibly reflect a humanistic attitude; showing compassion and respect

Keeping close watch of personal attitudes

Silence

Use of silence can also be a therapeutic intervention. Silence is an expressive, nonverbal response:

It is not absence of activity.

It is a natural conclusion of verbally transmitted thoughts.

It allows time to think.

It can help in finding solutions to problems and answers to questions.

It is a way of conveying feelings.

It promotes acceptance.

It may indicate anxiety in both the talker and the listener.

It can be used for pacing, timing, closeness, alienation, resistance, reflection, or relaxation.

Listening

Listening is a way of seeing the concerns of the patient. It may relieve some of the patient's anxieties and facilitate the collection of information. The patient should be allowed to take the conversational lead whenever possible. Listening is an active, physically visible process even when there is limited verbal activity on the part of the listener. A listening attitude is a learned skill. The patient's verbalizations should be responded to with a sense of listening. Some comments that would encourage the patient to verbalize his thoughts and feelings are, "Go on," "I see," "Uh-huh," "Tell me more," "Tell me how that happened," "What made you come to the hospital today?" and "This must be really important to you."

Questions

The basic question-answer pattern does little to develop a positive relationship. Questions are necessary to gather specific information but can limit therapeutic communication.

DON'TS IN QUESTIONING

Don't ask too many questions.

Don't ask "why" questions. They cause feelings of blame.

Don't use "you" or "who" to begin questions.

Don't ask double questions.

Don't ask long, elaborate questions.

Don't ask closed or direct questions except in seeking specific information.

Types of questions

After asking a question, the care giver must listen to the answer. There are several types of questions:

Leading questions: "Don't you know better than to not take your medications?"

This contains a suggested answer.

It restricts the respondent.

It implies the asker's judgment.

It elicits nonverbal clues.

No-choice questions: "You're ready for me to start this IV, aren't you?"

This implies a command.

It shows authority and may be interpreted as "one-upsmanship."

Closed questions: "Where is your pain?"

This elicits a specific response.

It asks for agreement or disagreement.

It can be responded to nonverbally, requiring little self-disclosure.

It can circumscribe the focus.

Limited-choice questions: "Do you want the injection in your hip or your arm?"

This gives the responder two choices.

It implies the responder's compliance in the situation.

Double questions: ''Was there any beer at the party? Are you saying that you don't drink beer?''

This consists of two questions asked in sequence, without pause.

It confuses both parties.

It requires the respondent to choose which question to answer.

It allows the respondent to avoid the subject.

Open-ended questions: ''What happened just before the accident?''

This conveys feelings and perceptions as well as thoughts.

It encourages elaboration, description, and comparison.

It allows freedom of response.

It assesses the reliability of the informant.

It begins with ''what,'' ''how,'' or ''tell me more.''

Indirect questions: ''Tell me about your home situation.''

This does not seem like a question.

It shows interest.

It has no question mark at the end.

It allows the other person to carry the conversational lead.

Communicating with children

When communicating with any child, especially a sick or injured child, a consistent, organized approach should be used. A child should not be treated as a miniature adult. A child is an individual person with very special needs and rights. It is important to remember that how a child and his illness are handled may have an effect on his growth and development. Being familiar with the stages of child growth and development will help in understanding a child's response to stress and may help him to cope with his situation in the emergency department.

In communicating with a child it is important to communicate also with' the family or friends who accompany him. Parents or friends may have feelings of guilt when a child becomes ill or is injured. Sometimes a child's situation will produce acute anxiety in his parents. It is important to work with the parents in a therapeutic fashion, as they may demonstrate their emotions much more than the child demonstrates his.

A child will react with anxiety and fears of separation, pain, or the unknown. Encourage a child to speak openly and to express his feelings appropriately. When speaking with the child, speak in open, direct language. Remember to use his first name frequently and not to ask too many questions. If the child asks a question, answer him honestly. Speak directly and state instructions as simple commands. Do not force a child to choose, as doing so may offer him an unacceptable alternative. Making choices also increases the child's anxiety. Use touching to aid in communication and convey the ideas of friendliness and caring.

Whenever possible, allow at least one of the parents to stay with the child. A child's way of coping may be to cry, sob, or scream, which is all right. Always remain calm and mildly authoritative in a way that demonstrates self-control.

Communicating with victims of trauma

When a major trauma occurs, the patient will usually present in some sort of crisis state. Sometimes this is true even in minor traumas. This state should be recognized, and appropriate crisis intervention should be provided as soon as possible. Patients who experience trauma may have high levels of anxiety. They may be afraid of disfigurement or death, and there may be a threat to their body image. Some of these patients may become angry and blame themselves or someone else for the accident. They may be angry that they were hurt while others were not. A type of depression in which the patient feels totally helpless and at the mercy of his rescuers may set in rapidly. The language of emergency medicine is foreign to most patients—the sounds of the monitors and the feel of the equipment are new. The feeling of helplessness may be overwhelming to the patient. Keep him informed of what is being done and the reasons why. Remember to talk with him frequently. The patient may have a tremendous feeling of guilt if he survives an accident in which others died. If he feels that he caused the accident he may be experiencing feelings of guilt over that as well.

It is important to explain why every therapeutic intervention is being made. Allow the patient to make choices—to be involved in his own care—whenever possible. Even offering small choices such as, ''I have to start an IV in your arm. Would you like it in the right arm or the left arm?'' helps to provide the patient with some level of autonomy, albeit a low one. Let him know that it is all right to feel frightened, anxious, angry, guilty, or whatever. Try to have the patient verbalize his feelings and help him to accept them. Help him to cope with his feelings of guilt or frustration. Do not try to second-guess the patient. If what he is trying to say is not clear, tell him so.

Never give a patient false reassurance or false hope. Be as open and honest as possible. Sometimes this candidness must come in small doses. Help the patient to realize that he will need help past the time of emergency department interventions. Help him to plan, even if it is only for a short time in the future.

Posttraumatic stress disorders

There are three very common types of posttraumatic stress disorders (''the development of characteristic symptoms following a psychologically traumatic event that is generally outside the range of usual human experience''[1]) following a major trauma. In the first the patient will relive the trauma through remembering the event and its details. He may have nightmares about the traumatic event or feel that it will happen again.

In the second, the patient becomes less involved with or oblivious to activities around him. He loses interest in things that were previously important to him or has little emotional response or feelings for those around him.

In the third there is the development of symptoms such as inability to sleep well, diminished concentration and memory, guilt about others who were injured or died in the same traumatic event, an overexaggerated startle response, avoidance of activities that may arouse memories of the trauma, and other symptoms that worsen when exposed to events representing or symbolizing the traumatic event.

This is why it is important to assure that both the patient and his family have long-term follow-up after the time of the emergency department and hospital stay.

Communicating with the survivors when a sudden death occurs

When a patient dies in the emergency care setting, staff involvement should go beyond the patient and reach to the family and friends. Staff personnel must become resource persons for the survivors. They will need empathy, support, and direction. The most common reaction to a sudden death is shock and disbelief. The next reactions are usually feelings of guilt, anger, and sorrow as the reality of the death of their loved one begins to set in. Finally, the survivors begin to work through their feelings of loss and return to their normal activities in life. Unfortunately for emergency care personnel, they rarely see the third stage. Emergency care personnel are the people directly involved in the shock and disbelief and guilt, anger, and sorrow stages of the grief process. Factors that can help a family cope with sudden death include being honest with them—helping them to realistically perceive the event. It is also important to be sure that there are adequate emotional supports available, such as hospital support personnel (e.g., chaplain service), other family, or friends. Also, the family should be allowed to cry and grieve in a quiet place, if the hospital has one.

As persons involved with the family of someone who has just died emergency care personnel must be able to assess the situation, intervene using the ideas just discussed, and anticipate what sort of referral or follow-up the family will need.

ASSESSING THE SITUATION

As soon as it becomes evident that a patient's death is imminent or his condition is critical, a member of the emergency care team should make contact with the family and remain with them throughout the resuscitation period if possible. This person can keep them informed along the way of the patient's condition. If no one can stay with the family the entire time, they should at least be checked with frequently. Listen to what the family is saying—they may need to talk. Keep in contact with the family's body language and nonverbal communication, which may also tell something about their needs. It may even be necessary to ask open-ended questions so that the family can begin to express their fears. Gently question about religious beliefs, as this may be important. Ask the family what happened, if they were present at the traumatic event. Pay attention to how they tell the story, as this may be a clue to how they should be dealt with. If possible keep the family informed of the patient's condition. If the patient is not doing well, tell the family.

After the death, help the family to realize that the event has actually happened but give them a little time to react to the news. If death occurs before the family arrives, a brief description of the events leading up to the death may be appropriate. If possible, limit the number of personnel in interaction with the family. Encourage the family to talk and to support each other.

Reactions to the death of a loved one may vary from crying and screaming, to being quite, to talking incessantly, or to any of a number of ways of showing emotion. Encourage healthy bereavement. Tell the grieving family, ''It's OK to cry.'' Avoid giving medications unless a prior history indicates that it would be most beneficial. Remember that a person who is crying hysterically will soon be fatigued. Giving medication to a hysterical family member may only delay the grief process.

Once the patient has died and the family has been made aware of the situation, allow them time to realistically perceive what has happened. Ask them if they would like to see the person who has died. Sometimes a few minutes alone with the family member who has died will help much in the grieving process. If the patient was badly disfigured in the accident the body should be covered, but the family should be allowed to see at least a part of the body that they can recognize—perhaps just a hand or a face. The family may be given some item that was removed from the patient, such as a ring or necklace, so that the death becomes a reality for them.

If an autopsy is necessary, help the family understand why. Tell them what is going to happen next, what kinds of papers they will have to sign, what will happen to the body, and so on. Encourage family members to make funeral arrangements together.

Discuss with the family some of the feelings that they may experience in the days to come. Encourage them to help each other. They may be given a call a couple of days after the death to see how they are doing. Most importantly, care givers should express some of their own feelings about the death. Emergency care personnel must work to keep their own emotional status healthy.

REFERENCE

1. American Psychiatric Association: Diagnostic and statistical manual of psychiatric disorders, ed. 3, Washington, D.C., 1980, The Association.

SUGGESTED READINGS

August, S.C.: Dealing with sudden death: the survivors. In Auerbach, P.S., and Budassi, S.A., editors: Cardiac arrest and CPR, ed. 2, Rockville, Md., 1983, Aspen Systems Corp.

Braverman, M.: Onset of psychotraumatic reactions, J. Forensic Sci. **25**:821, 1980.

Caplan, G.: Mastery of stress: psychosocial aspects, Am. J. Psychiatry **138**:413, 1981.

Geerts, A.E., and Rechardt, E.: Colliquium on trauma, Int. J. Psychoanal. **59**:365, 1978.

Graham, N.: Crisis intervention: rescue and self rescue. Speech presented at the Seventh Annual Scientific Assembly of Emergency Health Care Professionals, Los Angeles, June 3, 1978.

Graham, N.: Psycho-traumatology: crisis therapy in the trauma room, Dig. Emerg. Med. Care **1**:5, Sept. 1981.

Horowitz, M., and Krupnick, J.: Recurring themes in stress response syndromes, Arch. Gen. Psychiatry **38**:485, Apr. 1981.

Johnson, D.H., and Eie, K.: Crisis intervention training for prehospital personnel, Top. Emerg. Med. **2**:83, 1980.

Krell, G.I.: Managing the psychosocial factor in disaster programs, Health Soc. Work **3**:139, Aug. 1978.

Lindemann, E.: Symptomatology and management of acute grief, Am. J. Psychiatry **101**:141, Sept. 1944.

Pisarcik, G.: Psychiatric emergencies. In Budassi, S.A., and Barber, J.M., editors: Emergency nursing: principles and practice, St. Louis, 1981, The C.V. Mosby Co.

Scanlon-Schlipp, A.M., and Levesque, J.: Helping the patient to cope with the sequelae of trauma through the self-help group approach, J. Trauma **21**:35, 1981.

Schnaper, N., and Cowley, R.A.: Psychiatric sequelae to multiple trauma, Am. J. Psychiatry **133**:883, 1976.

Selverston, H.: Stress and the critical care team, Crit. Care Update, **4**:1, Jan. 1977.

Titchner, J.: Management and study of psychological response to trauma, J. Trauma **10**:974, 1970.

CHAPTER 2 Assessing, reporting, and biomedical communications

Accurate initial assessment in the field or emergency department and precise reporting are the keys to effective emergency care. Situations in which the patient and his past history are not known, the lighting is poor, the sounds of the street are loud, or the care giver is alone in the emergency department can make effective care difficult to say the least.

After assessment of the patient (and perhaps intervention for life-threatening conditions), a good report is essential. All data must be collected. It is difficult to give a complete report with incomplete information. Once the report is given and recorded, the data should be interpreted. In the case of prehospital care, data should be interpreted by a mobile intensive care nurse or a base station physician. In some cases data are interpreted by the prehospital care team, who function under established protocols. Once data are interpreted, therapeutic intervention should take place. Often data are interpreted as therapeutic intervention is concurrently performed. This is true especially in the case of the critically ill or injured patient, in which there is no time to complete the assessment before therapeutic intervention is applied.

HOW TO COLLECT DATA

To collect data it is necessary to be an astute observer. Before assessing the patient the emergency care giver must assess the environment to assure that it is safe for the rescuers and then that it is safe for the patient (e.g., the patient is inside a burning automobile). Once it is assured that the environment is safe, assessment of the patient should begin. *Always* begin with a 60-second survey (primary survey) that includes assessment of the airway, breathing, and circulation. The rest of the 60-second survey includes a gross survey of vital signs, including assessments of pulse (rhythm and rate), respirations (rhythm, rate, tidal volume, and gross lung sounds), blood pressure (by auscultation, palpation, or flush method), and skin (color, temperature, and moistness) and a brief neurologic examination.

After the 60-second primary survey is complete, immediate transport with interventions en route may be necessary. Immediate transport, also known in some emergency care systems as "load and go" or "scoop and run," involves those patients who would not benefit from prehospital care. Such patients are in immediate need of the definitive

11

care that only the emergency department or the hospital can provide. These patients include those who are experiencing deterioration of level of consciousness, respiratory failure, or shock as a result of trauma. In all of these cases, any stabilization efforts on the part of the prehospital care team should be performed en route.

If immediate transport is not necessary, the patient is assessed completely after the primary survey. If the chief complaint is pain, focus on this. A good mnemonic to use with the patient with a chief complaint of pain is PQRST:

P = Provokes

What provokes the pain? What makes it better? What makes it worse?

Q = Quality

What does the pain feel like? Is it sharp? Dull? Burning? Crushing?

R = Radiates

Where does the pain radiate? Is it in one place? Does it go any other place?

Brief neurologic examination

Determine depth of coma:
First use verbal stimuli, then painful stimuli.
Describe the patient in terms of stimulus response rather than with words such as "comatose" or "lethargic," which may mean different things to different people.
Examples of stimulus/response:
Patient responds to verbal stimuli by answering appropriately.
Patient does not respond to verbal stimuli.
Patient responds to painful stimuli by pushing away the source (purposeful movement).
Patient responds to painful stimuli by demonstrating decerebrate posturing.
Patient does not respond to painful stimuli.
Once it is determined that the patient can respond to questions, see if he is oriented to time (what day it is), place (where he is), person (who he is), and purpose (what happened to him).
Check the patient's eyes:
Pupil size
Pupil reaction to light and accommodation
Equality
Recheck the patient's respirations:
Rate
Rhythm
Depth
Check for motor activity:
Movment in all extremities
Any tingling or loss of sensation
An easy way to remember the procedure for a brief neurologic check is to use the mnemonic DERM, in which D = depth of coma, E = eyes, R = respirations, M = motor movement.

S = Severity

How severe is the pain? On a scale of 1 to 10 with 1 being the least pain and 10 being the worst, what rating would you give the pain?

T = Time

When did it start? How long did it last?

With the trauma patient, do a head-to-toe survey (see Chapter 23). With other chief complaints, assessments are made specific to that complaint (see individual chapters).

Be sure to obtain information such as the patient's name, age, past illnesses and medications, allergies, approximate weight, and any symptoms (what the patient describes) or signs (what can be seen).

REPORTING AND RECORDING DATA

Remember to report all findings, both positive and negative. If a certain parameter could not be assessed, state the reason why. This assures that errors of omission will not occur. Be sure to include all information in the written report as well. If something is not recorded it will be assumed that it was not noted. When giving your report, have an organized method of presentation that is comfortable for you. Here is an example of one form of reporting:

MOBILE INTENSIVE CARE UNIT
REPORTING FORMAT

Call Code Base Station Name

Mobile Unit your number designation

Location describe where (in general)

Age and Weight (estimate)   **Sex**

Problem severity mild—moderate—severe

Chief Complaint (or problem)

History and Medications—determine and describe
  (1) Any previous similar problem?
  (2) Any serious or chronic illness at present?

Initial Vital Signs
  General appearance—describe
  Level of consciousness—patients response to a stimulus
  Skin color and temperature
  Pulse—rate and rhythm
  Respirations—rate and rhythm
  Pupils—(if appropriate) size, reactivity to light, equal
  Blood pressure

Format developed by Stewart, R.D., Center for Emergency Medicine, University Health Center of Pittsburgh, Pittsburgh, Pa.

In the emergency department be sure to write detailed nurse's notes, including a triage note stating the time the patient arrived, the condition he was in on arrival, initial assessment of vital signs, and a statement of the chief complaint.

Once the data are collected decide which conditions take priority over others and which conditions are the most serious. Also, decide what is not normal in the findings of the primary and secondary surveys of the patient.

When therapeutic intervention is applied, self-confidence is important for the care giver. Give the patient some reassurance, keep him informed of what is being done and why, and practice a good bedside manner (even in an emergency). The care giver must use all psychologic, manual, and technical skills to the best of his or her ability.

BIOMEDICAL COMMUNICATIONS

Biomedical communications is the art of sending medical information from one point to another using radio, telephone, or television. There are three elements necessary for effective biomedical communication:

1. There must be people to relay and receive information.
2. There must be knowledge of both medical and technical aspects of patient care.
3. There must be proper equipment to relay the information.

Knowledge of medical aspects of care includes:

Skills in field assessment and early emergency department assessment

Thorough understanding of the local emergency medical services system

Knowledge of the limits and liabilities of individual roles (e.g., MDs, RNs, paramedics, EMTs)

Knowledge of personnel involved in the system and their expectations

Appreciation of unique circumstances found in prehospital care situations

Ability to evaluate the performance of self and others

Technical knowledge includes knowledge of the communications equipment used in the system.

Uses of biomedical communication include:

Check radio function on a daily basis.

Be familiar with management of a multiple call situation.

Be familiar with management of a multiple patient situation.

Have an alternate method of communicating with the base station in the event of co-channel interference.

Keep accurate records on all communications, including communication problems.

Radio courtesy and common sense

Use simple terms.

Speak clearly and slowly.

Be familiar with the aural brevity code.

Do not break into a transmission except in an absolute emergency.

Be as brief as possible without sacrificing information about the patient (i.e., avoid wordiness).

Be sure that the message is received; if uncertain, ask for a repeat of the message.

Always use professional language; never use profanity.

Frequently used radio terms
come in—Used in asking for acknowledgement of transmission.
go ahead—Proceed with your message.
repeat/say again—The message was not understood.
OK—Used in acknowledging that the message is received and understood.
ETA—Estimated time of arrival.
spell out—Used in asking sender to spell out phonetically words that are unclear.
stand by—Please wait.
landline—Telephone communication.
over—End of message.
clear—End of transmission.

The International Phonetic Alphabet

A	Alpha	**J**	Juliet	**S**	Sierra
B	Bravo	**K**	Kilo	**T**	Tango
C	Charley	**L**	Lima	**U**	Uniform
D	Delta	**M**	Mike	**V**	Victor
E	Echo	**N**	November	**W**	Whiskey
F	Foxtrot	**O**	Oscar	**X**	X-ray
G	Golf	**P**	Papa	**Y**	Yankee
H	Hotel	**Q**	Quebec	**Z**	Zebra
I	India	**R**	Romeo		

Federal Communications Commission Aural Brevity Code (The "10" Codes)

10-1	Signal weak	**10-21**	Call _____ by phone
10-2	Signal good	**10-22**	Disregard
10-3	Stop transmitting	**10-23**	Arrived at scene
10-4	Affirmative (OK)	**10-24**	Assignment completed
10-5	Relay to	**10-25**	Report to _____
10-6	Busy	**10-26**	Estimated time of arrival
10-7	Out of service	**10-27**	License/permit information
10-8	In service	**10-28**	Ownership information
10-9	Repeat	**10-29**	Records check
10-10	Negative	**10-30**	Danger/caution
10-11	_____ on duty	**10-31**	Pick up _____
10-12	Stand by (stop)	**10-32**	_____ units of blood needed (specify type)
10-13	Existing conditions	**10-33**	Need help quick
10-14	Message/information	**10-34**	Time
10-15	Message delivered	**10-35**	Reserved
10-16	Reply to message	**10-36**	Reserved
10-17	En route	**10-37**	Reserved
10-18	Urgent	**10-38**	Reserved
10-19	In contact	**10-39**	Reserved
10-20	Location		

Identify yourself with each transmission.
Always identify the party being addressed.
Always sign off at the end of the total transmission.
Acknowledge each transmission, even if there is no comment to make about it.

Always order medications by specific dose and route of administration.

Know what to do in the event of a multiple call situation.

Do not request or send continuous ECG strips, as doing so may tie up the frequency or make it difficult to override a transmission.

ECG transmissions should be short and intermittent.

Each ECG strip should be interpreted by both the sender and the receiver.

If information is being sent to the field that would be better if heard in privacy by the prehospital care team, ask if the base has a mute button to restrict the transmission to a hand-held receiver only.

If a transmission is not being received or if the transmission is broken up, inform the sender *immediately*.

Be familiar with field hospital personnel and their capabilities.

Be familiar with equipment carried by field personnel.

What to do in the event of a multiple call situation

A multiple call situation means that there is more than one unit attempting to make contact with the base at one time. In this situation it is especially important to assure that proper radio communication techniques are practiced. In multiple call situations the base hospital person is the one who controls the situation. If a landline is available the base hospital person may request that one of the units call on it. (This is after first assuring that the situation is not critical, and there is time to break radio communications to make the phone call.) If there is another base hospital available in the area, the original base may request that the prehospital care team call the other base. If neither of these options is possible, the calls must be directed simultaneously. It is absolutely essential that strict attention be paid to detail in such a situation.

The instant a multiple run or call situation arises, all parties in contact with the base station must be notified. It would be a good idea to remind all parties to be especially careful to identify themselves with each transmission. All parties should also verify therapeutic intervention orders by repeating them to the sender. This provides a double check to be sure that the right team receives the right orders. When sending a transmission it is important to state to whom the transmission is going. A multiple run situation should be handled calmly. With care, multiple run situations can be handled with ease.

SUGGESTED READINGS

Abbott, J., et al.: Protocols for prehospital emergency medical care, Baltimore, 1980, The Williams & Wilkins Co.

Budassi, S.A., and Barber, J.M.: Emergency nursing: principles and practice, St. Louis, 1982, The C.V. Mosby Co.

Caroline, N.: Ambulance calls, Boston, 1980, Little, Brown & Co.

Caroline, N.: Emergency care in the streets, Boston, 1979, Little Brown & Co.

Los Angeles County Paramedic Training Manuals, (4 vols.), Los Angeles, 1976, Los Angeles County Paramedic Training Institute.

McElroy, C.R., and Eie, K.: The prehospital care system, Top. Emerg. Med. **1:**4, 1980.

Miller, R.H., and Cantrell, J.R.: Basic emergency medicine, ed. 2, St. Louis, 1979, The C.V. Mosby Co.

Orban, D.J., and McElroy, C.R.: Controversies in emergency medicine, Top. Emerg. Med. **3:**2, 1981.

Stephenson, H.E.: Immediate care of the acutely ill and injured, ed. 2, St. Louis, 1978, The C.V. Mosby Co.

CHAPTER 3 **Basic and advanced life support**

There is no more vital function that a rescuer will perform than basic and advanced life support. As was once stated (source unknown), ''In your hands is the pulse of life . . . in your lungs is the breath of life.'' More than 650,000 people die of myocardial infarction each year in the United States. More than half of these (350,000) die in the first 2 hours of the attack, many before reaching the hospital.[1] This fact was recognized in the late 1960s, and the need for availability of sophisticated prehospital cardiac care became evident. Through the efforts of a few caring physicians, nurses, and politicians, the first paramedic units were trained and placed in service in 1969. Many systems have grown from these early ones, bringing advanced care to the public where they live, work, or play. It has also been recognized that basic and advanced care is needed by others besides the cardiac patient—the accident victim, the near-drowning victim, the smoke inhalation victim, and so on. Thus basic and advanced care became the standard for care for all patients, no matter what their complaint.

In 1973 the American Heart Association and the National Research Council sponsored a conference on cardiopulmonary resuscitation and emergency cardiac care. The classic article ''Standards and Guidelines for Cardiopulmonary Resuscitation (CPR) and Emergency Cardiac Care (ECC),'' was published as a result of this conference.[2] A vast amount of research on cardiopulmonary resuscitation (CPR) has caused rapid changes in basic and advanced life support, and there have been many updates and appraisals of the state of the art. The most recent is the American Heart Association and National Research Council's 1980 ''Standards and Guidelines for Cardiopulmonary Resuscitation (CPR) and Emergency Cardiac Care (ECC).''[1] The 1980 standards are much more comprehensive than the 1974 standards. In the 1980 standards there is much emphasis on the role of the citizen and citizen CPR. Courses in CPR are offered by the American Heart Association and the American Red Cross and at various fire departments and civic association meeting places around the country. The 1980 standards also stress early recognition of warning signs of cardiac problems and gaining entry into the emergency medical care system.

THE COMPONENTS OF BASIC LIFE SUPPORT

Basic life support is actually the first component of advanced life support. It consists of recognizing unconsciousness, opening an airway, and maintaining the airway. The rescuer must assure that breathing is present or apply artificial respirations and assure that circulation is present or apply chest compressions.

Airway management

There is much more emphasis on airway management in the 1980 standards than there were before. The currently accepted method for early airway management in the patient not suspected of having cervical spine trauma is the head tilt–chin lift maneuver (Fig. 3-1), which replaces the head tilt maneuver (Fig. 3-2). In head tilt–chin lift maneuver the head is tilted back and the chin is lifted almost far enough to close the mouth. An alternative to this that is used in cases of suspected cervical spine fracture is the jaw-thrust maneuver, in which the head remains in a neutral position while the jaw is pushed forward with the thumbs or fingers (Fig. 3-3). Either of these maneuvers may be enough to pull the tongue away from the posterior pharynx and open the airway, and the patient may begin to breathe spontaneously. Remember, however, that if one of these procedures opens the airway, it must be maintained until the patient is capable of doing so himself, or the airway is maintained by some other means, such as endotracheal intubation.

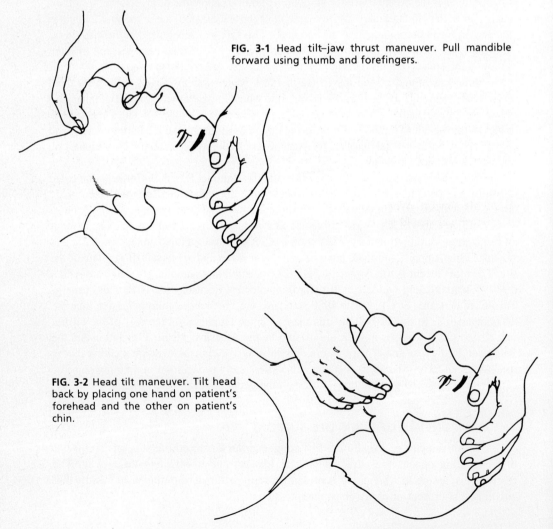

FIG. 3-1 Head tilt–jaw thrust maneuver. Pull mandible forward using thumb and forefingers.

FIG. 3-2 Head tilt maneuver. Tilt head back by placing one hand on patient's forehead and the other on patient's chin.

FIG. 3-3 Jaw thrust maneuver.

Breathing

Once the airway is established the rescuer must assure that breathing is present. If it is not, the rescuer must provide breaths for the patient. The most rapid method of establishing breathing for a patient is mouth-to-mouth breathing. It requires no special equipment—the rescuer delivers air to the patient's lungs through his own mouth. In an adult the rescuer places his mouth over the mouth of the patient. The patient's nose must be pinched shut to make sure no air escapes through it. A tight seal is made, and the rescuer breathes into the victim's mouth (Fig. 3-4), initially using four rapid breaths in succession. This provides the volume of oxygen necessary before proceeding to the next step of basic life support. When breathing into the victim's mouth the rescuer should meet no resistance and should see the victim's chest rise.

FIG. 3-4 Mouth-to-mouth breathing. Blow into victim's mouth, observing chest rise.

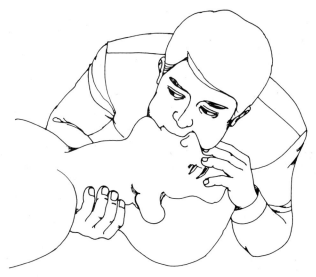

If there is a reason that mouth-to-mouth breathing cannot be done (e.g., facial trauma) the rescuer may elect to perform mouth-to-nose breathing. If mouth-to-nose breathing is used, the rescuer holds the patient's mouth closed. The patient's nose is covered with the rescuer's mouth. The rescuer then breathes into the patient's nose. In either mouth-to-mouth or mouth-to-nose breathing, the rescuer allows passive exhalation by removing the mouth from the patient's nose or mouth.

The rescuer breathes for the patient once every 5 seconds (12 times/minute) until other means of ventilation become available or until the patient is breathing on his own.

When managing an airway and breathing for an infant or small child, the rescuer is careful not to hyperextend the neck too much, as the cervical spine of a child is very flexible. Hyperextension may actually block the airway from the posterior aspect When breathing for an infant or small child, the rescuer's mouth covers the child's entire nose and mouth, allowing for smaller breaths in accordance with the size of the child. Breaths should be given at 3-second intervals (20 times/minute).

THE OBSTRUCTED AIRWAY

If when attempting to ventilate the patient the rescuer finds that the airway is blocked, the cause of the obstruction must be removed before any breathing maneuver can be performed. The first thing the rescuer does is reposition the airway; occasionally, in the fury of the rescue effort, good airway position may be lost. Once the airway is repositioned, the rescuer attempts to breathe for the patient once again. If efforts are still met with resistance the rescuer should suspect that there is a foreign body present. The rescuer turns the patient on his side and applies four back blows in rapid succession. The rescuer then applies four manual abdominal thrusts (Fig. 3-5). The rescuer sweeps a finger along the back of the throat to see if the back blows or abdominal thrusts caused the foreign body to be dislodged into the throat and then attempts to breathe for the patient once again. If the airway is still blocked, the rescuer repeats the entire sequence.

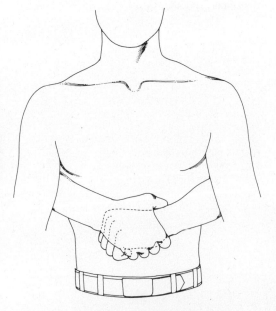

FIG. 3-5 Heimlich (abdominal thrust) maneuver. Place both arms around victim's waist; place fleshy part of fist below xiphoid and above navel. Place other hand on top. Apply quick firm upward and inward motion.

The abdominal thrust maneuver may be applied with the patient in a supine position and the rescuer straddling him. The rescuer kneels facing the patient's head. The heels of the rescuer's hands are placed at the halfway point between the umbilicus and the xiphoid. In a standing patient abdominal thrusts are performed by standing behind the patient. The rescuer's arms circle the patient, and the heels of the rescuer's hands are in the halfway position between the patient's umbilicus and xiphoid. In any instance, pressure should be applied in an inward and upward motion. This increases intrathoracic pressure and may dislodge the foreign body if there is a total airway obstruction.

Circulation

Once airway and breathing are established, the rescuer checks to see if a pulse is present. The best places to check for a pulse in an adult patient are the carotid and the femoral areas. In a child it is best to check the brachial pulse. *Do not* attempt to initiate circulation before establishing an airway and breathing. Doing so only circulates unoxygenated blood, which is useless. If no pulse can be found, the rescuer provides circulation by performing chest compressions.

The first step in chest compression (also known as cardiac compression or external compression) is to assure proper hand placement. Locate the xiphoid process and place the heel of one hand two fingers above the xiphoid, on the lower half of the sternum. Place the heel of the other hand on top of the first one. Lock the fingers and make sure that they do not touch the chest wall. Kneel with legs slightly separated and in as close to the patient as possible. Keep the elbows straight and in a locked position. Begin compressions with a smooth downward motion, compressing the sternum (Fig. 3-6). This should be followed

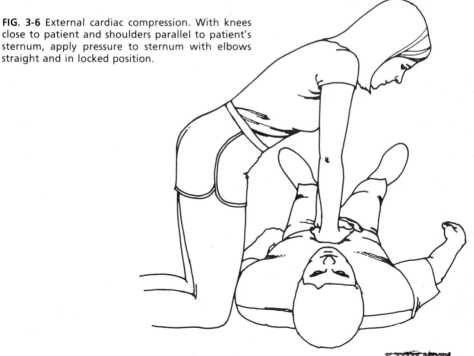

FIG. 3-6 External cardiac compression. With knees close to patient and shoulders parallel to patient's sternum, apply pressure to sternum with elbows straight and in locked position.

Differential diagnosis in cardiopulmonary arrest

There are many causes of cardiopulmonary arrest in addition to primary cardiac abnormalities. It is important for the rescuer to be familiar with these causes and to be alert to their signs and symptoms, as identification of these may modify the type of therapeutic intervention given. Listed below are some of the conditions that may lead to cardiopulmonary arrest that are not primary cardiac abnormalities. *All therapeutic interventions listed are in addition to basic and advanced cardiac life support measures.*

Causes	Specific	Signs and symptoms	Therapeutic intervention	Notes
Metabolic	Hypoglycemia	Physical signs of insulin or oral hypoglycemic agent usage; tachydysrhythmias; seizures; aspiration	Dextrose, 50%	Consider this a strong possibility in patients who have a history of diabetes
	Hyperkalemia	ECG: prolonged Q-T interval; peaked T waves; loss of P waves; wide QRS complexes	Calcium chloride; sodium bicarbonate	Often seen in hemodialysis and renal failure patients; also seen in patients on Aldactone
Drug induced	Tricyclic antidepressants (e.g., Elavil, Triavil, Tofranil, Etrafon, Sinequan, Vivactil)	Tachydysrhythmias	Sodium bicarbonate (to keep pH at 7.50); physostigmine (however, there has been some question as to efficacy)	Causes direct cardiac toxicity; often delayed toxicity in adults
	Narcotics	Bradydysrhythmias; heart blocks	Naloxone (Narcan)	There is a question of direct cardiac toxicity
	Propanolol	Cardiac: Heart blocks Bradydysrhythmias, PVCs	Isuprel Atropine	PVCs may be rate-related
		Respiratory: Bronchospasm	Aminophyline	
		Metabolic: Hypoglycemia	Dextrose, 50%	
Pulmonary (any disease causing severe hypoxia)	Asthma	Severe bronchospasm causing hypoxia and respiratory acidosis; ECG: tachydysrhythmias (especially ventricular fibrillation)	Endotracheal intubation and ventilatory support	Abuse of sympathomimetic inhalants

Pulmonary embolus	Pleuritic chest pain; shortness of breath in high-risk patients (e.g., postoperative, birth control pills); syncope (recent study shows 60% have syncope as part of initial complaint); tachydysrhythmias	Good ventilatory support	Pathophysiology: acute hypoxia and cor pulmonale leading to tachydysrhythmias
Tension pneumothorax	Distended neck veins; tracheal deviation; asymmetric chest expansion; ECG: often electrical mechanical dissociation	Needle thoracotomy; chest tube	Often seen in patients with blunt chest trauma; often occurs during CPR due to chest compressions (especially patients with COPD)
Neurogenic	Increased intracranial pressure from any cause (e.g., subarachnoid hemorrhage; subdural hematoma)	Central neurogenic breathing; dilated pupil(s); decerebrate decorticate posturing; ECG: wide range of dysrhythmias, especially heart blocks	Central neurogenic hyperventilation (causes respiratory alkalosis which causes cerebral vasoconstriction); steroids; diuretic agents; surgery	Pathophysiology: damage to brainstem and autonomic centers
Hypovolemic	Anything that causes volume loss such as GI bleeding, severe trauma with organ damage, ruptured ectopic pregnancy, dissecting/leaking aneurysm	Tachycardia; decreasing blood pressure; skin cool, clammy, pale; obvious signs of external blood loss	IV fluids; medical antishock trousers (MAST); shock position; surgery	A major cause of cardiopulmonary arrest that may be unrecognized
Other cardiac causes	Pericardial tamponade	Distended neck veins; decreasing blood pressure; distant heart sounds; ECG: electrical mechanical dissociation or bradydysrhythmias	IV fluids; MAST; atropine; Isuprel; pericardiocentesis; thoracotomy; widening pulse pressure	Look for it, especially in patients with blunt chest trauma or prolonged CPR efforts

SPECIAL NOTE FOR PREHOSPITAL CARE: Consider early transport for young patients in cardiac arrest as definitive therapeutic intervention will most likely include procedures not performed in the field situation.

From Budassi, S.A.: J.E.N. 7(2):79, 1981.

by a smooth upward motion. The ratio of downward to upward motion should be 1:1, or 50% downward and 50% upward. Avoid sharp, jabbing motions. Use the back to provide effortless compressions with a rocking motion. Compress to a depth of 1½ to 2 inches. Remember that this depth may vary from patient to patient.

If performed properly, chest compression may achieve cardiac outputs from one-third to one-half the normal individual's cardiac output and may generate a systolic blood pressure of up to 100 mm Hg. Research projects have demonstrated that increased intrathoracic pressure, and not compression of the left ventricle between the sternum and the vertebrae, is what causes cardiac output.[3] This means that chest compression and ventilation performed simultaneously will produce an increased cardiac output. However, more research is necessary to determine the effects of this technique on the respiratory parameters of pH and P_{CO_2} before the technique can be recommended as a method of CPR.

Studies have shown that circulation can be maintained during ventricular fibrillation and ventricular tachycardia by having the patient cough. This is probably related to changes in intrathoracic pressure that increase cardiac output.[4]

According to the 1980 standards, chest compression should be repeated at a rate of 80 times/minute in one-person CPR (allowing time for ventilations) and 60 times/minute in two-person CPR. In one-person CPR, one rescuer compresses the chest 15 times followed by two quick breaths. The rescuer repeats the cycle until another rescuer comes to the scene. In two-person CPR, the first rescuer compresses the chest five times and the second rescuer administers a breath on the fifth upstroke of the chest compressions.

In the resuscitation of infants and children, the ratio of chest compressions to ventilations is 5:1 no matter the number of rescuers. In compressing the chest of an infant or child one can use either the index and middle fingers of one hand or the thumbs (on an infant) or the heel of one hand (on a small child). As the ventricles are higher anatomically in a child than in an adult, compressions should be performed on the center of the sternum. The depth will vary from ½ to 1½ inches, depending on the child's size. Compressions should be slightly faster for children than for adults—80 to 100 times/minute.

Remember that most cardiopulmonary arrests in children begin primarily as respiratory arrests. So pay strict attention to the airway and ventilation throughout the resuscitation effort.

ADVANCED LIFE SUPPORT
Myocardial ischemia and cardiopulmonary arrest

Cardiac arrest is most commonly preceded by myocardial infarction or a major cardiac dysrhythmia (e.g., premature ventricular beats, ventricular tachycardia, or ventricular fibrillation). Cardiopulmonary arrest has a 75% to 85% mortality even with the best of resuscitation efforts. Cardiovascular disease is the leading cause of death in persons over 40 in the United States. It is interesting to note that 20% of persons who die of cardiopulmonary arrest had seen a physician 2 to 4 weeks before the terminal event.[5] Let us examine the symptom complexes that may terminate in cardiopulmonary arrest.

Any patient who demonstrates symptoms of poor cardiac output or decreased coronary circulation should be treated immediately. The first concern is gaining access to the circulation by establishing an IV line. This assures ready access to the circulation to attempt to prevent dysrhythmias, infarction, or heart failure. Concurrently, administer supplemental oxygen via a nasal cannula. Do not use a face mask so as to avoid inhalation of expired carbon dioxide. Determine vital signs and skin vital signs (color, temperature, and moistness). Examine a rhythm strip (lead II or MCL_1) for the presence of dysrhythmias. Further examine the chief complaint and obtain a brief history (Fig. 3-7).

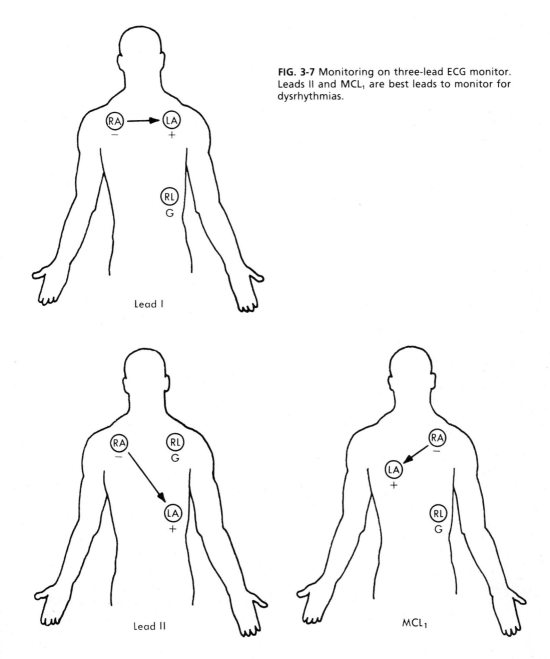

FIG. 3-7 Monitoring on three-lead ECG monitor. Leads II and MCL_1 are best leads to monitor for dysrhythmias.

Lead I

Lead II

MCL_1

If the chief complaint is chest pain, or any kind of pain for that matter, use the PQRST mnemonic to assist in gathering facts about the pain.

P = Provokes

What provokes the pain? What makes it better? What makes it worse?

Q = Quality

What does it feel like? Is it sharp? Dull? Burning? Stabbing? Crushing? (Try to let the patient describe it before offering choices.)

R = Radiates

Where does the pain radiate? Is it in one place? Does it go to any other place?

S = Severity

How severe is the pain? On a scale of 1 to 10 with 1 being the least pain and 10 being the worst, what rating would you give the pain? (Watch for nonverbal clues with this question. A patient may be writhing in pain and tell you the pain is a 2, or a patient may sit there very calmly and quietly and tell you the pain is a 10.)

T = Time

When did it start? How long did it last?

Find out if the patient has a history (or a family history) of heart disease, lung disease, or stroke. Ask if he is taking any medications. (Use words such as "heart pills" or "water pills" if necessary.) Ask if it hurts to take a deep breath. Find out what he was doing when the pain began. Ask if he has ever had this pain before. Ask if it is different this time.

Quickly check the patient for level of consciousness. Check his pupils for equality, reaction to light, and accommodation. (Remember that 10% of the population has unequal pupils.) Examine the neck veins for distention, and check the trachea to see that it is in a midline position. Inquire as to a recent history of trauma.

It is our belief that the initial intravenous fluid should be a crystalloid solution. It should be at a "keep-open" rate. Should fluid be required rapidly for hypotensive states associated with bradydysrhythmias, venodilation, or transient pump failure, time will not be wasted changing the IV solution. The rescuer must be extremely cautious with the patient who has a combination of rales, diaphoresis, cyanosis, and hypotension or who has hypertensive pulmonary edema, as an excess of fluids would not be advisable in these situations. In these early phases of myocardial infarction it is essential to pay particular attention to the relief of pain and the prevention of dysrhythmias.

NITROGLYCERIN

Nitroglycerin is a nitrate that is very effective in dilating the peripheral circulation. This causes a decrease in blood return to the heart and a consequent reduced workload. A reduced myocardial oxygen demand results.[6] Nitroglycerin also causes coronary artery dilation and may increase perfusion in the coronary arteries. This produces a relief of chest pain, particularly chest pain caused by angina pectoris. Nitroglycerin is given in an initial dosage of 0.4 mg or 1/150 Gr. Blood pressure should be monitored before nitroglycerin administration. Nitroglycerin is not administered unless systolic blood pressure is above 100 mm Hg. If the initial dose is not effective the rescuer may choose to administer an additional tablet (again, assuring that the patient's systolic pressure is greater than 100 mm Hg). If hypotension does occur as a result of nitroglycerin administration, the rescuer elevates the patient's legs to increase venous return to the central circulation. If this is ineffective, the rescuer considers volume replacement (a fluid challenge) or use of the military antishock trousers (MAST).

TRANSDERMAL NITROPASTE

Transdermal nitropaste is an alternative to nitroglycerin tablets. It is applied to the chest wall, usually over the left side of the chest, in a ½ to 1-inch area. Remember that the onset of action with nitropaste is a bit slower than with tablets and that the duration of action is longer than with tablets. If the patient develops an adverse reaction, this too will be longer in duration.

Both nitroglycerin and nitropaste can lose potency over time. If the patient tells the rescuer that he has taken several of his own nitroglycerin tablets or applied his own nitropaste without effect, the rescuer may choose to administer nitroglycerin from a fresh supply to assure potency.

MORPHINE SULFATE

Morphine sulfate is the "classic" drug of choice for chest pain of possible or probable myocardial origin. Besides relieving pain as a narcotic-analgesic morphine sulfate reduces preload and decreases myocardial oxygen demand. It should be administered slowly intravenously at a dosage of 2 to 10 mg, titrated to effect. It should not be given if systolic blood pressure is below 90 mm Hg. If hypotension should occur, the patient's legs should be elevated to facilitate venous return to the central circulation, as for nitroglycerin-induced hypotension. If there is respiratory depression, naloxone hydrochloride (Narcan) 0.8 mg IV should be administered. Naloxone acts rapidly and reverses the effects of morphine sulfate. The presence of chronic obstructive pulmonary disease is a relative contra-indication to the use of morphine sulfate.

NALBUPHINE HYDROCHLORIDE (NUBAIN)

Although relatively new, nalbuphine hydrochloride appears to have properties similar to those of morphine sulfate. It is a synthetic narcotic agonist-antagonist analgesic. In doses greater than 10 mg it is said to have endogenous narcotic (endorphin-like) self-limitation. This means that no further respiratory depression will occur past this dosage. Administration is similar to morphine sulfate—2 to 10 mg by IV push.

NITROUS OXIDE (NITRONOX, ENTONOX)

Administration of nitrous oxide in a mixture of 50% with 50% oxygen at a flow of 2 liters of nitrous oxide and 2 liters of oxygen/minute has a positive effect in the relief of chest pain without any demonstrable hemodynamic or cardiac consequences. It is self-administered by the patient through a hand-held mask. When the patient has received enough of the gases, his hand will fall away from his face. It acts rapidly (3 to 4 minutes) and reverses in about the same amount of time. It is currently being used in several prehospital care systems throughout the United States. It has been widely used in Ireland for many years under the direction of Dr. Peter Baskett.

Dysrhythmia management

The most common dysrhythmia that occurs in the patient experiencing acute myocardial infarction is premature ventricular contraction (PVC). Approximately 85% of patients who experience myocardial infarction have PVCs. Criteria for identification of "significant" PVCs have been widely published and generally adopted. These criteria include PVCs at a rate of six per minute or greater, PVCs that occur multiply, PVCs of multifocal origin, and PVCs that represent the R-on-T phenomenon. Recently it has also been discovered that ventricular tachycardia, ventricular fibrillation, and electricomechanical dissociation may not be preceded by warning dysrhythmias.[7-9] Many practitioners currently advocate the administration of prophylactic lidocaine for acute possible myocardial infarction with or without dysrhythmias.[8-10] Prophylactic lidocaine is given by bolus-bolus method, bolus–IV drip method, or rapid injection technique. When given by bolus-bolus method, the initial dose should be 1 to 2 mg/kg given slowly over 1 to 2 minutes. If lidocaine is given too rapidly, seizure may occur. The initial bolus is followed by an additional bolus of 50 mg 5 minutes later. Repeat the 50 mg bolus every 10 minutes up to a total dosage of 325 mg. This method of administration should be considered especially in the prehospital setting, because it is difficult to control an IV drip rate in a moving rescue vehicle. Lidocaine can also be given by slowly administering an initial bolus of 1 to 2 mg/kg IV, followed by a drip of 2 g lidocaine in 500 ml of D5W running at a rate of 1 to 4 mg/minute to maintain a constant blood level. Lidocaine should not be given without an initial loading-dose bolus. If an IV drip is started before a loading-dose bolus is given, an effective blood level of lidocaine may take a long time to reach or may never be attained.

A third method of lidocaine administration is intramuscular injection. If this method is chosen, a LidoPen should be used so that deep penetration of the muscle is attained. Lidocaine is given intramuscularly in a dosage of 300 mg.

Remember that if third-degree infranodal block is present in a patient having an acute myocardial infarction, lidocaine is not administered. If a patient has a history of liver disease the dosage of lidocaine should be reduced by half, or an alternate antidysrhythmic therapy should be considered. One alternate therapy is procainamide (Pronestyl) given in a dosage of 250 mg to 1 g by IV bolus slowly (not over 50 mg/minute of administration).

There are several new drugs currently being investigated for the management of ventricular dysrhythmias. These include aprindine hydrochloride, tocainide, amiodarone, mexiletene, lorcainide hydrochloride, encainide hydrochloride, and flecainide acetate.[12]

The next most common dysrhythmia seen in patients having acute myocardial infarction is bradycardia. It can be found in about 65% of these patients, especially those experiencing inferior wall infarctions. The therapeutic intervention for bradycardia includes the administration of oxygen and atropine sulfate, a parasympatholytic drug. Atropine is given in bolus form at a dosage of 0.5 to 1.0 mg IV if the heart rate is less than 60 beats/minute and the victim is demonstrating PVCs that are probably rate related or if the heart rate is less than 45 beats/minute even without PVCs. Atropine should also be given if there is a heart rate of 60 beats/minute or less, and there is associated hypotension. Atropine should never be administered in a dose of less than 0.3 mg, as this may produce a paradoxic effect and further decrease heart rate and blood pressure.

Atrioventricular (AV) blocks are not uncommon in acute myocardial infarction. They may be caused by parasympathetic overactivity, toxic levels of cardiac medications such as digitalis or propranolol, ischemia of the sinoatrial or atrioventricular nodes of the conduction system, or overdrive suppression caused by the termination of supraventricular tachycardia. First degree AV block, which is demonstrated by a prolongation of the P-R interval, and second degree block (Mobitz type I or Wenckebach phenomenon), which is demonstrated by a gradually prolonged P-R interval that results in a drop in ventricular conduction, need not be treated in acute inferior myocardial infarction. If, however, these dysrhythmias accompany acute anterior myocardial infarction the placement of a demand pacemaker should be strongly considered, as the chance of progression to complete heart block is very strong.[12]

Second degree AV block (Mobitz type II) should also be considered as a possibility in both inferior and anterior myocardial infarction. In inferior myocardial infarction, the block probably occurs at the AV node above the bundle of His. The escape beats will originate above the bifurcation of the Bundle of His, making this a relatively stable condition. With anterior myocardial infarction, both bundle branches may be involved, making the escape focus come from below the Bundle of His. This condition is an unstable one. In this instance a pacemaker should be strongly considered.

Third degree (complete) heart block usually requires the immediate placement of a pacemaker. In all block conditions, atropine, isoproterenol (as a time-buying measure), and a pacemaker if indicated should be considered.

Tachycardias are commonly seen in acute myocardial infarction. Supraventricular tachycardia may indicate myocardial ischemia or acute myocardial infarction. Tachycardia is often associated with chest pain but may also be seen in the absence of chest pain. Tachycardia increases myocardial oxygen consumption and may actually increase the size of the infarct. Therapeutic intervention varies depending on the clinical findings. If the patient is demonstrating severe chest pain and/or severe hypotension, cardioversion should be attempted (25 to 50 watt-seconds). (The patient who is taking digitalis should not receive electrical cardioversion if possible.) If he is hemodynamically stable and has no chest pain the rescuer may choose to try vagal maneuvers such as the Valsalva maneuver, carotid sinus massage, or having the patient hold his breath and bear down.

Verapamil, a calcium channel antagonist, is currently the drug of choice for supraventricular tachycardia. It works by prolonging conduction through the AV node and the sinoatrial (SA) node, decreasing contractility (inotropy), and peripherally vasodilating and dilating coronary arteries. It is given in a dosage of 0.15 mg/kg over 1 minute. The onset of action of verapamil is less than 2 minutes, with the peak effect at about 10 to 15 minutes. If the initial dose is not effective it may be repeated in 30 minutes. Verapamil has been reported as effective in treating 90% to 95% of cases of supraventricular tachycardia.

If a patient demonstrates a systolic blood pressure of below 85 mm Hg the rescuer may elect to use metaraminol, an alphapressor, to titrate the systolic blood pressure to an acceptable level.

Other agents that should be considered in the treatment of supraventricular tachycardia are propranolol, procainamide, digoxin, edrophonium chloride, and pacemaker therapy.

Atrial flutter in association with acute myocardial infarction may be caused by congestive heart failure, SA node ischemia, infarction, pericarditis, cardiogenic shock, vagal reaction, or sympathetic nerve activity increase. Although there is no mortality directly associated with this rhythm, death may be caused by the condition that caused the dysrhythmia (e.g., myocardial infarction). Atrial flutter can be treated with digoxin or quinidine.

CARDIOPULMONARY ARREST PHASE AND ADVANCED LIFE SUPPORT

Cardiopulmonary arrest may be caused by any of a number of conditions. The most common dysrhythmias seen are ventricular tachycardia, ventricular fibrillation, electromechanical dissociation, idioventricular rhythm, and asystole. If these rhythms occur the rescuer should immediately apply basic life support techniques. If there is enough help in the form of trained personnel present, the rescuer should also apply advanced life support principles, such as airway adjuncts, circulatory assist devices, fluids and medications, electric intervention, and transport if needed. Besides giving basic and advanced life support the rescuer should be alert for clues as to the cause of the arrest that must be treated with interventions specific to that cause (e.g., placement of an anterior chest wall needle or a chest tube for tension pneumothorax, or pericardiocentesis for pericardial tamponade).

Remember that airway management is essential in the arrest phase, and that the patient must be assured of receiving a maximum amount of oxygen.

In this section the four most common dysrhythmias seen in cardiopulmonary arrest will be reviewed. These are ventricular fibrillation, asystole, electromechanical dissociation, and idioventricular rhythm. Ventricular fibrillation is the most common of these. The therapy for ventricular fibrillation is defibrillation. An initial dosage of 200 to 300 watt-seconds should be given, followed by the initiation of an IV line. Basic life support should be continued throughout the rescue effort. Once the IV line is established epinephrine, 5 to 10 ml of a 1:10,000 solution, and sodium bicarbonate, 1 mEq/kg initially followed by 0.5 mEq/kg every 10 minutes, should be administered until arterial blood gas results are available. At that time the drugs are administered in accordance with blood gas values. Also, these drugs will need time to circulate if they are given intravenously; circulation takes 60 to 90 seconds. Once the initial doses of epinephrine and bicarbonate are given, defibrillation may once again be attempted, this time using a 300 to 400 watt-second dose. If these attempts fail, a higher watt-second dose, a double defibrillation (two defibrillation attempts in rapid succession), or defibrillation using anterior-posterior paddle placement may be tried. If these fail there are several other therapeutic interventions that may be used. Atropine 1 to 2 mg may be administered with the thought that there may be excess vagal tone preventing the patient from returning to a normal rhythm.

Lidocaine is not routinely given in cases of ventricular fibrillation, but it may be given with the thought that will suppress any ventricular ectopic foci that may have caused the ventricular fibrillation.

Bretylium tosylate has now been approved by the FDA for use in cases of ventricular fibrillation and ventricular tachycardia that are unresponsive to other antidysrhythmic agents. It is given in a dose of 5 mg/kg for this condition. If the ventricular fibrillation persists after this dosage doubling the dosage to 10 mg/kg and repeating this dosage as necessary may be considered. Bretylium may not take effect for up to 10 minutes. It is important to continue CPR during this time.

The presence of asystole may indicate that the patient was in an arrest situation for a time before the rescue team's arrival. Resuscitation is rare, and even if the patient can be resuscitated, brain damage has frequently already occurred. Therapeutic intervention includes high doses of oxygen, correction of the acidotic state by administering sodium bicarbonate, and the administration of intravenous epinephrine. If the IV route is not available, epinephrine may be administered via the endotracheal route. These drugs must be circulated for 60 to 90 seconds to allow them to reach the coronary circulation. Defibrillation would be useless; there is no need for electric interruption, as there is no electric activity in asystole. If the initial sodium bicarbonate and epinephrine are unsuccessful, atropine 1 mg IV should be administered. As described previously, atropine may decrease vagal tone, which may be the reason the initial drugs were ineffective. Administration of a bolus of isoproterenol or the insertion of a pacemaker may also be tried.

There is a very poor prognosis for patients who exhibit an idioventricular rhythm. Idioventricular rhythm may indicate that there has been a major infarction and that there is much myocardial damage. Naloxone hydrochloride 0.8 mg and 50 ml of 50% dextrose may be administered for idioventricular rhythm that was caused by a narcotic overdose or a metabolic phenomenon. Occasionally it is difficult to distinguish an idioventricular rhythm from a nodal rhythm with a bundle branch block. To assure that the rhythm is truly an idioventricular rhythm, atropine may be administered. If a junctional rhythm is present, the atropine may cause it to accelerate. At the same time, if the rhythm is idioventricular, atropine may decrease excess vagal tone and abolish the idioventricular rhythm. A dose of 0.5 mg of atropine is given initially. This dose is repeated until a total dosage of 2 mg has been administered. If atropine does not effectively increase the rate isoproterenol may be administered at a dosage of 2 to 20 μg/minute. The drip should be started at a rate of 1 to 2 μg/minute and titrated up to the point at which the rhythm is 60 to 80 beats/minute. A fluid challenge of 200 to 500 ml of an isotonic fluid may also be given to fill the vascular spaces created by vagal tone.

Pacemaker insertion should be considered after the administration of isoproterenol. The pacemakers of choice in this instance are a transthoracic pacemaker or a transvenous floating pacemaker. Occasionally thoracotomy should be considered in the hope that open chest massage will improve coronary perfusion and increase cardiac output.

Electromechanical dissociation is the production in the heart of an organized electrical impulse without the presence of muscular response. The mortality from this dysrhythmia is 95%. The goal of therapeutic intervention is to assist inotropic qualities of the heart. Sometimes electromechanical dissociation is caused by cardiac tamponade or tension pneumothorax, both of which are reversed rapidly if signs and symptoms are recognized and rapid therapeutic intervention is applied. Intervention should include a fluid/volume challenge to improve pulmonary capillary wedge pressure, application of military anti-shock trousers (MAST) to augment volume status by autotransfusion and increase peripheral vascular resistance, and use of pressor agents if blood pressure does not respond to volume increase and MAST application. The pressor of choice is dopamine, which is capable of both alpha- and beta-adrenergic effects depending on dose. Low doses of dopamine, 2 to 5 μg/kg/minute, stimulate cardiac beta receptors and dilate renal and mesenteric vasculature. Intermediate doses of 5 to 10 μg/kg/minute stimulate the release of norepinephrine and accelerate alpha-adrenergic effects. High doses of greater than 10 μg/kg/min cause increased alpha effects. Renal and mesenteric arteries constrict, which results in a maximum blood pressure. However, atrial and ventricular tachydysrhythmias may occur at this dosage. Dobutamine, another pressor agent, stimulates myocardial beta receptors and causes an increase in myocardial contractility without increasing heart

Oxygen

Major actions
Decreases ventilatory and myocardial effort to maintain alveolar and arterial oxygen tensions, respectively.
Increases alveolar oxygen tensions.

Primary emergency uses
Shock states.
Head injuries.
Cardiac or pulmonary complaints.
Poisonings or toxic states resulting in respiratory depression, acidosis, or decreased levels of consciousness.
Sickle cell anemia crisis.
Agitation and confusion which may be the result of cerebral hypoxia.
Cardiac or pulmonary arrest.

Notes on administration
Humidify oxygen if possible since it has a rapid drying effect on nasal and pulmonary mucosa. This is a crucial consideration when an artificial airway is in use.
Do not attempt to supply humidity when using a bag-mask device for assisting breathing since water can be aspirated into the tubing and valve mechanisms of the bag, thus interfering with gas delivery.
Oxygen, even 100% concentration, has no adverse effects for brief periods in emergency situations. Do not withhold oxygen during initial transportation or resuscitation while waiting for arterial blood gas analysis or the ruling out of chronic obstructive pulmonary states. The detrimental and often irreversible effects of hypoxia and hypoxemia develop quickly. Most adverse effects of excessive oxygen delivery (e.g. oxygen toxicity) develop slowly—usually after 24 hours of therapy. When in doubt, employ concentrations of less than 50% for supportive management of the cardiopulmonary mechanisms while awaiting results of arterial blood gas analyses and other clinical validation.
Ensure airway efficiency by proper positioning, suctioning, and employment of an adjunctive device if necessary.
Never deliver less than 5 liters by mask. Expired air can accumulate in the device and be rebreathed, thus increasing carbon dioxide inhalation and resulting in a concurrent decline in oxygen delivery.
Low flow oxygen delivery (less than 35%) should be reserved for patients with regular, consistent ventilations of normal volume and a rate less than 25 per minute.
High flow oxygen delivery (greater than 60%) is usually reserved for patients with primary cardiopulmonary disease or those who cannot maintain a consistent ventilatory pattern.
Never discontinue oxygen at the same time that mechanical ventilatory support is discontinued. When oxygen therapy is no longer indicated, administration should be gradually reduced while carefully monitoring ventilatory indices and cardiac activity.

Guide to oxygen therapy

Device	Liter flow	Concentration delivered in %	Notes
Nasal cannula or catheter	1	21	Same concentration as room air.
	2	24	
	4	36	
	6	44	Most patients will not tolerate flow in excess of 6 liters.
Mask			Do not use less than 5 liters by mask since exhaled carbon dioxide would accumulate in the mask and be inspired again.
	5-6	40	
	6-7	50	
	7-8	60	Fills maximum anatomic reservoir.
Mask with reservoir bag	6	60	
	8	80	
	10	99	
Self-inflating bag mask (2 liter capacity)	15	40-80	Do not use humidity.

From Barber, J.M.: J.E.N. **4**(3):53, 1978.

rate. It does not, however, have any effect on blood pressure and has not been found to be useful in therapeutic intervention for electromechanical dissociation.

There have been some attempts to restore blood pressure using dexamethasone. Some of the results have been favorable. It is important to remember that many more cases must be studied before dexamethasone administration can be universally recommended.

In the past, calcium chloride administration has been recommended to improve myocardial contractility, though there has been very little evidence that calcium chloride actually has any effects. One should consider, however, that arrest that occurs after massive blood transfusion may be caused by the citrate found in banked whole blood, which binds the patient's free calcium. In this case, the administration of calcium chloride would be the therapeutic intervention of choice.

A = airway

Of number one importance in any resuscitation effort is airway management. If a patent A = airway is *not* present, B = breathing will not take place and C = circulation will soon cease. Besides the basic maneuvers of basic life support (the head-tilt, jaw-thrust, and jaw-lift maneuvers), it is sometimes necessary to employ the advantages of an airway adjunct. The following describes commonly used airway adjuncts.

Type of airway	Use	Placement
Oropharyngeal airway	Unconscious patients who may have good respiratory effort	Inserted upside down with curved side facing tongue, rotating 180° while advancing until curve is over tongue and distal opening is in posterior pharyngeal area; alternate placement: use tongue blade to move tongue to one side and visualize placement
Nasopharyngeal airway	Adult unconscious or conscious patients	Lubricate tip with water-soluble anesthetic lubricant; insert through nostril until distal opening reaches posterior pharyngeal area
Esophageal obturator airway	Unconscious, apneic patients	Grasp lower jaw and lift forward, keeping head and neck in neutral or "sniffing" position; advance lubricated tip through mouth past posterior pharyngeal area with tip pointing toward hard palate; rotate tube 180° as it is advanced past tongue and posterior pharyngeal area into esophagus until mask rests firmly against the face; blow into end of tube to assure proper placement; inflate balloon with 30 cc of air
Endotracheal tube	Unconscious or conscious patients (conscious patients will probably require muscle relaxant)	Hold laryngoscope in left hand; insert into mouth along left side; advance until glottic opening can be seen, lifting lower jaw while this is being accomplished; advance endotracheal tube into mouth and down past vocal cords into trachea; inflate balloon/cuff; attach to bag-valve-mask device and inflate lungs, auscultating as this is done to assure proper placement

From Budassi S.A.: J.E.N. **7**(3):127, 1981.

Advantages	Disadvantages	Notes
Rapid access to upper airway; can suction through it; can be used with bag-valve-mask device; may also be used in conjunction with endotracheal intubation to prevent patient from biting on tube	Cannot be used in conscious patient; if improperly placed, may actually push tongue into airway; may induce vomiting if gag reflex present	Once placed, must maintain head-tilt, jaw-thrust, or jaw-lift maneuver
Rapid access to airway; can suction through it; can be used with bag-valve-mask device	May induce vomiting	Once placed, must maintain head-tilt, jaw-thrust, or jaw-lift maneuver
Requires minimal training time; no need to stop chest compressions; prevents aspiration; can administer positive pressure through it; may be used with cervical-spine injury; can endotracheally intubate around it; may be used with bag-valve-mask device, manually operated positive pressure device, or ventilation; may administer 100% O_2	Cannot be used in conscious victims; may pass into trachea; may perforate esophagus; not acceptable for long-term ventilation	Prior to removal deflate balloon and have suction ready; cannot be used in children or adults with esophageal problems
May be placed with esophageal obturator airway in place; may be used with bag-valve-mask device or other positive pressure device; may give positive pressure; may be used for longer period of time than esophageal obturator airway; decreases likilhood of aspiration; may administer 100% O_2; can suction through it	Requires much skill to place; blind nasotracheal intubation difficult on selected patients (e.g., patients with cervical spine injuries); tube may be placed into one of mainstem bronchi; tube may pass into esophagus; chest compression must be interrupted during insertion	Obtain chest x-ray film—if in one of mainstem bronchi must be pulled back until in trachea; in child, use tube the diameter of child's finger

Continued.

A = airway, cont'd

Type of airway	Use	Placement
Transtracheal catheter	Rapid access into blocked upper airway	Locate cricothyroid membrane; prep skin; perforate skin and cartilage with catheter at 45°-angle caudad; advance catheter with negative pressure on syringe until air flows freely and catheter is in trachea
Cricothyrotomy	Rapid access to blocked upper airway	Locate cricothyroid membrane; prep area; spread skin taut; make incision over cartilage through skin; make horizontal puncture into cricothyroid cartilage; rotate scalpel 90° to spread cartilage; insert small tube into opening

AIRWAY MANAGEMENT

Of supreme importance in any emergency situation are the ABCs—airway, breathing, and circulation. As the basic positions of head tilt and chin lift for airway management have been previously discussed, this section will deal with adjuncts for airway management (see pp. 34-37).

Oropharyngeal airway (Fig. 3-8)

The oropharyngeal airway is a curved piece of equipment made of plastic, rubber, or metal. It is inserted over the tongue and into the posterior pharyngeal area. Its primary use is to prevent the tongue from slipping back into the posterior pharyngeal area and thereby occluding the airway. It should be placed either by inserting it upside down with the curved portion facing the tongue and then rotating it as it is advanced into the posterior pharyngeal area or by using a tongue blade or similar piece of equipment to move the tongue out of the way while the airway is being placed.

Remember that if the oropharyngeal airway is not placed properly it may actually push the tongue into the posterior pharyngeal area and cause an airway obstruction. This airway is recommended for use in the unconscious patient who has an adequate respiratory effort. It should not be used in the conscious patient, as it may induce vomiting. Once the airway is in place, strict attention must be paid to maintenance of proper head tilt position or the jaw thrust maneuver.

Advantages	Disadvantages	Notes
Rapid access into blocked airway; may be attached to positive pressure device; can be accomplished without interrupting chest compressions; endotracheal intubation, cricothyrotomy, or tracheostomy can be performed while patient is being ventilated	Cannot suction airway through it; difficult to have passive exhalation; may cause hemorrhage; may perforate thyroid or esophagus; subcutaneous emphysema or mediastinal emphysema	Requires special attachment for positive pressure device
Rapid access into blocked airway; may be attached to positive pressure device if cuffed tube used; may give 100% O_2; can be accomplished without interrupting chest compression; tracheostomy can be performed while patient is being ventilated.	Hemorrhage; may lacerate esophagus; subcutaneous or mediastinal emphysema (later, tracheal stenosis)	Any type of object which will keep airway open may be used (e.g., a drinking straw, barrel of pen)

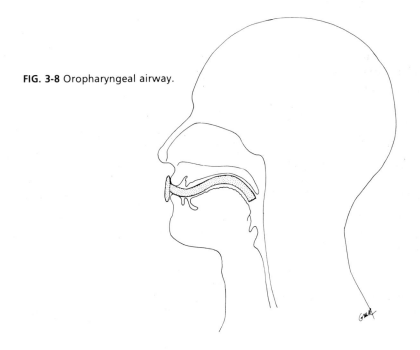

FIG. 3-8 Oropharyngeal airway.

Nasopharyngeal airway (Fig. 3-9)

The nasopharyngeal airway, or trumpet tube (Fig. 3-9) is a soft rubber tube about 6 inches in length. It is inserted through a nostril, using a topical anesthetic lubricant, into the posterior pharyngeal area, posterior to the tongue (Fig. 3-9). This airway is tolerated much better by the alert, oriented patient.

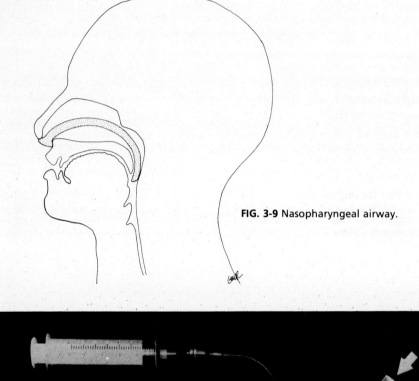

FIG. 3-9 Nasopharyngeal airway.

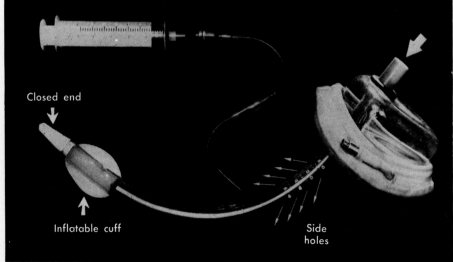

Closed end

Inflatable cuff

Side holes

FIG. 3-10 Esophageal obturator airway. (Brunswick Manufacturing Co., North Quincy, Mass.) (From Stephenson, H.E., Jr.: Cardiac arrest and resuscitation, ed. 4, St. Louis, 1974, The C.V. Mosby Co.)

Esophageal obturator airway

The esophageal obturator airway should only be used on the apneic, unconscious patient. It requires little technical skill and can be inserted by field and emergency personnel untrained in endotracheal intubation. It is a quick and safe procedure and can easily be taught to ambulance personnel and lifeguards.

The esophageal obturator airway has three main parts: (1) the mask, used to seal off the nose and mouth; (2) the tube (with a blocked distal end), which contains perforations in the area of the pharynx (when placed) and through which air escapes and is forced into the trachea (the only unobstructed opening); and (3) the balloon, which, when inflated, prevents aspiration of vomitus and inflation of the stomach (Fig. 3-10).*

INSERTION

1. Grasp the patient's tongue and lower jaw between the index finger and thumb and lift straight forward.
2. Advance the lubricated tube into the posterior pharyngeal area with the tip of the tube pointing upward toward the hard palate.
3. Advance the tube carefully behind the tongue, past the pharynx. Rotate the tube 180° and into the esophagus.
4. Stop when the mask reaches the face; press it firmly against the face with both hands.
5. Blow into the end of the tube with a deep breath. If the tube is in the esophagus, the chest will rise (Fig. 3-11). If the chest does not rise, either there is not a tight seal with

*A modified version with a one-way valve allowing for nasogastric tube placement is currently available.

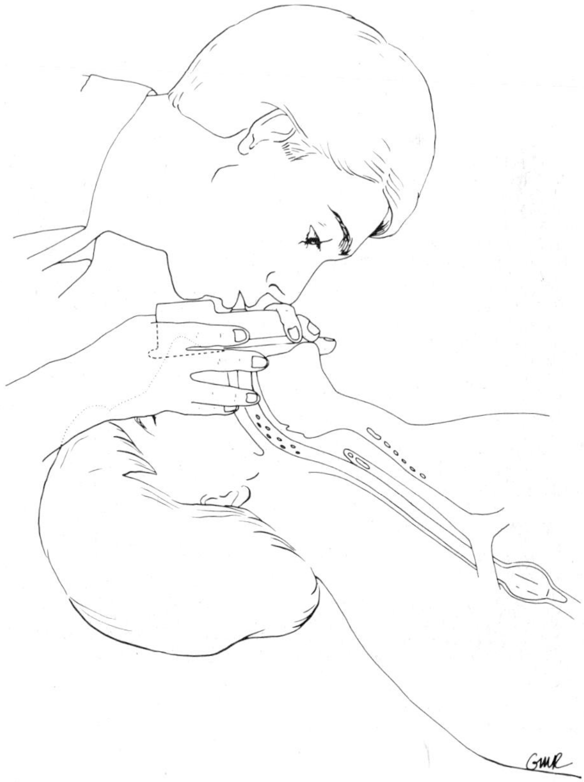

FIG. 3-11 Esophageal obturator airway in place.

the mask or the tube is in the trachea. If the latter is true, remove the tube immediately and make a second attempt.

6. Once the airway is in place, auscultate the chest bilaterally to assure both right and left lung ventilations.
7. Inflate the cuff between ventilations with 35 ml of air via a syringe through the one-way valve.
8. Ventilate the patient.

REMOVAL

1. If the patient is unable to maintain his own respirations, insert an endotracheal tube around the esophageal obturator airway. If the patient has effective spontaneous respirations and a gag reflex, turn him on his side (not necessary with an endotracheal tube).
2. Deflate the cuff.
3. Withdraw the airway. (*Never* withdraw it without first deflating the cuff.)
4. Have suction apparatus available and functioning.

ADVANTAGES

It is easily used; it requires no special insertion equipment and little training. (Personnel may be trained with a mannequin in 15 minutes.)
It may be used in patients with cervical spine injury for whom hyperextension of the neck is contraindicated; placement of the tube can take place with the head and neck in a neutral position.
An endotracheal tube may be placed with the airway in place; endotracheal tube placement may actually be easier.
It prevents aspiration of stomach contents.
It prevents air (from resuscitation) from entering the stomach.
The volume of air delivered is superior to the volumes delivered by bag-valve-mask devices.
The air intake is equal to that provided by endotracheal intubation.
It can be inserted quickly (5 to 30 seconds).

CONTRAINDICATIONS

It cannot be used on conscious or semiconscious patients.
It cannot be used on infants and children. (However, pediatric-size esophageal obturator airways are currently being developed.)
It cannot be used in patients with a history of caustic poison ingestion.
It cannot be used in patients with a history of esophageal disease.
It cannot be used if there is a foreign body in trachea. (Endotracheal intubation is preferable.)

DANGERS

Passing of the airway into the trachea (easy to correct)
Perforation of the esophagus (rare)

Endotracheal intubation (Fig. 3-12)

An endotracheal tube is passed directly into the trachea. Endotracheal intubation requires a great deal of technical skill and may be accomplished in the prehospital

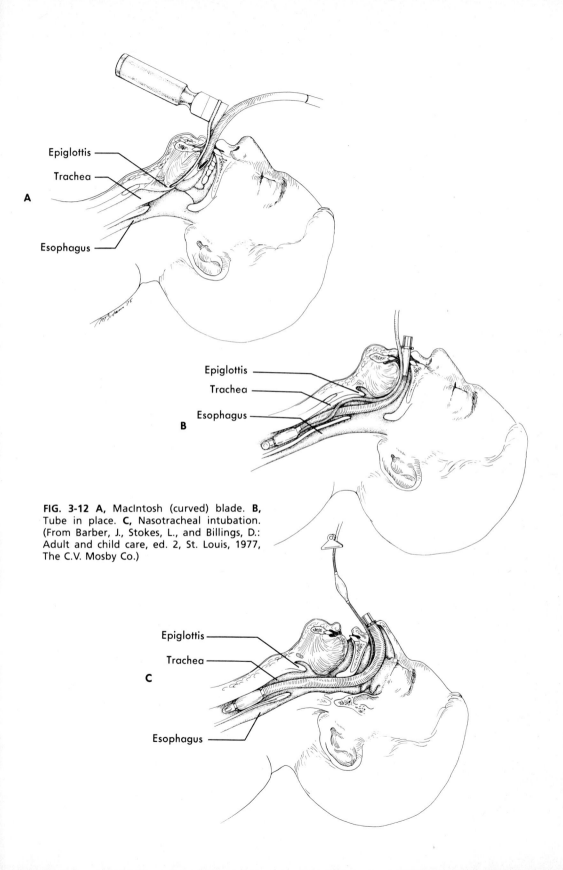

Epiglottis

Trachea

A

Esophagus

Epiglottis

Trachea

Esophagus

B

FIG. 3-12 A, MacIntosh (curved) blade. **B,** Tube in place. **C,** Nasotracheal intubation. (From Barber, J., Stokes, L., and Billings, D.: Adult and child care, ed. 2, St. Louis, 1977, The C.V. Mosby Co.)

Epiglottis

Trachea

C

Esophagus

situation (in accordance with state laws) or in the hospital by trained, skilled individuals. The endotracheal tube is a tube that is open at both ends. It consists of:

Standard 15 mm adapter for use with a bag-valve-mask or other type of resuscitation device

Tube

Cuff, which is located near the distal end of the tube

Other equipment is required for endotracheal intubation, including:

Malleable stylette

Laryngoscope with curved or straight blade

Suction equipment

INSERTION

1. Prepare the equipment.
   a. Insert the malleable stylette into the tube and shape it to the configuration desired, assuring that the stylette does not slip beyond the end of the tube.
   b. Prepare the laryngoscope by connecting the blade to the handle, assuring that the batteries are charged and the light is working.
   c. Ready the suction equipment.
   d. Ready the bag-valve-mask device or respirator.
2. Align the three axes of the mouth, pharynx, and trachea to allow for visualization of the vocal cords (Fig. 3-13) by flexing the neck forward and extending the head back. (Do *not* hang the head over the end of the bed or table.)
3. Insert the laryngoscope blade into the mouth, following the natural curves of the upper airway.
4. Insert the blade just to the right of the midline.
5. Lift up on the laryngoscope to elevate the tongue and shift it to the left side of the mouth. The blade should be in the midline position.

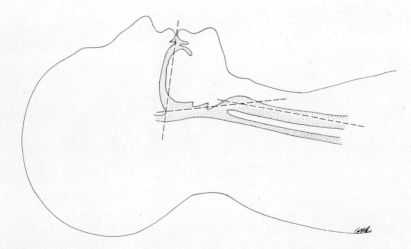

FIG. 3-13. Normal anatomic alignment of upper airway demonstrating the three axes.

6. Advance the laryngoscope until the glottic opening can be seen by placing the curved laryngoscope blade into the space between the base of the tongue and the epiglottis (the vallecula) or by placing the straight laryngoscope blade under the epiglottis. Do *not* pry the laryngoscope against the upper teeth.
7. Hold the laryngoscope in the left hand and advance the endotracheal tube with the right hand, from the right side of the mouth into the trachea.
8. Once the endotracheal tube is in place, inflate the balloon and blow into the airway to check proper positioning; watch to see that the chest rises and auscultate bilateral breath sounds.
9. Deflate the balloon on the esophageal obturator airway and remove it.
10. Attach the tube to the bag-valve-mask device or the respirator.
11. Secure the tube to the patient's face, using tincture of benzoin and adhesive tape.
12. Obtain a portable anterior-posterior chest x-ray film to ensure proper positioning of the tube. If the tube is found to be in the right mainstem bronchus, pull back on it slightly.

If the patient has had spontaneous respirations for 8 hours, the endotracheal tube may be removed (provided arterial blood gases are also at an acceptable level).

REMOVAL

1. Suction the tube and the patient's mouth and posterior pharyngeal area.
2. Deflate the cuff.
3. Withdraw the airway. (*Never* withdraw the airway without deflating the cuff.)
4. Always have suction apparatus ready.
5. Monitor the patient for cardiac dysrhythmias.

ADVANTAGES

It provides control of the airway.
The patient is protected from aspiration.
Intermittent positive pressure breathing with 100% oxygen can be given.
The trachea is easy to suction.
It causes less gastric distention.
Chest compression can be continued after insertion.

DISADVANTAGES

It can easily pass into the esophagus.
A skilled technician is required to place it.
It may cause hypoxia during prolonged insertion.
Chest compression must be interrupted during insertion.

Surgical techniques for airway management

If attempts at airway management with previously mentioned techniques and equipment are not successful and if airway obstruction is present, a surgical procedure for airway management may be attempted. Remember that an airway must be established rapidly for it to be a life-saving technique. There are three surgical procedures that may be used for airway management.

Transtracheal catheter ventilation

If airway obstruction is present, a rapid means of access to the airway is via transtracheal catheter ventilation.

EQUIPMENT

14-gauge (or larger) plastic IV catheter needle
IV extension tubing
Hand-operated release valve
Oxygen source (50 psi)
10 ml syringe
Alcohol swabs

PROCEDURE

1. Locate the cricothyroid membrane.
   a. It extends from the cricoid cartilage to the thyroid cartilage.
   b. Palpate by placing a finger on the Adam's apple and moving the finger downward 3 cm or placing a finger on the thyroid cartilage and moving the finger upward 2 cm.
2. Prepare the area with alcohol or other antiseptic solution.
3. Perforate both skin and cartilage with the catheter attached to the syringe, by directing the catheter down and toward the feet at a 45° angle (Fig. 3-14).

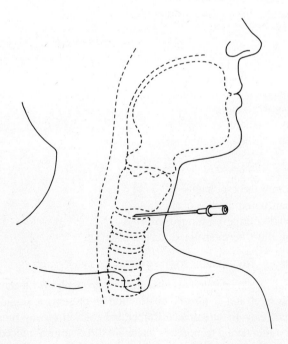

FIG. 3-14 Technique for performing needle cricothyrotomy.

4. Apply negative pressure to the syringe plunger while the catheter is being advanced. When the catheter is in the trachea, air will enter the syringe.
5. Advance the catheter over the stylette.
6. Remove the stylette and the syringe.
7. Attach the IV extension tubing to the catheter.
8. Attach the other end of the IV extension tubing to the oxygen release valve.
9. Press the release valve and introduce oxygen into the trachea. The lungs should inflate, and the chest should rise.
10. When chest rise is seen, release the valve and allow for passive exhalation.
11. Use only the minimum pressure necessary to inflate the lungs.

ADVANTAGES

Intubation can be accomplished during chest compression.
The procedure takes only seconds.
Endotracheal intubation or tracheostomy can be performed while patient is being continuously ventilated.

COMPLICATIONS

Hemorrhage
Perforation of thyroid
Perforation of esophagus
Subcutaneous emphysema
Mediastinal emphysema

Cricothyrotomy

Cricothyrotomy is an alternate method of quick access to a blocked airway, in which a scalpel or other such instrument is used to perforate the cricothyroid membrane to create an opening into the airway.

EQUIPMENT

Alcohol swabs or other antiseptic solution
Scalpel and blade
Suction device
Small airway tube (or other such instrument)

PROCEDURE

1. Identify the cricoid membrane. (See procedure for transtracheal catheterization.)
2. Prepare the skin with alcohol or other antiseptic solution.
3. Spread the overlying skin to make it taut.
4. Make a small incision over the cartilage through the skin using the scalpel.
5. Once the skin is invaded, make a horizontal puncture hole into the cricoid cartilage. (A little bleeding may occur, but usually it is not excessive.)
6. Rotate the scalpel 90° to spread the cartilage (Fig. 3-15).
7. Insert a small tube, such as a No. 6 tracheostomy tube, into the opening. (If a tube is not available, use whatever means is available to maintain an opening.)

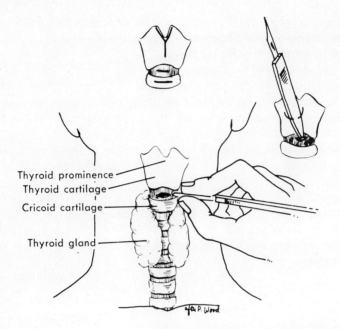

Thyroid prominence
Thyroid cartilage
Cricoid cartilage
Thyroid gland

FIG. 3-15 Cricothyrotomy incision, frontal view. (From Miller, R.H., and Cantrell, J.R.: Textbook of basic emergency medicine, St. Louis, 1975, The C.V. Mosby Co.)

8. Supply oxygen via the opening. (If the patient is apneic, there is need for a cuffed tracheostomy tube and positive pressure breathing.)

ADVANTAGES

It provides rapid entrance into an obstructed airway.
A cuffed tracheostomy tube can be placed quickly for the apneic patient.
An endotracheal tube can be placed while the patient is being continuously ventilated.

COMPLICATIONS

Hemorrhage
Laceration of the esophagus
False passage of the tube
Subcutaneous emphysema
Mediastinal emphysema
Tracheal stenosis (later)

Tracheostomy

Tracheostomy is performed when other attempts at ventilation have failed, and when the rescuer has been unable to obtain control of the airway, usually because of laryngeal edema, foreign body, or tumors.

EQUIPMENT

Tracheostomy tube of appropriate size (available in French sizes 13 to 38 and Jackson
   sizes 00 to 9)
Tracheostomy tape
20-ml syringe
Scalpel handle and blade
Kelly clamp with rubber-coated tips
Scissors
Hemostats
Vein retractor
Suture materials
Tissue forceps
Sterile 4 × 4 inch gauze
Sterile drapes
Suction
Gloves and mask (gown and cap if time permits)
Antiseptic solution
Crash cart (including monitor and defibrillator)

PROCEDURE

 1. Position the patient with a pillow under his shoulders and his neck in extension.
 2. Ventilate the patient via an endotracheal tube, cricothyrotomy, or other method.
 3. Prepare the skin (chin to nipples).
 4. Drape the patient.
 5. Locate the area for the incision, usually the third or fourth tracheal ring in an adult.
 6. Make an incision into the skin. It may be a flap or a horizontal or vertical incision;
    usually a vertical incision is used to avoid arteries, veins, and nerves on the lateral
    borders of the trachea.
 7. Control the bleeding.
 8. Dissect down through the subcutaneous fat and platysma muscle.
 9. Retract the midline muscles.
10. Expose the tracheal rings. Retract the thyroid isthmus cephalad.
11. Inject local anesthesia into the tracheal lumen to decrease the cough reflex.
12. Create a stoma by removing 1 cm^2 of cartilage.
13. Continuously suction to remove blood and secretions.
14. Insert the tracheostomy tube.
15. Assure correct tube position by checking for air movement.
16. Attach the tube to a ventilation device.
17. Auscultate the lungs.
18. Inflate the cuff.
19. Suture the corners of the incision loosely.
20. Secure the tube with tracheostomy tape.
21. Dress the wound.
22. Obtain a follow-up chest x-ray film.

ADVANTAGES

It reduces physiologic dead space.
It allows for prolonged positive pressure breathing.
It allows direct access to the respiratory tract for secretion removal.

COMPLICATIONS

Inaccurate tube placement	Perforation of the esophagus
Laceration of arteries, veins, and nerves	Subcutaneous emphysema
Hemorrhage	Mediastinal emphysema
Pressure necrosis from cuff	

BREATHING

There are various devices available for oxygen administration. The most commonly used of these is the *nasal cannula*. This device can only be used on a patient who is breathing spontaneously. At a flow rate of 6 liters/minute an oxygen concentration of 25% to 40% can be achieved.

Face mask (Fig. 3-16)

Face masks are usually tolerated well, except by patients who are experiencing severe dyspnea and the feeling of suffocation. A flow rate of 10 liters/minute can provide an oxygen concentration of 50% to 60%.

Oxygen reservoir mask

The oxygen reservoir mask is equipped with a plastic bag reservoir. While the patient is exhaling, the bag fills with 100% oxygen; at a flow rate of 10 to 12 liters/minute, when the patient inspires, he may receive a concentration of approximately 90% oxygen (if the mask has a tight seal).

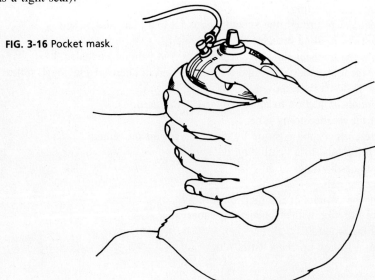

FIG. 3-16 Pocket mask.

Venturi mask

The Venturi mask should be used on a patient who has a history of chronic obstructive pulmonary disease, who is currently experiencing respiratory distress, and who may experience respiratory depression if given too high a concentration of oxygen. The Venturi mask allows for delivery of a fixed oxygen concentration. By adjusting the oxygen flow rate and the meter on the mask; one can achieve the following oxygen concentrations:

4-liter oxygen flow: 24% and 28% oxygen delivery

8-liter oxygen flow: 35% and 40% oxygen delivery

The 24% oxygen concentration setting is used initially and the patient is observed closely for respiratory depression. If the patient appears to be tolerating the 24% concentration well, the oxygen concentration is increased to 28%, and so on.

Pocket mask

The pocket mask can be carried by the rescuer in a compact form. It has an opening in the top to allow for mouth-to-mask breathing. The mask is fit snugly onto the patient's face, using two hands. The head is tilted back and the jaw is pulled forward, with the mouth slightly open. The rescuer then blows into the mask.

Supplemental oxygen may be given by attaching the oxygen source to the one-way valve nipple in the mask. A flow of 10 liters/minute provides an oxygen concentration of about 50%.

The mask may be turned upside down to allow for pediatric use, with the wide end at the top of the child's head and the narrow end just below his mouth.

Bag-valve-mask

Bag-valve-mask devices deliver room air (21% oxygen) to the patient. An additional oxygen source of 12 liters/minute can provide an oxygen concentration of 40%. By adding a plastic cap and a reservoir of 3 feet of corrugated tubing with an open end, an oxygen concentration of approximately 90% can be achieved (Fig. 3-17). The mask is

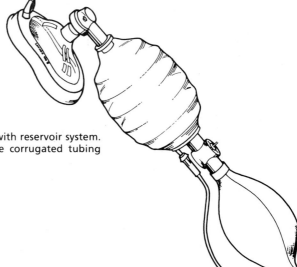

FIG. 3-17 Bag-valve-mask device with reservoir system. Some bag-valve-mask devices use corrugated tubing instead of reservoir bag.

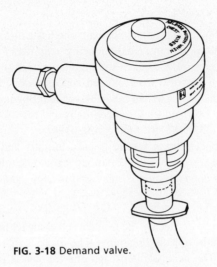

FIG. 3-18 Demand valve.

applied in the same way as the pocket mask. An oropharyngeal or nasopharyngeal airway would be appropriate to use in conjunction with the bag-valve-mask.

Although there are several commercial brands of bag-valve-mask devices on the market, a transparent device is recommended. This allows for observation and rapid intervention should emesis occur.

Oxygen-powered devices

One hundred percent oxygen delivered at a rate of 100 liters/minute may be delivered by an oxygen-powered breathing device to a mask, an esophageal obturator airway, an endotracheal tube, or a tracheostomy tube. The key to successful use of this device is timing and length of oxygen delivery time by manual triggering (Fig. 3-18). This device should *not* be used in children under 12 years of age unless a special low-flow control adapter is available.

CIRCULATION

When initiating chest compression during cardiopulmonary resuscitation, be sure that the patient is on a firm surface. The victim may have to be removed from a bed and placed on the floor or another firm surface, or a cardiac board may be placed under him in bed. If this is not done, pressure exerted to compress the chest will be transmitted into the soft surface, and very little chest compression will occur. The use of a mechanical chest compressor may be considered. There are several types of chest compressors commercially available. One manually operated compressor has a hinged device, at one end of which is a plunger that can be adjusted to provide a given chest-compression depth. An automatic gas-powered chest compressor is available in which the compressor plunger is powered by compressed gas. This plunger may also be adjusted to the desired depth of chest compression.

As time goes on there will be more and more resuscitation "aids" available. Several

TABLE 3-1 Summary of oxygen assist devices

Type of breathing device	Oxygen flow rate	Oxygen concentrations	Advantages	Disadvantages
Nasal cannula	2-6 liters/min	25%-40%	No rebreathing of expired air	Can only be used on patients who are breathing spontaneously
Face mask	10 liters/min	50%-60%	Higher oxygen concentration than nasal cannula or face mask	Not tolerated well by severely dyspneic patients; can only be used on patients who are breathing spontaneously
Oxygen reservoir mask	10-12 liters/min	90%	Higher oxygen concentration than nasal cannula or face mask	Must have tight seal on mask; can only be used on patients who are breathing spontaneously
Venturi mask	4 liters/min 8 liters/min	24%-28% 35%-40%	Fixed oxygen concentration	Can only be used on patients who are breathing spontaneously
Pocket mask	10 liters/min	50%	Avoids direct contact with patient's mouth; may add oxygen source; may be used on apneic patient; may be used on child	Rescuer fatigue
Bag-valve-mask	Room air 12 liters/min	21% 40%-90%	Quick; oxygen concentration may be increased; rescuer can sense lung compliance; may be used on both apneic and spontaneously breathing patients	Air in stomach; low tidal volume
Oxygen-powered breathing device	100 liters/min	100%	High oxygen flow, positive pressure	Gastric distention; overinflation; standard device cannot be used in children without special adapter

items are currently being evaluated for use. Among these is the abdominal belt, which can inflate and deflate a set number of times each minute to increase intrathoracic pressure. Another item, called CPR vest also inflates and deflates at a set rate every minute to increase intrathoracic pressure.

Dysrhythmia management

During a cardiopulmonary arrest situation it is important to be able to interpret cardiac dysrhythmias and apply therapeutic interventions accurately and rapidly. It is important, however, to develop a method of dysrhythmia interpretation that allows for speed and accuracy. First assess the rhythm. Is it regular, irregular, or regularly irregular? Next, assess the rate. Is it fast, slow, or normal? Next, check for the presence or absence of P waves. If they are present, are they the same or different in configuration? Check the QRS complex. Is it present or absent? If it is present, is it wide or narrow? Is it a positive inflection or a negative deflection? Is the direction of the QRS correct for the lead being observed? Next, check to see if there is a relationship between the P waves and the QRS complexes. Is there a P wave for each QRS? Is there a QRS for each P wave? Finally, check the PR interval.

Dysrhythmia interpretation is important, but do not forget to observe the patient—treat the patient and not just the dysrhythmia. *Text continued on p. 77.*

Cardiac dysrhythmias
DYSRHYTHMIAS ORIGINATING IN THE SINUS NODE
Normal sinus rhythm

Rate	60 to 100 beats/minute
Rhythm	Regular
P waves	Present
QRS complex	Present; normal duration
P/QRS relationship	P wave preceding each QRS complex
PR interval	Normal

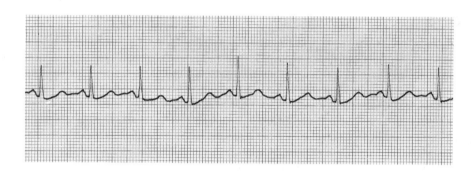

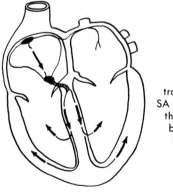

Impulse
travels from
SA to AV node
through His
bundle to
Purkinje
fibers

Significance: The SA node is the normal pacemaker of the heart; it is influenced both by the parasympathetic and the sympathetic branches of the autonomic nervous system.
Therapeutic intervention: None required.

Sinus tachycardia

Rate	>100 beats/minute
Rhythm	Regular
P waves	Present
QRS complexes	Present, normal duration
P/QRS relationship	P wave preceding each QRS complex
PR interval	Normal

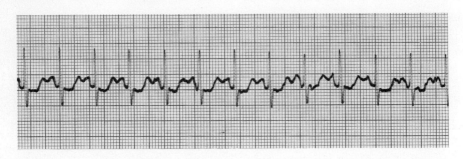

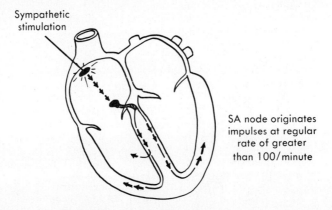

Sympathetic stimulation

SA node originates impulses at regular rate of greater than 100/minute

Significance: The normal pacemaker of the heart is firing at an increased rate because of anxiety, fever, pain, exercise, smoking, hyperthyroidism, heart failure, volume loss, or other reasons that may cause increased tissue oxygen demands. This condition may also be caused by decreased vagal tone (parasympathetic decrease), which allows the sinus node to increase its rate.

Therapeutic intervention: Treat the cause. There is no specific drug given for sinus tachycardia except in the face of congestive heart failure; then digitalis is usually the drug of choice. If sinus tachycardia is the dysrhythmia seen following cardiopulmonary arrest, a Swan-Ganz catheter should be placed and the wedge pressure should be maintained at 15 to 18 mm Hg.

Sinus bradycardia

Rate	<60 beats/minute
Rhythm	Regular
P waves	Present
QRS complexes	Present; normal duration
P/QRS relationship	P wave preceding each QRS complex
PR interval	Normal

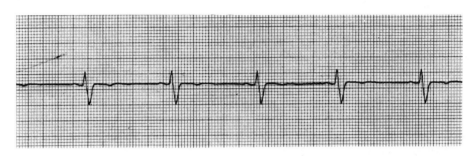

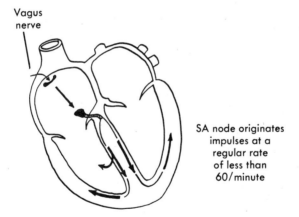

Vagus nerve

SA node originates impulses at a regular rate of less than 60/minute

Significance: The normal pacemaker, the SA node, is slowed by increased vagal tone (parasympathetic stimulation); causes include sleep, a normal athletic heart, anoxia, hypothyroidism, increased intracranial pressure, acute myocardial infarction, and vagal stimulation (such as vomiting, straining at stool, carotid sinus massage, or ocular pressure). It may also be caused by beta-blocker medications or may occur after cardioversion.

Therapeutic intervention: Observe the patient for symptoms such as a decrease in blood pressure, a decreasing level of consciousness, syncope, shock, or acidosis.

1. Stop digitalis administration and concurrently administer oxygen.
2. Treat with atropine or isoproterenol (Isuprel) or a pacemaker if the patient develops symptoms (e.g., severe hypotension).

Sinus dysrhythmia

Rate	60 to 100 beats, but this may increase with inspiration and decrease with expiration
Rhythm	Irregular
P waves	Present
QRS complexes	Present; normal duration
P/QRS relationship	P wave preceding each QRS complex
PR interval	Normal

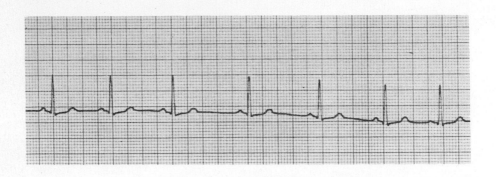

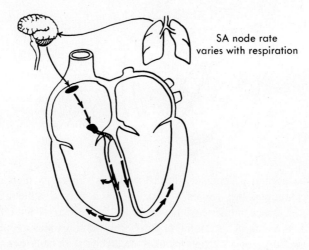

SA node rate
varies with respiration

Significance: This dysrhythmia is a normal finding in children and young adults in whom there is a variation of vagal tone in response to respirations. For this variance to be considered a dysrhythmia, the variation must exceed 0.12 second between the longest and shortest cycles.

Therapeutic intervention: None required.

DYSRHYTHMIAS ORIGINATING IN THE ATRIA
Premature atrial contractions (PACs, extrasystoles)

Rate	Usually 60 to 100 beats/minute
Rhythm	Usually regularly irregular
P waves	Present, but premature P wave may appear different in configuration (because it did not originate in the SA node)
QRS complexes	Present; normal duration
P/QRS relationship	P wave preceding each QRS complex
PR interval	Usually normal

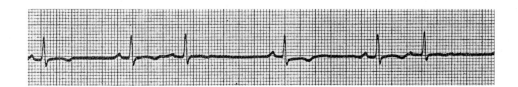

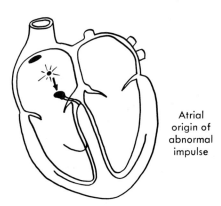

Atrial
origin of
abnormal
impulse

Significance: PACs are the result of an irritable ectopic focus that may be caused by fatigue, alcohol, coffee, smoking, digoxin, congestive heart failure, or ischemia; sometimes the etiology is unknown. They may be a prelude to atrial fibrillation, atrial flutter, or paroxysmal atrial tachycardia.

Therapeutic intervention: Treatment is usually unnecessary but should be given if more than 6 PACs occur per minute and the patient is becoming symptomatic. Oxygen should be the drug of choice, followed by quinidine, procainamide, or digitalis. If alcohol, coffee, or tobacco is the cause, advise the patient to eliminate it.

Wandering atrial pacemaker

Rate	Usually 60 to 100 beats/minute
Rhythm	Usually regular or slightly irregular
P waves	Present; configuration varies
QRS complexes	Present; normal duration
P/QRS relationship	P wave preceding each QRS
PR interval	Normal

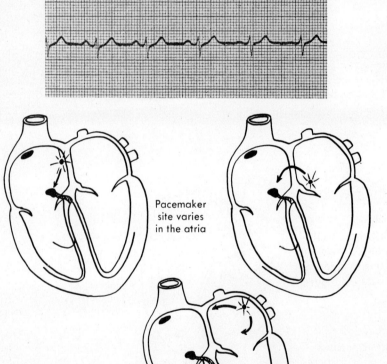

Pacemaker site varies in the atria

Significance: Either the SA node is suppressed or other atrial foci become excited and take over the pacemaker function of the heart.

Therapeutic intervention: Treatment is usually unnecessary. If the patient is receiving digitalis, it may be wise to withhold the digitalis and obtain a serum digoxin level.

Paroxysmal atrial tachycardia (PAT)

Rate	160 beats/minute
Rhythm	Regular
P waves	May be hidden in T wave of previous beat
QRS complexes	Present; normal duration
P/QRS relationship	P wave preceding each QRS complex, but it may be difficult to see; if there is PAT with block, there will not be a QRS complex following each P wave
PR interval	Normal

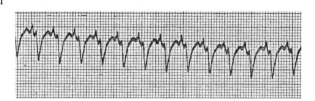

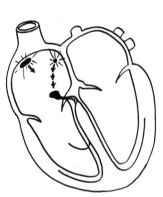

Irritable
focus in
atrial wall
beats regularly
at rate of
160-240/minute

Significance: The onset of this dysrhythmia is usually sudden, as is its cessation. A pacemaker cell in the atrial wall becomes irritable and fires at a rate of 160 to 240 beats/minute, involving reentry in the AV node or a persistent ectopic focus. The danger of this dysrhythmia is that continuous rapid firing could lead to decreased ventricular filling and, consequently, decreased coronary artery filling and perfusion. This is an extremely dangerous event for those who have a history of coronary artery disease, as myocardial infarction may result. PAT may also cause pulmonary edema, congestive heart failure, or shock associated with left ventricular failure. Common causes of this dysrhythmia include digitalis toxicity, Wolff-Parkinson-White syndrome, chronic obstructive pulmonary disease (COPD), rheumatic heart disease, and ischemic heart disease.
Therapeutic intervention: Therapeutic intervention includes the administration of oxygen, an IV of D5W TKO, and vagal stimulation using carotid sinus massage (first checking for bruits), Valsalva maneuver, or immersion of the face in ice water. In addition, pharmacologic intervention could include the administration of verapamil, a calcium channel blocker; edrophonium chloride (Tensilon); or metaraminol (Aramine). If these therapeutic interventions fail and the patient is becoming severely symptomatic, application of synchronous cardioversion should be considered. If synchronous cardioversion is not successful atrial pacemaker insertion should be considered. NOTE: If PAT is present in conjunction with a cardiac aberrancy the resultant rhythm may be mistaken for ventricular tachycardia. Remember: treat the patient.

Atrial flutter

Rate	Atrial rate of 240 to 360 beats/minute
Rhythm	Regular or irregular
P waves	Saw-toothed pattern
QRS complexes	Present; normal duration
P/QRS relationship	Because of rapid atrial rate, ventricular response will vary; there may be a regular or an irregular response
PR interval	Irregular

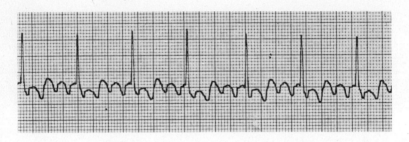

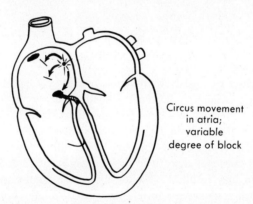

Circus movement
in atria;
variable
degree of block

Significance: An irritable focus in the atria is responsible for this dysrhythmia. The atrial pacemaker fires at such a rapid rate that there is a variable block at the AV node, so that only every other, every third, or every fourth impulse reaches the ventricles. The ventricular response may be regular or irregular. Atrial flutter is a dangerous dysrhythmia in that ineffective atrial contraction may cause mural clots to form in the atria and consequently break loose, forming pulmonary or cerebral emboli. Atrial flutter may be seen in coronary artery disease, rheumatic heart disease, and hyperthyroidism.

Therapeutic intervention: Check the apical and radial pulses for perfusion. The treatment of choice is usually digitalization following synchronous cardioversion. Quinidine may be administered following reduction of the ventricular response by digitalis. Procainamide or propranolol (Inderal) may be given.

Atrial fibrillation

Rate	Atrial rate 400 to 800 beats/minute; ventricular rate varies
Rhythm	Ventricular rhythm *always* irregular
P waves	Irregular, rapid; appears like fibrillating baseline; P waves indistinguishable
QRS complexes	Irregular rhythm, but normal duration
P/QRS relationship	Indistinguishable P waves; irregular ventricular response
PR interval	Indistinguishable

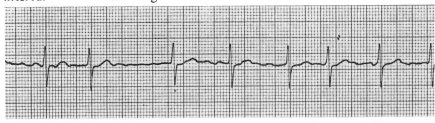

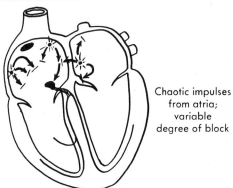

Chaotic impulses
from atria;
variable
degree of block

Significance: Multiple atrial pacemakers fire chaotically in rapid succession. The atria never firmly contract. The ventricles react in a sporadic fashion. Because of poor atrial emptying there is danger of mural clot formation and embolism. Cardiac output drops 15% to 20% because of lack of atrial kick. This dysrhythmia is frequently seen in the presence of coronary artery disease, pericarditis, congestive heart failure, rheumatic heart disease, infection, pulmonary embolus, and hyperthyroidism and with the use of propranolol and verapamil and, most commonly, with digitalis toxicity.

Therapeutic intervention: Check the ventricular response, both on the monitor and by checking peripheral pulses. Check the patient's blood pressure. If the patient is severely symptomatic (syncope, altered level of consciousness, deteriorating vital signs, and chest pain) synchronous cardioversion should be administered. If the patient has been on digitalis therapy, a serum digoxin level should be obtained before cardioversion. If the patient has not been on digitalis therapy before the onset of this dysrhythmia, he may be treated with digitalis or quinidine following a successful synchronous cardioversion. On occasion this dysrhythmia may be converted by placing the patient on bed rest and sedating him.

DYSRHYTHMIAS ORIGINATING IN THE AV NODE
Nodal (junctional) rhythm

Rate	Usually 40 to 60 beats/minute
Rhythm	Regular
P waves	May appear inverted or may not be present
QRS complexes	Regular; normal duration
P/QRS relationship	P wave may appear inverted before or after the QRS complex or may be entirely absent
PR interval	Less than 0.12 when P wave is present preceding QRS

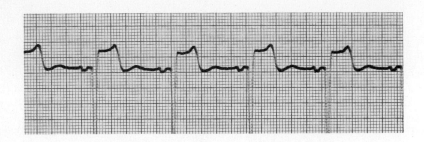

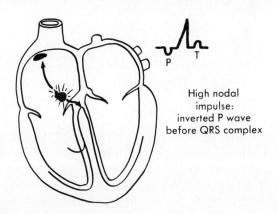

High nodal
impulse:
inverted P wave
before QRS complex

Significance: Usually when higher pacemakers in the atria fail, the AV node takes over as the pacemaker of the heart.

Therapeutic intervention: If the patient has been on digitalis therapy, withhold digitalis and obtain a serum digoxin level to check for digitalis toxicity. There is no specific therapy for this dysrhythmia. If the patient becomes symptomatic (syncope, altered level of consciousness, and chest pain) as a result of the slow heart rate, give atropine sulfate. If the atropine is found to be unsuccessful, isoproterenol would be the next drug of choice, given by IV drip. If both of these drugs are unsuccessful, pacemaker insertion would then be indicated.

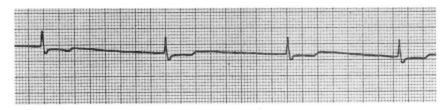

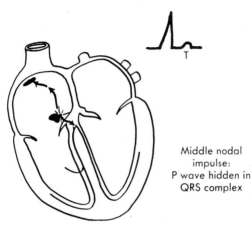

Middle nodal
impulse:
P wave hidden in
QRS complex

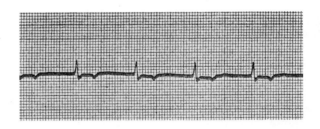

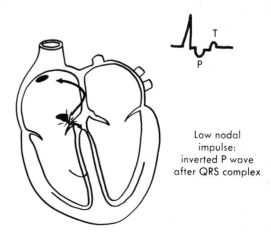

Low nodal
impulse:
inverted P wave
after QRS complex

Premature nodal contractions (PNCs)

Rate	Usually normal or bradycardic
Rhythm	Irregularly irregular
P waves	May appear inverted or may not be present
QRS complexes	Regular; normal duration
P/QRS relationship	P waves may appear inverted before or after the QRS complex or may be absent; entire P/QRS complex is early
PR interval	Less than 0.12 when P wave is seen in premature beat

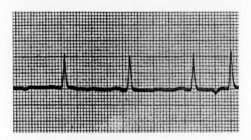

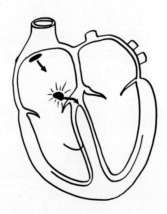

Significance: The AV junction is the pacemaker. The dysrhythmia is less frequently seen than PACs or PVCs; it may precede first, second, or third degree heart block.

Therapeutic intervention: If the patient is on digitalis therapy, withhold digitalis and obtain a serum digoxin level. Observe closely. Pharmacologic therapy may include quinidine or procainamide. Alcohol, coffee, and tobacco should be held from the patient's daily routine.

Nodal tachycardia (junctional tachycardia)

Rate	100 to 180 beats/minute
Rhythm	Regular
P waves	May appear inverted or may not be present
QRS complexes	Regular; normal duration
P/QRS relationship	P waves may appear inverted before or after the QRS complex or may be absent
PR interval	<0.12 when P wave is present

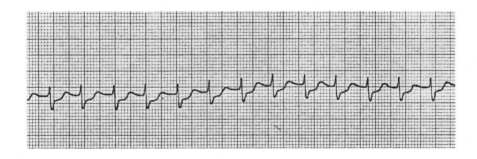

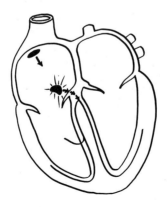

Significance: An irritable nodal focus takes over as the heart's pacemaker.
Therapeutic intervention: Check vital signs; if the patient is on digitalis therapy, withhold digitalis and obtain a serum digoxin level. Usually no other treatment is necessary.

First degree AV block

Rate	Usually 60 to 100 beats/minute
Rhythm	Usually regular
P waves	Present
QRS complexes	Regular; normal duration
P/QRS relationship	P wave preceding each QRS complex
PR interval	>0.20 seconds

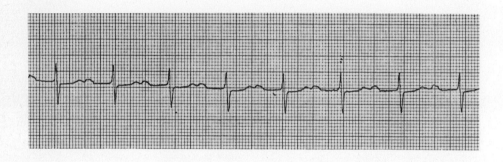

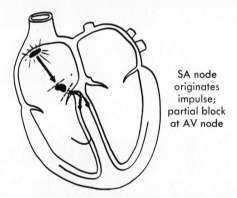

SA node
originates
impulse;
partial block
at AV node

Significance: The SA node initiates an impulse that is delayed through the AV node. This may be caused by anoxia, ischemia of the myocardium, AV node malfunction, edema following open heart surgery, myocarditis, thyrotoxicosis, rheumatic fever, and certain drugs, including digitalis, clonidine, and tricyclic antidepressants.

Therapeutic intervention: Treat the underlying cause. If the patient is on digitalis therapy, withhold digitalis and obtain a serum digoxin level. Administer oxygen and observe the patient for a higher degree of block. If the patient becomes symptomatic (syncope, altered level of consciousness, chest pain), administer atropine. If atropine administration is unsuccessful, administer isoproterenol via IV drip. If isoproterenol administration is unsuccessful, prepare for pacemaker placement.

Second degree AV block—Mobitz type I (Wenckebach phenomenon)

Rate	Usually normal
Rhythm	Regularly irregular
P waves	One preceding each QRS complex except for regular dropped ventricular conduction at intervals
QRS complexes	Cyclic missed conduction; when QRS complex is present, it is of normal duration
P/QRS relationship	P wave before each QRS complex except for regular dropped ventricular conduction at intervals
PR interval	Lengthens with each cycle until one QRS complex is dropped, then repeats

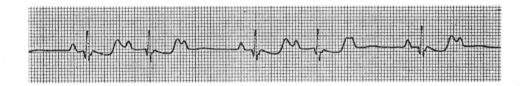

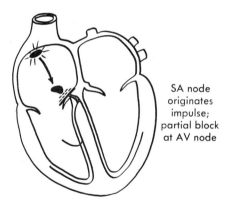

SA node
originates
impulse;
partial block
at AV node

Significance: Each atrial impulse takes longer to travel through the AV node, until a beat is finally dropped, and the entire cycle repeats itself. Although its cause is not well understood, this dysrhythmia is commonly seen following inferior wall myocardial infarction or any other disorder that affects conduction through the AV node or the bundle of His, such as digitalis intoxication or myocarditis.

Therapeutic intervention: If the patient is on digitalis therapy, withhold digitalis and obtain a serum digoxin level. Observe for further dysrhythmia development. If perfusion is impaired or serious dysrhythmias result from bradycardia, consider pacemaker placement.

Second degree AV block—Mobitz type II

Rate	Atrial rate usually 60 to 100 beats/minute; ventricular rate usually slow
Rhythm	Regularly irregular (usually)
P waves	Two or more for every QRS complex
QRS complexes	Normal duration when present
P/QRS relationship	Two or more nonconducted impulses appearing as P waves without QRS complexes following
PR interval	Normal or delayed on the conducted beat; but remains same throughout the dysrhythmia

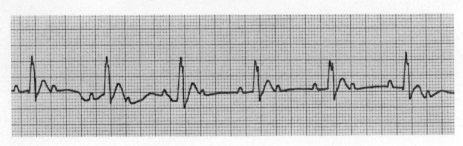

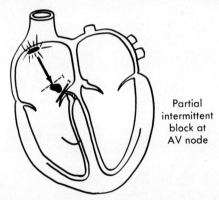

Partial
intermittent
block at
AV node

Significance: One or more atrial impulses is not conducted through the AV node to the ventricles. This is usually the result of an anterior wall myocardial infarction but may also be caused by anoxia, digitalis toxicity, edema following open heart surgery, or hyperkalemia.

Therapeutic intervention: If the patient is symptomatic or in danger of developing a higher degree of block, administer atropine. If atropine is unsuccessful, administer isoproterenol. If isoproterenol is unsuccessful, prepare for pacemaker insertion. If the patient is on digitalis therapy, withhold digitalis and obtain a serum digoxin level. If hyperkalemia is the cause of the dysrhythmia, administer sodium polystyrene sulfonate (Kayexalate) enema. Always administer supplemental oxygen.

Third degree AV block—Stokes-Adams syndrome

Rate	Atrial rate 60 to 100 beats/minute; ventricular asystole
Rhythm	Irregular
P waves	Occur regularly
QRS complexes	Absent during episode
P/QRS relationship	P waves present; absence of QRS complex during episode
PR interval	None during episode

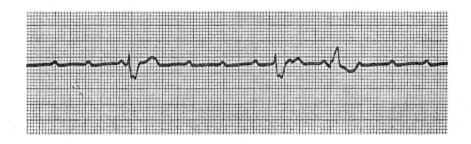

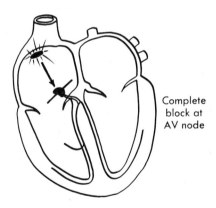

Complete block at AV node

Significance: The SA node initiates an impulse that is not conducted through the AV node. The ventricles do not contract, and there is no cardiac output during the episode, resulting in poor peripheral perfusion and cerebral ischemia, which results in a syncopal episode. This syncopal episode may be followed by asystole if the temporary asystole lasts for more than just a few seconds.

Therapeutic intervention: Take precautions against seizures; prepare to perform basic and advanced cardiac life support if asystole lasts for more than a few seconds. The patient should be treated with isoproterenol followed by pacemaker insertion. Also give an initial bolus of atropine while the isoproterenol drip is being prepared.

Third degree AV block—complete heart block

Rate	Atrial rate, 60 to 100 beats/minute; ventricular rate usually <60 beats/minute
Rhythm	Usually normal
P waves	Occur regularly
QRS complexes	Slow; usually wide (0.10 second)
P/QRS relationship	Completely independent of each other
PR interval	Inconsistent

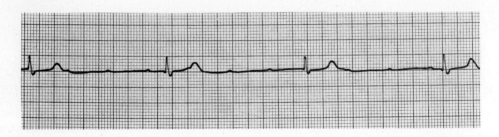

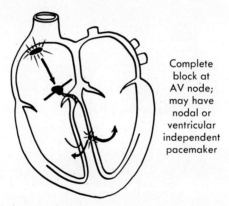

Complete block at AV node; may have nodal or ventricular independent pacemaker

Significance: In this dysrhythmia there is no conduction of the SA node impulse through the AV node. The ventricle begins to initiate its own impulse; the atria and ventricles beat independently of each other. Causes may include digitalis toxicity, diaphragmatic or anterior myocardial infarction, myocarditis, or accidental injury during open heart surgery.

Therapeutic intervention: If the patient is on digitalis therapy, withhold digitalis and obtain a digoxin level. Observe the ventricular rate closely. If the ventricular rate is slow, the patient will most likely be symptomatic (syncope, altered level of consciousness, and chest pain), and cardiac failure may soon result. Therapeutic intervention is the placement of a pacemaker. Atropine or isoproterenol may be an effective temporary measure until the pacemaker is in place. Be prepared to perform both basic and advanced life support.

Rapid AV dissociation

Rate	May or may not be normal
Rhythm	QRS complexes regular
P waves	Vary; may be sinus, atrial, or nodal
QRS complexes	Usually regular; normal duration or wide
P/QRS relationship	Varies; usually no relationship
PR interval	Inconsistent

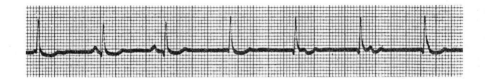

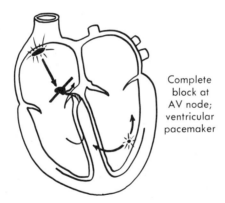

Complete block at AV node; ventricular pacemaker

Significance: The sinus node initiates an impulse but it is blocked by the AV node. The AV node also initiates impulses, as does the ventricular pacemaker(s). The AV node is so irritated that the P wave may actually pass through the QRS complex and the impulse is conducted in a retrograde fashion.

Therapeutic intervention: Observe the patient carefully. If he is symptomatic (syncope, altered level of consciousness, and chest pain) prepare for pacemaker insertion. Administer atropine IV followed by isoproterenol by IV drip while preparing pacemaker equipment. Withhold digoxin preparations.

DYSRHYTHMIAS ORIGINATING IN THE VENTRICLES
Premature ventricular contractions (premature ectopic beats, extrasystoles, PVCs, PVBs, VPBs)

Rate	Usually 60 to 100 beats/minute
Rhythm	Irregular
P waves	Present with each sinus beat; do not precede PVCs
QRS complexes	Sinus-initiated QRS complex normal; QRS of PVC wide and bizarre, >0.10 second; full compensatory pause
P/QRS relationship	P wave before each QRS complex in normal sinus beats; no P wave preceding PVC
PR interval	Normal in sinus beat; none in PVC

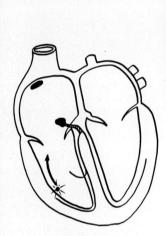

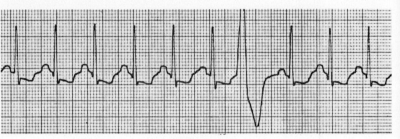

Single PVC

Significance: PVCs are indicative of an irritable ventricle. PVCs come from an impulse initiated by a ventricular pacemaker cell. They may occur as a result of hypoxia, hypovolemia, ischemia, infarction, hypocalcemia, hyperkalemia, or acidosis or the use of alcohol, tobacco, coffee, or many other drugs. PVCs may originate from the same focus (unifocal PVCs) or from various foci (multifocal PVCs). Multifocal PVCs appear to be of different configurations. PVCs may occur in repetitious patterns. If they occur every other beat the condition is called bigeminy. If they occur every third beat it is called trigeminy. If they occur in a pair they are called a couplet. If three occur together they are called a triplet. A series of six or more consecutive PVCs is commonly known as ventricular tachycardia.

Therapeutic intervention: If the cause of the PVCs is known, treat the cause. If the patient is hypoxic, administer oxygen. If the patient is hypovolemic, initiate volume replacement. If the cause is a serum electrolyte imbalance, correct the imbalance. If the cause cannot be isolated, administer lidocaine in the form of an IV bolus followed by additional boluses or an IV drip. Other drugs that may be administered are atropine (if the PVCs are rate related), procainamide, quinidine, phenytoin, bretylium, or propranolol.

Ventricular tachycardia (V tach)

Rate	150 to 250 beats/minute
Rhythm	May be only slightly irregular
P waves	Not seen
QRS complexes	Wide and bizarre
P/QRS relationship	None
PR interval	None

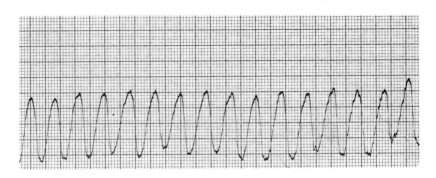

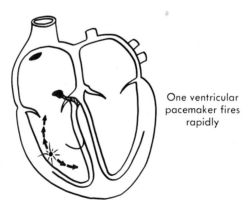

One ventricular
pacemaker fires
rapidly

Significance: This rhythm is actually several PVCs consecutively. It cannot be tolerated for long periods of time. If it does not dissipate by itself, it will deteriorate to ventricular fibrillation. Because the ventricular rate is so fast, there is essentially little cardiac output, and cardiac arrest will soon result.

Therapeutic intervention: If a defibrillator is close by, immediately begin defibrillation or synchronous cardioversion (opinions vary as to the dosage). If the patient appears to be tolerating the dysrhythmia relatively well, administer a bolus of lidocaine before defibrillation. Administer oxygen as well. If attempt(s) to defibrillate are unsuccessful and the patient becomes unconscious, pulseless, and apneic, immediately begin basic and advanced cardiac life support.

Ventricular fibrillation

Rate	Rapid, disorganized
Rhythm	Irregular
P waves	Not seen
QRS complexes	Sometimes not seen; other times extremely bizarre, wide patterns, appearing like baseline oscillations
P/QRS relationship	None
PR interval	None

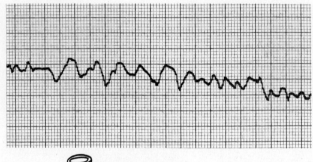

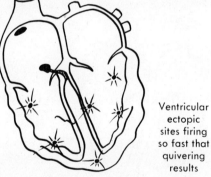

Ventricular
ectopic
sites firing
so fast that
quivering
results

Significance: This is the most common dysrhythmia seen in cardiopulmonary arrest. It produces essentially no cardiac output; death will result if it is allowed to persist for more than 4 to 6 minutes. It is often initiated by ventricular tachycardia.

Therapeutic intervention: Begin basic and advanced cardiac life support immediately. Administer oxygen at 100% concentration under positive pressure; administer epinephrine IV and sodium bicarbonate IV. Allow the drugs to circulate for 90 seconds and reevaluate the rhythm—if it is the same, defibrillate the patient at 400 watt-seconds. If this is unsuccessful, the following treatments may be tried: (1) bretylium, (2) two electric discharges in rapid succession, (3) increased paddle size, (4) anterior-posterior paddle placement, (5) atropine 1 mg by IV push (to decrease vagal tone), (6) calcium chloride, and (7) isoproterenol. If ventricular fibrillation is recurrent, the following may be given: (1) atropine, (2) lidocaine (''slow bolus''), or (3) procainamide. If resuscitation is successful, the underlying cause of the arrest must be corrected.

Asystole (ventricular standstill)

Rate	None
Rhythm	None
P waves	May or may not appear
QRS complexes	None
P/QRS relationship	None
PR interval	None

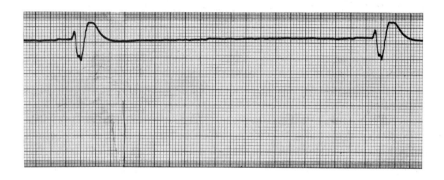

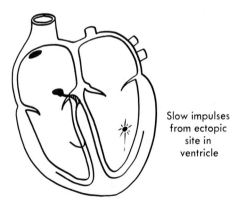

Slow impulses
from ectopic
site in
ventricle

Significance: Asystole often implies that the patient has been in cardiopulmonary arrest for a prolonged period; mortality is high (greater than 95%).

Therapeutic intervention: Do *not* defibrillate. Give 100% oxygen under positive pressure, IV or intracardiac epinephrine, calcium gluconate or calcium chloride, and sodium bicarbonate IV; allow the first two drugs to circulate for 90 seconds. If this is unsuccessful, repeat the treatment and give atropine (to decrease vagal tone increased by myocardial infarction and maneuvers such as defibrillation and intubation). Isoproterenol by IV bolus or intracardiac or pacemaker insertion may be tried.

Idioventricular rhythm

Rate	Usually less than 20 beats/minute
Rhythm	Regular or irregular
P waves	None
QRS complexes	Wide and bizarre
P/QRS relationship	None
PR interval	None

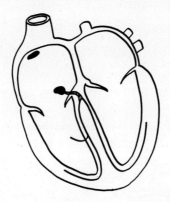

Significance: This dysrhythmia is associated with a poor prognosis; it probably indicates a large myocardial infarction with concurrent loss of a large amount of ventricular mass.
Therapeutic intervention: Give atropine; repeat if unsuccessful. Give isoproterenol. Administer a fluid challenge (200 ml IV over 2 to 5 minutes). Consider pacemaker insertion or open chest massage.

Intratracheal administration of medications in cardiac arrest

The intravenous route of drug administration is preferred during cardiopulmonary arrest. If there is difficulty obtaining vascular access the rescuer may wish to consider administering medication via the endotracheal route. This route is particularly beneficial for children, in whom much time may be consumed attempting to find an IV route.

The lungs absorb medications rapidly, and the entire cardiac circulation passes through them, making the absorption of medications by the cardiovascular system rapid. It is interesting to note that the onset of action of atropine, epinephrine, and lidocaine given intratracheally to animals in cardiopulmonary arrest was 70% to 80% more rapid than the onset with IV drugs.[13]

The following medications have been found to be readily absorbed via the intratracheal route:

Lidocaine
Atropine sulfate
Naloxone (Narcan)
Epinephrine (Adrenalin)

The following medications should *not* be given via the intratracheal route:

Sodium bicarbonate; because of alkalinity and volume
Norepinephrine (Levophed); causes tissue necrosis and sloughing
Calcium chloride; causes tissue necrosis and sloughing

When administering intratracheal drugs, place them as far into the tracheobronchial tree as possible. A long, small-bore catheter placed down the endotracheal tube may be used to accomplish this. Following drug instillation four or five positive pressure ventilations should be administered to assure distribution of the medication. The medication must be diluted with 5 to 10 ml of saline solution or distilled water before administration.

Defibrillation

Ventricular fibrillation is a catastrophic event that will cause death if not corrected. Defibrillation is spontaneous fibrillation of all cells of the myocardium at the same time in the hope that this will be followed by spontaneous repolarization of the cells in a simultaneous fashion. When this occurs there is a possibility that one of the higher pacemaker cells such as the SA or AV node will assume the pacemaker function of the heart and produce a life-sustaining rhythm.

On discovering a patient to be in ventricular fibrillation, the rescuer may elect to defibrillate immediately. If the initial defibrillation is unsuccessful, it may be because the myocardium is hypoxic. It is essential to begin basic cardiopulmonary resuscitation techniques and then use advanced life support techniques and medications to oxygenate the myocardium and prepare it for another defibrillation attempt. The drugs used are usually sodium bicarbonate and epinephrine.

Except on some newer machines, the watt-second reading is that of stored energy in the machine and not the energy actually delivered to the patient. Defibrillators should be tested monthly for actual delivered-energy amounts. These test figures should be recorded and listed directly on the machine.

The defibrillation threshold is the amount of energy it takes to defibrillate the ventricles on the first attempt. The defibrillation threshold can be reduced by rapidly discharg-

TABLE 3-2 Crash cart drugs

Drug	Category	Use	Dosage	Other
Atropine sulfate	Parasympatholytic agent	Increases rate of SA node discharge and increases conduction through AV node; indicated for bradydysrhythmias producing hemodynamic deterioration; given in asystole to decrease vagal tone	0.5-1.0 mg slow IV bolus; may be repeated at 5-minute intervals to a maximum dose of 2 mg	At doses lower than 0.3 mg, paradoxic slowing may occur; do not give for heart rate over 60/min
Bicarbonate (Sodium bicarbonate)	Alkalotic agent	Used to combat acidosis during cardiac arrest	Use blood gas values; in unwitnessed arrest give 1 mEq/kg initially, then half this dose every 10 minutes thereafter	Low arterial pH caused by respiratory acidosis should first be corrected by improving the patient's ventilatory status
Bretylium tosylate (Bretylol)	Adrenergic nerve-blocking agent; an antidysrhythmic agent	Used to treat ventricular dysrhythmias	In ventricular fibrillation: 5 mg/kg by rapid IV push; may be repeated at 10 mg/kg as necessary. In ventricular tachycardia: 500 mg bretylium diluted in 50 ml IV solution given at 5-10 mg/kg over 10 minutes; a second dose of 5-10 mg/kg may be repeated in 1-2 hours; may also be given as continuous IV drip at 1-2 mg/min	Usually recommended following lidocaine and countershock; perhaps should be considered earlier
Calcium chloride	Myocardial stimulator	Used to increase inotropic state; administered during asystole and electromechanical dissociation	2.5-5 ml of 10% solution IV bolus; may be repeated every 10 minutes	There is currently much debate in the literature as to the actual efficacy of this agent
Dopamine (Intropin)	Alpha- and beta-adrenergic stimulator; catecholamine	Used to treat hypotensive states not caused by volume depletion; may be used as an adjunct to volume replacement	400 mg in 500 ml D5W given at a drip rate of 2-10 μg/kg/min (see dosage chart in Appendix)	Increases renal flow and mesenteric blood flow at doses that do not increase heart rate; clinical effects will vary according to dosage

Drug	Description	Indications	Dosage	Comments
Epinephrine (Adrenalin)	Endogenous catecholamine with both alpha and beta-adrenergic properties	Used to increase perfusion pressure, decrease fibrillatory threshold, and cause myocardial stimulation in asystole and idioventricular rhythms	1.0 mg IV bolus (10 ml of 1:10,000 solution) every minute during arrest; if IV route not available, give via endotracheal route or intracardiac route	Remember to allow about 90 seconds circulation time between epinephrine administration and defibrillation
Furosemide (Lasix)	Diuretic agent	Used to treat congestive heart failure and acute pulmonary edema; can also be used to reduce cerebral edema in head trauma	40 mg slow IV bolus (over 2 minutes)	Significant diuresis may cause severe volume depletion; monitor urinary output closely
Isoproterenol (Isuprel)	Synthetic sympathomimetic agent that stimulates beta-adrenergic receptors	Used to treat bradydysrhythmias not responsive to atropine; may also be used in asystolic states	2 mg in 500 ml D5W at a rate of 2-4 μg/min; may also be given 0.2 mg IV endotracheal or intracardiac bolus	Increases myocardial O_2 consumption and may cause increased ischemia or infarct
Norepinephrine (Levophed)	Alpha- and beta-adrenergic stimulator; a catecholamine	Used as a vasopressor in the setting of clinical shock; used especially when alpha-adrenergic stimulation is required	0.1-0.2 μg/kg/min titrated; normally given between 2-4 μg/min to maintain blood pressure between 90 and 100 mm Hg systolic	Use has diminished since advent of dopamine
Lidocaine (Xylocaine)	Antidysrhythmic	Used to suppress ventricular ectopy, especially in the setting of myocardial infarction; used to abolish premature ventricular contractions and ventricular tachycardia and to prepare the heart for defibrillation in the setting of ventricular fibrillation	1 mg/kg as an initial dose followed by repeated boluses of 50 mg, one given 5 minutes following initial bolus then every 10 minutes thereafter or followed by a drip of 2 lidocaine in 500 ml D5W run at 1 to 4 mg/min.; if IV route not available give by rapid IM injection (Lidopen) 300 mg.; total dosage of IV lidocaine should not exceed 225 mg	If bolus given too rapidly, seizures may develop; in presence of hepatic failure, give half the suggested dosage

Continued.

TABLE 3-2 Crash cart drugs—cont'd

Drug	Category	Use	Dosage	Other
Metaraminol (Aramine)	Alpha-adrenergic agent	Used to cause peripheral vasoconstriction and increased cardiac contractility; used to improve blood pressure	200 mg in 500 ml D5W at 0.5-1 ml/min (200-400 μg/min) titrated to desired blood pressure; may also be given IM 2-10 mg	Occasionally used to treat supraventricular tachycardias
Morphine sulfate	Narcotic analgesic	Used in the setting of acute myocardial infarction for pain relief; used in acute pulmonary edema to cause venodilation and peripheral pooling of blood reducing venous return to right side of the heart	2-10 mg IV slowly titrated to effect; may also be given IM	May cause respiratory depression if given too rapidly or in too large a dose; have 0.8 mg naloxone ready in case of respiratory problems
Naloxone (Narcan)	Opiate antagonist; synthetic narcotic antagonist	Used to reverse the effects of a narcotic agent or natural synthetic narcotic agent	0.4-0.8 mg IV, intratracheally or injected into the sublingual area; may be given in larger doses if required	Also being used in septic and hypovolemic shock
Procainamide (Pronestyl)	Antidysrhythmic agent	Used to treat ventricular ectopy, tachycardia, atrial fibrillation, and PAT	250 mg by slow IV bolus; wait 3 min. and repeat until desired effect seen; total dose not to exceed 1 G	Used to treat dysrhythmias refractory to lidocaine; contraindicated in heart block
Propranolol (Inderal)	Beta-adrenergic blocking agent	Used to treat tachydysrhythmias following acute myocardial infarction and digitalis toxicity; used to treat dysrhythmias not responsive to other drugs	1 mg by IV bolus, repeated every 2-3 minutes; total dose not to exceed 3 mg	May cause bronchoconstriction and severe asthma
Verapamil (Isoptin)	Calcium channel antagonist	Used to treat paroxysmal supraventricular tachycardia	5-10 mg by slow IV bolus; may be repeated to 0.15 mg/kg 30 min after initial dose	May cause a transient reduction in arterial pressure; may worsen underlying congestive heart failure

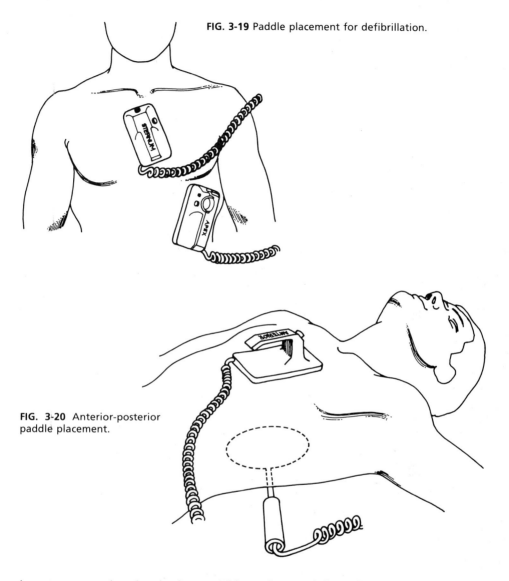

FIG. 3-19 Paddle placement for defibrillation.

FIG. 3-20 Anterior-posterior paddle placement.

ing two consecutive electric charges. This works especially well in the large patients in whom preceding defibrillation attempts have been unsuccessful.

In external defibrillation paddle placement and resistance across the chest are important factors to consider. Using larger electrode paddles can diminish the resistance of the thorax. Although the anterior-lateral paddle placement is most commonly used (Fig. 3-19), anterior-posterior paddle placement is actually more effective (Figs. 3-20). Also remember that resistance will be lowered with each consecutive shock.

A coupling agent should be placed on the defibrillator paddles. *Never* administer a countershock without first applying a coupling agent, even in the case of an extreme emergency. Saline-soaked 4 × 4 inch gauze, commercially available electrode jelly or paste, and commercially available disposable prejelled electrodes may all be used in defibrillation. *Never* use alcohol-soaked pads, as alcohol will ignite.

The recommended dosage for defibrillation varies greatly in the literature. We recommend a dosage of 2 watt-seconds/kg in a child, 3.5 to 6 watt-seconds/kg in a small adult (under 50 kg), and the full energy output of the machine (usually 300 to 400 watt-seconds) in an adult weighing over 50 kg.

Ventricular fibrillation is treated with defibrillation. Ventricular tachycardia should be treated with synchronous cardioversion (see pp. 84-85) but may be treated with defibrillation when the synchronous mode is not available. The atrial dysrhythmias, atrial fibrillation, atrial flutter, and atrial tachycardia are all treated with synchronous cardioversion.

Remember that cardioversion may produce dysrhythmias as well as correct them. Transient mild dysrhythmias are common following defibrillation and cardioversion.

EXTERNAL DEFIBRILLATION

1. Turn the machine on.
2. Check that the "synchronous/defibrillate" switch is in the defibrillate mode.
3. Apply a coupling agent to the paddles.
4. Select the dosage level.
5. Apply the electrodes in the proper positions.
6. Reconfirm the dysrhythmia on the scope.
7. Apply 20 pounds of pressure to the paddles to assure good contact.
8. Assure that all personnel are standing clear of the victim, the gurney, and the electrical equipment.
9. Press the discharge buttons and discharge the current.
10. Quickly interpret the rhythm and assess pulses and breathing status; if these are not acceptable, resume cardiopulmonary resuscitation.

INTERNAL DIFIBRILLATION

1. Replace the external paddles with internal paddles.
2. Turn the machine on.
3. Assure that the "synchronous/defibrillate" switch is in the defibrillate mode.
4. Use sterile saline-soaked sponges as a coupling agent; place them on the surfaces of the electrodes.
5. Select the dosage level (usually 25 to 50 watt-seconds in an adult).
6. Apply the electrodes to the surface of the fibrillating ventricles.
7. Assure that all personnel are standing clear of the victim, the gurney, and the electrical equipment.
8. Press the discharge buttons and discharge the current.
9. Quickly interpret the rhythm and assess pulses and breathing status; if these are not acceptable, resume internal massage and continue ventilation.

Open chest message

Thoracotomy and open chest massage (direct cardiac massage) may be required in cases of penetrating wounds to the heart, repeat pericardial tamponade not relieved by pericardiocentesis, tension pneumothorax, crush injuries to the chest, or any other incident for which ready access to the intrathoracic cavity is desired. Other examples include patients in arrest with chest wall deformities such as those found in patients with COPD and barrel chest.

EQUIPMENT

Gloves	Antiseptic solution
Scalpel and blade	Sterile towels or drapes
Rib retractor	Suture material
Forceps	Needle holder
Scissors	Vascular clamps
Good suction	Good lighting
Defibrillator with internal paddles	Povidone-iodine
4 × 4 inch gauze soaked in saline	

PROCEDURE

1. Place patient in supine position.
2. Assure that patient is being ventilated.
3. Assure placement of two large-bore IV lines.
4. Cleanse skin rapidly with povidine-iodine.
5. Apply simple skin draping.
6. Make a curvilinear incision 2 to 3 cm lateral to the left sternal border, extending to the midaxillary line in the fourth or fifth intercostal space.
7. Spread the ribs and retract the lungs.
8. Introduce a gloved hand into the chest cavity.
9. Open the pericardial sac if necessary.
10. Massage the heart gently.
11. Determine if there is volume in the heart.
12. Determine if there is an injury and repair it if possible.
13. It may be necessary to cross-clamp the aorta if there is massive bleeding.
14. Once the procedure has been accomplished, transport the patient to the operating suite for irrigation, repair, closure, chest tube placement and so on.

Thoracotomy is of limited usefulness in medically caused cardiopulmonary arrest. Thoracotomy should only be performed by a trained physician.

Carotid sinus massage

Carotid sinus massage is the procedure usually chosen before pharmacologic or electric intervention for patients who are experiencing PAT and demonstrating signs and symptoms of cardiovascular compromise (decreasing blood pressure, syncope). The procedure is performed to place pressure on the carotid bodies located in the carotid arteries. This pressure is interpreted by the body as an increase in total body blood pressure (even though the pressure is localized to the carotid area), and the autonomic nervous system is activated, causing vagal nerve stimulation. As a result, the heart rate slows in an attempt to lower the blood pressure.

PROCEDURE

1. Place the patient in a supine position.
2. Administer oxygen via nasal cannula at 4 to 6 liters/minute.
3. Initiate IV D5W TKO.
4. Monitor the patient continuously.
5. Auscultate the carotids for the presence of bruits (murmurs); do not perform the massage if bruits are present.
6. On the patient's right side locate the carotid pulse.
7. Press the carotid artery between the fingers and the transverse processes of the vertebrae.
8. Pressure should be in a small, circular motion, backward and medially.
9. Pressure should last no more than 5 to 10 seconds (or less if a rhythm change is seen).
10. Carotid sinus massage may be repeated if it is unsuccessful the first time.

SPECIAL NOTES

Have a crash cart standing by during the procedure.

Stop the procedure if there is a rhythm change.

Never massage both sides at once.

Do *not* use this procedure in atrial flutter, as the block may increase.

Successful conversion is often preceded by short periods of asystole followed by a few PVCs before normal sinus rhythm resumes.

If the procedure is successful, continue to monitor the patient.

COMPLICATIONS

Dysrhythmias (ventricular tachycardia, ventricular fibrillation, asystole)
Cerebral occlusion (CVA)
Cerebral anoxia
Seizures

OTHER METHODS USED TO STIMULATE THE VAGUS NERVE

Drug therapy—norepinephrine or metaraminol (Aramine)
Valsalva maneuver
Emesis
Ocular pressure (may cause detached retina)
Facial immersion in ice water ("seal diving reflex")

Cardioversion (synchronous electrical countershock)

Cardioversion is used as an emergency procedure in supraventricular tachycardia with aberrant conduction and in ventricular tachycardia. Cardioversion is the fastest and most effective means of converting non-digitalis-induced ectopic tachycardias.

Cardioversion may also be used as an elective procedure in patients with long-term atrial flutter or atrial fibrillation or symptomatic patients with either of these dysrhythmias. It may also be used in non-digitalis-induced PAT with block.

This procedure should only be undertaken by adequately trained personnel who will not only be able to perform the procedure but who will be able to manage any emergency situation that may arise as a result of the cardioversion.

NONEMERGENT PROCEDURE

1. Explain the procedure to the patient.
2. Obtain written consent from the patient.
3. Anticoagulation therapy may be begun up to 3 months before the procedure.
4. The patient is often given a quinidine reaction test; he may be placed on quinidine therapy after the procedure.
5. Withhold digitalis for 24 to 72 hours before the procedure; a safe digitalis level in atrial fibrillation may be a toxic level in normal sinus rhythm.
6. Give the patient nothing by mouth (NPO) for 12 hours before the procedure to prevent emesis and aspiration.
7. Determine the serum potassium level; hypokalemia predisposes the patient to ventricular fibrillation.
8. Ask the patient to void.
9. Remove the patient's dentures.
10. Continue at No. 4 of emergent procedure.

EMERGENT PROCEDURE

1. Give a brief explanation of the procedure to the patient and/or family.
2. Obtain consent from the patient or family if possible; if not, responsibility is assumed by two physicians.
3. Remove the patient's dentures.
4. Draw blood for a serum digoxin level; if the patient is known to be receiving digitalis, a lower voltage level should be used.
5. Keep the room very quiet and dim (usually less diazepam will be required).
6. Have a crash cart and inhalation equipment standing by.
7. Give D5W IV TKO with an 18-gauge or larger cannula.
8. Have up to 20 mg diazepam (Valium) ready in bolus form; administer it slowly by IV push at small increments until the patient is no longer awake and alert.
9. Have 100 mg lidocaine ready in bolus form.
10. Assure that the patient is disconnected from all other electric equipment *and oxygen.*
11. Turn on the oscilloscope and synchronous unit.
12. Cover the electrodes of the ECG machine with conduction medium and apply them to limbs.
13. Obtain a precardioversion 12-lead ECG and have it read by a physician; mark the strip with name, date, and time.
14. Turn on "synchronous" button.
15. Test the "synchronous" mode by running the ECG machine, setting the synchronous unit on 10 watt-seconds, placing the paddles together and releasing the energy; a synchronous spike should appear on the ECG strip at the QRS complex. If the spike appears on the T wave, the machine is not synchronizing and should *not* be used.
16. Set the energy level between 25 and 200 watt-seconds depending on the amount of

energy previously used to cardiovert the patient or according to the physician's orders.

17. Run an ECG strip throughout the procedure.
18. Cover the paddle surfaces with conduction medium. (*Never* use alcohol-soaked pads—they will explode!)
19. Place the paddles just to the right of the sternum in the third or fourth intercostal space and in the fifth intercostal space in the midaxillary line.
20. Quickly double-check the room to assure that all other equipment is disconnected from the patient and that all personnel are standing clear of the bed.
21. Give a verbal command and discharge the impulse.
22. Observe the patient closely for respiratory rate and observe the ECG for the resulting rhythm.
23. If the procedure is unsuccessful, repeat it using a higher voltage level; the paddles may also be switched to the anterior-posterior position.
24. If the procedure is successful, run a postcardioversion ECG and mark the strip with date, name, time.

CARE OF PATIENT AFTER CARDIOVERSION

Check the signs every 15 minutes for 1 hour, then every 30 minutes for 2 hours, then every 2 hours.
Monitor the cardiac rhythm and document any dysrhythmias.
Tend to burns that may have been produced by paddles.
The patient should remain for observation for 24 hours.
If there are no problems, the patient may be discharged.

EARLY COMPLICATIONS

Asystole
Junctional rhythm
Premature ventricular contractions

Ventricular tachycardia
Embolization

LATE COMPLICATIONS

Reversion to atrial fibrillation or atrial flutter
Embolization

Pacemakers

A pacemaker is an artificial form of electric excitation used to provide low-voltage stimulation to the myocardium. A temporary pacemaker should be placed if the patient's clinical condition is deteriorating (e.g., severe hypotension, congestive heart failure, or cardiopulmonary arrest) because of a dysrhythmia that cannot be converted by any other means, if the patient is demonstrating syncope or chest pain that could be corrected by using a pacemaker, if there is potential of a rapid deterioration because of an underlying condition, or if the risks of inserting a pacemaker far outweigh the risks not placing it.

A pacemaker should be placed for the following[14]:

1. In cardiac arrest
   a. With bradycardia
      (1) From high degree of AV block with slow ventricular response

   (2) A very slow sinus bradycardia
   (3) A very slow junctional bradycardia
   b. With tachydysrhythmias refractory to therapy
   c. With asystole
2. In myocardial infarction
   a. With symptomatic bradydysrhythmias
      (1) Demonstrating a high degree of AV block
      (2) With a very slow rate
      (3) Demonstrating an idioventricular rhythm
   b. When tachydysrhythmias recur
   c. For prophylactic reasons
      (1) With right bundle branch block
      (2) With bifascicular block
      (3) With alternating bundle branch block
      (4) With Mobitz type II block
3. With recurrent/refractory tachydysrhythmias
4. With digitalis toxicity causing severe bradydysrhythmias
5. With sick sinus syndrome causing a bradycardia-tachycardia syndrome
6. With a prolonged QT interval
7. With any dysrhythmia causing a hemodynamic compromise that is making the patient symptomatic

TYPES OF PACEMAKER WIRES
Transthoracic

Electrodes can be introduced directly through the chest wall and into the myocardium via a transthoracic wire. The transthoracic wire is straight with the negative electrode located in its tip and the positive electrode a short distance proximal. This pacemaker wire is inserted via a sharp cannula. The proximal end of the wire may be attached to the V lead of an ECG machine with an alligator clip. When the wire passes through the myocardium a "current of injury" will be recorded on the ECG machine.

Transvenous

In the transvenous approach a venous cutdown is performed, and a bipolar electrode wire is introduced into the right antecubital vein or the jugular vein and floated, with the help of a balloon, into the right ventricle. There is a variation of this catheter that is stiffer and has no balloon. This catheter is usually placed with the aid of fluoroscopy. As with the transthoracic pacemaker wire, when the wire reaches the endocardium a "current of injury" will appear on ECG if the end of the wire is attached to the ECG machine with an alligator clip.

The energy generator

A temporary pacemaker generator functions in the bipolar mode. It has a rate control, an energy output control, and a sensitivity control. The sensitivity control determines the amplitude of the signal it will accept from the patient before it will administer electric stimulation.

COMPLICATIONS
From placement

Pneumothorax

Arterial puncture

Thrombosis

Sepsis

Dysrhythmias

Pericardial tamponade

Myocardial laceration

Coronary artery laceration

Air embolism

Hiccups

From the generator or wire

Weak batteries

Electrode failure

Generator failure

TYPES OF PACEMAKERS
Demand

The demand pacemaker (Fig. 3-21) is generally used when there is some sort of electrical conduction present. It senses the patient's own QRS impulse and fires only if no QRS impulse is present after a set period of time (usually 0.8 second). Problems with this type of pacemaker include false sensing of QRS complexes near microwave ovens, in electrical storms, near electric motors, and in areas covered by radar. Demand pacemakers may also malfunction by initiating an impulse on the T wave of the patient's own cardiac cycle, causing the patient to go into ventricular tachycardia. Electromechanical dissociation may also occur when a QRS complex appears on the monitor and no pulse is generated.

Fixed-rate

Also known as the conventional pacemaker, the fixed-rate pacemaker is set at a predetermined rate. No matter what the patient's own heart is doing, the pacemaker will continue to fire at the fixed rate. The problem with this type of pacemaker is that its paced beats may compete with the patient's supraventricular beats, causing ventricular fibrillation.

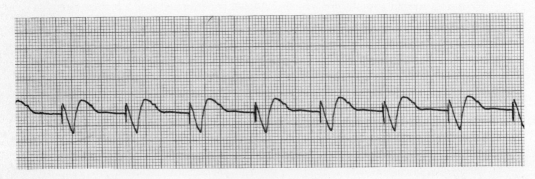

FIG. 3-21 Demand pacemaker.

Atrial synchronous

If the ventricles do not respond to the heart's supraventricular pacemakers, an atrial synchronous pacemaker may be used. It fires an impulse after the P wave to cause a ventricular contraction. This type of pacemaker is placed via the transthoracic route.

Paired-pacing

The paired-pacing method is also known as "paired-coupling pacing." It is used for tachycardia or for states of decreased myocardial contractility. The pacemaker fires at the absolute end of the refractory systole, so that there is no mechanical systolic response. The heart is unresponsive to this stimulus for a period twice as long as normal, producing an increased contractile force on the next contraction. A complication of this type of pacemaker is ventricular fibrillation.

CARE OF THE PATIENT WITH A PACEMAKER PROBLEM

1. Locate the pacemaker generator and check for trauma near the site.
2. Ask when the batteries were last changed.
3. Check both central and peripheral pulses.
4. Record an ECG strip and observe for the presence and location of a pacemaker in the department.
5. Set up for possible pacemaker replacement.

Pulsus alternans

Pulsus alternans is a phenomenon in which the heart beats regularly but with alternating strong and weak impulses as a result of an alteration in the contractile force of the left ventricle. Pulsus alternans is easier to detect in peripheral pulses than in central pulses, and it is often detected when auscultating blood pressure. It can be seen on the cardiac monitor as alternating tall and short impulses. The following are possible causes of pulsus alternans:

Digitalis toxicity	Paroxysmal atrial tachycardia
Atrioventricular block	Aortic insufficiency
Left ventricular failure	Cardiac tamponade
Hypotension	

Electromechanical dissociation

Electromechanical dissociation is a phenomenon in which ECG complexes are seen (the SA or AV node sends out an impulse), but there is essentially no contraction and thus no cardiac output and no pulse. The patient is essentially in cardiac arrest. Death almost always follows electromechanical dissociation, although there is some survival from certain causes if recognized and treated early in the process.

CAUSES

1. A decreased preload:
   a. Severe hypovolemia
   b. Cardiac tamponade
   c. Atrial myoma

2. An increased afterload:
   a. Severe pulmonic or aortic stenosis
   b. Tension pneumothorax
   c. Massive pulmonary embolus
3. A decreased pump action:
   a. Massive myocardial infarction
   b. Severe electrolyte imbalance
   c. Ruptured papillary muscle
   d. Ruptured intraventricular septum

THERAPEUTIC INTERVENTION

Identify the cause.

Apply intervention specific to the cause.

Application of the MAST has been used in electromechanical dissociation from hypovolemic causes with some favorable results. Hypovolemia is often the cause of electromechanical dissociation, especially in children.

CARDIOPULMONARY ARREST AND RESUSCITATION IN INFANTS AND CHILDREN

Although the principles of basic and advanced cardiopulmonary resuscitation are the same for adults as for infants and children, it is essential to be familiar with certain aspects of resuscitation of infants and children that are different. In the majority of infants and children, respiratory arrest is followed by cardiac arrest. It is therefore essential that strict attention be paid to the airway throughout the resuscitation effort.

Airway

Do not hyperextend the neck of an infant or child to open the airway. The vertebrae are so supple that hyperextension may actually block the airway from behind.

The best airway to use on an apneic infant or child is an endotracheal tube. The esophageal obturator airway is not yet available in pediatric sizes. To effectively intubate an infant or child the rescuer must be familiar with some anatomic differences between an adult and a child. A child has very small nares and a large tongue. His glottis is high, his vocal cords slant, and his cricoid ring is narrow. In neonates and infants it is recommended to use a straight (Miller) laryngoscope blade and in larger children a curved (MacIntosh) blade.

AIRWAY OBSTRUCTION

One of the most common causes of respiratory arrest in children is upper airway obstruction. If upper airway obstruction from a foreign body is suspected the child should be turned upside down with the head dependent, and four back blows should be given. Then manual thrusts should be given with the child still in a dependent (head-down) position. The rescuer must be aware that airway obstruction in a child may be the result of an infectious process, an allergic reaction, or trauma.

Age of the child/size of the endotracheal tube

Age	Weight (kg)	Tube size (interior diameter)
Newborn	Less than 1	2.5-3.0
Newborn	More than 1	3.0-4.0
6 months	7	3.5-4.5
1 year	10	4.0-5.0
3 years	15	4.5-5.5
5 years	20	5.0-6.0
6 years	22	5.5-6.5
8 years	25	6.0-6.5
10 years	30	6.5-7.0
12 years	40	6.5-7.0
16 years	50	7.0-7.5

Adapted from American Heart Association: JAMA **227**(suppl.): 837, 1974.

Breathing

In establishing respirations for a newborn or infant, the rescuer uses small puffs of air at a rate of 20 per minute. The rescuer's mouth covers the entire nose and mouth of the child. If the only mask available for a bag-valve-mask device or a pocket mask is an adult size, the rescuer turns the mask upside down and places the pointed end at the child's chin and the wide area at the child's forehead.

If mouth-to-mouth breathing is being performed and supplemental oxygen is available, the rescuer should apply a nasal cannula to his or her own nose, breathe in through the nose, and give the child a breath through the mouth. This will add supplemental oxygen to the air mixture given to the child.

Circulation

The rescuer places the index and middle fingers of one hand or both thumbs in the center of the sternum to provide circulation for an infant. The rescuer uses the heel of one hand in the center of the sternum on a larger child. Compressions are delivered at the rate of 100 times/minute for an infant and 80 to 100 times/minute for a larger child. The depth of compressions should be ½ to 1 inch for a newborn and 1 to 1½ inches for a larger child. In a small child, the rescuer palpates the brachial pulse during compressions. In a larger child, the rescuer monitors the carotid or femoral pulse. A breath is given at every fifth compression.

Blood pressure measurement

It is important to use the proper cuff size when attempting to obtain a blood pressure measurement in a child. A rough estimate of the proper blood pressure for a given age can be gotten by multiplying the child's age by 2 and adding 80. The resulting figure indicates about what the child's systolic blood pressure should be. For example, the equation is as follows for a child who is 8 years old:

$$8 \times 2 = 16$$
$$16 + 80 = 96$$

Therefore the child's systolic blood pressure should be somewhere around 96 mm Hg.

IV lines

Establishing an IV line in an infant or small child can be difficult and frustrating. It is our recommendation that an IV be attempted if the rescuer feels he or she may be able to initiate it. Do not waste time. Small needles should be used—21- to 23-gauge "butterfly" catheters or small 20- to 22-gauge catheter-over-needle devices. The best access sites in an emergency are the dorsum of the hand, the scalp, and the dorsum of the foot. In the emergency department a central line or cutdown can be placed. If all else fails the rescuer may elect to use the femoral vein.

Drugs

It is important to know or be able to estimate weight in an infant or child as medications are given on a per-kilogram basis during arrest.

Defibrillation

Paddles that are of appropriate size should be used when administering defibrillation to an infant or child. Paddles measuring 4.5 cm in diameter should be used for infants and paddles measuring 8 cm in diameter should be used for children. If pediatric-size paddles are not available, adult-size paddles should be used in the anterior-posterior position to avoid contact and arcing between the paddles. The watt-second dosage recommended for an infant or small child is an initial dose of 2 watt-seconds/kg (roughly 1 watt-second/pound). If the initial dose fails, subsequent doses should be increased to 4 watt-seconds/kg (2 watt-seconds/pound). There have been no established guidelines for watt-second

---

Guide to estimating weight by age in children

Age (years)	Weight (kg)	Pounds
Newborn	3-5	6-11
1	10	22
3	15	33
5	20	44
8	25	55
10	30	66
15	50	110

From Melker, R.: Resuscitation of neonates, infants and children. In Auerbach, P.A., and Budassi, S.A., editors: Cardiac arrest and CPR, ed. 2, Rockville, Md., 1983, Aspen Systems Corp.

TABLE 3-3 Basic medications for pediatric CPR

Medication	How supplied	Dose	Remarks
Sodium bicarbonate	0.89 mEq/ml (7.5%) or 1 mEq/ml (8.4%)	Newborn 1-2 mEq/kg Children 1 mEq/kg	Diluted 1:1 with D5W Undiluted q 10 min
Epinephrine	1:1,000 (1 mg/ml)	0.01 mL/kg	For subcutaneous use only Do not exceed 0.3 ml
	1:10,000 (0.1 mg/ml)	0.1 ml/kg	For IV use
Atropine	0.1 mg/ml	0.01-0.03 mg/kg	Minimum dose—0.1 mg
Calcium chloride	100 mg/ml (10%)	0.3 ml/kg	*Push slowly!*
Lidocaine	5 mg/ml (5%) 10 mg/ml (10%)	0.5-2.0 mg/kg	
Naloxone	0.4 mg/ml (adult) 0.02 mg/ml (newborn)	0.01 mg/kg	
Isoproterenol	1:5,000 (0.2 mg/ml)	0.1-0.5 μg/kg/min	Add 1 mg to 250 or 500 ml fluid—avoid overload
Dopamine		2-50 μg/kg/min	Titrate
Aminophylline	250 mg/10 ml	7 mg/kg loading dose then, 4 mg/kg q4-6H	Over 20-30 min

From Melker, R.: Resuscitation of neonates, infants and children. In Auerbach, P.A., and Budassi, S.A., editors: Cardiac arrest and CPR, ed. 2, Rockville, Md., 1983, Aspen Systems Corp.

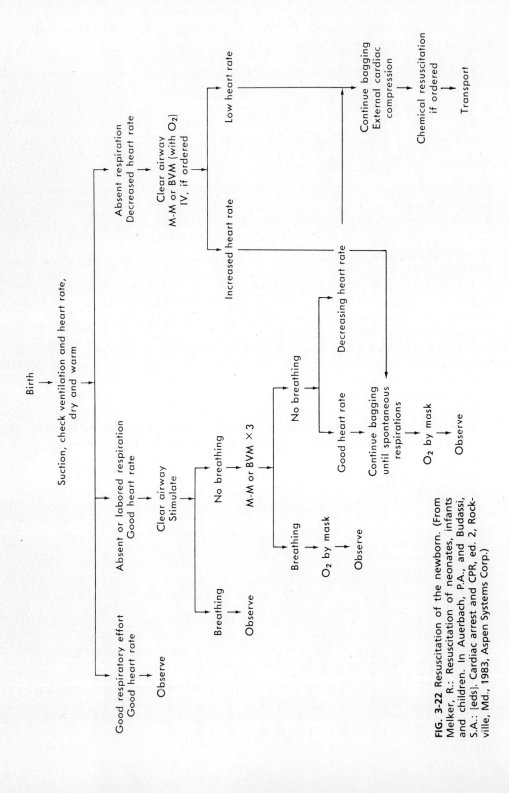

FIG. 3-22 Resuscitation of the newborn. (From Melker, R.: Resuscitation of neonates, infants and children. In Auerbach, P.A., and Budassi, S.A.: [eds]. Cardiac arrest and CPR, ed. 2, Rockville, Md., 1983, Aspen Systems Corp.)

dosage for children. It is assumed that the dosage should be lowered. Defibrillation should never be attempted for an unwittnessed, unmonitored arrest in a child.

Some special notes on resuscitation of newborns

Remember that newborns are obligate nosebreathers. Therefore it is important to suction the nose first, then the mouth. If the mouth were to be suctioned first the newborn would take a breath through the nose and could possibly aspirate material in the nose.

If a newborn is breathing spontaneously and the heart rate is over 110 beats/minute keep the infant warm and continue to observe him. If breathing is absent or labored but the heart rate remains above 100 beats/minute, suction the airway and stimulate the infant. Most infants will then begin to breathe spontaneously. If there is still no breathing, begin mouth-to-mouth or mouth-to-nose breathing by giving three to four quick breaths. The newborn will probably then begin to breathe. If not, continue breathing for the child and check for a pulse. Use supplemental oxygen when breathing for the child and apply an endotracheal tube when possible. Breaths should continue to be given at a rate of 20 to 30/minute.

If breathing is absent or labored and the pulse rate is less than 11 beats/minute, open the airway, suction the airway, and use mouth-to-mouth or mouth-to-nose breathing. If respirations and heart rate continue to decrease, continue to ventilate the child. If a pulse cannot be palpated, begin chest compressions at a rate of 100/minute and institute advanced life support measures. The initial steps in the resuscitation of a newborn are:

1. Airway management
2. Breathing with supplemental oxygen
3. Circulation
4. Establishment of an IV line (usually via the umbilical vein)
5. Administration of sodium bicarbonate (2 mEq/kg diluted 1:1) by IV push
6. Administration of epinephrine (0.1 ml/kg of a 1:10,000 solution)

Remember that hypothermia can be detrimental to the resuscitation of newborns, infants, and children of all ages—therefore keep the patient warm.

REFERENCES

1. American Heart Association: Standards and guidelines for cardiopulmonary resuscitation (CPR) and emergency cardiac care (ECC), JAMA **244**(suppl): 485, 1980.
2. American Heart Association: Standards and guidelines for cardiopulmonary resuscitation (CPR) and emergency cardiac care (ECC), JAMA **277** (suppl.), 1974.
3. Wolf Creek Conference, Critical care medicine, 1981.
4. Criley, J.M., Blaufuss, A.H., and Kissel, G.L.: Cough-induced cardiac compression: self administered form of cardiopulmonary resuscitation, JAMA **236**:1246, 1976.
5. Epstein, S.: Protection of the ischemic myocardium by nitroglycerine: experimental clinical results. In Brunwald, E., editor: AHA Monograph #48, Dallas, 1976, American Heart Association.
6. Helifant, R.: Nitroglycerine: new concepts about an old drug, Am. J. Med. **60**:905, 1976.
7. Bennett, M.A., and Pentecost, B.L.: Warning of cardiac arrest due to ventricular fibrillation and tachycardia, Lancet **1**:1351, 1972.
8. Koch-Weser, J.: Antiarrhythmic prophylaxis in acute myocardial infarction, N. Engl. J. Med. **285**:1024, 1971.
9. Raizes, G., Wagner, G.S., and Hachel, D.B.: Instantaneous nonarrhythmic cardiac death in acute myocardial infarction, Am. J. Cardiol. **39**:1, 1977.

10. Chopra, M.P.: Lidocaine therapy for ventricular ectopy after acute myocardial infarction: a double-blind trial, Br. Med. J. **3:**668, 1971.
11. Nademanee, K., and Singh, B.N.: Advances in antiarrhythmic therapy: the role of newer antiarrhythmic drugs, JAMA **247:**217, 1982.
12. Chait, L.O.: Management of bradydysrhythmias in acute myocardial infarction, Pract. Cardiol. **7:**78, 1981.
13. Elam, J.O.: The intrapulmonary route for CPR drugs. In Safar, P., editor: Advances in cardiopulmonary resuscitation, New York, 1977, Springer-Verlag New York, Inc.
14. Morelli, R.L.: The temporary pacemaker in cardiac arrest. In Auerbach, P.A., and Budassi, S.A., editors: Cardiac arrest and CPR, ed. 2, Rockville, Md., 1983, Aspen Systems Corp.

SUGGESTED READINGS

Ahlgren, E.W.: Pediatric resuscitation equipment and techniques. In Wasserberger, J., and Eubanks, D.H., editors: Practical paramedic procedures, ed. 2, St. Louis, 1981, The C.V. Mosby Co.

Akhtar, M.: Management of ventricular dysrhythmias, JAMA **247:**1178, 1982.

American Heart Association: Textbook of advanced cardiac life support, Dallas, 1981, Office of Communications.

Amey, B.D., et al.: Paramedic use of intracardiac medications in pre-hospital sudden cardiac death, J.A.C.E.P. **7:**130, 1978.

Auerbach, P.A., and Budassi, S.A., editors: Cardiac arrest and CPR, ed. 2, Rockville, Md., 1983, Aspen Systems Corp.

Baker, C.C., Thomas, A.N., and Trunkey, D.D.: The role of emergency room thoracotomy in trauma, J. Trauma **20:**848, 1980.

Bishop, R.L., and Weisfelt, M.L.: Sodium bicarbonate administration during cardiac arrest, JAMA **235:**506, 1976.

Budassi, S.A., and Barber, J.M.: Emergency nursing: principles and practice, St. Louis, 1981, The C.V. Mosby Co.

Chamedes, L.: Guidelines for defibrillation in infants and children, Circulation **56:**502, 1977.

Committee on Emergency Medical Services, Assembly of Life Sciences, National Research Council: Report on emergency airway management, Washington, D.C., 1976, National Academy of Sciences.

Davidson, R., et al.: Intracardiac injections during cardiopulmonary resuscitation: a low risk procedure, JAMA **244:**1110, 1980.

DeBard, M.L.: Cardiopulmonary resuscitation: analysis of six years of experience and a review of the literature, Ann. Emerg. Med. **10:**408, 1981.

Diamond, N.J., Schofferman, J., and Elliott, J.W.: Factors in successful resuscitation by paramedics, J.A.C.E.P. **6:**42, 1977.

Elam, J.O.: The intrapulmonary route for CPR drugs. In Safar, P., editor: Advances in cardiopulmonary resuscitation, New York, 1977, Springer-Verlag New York, Inc.

Gillette, P.C.: Ventricular arrhythmias. In Roberts, N.K., and Gelband, H., editors: Cardiac arrhythmias in the neonate, infant and child, New York, 1977, Appleton-Century-Crofts.

Goldberg, L.I.: Dopamine: clinical uses of an endogenous catecholamine, N. Engl. J. Med. **291:**707, 1974.

Greenberg, M.I.: Endotracheal medication in cardiac emergencies. Abstracts of the Fourth Purdue Conference on Cardiac Defibrillation and Cardiopulmonary Resuscitation, 1981.

Greenberg, M.I., Roberts, J.R., and Baskin, S.I.: Endotracheal naloxone reversal of morphine-induced respiratory depression in rabbits, Ann. Emerg. Med. **9:**289, 1980.

Greenberg, M.I., Roberts, J.R., and Baskin, S.I.: Use of endotracheally administered epinephrine in a pediatric patient, Am. J. Dis. Child. **135:**767, 1981.

Gutgesell, H.P.: Energy dose for ventricular fibrillation of children, Pediatrics **58:**898, 1976.

Harrison, E.E.: Diluent of choice for ET epinephrine, J.A.C.E.P. **8:**292, 1978.

Hazard, P.B., Benton, C., and Milnor, J.P.: Cardiac pacing in cardiopulmonary resuscitation, Crit. Care Med. **9:**666, 1981.

Hindman, M.C., et al.: Clinical significance of bundle branch block complicating myocardial infarction: indications for temporary and permanent pacemaker insertion, Circulation **58:**689, 1981.

Hinkle, L.E.: The antecedents of sudden death: prospective studies. In Report to the National Heart, Lung and Blood Institute, Springfield, Va., 1979, National Technical Information Service.

Iseri, L.T., Humphrey, S.B., and Siner, E.J.: Pre-hospital bradyasystolic cardiac arrest, Ann. Intern. Med. **88:**741, 1978.

Keszler, H., and Carroll, G.C.: Intracardiac injections during resuscitation, JAMA **246:**123, 1981.

Kluger, J.: Sudden death: prediction and prevention, Cardiovasc. Rev. Rep. **3:**106, 1982.

Kuller, L.H.: Sudden death: definition and epidemiological considerations, Prog. Cardiovasc. Dis. **23:**1, 1980.

Lang, R., et al.: The use of the balloon-tipped floating catheter in temporary transvenous cardiac pacing, PACE **4:**491, 1981.

Lie, K.J., and Durrer, D.: Conduction disturbance in acute myocardial infarction. In Narula, O., editor: Cardiac arrhythmia: electrophysiology, diagnosis and management, Baltimore, 1979, The Williams & Wilkins Co.

Lim, R.C., Jr., and Baker, C.C.: Assuming responsibility for emergency thoracotomy, E.R. Reports **2:**6, 1981.

Lown, B.: Cardiovascular collapse and sudden death. In Braunwald, E., editor: Heart disease, Philadelphia, 1980, W.B. Saunders Co.

MacWilliams, J.A.: Electrostimulation of the heart in man, Br. Med. J. **1:**348, 1889.

McElroy, C.R., and Auerbach, P.A.: Arrhythmias of arrest. In Auerbach, P.A., and Budassi, S.A., editors: Cardiac arrest and CPR, ed. 2, Rockville, Md., 1983, Aspen Systems Corp.

McSwain, N.E., Jr.: Intracardiac injections of medications, J.A.C.E.P. **7:**170, 1978.

Melker, P.: The pre-hospital care of the pediatric patient. In Los Angeles County paramedic training manuals, Los Angeles, 1977, Los Angeles County Paramedic Training Institute.

Melker, R.: Development of the pediatric esophageal obturator airways. Paper presented at Annual Meeting of the University Association of Emergency Medicine, San Francisco, May 8-20, 1978.

Melker, P., Cavallaro, D., and Kirscher, J.: Development of a pediatric esophageal gastric tube airway, Crit. Care Med. **9:**426, 1981.

Mildikan, J.S., et al.: Temporary cardiac pacing in traumatic arrest victims, Ann. Emerg. Med. **9:**591, 1980.

Morgan, M.T.: Ventricular defibrillation. In Auerbach, P.A., and Budassi, S.A.: Cardiac arrest and CPR, ed. 2, Rockville, Md., 1983, Aspen Systems Corp.

Moss, A.J., and Schwartz, P.J.: Delayed repolarization (QT or QTU prolongation) and malignant ventricular arrhythmias, Mod. Concepts Cardiovasc. Dis. **51:**85, 1982.

Mueller, H.S., Evans, R., and Ayers, S.: Effects of dopamine on hemodynamics and myocardial metabolism in shock following acute myocardial infarction in man, Circulation **57:**361, 1978.

Orlowski, J.P.: Cardiopulmonary resuscitation in children, Pediatr. Clin. North Am. **27:**495, 1980.

Pelton, D.A., and Whelan, J.S.: Airway obstruction in infants and children, Int. Anesthesiol. Clin. **10:**123, 1972.

Roberts, J.R., and Greenberg, M.I.: Emergency transthoracic pacemaker, Ann. Emerg. Med. **10:**600, 1981.

Roberts, J.R., Greenberg, M.I., and Baskin, S.I.: Endotracheal epinephrine in cardiorespiratory collapse, J.A.C.E.P. **8:**515, 1979.

Roberts, J.R., et al.: Blood levels following intravenous and endotracheal epinephrine administration, J.A.C.E.P. **8:**53, 1979.

Roberts, J.R., and Price, D.: Transthoracic pacing during CPR (letter), Ann. Emerg. Med. **10:**394, 1981.

Rockswald, G., et al.: Follow-up of 514 consecutive patients with cardiopulmonary arrest outside the hospital, J.A.C.E.P. **8:**216, 1979.

Safar, P.: Resuscitation of the arrested brain. In Safar, P., editor: Advances in cardiopulmonary resuscitation, New York, 1977, Springer-Verlag New York, Inc.

Sanna, G., and Arcidiacond, R.: Chemical ventricular defibrillation of the human heart with bretylium tosylate, Am. J. Cardiol. **32:**982, 1973.

Schaeffer, W.A., and Cobb, L.A.: Recurrent ventricular fibrillation and modes of death in survivors of out-of-hospital ventricular fibrillation, N. Engl. J. Med. **293:**259, 1975.

Schanker, L.S.: Drug absorption from the lung, Biochem. Pharmacol. **27:**381, 1978.

Scheinman, M.M., and Gonzales, R.: Fascicular block and acute myocardial infarction, JAMA **244:**2646, 1980.

Sheldon, R.E.: Management of perinatal asphyxia and shock, Pediatr. Ann. **6:**227, 1977.

Tintinalli, J.E., and While, D.C.: Transthoracic pacing during CPR, Ann. Emerg. Med. **10:**113, 1981.

Todres, I.D., and Rogers, M.C.: Methods of external cardiac massage in the newborn infant, J. Pediatr. **86:**781, 1975.

Vincent, J.L., et al.: Clinical and experimental studies on electrical-mechanical dissociation, Circulation **64:**18, 1981.

Wheatley, G.M.: Childhood accidents: prevention and treatment, Pediatr. Ann. **6:**688, 1977.

Yakaitis, R.W.: Intracardiac injections during resuscitation, JAMA **246:**123, 1981.

Yakaitis, R.W., Otto, C.W., and Blitt, C.D.: Relative importance of alpha and beta-adrenergic receptors during resuscitation, Crit. Care Med. **7:**293, 1979.

CHAPTER 4 Intravenous therapy and collection of laboratory specimens

The purpose of initiating an intravenous (IV) line is to allow for the administration of fluids, medications, and blood and blood substitutes into the vascular system. To initiate an IV line appropriately care givers must be familiar with the anatomy and physiology of the vascular system. They must also be able to determine which site is best for the purpose the IV is being initiated. In the emergency situation, anatomic considerations may take second place if the IV line must be initiated as quickly as possible for life-saving reasons. Care givers must be aware that vein size, location, and resilience may play major roles in the efficacy of fluid therapy. They must also be familiar with the physiology of the venous system and the use of vasoconstrictors to decrease the size of a vein and vasodilators to increase the size of a vein. Care givers should also be familiar with what causes and what relieves venospasm.

When initiating an IV line, consider the patient. Try to make the procedure as painless as possible. Also be familiar with complications of IV therapy and practice as many preventive measures as possible.

COMPLICATIONS OF IV THERAPY

Hematoma
Fluid extravasation outside the vein and into the tissues
Phlebitis
Clot embolism
Catheter fragment embolism
Cellulitis
Sepsis
Fluid overload

THE CIRCULATORY SYSTEM OF THE BODY

There are two main systems for circulation in the human body, the pulmonary system and the systemic system. The pulmonary system circulates blood from the right side of the heart, through the pulmonary system, and back to the left side of the heart for circulation to the systemic circulation. The systemic system begins at the aorta and leads through the arteries, arterioles, capillaries, venules, veins, and the inferior and superior venae cavae to the right side of the heart. Intravenous therapy directly involves the systemic circulation and indirectly involves the pulmonary system. The systemic system includes systemic veins that are either superficial or deep. The superficial veins are those most often used in IV therapy as they are close to the body's surface in the superficial fascia and are usually easy to cannulate. Rapid infusion of cold blood products or fluids can cause vasoconstriction, which increases venous spasm and causes a decreased blood flow.

Veins consist of three layers:
1. The tunica intima (inner layer), which is elastic; it is the same material that forms valves in the veins.
2. The tunica media (middle layer), which is muscular and elastic; it can contract or relax in accordance with impulses from the medulla.
3. The tunica adventitia (outer layer), which is made from areolar connective tissue that supports the vessel.

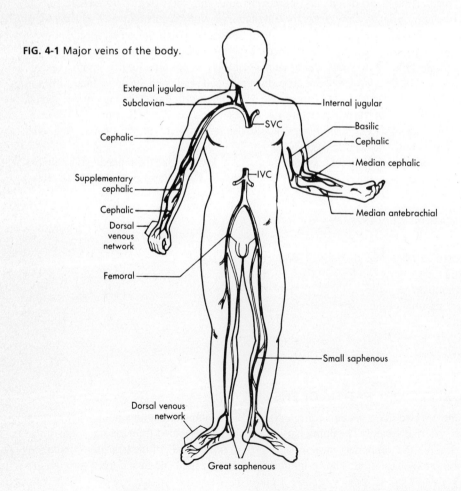

FIG. 4-1 Major veins of the body.

External jugular
Subclavian
Cephalic
Supplementary cephalic
Cephalic
Dorsal venous network
Femoral

SVC
IVC

Internal jugular
Basilic
Cephalic
Median cephalic
Median antebrachial

Small saphenous

Dorsal venous network
Great saphenous

PERIPHERAL IV SITES IN THE ADULT

The most common sites for the initiation of IV lines in the adult patient are in the upper extremities (Fig. 4-1). The choice of an IV site depends on:

The condition of the vein

The length of time the IV will be in place

The clinical condition of the patient

The age of the patient

The size of the patient

The purpose of the IV line

The superficial veins of the upper extremities

The digital veins   These are located on the dorsal portions of the fingers. They can be cannulated with a scalp vein needle and should only be used in an absolute emergency when no other IV site is attainable. Large volumes of fluid cannot be given via these sites.

The metacarpal veins   Three metacarpal veins (Fig. 4-2) are formed by the junction of the digital veins; these are good IV sites, because they are located between the metacarpal bones of the hand, which form natural splints. They are especially useful if long-term IV therapy is indicated, because future IVs can be initiated above the site. This site should be avoided in the elderly,

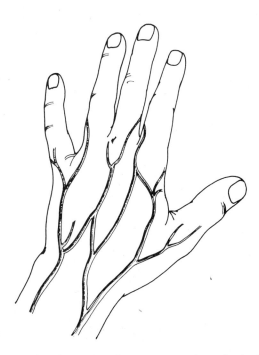

FIG. 4-2 Dorsal and metacarpal venous networks on back of hand.

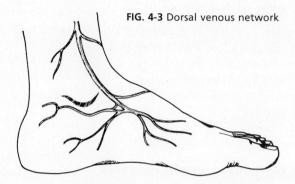

FIG. 4-3 Dorsal venous network

however tempting it may be, because the skin of elderly people is very thin, and blood may extravasate into the hand.

The cephalic veins

These are located in the radial aspect of the dorsal venous network. They are formed by the union of the metacarpal veins on the radial aspect of the forearm. They are large and in good locations and can accommodate a large-bore cannula. Their locations provide natural splints.

The accessory cephalic vein

This vein originates from the union of the dorsal veins and joins the cephalic vein below the elbow. It can accommodate a large-bore cannula and is a good vein to use for the administration of blood.

The basilic vein

This vein originates from the union of the dorsal veins on the ulnar aspect of the arm. It has a large capacity but is often not chosen as an IV site because it is not readily accessible. This vein can be visualized by flexing the arm at the elbow and elevating it.

The median veins

The median antebrachial vein

This vein originates from the union of many veins on the palm of the hand. It ascends along the ulnar aspect of the arm and can sometimes be difficult to find.

The median cephalic/ median basilic vein

This vein is located in the antecubital fossa. It is large and is frequently used to withdraw blood for laboratory specimens. It is also frequently used as an IV site in extreme emergency situations, such as cardiopulmonary arrest or multiple trauma, because there is usually very easy access, and the vein can accommodate a very large-bore cannula. It is important to remember that the brachial artery lies just behind this view.

The peripheral veins of the lower extremities

The saphenous vein

The small saphenous vein terminates at the deep popliteal vein, which enters the great saphenous vein, which terminates at the femoral vein. It is important to be aware that there is great danger of embolism when an IV is initiated at this site; it should only be used in cases of extreme emergency. If an IV is initiated at this site and the MAST is applied, a pressure bag must be placed over the IV bag, and the pressure must exceed that of the MAST to run.

The peripheral veins of the neck

The external jugular vein

This vein is often overlooked. It is very large and easy to cannulate. It should be considered as an IV site in cardiopulmonary arrest and multiple trauma, especially for cases in which large amounts of fluids are to be administered over a short period of time. This vein has the capacity for a very large-bore cannula.

PERIPHERAL IV SITES IN INFANTS AND CHILDREN

The IV sites of choice in an infant or small child are the dorsum of the hand, the dorsum of the foot, and the scalp (in an infant). In the newborn, the umbilical vein should not be overlooked. Be sure to anchor an IV extra securely in an infant or a small child, as movement may dislodge it.

Venous cutdown

A venous cutdown is a minor surgical procedure that is used if a peripheral IV site cannot be located or if it is desired to administer a large volume of fluid over a short period of time. Many trauma centers recommend cutdowns as opposed to peripheral IV lines. A cutdown is usually done on the basilic vein (just above the elbow) or the saphenous vein (above the ankle). The saphenous vein is usually chosen for a cutdown performed on a child (Fig. 4-4).

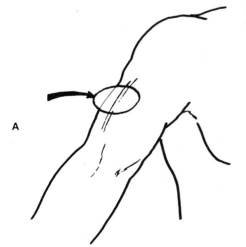

FIG. 4-4 Common sites of venous cutdown. **A,** Cephalic vein. **B,** Saphenous vein.

A

B

EQUIPMENT

Surgical gloves
Surgical mask
Scalpel handle and blades (11- or
    15-gauge)
Vascular scissors
Suture scissors
Lidocaine (1% or 2%)
Suture material
Forceps
4 × 4-inch gauze squares
Sterile towels

Catheter (may use infant-feeding tube
    or IV connector)
Antiseptic solution
Hemostats
Syringe and needle (25-gauge)
Antibiotic ointment
IV setup
Tape
Small vein retractor

PROCEDURE

1. Prepare the extremity with antiseptic solution.
2. Drape the limb.
3. Apply a local anesthetic.
4. Make a transverse incision.
5. Dissect the tissue down to the vein.
6. Lift the vein (Fig. 4-5).

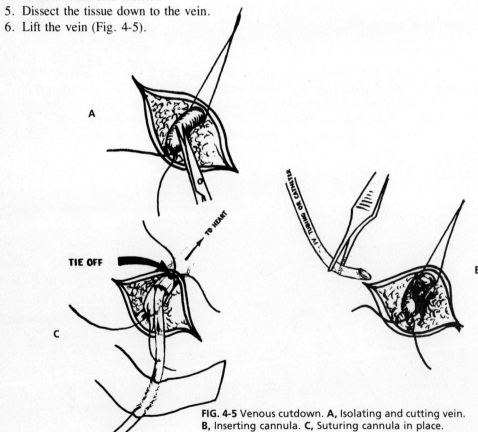

FIG. 4-5 Venous cutdown. **A,** Isolating and cutting vein.
B, Inserting cannula. **C,** Suturing cannula in place.

7. Nick the vein with a scalpel.
8. Insert the cannula.
9. Secure the cannula with a suture.
10. Suture the wound around the cannula.
11. Apply antibiotic ointment.
12. Tape the cannula in place.
13. Label the IV site (gauge and type of cannula, date, time, initials).

Central veins

Catheterization of the subclavian vein is used to provide large volumes and to enable measurement of the central venous pressure. Catheterization of the internal jugular vein is used to provide large volumes over a short period of time. It should be remembered that catherizing these sites carries a risk of pneumothorax. They should only be used in urgent situations.

SUBCLAVIAN VEIN

This vein is located in the neck between the median and middle thirds of the clavicle and the sternal notch (Fig. 4-6).

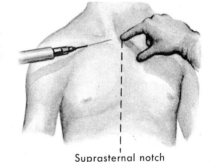

FIG. 4-6. Technique of percutaneous intraclavicular subclavian catheterization. Needle, inserted under midclavicle and aimed in three dimensions at top of posterior aspect of sternal manubrium (indicated by fingertip in suprasternal notch), lies in a plane parallel with frontal plane of patient and will enter anterior wall of subclavian vein. (From Needle and cannula techniques, Chicago, 1971, Abbott Laboratories.)

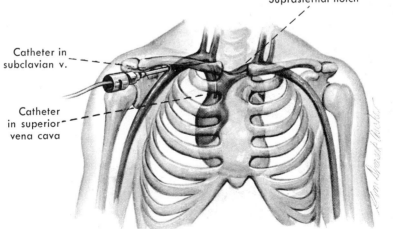

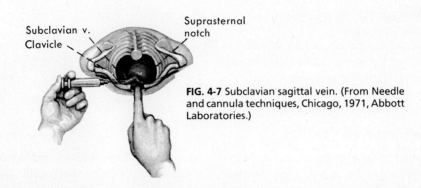

Subclavian v.
Clavicle

Suprasternal
notch

FIG. 4-7 Subclavian sagittal vein. (From Needle and cannula techniques, Chicago, 1971, Abbott Laboratories.)

1. Place the patient in Trendelenburg's position to increase the size of the vein and decrease the possibility of air embolism.
2. Place a rolled towel between the patient's shoulderblades to provide a better angle.
3. Prepare the neck and upper chest with an antiseptic solution.
4. Anesthetize the area (use 1% lidocaine) at the inferior edge of the clavicle where the medial and middle thirds join.
5. Insert a 14-gauge or larger cannula (with a syringe on the end to avoid air embolism), aiming toward the suprasternal notch and keeping the cannula just under the clavicle (Fig. 4-7).
6. Aspirate as the needle is advancing; if nonpulsating blood is drawn, the vein has been cannulated.
7. Advance the catheter through the needle; do not pull back on the catheter as it may be sheared off.
8. When the catheter is in place, withdraw the needle.
9. Clip on the catheter guard so that the needle will not shear off the catheter.
10. Suture the catheter and guard in place.
11. Apply antibiotic ointment to the puncture site.
12. Apply a dry sterile dressing.
13. Apply a waterproof dressing.
14. Label the cannulation site.

INTERNAL JUGULAR VEIN

1. Place the patient in Trendelenburg's position to increase the size of the vein and decrease the possibility of air embolism.
2. Place a rolled towel between the shoulder blades to provide a better angle.
3. Prepare the neck and upper chest with an antiseptic solution.
4. Drape the neck and upper chest area.
5. Anesthetize the area with 1% lidocaine at the junction of the middle and lower thirds of the anterior border of the sternocleidomastoid muscle.
6. Insert a #14 or larger cannula (with a syringe on the end to avoid air embolism) close behind the sternocleiodmastoid muscle, aimed toward the space formed by the clavicular and sternal heads.

7. Aspirate as the needle is advancing; if nonpulsating blood is drawn, the vein has been cannulated.
8. Advance the catheter through the needle; do not pull back on the catheter as it may be sheared off.
9. When the catheter is in place, withdraw the needle carefully.
10. Clip the catheter guard so that the needle will not shear off the catheter.
11. Suture the catheter and guard in place.
12. Apply antibiotic ointment to the puncture site.
13. Apply a dry sterile dressing.
14. Apply a waterproof dressing.
15. Label the cannulation site.

CENTRAL VENOUS PRESSURE

The central venous pressure (CVP) measures the right-sided pressures of the heart, blood volume, effectiveness of pump, and vascular tone.

PROCEDURE

1. Place the patient in a supine (flat) position.
2. Measure at the midaxillary line (5 cm from the top of the chest) in the fourth intercostal space at the level of the right atrium.
3. Place the manometer zero reading at this point.
4. Fill the manometer from the attached IV solution (do not let it overflow).
5. Turn the stopcock on the IV line open to the patient and the manometer. The fluid level will fall and fluctuate (decreasing on inspiration and increasing on expiration).
6. When the fluid level appears stable, note where the top of the fluid column reaches.
7. Record this reading as the CVP.
8. Adjust the stopcock to close the manometer and open the IV line to the patient (make sure to readjust the IV solution).

The normal range of CVP is 4 to 10 cm of water pressure. A value greater than 10 cm may indicate tamponade, right heart failure, fluid overload, pulmonary edema, tension pneumothorax, or hemothorax. A value below 4 cm may indicate hypovolemia, vasodilation, dehydration, septic shock, or drug-induced shock.

PULMONARY ARTERY WEDGE PRESSURE

Pulmonary artery wedge pressure (PAWP) is a reflection of left ventricular pressure. It is measured with a Swan-Ganz catheter (Fig. 4-8), which may be placed by a percutaneous or cutdown approach. A normal PAWP value is 6 to 12 cm of water.

PROCEDURE

1. The catheter is inserted into the superior vena cava.
2. The balloon is inflated with air to let blood flow carry it into the right atrium and right ventricle into the pulmonary artery.

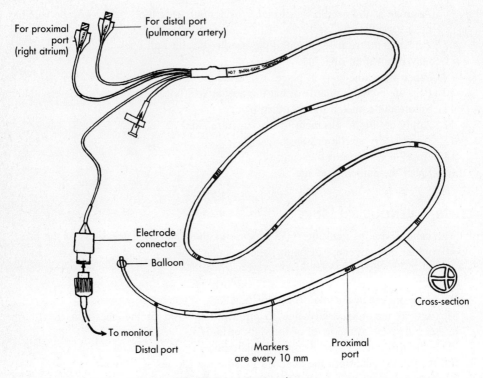

FIG. 4-8 Swan-Ganz catheter.

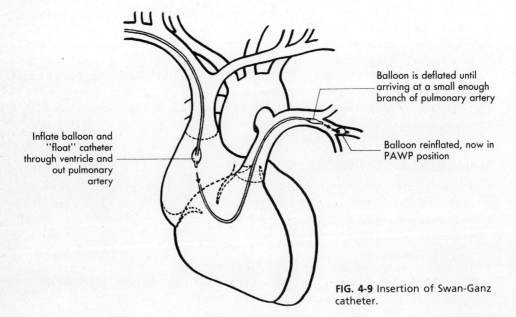

FIG. 4-9 Insertion of Swan-Ganz catheter.

3. Once the catheter arrives at the pulmonary artery, the balloon is deflated.
4. The catheter is advanced a few centimeters more into a small branch of the artery.
5. When the balloon is once again inflated, it occludes the artery and the tip of the catheter transmits a pressure that is reflective of left ventricular pressure (Fig. 4-9).

INTRAARTERIAL LINE

Intraarterial lines may be established via a percutaneous puncture or cutdown. Before puncture of the limb, the collateral circulation should be checked. Circulation in the forearm is checked by the Allen test.

Allen test*

To assess for the Allen sign, palpate both the radial and ulnar pulses. Occlude both arteries with firm pressure and raise the arm to blanch the hand. Release the ulnar artery and assess for return of color to the hand. If the hand does not perfuse (negative Allen sign), this indicates that the ulnar artery is not capable of maintaining circulation to the hand. Therefore do not attempt a radial artery puncture in this wrist.

GENERAL PRINCIPLES OF IV THERAPY

In emergency situations, look for a site that is easy to cannulate.

The vein to be cannulated should be large enough to hold the cannula that will be introduced.

If the purpose of the IV line is to provide a vehicle to administer large volumes of fluid over a short period of time, be sure to initiate the largest-bore cannula possible.

Whenever possible, try not to initiate the IV in the patient's dominant arm.

Be sure to have all equipment ready ahead of time (including tape strips).

IV administration of medications is preferable to intracardiac injections in cardiopulmonary arrest.

If a patient is in shock, perfusion is decreased and medication absorption is erratic; IV administration of medications is much more reliable than other routes of administration.

Cannula and needle sizes for fluid and medication
ADMINISTRATION

Blood and blood products—18-gauge or larger
Colloids (plasma or albumin)—20-gauge or larger
Crystalloids—21-gauge or larger

To give large volumes of fluid use at least a 16-gauge or larger needle.

TYPES OF CANNULAS USED IN IV THERAPY

hollow needle—A sharpened stainless steel or aluminum cannula (Fig. 4-10).
winged needle—Otherwise known as a "scalp vein" or a "butterfly"; a stainless steel

---

*Modified from Budassi, S.A.: J.E.N. **3:**24, 1977.

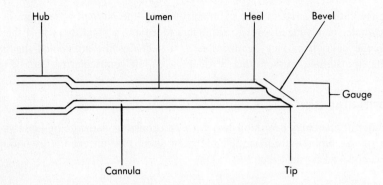

FIG. 4-10 Hollow metal needle.

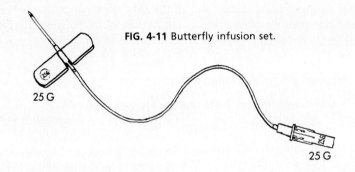

FIG. 4-11 Butterfly infusion set.

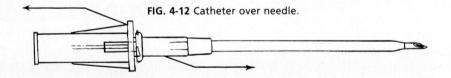

FIG. 4-12 Catheter over needle.

needle with two winglike plastic projections mounted where the needle meets the catheter for facilitation of placement and anchoring (Fig. 4-11).

indwelling catheter—Made of polyethylene, polyvinyl chloride, Silastic, or Teflon; better than a metal cannula for long-term use.

plain plastic catheter—Without a needle tip; used when cutdown is performed.

catheter-over-needle—A tapered catheter fitted over a needle; the needle is used to puncture the skin and the vein; the catheter is advanced over the needle; the needle is removed from the patient (Fig. 4-12).

catheter-inside-needle—A sharp hollow needle with a catheter inside the lumen; the needle punctures the skin and the vein; the catheter is advanced through the needle; the needle is removed from the patient but remains outside, over the end of the catheter, secured by an outer plastic clip; this type of device is often used for placement of a central venous pressure line, most often a subclavian line (Fig. 4-13).

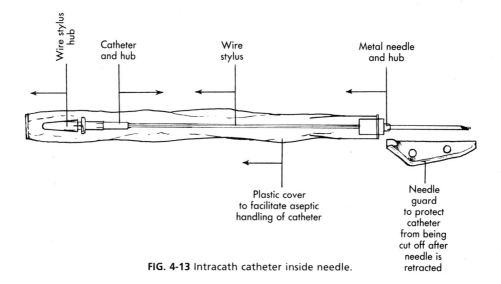

FIG. 4-13 Intracath catheter inside needle.

SITE PREPARATION

1. Apply a proximal tourniquet to sites in extremities to distend the vein, using rubber tubing, a wide (commercially available) tourniquet, or a blood pressure cuff (most comfortable and most effective) (Fig. 4-14).
2. Keep the tourniquet in place for 5 minutes or just until the vein dilates enough; if the vein does not dilate enough for cannulation:
   Rub the vein
   Tap the vein
   Hold the limb in a dependent position
   Apply heat via a hot pack or warm towel
   Have the patient open and close his fist
3. Apply a 10% povidone and iodine (Betadine) solution (Fig. 4-15).
4. Make a wheal with 2% lidocaine over the puncture site if a large-bore needle is to be used.

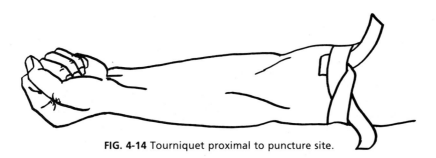

FIG. 4-14 Tourniquet proximal to puncture site.

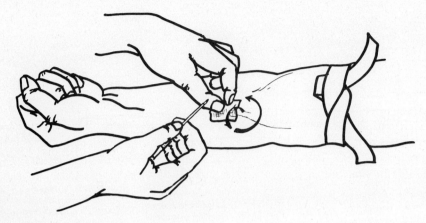

FIG. 4-15 Just before venipuncture, antiseptic solution is applied to area of needle insertion.

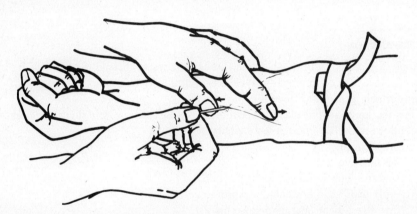

FIG. 4-16 Proper handling and alignment of needle with axis of vein contributes to successful venipuncture.

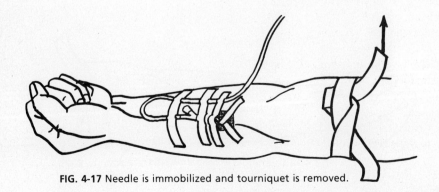

FIG. 4-17 Needle is immobilized and tourniquet is removed.

PERIPHERAL VENIPUNCTURE TECHNIQUE

1. Stabilize the vein (Fig. 4-16).
2. Use the smallest angle possible between the needle and the vein.
3. Puncture the skin and the vein with the bevel of the needle facing upward.
4. Advance the needle slowly.
5. Check for a blood return (''flashback'').
6. Remove the tourniquet.
7. Slowly advance the needle as far as possible; it is often helpful to have the IV solution running while doing this to help float the catheter in and dilate the vein.
8. Place a small dab of antibiotic ointment at the puncture site.
9. Cover the site with sterile 2 × 2-inch gauze.
10. Secure the cannula with tape.
11. Make a loop with the IV tubing and secure it (Fig. 4-17).
12. Label the IV site (type, gauge, time, date, initials).
13. Mark the drip rate and whether or not any medications have been added on the solution container.

HEPARIN LOCK

A heparin lock is a peripheral IV cannula without IV tubing attached. The distal end of the cannula is plugged. The purpose of this lock is to have ready access to a vein should the need arise or to have brief access to a vein should an intravenous medication be given. The cannula should be filled with a heparin solution so that it will not clot while it is not in use. It can be used if the patient does not require massive volume replacement and medications do not have to be diluted in large amounts of solution.

Drawing blood for blood gas measurement*
SELECTION OF SITE

Choose the radial, brachial, or femoral artery (Figs. 4-18 to 4-20)
Avoid limbs that demonstrate poor circulation.
Avoid limbs where hematomas are present.
If the radial artery is selected, check for the presence of a positive Allen test.

SUGGESTED EQUIPMENT

Container of crushed ice (plastic bag or emesis basin is fine)
Rubber or cork stopper or commercial blood gas cap
5 ml *glass* syringe
Two 22-gauge 1.5-inch needles
Two alcohol swabs
Sodium heparin, 0.5 ml (1,000 units/ml)
One small dry gauze pad
Gummed label for syringe
Laboratory requisition slip with the following information: concentration of O_2 patient is receiving and by what route (FIO_2) and patient's rectal temperature at the time the specimen is collected (Both parameters affect calculation of values.)

---

*Modified from Budassi, S.A.: J.E.N. 3(2):24, 1977.

FIG. 4-18 Brachial artery, a continuation of axillary artery. *Advantages:* Easy to locate, not much arterial spasm, and easy to immobilize. *Disadvantages:* Radial and medial nerves in close proximity and venous system in close proximity making venous sampling possible. (From Budassi, S.A.: J.E.N. **3**[2]:24-27, 1977.)

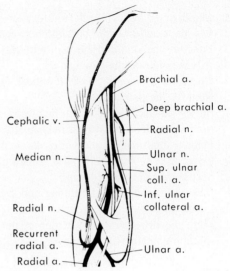

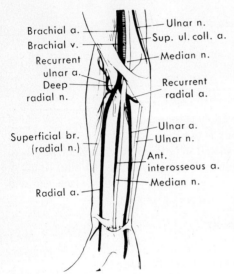

FIG. 4-19 Radial artery extends from neck of radius to median side of styloid process. *Advantages:* No close proximity to nerves and no close proximity to veins; thus venous sampling is unlikely. *Disadvantages:* Puncture may produce spasm and artery is very small. (From Busassi, S.A.: J.E.N. **3**[2]:24-27, 1977.)

DRAWING THE SPECIMEN

1. Explain the procedure to the patient.
2. Draw up 0.5 ml heparin into a *glass* syringe.
3. Flush the syringe with heparin (expel all air bubbles).
4. Replace the needle.
5. Select the puncture site.
6. Straighten the limb of the selected puncture site, and position it on a firm surface.
7. Palpate the artery: assess the pulse and position of the artery.
8. Cleanse area over the puncture site with an alcohol swab (be sure to use plenty of friction and allow the alcohol to dry before the actual puncture).

FIG. 4-20 Femoral artery branches from abdominal aorta and branches to superficial epigastric, superficial circumflex iliac, external pudendal, deep femoral, and descending genicular arteries. *Advantages:* Easily accessible. *Disadvantages:* May have large amount of interstitial bleeding before it is noticed. Close proximity to vein makes venous sampling possible. (From Budassi, S.A.: J.E.N. **3**|2|:24-27, 1977.)

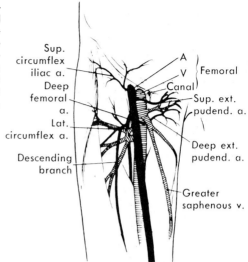

FIG. 4-21 Puncture of radial artery. (From Budassi, S.A.: J.E.N. **3**|2|:24-27, 1977.)

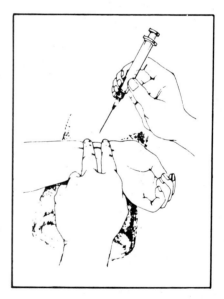

9. Immobilize the artery between two fingers (be careful not to contaminate the puncture site).
10. Penetrate both the skin and the artery at a 45° to 90° angle, holding the syringe like a pencil (Fig. 4-21).
11. If the syringe begins to fill and the plunger begins to move spontaneously, this is usually an indication that the needle is in the artery.
12. If the syringe does not begin to fill spontaneously, withdraw the needle slightly (it may have gone all the way through the artery).

13. If systolic blood pressure is less than 100 mm Hg, the syringe may not fill spontaneously and it may be necessary to manually withdraw the plunger (e.g., during CPR).
14. If the blood sample is not bright red or is bluish in color, this may indicate that the specimen is venous, and another attempt at an arterial specimen should be made.
15. Obtain 3 to 5 ml of arterial blood sample (some laboratories will accept less for analysis).
16. Withdraw the needle quickly.
17. Apply direct pressure with dry gauze.
18. Maintain pressure for 5 minutes (make certain to time it on your watch or the wall clock—it is difficult to estimate 5 minutes).

CARE OF THE SPECIMEN

1. Expel all air bubbles from the sample.
2. Stick the needle into a cork or rubber stopper or remove the needle and cap the syringe.
3. Place the gummed label (containing patient's name and hospital number) on the syringe.
4. Place the syringe into the container of ice.
5. Send to laboratory immediately along with completed laboratory request form. (If the specimen is being sent to a small laboratory, it frequently is helpful to call the laboratory before obtaining the arterial specimen so that the blood gas analyzer can be calibrated before the arrival of the specimen in the laboratory.)

AFTERCARE

Assure that pressure is maintained over the puncture site for at least 5 minutes (sandbags will not do—use fingers!).

Do not use dressings or band-aids that interfere with visualization of the puncture site. Patients with blood dyscrasias or who are anticoagulated may require a longer period of pressure to ensure that bleeding has ceased.

Observe the puncture site for at least 1 minute following removal of manual pressure for formation of a hematoma.

Reassess pulse.

INTERPRETATION OF ARTERIAL BLOOD GAS VALUES

Notice the pH value: 7.35 to 7.45 = normal; above 7.45 = alkalosis; below 7.35 = acidosis.

Notice the bicarbonate level: 22 to 26 mEq = normal; above 26 mEq = metabolic alkalosis; below 22 mEq = metabolic acidosis.

Notice the P_{CO_2} value: 35 to 40 mm Hg = normal; above 45 mm Hg = respiratory acidosis; below 35 mm Hg = respiratory alkalosis.

Make an acid-base "diagnosis" based on these criteria. Consider the effect on blood gas values of compensatory mechanisms. While the values are abnormal, they may not all fit the criteria. The variance is caused by the compensatory action—see the examples that follow.

	pH	CARBONIC ACID	BICARBONATE
ACIDOSIS	Low	Increase	Decrease
ALKALOSIS	High	Decrease	Increase

Acid-base balance is normally maintained by three different body systems: the respiratory system, the renal system, and the buffer system.

BLOOD GASES QUICK REFERENCE CHART

	Respiratory acidosis	Respiratory acidosis with metabolic compensation	Metabolic acidosis	Metabolic and respiratory acidosis	Metabolic alkalosis	Metabolic alkalosis with respiratory compensation	Respiratory alkalosis	Metabolic and respiratory alkalosis
pH	↓	↓	↓	↓	↑	↑	↑	↑
pCO$_2$	↑	↑	Normal	↑	Normal	↑	↓	↓
Bicarb	Normal	↑	↓	↓	↑	↑	Normal	↑

Possible causes:
Emphysema, pneumonia, drug overdose;
Diabetes, shock, renal failure;
Cardiac arrest;
Usually iatrogenic: hypokalemia, diuresis, vomiting, bicarbonate administration, NG suctioning, hypoxia;
Hyperventilation, fever, anxiety, hyperthyroidism;
"bucking" respirator

FIG. 4-22 Quick reference chart for blood gases. (From Budassi, S.A.: J.E.N. 3[2]:24-27, 1977.)

Definitions

acid—A hydrogen ion donor; carbonic acid (H_2CO_3) is an acid.

base—A hydrogen ion acceptor; bicarbonate (HCO_3) is a base.

acidosis—Increased acid concentration and/or decreased base concentration. A pH of less than 7.4 is considered acidosis. A pH less than 7.3 is considered within the "danger range." Severe alkalosis is a central nervous system depressant.

Signs and symptoms: judgment errors, lethargy, disorientation

alkalosis—Increased base concentration and/or decreased acid concentration. A pH greater than 7.4 is considered alkalosis. A pH greater than 7.6 is considered within the "danger range." Severe alkalosis is a central nervous system excitant.

Signs and symptoms: tingling of fingertips, muscle spasms, seizures

pH—The hydrogen ion concentration of a solution; the relationship of carbonic acid (H_2CO_3) and bicarbonate (HCO_3) determines the pH of human serum. Acid-base balance is a function of the ratio of carbonic acid (H_2CO_3) to bicarbonate (HCO_3).

IV SOLUTIONS
Dextrose (5%) in water (D5W)

A hypotonic solution of dextrose in water containing 50 g dextrose monohydrate/liter

Use: TKO IV lines and nonelectrolyte fluid replacement, medical lines (emergency and other)

Contraindications: Head injuries; may increase intracranial pressure

Normal saline

A crystalloid, isotonic solution containing
9.0 g NaCl/liter
145 mEq Na/liter
145 mEq Cl/liter

Use: Restoration of water and salt loss in hypovolemic states; as irrigation solution

Contraindications: Congestive heart failure, pulmonary edema, renal impairment, edematous states with sodium retention

Dextrose (2.5%) and half normal saline

An isotonic solution containing
25 g dextrose monohydrate/liter
4.5 g NaCl/liter

Use: Maintenance fluid

Contraindications: Congestive heart failure, renal impairment, edema with sodium retention

Dextrose (5%) and Ringer's lactate

A hypertonic solution containing

50 g dextrose monohydrate	300 mg KCl/liter
8.6 g NaCl/liter	330 mg CaCl/liter

TABLE 4-1. Fluid resuscitation choices in hemorrhagic shock*

Solution	Advantages	Disadvantages	Use
Crystalloids: *low molecular weight electrolyte or carbohydrate solutions; flow freely between intravascular and interstitial fluid components*			
Lactated Ringer's (Hartmann's) solution	Stable when stored at room temperature	Must infuse 2-4 times the amount lost; possibility of fluid overload and respiratory complications	Rapid expansion of extracellular fluid space with resultant plasma volume expansion
Normal saline	Inexpensive		Correction of interstitial sodium and fluid deficits
5% dextrose in normal saline	Nontoxic	Non-oxygen carrying	To replace blood loss of 1,000 ml or more
5% dextrose in Ringer's	Electrolyte concentration similar to plasma	Lacks plasma-specific osmotic activity	
		Reduces buffering ability of blood	
		Dilutes red cells and protein	
		Volume expansion is transient	
Colloids: *solutions containing high molecular weight particles; remain in intravascular fluid compartment, exerting osmotic pressure to expand plasma volume*			
Whole blood	Oxygen-carrying capacity	Hepatitis risk	To replace blood loss of 1,000 ml or more
	Provides plasma proteins	Expensive	
	Restores some clotting factors if fresh	Limited supply	
	Very fresh blood contains viable platelets	21-day storage life	
		Deficient in clotting factors and platelets	
		High potassium and acid content	
		Degenerated platelets and white blood cells have been blamed for wet lung and disseminating intravascular coagulopathy	
		Cold blood requires warming	
		Citrated stored blood binds ionized calcium	
		Typing and cross-matching necessary except in dire emergencies, in which O− uncross-matched or type-specific un-cross-matched blood is used; O+ can also be used for men and women past child-bearing age if O− unobtainable	
		Possible transfusion reactions	

*From J.E.N. 3(5):51, 1977.

Continued.

TABLE 4-1. Fluid resuscitation choices in hemorrhagic shock—cont'd

Solution	Advantages	Disadvantages	Use
Active blood component therapy Albumin	No hepatitis risk Easily stored Exerts osmotic pressure	Infuses slowly Massive hemorrhage would require a large amount Non–oxygen carrying Does not provide clotting factors Transient effect if used alone Increases tendency toward respiratory failure	Concurrently with crystalloids as a blood volume expander To increase colloidal osmotic pressure
Packed cells	More red blood cell masses than white Oxygen-carrying capacity Less acid and potassium load than whole blood Increased hematocrit Minimum antigen-antibody level	Expensive Some hepatitis risk Deficient in clotting factors 21-day storage limitation	To replace red blood cell mass To improve use of blood products
Plasma (single donor or pooled)	Exerts osmotic pressure Physiologically similar to body plasma	Expensive Hepatitis risk great Deficient in clotting factors Non–oxygen carrying	Plasma volume expander To replace plasma lost in burns To combat hemorrhage when blood is not immediately available
Fresh frozen plasma	Physiologically similar to body plasma Exerts osmotic pressure Has clotting factors (except platelets)	Expensive Takes 20 minutes to thaw Decreased factor V levels after 2 months Hepatitis risk Non–oxygen carrying Thrombocytopenic bleeding can occur	Plasma volume expander To provide clotting factors
Plasma protein fraction (Plasmanate)	Easily stored Physiologically similar to body plasma A source of protein Prolonged blood volume expansion	Expensive Non–oxygen carrying Platelet deficient	Same as plasma

Artificial colloids: *colloidlike solutions of large carbohydrate molecules that stay in the intravascular space, exerting osmotic pressure to expand plasma volume*

Dextran 70 (Macrodex), Gentran, Expandex Dextran 40 (low molecular weight dextran, Rheomacrodex)	Effective plasma volume expander Shelf storage Inexpensive Some evidence of reducing sludging of red blood cells and increasing blood flow to microcirculation units	May cause clotting deficiencies Possibility of renal toxicity Possibility of allergic reaction Interferes with coagulation and testing for coagulation defects Interferes with typing and cross-matching procedures May cause increased hemorrhage and hematoma formation by reducing platelet aggregation; should not be used in patients with known bleeding tendencies, clotting factor deficiency, or oliguria Dextran 40 may create fluid overload due to rapid volume expansion; contraindicated for patients with overhydration or congestive heart failure	Last choice of available blood substitutes As supplement to crystalloid infusion for plasma volume expansion Dextran 40 exerts osmotic pressure for 6-8 hours, Dextran 70 for 24 hours Dextran 70 useful to reduce transcapillary fluid leak into interstitial spaces during sepsis; expands volume slightly in excess of volume infused; maximum recommended infusion is 500 ml for 24 hours Dextran 40 expands volume by twice the volume infused; improves tissue perfusion by expanding intravascular volume and by decreasing blood viscosity

Use: To replace fluid and electrolyte loss
Contraindications: Congestive heart failure, renal impairment, edema with sodium retention

Ringer's lactate

A crystalloid isotonic polyelectrolyte solution equaling the electrolyte concentration in human plasma and containing

13.0 mEq Na/liter	109 mEq Cl/liter
4 mg K/liter	2.8 mEq lactate/liter

Use: In hypovolemia for volume replacement
Contraindications: Congestive heart failure, renal impairment, edema with sodium retention, head injury, liver disease, respiratory alkalosis

Dextran 75

A colloid solution containing
  6% Gentran in 0.7% NaCl
Should be administered through a blood filter

Use: Treatment of shock, hemorrhage, burns
Contraindications: Bleeding disorders, congestive heart failure, renal impairment

Plasma

A colloid solution and the liquid fraction of unclotted whole blood containing

135 to 150 Na/liter	98 to 106 Cl/liter
3.5 to 5.0 K/liter	22 to 30 HCl_3/litr

Should be administered through a blood filter

Use: Volume replacement
Contraindications: Congestive heart failure, pulmonary edema

Plasmanate

A colloid and commercial IV solution containing
  Human albumin, 88%
  Alpha globulin, 7%
  Beta globulin, 5%
  Polyelectrolyte solution
    100 mEq Na/liter
    50 mEq Cl/liter
Should be administered through a blood filter

Use: Blood volume expansion
Contraindications: Congestive heart failure, pulmonary edema

Salt-poor albumin

A colloid solution containing
  Normal human albumin, 25%

Alpha globulin, 7%

Protein, 12.5%

Should be administered through a blood filter

Use: Urgent fluid volume replacement because of trauma or burns; rarely used in trauma management today

Contraindications: Congestive heart failure, pulmonary edema

Special fluid needs

Patients with special fluid needs in the emergency setting include those with hypovolemia caused by gastrointestinal bleeding, trauma, dehydration, or septic shock.

For gastrointestinal loss administer:

0.45% normal saline with 20 mEq KCl for gastric content loss

0.45% normal saline with 30 to 40 mEq KCl for fluid and electrolyte loss from diarrhea

For hypovolemia caused by trauma administer:

Ringer's lactate or normal saline (warmed to 40° C) up to 8 liters, with whole blood given as soon as available; give 1 unit of fresh-frozen plasma for every 4 units of whole blood

If citrated whole blood is being used, administer 10 ml of 10% calcium chloride solution for every 4 units of whole blood (through an alternate IV line); citrate in banked blood binds the patient's free calcium, and therefore additional calcium must be given

BLOOD AND BLOOD COMPONENTS

GENERAL PRINCIPLES

If a patient is losing blood, he is losing *all* components.

Blood replacement with fresh whole blood cells is best, but it is difficult to obtain large amounts.

It requires 30 to 45 minutes to type and cross-match blood properly.

If the need is urgent, type-specific (A, B, AB, or O) unmatched blood can be given to decrease the hazard of reaction.

COMPLICATIONS

Mismatched blood

Hypothermia

Hypocalcemia

Hyperkalemia—potassium levels increase in stored blood by 1 mEq/liter/day

Acid-base problems—stored blood has a pH of 6.4 to 6.8; check arterial blood gases and give $NaHCO_3$ accordingly

Coagulation defects—especially disseminated intravascular coagulation (DIC)

CARE OF THE PATIENT RECEIVING VOLUME REPLACEMENT

Check the airway frequently

Auscultate the lungs

TABLE 4-2 Transfusion reactions*

Reaction	Cause	Prevention	Assessment	Intervention
Hemolytic	Blood incompatibility	Type and crossmatch; infuse first 50 ml slowly	Fever; chills; dyspnea; tachypnea; lumbar pain; fever; oliguria; hematuria; tightness in chest; collect blood and urine samples	Discontinue immediately; fatality may occur after 100 ml infused
Allergic	Antibody reaction to allergens	Screen donors for allergy; antihistamines before transfusion	*Mild:* chills; hives; wheezing; vertigo; angioneurotic edema; itching *Severe:* dyspnea; bronchospasm	*Mild:* slow infusion; give antihistamine as ordered *Severe:* stop infusion; epinephrine may be ordered
Pyrogenic	Infusing chilled blood	Screen donors; use aseptic technique in administration	Fever; chills; nausea; lumbar pain	Stop infusion
Hypothermic	Infusing chilled blood	Give at room temperature; use warming coils for rapid infusion	Chills	Slow infusion; cover client
Circulatory overload	Infusion of large amounts of blood especially to clients with cardiac disease or extremes of age	Infuse slowly; check drip rate frequently	Rales; cough; dyspnea; cyanosis; pulmonary edema; increased CVP	Stop infusion; treat pulmonary edema; apply rotating tourniquets
Air embolism	Entry of air in vein	Use proper infusion technique; avoid giving under pressure; check connections to tubings; avoid Y-tubes; use filter; use plastic containers	Chest pain; dyspnea; hypotension; venous distention	Stop infusion; position on left side; give oxygen; embolectomy may be performed
Hypocalcemic	Precipitate from ACD	Use blood immediately	Numbness; tingling in extremities	Stop infusion; give calcium as ordered
Hyperkalemic	Hemolysis of red blood cells releases potassium	Use blood immediately	Nausea; vomiting, muscle weakness; bradycardia	Stop infusion

*From Barber, J., Stokes, L., and Billings, D.: Adult and child care: a client approach to nursing, ed. 2, St. Louis, 1977, The C.V. Mosby Co.

Monitor the ECG
Check urinary output
Check temperature
Check electrolytes
Check hematocrit

THE COLLECTION OF LABORATORY SPECIMENS
The collection of blood

Most patients have blood samples collected at some time during their emergency department visit. These blood values may be used to establish a baseline, identify trends, or diagnose a particular condition. Always explain to the patient that blood is going to be drawn for some tests. If the patient asks what the tests are for, try to explain. The patient should be lying or sitting while the specimen is being collected.

SELECTION OF THE SITE

Usually the median cephalic vein, located in the antecubital fossa, is used for the collection of blood. The care giver may, however, use any other peripheral site that is readily accessible. If an IV line must also be initiated, the care giver may consider establishing the IV line and withdrawing a blood sample from that line before connecting the IV solution. This will save the patient from an additional puncture and may also save time.

A tourniquet may be applied first to observe for a suitable vein. Remember that the care giver is not committed to search for a vein with a needle if one cannot be located by sight. The care giver may choose to search for an alternate access site, perhaps in another extremity.

METHODS TO FIND A VEIN

Apply a tourniquet and leave it in place for 5 minutes.
Lower the extremity, causing the site from which the specimen is to be collected to be dependent.
Apply warm soaks to the area.
Have the patient open and close his hand.
Use good direct lighting.
Feel for a vein with the fingers; sometimes good large veins are a bit deeper and cannot be visualized but can be palpated.

In an absolute emergency situation, when a site for drawing blood cannot be located, the specimen may be drawn from the femoral vein. This site is not routinely recommended because of the increased incidence of infection and/or embolization.

PROCEDURE

Once the site has been identified, cleanse it with an antiseptic solution such as alcohol or an iodine-based solution (be sure to check to see if the patient is allergic to any of these preparations). Then:
Palpate the site above the proposed needle entry point; do not touch the actual site.

Have the patient open and close his fist to allow for venous filling.

Stabilize the vein with a thumb.

Draw the skin taut below the site to prevent the vein from moving during puncture.

Insert the needle at a 30° angle with the bevel facing up.

    If using a Vacutainer, insert the laboratory tube at this point.

    If using the needle-and-syringe technique, begin to pull back on the plunger of the syringe at this point.

Once the correct amount of blood has been collected, release the tourniquet.

Place a dry, sterile 2 × 2-inch gauze square over the needle insertion site and withdraw the needle.

Place a slight amount of pressure over the puncture site.

Place specimens into the correct laboratory tubes if the needle-and-syringe technique was used.

Do not force blood with pressure through the needle and into the laboratory tube.

Be sure to carefully agitate tubes containing any type of preservative or chemical to allow for its dissemination.

Label all tubes carefully using the patient's name, hospital number, the date, and the care giver's initials.

Do not have the patient bend his arm at the elbow to decrease bleeding; rather, have the patient elevate his arm.

BLOOD SAMPLING IN PEDIATRIC PATIENTS

Be sure to restrain children before attempting to draw blood. Specimens may be obtained by finger-stick, heel-stick, or regular venipuncture technique, depending on the nature of the specimen required. If using conventional venipuncture technique, the appropriate size needle for collection would be between 19 and 23 gauge. Pediatric-size vacuum tubes are available in 3 and 5 ml sizes.

Finger-stick technique

This should be done on the ring finger of the nondominant hand.

Cleanse the site.

Apply a small sterile dressing at the completion of the procedure.

Heel-stick technique

This should be done on the lateral aspect of the heel. Use a lancet or the tip of a #11 scapel blade.

BLOOD FOR BLOOD CULTURES

Particular care must be taken when obtaining specimens for blood culture:

1. Separate containers are required for specimens for aerobic, anaerobic, and fungal cultures.
2. The stopper of a culture medium container must be cleansed using a 70% alcohol solution, a dry wipe and/or air drying, and tincture of iodine, followed by dry wiping or air drying.
3. It is recommended that the care giver wear a sterile glove when obtaining the specimen to avoid contamination of the puncture site.

4. The site must also be prepared in the same way as the culture medium stopper.
5. The needle must be changed each time a culture medium is inoculated.
6. The ratio of blood to medium should be 1:10
7. The laboratory slip is labeled with the patient's name, hospital number, date, time, and body temperature, and any antibiotics the patient is taking are listed.
8. The culture medium container is labeled with the patient's name, the hospital number, date, time, and care giver's initials; also include the patient's hospital/emergency department number.

SPINAL FLUID

Usually three to five specimens are sent to the laboratory following a spinal tap.
1. Number the tubes serially during collection.
2. If only one tube is collected, this tube should be sent to the microbiology section of the laboratory for division of the specimen under aseptic conditions following examination for necessary cultures.
3. Transport specimens to the laboratory immediately following collection; do not allow these specimens to sit in the department for prolonged periods.

URINE SPECIMENS

All urine specimens collected in the emergency department should be obtained by at least a midstream clean catch. On occasion it will be necessary to obtain a urine specimen by catherization of the bladder.
1. Use sterile containers.
2. If the physician orders a urinalysis, split the urine and save a specimen (refrigerated) in case a culture and sensitivity test is ordered later.
3. Do not allow specimens to remain at room temperature for more than 30 minutes.

PERCUTANEOUS FLUID OR WOUND DRAINAGE SPECIMENS

Fluids from body cavities or wounds should be collected in a sterile syringe and then transferred to a sterile test tube or bottle. Be sure that specimens collected for anaerobic testing are free of air bubbles before being sent to the lab. If the patient is taking any type of medication, be sure to indicate what it is on the laboratory slip.

EMESIS AND GASTRIC LAVAGE MATERIAL

At certain times it will be necessary to collect an emesis specimen for laboratory analysis. Vomitus should be collected and sent in a clean container.

If the specimen is to be collected from gastric lavage, be sure to send the sample from the initial aspirate. If it is known or suspected what the ingested substance is or if there is an unusual smell about the patient, be sure to indicate this on the laboratory slip as it may aid in identification of toxic material.

STOOL SPECIMENS

If stool is to be sent to the laboratory for culture it should be warm and newly evacuated. It should be sent to the laboratory in a sterile container. If the specimen is obtained by rectal swabbing, be sure that there is particulate matter on the swab. Do not add saline or any other liquid to the specimen, as this may destroy certain parasites.

THROAT SWABS AND SPUTUM SPECIMENS

A throat culture is usually obtained via the oropharyngeal route using a long, sterile, cotton-tipped swab. The swab should then be placed in a sterile culture tube and transported to the laboratory as soon as possible.

Sputum can be collected directly into a dry, sterile container. The specimen should come from deep within the tracheobronchial tree. Saliva is not an acceptable sputum specimen. The specimen should be taken to the laboratory immediately. If the patient cannot cough or is unconscious, it may be necessary to obtain a specimen by suctioning the tracheobronchial tree.

SUGGESTED READINGS

Budassi, S.A., and Barber, J.M.: Emergency nursing: principles and practice, St. Louis, 1981, The C.V. Mosby Co.

Garcia, J.M., Misperita, L.A., and Pinto, R.V.: Percutaneous subclavicular superior vena cava cannulation, Surg. Gynecol. Obstet. **134:**839, 1977.

Kaye, W.E.: Intravenous lifeline techniques. In ACLS textbook, New York, 1981, American Heart Association.

Plumer, A.L.: Principles and practice of IV therapy, ed. 2, Boston, 1975, Little, Brown and Co.

Wilson, R.F.: Lifelines, Emerg. Med. **10:**25, 1978.

Wilson, R.F.: Securing of the lifeline, Emerg. Med. **10:**43, 1978.

CHAPTER 5 Shock

Shock results when there is a lack of oxygen or nutrients available to the cells for use. It may be caused by hypoxia or poor cellular perfusion that occurs for a variety of reasons. There are four main areas responsible for supplying the cells with nutrients and oxygen:

Heart (the pump)

Blood (the fluid)

Vascular system (the pipes)

Capillaries (the gas-exchange area)

There are five types of shock:

hypovolemic—Caused by trauma, hemorrhage, burns, and dehydration.

cardiogenic—Caused by myocardial infarction, cardiac tamponade, and pulmonary embolus.

septic—Caused by massive infection and endotoxin release.

anaphylactic—Caused by a severe allergic reaction that results in the release of histamines, increased capillary permeability, and dilation of arterioles and capillaries.

neurologic (spinal)—Caused by loss of sympathetic tone, which results in dilation of arterioles and venules, which causes decreases in circulating blood supply and blood pressure.

All of the types of shock will be discussed later in this chapter in further detail.

The first hour of therapeutic intervention for shock is the most important. Management is difficult and mortality is high. It is most important to determine if the cause is a volume-deficit problem or a pump-failure problem.

SIGNS AND SYMPTOMS OF SHOCK (IN GENERAL)

Decreased blood pressure

Elevated pulse

Rapid, shallow respirations

Pale, cool, clammy skin

Anxiety

Restlessness

Unconsciousness

Decreased capillary refill (greater than 2 seconds)

DIAGNOSTIC AIDS

Blood pressure (be sure to use appropriate size cuff)

Pulse

TABLE 5-1 Causes of hypotension*

Volume deficits
Whole blood loss
Plasma loss
Interstitial fluid loss or shift
Water deficit
	Endocrine causes
	Adrenocortical insufficiency
	Adrenomedullary dysfunction (e.g., shock
	   before and following resection of pheo-
	   chromocytoma)
	Thyroid crisis
	Hyperinsulinism
	Diabetic coma

Electrolyte deficits or excesses Na, K, Cl, Ca, Mg	

Acid-base imbalance
Respiratory acidosis
Metabolic acidosis
Respiratory alkalosis
Metabolic alkalosis
	Shock during operation
	Hypovolemia (from anesthetic vasodilation
	   and preexisting blood-volume deficit, or
	   acute blood loss)
	Heart failure
	  Hypoxia

Sepsis
Septicemia
Infection with fluid shift (peritonitis)
	Hypercapnia
	  Myocardial ischemia
	  Arrhythmia
	Miscellaneous other causes

Respiratory insufficiency
Hypoxia
Hypercapnia
Right-to-left pulmonary shunts (atelectasis,
   pneumonia, lung contusion)
Pneumothorax
Mechanical disturbances caused by trauma
   (flail chest, tracheolaryngeal injury)
Pulmonary embolism
	Shock in recovery room
	Hypovolemia
	Cardiac failure
	  Hypoxia
	  Hypercapnia (caused by inadequate ventila-
	   tion)
	  Coronary insufficiency
	  Arrhythmia
	  Electrolyte imbalance
	Endotoxin shock
	Pulmonary embolus
	Excessive medication

Cardiac causes Cardiac arrest or fibrillation Coronary occlusion Pericardial tamponade Cardiac arrhythmia Myocardial failure Cardiac contusion	
	Miscellaneous Drug reactions Transfusion reactions Fat embolism Hepatic failure Anaphylaxis
Central nervous system causes Brain injury Increased intracranial pressure Reflex vagal stimuli Psychic stimuli Brainstem and spinal cord injury	

*From Gurd, with modifications and additions. Adapted from Hardy, J.D.: Shock and cardiac arrest. In Hardy, J.D.: Critical surgical illness. Philadelphia, 1971. W.B. Saunders Co.

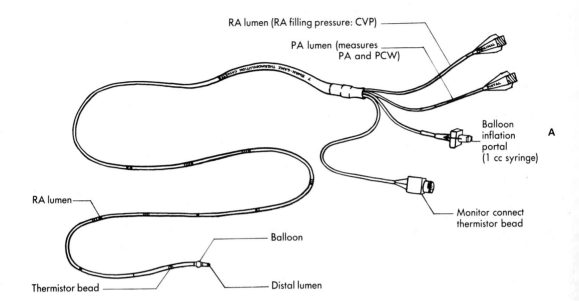

RA lumen (RA filling pressure: CVP)

PA lumen (measures PA and PCW)

Balloon inflation portal (1 cc syringe)

A

Monitor connect thermistor bead

RA lumen

Balloon

Thermistor bead

Distal lumen

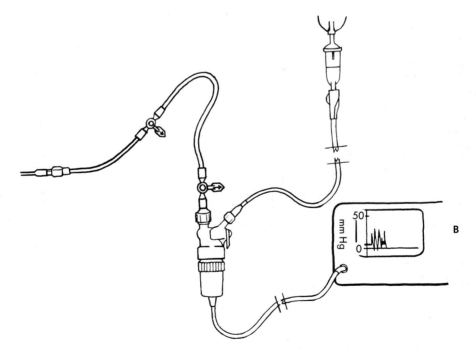

50

mm Hg

0

B

FIG. 5-1 A, Swan-Ganz thermodilution catheter. **B,** Arterial or Swan-Ganz line set up with pressure transducer.

Respirations

Temperature

Neurologic examination (using DERM mnemonic—see Chapter 7)

Skin vital signs (color, temperature, and moistness)

Capillary refill

Jugular venous pressure

Neck veins—distended neck veins indicate cardiogenic or pulmonary causes, such as tamponade, myocardial infarction, pulmonary embolus, or tension pneumothorax; flat neck veins indicate hypovolemic causes, such as trauma or severe dehydration

Urinary output (measure hourly via indwelling catheter)

Arterial pressure (via radial, femoral, or brachial arteries; much more reliable than cuff reading) (Fig. 5-1)

Arterial blood gases

Central venous pressure

Oxygen consumption

Pulmonary capillary wedge pressure (via Swan-Ganz line; greater than 17 mm Hg indicates pulmonary congestion; greater than 25 mm Hg indicates pulmonary edema)

Cardiac output (using thermodilution line in Swan-Ganz line; poor prognosis if cardiac output is less than 2.5 liters/minute/meter^2)

PROBLEMS IN THE FIVE VITAL ORGANS ASSOCIATED WITH SHOCK

The heart Decreased coronary artery perfusion causes decreased function of the heart as a pump; stroke volume and blood pressure decrease.

The brain If oxygen and nutrient supplies are low, brain function will diminish.

The lungs As the partial pressure of oxygen decreases because of decreased blood volume, gas exchange does not take place at the capillary membrane level.

The liver Glycogen stores are depleted by an excess of circulating epinephrine; also, metabolic acids that are normally detoxified in the liver cause acidosis.

The kidneys A decrease in cardiac output causes a decrease in blood flow through the kidneys; a decreased urinary output and renal failure result.

BLOOD PRESSURE

Blood pressure is a result of cardiac output multiplied by peripheral vascular resistance (BP = CO × PVR). When either decreases, blood pressure will decrease. When either rises, blood pressure will rise. Cardiac output is determined by preload, contractility, afterload, and heart rate.

Preload is the length and the force of myocardial contraction. Contractility is the force of myocardial muscle contraction. Afterload is the amount of pressure in the left ventricle required to cause the muscle to contract (an increased afterload causes stroke volume and cardiac output to decrease). Heart rate is the number of heartbeats per minute caused by pacemaker stimulation of the conducting system of the heart.

PULMONARY ARTERY WEDGE PRESSURE

The pulmonary artery wedge (PAW) pressure provides a rather precise indication of left ventricular function for early detection of limitations of cardiac competence and provides a guide for fluid replacement. A flow-directed balloon-tipped catheter is usually used (Fig. 5-2).

1. Position the patient in Trendelenburg's position if insertion is into the internal jugular, external jugular, or subclavian vein.

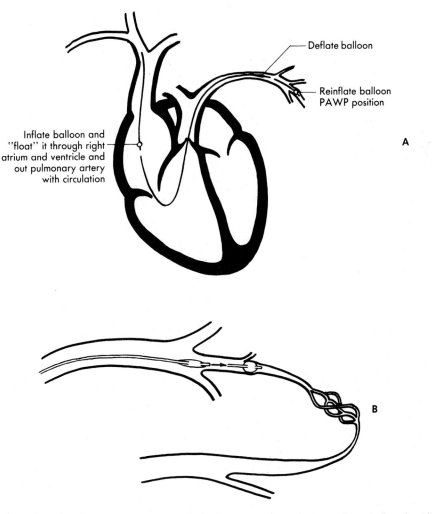

FIG. 5-2 A, Position of Swan-Ganz catheter in heart and great vessels. **B,** Balloon inflated and floated into wedge position.

2. Prepare a percutaneous insertion site by scrubbing with antiseptic solution and drying, or do a surgical cutdown (see pp. 103-104) to gain access to a peripheral vein. Acceptable sites include:
   Internal jugular vein
   Supraclavicular or infraclavicular subclavian vein (infraclavicular approach has higher risk of pneumothorax)
   Brachial vein
   Antecubital vein
   Femoral vein
3. Enter the vein with a suitable needle and/or catheter introducer with spring guide, thin-walled sheath, and a tapered perforating catheter. When the catheter introducer is in place, remove the spring guide and perforating catheter, leaving the sheath in place, through which to advance the monitoring catheter. When this has been accomplished, withdraw the sheath over the catheter.
4. When the catheter is in the vena cava, inflate the balloon at the tip (with air or carbon dioxide) and advance the catheter through the right atrium and ventricle into the pulmonary artery. *Observe for dysrhythmias,* especially when the catheter passes through the right ventricle.
5. Advance the catheter smoothly to retard venospasm.
6. When the catheter ceases to advance, deflate the balloon and advance the catheter slightly.
7. Position the catheter tip so that the pulmonary artery (PA) pressure reading is obtained with the inflated balloon.
8. Secure the catheter with a suture and close the incision. Apply a sterile dressing to the site. Tape the site securely to protect the catheter and dressing.

Measurement with the standard strain gauge pressure transducer*

The following method is used for obtaining PA and PAW pressure readings with the standard strain gauge pressure transducer:

1. Deflate the balloon to obtain the PA pressure. After calibrating and zeroing the pressure monitor, close the two-way stopcock of the transducer to room air to enclose the pressure. Then close the three-way stopcock to the IV drip; this closing off of the IV fluid opens the catheter pressure to the transducer. Observe the oscilloscope for the characteristic PA pressure wave form. Take a pressure reading and record it.
2. To obtain a PAW pressure, inflate the balloon until the wave form changes to the PAW pressure wave form. *Inflate the balloon only enough to change the wave form.* Overinflation causes damping of the pressure wave form and may cause intrapulmonary hemorrhage. Take a pressure reading and record it. Inflate the balloon for only a few minutes at a time to prevent the development of pulmonary infarction.
3. Deflate the balloon after the PAW pressure reading is obtained.

---

*From Schroeder, J.S., and Daily, E.K.: Techniques in bedside hemodynamic monitoring, St. Louis, 1976, The C.V. Mosby Co.

4. After recording pressures, first close the three-way stopcock to the transducer; then open the two-way stopcock to room air. Adjust the IV drip to maintain catheter patency. If the PA pressure is extremely high (>40 or >50 mm Hg), it may be necessary to use a pressure bag to maintain a continuous IV drip.
5. If the wave form is damped on the oscilloscope or the IV solution is not dripping well, the catheter may be excessively wedged or have a thrombus occluding the tip. Pull back the catheter first and flush it if the pressure tracing remains damped.

Measurement with the miniature strain gauge pressure transducer*

The miniature strain gauge pressure transducer facilitates bedside hemodynamic monitoring because of its durability, convenience, and very small size. It is based on the same fluid displacement principle as the standard model but requires a small volume displacement, so that it is small enough to connect directly to the catheter. This feature eliminates the need for connecting tubes from the catheter to the transducer. Fig. 5-3 illustrates its placement on the catheter, connections to the IV system, and a continuous flush (Sorenson Intraflo) device that can be used if desired. A Luer-Lok stopcock is placed between the catheter and the Intraflow device to facilitate blood sampling and for room air reference for zeroing of the amplifiers. The transducers also have a release valve so that inadvertent

---

*From Schroeder, J.S., and Daily, E.K.: Techniques in bedside hemodynamic monitoring, St. Louis, 1976, The C.V. Mosby Co.

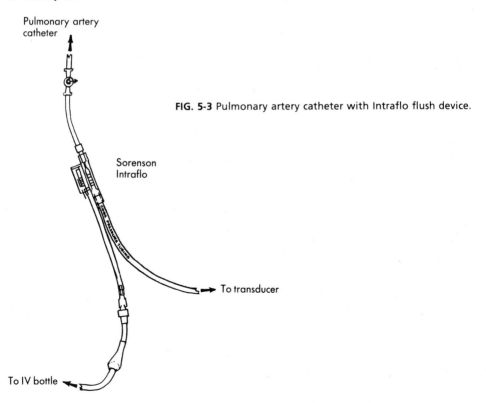

Pulmonary artery catheter

Sorenson Intraflo

FIG. 5-3 Pulmonary artery catheter with Intraflo flush device.

To transducer

To IV bottle

pressure injection into the transducer system without the catheter being open will not damage the sensitive transducer dome.

The following method is used with the miniature transducer:

1. Attach a three-way Luer-Lok stopcock to the fluid-filled Intraflow device.
2. With the stopcock open and the IV fluid flowing out the port, attach the stopcock to the catheter.
3. Loosen the retaining nut of the transducer one quarter of a turn.
4. Flush IV fluid through the dome of the transducer, expelling all the air.
5. Tighten the retaining screw and attach the transducer to the remaining end of the Intraflow device.
6. Turn the Luer-Lok stopcock to open the transducer to room air and attach the transducer cable to the pressure amplifier.
7. Adjust the amplifier at zero and perform the appropriate calibration procedure.
8. Adjust the heights of the arm and the transducer to the level of the heart. This adjustment is necessary so that hydrostatic pressure differences of the fluid column between the heart and the transducer will not give falsely high or low measurements.
9. Turn the stopcock to open the pathway from the catheter to the transducer to record pressures.

Each miniature transducer must be calibrated according to a specific procedure before it is used.

After each use, the transducer should be cleaned by flushing with activated dialdehyde solution or by gas sterilization as previously described. Care should be taken during cleaning to keep the electrical connector cable of the transducer dry at all times.

Defibrillation during a cardiac arrest may cause irreparable damage to the transducer if it is connected to the patient. If the transducer is not electrically isolated, it is necessary to remove it from the catheter before electrical defibrillation.

HYPOVOLEMIC SHOCK

Hypovolemic shock is the result of an intravascular volume deficit (greater than 15% to 25% blood loss). The degree of shock depends on several factors:

The volume lost

The rate of volume lost

The age of the patient

The patient's general physical condition

The patient's compensatory mechanisms

The average 70 kg (150-pound) person, there is approximately 5,000 ml (5 liters) of circulating blood volume. If there is a blood loss of 1,500 ml (1.5 liters) severe hypovolemic shock will usually occur.

SIGNS AND SYMPTOMS

anxiety and restlessness or coma—Caused by catecholamine stimulation of the cerebrum and hypoxia.

decreased blood pressure—Caused by decreased blood volume; a blood loss of 10% to

Postural vital signs

Assessment

Indications: Postural vital signs should be assessed on all patients with (1) evidence of significant fluid loss through bleeding, vomiting, diarrhea, perspiration, or wound drainage; (2) unexplained tachycardia; (3) hypotension without tachycardia; (4) history or suspicion of chronic or concealed bleeding; or (5) blunt abdominal or chest trauma.

Contraindications: Postural vital signs are *not* indicated if other injuries or the patient's general condition preclude safe administration of the test.

Rationale for test: When a patient assumes a vertical position, gravity tends to cause sequestration (pooling) of blood in the capacitance vessels of the legs and trunk. Normally, individuals adapt readily to this postural change through rapid vasoconstriction of the vessels in which the blood tends to pool. This adjustment is not possible for the volume-depleted patient whose vasoconstrictor potential has already been maximimally utilized.

Interpreting results: Postural changes (from lying to sitting or standing) resulting in a *decrease* of 20 mm Hg or more in the systolic or diastolic blood pressure or *increase* of 20 beats or more per minute in the pulse rate is a *positive* test result, and the patient should be considered *hypovolemic* until proved otherwise.

CAUTION! The patient may experience weakness, dizziness, visual disturbances, or fainting during the test. These symptoms are promptly eliminated in most instances when the patient lies down again. Be certain to protect the patient during the assessment of postural vital signs to prevent injuries.

Test*

1. With the patient supine, take and record the blood pressure and pulse as a baseline against which changes of both measures taken after position changes can be evaluated.
2. Have the patient sit up to a 90° position and again record the blood pressure and pulse.
3. Have the patient stand if possible, and again record the blood pressure and pulse. If significant changes occur, or if the patient's symptoms become acute during the sitting portion of the test, the third step may be eliminated and the results of the sitting portion considered positive.

Correct charting of the results is done in the following manner:

BP 120/80, P 88   BP 110/60, P 100   BP 90/50, P 120

*From Bookman, L.B., and Simoneau, J.K.: J.E.N. **3**:43, 1977.

15% will cause blood pressure to decrease and pulse to rise orthostatically; a blood loss of greater than 30% will cause blood pressure to decrease and pulse to rise when the patient is supine.

elevated pulse—A compensatory mechanism for blood loss.

rapid, shallow respirations—An attempt to decrease acidosis and improve the hypoxic state by blowing off CO_2.

pale, cool, clammy skin—Caused by vasoconstriction.

decreased capillary refill time—Caused by decreased blood volume.

increased thirst—Caused by intracellular and intravascular volume depletion.

decreased urinary output—Caused by decreased blood flow through kidneys.

decreased hematocrit—Initially is normal; then, because of fluid shift to intravascular space (a compensatory mechanism), a dilutional effect and thus a drop in hematocrit occur.

decreased central venous pressure—Caused by volume depletion; less than 5 cm water.

decreased pulmonary capillary wedge pressure—Caused by volume depletion; less than 4 mm Hg.

DEGREES OF HYPOVOLEMIC SHOCK

Mild—10% to 20% blood loss
Moderate—20% to 40% blood loss
Severe—greater than 40% blood loss

COMPENSATORY MECHANISMS IN HYPOVOLEMIC SHOCK

Compensatory mechanisms will assist in maintaining blood pressure in most patients up to about a 30% blood loss.

sympathetic discharge—This mechanism can compensate for up to about a 10% to 25% blood loss; it causes the small veins and venules to constrict, diverts blood to the vital organs and increases heart and respiratory rates.

renin-angiotensin mechanism—Because of a decreased blood flow through the kidneys, renin is released from the kidneys causing the release of angiotensin I and II. This causes aldosterone to be released, which increases sodium resorption from the renal tubules and subsequently increases vascular volume.

antidiuretic hormone (ADH)—ADH is released by the anterior pituitary gland, causing increased water resorption at the renal tubules. This results in increases in vascular volume, mean systolic pressure, cardiac output, and venous return.

fluid shift—Fluid shifts from the intracellular space to the intravascular space to provide volume.

COMPLICATIONS OF HYPOVOLEMIC SHOCK

hypoxia—Tissue hypoxia; caused by stimulation of chemoreceptors, which causes increased respiratory rate and increased peripheral vascular resistance.

metabolic acidosis—Caused by hypoperfusion and hypoxia, which cause anerobic metabolism.

respiratory acidosis—Caused by decreased gas exchange at the alveolar capillary membrane level and by metabolic acidosis.

myocardial infarction—Caused by decreased coronary artery perfusion.

renal failure—Caused by decreased renal artery perfusion.

cerebral edema—Caused by decreased cerebral perfusion.

sepsis—Caused by intestinal mucosa damage and reticular endothelial system damage.

adult respiratory distress syndrome (ARDS)—Caused by intravascular volume decrease, decreased blood pressure, and decreased colloid osmotic pressure.

disseminated intravascular coagulation (DIC)—Caused by acidosis that results in increased coagulation. This causes blockage of the small vessels and resultant congestion at the postcapillary sphincters and relaxation of the precapillary sphincters. An aggregation of platelets and DIC result.

THERAPEUTIC INTERVENTION

Oxygen

MAST application

IVs with Ringer's lactate or normal saline solution; can give crystalloids up to 8 liters

Consider blood products:

O— if blood is needed immediately

Type-specific blood can be ready in 20 minutes

Whole blood is preferable but may take 1 to 2 hours to type and cross-match

Autotransfusion

Control bleeding

Treat trauma (see Chapter 23)

Psychologic support

Possible surgical intervention

AUTOTRANSFUSION

Autotransfusion is a technique for managing massive hemorrhage by the collection of blood shed by the patient and the return of this blood after processing (filtering and defoaming via an autotransfuser pump). Emergency candidates for autotransfusion include patients with:

Exsanguinating hemorrhage

Religious beliefs that oppose use of another individual's blood via transfusion

Hemorrhage in which banked blood is not readily available, that is, extremely urgent cases in which there is not time for pretransfusion laboratory tests or delivery of blood from a distant site

Difficult blood to type and cross-match for which no suitable banked blood is available

History of previous transfusion reactions

Contraindications include patients with:

Wounds more than 4 hours old

Gross contamination of shed blood by leakage of abdominal contents

Inadequate liver or kidney function

Autotransfusion requires that all members of the core emergency team be well versed in the use of the autotransfuser and understand the procedures involved in preparing both the patient and the equipment for the autotransfusion. Since the procedure is only an interim adjunct to management of shock from hemorrhage, the surgical personnel should be alert at once regarding this patient.

EMERGENCY MANAGEMENT

1. Prehospital personnel should alert the emergency department that they are en route with a candidate for autotransfusion so that hospital personnel can ready the equipment and supplies. (Other prehospital care, of course, is carried out as usual.)
2. Obtain a urine sample for urinalysis and venous blood for testing:
   Partial thromboplastin time (PTT)
   Thrombin time
   Prothrombin time
   Fibrinogen level
   Fibrinogen split products
   Free plasma hemoglobin
   Potassium
   Calcium
   Creatinine
   BUN
   Complete blood count
   Platelet count
3. Draw blood for arterial blood gas testing.
4. Proceed with autotransfusion* after taking baseline vital signs and ensuring that basic life support needs have been met, including delivery of high-flow oxygen and regular administration of resuscitative fluids (i.e., other than autotransfused blood, such as plasma protein fraction [Plasmanate]). At least two IV lines must be established, and monitoring the CVP is recommended.
5. Record the approximate amount of shed blood collected and retransfused along with the type and amount of any anticoagulants. Note the source of blood collected.
6. Monitor the patient for complications.
   a. Air or fat embolus (see Chapter 26)
   b. Bleeding caused by coagulation defects
   c. Hypothermia
   d. DIC
   e. Hemolysis of red cells
   f. Sepsis
7. After the transfusion continue to monitor previously cited laboratory values and vital signs.
8. Consider the use of platelet transfusions and forced diuresis if indicated.
   The main advantage of autotransfusion is rapid availability of warm, perfectly typed and cross-matched (the patient's own) whole blood.

Disadvantages of autotransfusion

1. A skilled person is required to run the pump. This person is involved in the autotransfusion procedure only and is not available for other tasks in the care of the patient.
2. There is a possibility of air embolism (extreme caution is required).
3. There may be a bleeding problem because of the necessity of anticoagulation with heparin or citratephosphodextrose (CPD).

*The procedure usually involves collecting blood via chest tubes. Details of the procedure vary with the bleeding site and the autotransfuser apparatus.

4. It has limited usefulness (i.e., it can only be used to collect blood from the chest cavity; abdominal blood is considered to be contaminated).

MILITARY ANTISHOCK TROUSERS (MAST)

The MAST is probably the single most important piece of equipment the emergency department can have for care of multiple-trauma patients or patients with hypovolemic shock of other causes. It is made of nylon and is waterproof, flame resistant, and radio-lucent. It has three separate chambers and inflates to a maximum pressure of 104 mm Hg. It has pop-off valves to avoid overinflation, and in-line gauges are available to measure actual pressures in each chamber. It comes in an adult and a pediatric size. The adult size fits people over 5 feet tall and the pediatric size fits people from 3½ to 5 feet tall. There is a problem using the MAST with people under 3½ feet and with very tall or very obese patients. There is an opening in the perineal area to allow for bladder catherization. There are also open foot areas to allow for palpation of pedal pulses, electrode placement, venous cutdowns, and so on.

How to apply the MAST

1. Place the unfolded unit under the patient.
2. Wrap the abdominal section around the patient just below the costal margin.
3. Wrap the leg sections.
4. Inflate the leg sections first, using the foot pump or an adapter attached to a demand-valve respirator.
5. Inflate the abdominal section.

How the MAST works

The MAST compresses peripheral circulation under the suit. It can return approximately 500 to 1,000 ml of blood to the central circulation (Fig. 5-4). Of the body's total blood volume, 20% to 30% is in the large vessels of the pelvis and lower extremities. This blood can be shunted to the central circulation where it is more essential. The MAST works by exceeding the patient's systolic pressure. The MAST can be applied in about 60 seconds, and the blood it delivers is the patient's own warm, perfectly typed, and cross-matched whole blood.

Application of the MAST is usually not definitive therapy, but it does "buy some time" so that other, definitive therapeutic interventions can be effective.

Advantages of the MAST

In addition to its autotransfusion and increased peripheral vascular resistance capabilities, the MAST has some other advantages. It tamponades bleeding sites by retarding arterial hemorrhage. The effect is direct on the lower extremities and indirect on the large abdominal vessels through increased intraabdominal pressure. Because of this it is especially useful in abdominal aneurysms and pelvic fractures. An additional advantage of the MAST is that it splints the lower extremities and the pelvis. It also distends upper limb veins, making intravenous line initiation less difficult.

For increasing peripheral vascular resistance, the MAST is much faster than the

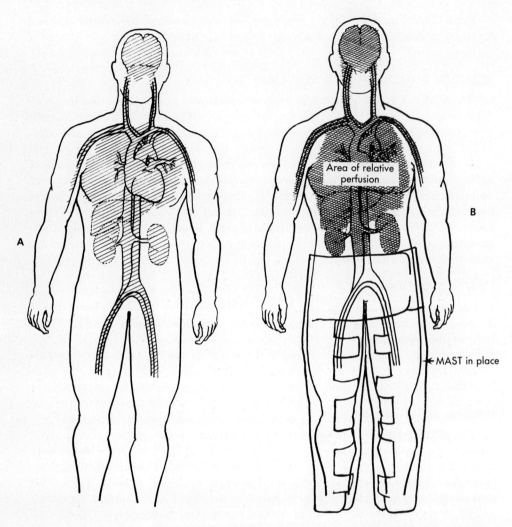

FIG. 5-4 A, Circulation before MAST inflation. **B,** Autotransfusion of blood to essential organs after MAST inflation.

administation of fluid via any size cannula. This autotransfused blood is also able to carry oxygen, a capability that crystalloid solutions do not have. Also, the MAST can be applied while the care giver is initiating IV lines and awaiting the arrival of blood from the blood bank.

When to use the MAST

The MAST can be used in trauma in which hypovolemia is a problem. Hypovolemia is considered to be a systolic blood pressure of less than 80 mm Hg. It is usually caused by the rupture of an organ or great vessel, pelvic fracture, femur fracture, or pericardial tamponade, in which it also has the effect of maximizing Starling's curve. It is also found to be useful in the treatment of hypovolemia caused by spinal shock. It can be used in medically caused hypovolemic states such as overdose, anaphylaxis, gastrointestinal bleeding, DIC, or bleeding after biopsy. The MAST has been found useful in obstetric cases such as postpartum hemorrhage and ruptured ectopic pregnancy. There have been reports in the literature of successful use in cardiac arrest from any cause and in cardiogenic shock.

Hindrances for use of the MAST

It may be impossible to place the MAST for mechanical reasons, such as severe flexion contractures or protrusion of bone fragments. If there is a potentially impaling object that makes the MAST impossible to place, the care giver must weigh the risks of not placing the MAST and leaving the impaling object in place versus the risks of removing the impaling object and placing the MAST. Usually, the systolic blood pressure measurement is the deciding factor—if the patient is severely hypotensive (i.e., has a systolic blood pressure of below 60 mm Hg) the care giver should consider placing the MAST.

Occasionally the size of the MAST may be incompatible with the size of the patient. If a patient is very cachectic, the care giver may consider wrapping both of the patient's legs in one chamber of the MAST. If the patient is very obese, the care giver may consider using the MAST in normal fashion but using tape instead of Velcro to fasten it. The care giver must then be cautious not to overinflate the MAST, as the tape will not release as Velcro does when pressures greater than 104 mm Hg are reached.

Another problem associated with use of the MAST is that emesis, micturition, or defecation may occur because of increased pressure on the abdomen and upward pressure by the diaphragm. Because of this the patient will complain of being uncomfortable. It is then important to provide him with constant reassurance.

Pay close attention to wounds and other abdominal signs before placing the MAST, because once the MAST is in place, these parameters will no longer be observable.

Pay particular attention to the fluid status of the patient. MAST application in combination with rapid fluid administration increases the risks of fluid overload. Therefore monitor blood pressure, pulse, and lung sounds carefully and frequently.

Contraindications

The only absolute contraindication to inflation of the MAST is decreased ventilatory capability caused by COPD or tension pneumothorax. In these instances, and if the patient is severely hypotensive, the care giver should consider inflation of the leg units only.

Debatable issues

There are some conditions for which use of the MAST is debatable. These include the following.

INTRATHORACIC INJURIES

COMMENT: If the patient is bleeding into the thoracic cavity, application of the MAST will cause further bleeding.

RESPONSE: It is better to take advantage of pooled venous blood from the lower extremities and pelvis than to have no blood in the central circulation at all. Remember, the MAST is used to "buy time."

INTRACRANIAL INJURIES

COMMENT: Application of the MAST will increase intracranial pressure.

RESPONSE: This may be true, but if the patient is severely hypotensive and hypovolemic chances are that this condition is not being caused by the head trauma (unless there is a large scalp laceration with massive bleeding). If hypovolemia is severe, the patient will die if not treated. Elevating blood pressure and providing circulation become priorities.

PREGNANCY

COMMENT: The MAST may impair fetal circulation.

RESPONSE: The effects of the MAST on fetal circulation are unknown. If the mother is severely hypotensive the status of the fetus will be compromised, as the mother's bodily response will be to shunt blood to her circulation at the expense of the fetus. At least consider inflation of the leg units and in severe hypovolemic states, maybe the entire MAST.

How effective is the MAST?

The MAST appears to elevate systolic pressure in the large majority of patients.

How to remove the MAST

The MAST should only be removed after vascular volume has been restored or when the patient is in the operating suite for surgery. It should be deflated slowly, one chamber at a time, beginning with the abdominal chamber. A small amount of air should be released, and a blood pressure measurement should be obtained. If blood pressure remains constant, another small amount of air should be released from the MAST. The procedure should be repeated until the entire abdominal section is deflated. If there is a drop in blood pressure, the section should be reinflated and fluid infusion increased. If blood pressure remains constant, the care giver should continue to deflate the two leg chambers individually, following the same procedure as for deflation of the abdominal chamber. The only exception to this removal procedure takes place occasionally in the operating suite. There the abdominal section of the MAST is removed rapidly, and the surgeon makes an abdominal incision without surgical scrub or other preparations. This of course would be used only in extreme emergency cases.

Current controversial areas for use

Cardiac Arrest—it is said that use of the MAST increases intrathoracic pressure by causing minimal diaphragmatic descent. The MAST does assist in resuscitation efforts.

Placenta previa and abruptio placentae—the effects of the MAST on these conditions are not known.

Air transport—The MAST may be used even in unpressurized cabins, because as gas expands and pressure in the MAST increases, pressures above 104 mm Hg will cause gas to escape via bleed-off valves. The care giver must, however, remember to reinflate the MAST on descent.

Electromechanical dissociation—It is recommended that the MAST be used in this condition, because it is often caused by hypovolemia (a cause that is reversible).

How long can the MAST be left inflated?

The optimal maximum time for leaving the inflated MAST in place is 2 hours, although the MAST has been used for many days at low pressures. There have been some favorable reports in the literature regarding the use of the MAST at low pressures (i.e., 30 mm Hg) in the treatment of DIC.

CARDIOGENIC SHOCK

Cardiogenic shock is a decrease in blood pressure (less than 90 mm Hg) in the setting of acute myocardial infarction caused by pump failure. Pump failure is the inability of the infarcted area to contract and produce adequate cardiac output. It usually involves greater than 15% of the left ventricular myocardium. When the infarcted area does not contract, stroke volume decreases and cardiac output drops, with a concurrent increase in left ventricular end diastolic pressure. This decrease in cardiac output will cause a decrease in tissue perfusion.

Cardiogenic shock occurs in 15% of myocardial infarction patients. There is an 85% to 90% mortality.

SIGNS AND SYMPTOMS

Decreased peripheral pulses
Increased respirations
Decreased blood pressure (if blood pressure increases it does so at the expense of myocardial ischemia)
Decreased cardiac output
Decreased level of consciousness (or anxiousness or restlessness)
Congestive heart failure
Myocardial infarction
Pale, cool, clammy skin
Decreased urinary output (less than 20 ml/hour)
Metabolic acidosis
ECG changes
Elevated cardiac enzyme levels
Elevated pulmonary capillary wedge pressure (pressure greater than 18 mm Hg)

THERAPEUTIC INTERVENTION

Oxygen
MAST
IVs

Inotropic agents to decrease left ventricular work load and increase cardiac output and coronary artery perfusion

Dopamine (Intropin)

Dobutamine (Dobutrex)

Vasodilators to decrease left ventricular outflow problems, peripheral vascular resistance, and left ventricular filling pressures and increase cardiac output

Sodium nitroprusside (Nipride)

Nitroglycerine

Corticosteroids to stabilize lysosomal membranes, increase lactate metabolism, and decrease systemic vascular resistance and the size of the infarct

Intraaortic balloon pump (IABP) to increase cardiac output, oxygen delivery, and blood flow to the coronary arteries and to decrease myocardial oxygen consumption

SEPTIC SHOCK

Septic shock is usually caused by an overwhelming infection that results in decreased tissue perfusion because of vasodilation. It may also be caused by immune system suppression, invasion of organs by toxic substances, or the failure of the immune system to react to bacteria. It is important to remember that blood volume in septic shock is essentially normal. The infection may come from a source such as an indwelling urinary catheter or a massive burn in which skin is severely disrupted, or it may occur as a postpartum complication. Mortality from septic shock is high—30% to 50%. Death from septic shock is more common in the very young and the very old.

The usual cause of the infection is a gram-negative enteric bacillus such as *Escherichia coli, Pseudomonas, Staphylococcus, Proteus, Salmonella,* or *Bacteroides.* It is occasionally caused by gram-positive cocci or, on rare occasions, fungi, viruses, or yeast. Bacteria enter the vascular system and cause endotoxin and exotoxin release into the circulation. This causes fluid leaks into the interstitial spaces, increased vascular permeability and vasodilation, and hypotension.

SIGNS AND SYMPTOMS

Decreased blood pressure

Elevated temperature

Elevated pulse

Chills

Tremors

Pink, warm, dry skin

Nausea and vomiting

Decreased level of consciousness

Diarrhea

Increased cardiac output

Initially peripheral vascular resistance decreases and vasodilation is minimal with increased cardiac output. This state is known as "warm shock." Later plasma volume decreases (as plasma leaks into interstitial tissues) and cardiac output drops because of a decreased preload and decreased cellular perfusion. This causes a stagnation of blood and resultant anaerobic metabolism and acidotic state.

THERAPEUTIC INTERVENTION

Oxygen
IV fluids
Antibiotics (be sure to culture any draining wounds first)
Inotropic agents and vasodilators
    Dopamine (Intropin)
    Dobutamine (Dobutrex)
Naloxone (Narcan—has been found to be useful in septic shock states)
Corticosteroids (controversial)

ANAPHYLACTIC SHOCK

Anaphylactic shock is an antigen-antibody reaction that occurs when a sensitized person is exposed to an antigen. It develops rapidly and may be caused by such events as a bee sting or ingestion of food-stuffs or medications. When the antigen-antibody reaction occurs, there is a histamine release that causes arterioles and capillaries to dilate. When the capillaries dilate, capillary permeability increases and intravascular fluid leaks into the interstitial spaces. This causes a form of relative hypovolemia and shock to occur.

SIGNS AND SYMPTOMS

Respiratory difficulty
Stridor
Bronchospasm
Wheezing
Airway obstruction (by enlarged tongue or laryngeal edema)
Warm skin
Urticaria/angioneurotic edema
Dysrhythmias
Cardiopulmonary arrest

THERAPEUTIC INTERVENTION

ABCs
Oxygen
IVs
Epinephrine 0.3 to 0.5 ml of 1:1,000 solution subcutaneously or intramuscularly *or*
Epinephrine 0.1 to 0.5 ml of 1:10,000 solution by *slow* IV push if there is profound
    vasoconstriction (may be repeated in 5 to 15 minutes if necessary)
Aminophylline for bronchospasm
Antihistamines—diphenhydramine (Benadryl)
Steroids

NEUROGENIC SHOCK

Neurogenic shock is caused by a decrease of sympathetic tone. This results in a dilation of arterioles and venules, which causes relative hypotension. Neurogenic shock may result from such causes as spinal anesthesia, spinal cord injury, or direct medullary damage.

SIGNS AND SYMPTOMS

Decreased blood pressure
Rapid, shallow respirations
Elevated pulse rate
Paraplegia or quadriplegia
Priapism

THERAPEUTIC INTERVENTION

ABCs
MAST
Fluids
Cervical spine protection
Thoracic and lumbar spine protection

SUGGESTED READINGS

Braunwald, E., Ross, J., Jr., and Sonnenblick, E.H.: Mechanisms of contraction of the normal and failing heart, Boston, 1968, Little, Brown & Co.

DaLuz, P.L., Weil, M.H., and Shubin, H.: Current concepts on mechanisms and treatment of cardiogenic shock, Am. Heart J. **92:**103, 1976.

DuPoint, H.L., and Spink, W.W.: Infections due to gram negative organisms: an analysis of 860 patients with bacteremia at the University of Minnesota Medical Center, 1958-1966, Medicine **48:**307, 1969.

Hardaway, R.M., et al.: Intensive study of shock in man, JAMA **199:**779, 1967.

Hathaway, R.G.: Hemodynamic monitoring in shock, J.E.N. **3:**37, 1977.

Hathaway, R.G.: The Swan-Ganz catheter: a review, Nurs. Clin. North Am. **13:**389, 1978.

Holaday, J.W., and Faden, A.L.: Naloxone reversal of endotoxin hypotension suggests role of endorphins in shock, Nature **275:**450, 1978.

James, P.N., and Meyers, R.T.: Central venous pressure monitoring: misinterpretation, abuses, indications and a new technique, Ann. Surg. **175:**693, 1971.

Jelenko, C., III, et al.: Shock and resuscitation II. Volume replacement with minimal edema using the halfed method, J.A.C.E.P. **7:**326, 1978.

Jelenko, C., III, et al.: Studies in shock and resuscitation I. Use of hypertonic albumin containing demand regiment (HALFD) in resuscitation, Crit. Care Med. **7:**157, 1979.

Knopp, R., and Dailey, R.: Central venous cannulation and pressure monitoring, J.A.C.E.P. **6:**358, 1977.

Kuhn, L.A.: Management of shock following acute myocardial infarction: drug therapy, Am. Heart J. **95:**529, 1978.

Kuhn, L.A.: Management of shock following acute myocardial infarction: mechanical circulatory assistance, Am. Heart J. **95:**789, 1978.

Perry, A.G., and Potter, P.A., editors: Shock: comprehensive nursing management, St. Louis, 1983, The C.V. Mosby Co.

Shubin, H., and Weil, M.H.: Bacterial shock, JAMA **235:**421, 1976.

Thal, A.P.: Septic shock. In Hardy, J.D.: Textbook of surgery, Philadelphia, 1977, J.B. Lippincott Co.

Thompson, W.L.: The patient in shock. From a clinical discussion from the proceedings of a Symposium on Recent Research Developments and Current Clinical Practices in Shock, Kalamazoo, Mich., 1977, Upjohn Co.

Wilson, R.F.: Shock. In A manual of practice and techniques in critical care medicine, Kalamazoo, Mich. 1976, Upjohn Co.

MEDICAL EMERGENCIES

CHAPTER 6

Cardiac and pulmonary emergencies

CHEST PAIN OF CARDIAC ORIGIN

Over 600,000 people die from disease of myocardial origin each year. Of these, over half die in the first 2 hours after the onset of symptoms. This is why prehospital care systems grew—to bring emergency cardiac care to the patient in his home or on the street. There are several factors that contribute to the incidence of coronary artery disease and myocardial infarction. Among them are smoking, hypertension, obesity, diabetes mellitus, stress, lack of exercise, increasing age, poor diet, and a family history of heart disease. The greater number of risk factors present in an individual, the greater that person's risk of developing a myocardial infarction.

Coronary artery disease has grown to epidemic proportions in this country. It has been estimated that more than 5.5 million people over the age of 18 have coronary artery disease. Coronary artery disease is actually atherosclerosis, which is a combination of two words, "atheroma," meaning lipid deposits, and "sclerosis," meaning smooth cell fibers.

Angina pectoris

When the myocardium becomes anoxic, a condition known as angina pectoris occurs. It is often described as a retrosternal discomfort. Angina pectoris usually occurs as a result of an increased cardiac output and an increased oxygen demand with an underlying diseased coronary artery system. The most common angina is caused by a partial occlusion of the coronary arteries, usually because of atherosclerosis. Angina may also be caused by arterial spasms, emboli, or a dissecting aortic aneurysm.

When a patient comes to the emergency department with a chief complaint of angina it is important to obtain an accurate history, as this may provide clues to diagnosis. Important items to ask about in gathering the history include:

What precipitated the pain?

What relieved the pain?

Did the pain come on suddenly?

How long did the pain last? Less than 5 minutes? More than 5 minutes?

What did the pain feel like? Was it sharp? Dull? Burning? Pressing? Choking? Tearing?

Where was the pain located? In one spot? Did it radiate?

Did you take any medications during the pain? Did you take nitroglycerin? Did it help?

151

Anginal pain is not usually sharply localized. The pain described in angina may differ from patient to patient but will be described the same way on different occasions by the same patient. Angina is often confused with gastrointestinal disorders on the basis of the description.

There are three main types of angina:

stable (typical)—The pain that occurs is predictable and follows events such as exercise, heavy work, or strain.

unstable (preinfarction)—Attacks are prolonged and more severe and occur more frequently.

Prinzmetal's (variant)—The pain occurs while the patient is at rest and usually at the same time each day; during the attack there may be an elevated ST segment; the prognosis is poor, with a 50% mortality the first year. In the early stages of the disease, if coronary catherization indicates it, coronary artery bypass surgery is usually recommended.

THERAPEUTIC INTERVENTION

Therapeutic intervention for angina is aimed at increasing coronary blood flow and/or reducing myocardial oxygen demand. The primary medication used to treat angina is nitroglycerin. It dilates coronary arteries, reduces afterload (causing a reduction in blood pressure), reduces preload (enhancing venous return to the right heart), and reduces left ventricular end diastolic pressure. The dose is one tablet administered sublingually (tablets come in 1/100, 1/150, and 1/200 Gr). Before administering nitroglycerin the care giver should measure the patient's blood pressure. If the systolic pressure is less than 100 mm Hg, the care giver should consider an alternate form of treatment, as the administration of nitroglycerin may cause a further drop in blood pressure. If nitroglycerin is administered, be sure to tell the patient that it may make him feel light headed. After administration of the tablet the care giver should read the patient's blood pressure again. If there is an abnormally large decrease, the care giver should consider giving a fluid challenge, elevating the patient's legs, or in severe cases applying the MAST.

Myocardial infarction

Myocardial infarction is a localized ischemic necrosis of an area of the myocardium caused by a narrowing of one or more of the coronary arteries. The narrowing may be caused by a thrombus, spasm, or hemorrhage. The size and location of the infarction depend on the location of the block in the coronary artery (Table 6-1).

Anterior wall myocardial infarction is caused by a block in the anterior descending branch of the left coronary artery. An anterolateral infarction is caused by a block in the circumflex branch of the left coronary artery. A posterior infarction is caused by a block in the right coronary artery. An inferior wall infarction is caused by a block in either the left anterior descending artery or the right coronary artery.

CLINICAL FINDINGS IN MYOCARDIAL INFARCTION

Pain is the most common finding in myocardial infarction. In one third of the victims, pain may be of sudden onset and last from several minutes to several days. Although the cause of the pain is not known for certain, it is speculated that it is caused by myocardial hypoxia, a buildup of lactic acid, and sensory responses of the hypoxic arteries. The pain

TABLE 6-1 Coronary arteries in myocardial infarction (MI)

Right coronary artery	Left coronary artery

Supplies:
  Right atrium
  Right ventricle
  Posterior surface of left ventricle
  50% to 60% of SA node
  Bundle of His

Block causes:
  Infarction of posterior wall of left ventricle
  Infarction of posterior half of interventricular septum

In inferior MI (leads II, III, aV$_F$) anticipate second degree heart block, Mobitz type I block, Wenckebach block

Left circumflex branch
Supplies:
  Left atrium
  Free wall of left ventricle
  40% to 50% of SA node
  8% to 10% of AV node
  Bundle of His
  Right bundle

Block causes:
  Lateral wall infarction
  Posterior wall infarction (near base)

Left anterior descending branch
  Supplies:
  Interventricular septum
  Block causes:
  Infarction of anterior wall of left ventricle
  Effect on papillary muscle (which attaches to mitral valve)
  Infarction of anterior wall of septum

In anterior MI (leads V$_1$, V$_2$, V$_3$) anticipate second degree heart block, Mobitz type II block

---

is usually localized in the substernal area and may radiate up into the jaw or down into the arm. It also may have an atypical presentation, such as a toothache or other painful sensation. The pain of myocardial infarction is frequently described as crushing, sharp, or burning or as a pressure, tightness, or choking.

Nausea and vomiting are frequent findings in myocardial infarction and hiccups may occur as a result of phrenic nerve stimulation. Blood pressure is usually decreased as a result of a drop in cardiac output, which is caused by poor pump action.

Edema, which is basically the retention of sodium and water, is caused by decreased cardiac output and increased venous pressure. Myocardial infarction causes a portion of the myocardium to become nonfunctional, which leads to ventricular failure. If ventricular failure reaches a certain extent, stroke volume will decrease and ventricular diastolic pressure will increase. The sympathetic nervous system will activate, causing a decrease in blood flow to the periphery. There will also be decreased blood flow and decreased pressure in the kidneys, causing a slowed glomerular filtration rate. Because of this, renal cells will be stimulated and will release a substance called renin. With an increased renin level, angiotensin will also be released. An elevated angiotensin level will cause the secretion of aldosterone. The combination of aldosterone release and the decreased glomerular filtration rate will cause the retention of sodium and water and edema will result.

Heart sounds in myocardial infarction will vary depending on the physiologic status of the myocardium. If there is decreased myocardial contractility, there will be a decreased first sound. If there is increased pulmonary artery pressure, there will be an increased second sound. If there is ventricular dilation and an increased ventricular filling pressure, there will be a third heart sound. There may also be a pericardial friction rub in systole, which may cause what will appear to be transient pericarditis. If there is left heart failure, there may be evidence of pulsus alternans.

Distended external jugular veins (in the neck) are caused by an increased pressure to the heart and a "congestion" of blood in the venous system. Neck veins are considered distended when the patient is at a 45° angle and the neck veins remain distended.

A number of different body systems will be affected and a number of different signs and symptoms will be displayed in myocardial infarction. When the patient's temperature is elevated during myocardial infarction it is usually because of inflammation or necrosis of the myocardial tissue. Cardiac enzyme elevation will be seen as a result of tissue damage and enzyme leak into the serum. Patients with myocardial infarction may be

TABLE 6-2 Differential diagnosis of angina

	Stable angina	Unstable ("preinfarction") angina
Location of pain	Substernal; may radiate to jaws and neck and down arms and back	Substernal; may radiate to jaws and neck and down arms and back
Duration of pain	1 to 5 minutes	5 minutes, occurring more frequently
Characteristic of pain	Ache, squeezing, choking, heavy; burning	Same as stable angina, but more intense
Other symptoms	None, usually	Diaphoresis; weakness
Pain worsened by	Exercise; activity; eating; cold weather; reclining	Exercise; activity; eating; cold weather; reclining
Pain relieved by	Rest; nitroglycerin; isosorbide (Isordil)	Nitroglycerin, Isordil may only give partial relief
ECG findings	Transient ST depression; disappears with pain relief	ST segment depression; often T-wave inversion; but ECG may be normal

diaphoretic. This is caused by an autonomic nervous system response. Anxiety may occur as a result of many things, such as pain, fear of the unknown, or fear of the known. Pulse rate increases as a sympathetic response to the low-output state. This is one of the compensatory mechanisms of the body. Cyanosis occurs when there is a decreased blood supply to the peripheral vascular system and a decreased amount of oxyhemoglobin available. A detailed discussion of therapeutic intervention for myocardial infarction can be found in Chapter 3.

PULMONARY EDEMA

The key to survival in pulmonary edema is prompt recognition and rapid therapeutic intervention on the part of the clinician. Pulmonary failure is also known as backward failure or circulatory overload. It is most often a result of backward pressure into the left side of the heart and lungs. This transmits an increased pressure into the pulmonary capillaries and produces a leak of material from the capillaries into the alveoli. This condition is commonly known as pulmonary edema. Normally the fluid content of the lungs is about 20% of their total volume. In acute pulmonary edema, the fluid content of the lungs can rise as high as 1,000% of normal.

The care giver should pay particular attention to the fact that pulmonary edema is a symptom complex, not a diagnosis. There are several diseases that may produce pulmonary edema. The most common of these are of cardiac origin. Pulmonary edema may be caused by any of the following:

Myocardial infarction (with left ventricular failure)

Aortic insufficiency

Mechanism of pulmonary edema of cardiac origin

Myocardial infarction
↓
Left ventricular failure
↓
Increased pressure in left ventricle
↓
Increased pressure in pulmonary venous system
↓
Loss of plasma oncotic pressure
↓
Leak of fluid into interstitial tissue
↓
Reflex spasm of airways (cardiac asthma) and pulmonary alveoli
↓
Pulmonary edema and interference with gas exchange
↓
Decreased Po_2 and acidosis

Aortic stenosis
Mitral stenosis
Myocarditis
Amyloidosis
Hypertension
Coronary artery disease
Dysrhythmias (tachycardias greater than 180 beats/minute and bradycardias less than 30 beats/minute)
Hyperthermia
Hyperthyroidism
Exercise
Severe congestive heart failure
Adult respiratory distress syndrome
Heroin overdose
Inhalation of pulmonary irritants
Pulmonary embolism
High altitude
Neurogenic causes
Volume overload
Anemia
Uremia
Disseminated intravascular coagulation (DIC)
Near-drowning
Renal impairment
Lymphatic obstruction
Bacteremic sepsis
Beriberi
General anesthesia
Acute pulmonary edema can exist for a very long time and may have sudden exacerbations. The chief complaints are shortness of breath and chest tightness. Other signs and symptoms may include:
Cough
Cyanosis (central and peripheral)
Rales, rhonchi, wheezing
Distended neck veins
Pink, frothy sputum
Peripheral edema
Tachycardia
Paroxysmal nocturnal dyspnea (PND) or orthopnea
Cheyne-Stokes respirations
S_3 gallop and decreased heart sounds

GOALS IN TREATMENT

Decrease hypoxia
Improve ventilation

Decrease pulmonary capillary wedge pressure

Improve myocardial contractility

MONITORING PARAMETERS

Assure ABCs.

Attempt to obtain a brief history.

Check vital signs.

Patient will usually be tachypneic, tachycardic, and hypertensive; 75% of patients with pulmonary edema and congestive heart failure are hypertensive.

Monitor for dysrhythmias.

A dysrhythmia may have precipitated the pulmonary edema, or the dysrhythmia may have been caused by the hypoxic condition.

Auscultate the lungs.

Rales and rhonchi will be heard.

Wheezing is suggestive of cardiac asthma caused by a reflex spasm of the airways.

Auscultate the heart.

There will often be distant, muffled heart sounds of an S_3 caused by ventricular distention.

Observe external jugular (neck) veins.

The jugular vein acts as the body's built-in manometer by reflecting the pressures found in the right atrium. To observe this, turn the patient's head to the right or left and observe the vein at the posterior border of the sternocleidomastoid muscle; the patient should be in semi-Fowler's position. Neck vein distention 2 inches above the sternal notch is suggestive of right atrial congestion.

Observe for peripheral edema.

Pay particular attention to dependent parts, such as the arms, legs, feet, and sacral area.

THERAPEUTIC INTERVENTION

The following therapeutic interventions will alter circulatory and ventilatory dynamics but may not alter the underlying disease process. Once the patient is out of a life-threatening condition, his status must be reevaluated to determine proper therapeutic intervention for the condition that caused the pulmonary edema.

Place the patient in high Fowler's position with legs dependent, if possible. Usually it is not necessary to encourage the patient to do this, as he is already doing it; these patients cannot tolerate lying down. High Fowler's position decreases venous return to the right heart, decreasing the work of breathing and increasing tidal volume.

Oxygen is used to treat hypoxia. Start by administering 6 to 8 liters of oxygen via a nasal cannula. Once the patient is in a controlled setting, administer 100% oxygen by mask, using positive pressure. Be sure that someone is explaining the procedures to the patient. He will need some direction as to what to do with the positive pressure device, which makes some patients feel as though they are suffocating.

An IV line should be initiated for the administration of medications. Either initiate a heparin lock or be sure that the cannula is attached to a controlled volume reservoir with a microdrip device to avoid accidental large-volume infusion.

Morphine sulfate (8 to 15 mg IV in 2 to 3 mg increments, slowly) is given to cause venous dilation and a decreased return to the right heart. It has the additional effect of acting as a sedative, which will calm the patient and allow for more efficient breathing. Be cautious with morphine, as it can cause respiratory depression—have naloxone drawn up into a syringe and close by.

Nitroglycerin is currently being used for pulmonary edema in several parts of the country. It causes venous pooling and dilated vasculature that produce a decreased venous return to the right heart. Provided that blood pressure is in an acceptable range, dose will vary from one to four tablets of 1/150 Gr sublingually.

Furosemide (Lasix) is given to produce diuresis and decrease intravascular volume. It should be given in a dose of 20 to 40 mg by IV push. The care giver can expect to see a response 5 to 15 minutes after Lasix administration. Particular caution should be used with the patient who has been digitalized or has been on previous diuretic therapy, as hypokalemia-induced dysrhythmias or hypotensive states caused by excessive diuresis may result from furosemide administration.

Digitalis is sometimes given to increase myocardial contractility and improve cardiovascular function.

Aminophylline is usually given for pulmonary edema patients with expiratory wheezing who have not responded to oxygen and morphine sulfate therapy. Aminophylline is a potent bronchodilator, a vasodilator that affects both the venous and arterial systems, an inotropic agent (increases myocardial contractility), and a short-acting diuretic. The standard recommended loading dose is 5 to 6 mg/kg over a 20-minute period.

Arterial blood gas analysis is essential. The following blood gas values are desirable: P_{O_2}: 80 mm Hg; P_{CO_2}: 30 to 40 mm Hg; pH: 7.45.

A Foley catheter should be placed if the patient is unable to control urination.

Probably the most important aspect of care of the patient with pulmonary edema is reassurance. These patients experience feelings of suffocation and doom. They need much verbal support and touch communication.

High-altitude pulmonary edema

High-altitude pulmonary edema (HAPE) usually occurs in patients who have made a rapid ascent to altitudes above 10,000 feet over sea level and have engaged in heavy physical activity for the first 3 days at that altitude. It can occur much sooner in patients with underlying pulmonary or cardiac disease. Symptoms may begin to occur from 6 to 36 hours after change of altitude. HAPE can also occur in patients who normally live at high altitudes but go to sea level for 2 or more weeks and then return to high altitude. It may be seen in patients with no history of cardiac or pulmonary disease who have marked hypertension. Therapeutic intervention is return to a lower altitude, oxygen therapy, and bed rest.

CONGESTIVE HEART FAILURE

When the heart fails to pump blood adequately, congestion occurs, and causes a decreased cardiac output and an increased systemic peripheral pressure. Congestive heart failure may be seen as an individual entity or in conjunction with pulmonary edema. The onset of symptoms may be gradual or sudden. There are several causes of congestive heart failure, which is a symptom complex and not a diagnosis. Some of the causes are:

Hypertension
Fluid overload
Increased intracranial pressure
Myocardial infarction with failure
Valvular heart disease
Coronary artery disease
Cardiomyopathy
Dysrhythmias
Tachycardia (more than 180 beats/minute)
Bradycardia (less than 30 beats/minute)
Fever from any cause
Hyperthyroidism
Post-pneumothorax
Adult respiratory distress syndrome (ARDS)
Oxygen toxicity
Uremic pneumonia
Intracranial tumors
Drugs such as methotrexate, busulfan, hexamethonium, and nitrofurantoin

SIGNS AND SYMPTOMS

Shortness of breath
Dyspnea
Weakness
Dependent edema
Distended neck veins
Hepatomegaly
Bilateral rales
Increased circulation time

MONITORING PARAMETERS

ABCs
Vital signs
Cardiac monitor
Auscultation of the lungs
Auscultation of the heart
Observation of neck veins
Observation for peripheral edema
Obtain a history and perform a brief physical examination

THERAPEUTIC INTERVENTION

Bed rest
High Fowler's position
Oxygen

Digitalis
Diuretics
IV D5W TKO
Note patient's weight and intake and output

ACUTE PERICARDITIS

Acute pericarditis is an inflammation of the pericardial sac. In the young patient it is usually a result of infection (e.g., with coxsackievirus, streptococci, staphylococci, or *Haemophilus influenzae*) or tuberculosis. In the older patient acute pericarditis is usually caused by infection, trauma, coronary artery disease, or tumor. It may also occur if there is pericardial effusion.

SIGNS AND SYMPTOMS

Severe chest pain that increases with respirations or activity
Fever and chills
Diaphoresis
Dyspnea
Tachycardia or other dysrhythmias
Pericardial friction rub (increased when patient leans forward)
Malaise
ST segment elevation of 1 to 3 mm in all ECG leads except aV_R and V_1
Decreased blood pressure (if effusion has occurred)

THERAPEUTIC INTERVENTION

Oxygen
Sedation or analgesia
Rest
Antibiotics
Much reassurance

CARDIAC TAMPONADE

Cardiac tamponade is a condition in which blood leaks into the pericardial sac. It may be caused by infection, neoplasm, and most commonly trauma. The tamponade may have both positive and negative effects. Its positive effect is that it produces a pressure that may reduce an underlying hemorrhage. Its negative effect is that it may compress the heart when the pericardial sac, which is not distensible, fills with blood. This prevents good venous return from the systemic circulation to the right side of the heart and does not allow the heart to take advantage of Starling's curve to produce maximum output. If compression and the volume of blood collected in the sac are great enough, the patient may develop profound shock.

Tamponade produces a decreased venous return to the right side of the heart, elevates central venous pressure, causes neck vein distention, and decreases cardiac output. This decrease in cardiac output causes a compensatory vasoconstriction and an increase in peripheral vascular resistance, which is responsible for an early hypertensive state. The patient may develop profound shock with as little as 150 to 200 ml of blood loss into the pericardial sac. Removal of as little as 10 to 20 ml of blood through pericardiocentesis may be life-saving.

SIGNS AND SYMPTOMS

Tachycardia ⎫ Immediately
Elevated CVP (greater than 15 mm Hg) ⎬ suspect
Decreased blood pressure* ⎭ tamponade
Distended neck veins*
Distant heart sounds*
Decreased arterial pressure
Weak, thready pulse
Cyanosis
Increased respiratory rate
Dyspnea
Paradoxic pulse
Restlessness
Loss of apical cardiac impulse
Shock
Widening cardiac silhouette

THERAPEUTIC INTERVENTION

Oxygen
MAST to increase venous return to the right side of the heart and correct hypovolemia
Pericardiocentesis
IV D5W TKO

Pericardiocentesis (Fig. 6-1)
EQUIPMENT

16-gauge spinal needle
50 ml syringe
Alligator clips
Kelly clamp
ECG machine
Three-way stopcock
Local anesthetic agent
Antiseptic solution
Gloves

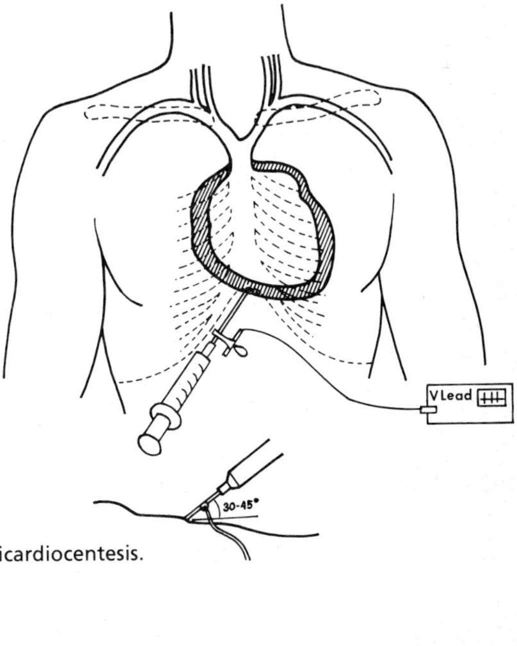

---

*Beck's triad.

FIG. 6-1 Pericardiocentesis.

PROCEDURE

1. Prepare the patient's chest at the left inferior costal margin and the xiphoid.
2. Administer a local anesthetic to the area.
3. Attach an alligator clip to the hub of the 16-gauge needle and the other end of the clip to the V lead of the ECG machine.
4. Attach the needle to the syring via the three-way stopcock.
5. Run the ECG machine on the V-lead setting.
6. Advance the needle in a subxiphoid approach between the left inferior costal margin and the xiphoid at a 30° to 45° angle to the body, advancing toward the tip of the right scapula.
7. Gently aspirate the syringe as the needle is advanced; if blood returns and there is no ST-segment elevation on the ECG, the needle has probably entered the pericardial sac. If an ST-segment elevation appears on the ECG, the needle has pierced the epicardium. If this occurs the needle should be withdrawn slowly until the ST segment returns to normal. If the needle has gone all the way through to the myocardium, a pulsation will be felt up through the needle and the syringe.
8. Once blood is being withdrawn from the pericardial sac, attach a Kelly clamp to the needle at the level of the skin to avoid accidental advancement of the needle.

NOTE: Blood withdrawn from the pericardial sac should not clot, as it has been defibrinated in the sac.

COMPLICATIONS

Laceration of a coronary artery
Laceration of the lung
Laceration of the ventricle
Cardiac dysrhythmias
Increased tamponade

PARADOXICAL PULSE

Paradoxical pulse is found in one third of patients experiencing acute pericardial tamponade. It will be noted by an abnormal fall in systolic blood pressure during inspiration.

PROCEDURE

1. Apply a blood pressure cuff to the patient's arm.
2. Inflate the cuff to a level above systolic pressure.
3. Deflate the cuff slowly until the first systolic sound is heard. During normal inspiration the systolic sound will disappear.
4. Deflate the cuff until all systolic sounds can be heard during both inspiration and expiration.
5. Note the point at which all systolic sounds can be heard.
6. The difference in millimeters of mercury between the pressure at which the systolic sound disappears during inspiration and the pressure at which all systolic sounds can be heard is called a paradox.

NOTE: A paradox of more than 10 mm Hg indicates a paradoxical pulse.

CHEST PAIN OF AORTIC ORIGIN
Aortic dissection and aortic rupture (Fig. 6-2)

There are four major presentations of aortic aneurysms, dissections, and ruptures. Dissection of the aorta will be discussed in this section. Aortic dissection occurs primarily in men. It is frequently seen in conjunction with arteriosclerotic heart disease and hypertension. Other causes of dissection are trauma and Marfan's syndrome, which are seen primarily in the young.

An aortic dissection is a tear in the intimal layer of the aorta that allows blood to leak between the intimal and medial layers. There are three types of aortic dissections:

type I—Dissection of the descending aorta to and beyond the aortic arch (occurs in two thirds of cases).

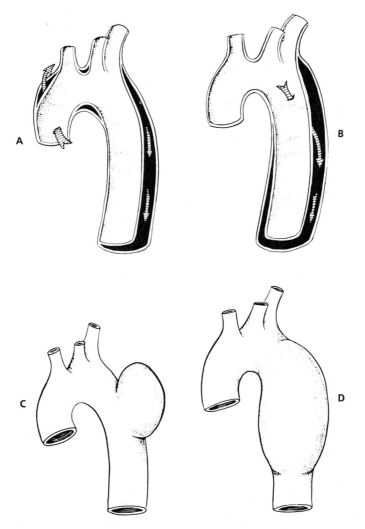

FIG. 6-2 Types of aneurysms. **A** and **B,** Dissecting. **C,** Saccular, **D,** Fusiform. (From Barber, J., Stokes, L., and Billings, D.: Adult and child care, ed. 2, St. Louis, 1977, The C.V. Mosby Co.)

type II—Dissection of the ascending aorta alone.
type III—Dissection from beyond the left subclavian artery.

Dissection may cause occlusion of major vessels that branch off of the aorta, such as the myocardial, cerebral, mesenteric, and renal vessels. Rupture of the dissection may have two results: (1) rupture into the pericardial sac causing pericardial tamponade and (2) rupture into the chest cavity causing exsanguination.

SIGNS AND SYMPTOMS

Chest pain—described as excruciating or tearing; anteroposterior in nature (may be confused with myocardial infarction, back pain, pericarditis, or peptic ulcer)
Dyspnea
Orthopnea
Diaphoresis
Pallor
Apprehension
Syncope
Tachycardia
Absence of major arterial pulses unilaterally
Blood pressure differences between arms
Hypertension
Pulse at the sternoclavicular joint
Murmur of aortic insufficiency (in type II)
Hemiplegia or paraplegia
Shock
Widened mediastinum

THERAPEUTIC INTERVENTION

High Fowler's position
Oxygen
IV D5W TKO
Nitroprusside (Nipride)
Propranolol (Inderal)
Much support and reassurance
Preparation for surgery
MAST if dissection is ruptured and patient is in shock

CHEST PAIN OF PULMONARY ORIGIN
Pulmonary embolus

Pulmonary embolus is one of the most difficult diagnoses to make in the emergency department. It is often confused with myocardial infarction, pneumothorax, and other conditions involving chest pain. Like many other conditions of the chest, pulmonary embolus is not a disease but rather a complication of a disease. It is caused by a free-flowing thrombus from the venous system of the legs, pelvis, or right side of the heart.

The thrombus lodges in a branch of the pulmonary artery, causing partial or total occlusion and sometimes infarction. An embolus may consist of clotted blood, fat, bone, air, or amniotic fluid.

CAUSES

Trauma
Long bone fractures
Surgery (especially abdominal or pelvic)
Obesity
Decreased peripheral circulation
Congestive heart failure with myocardial infarction
Thrombophlebitis
Cardiac disease
Atrial fibrillation
Prolonged immobilization
Acute infections
Blood dyscrasias
Amniotic fluid emboli (in childbirth)
Air emboli (from scuba diving or poor IV technique)
Oral contraceptives
Neoplasms

PREVENTION

Frequent ambulation on long trips
Avoiding long periods of standing
Early postoperative ambulation
Elastic stockings for those on bed rest
Range of motion exercises for those on bed rest
Good IV technique
Careful management and movement of severely traumatized patients
Prophylactic anticoagulants for high-risk patients

SIGNS AND SYMPTOMS

There may be absolutely no prodromal signs or symptoms preceding a terminal event.

When signs and symptoms do appear they may be vague. The following is a list of some of the more commonly seen signs and symptoms:

Shortness of breath
Tachypnea
Tachycardia
Angina-like chest pain
Pallor or cyanosis
Anxiety
Occasionally decreased blood pressure
Possible wheezing

Right bundle branch block with right axis deviation, peaked T waves in limb leads, and depressed T waves in the right precordial leads (V_1, V_2, V_3)

THERAPEUTIC INTERVENTION

ABCs
Oxygen at high flow rate
IV D5W TKO
Analgesia (usually meperidine—avoid morphine)
Bronchodilators
Treatment of dysrhythmias
Heparin (7,500 to 10,000 units IV initially, then 500 units every 4 hours); monitor clotting times carefully
Posteroanterior and lateral chest x-ray films
Much reassurance

When 60% of the pulmonary vasculature is blocked, cardiac function is compromised. If a large pulmonary embolus lodges in the main, right, or left pulmonary artery, sudden death may occur.

Spontaneous pneumothorax

Spontaneous pneumothorax may occur in the absence of trauma. It occurs most often in younger persons (16 to 26 years) and is more commonly associated with males than females. The usual cause in young people is a ruptured congenital bleb. In older people spontaneous pneumothorax is usually a result of a ruptured bleb or bulla that has developed from chronic obstructive pulmonary disease. Other causes of spontaneous pneumothorax include:

Mechanical ventilation pressures that are too great
Rupture of a cyst
Abscess
Fungal disease
Cancer
Tuberculosis
Trauma
Chest compression in cardiopulmonary resuscitation
Tracheostomy
Subclavian puncture

SIGNS AND SYMPTOMS

The signs and symptoms of spontaneous pneumothorax may be minimal. Classic signs and symptoms are usually associated with pneumothorax of 40% or greater.

Dyspnea
Tachypnea
Cyanosis
Sudden onset of pleuritic chest pain
Agitation
Decreased breath sounds

Severe signs and symptoms of tension pneumothorax include:
Decreased motion of chest wall
Mediastinal shift
Distended neck veins
Deviated trachea
Tympany on percussion
Shock

The absolute diagnosis of pneumothorax is made by chest x-ray examination. If symptoms are severe, however, therapeutic intervention should not be delayed until a chest x-ray film is available.

THERAPEUTIC INTERVENTION

Therapy is aimed toward reexpansion of the collapsed lung. (See Chapter 20 for more detailed information.)
Oxygen at high flow
Needle placement in the anterior chest wall or chest tube
IV D5W TKO
Bed rest in high Fowler's position
Much reassurance

Pleurisy

Pleurisy is an inflammation of the lining of the chest cavity. It may be caused by pneumonia, tuberculosis, trauma, or tumors.

Dry pleurisy

Dry pleurisy is also known as fibrinous pleurisy.

SIGNS AND SYMPTOMS

Sharp chest pain that increases with inspiration
Short, quick breaths
Patient will lay on affected side

THERAPEUTIC INTERVENTIONS

Bed rest
Analgesia
Sedation
Oxygen

Exudative pleurisy with effusion

Exudative pleurisy with effusion is often caused by an infectious process.

SIGNS AND SYMPTOMS

Dyspnea
Elevated temperature
History of dry pleurisy

THERAPEUTIC INTERVENTION

Bed rest
Thoracentesis to remove fluid
Analgesia

Antipyretics
Oxygen

Pneumonia

Pneumonia results from a bacterial, viral, or fungal infection. The patient will often offer a history of recent upper respiratory tract infection, otitis media, or conjunctivitis. Often, however, the patient will give a history of no known medical problems before the onset of the pneumonia. Pneumonia frequently appears in very young or very old people who are debilitated in some way.

Pneumonia is classified according to the organism that causes it (pneumococcal, streptococcal, or viral) and according to its location (bronchial or lobar). Some of the more common causes of pneumonia are:

Debilitation
Underlying cardiovascular disorder
Underlying pulmonary disorder
Rapid environmental temperature changes
Smoking
Diabetes mellitus
Steroids
Immunosuppression
Aspiration (frequently seen in alcohol or drug abusers or those
    with head injury)
Foreign body

SIGNS AND SYMPTOMS OF BACTERIAL PNEUMONIA

Dyspnea
Sudden onset
Chills
Fever 39.4° to 40° C (103° to 104° F)
Toxicity
Productive cough and purulent sputum
Chest pain (may be referred diaphragmatically and be mistaken for a gastrointestinal
    disorder)
Diaphoresis
Tachypnea
Nausea and vomiting
Cyanosis
Rales
Otitis media
Conjunctivitis
Apprehension
Abdominal distention

SIGNS AND SYMPTOMS OF NONBACTERIAL PNEUMONIA

Same symptoms as bacterial pneumonia   Myalgia
Insidious onset   Headache
Preceded by upper respiratory infection   May have seasonal pattern

THERAPEUTIC INTERVENTION

Oxygen
High Fowler's position
Pneumococcal—penicillin G (600,000 units every 12 hours)
Staphylococcal—methicillin (1 g every 4 to 6 hours IV)
Gram-negative—gentamicin (1.7 mg/kg every 8 hours)
Mycoplasmal—erythromycin, tetracycline, doxycycline (Vibramycin)
Aspiration—penicillin G (1,200,000 units every 6 hours)

COMPLICATIONS

Rupture of pneumatocele producing pneumothorax
Empyema
Therapeutic intervention for both of these complications is placement of a chest tube.

CHEST PAIN OF OTHER ORIGINS
Hyperventilation

Hyperventilation is one of the most commonly seen conditions in the emergency department. Extreme caution must be used with patients who are hyperventilating. Hyperventilation may occur as a result of anxiety, or it may be caused by a disease process such as salicylate overdose, myocardial infarction, or intracerebral bleeding. The care giver should pay close attention to associated signs and symptoms that may lead to the discovery of an underlying disorder. The care giver must avoid "tunnel vision" and must keep his or her mind open to all possibilities for the cause. It is important to remember that hyperventilation may be a response to a disease process that, when treated with the traditional breathing into a paper bag, could cause serious complications. Medical illness must be ruled out before assuming that the hyperventilation is caused by anxiety or a hysteric response.

CAUSES

Anxiety   Thyrotoxicosis
Pregnancy   Pulmonary hypertension
Fever from any cause   Pulmonary edema
Trauma   Smoke inhalation
Pain   Anemia
Liver disease   Intracerebral bleeding and increased intracranial pressure
Pulmonary embolus   Central nervous system lesion
Stress   Fibrosis of lung tissue
Diabetic ketoacidosis   Exercise
High altitude   Fatigue

TABLE 6-3 Differential diagnosis of chest pain

Cause	Onset of pain	Characteristic of pain	Location of pain
Acute myocardial infarction	Sudden onset; lasts more than 30 minutes to 1 hour	Pressure, burning, aching, tightness, choking	Across chest; may radiate to jaws and neck and down arms and back
Angina	Sudden onset; lasts only few minutes	Aches, squeezing, choking, heaviness burning	Substernal; may radiate to jaws and neck and down arms and back
Dissecting aortic aneurysm	Sudden onset	Excruciating, tearing	Center of chest; radiates into back; may radiate to abdomen
Pericarditis	Sudden onset or may be variable	Sharp, knifelike	Retrosternal; may radiate up neck and down left arm
Pneumothorax	Sudden onset	Tearing, pleuritic	Lateral side of chest
Pulmonary embolus	Sudden onset	Crushing (but not always)	Lateral side of chest
Hiatal hernia	Sudden onset	Sharp, severe	Lower chest; upper abdomen
Gastrointestinal disturbance or cholecystitis	Sudden onset	Gripping, burning	Lower substernal area, upper abdomen
Degenerative disk (cervical or thoracic spine) disease	Sudden onset	Sharp, severe	Substernal; may radiate to neck, jaw, arms and shoulders
Degenerative or inflammatory lesions of shoulder, ribs, scalenus anterior	Sudden onset	Sharp, severe	Substernal; radiates to shoulder
Hyperventilation	Sudden onset	Vague	Vague

History	Pain worsened by	Pain relieved by	Other
Age 40 to 70 years; may or may not have history of angina	Movement, anxiety	Nothing; no movement, stillness, position, or breath holding; only relieved by medication (morphine sulfate)	Shortness of breath, diaphoresis, weakness, anxiety
May have history of angina; circumstances precipitating; pain characteristic; response to nitroglycerin	Lying down, eating, effort, cold weather, smoking, stress, anger, worry, hunger	Rest, nitroglycerin	Unstable angina appears even at rest
Nothing specific except that pain is usually worse at onset			Blood pressure difference between right and left arms, murmur of aortic regurgitation
Short history of upper respiratory infection or fever	Deep breathing, trunk movement, maybe swallowing	Sitting up, leaning forward	Friction rub, paradoxic pulse over 10 mm Hg.
None	Breathing		Dyspnea, increased pulse, decreased breath sounds, deviated trachea
Sometimes phlebitis	Breathing		Cyanosis, dyspnea, cough with hemoptysis
May have none	Heavy meal, bending, lying down	Bland diet, walking, antacids, semi-Fowler's position	
May have none	Eating, lying down	Antacids	
May have none	Movement of neck or spine, lifting, straining	Rest, decreased movement	Pain usually on outer aspect of arm, thumb, or index finger
May have none	Movement of arm or shoulder	Elevation and arm support to shoulder postural exercises	
Hyperventilation, anxiety, stress, emotional upset	Increased respiratory rate	Slowing of respiratory rate	Be *sure* hyperventilation is from nonmedical cause!

No matter what the cause of hyperventilation, it is accompanied by a fall in P_{CO_2} (hypocapnia), which causes constriction of cerebral vasculature, respiratory alkalosis, and symptoms of tetany. P_{CO_2} may drop to as low as 15 mm Hg.

SIGNS AND SYMPTOMS

Anxiety or panicky appearance
Shortness of breath
Tingling of fingers and toes
Periorbital numbness
Carpopedal spasm
Syncope
Confusion

THERAPEUTIC INTERVENTION

Therapeutic intervention for hyperventilation syndrome should only be undertaken after medical disease and trauma have been ruled out as the cause of the hyperventilation.

1. Speak with the patient; make him aware of what he is doing.
2. Have the patient talk. (It is difficult to hyperventilate while talking.)
3. Act in a calm, reassuring manner; never be demanding or demeaning.
4. Demonstrate proper breathing for the patient and say, "Breathe like I am breathing."
5. Once the patient seems to be aware of what he is doing, have him watch a clock with a second hand and breathe once every 5 seconds.
6. If none of these seem to be working, have the patient rebreathe into a paper bag (carbon dioxide rebreathing).

Always remember to look for underlying causes of hyperventilation other than anxiety or hysteria.

Chest pain may originate from the gastrointestinal region (hiatal hernia, gastric or peptic ulcer, pancreatitis, esophageal spasm), from Mallory-Weiss syndrome, or from Borhave's syndrome. Chest pain can also result from musculoskeletal problems involving trauma, degenerative disk disease, or other miscellaneous causes, such as xiphoidalgia, costochondritis, Mondor's disease, or postherpetic syndrome.

PULMONARY EMERGENCIES PRESENTING WITH OTHER THAN CHEST PAIN

When dealing with pulmonary emergencies, it is important to be able to give at least a rough estimate of tidal volume (the amount of air breathed in on each normal breath). To assess tidal volume, the care giver places his or her hands on the lower costal margins of the patient's chest and feels for movement. The care giver should be able to estimate tidal volume roughly, by estimating the amount of chest movement in terms of cc of air, once this procedure has been practiced a few times.

Other assessment parameters in the patient with a pulmonary disorder are:
ABCs
Listen for noises; remember, "noisy breathing is obstructed breathing"
Check level of consciousness

Check skin vital signs (color, temperature, and moistness)
Check character of respirations
Check for use of accessory muscles
Check for paradoxical chest movement

Dyspnea

Severe dyspnea is a common chief complaint in the emergency setting. It is not uncommon to find that the patient has no history of pulmonary problems and the present history does not correlate with the dyspnea found in COPD or asthma. The care giver should be able to assess the seriousness of this problem rapidly and accurately and be able to apply appropriate therapeutic interventions without delay. Questions to ask to assist with a diagnosis include:

When did this begin?
What brought it on? What were you doing when it started?
Did it come on gradually or suddenly?
Is it difficult to get air in?
Is it difficult to get air out?
Has this ever happened before?
Is it extremely difficult to breathe?
Have you ever had lung disease? Heart disease? Asthma? High blood pressure?
Do you smoke?
Are you taking any medications? For your heart? For retained water?
Do you have difficulty walking up stairs?

SIGNS AND SYMPTOMS

Apparent respiratory distress
Flaring of nostrils
Cyanosis
Pallor
Use of accessory muscles of respiration
Diaphoresis
Possible loss of consciousness

THERAPEUTIC INTERVENTION

ABCs
High Fowler's position
Oxygen (if no history of chronic obstructive pulmonary disease, administer at 6 to 8 liters/minute)
IV D5W TKO
Aminophylline (250 mg in 25 ml D5W over 5 to 10 minutes)

Asthma

Asthma is reversible obstructive airway disease. It is estimated that 6 to 8 million Americans have asthma. It is an obstruction of air flow caused by one or more of the following ("the three S's").

Spasm
Swelling
Secretions

These produce bronchospasm, hypoxia, and anxiety. It is interesting to note that between attacks the lungs and bronchial tree are normal. Asthma may occur at any age and may be the result of bronchial-tree sensitivity to inhalants such as dust, pollen, mold, animal dander, gases, or insecticides or ingestion of foods such as shellfish, milk, or chocolate that have a high sensitivity factor. Asthma may also be caused by:

Stress and depression
Exercise
Smoking
Pulmonary emboli
Allergies
Cardiogenic causes
Nasal polyps
Hiatal hernia
Mechanical obstructions (such as tumors)

SIGNS AND SYMPTOMS

Wheezing (most commonly expiratory, but may also be inspiratory); remember that in
    severe bronchospasm there may be no wheezing, as there may be no air movement
Dyspnea
Cough
Tachycardia
Hypertension
Mild cyanosis
Use of accessory muscles of respiration
Possible history of asthma
Usually a history of upper respiratory infection

THERAPEUTIC INTERVENTION

High Fowler's position
Epinephrine 0.1 to 0.3 ml of 1:1,000 solution subcutaneously (adult dosage)
Oxygen
IV D5W TKO
Aminophylline (500 mg in 50 ml D5W over 5 to 10 minutes followed by 500 mg in 1,000
    ml D5W at slow drip rate)
Sodium bicarbonate if indicated by blood gas values
Fluid and electrolyte replacement
Much verbal reassurance
Treatment of dysrhythmias

Status asthmaticus

Status asthmaticus is severe asthma that does not respond to epinephrine (1:1,000 solution). The diagnosis is usually made through the patient's history.

SIGNS AND SYMPTOMS

Dyspnea (usually increases gradually over a few days)
Chest tightness
Tachycardia
Nonproductive cough
Wheezing on inspiration and expiration (if bronchospasm is severe there may be no wheezing, as there may be no air movement)
Anxiety
Sitting forward, using accessory muscles of respiration
Possible overmedication with isoproterenol that is self-administered via inhalation device
Mild cyanosis
Distended neck veins in expiration

THERAPEUTIC INTERVENTIONS

Arterial blood gas determinations
Humidified oxygen
IV D5W TKO
Epinephrine 0.4 ml of 1:1,000 solution every ½ hour for three to five doses
Aminophylline 500 mg in 50 ml D5W over 5 to 10 minutes (adult) or 3 to 4 mg/kg every 8 hours, not to exceed 12 mg/kg (child)
Intermittent positive-pressure breathing (IPPB) with bronchodilator
Intubation if severe
Sodium bicarbonate in accordance with blood gas values
Steroids
Chlordiazepoxide (5 to 10 mg every hour if sedation is needed)

Aftercare instructions for the asthmatic

Rise slowly in the morning.
Take deep breaths frequently throughout the day.
Maintain good posture.
Take medications as ordered, but don't overuse your Medihaler; avoid using your Medihaler whenever possible.
Gradually increase your physical activity.
Learn to relax.
Drink lots of fluids (at least 4 quarts a day).
Do not overeat.
Avoid:
    Smoking and people who smoke
    Fumes and exhaust
    Aerosol sprays (including your Medihaler)
    Extreme changes in temperature
    Other things that you know make you wheeze

Antacids
Expectorants
Accurate recording of intake and output

Bronchitis

Bronchitis is a syndrome in which there is a frequent and productive cough. The cause of bronchitis is believed to be chronic irritation of the bronchial mucosa by such things as smoking, air pollution, or chronic inhalation of irritant substances. It is a precursor to emphysema and is commonly found in middle-aged persons. It appears to be more common in men than women.

SIGNS AND SYMPTOMS

Dyspnea
Productive cough that worsens in the evenings or when there is damp weather

THERAPEUTIC INTERVENTION

Remove the cause (the source of the irritation)
Move to a climate where there is warm, dry, dust-free air if possible
Rest
Relaxation
Bronchodilators
Expectorants
Antibiotics
Fluids (at least 4 liters/day by mouth)

Chronic obstructive pulmonary disease (emphysema)

Chronic obstructive pulmonary disease (COPD) is a process in which there is an enlargement of the alveoli in the lungs, a loss of elasticity in the lung tissue, and destruction of the alveolar wall. The patient with COPD will have much difficulty exhaling and will have difficulty with gas exchange at the alveolar level. The specific cause of COPD is not known, but smoking appears to contribute to it (90% of COPD patients have a history of heavy smoking—more than 1 pack per day). Other causative factors may include pollution, industrial inhalants such as silicon, and tuberculosis.

SIGNS AND SYMPTOMS

Patient states that he has emphysema
Severe dyspnea that increases over a number of days
Cyanosis (especially of the lips, nailbeds, and earlobes)
Clubbing of fingers
Faint breath sounds, wheezes, or rales
Prolonged expiratory phase of respiration
Use of accessory muscles of respiration
Subclavicular and tracheal drawing-in on inspiration
Productive cough
History of smoking
Barrel chest

THERAPEUTIC INTERVENTION

High Fowler's position

IV D5W TKO

Aminophylline (250 mg in 25 ml D5W given over 5 to 10 minutes)

Oxygen at 2 liters/minute; observe the patient carefully; do not hesitate to give oxygen if the patient is hypoxic; the most severe life-threatening problem for these patients is hypoxemia

Adequate hydration

Smoke inhalation

The inhalation of smoke and other noxious fumes usually occurs during a fire in an enclosed space. Although a patient may have only minor burns, smoke inhalation may be severe. Respiratory tract burns are difficult to distinguish from pure smoke inhalation. In either case, severe pulmonary damage, such as chemical pneumonitis or asphyxia caused by increased levels of carboxyhemoglobin, may result. The burning of synthetic materials produces noxious chemicals that produce additional problems in the respiratory tract (Table 6-4).

When caring for the victim of smoke inhalation it is important to ask a few questions:

How long were you exposed?

Were you in a confined space?

What type of material burned?

How much of the material burned?

The primary manifestation of smoke inhalation is pulmonary edema. This may not appear for 24 to 48 hours.

TABLE 6-4 Toxic products of combustion*

Material	Use	Major toxic chemical products of combustion†
Polyvinyl chloride	Wall and floor covering, telephone cable insulation	Hydrogen chloride (P), phosgene (P), carbon monoxide
Polyurethane foam	Upholstery	Isocyanates, (toluene-2,4-diisocyanate) (P), hydrogen cyanide
Lacquered wood veneer, wallpaper	Wall covering	Acetaldehyde (P), formaldehyde (P), oxides of nitrogen (P), acetic acid
Acrylic	Light diffusers	Acrolein (P)
Nylon	Carpet	Hydrogen cyanide, ammonia (P)
Acrilan	Carpet	Hydrogen cyanide, acrolein (P)
Polystyrene	Miscellaneous	Styrene, carbon monoxide

*From Genovesi, M.G., Tashkin, D.P., Chopra, S., Morgan, M., and McElroy, C.: Chest **71**:441, 1977.
†P indicates a pulmonary irritant.

SIGNS AND SYMPTOMS

Mild irritation of the upper airways or burning pain in the throat or chest
Singed nasal hairs
Hypoxia
Facial burns
Sputum that contains carbon
Rales
Rhonchi
Wheezes
Dyspnea
Restlessness or agitation
Cough
Hoarseness
Other signs of pulmonary edema (usually appear hours later)

THERAPEUTIC INTERVENTION

ABCs
Humidified oxygen
IV D5W TKO
Arterial blood gas values and appropriate therapy
Coughing, chest physical therapy, suctioning
Admission and observation for 24 to 48 hours
Endotracheal intubation, cricothyrotomy, or tracheostomy if indicated
Bronchodilators
Nasogastric tube
Steroids

Adult respiratory distress syndrome

Adult respiratory distress syndrome (ARDS) (otherwise known as shock lung, pulmonary contusion, congestive atelectasis, posttraumatic lung, and traumatic wet lung) is a pulmonary insult caused by a sudden pulmonary congestion and atelectasis with hyaline membrane formation resulting from loss of surfactant and buildup of mucus along the alveoli. It is a syndrome of acute progressive failure caused by a variety of insults, such as:

Cardiopulmonary bypass	Lung contusion
Infection	Massive fat emboli
Pulmonary edema	Aspiration
Inhaled toxins	Overdose
Hemorrhagic shock	Eclampsia
Massive transfusions	Disseminated intravascular coagulation

Initially the lung appears normal. Then there is progressive atelectasis, increased interstitial and alveolar edema, and marked interstitial and alveolar edema, and marked ventilation-perfusion abnormalities that result in progressive hypoxemia and difficulty in breathing as lung compliance decreases.

SIGNS AND SYMPTOMS

Dyspnea
Tachypnea
Cyanosis
Hypoxemia
Hypocapnea
Pulmonary hemorrhage
Hypotension

THERAPEUTIC INTERVENTION

ABCs
Intubation—endotracheal or tracheostomy
Ventilation with volume-cycled ventilator and positive-end expiratory pressure (PEEP)
Dehydration with diuretics and fluid restriction
Medication, possibly with steroids to enhance surfactant production; perhaps heparin
Suction

Benefits of PEEP

Prevents the collapse of alveoli
Increases functional residual capacity
Improves VQ relationship
Combats pulmonary edema
Enhances FIO_2

Dangers of PEEP

Oxygen toxicity
Fluid overload
Decreased cardiac output
May cause pneumothorax (especially in patients with COPD)
Infection

If PEEP fails, hyperbaric oxygenation may be used if a chamber is readily available. The care giver may also elect to use a bypass oxygenator as a last-ditch effort.

Near-drowning

There are more than 8,000 drowning deaths in the United States each year and more than 140,000 worldwide. More than half of these occur in backyard swimming pools. Drowning is the second leading cause of accidental death in the United States. It is the fourth leading cause of death in children. It accounts for 10% of all accidental deaths with 47% of those in children under 4 years of age. The highest incidence of drowning and near-drowning occurs in the 15- to 19-year age group. The incidence is five times higher in men than women.

Drowning or near-drowning occurs when an individual cannot stay afloat because he is fatigued, lacks skill as a swimmer, panics, experiences an acute medical incident while in the water (e.g., a myocardial infarction or a seizure), is traumatized, or hyperventilates in preparation for a long-distance swim underwater. A near-drowning may also be a suicide attempt.

Basically there are three categories of near drowning and drowning:

dry drowning—Occurs in 10% to 20% of cases. Asphyxiation is caused by decreased oxygen as a result of laryngotracheal spasm (prevents entrance of water as well as oxygen into trachea). This causes cerebral anoxia, edema, and unconsciousness. Near-drowning victims who experience dry drowning have the best chance of survival.

wet drowning—Occurs in 80% to 90% of cases. When the victim makes a desperate respiratory effort, the lungs fill with fluid rather than air.

secondary drowning—This is the recurrence of respiratory distress (usually in the form of pulmonary edema or aspiration pneumonia) that occurs following successful resuscitation from the initial near-drowning incident. It can occur anywhere from 3 to 4 minutes to several days after the incident. Pulmonary edema is common following both fresh-water and saltwater near-drownings.

Seawater

Seawater is a hypertonic solution; fluid transverses into the alveoli because of an osmotic pull across the alveolar capillary membrane that results in pulmonary edema; it also causes hemoconcentration and hypovolemia.

Fresh water

Fresh water is a hypotonic solution; fluid transverses rapidly out of the alveoli into the blood by diffusion. Because the fresh water contains contaminants such as chlorine, algae, and mud, surfactant breakdown occurs and fluid begins to seep into the alveoli once again, resulting in pulmonary edema; it also causes hemodilution and hypervolemia.

Pulmonary edema in both fresh-water and salt-water near-drowning is worsened by inflammatory responses of the body.

SIGNS AND SYMPTOMS

History of immersion
Dyspnea that progresses
Wheezing
Rales
Rhonchi
Cough (sometimes with pink, frothy sputum)
Tachycardia
Cyanosis
Elevated temperature (but cold water may cause hypothermia)
Chest pain
Mental confusion
Seizure
Increased muscle tone
Unconsciousness
Respiratory or cardiac arrest

THERAPEUTIC INTERVENTION

ABCs
Protection of cervical spine

Plasma IV
IPPB with 100% oxygen

TABLE 6-5 Significant differences between saltwater and fresh-water aspiration*

Saltwater	Fresh water
Hypoxia	
Greater degree of hypoxia; fluid in alveoli interferes with ventilation	Alteration of normal surface tension properties of surfactant with subsequent collapse of the alveoli; atelectasis; uneven ventilation and recurrent collapse continue until surface-active material regenerates
Blood volume	
Hypertonic fluid draws water into the alveolar spaces causing a persistent hypovolemia; increase in blood osmolarity and viscosity	Hypotonic water rapidly absorbed into the circulation; transient hypervolemia; decrease in blood osmolarity and viscosity; elevated CVP
Serum electrolytes	
Changes usually insignificant; hyperkalemia may result from severe hypoxia and acidosis	
Picture may be complicated by ingestion of large amounts of saltwater	
Hemoglobin	
Hemolysis occurs after aspiration of at least 11 ml of fluid/kg body weight, with a possible decrease in hemoglobin	
Hematocrit	
Technical problems make correct measurements almost impossible and interpretation difficult	
Cardiac changes	
Sufficient water to cause ventricular fibrillation is seldom aspirated	
Central venous pressure	
An increase in CVP coincides with hyperventilation; falls rapidly to normal when only small amounts of liquid have been aspirated	
Aspiration of large amounts of fluid results in initial rise in CVP, followed by a rapid drop to zero	Aspiration of large quantities of fluid results in a persistent rise in CVP
Neurologic effects	
When seawater is ingested in large quantities, the magnesium ion may cause lethargy, drowsiness, and coma	
Urinary system	
Acute renal failure due to tubular necrosis resulting from hypoxia and hypotension	Acute renal failure due to hemolysis and hypotension

*From Orris, W.L.: In Warner, C.G., editor: Emergency care: assessment and intervention, ed. 2, St. Louis, 1978, The C.V. Mosby Co.

PEEP

Frequent suctioning

Correction of acid-base imbalances

Antibiotics

Steroids

Isoproterenol for bronchospasm

Nasogastric tube

Central venous pressure line, arterial pressure line, or pulmonary capillary wedge pressure line

Admission for a minimum of 24 hours of observation

NOTE: Do not attempt to drain fluid from the lungs at the time of the incident, as this would waste time that could be used in the rest of the resuscitation effort.

ECG MONITORING AND PLOTTING AN AXIS
ECG monitoring

Monitoring on a four-lead monitoring system (with an automatic lead switch button) is shown in Fig. 6-3.

When monitoring on a three-lead ECG monitor (without an automatic lead switch button) the best lead placement to use is Lead II or MCL_1. Leads II and MCL_1 are the best leads to monitor for dysrhythmias.

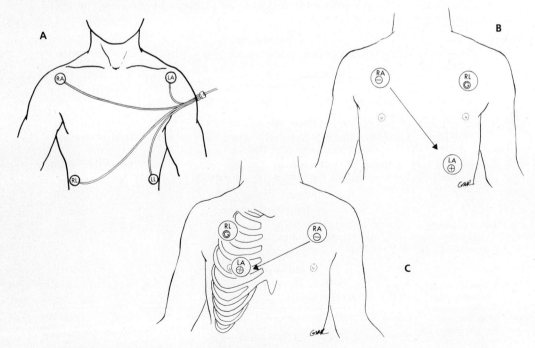

FIG. 6-3 Lead placement for four-lead monitoring system (with automatic lead switch button), **A.** Monitoring on three-lead system (without automatic lead switch button, **B,** Lead II. **C,** Lead MCL_1.

Standard 12-lead ECG

The standard 12-lead ECG takes 12 views of the heart's electrical activity and records it on a wax-coated, standardized ECG paper.

BEFORE BEGINNING

1. Check to be sure that all leads are placed correctly.
   a. "Green and white on the right, Christmas trees (red and green) below the knees" is a helpful memory aid.
   b. Assure that there is a conduction medium between the electrodes and the patient.
   c. Avoid placing the electrodes over large muscle masses.
2. Assure that lead wires are not touching anything metal (this will cause 60-cycle interference).
3. Explain what you are doing to the patient.

WHEN BEGINNING

1. Standardize the machine at the beginning of each lead.
2. Record at least four complexes in each lead.
3. If 60-cycle interference occurs, check for the following:
   a. Loose leads.
   b. Leads and wires against metal.

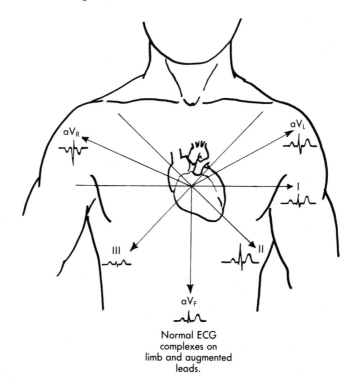

Normal ECG
complexes on
limb and augmented
leads.

FIG. 6-4 The six limb leads.

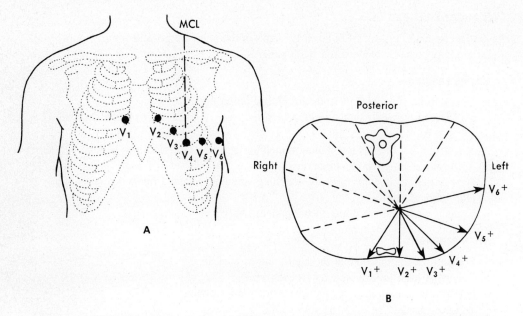

FIG. 6-5 A, Electrode positions of the precordial leads: V_1, fouth intercostal space at right sternal border; V_2, fourth intercostal space at left sternal border; V_3, halfway between V_2 and V_4; V_4, fifth intercostal space at midclavicular line; V_5, anterior axillary line directly lateral to V_4; V_6, midaxillary line directly lateral to V_5. **B,** Precordial reference figure. Leads V_1 and V_2 are called right-sided precordial leads; leads V_3 and V_4, midprecordial leads; and leads V_5 and V_6, left-sided precordial leads. (Modified from Andreoli, K., et al.: Comprehensive cardiac care: a text for nurses, physicians, and other health practitioners, ed. 4, St. Louis, 1979, The C.V. Mosby Co.)

    c. Other electrical machines that could be unplugged.

4. If the patient will be transferred to a coronary care or intensive care unit where daily a ECG will be done, mark the chest where the chest leads are placed (with methylene blue or another dye) to ensure that the leads will have the same placement each time the ECG is recorded.

5. Attempt to maintain the patient's modesty.

AT THE CONCLUSION

1. End the ECG with at least 15 seconds of lead II recording (used for dysrhythmia detection).

2. Record the patient's name, the date, and the time the ECG was taken directly on the ECG strip.

3. Interpret the strip or relay it to the appropriate individual for interpretation.

Interpretation

    When current flows toward a lead (arrowheads, positive electrode), an upward ECG deflection occurs. When current flows away from a lead (arrowhead, positive electrode), a downward deflection of the ECG occurs. When current flows perpendicular to a lead (arrowhead, positive electrode), diphasic deflection of the ECG occurs.

When examining a 12-lead ECG, examine each of the 12 leads individually and note any of the following:

 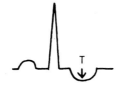 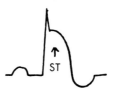 

Normal

Ischemia
Decreased blood supply
T wave inversion
May indicate ischemia
without myocardial infarction

Injury
Acute or
recent; the
more elevated
the ST segment,
the more recent
the injury

Infarct
Significant Q wave
greater than 1 mm
wide and half the
height + depth of
the entire complex
Indicates myocardial
necrosis

The leads directly recording the area of infarct will demonstrate changes. An anterior wall myocardial infarction appears in leads V_1, V_2, and V_3.

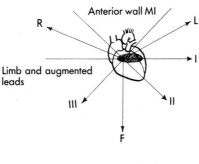

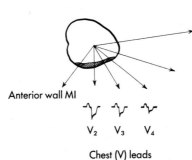

Chest (V) leads

An inferior wall myocardial infarction appears in leads II, III, and aV_F.

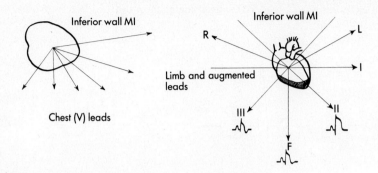

A lateral wall myocardial appears in leads I, aV_L, V_5, and V_6.

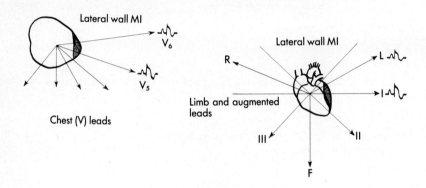

A posterior wall myocardial infarction appears in leads V_1 and V_2. The first R wave is tall, there is a depressed ST segment, and there is an elevated T wave.

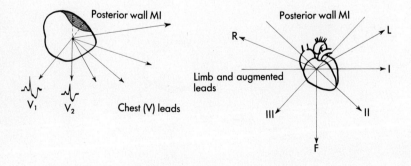

Plotting a simple axis

An axis is a graphic representation of the main vector in the heart.

EQUIPMENT

12-lead ECG
Graph paper
Ruler
Writing instrument

PROCEDURE

1. Draw leads I and aV_F lines on graph paper.

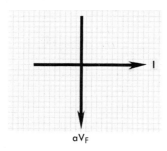

2. Examine lead I of the ECG.
   a. Determine if it is positive or negative.
   b. Determine by how much.

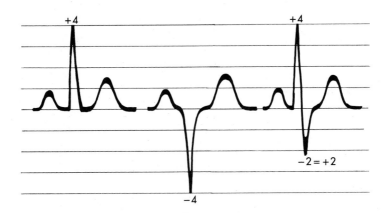

3. Plot the positive inflection or negative deflection on the graph paper by drawing a perpendicular line.
   a. Positive goes *toward* the lead.
   b. Negative does *away from* the lead.

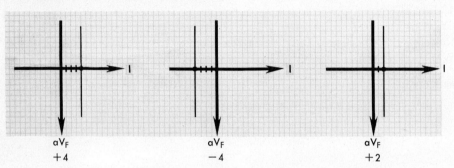

4. Examine lead aV_F of the ECG.
   a. Determine if it is positive or negative.
   b. Determine by how much.

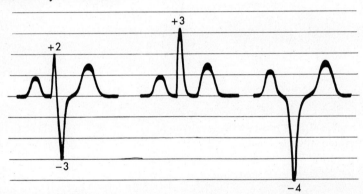

5. Plot the positive inflection or negative deflection on the graph paper by drawing a perpendicular line.
   a. Positive goes *toward* the lead.
   b. Negative goes *away from* the lead.

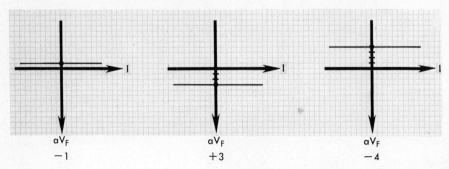

6. The intersection of the plots of leads I and aV_F is the axis.

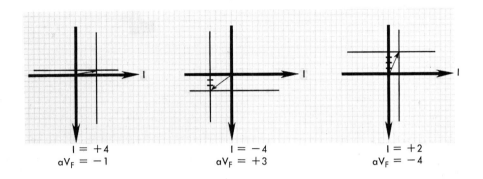

| $I = +4$ | $I = -4$ | $I = +2$ |
| $aV_F = -1$ | $aV_F = +3$ | $aV_F = -4$ |

7. Superimpose a protractor compass over the graph paper to determine the exact degree of axis or estimate the degree of axis by quadrants.

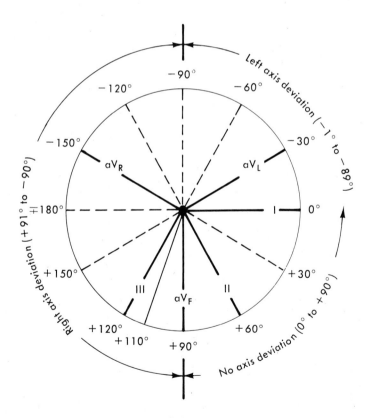

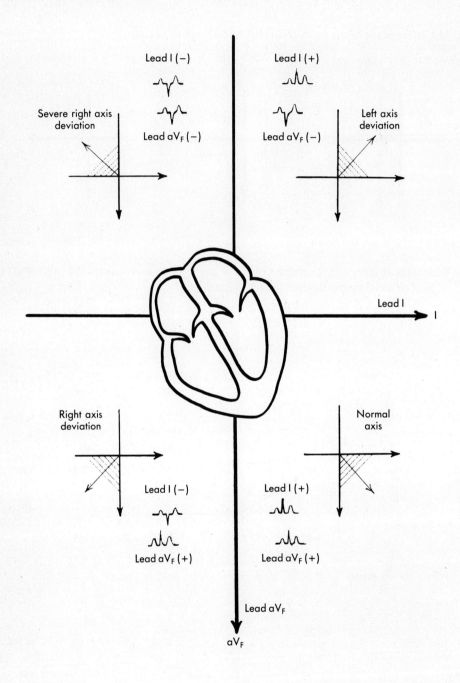

Lead I (−)

Lead I (+)

Severe right axis deviation

Lead aV_F (−)

Lead aV_F (−)

Left axis deviation

Lead I

I

Right axis deviation

Normal axis

Lead I (−)

Lead I (+)

Lead aV_F (+)

Lead aV_F (+)

Lead aV_F

aV_F

SUGGESTED READINGS

Anagnostopoulos, C.F.: Acute aortic dissection, Baltimore, 1975, University Park Press.

Bache, R.J.: Effect of nitroglycerine and arterial hypertension on myocardial blood flow following acute coronary artery occlusion in the dog, Circulation **57**:557, 1978.

Bendersky, R., et al.: Dobutamine in chronic ischemic heart failure: alterations in left ventricular function and coronary hemodynamics, Am. J. Cardiol. **48**:555, 1981.

Berte, J.B.: Pulmonary emergencies, Philadelphia, 1977, J.B. Lippincott Co.

Biddle, T.L.: Acute pulmonary edema, Hosp. Med. **13**:56, 1977.

Braunwald, E., and Sobel, B.E.: Coronary blood flow and myocardial ischemia. In Braunwald, E., editor: Heart disease, Philadelphia, 1980, W.B. Saunders Co.

Burch, G.E., and DePasquale, N.P.: Congestive heart failure: pulmonary edema. In Weil, M.H., and Shabin, H., editors: Critical care medicine, New York, 1976, Harper & Row Publishers, Inc.

Clarke, E.B., and Higgeman, E.H.: Near-drowning, Heart Lung **4**:946, 1975.

Dack, S.: Acute pulmonary edema, Hosp. Med. **14**:3, 1978.

Epstein, S., et al.: Reduction of ischemic injury by nitroglycerine during acute myocardial infarction, Physiolog. Med. **292**:29, 1975.

Fowler, N.O.: Pericardial disease. In Hurst, J.W., editor: The heart, ed. 3, New York, 1974, McGraw-Hill Book Co.

Fuchs, M.F.: Respiratory crisis. In Nursing Skillbook Series: Giving emergency care competently, Horsham, Pa., 1978, Intermed Communications.

Greenburg, M.I., and Walter, J.: Axioms in smoke inhalation, Hosp. Med. **14**:100, 1978.

Gunther, S., et al.: Therapy of coronary vasoconstriction in patients with coronary artery disease, Am. J. Cardiol. **47**:157, 1981.

Hancock, E.W.: Constrictive pericarditis: clinical clues to diagnosis, JAMA **232**:176, 1975.

Harrison, D.C.: Should lidocaine be administered routinely to all patients after acute myocardial infarction? Circulation **58**:581, 1978.

Hopewell, P.C.: The adult respiratory distress syndrome, Annu. Rev. Med. **27**:343, 1976.

Leier, C.V., Webel, J., and Bush, C.A.: The cardiovascular effects of the continuous infusion of dobutamine in patients with severe cardiac failure, Circulation **56**:468, 1977.

Madias, J.E., and Hood, W.B., Jr.: Reduction of ST segment elevation in patients with anterior myocardial infarction by oxygen breathing (brief communication), Circulation **53**(suppl. 1):198, 1976.

Maroko, P.R., et al.: Reduction of infarct size by oxygen inhalation following acute coronary occlusion, Circulation **52**:360, 1976.

Mason, D.T.: Congestive heart failure: mechanisms, evaluation and treatment, New York, 1976, Dun-Donnelly Publishing Corp.

Raffin, R.A., and Theodore, J.: Separating cardiac from pulmonary dyspnea, JAMA **238**:2066, 1977.

Rude, R.E., Muller, J.E., and Brunwald, E.: Efforts to limit the size of myocardial infarcts, Ann. Intern. Med. **95**:736, 1981.

Shibel, E.M., and Moser, K.M.: Respiratory emergencies, St. Louis, 1977, The C.V. Mosby Co.

Shoemaker, W.C.: Algorhythm for early recognition and management of cardiac tamponade, Crit. Care Med. **3**:39, 1975.

Vismara, L.A.: Identification of sudden death risk factors in acute and chronic coronary artery disease, Am. J. Cardiol. **39**:821, 1977.

Warren, J., and Lewis, R.: Beneficial effects of atropine in the pre-hospital care phase of coronary care, Am. J. Cardiol. **37**:68, 1976.

Wilson, A.F.: Drug treatment of acute asthma, JAMA **237**:1141, 1977.

Wyman, M.G., et al.: Multiple bolus technique for lidocaine administration during the first hours of an acute myocardial infarction, Am. J. Cardiol. **41**:313, 1978.

CHAPTER 7 Neurologic emergencies and the unconscious patient

A variety of patients come to the emergency department with a chief complaint that seems to be neurologic in nature. Several of the more common of these chief complaints are presented in this chapter. For a more thorough review of neurologic emergencies, the reader is referred to the suggested readings found at the end of the chapter.

HEADACHE

Headache is a common chief complaint. It is a symptom of some underlying disorder and not a diagnosis in itself. Patients who come to the emergency department with a chief complaint of headache should be carefully evaluated. Headache may indicate intracranial involvement, especially if it is sudden in onset and there is no previous history of headaches. Intracranial involvement should also be considered if the patient has a history of chronic headaches but reports that this one is different.

The diagnosis of migraine or tension headache is based on the patient's history. History is important:

Is this the first headache?
When did it start?
Was there any trauma?
Have there been any personality changes since the onset?
Has there been any memory loss?
Have there been any recent infections?
Have there been any recent eye problems?
Have there been any recent neurologic problems?
Has there been an elevated blood pressure? For how long?
Have there been any emotional problems?
Is the patient currently taking any medications?
Has the patient ever had any seizures? Recently?

Using the PQRST mnemonic, assess the pain:

P = Provokes: What makes the pain better? What makes it worse?
Q = Quality: What does the pain feel like? Describe it.
R = Radiates: Where is the pain? Where does it go?

S = Severity: How bad is the pain? (This is not a good index item for assessing headache.)

T = Time: When did it start? When did it end? How long did it last?

There are many causes of headache. Some of the causes include:

Systemic illness
Intracranial hemorrhage
Intracranial tumor
Intracranial inflammations
Vascular problems
Temporal arteritis

SIGNS AND SYMPTOMS OF MIGRAINE HEADACHES

Recurrent pain
Severe pain
Pulsatile pain
Motor and vision problems
Anorexia
Nausea and vomiting
Emotional irritability
Syncope
Diaphoresis
Photophobia
Gastrointestinal disturbances
May be preceded by "aura"
Possible family history of migraines

SIGNS AND SYMPTOMS OF CLUSTER HEADACHES

Unilateral pain
Severe pain
Pain usually in side of face or in one eye
Nasal congestion
Lacrimation
Ptosis
Diaphoresis

A cluster headache is a form of migraine headache. Migraine headaches are probably caused by extracerebral cranial artery dilation.

THERAPEUTIC INTERVENTION

Pain relief
    Usually with ergotamine tartrate, a vasoconstrictor
    Possibly with a narcotic analgesic
Nausea and vomiting relief
    With antiemetics
Anxiety relief
    With a sedative

Tension headaches

Tension headaches usually occur during times of emotional distress. The pain is believed to be caused by contraction of the scalp and the muscles of the cervical area.

SIGNS AND SYMPTOMS

Dull headache (a tight, constricting feeling)
Bilateral pain (frontal or occipital)

THERAPEUTIC INTERVENTION

Mild analgesics
Identify the cause of the pain and treat it

Traumatic headaches

When there is local tissue damage from trauma, the result may be a headache. Trauma may cause muscle contractions and tension on the extracranial vasculature. Concussions and contusions are frequently followed by headaches. Headaches are also often found in cases of intracerebral bleeding (see Chapter 16).

Extracranial headaches

There are many causes of extracranial headaches. These may include:
Glaucoma (see Chapter 19)
Toothaches (see Chapter 19)
Ear problems (see Chapter 19)
Sinus congestion
These headaches are treated in accordance with their cause.

Temporal arteritis

Temporal arteritis is a condition in which there is a severe headache in one temporal area. The pain may also involve the neck or jaw area or both.

SIGNS AND SYMPTOMS

Severe headache
Patient is usually over 50 years old
Pain when temporal area is touched
Visual disturbances
History of polymyalgia rheumatica

THERAPEUTIC INTERVENTION

Steroids
Biopsy

HYPERTENSION

Hypertension is a product of cardiac output multiplied by peripheral vascular resistance. A systolic blood pressure between 140 and 160 mm Hg is considered in ''the gray zone." The patient with hypertension should be referred for follow-up care and reevaluation. A patient with a blood pressure of 160/90 or over should be considered to have hypertension. If there is hypertension with any of the following, it is considered an absolute emergency:

Cerebrovascular accident

Myocardial infarction

Grade III or IV retinopathy

Angina pectoris

Congestive heart failure

Renal insufficiency

Aortic dissection

According to studies, the systolic reading is just as important as the diastolic for diagnosing hypertension. An elevated blood pressure can be diagnosed in the following ways:

On physical examination (especially with sustained abdominal bruit)

In accordance with family history

By age; if the patient is less than 25 years old and has hypertension, he probably has renal vascular disease

By laboratory examination; urinalysis, BUN, creatinine, electrolytes, uric acid, calcium, lipids, and glucose

By chest x-ray examination

By ECG

By intravenous pyelogram

Some patients will have an elevated blood pressure but no evidence of end-organ damage. This may be because the blood pressure increase is secondary to some other problems, such as:

Drug withdrawal (especially clonidine or propranolol [Inderal])

Drug interactions (such as the combination of monoamine oxidase inhibitors and Chianti wine)

Direct drug effects (such as from amphetamines, tricyclics, or phencyclidine)

Pheochromocytoma

Head trauma

Guillain-Barré syndrome

Therapeutic intervention is to treat the underlying cause.

Essential hypertension usually originates from the kidneys, adrenal glands, neurogenic causes, coarctation of the aorta, and toxemia.

SIGNS AND SYMPTOMS

Headache	Tinnitus
Epistaxis	Syncope

COMPLICATIONS
Minor

Coronary hypertrophy	Abnormal ECG or dysrhythmias
Left ventricular hypertrophy	Conduction disturbances
Grade III retinopathy	

TABLE 7-1 Comparison of benign and malignant hypertension

	Benign (gradual phase)	Malignant (accelerated phase)
Duration	More than 10 years	Less than 2 years
Onset	Gradual; frequently asymptomatic	Sudden; symptomatic
Encephalopathy	Rarely	Often

TABLE 7-2 Stages of complications of hypertension

	I	II	III	IV
Fundi	Vascular spasms	Vascular sclerosis	Hemorrhage and/or exudates	Papilledema
Heart	Left ventricular hypertrophy	Congestive heart failure	Myocardial ischemia	Myocardial infarction
Aorta and branches	Atherosclerosis	Aneurysm with or without rupture	Dissection of aneurysm	Rupture of aneurysm
Brain	Cerebrovascular insufficiency	Encephalopathy	Cerebral thrombosis	Intracranial or subarachnoid hemorrhage
Renal	Benign nephrosclerosis	Malignant nephrosclerosis	Impaired renal function; low specific gravity; proteinuria; hematuria	Elevated creatinine and BUN

Major

Cerebrovascular accident
Aortic dissection
Congestive heart failure
Renal insufficiency
Encephalopathy

Grade IV retinopathy
Myocardial infarction
Cerebral thrombosis
Peripheral vascular insufficiency
Sudden death

HYPERTENSIVE CRISIS

A diastolic blood pressure greater than 130 mm Hg is considered to be a hypertensive crisis. Several complications occur and are discussed here.

Hypertensive encephalopathy
SIGNS AND SYMPTOMS

Fluctuating levels of consciousness or coma
Headaches

Seizures
Grade IV retinopathy

THERAPEUTIC INTERVENTION

Diazoxide
Sodium nitroprusside
Treat underlying condition

Hypertensive cerebrovascular syndromes (transient ischemic attacks and hemorrhages)
SIGNS AND SYMPTOMS

Headache
Decreased level of consciousness

THERAPEUTIC INTERVENTION

For intracerebral bleeding
    Oxygen
    Furosemide
    Consider surgery

For CVA
    Sodium nitroprusside

Toxemia
SIGNS AND SYMPTOMS

Elevated blood pressure
Peripheral edema
Proteinuria
Seizures
Decreased level of consciousness

THERAPEUTIC INTERVENTION

Immediate delivery (via induction of labor or cesarean section)
Diazoxide
Sodium nitroprusside
Magnesium sulfate for seizures

Left ventricular failure
SIGNS AND SYMPTOMS

Dyspnea
Pink, frothy sputum
Rales
Bronchospasm

THERAPEUTIC INTERVENTION

Antihypertensive agent

Aortic dissection (see Chapter 6)
SIGNS AND SYMPTOMS

Chest pain that radiates to back
Hypertension

Blood pressure discrepancies between arms
Pulse discrepancies between femoral areas

THERAPEUTIC INTERVENTION

Sodium nitroprusside
Beta blockade

Drug overdose
THERAPEUTIC INTERVENTION

Sodium nitroprusside

Drug withdrawal
THERAPEUTIC INTERVENTION

Clonidine (Catapres)—alpha and beta blockade
Propranolol (Inderal)—bed rest, nitroglycerin, Inderal

Pulmonary edema
THERAPEUTIC INTERVENTION

Morphine sulfate
Nitroglycerin
Oxygen

Furosemide
High Fowler's position
Aminophylline

MAO inhibitors
THERAPEUTIC INTERVENTION

Phentolamine (Regitine)
Phenoxybenzamine (Dibenzylene [alpha blockade])

Glomerulonephritis
THERAPEUTIC INTERVENTION

Hydralazine
Diazoxide
Furosemide

Hyperthyroidism
THERAPEUTIC INTERVENTION

Alpha and beta blockade
Iodine
Propylthiouracil

SEIZURES

Seizure is one of the most commonly seen chief complaints in the emergency department. Seizures affect 1% to 2% of the population of the United States. It is important to remember that seizure is a symptom, not a disease. A seizure is a period of abnormal electrical activity in the brain. There are three types of seizures: grand mal, petit mal, and focal.

TABLE 7-3 Rapid-acting antihypertensive agents

Drug	Route	Dose	Onset	Notes	Given for
Sodium nitroprusside (Nipride)	IV	Titrate 50 mg in 500 ml D5W (100 μg/ml); run at 3 μg/kg/min	1-2 minutes	Requires constant monitoring; most effective; most controllable; relaxes smooth muscle and increases venous capacity; decomposes in light; no direct heart action; requires concomitant diuretic	Aneurysm; drug-induced pheochromocythemia; acute encephalopathy; hypertension with acute or chronic glomerulonephritis; malignant hypertension; eclampsia; hypertension with left ventricular failure; intracranial hemorrhage
Trimethaphan camsylate (Arfonad)	IV	Titrate 1 g in 1,000 ml D5W; run at 1-2 mg/min	3-4 minutes	An automatic ganglionic blocking agent; decreases cardiac output; requires constant monitoring; requires CircOlectric bed; may cause tachyphylaxis; no direct heart action; requires concomitant diuretic	Aneurysm; acute encephalopathy; malignant hypertension; intracranial hemorrhage; hypertension with left ventricular failure; DO NOT USE in acute or chronic hypertension with glomerulonephritis or eclampsia
Diazoxide (Hyperstat)	IV	300 mg (5 mg/kg) rapidly	1-2 minutes	May cause hypercalcemia and sodium retention; give concurrently with diuretic; may cause nausea and vomiting; BP will fall initially, then rise slightly	Acute encephalopathy; hypertension with acute or chronic glomerulonephritis; intracranial hemorrhage; malignant hypertension; DO NOT USE in eclampsia, left ventricular failure, or aneurysm
Hydralazine (Apresoline)	IV, IM	10-20 mg	15-20 minutes	Relaxes smooth muscle, causing peripheral vascular dilation and reflux tachycardia; causes headache and flushing; less rapid than other drugs; consider propranolol; requires concomitant diuretic	Eclampsia; malignant hypertension; hypertension with acute or chronic glomerulonephritis; DO NOT USE in left ventricular failure or aneurysm
Reserpine (Serpasil)	IM	2.5 mg	1½-2 hours	Depletes catecholamines; may cause drowsiness; lack of precise control	Malignant hypertension; DO NOT USE in hypertensive encephalopathy or intracranial bleeding
Methyldopa (Aldomet)	IV	500 mg in 50 ml D5W over 30-60 minutes	30-60 minutes (maximum 3-6 hours)	Decreases cardiac output and peripheral vascular resistance; response is variable; may cause drowsiness	Hypertension with acute or chronic glomerulonephritis; malignant hypertension; DO NOT USE in hypertensive encephalopathy or intracranial bleeding

Grand mal seizures

In grand mal seizure there is a sudden loss of organized muscle tone. This causes a severely decreased level of consciousness, extensor muscle spasms, and apnea and then bilateral clonic movements. The patient fades into a postictal state in which there is muscle relaxation, deep breathing, and a depressed level of consciousness. The seizures may be idiopathic or may be caused by an easily identifiable condition, such as hypoxia.

THERAPEUTIC INTERVENTION

Protect airway patency
Protect patient from injury
Administer naloxone 0.8 mg and dextrose 50% 50 ml IV if cause is unknown

Petit mal (absence) seizures

Petit mal seizures are usually caused by a cortical lesion and generally occur in children between 4 and 12 years old. The child may appear confused and disinterested, have a glassy stare, blink, and make lip-smacking movements. During the seizure he may respond to verbal commands.

THERAPEUTIC INTERVENTION

Diazepam IV *or*
Ethosuximide IV

Focal (jacksonian) seizures

Focal or jacksonian seizures usually occur unilaterally and are caused by a focal brain lesion such as a tumor, abscess, infarction, or eschar. This type of seizure is usually not life threatening but neither does it respond well to anticonvulsant medications.

THERAPEUTIC INTERVENTION

Diazepam or phenobarbital (although they may not work)
Be sure to do a brief neurologic examination on all seizure patients once the postictal period has passed. (Use the DERM mnemonic—see Chapter 2.) Also, find out if there is a history of seizures, what happened preceding the seizure, and what the patient's vital signs are. Check for a Medic Alert tag or some other type of medical identification, and check the patient for trauma.

Status epilepticus

Status epilepticus is a series of consecutive seizures or a continuous seizure that is not responsive to traditional therapeutic interventions.

THERAPEUTIC INTERVENTION

Try to find out the cause of the seizure once the status is controlled
Treat the cause if possible
Airway
Oxygen (consider 100% oxygen and endotracheal intubation if seizure is prolonged)

IV
Naloxone
Dextrose 50% 50 ml
Thiamin 50 to 100 mg if possibility of alcoholism
Diazepam (Valium) 2.5 mg increments IV (to 15 mg) adult dose
Phenytoin (Dilantin) 25 to 50 mg/minute loading dose (to 1 g) adult dose; be sure to give
   phenytoin via normal saline solution, not D5W
Consider phenobarbital 130 mg every 10 to 15 minutes (to 1 g) adult dose
Consider paraldehyde 1 to 4 ml IV or 5 to 10 ml IM adult dose
Consider general anesthesia if status has not responded to any of these

Febrile seizures

Febrile seizure will be discussed as a pediatric emergency (see Chapter 26).

CEREBROVASCULAR ACCIDENT

Cerebrovascular accident (CVA) is a commonly seen chief complaint in the emergency department. It is caused by the occlusion or rupture of a cerebral blood vessel by:

embolus—From the heart or large arteries caused by atrial fibrillation, myocardial infarction, or surgery; sudden in onset.
thrombosis—Often the cause of a transient ischemic episode; gradual onset.
intracerebral bleeding—Sudden steady onset.
subarachnoid bleeding—Usually caused by the rupture of a berry aneurysm or an AV malformation; sudden in onset.

It is important to obtain the patient's history. Be sure to collect all of the following signs and symptoms:
Headache
Nausea and vomiting
Sudden neurologic deficit
Unequal pupils
Hemiparesis
Aphasia
Decerebrate posturing
Sleepiness
Coma
Decreased BP on left side (left subclavian artery occlusion)
Frequently occurs in early morning
Find out if the patient has a history of any of the following:

Hypertension	Subacute bacterial endocarditis
Hyperlipidemia	Prosthetic heart valves
Diabetes	Collagen disease
Smoking	Use of birth control pill
Heart problems	Recent neck trauma
Atrial fibrillation	

THERAPEUTIC INTERVENTION

ABCs
Decrease blood pressure to normal
Correct dysrhythmias
Consider anticoagulants
Consider aspirin

Consider surgery
Consider mannitol
Consider steroids
Consider antipyretics

TRANSIENT ISCHEMIC ATTACK

A transient ischemic attack (TIA) is a neurologic deficit that lasts for less than 12 hours. Most last only about 5 to 30 minutes. There are two causes, thrombosis and embolus. A TIA may be a prodrome to a cerebrovascular accident.

THERAPEUTIC INTERVENTION

ABCs
Consider anticoagulants
Consider antiplatelet therapy (seems to only work in males)
Consider surgery

COMA (UNCONSCIOUSNESS)

Unconsciousness is by definition the opposite of consciousness. It is the depression of consciousness or the total lack of awareness of the self or anything surrounding the self. This condition continues despite attempts at providing a stimulus. There are two causes of coma, structural lesions and metabolic or toxic states.

Examine the patient to determine if the coma is focal or diffuse and if it seems to be organic (as it is 95% of the time) or functional. Ascertain whether the patient is improving or getting worse with each passing minute. At this point, besides paying strict attention to the ABCs, it is important to do a brief neurologic examination (see Chapter 2).

THERAPEUTIC INTERVENTION

The main therapeutic intervention is trying to isolate the cause. Others include:
ABCs
Naloxone 0.8 mg IV
Dextrose 50% 50 ml IV
Thiamin 50 to 100 mg IV (if alcohol abuse is suspected)
Left lateral swimmer's position with head dependent
Cervical spine precautions
Hyperventilate with 100% oxygen if trauma is suspected as the cause
Other treatment depends on findings

The causes of coma can be remembered using a simple mnemonic:

A = Alcoholism
E = Epilepsy
I = Insulin (too much or too little)
O = Overdose (or underdose)

U = Uremia (or other metabolic causes)
T = Trauma or tumors
I = Infection or ischemia
P = Psychiatric
S = Stroke (i.e., CVA or other neurologic cause)

In the differential diagnosis process, be sure to assess the following:

Temperature	Presence of paralysis
Respirations	Occurrence of trauma
Blood pressure	Abdomen
Pulse	Extremities
Skin vital signs (color, temperature, moistness)	Presence of Babinski's reflex
Pupils	Presence of Battle's sign
Breath odor	Presence of hemotympanum
Presence of needle tracks	Presence of raccoon eyes
Presence of petechiae	Presence of Brudzinski's sign
Lung sounds	Presence of Kernig's sign
Deep tendon reflexes	Presence of incontinence
Presence of posturing	Presence of tongue lacerations

Consider the following laboratory tests to assist with diagnosis:

CBC	Urinalysis
Platelet count	Monitor:
Electrolyte levels	ECG
Glucose levels (serum and urine)	Cerebrospinal fluid pressure
BUN	X-ray examinations:
Creatinine levels	Skull
Toxicology screen	Face
Cholesterol level	Chest
Magnesium level	Abdomen
Calcium level	Scan:
Phosphorus level	Head
Bilirubin level	Lungs

BOTULISM

Botulism is caused by the ingestion of foods that have been improperly canned (high bacteria content before canning). It can occur in infants who have been given raw honey.

SIGNS AND SYMPTOMS

Dilated fixed pupils	Difficulty chewing
Dry mouth	Nasal tone to voice
Diplopia	Respiratory paralysis
Urinary retention	Patient remains awake and alert throughout
Distended abdomen	
Postural hypotension	
Difficulty swallowing	

THERAPEUTIC INTERVENTION

ABCs (especially good respiratory support)
Gastric lavage
Antitoxin

GULLAIN-BARRÉ SYNDROME

Gullain-Barré syndrome is an acute paralytic disease that causes a decrease of myelin in the nerve roots and the peripheral nerves.

SIGNS AND SYMPTOMS

Tingling sensation in the extremities (for hours to weeks)
Severely decreased deep tendon reflexes
Symmetrical paralysis, usually beginning in lower extremities and gradually ascending to respiratory muscles

THERAPEUTIC INTERVENTION

ABCs (consider endotracheal intubation and ventilator)
General supportive care

MYASTHENIA GRAVIS

Myasthenia gravis is a defect in neuromuscular transmission. It can occur at any age but is most common in those in their 20s and 30s. It is seen more frequently in females than males. In myasthenia crisis there is a sudden onset, and this may cause respiratory paralysis.

SIGNS AND SYMPTOMS

Increasing fatigue
Delayed recovery of muscle strength
Weak eye muscles
Weak facial muscles
Weak jaw muscles

Weak pharyngeal muscles
Diplopia
Dysphagia
Inability to handle secretions
Possible aspiration

Muscles below the neck are rarely affected.

THERAPEUTIC INTERVENTION

ABCs (consider endotracheal intubation)
Neostigmine (Prostigmin) 1 mg IV in myasthenia crisis
Medications that precipitate myasthenia include:

Barbiturates
Opiates
Quinidine
Quinine
Any muscle relaxants

Adrenocorticotropic hormone (ACTH)
Steroids
Aminoglycosides
Certain antibiotics

PARALYTIC SHELLFISH POISONING

Saxitoxin is a toxin produced by marine protozoans that interferes with neuron membrane permeability to sodium ions. The toxin is consumed by shellfish such as oysters, clams, and sea snails that produce the phenomenon known as *red tide*. When these shellfish are consumed by humans they cause paralytic shellfish poisoning.

SIGNS AND SYMPTOMS

Paresthesias (progressive)
Paresthesias of the mouth and head
Dysphagia
Tremors
Vertigo
Flaccid quadriplegia
Dysarthria
Respiratory paralysis

THERAPEUTIC INTERVENTION

ABCs (consider endotracheal intubation and ventilator)
Good supportive care
　　The prognosis for paralytic shellfish poisoning is usually good after 24 hours.

SUGGESTED READINGS

Behrens, M.M.: Headaches associated with disorders of the eye, Med. Clin. North Am. **62:**507, 1978.

Budassi, S.A.: Wernicke-Korsakoff syndrome, J.E.N. **8**(6):295, 1982.

Budassi, S.A., and Barber, J.M.: Emergency nursing: principles and practice, St. Louis, 1981, The C.V. Mosby Co.

Dimant, J., and Grob, D.: EKG changes and myocardial damage in patients with acute CVA, Stroke **8:**449, 1977.

Friedman, A.P.: Clinical approach to the patient with headache, Med. Clin. North Am. **62:**443, 1978.

Froscher, W.: Treatment of status epilepticus, Baltimore, 1979, University Park Press.

Lee, C.H., and Lance, J.W.: Migraine stupor, Headache **17:**32, 1977.

Plum, F., and Posner, J.B.: The diagnosis of stupor and coma, ed. 3, Philadelphia, 1980, F.A. Davis Co.

Ram, C.V.S.: Hypertensive encephalopathy, Arch. Intern. Med. **138:**1851, 1978.

Wasslis, W.E., Willoughby, E., and Baker, P.: Coma in Wernicke-Korsakoff syndrome, Lancet **2:**400, 1978.

CHAPTER 8 Abdominal pain

Abdominal pain may be the result of a chronic, long-standing condition or an acute process. There are three types of abdominal pain: visceral, somatic, and referred. Visceral pain may be caused by the stretching of a viscus. It is usually referred to by the patient as cramping pain or gas pains. It is pain that intensifies and then decreases and that is usually centered around the midline of the abdomen. The pain is diffuse and difficult to localize on examination. In response to the pain the patient may be diaphoretic and have nausea and vomiting, a decreased blood pressure, tachycardia, and spasms of the abdominal wall muscles. Many inflammatory conditions begin with signs and symptoms of visceral pain. Some of these conditions are:

Appendicitis

Cholecystitis

Pancreatitis

Intestinal obstruction

Somatic pain occurs when nerve fibers in the parietal perineum are irritated by bacteria or chemicals. Thus somatic pain is described as sharp. It can usually be localized to the area in which the problem is occurring. This patient will lay with his thighs flexed and his knees pulled up toward his chest. This is to avoid any stimulation to the peritoneal area that may increase pain. There will be involuntary guarding and rebound tenderness.

Referred pain (Figs. 8-1 and 8-2) is felt away from the original source of the pain. One theory is that this is because of fetal development of nerve patterns.

It is important to remember that pain is a symptom, not a diagnosis, and that different people react differently to pain. In general, elderly people do not seem to react to pain as much as young people. The care giver must also consider the sex of the patient; men have a tendency to hide the fact that they have pain, since the expression of pain is not considered masculine. The care giver must also consider the ethnic background of the patient; there are some cultures in which pain is almost never expressed and others in which even the smallest pain is expressed.

There are three main points to consider when examining a patient with abdominal pain. The first is to determine the probable diagnosis, the second is to decide if the patient needs immediate surgery, and the third is to decide if the patient requires hospital admission.

ASSESSMENT OF THE PATIENT WITH ABDOMINAL PAIN

History is an important assessment parameter in the patient with abdominal pain. Questions to ask when obtaining a history include:

206

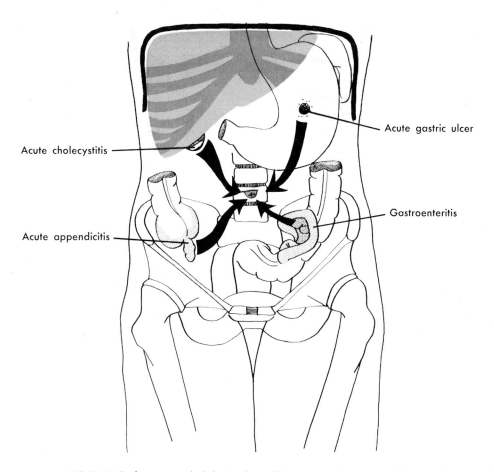

FIG. 8-1 Pain from several abdominal conditions can radiate to umbilicus.

When did the pain start?
Did it wake you from sleep?
Is there anything that makes it better?
Is there anything that makes it worse?
What kind of pain is it? Sharp? Dull? Pressing?
Where is the pain located? Does it radiate anywhere?
How bad is it?
Are there any other symptoms (e.g., nausea and vomiting)?

Pain of a sudden onset is usually associated with a rupture, torsion, strangulation, or vascular problem. If the sudden pain is caused by an event in the hollow viscus the patient will probably describe the event as feeling like being "punched in the gut."

Pain that is gradual in onset is usually caused by an inflammatory or obstructive process, such as appendicitis or intestinal obstruction.

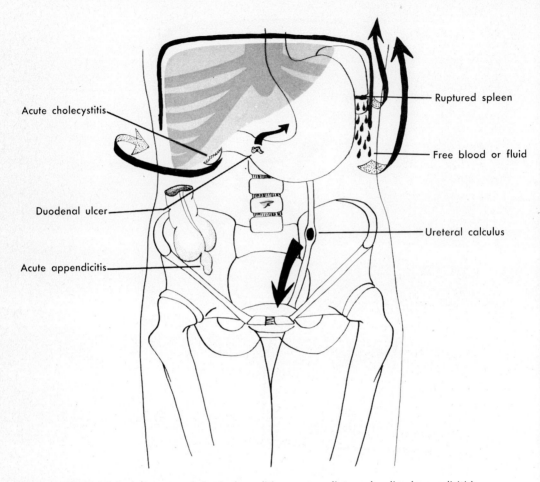

Acute cholecystitis

Duodenal ulcer

Acute appendicitis

Ruptured spleen

Free blood or fluid

Ureteral calculus

FIG. 8-2 Pain from acute abdominal conditions may radiate or localize (appendicitis).

Generally, the more acute the underlying process, the more acute the pain. If there is a blood loss of large volume, the signs and symptoms of hypovolemia may overshadow the abdominal pain.

Location of the pain may offer some useful information, though it is not always reliable. It is often helpful to find out where the original pain occurred because, if peritonitis has occurred, there will be diffuse pain. There are certain conditions for which specific location of pain is accurate. Stomach pain is almost always located in the epigastric region, pain from the gallbladder is almost always located in the right upper quadrant, and the pain of appendicitis is usually located in the right lower quadrant. Intestinal pain usually appears more diffuse.

Pain in the four quadrants of the abdomen

RIGHT UPPER QUADRANT

Cholecystitis
Hepatic abscess
Hepatitis
Hepatomegaly
Pancreatitis
Duodenal ulcer perforation
Right renal pain
Myocardial infarction
Pericarditis
Right-lung pneumonia

LEFT UPPER QUADRANT

Pancreatitis
Splenic rupture
Myocardial infarction
Gastritis
Left renal pain
Left lung pneumonia
Gastric ulcer perforation
Aortic aneurysm dissection or rupture
Colon perforation

RIGHT LOWER QUADRANT

Appendicitis
Cholecystitis
Perforated ulcer
Intestinal obstruction
Meckel's diverticulum
Diverticulitis or perforation of the cecum
Abdominal aortic dissection or rupture
Ruptured ectopic pregnancy
Twisted ovarian cyst
Pelvic inflammatory disease
Endometriosis
Right ureteral calculi
Incarcerated hernia

LEFT LOWER QUADRANT

Appendicitis
Intestinal obstruction
Diverticulum of the sigmoid colon
Ruptured ectopic pregnancy
Twisted left ovary
Ovarian cyst
Pelvic inflammatory disease
Endometriosis
Left ureteral calculi
Left renal pain
Incarcerated hernia
Perforated descending colon
Regional enteritis

There are certain conditions for which referred pain may be the clue to diagnosis.

Problem area	Pain referred to
Fluid collection under diaphragm	Top of shoulder
Ruptured peptic ulcer	Back
Pancreas	Midline back or directly through to the back
Biliary tract	Around right side to the scapula
Dissecting or ruptured aneurysm	Low back and thighs
Renal colic	Groin and external genitalia
Appendix	Maybe epigastric region
Uterine disease	Low back
Rectal disease	Low back

Pain description can also offer clues to diagnosis:

Severe, sharp pain	Infarction or rupture
Severe pain controlled by medication	Pancreatitis, peritonitis, small bowel obstruction, renal colic, biliary colic
Dull pain	Inflammation, low-grade infection
Intermittent pain	Gastroenteritis, small bowel obstruction

ASSOCIATED SIGNS AND SYMPTOMS

Nausea and vomiting and anorexia

The care giver should pay close attention if the patient is experiencing nausea and vomiting or anorexia, as these findings may also offer clues to the diagnosis. When nausea and vomiting appear to be the highlights of the findings, the most likely causes are gastroenteritis, acute gastritis, pancreatitis, or an obstruction located high in the intestinal structure. If vomiting is intractable or there is feces present in the vomitus, this is evidence of an intestinal obstruction in progress. If there is blood in the vomitus, this is suggestive of gastritis or gastric ulcer. If pain precedes vomiting, this suggests appendicitis.

Diarrhea and constipation

When there is abdominal involvement in an emergency situation it is often accompanied by a change in bowel content.

Diarrhea	Inflammatory disease (e.g., gastroenteritis)
Constipation (or failure to pass flatus)	Dehydration, paralytic ileus, intestinal obstruction
Clay-colored stool	Biliary obstruction
Melena (black tarry stool)	High intestinal bleeding
Bright red blood	Low intestinal bleeding
Bloody diarrhea	Amebic dysentery, Crohn's disease, ulcerative colitis

Fever and chills

Fever and chills can offer clues to diagnosis. Repeated fever and chills indicate bacterial infection, pyelonephritis, or appendicitis. Intermittent fever and chills may indicate acute cholecystitis.

Urinary tract symptoms

A burning sensation on urination indicates urinary tract infection. Pain on urination usually indicates an obstruction somewhere along the urinary tract. Hematuria or dysuria indicates urinary tract infection or renal colic.

Gynecologic symptoms

Most gynecologic symptoms signal gynecologic problems. Pain may be indicative of pelvic inflammatory disease or a ruptured ectopic pregnancy, ovarian cyst, or corpus luteum. Vaginal bleeding may indicate miscarriage or many other gynecologic disorders (see Chapter 25).

Gastrointestinal upset

If a meal was consumed by several people but only one complains of associated signs and symptoms, the care giver would rule out the possibility of gastroenteritis. If there is a history of ingestion of fatty foods followed by abdominal pain, this may indicate acute cholecystitis. If there is a history of alcohol abuse, the care giver must be sure to rule out pancreatitis. If abdominal pain starts just before eating and is relieved by eating, the care giver would assume that the problem is probably caused by a gastric ulcer or associated gastric disorder.

Age

The age of the patient may offer a clue to the diagnosis. For example, intussusception is rarely seen in those beyond the age of 2 years, intestinal obstruction is usually found in those over the age of 40, and appendicitis is usually seen in those between the ages of 5 and 45.

Physical examination and laboratory analysis

Look at the patient. Sometimes his physical appearance will offer clues to the diagnosis. What position is he lying in to relieve the pain? Vital signs are important early parameters to obtain. If there is an acute condition, body temperature may be normal for a while then elevate in the course of the disease process. Be sure to take all temperatures rectally to assure accuracy. Temperature will rise if there is rupture or peritonitis or when infection is fulminant.

When assessing the pulse, assume that it will probably demonstrate tachycardia, although occasionally there is a reflux bradycardia.

It is also important to assess respirations. If a patient has peritonitis his respirations will be shallow, and there will be very little motion of the abdominal wall. Rapid respirations may indicate shock, pancreatitis, or peritonitis.

If there is hypotension, consider the possibility of rupture or an acute condition requiring surgery.

INSPECTION

Observe the patient's abdomen. See if there is much movement. If there is not, this suggests extensive peritonitis. If the patient has his hips flexed and knees drawn up toward the chest, this is highly suggestive of acute appendicitis, a pelvic abscess, or a psoas abscess. If the care giver can actually see peristaltic movements or abdominal distention, this may suggest intestinal obstruction. Liver disease may offer the clue of ascites. If there is an abdominal aneurysm there may be a visible and palpable abdominal mass. Check for abdominal distention, which may be a clue to ascites.

PALPATION

Palpate the abdomen as gently as possible. Check for spasm, tenderness, and any masses. Be sure to observe the patient's face during the examination, as it may also offer clues as to when pain is worse or better.

PERCUSSION

Percussion is probably the least useful of all examination tools, as it is often difficult to assess the findings. The one finding that is useful is tympany. Tympany is a sign that gas is present. Areas that are normally dense will normally produce dull sounds. If a tympanic sound is heard where a dull sound is normally heard, air may be present in that area. Conditions that offer this finding are appendicitis and sigmoid obstruction. Ascites (shifting dullness) is the presence of fluid where it normally should not be. Ascites can also suggest a tumor, congestive heart failure, or blood in the peritoneal cavity. Urinary retention will offer the sign of dullness over the suprapubic area.

AUSCULTATION

Bowel sounds are difficult to assess in the emergency situation because it takes a full 3 to 5 minutes of auscultation before the absence of bowel sounds can be established. Normally there are 10 to 20 peristaltic sounds each minute.

LABORATORY TESTS AND X-RAY EXAMINATIONS

The following laboratory tests should be performed on the patient with abdominal pain:

Electrolytes
Serum amylase
Urinalysis
Urine amylase
Complete blood count (include hematocrit and hemoglobin)
BUN

The following x-ray studies should be taken:

Upright chest film
Upright abdominal film
Left lateral decubitus film
Plain abdominal film
Intravenous pyelogram (IVP) if indicated
Intravenous cholangiogram if indicated
Upper GI series if indicated
Lower GI series if indicated

Conditions that require surgery be considered include:

Appendicitis
Bowel obstruction/infarction
Ruptured ectopic pregnancy
Ureteral stone
Peritonitis
Diverticulitis

Cholecystitis
Pancreatitis
Salpingitis
Perforation of viscus
Ruptured intraabdominal aneurysm
Massive GI bleeding

Chronic conditions that may have abdominal pain as a symptom include:

Ulcerative colitis
Crohn's disease
Reflux esophagitis
Irritable bowel syndrome
Regional enteritis

Conditions outside of the abdomen that may have abdominal pain as a symptom include:

Hepatitis
Rheumatic fever
Myocardial infarction
Pneumothorax
Pneumonia
Empyema

Pleurisy
Hip joint disease
Spinal tumors

INFLAMMATORY CONDITIONS CAUSING ABDOMINAL PAIN
Acute appendicitis (Fig. 8-3)
SIGNS AND SYMPTOMS

Anorexia

Nausea and vomiting

Pain in right lower quadrant

Afebrile (unless ruptured)

Guarding posture (fetal position)

Patient has hips flexed and knees drawn up

Pain at McBurney's point

Elevated white count on CBC

THERAPEUTIC INTERVENTION

IV Ringer's lactate TKO or faster if condition indicates preparation for surgery

If ruptured:

Nasogastric tube

Rectal aspirin or acetaminophen for fever control

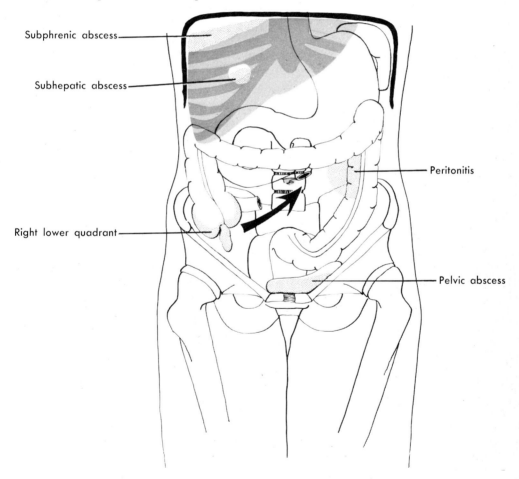

FIG. 8-3 Acute appendicitis can lead to abscess formation all over abdominal cavity.

Acute pancreatitis

SIGNS AND SYMPTOMS

Severe epigastric pain after ingestion of alcohol or large amounts of food
Nausea and vomiting
Abdominal distention
Abdominal tenderness
Abdominal rigidity

THERAPEUTIC INTERVENTION

IV Ringer's lactate
Analgesia for pain management
Nasogastric tube
Antibiotics
Chest x-ray film (20% to 50% of patients with pancreatitis have associated pulmonary complications)

DIAGNOSTIC AIDS

CBC
Serum electrolytes
Alkaline phosphatase
Serum glucose
Serum amylase

Bilirubin
Cardiac monitor
Central venous pressure measurement
Foley catheter and hourly urinary output

Ulcerative colitis

SIGNS AND SYMPTOMS

Bloody diarrhea
Frequent stools (usually more than 20 per day)
Abdominal cramps
Weight loss
Weakness

If perforated:
    Fever
    Tachycardia
    Generalized signs of sepsis

DIAGOSTIC AIDS

CBC
Electrolytes
Amylase
BUN and creatinine
Serum glucose
Bilirubin

Cardiac monitor
Central venous pressure measurement
Foley catheter and hourly urine measurement
Abdominal x-ray film series

THERAPEUTIC INTERVENTION

IV Ringer's lactate or normal saline
Antibiotics
Hospital admission

Toxic megacolon

Toxic megacolon is a severe dilation of the colon associated with colitis.

SIGNS AND SYMPTOMS

Fever
Explosive blood diarrhea
Quiet abdomen
Prostration
Possible shocklike state

THERAPEUTIC INTERVENTION

IV Ringer's lactate
Hospital admission

Esophagitis

Esophagitis is an inflammation of the hiatal esophagus usually caused by the regurgitation of gastric acids. It is often accompanied by hiatal hernia or gastric ulcer. It may also be caused by the ingestion of a caustic substance such as lye or another strong alkali or acid.

SIGNS AND SYMPTOMS

Steady, substernal pain that is increased by swallowing
Occasional vomiting
Weight loss
Obstruction
Bleeding
Foul breath

DIAGNOSTIC AIDS

Upper GI x-ray film series
15 ml viscous lidocaine (Xylocaine) and 20 ml antacid (if the patient has esophagitis, there will be instant relief of pain)

THERAPEUTIC INTERVENTION

Bland diet
Antacids
Surgery to correct anatomic defect
If caused by caustic ingestion:
    ABCs
    Dilation of the esophagus
    Antibiotics

Gastritis

Gastritis is an inflammation of the gastric mucosa. It can occur as a result of ingestion of a gastric irritant, hyperacidity, bile reflux, or shock.

SIGNS AND SYMPTOMS

Epigastric pain
Nausea and vomiting
Mucosal bleeding
Epigastric tenderness on palpation

DIAGNOSTIC AIDS

Antacids (if they bring pain relief, diagnosis of gastritis may be made)
Gastroscopy
Upper GI x-ray film series

THERAPEUTIC INTERVENTION

Antacids
Bland diet
Sedative (if nausea is severe)

Nasogastric tube
Fluid replacement
Anticholinergic medications

Peptic ulcer

A peptic ulcer can occur in the stomach and the duodenum. It is usually caused by hyperacidity.

SIGNS AND SYMPTOMS

Burning pain in epigastric region, usually occurring early in the morning and just before
    meals
Pain is relieved by antacids, bland foods, or vomiting
Symptoms may occur during stressful periods when there is increased production of
    gastric acids

DIAGNOSTIC AIDS

Upper GI x-ray film series
Gastroscopy
Antacids

THERAPEUTIC INTERVENTION

Antacids
Bland diet (several small feedings)
Sedation
Nasogastric tube (for severe vomiting)
Fluid replacement (with electrolytes)

OBSTRUCTIVE CONDITIONS CAUSING ABDOMINAL PAIN
Intestinal obstruction (Fig. 8-4)

Intestinal obstruction can be caused by a large variety of syndromes. Intestinal obstruction may be caused by hernia, fecal impaction, adhesion, tumor, paralytic ileus,

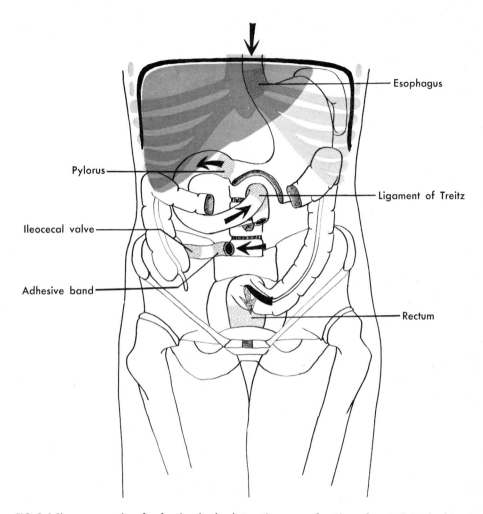

FIG. 8-4 Six common sites for foreign body obstruction or perforation of gastrointestinal tract.

intussusception, regional enteritis, volvulus, gallstone, abscess, and hematoma. There may be a primary mechanical obstruction or a secondary obstruction caused by an inflammation or nervous system problem (Figs. 8-5 and 8-6). The primary danger of intestinal obstruction is dehydration. Other dangers include infarction and perforation of the bowel.

SIGNS AND SYMPTOMS

Nausea and vomiting (may vomit fecal material)
Abdominal pain
Constipation/obstipation
Abdominal distention

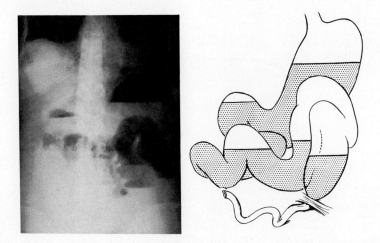

FIG. 8-5 Mechanical bowel obstruction. Localized air-fluid levels seen on upright film of abdomen. Diagram shows dilated proximal bowel and stomach air-fluid levels, and adhesive band causing obstruction. (From Liechty, R.D.: In Liechty, R.D., and Soper, R.T.: Synopsis of surgery, ed. 4, St. Louis, 1980, The C.V. Mosby Co.)

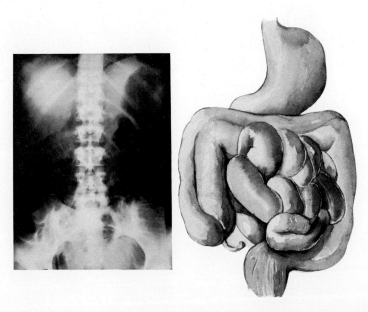

FIG. 8-6 Paralytic ileus. Upright film of abdomen shows dilated small and large intestine. Gas is scattered diffusely throughout intestinal tract. Diagram shows diffuse intestinal dilation. (From Liechty, R.D.: In Liechty, R.D., and Soper, R.T.: Synopsis of surgery, ed. 4, St. Louis, 1980, The C.V. Mosby Co.)

DIAGNOSTIC AIDS

X-ray films—fluid-filled loops proximal to block more than two fluid-air levels
Serum electrolytes
Serum amylase
CBC
Serum glucose
Urinalysis

TABLE 8-1 X-ray and clinical evidence of specific bowel obstructions

Type	X-ray findings	Clinical signs and symptoms
Bowel obstructions (general	Air-fluid levels may appear as a "string of beads" and thus serve as important diagnostic clue to mechanical obstructions. More than two fluid-air levels present reflect mechanical obstruction and/or adynamic ileus. Fluid-filled loops form proximal to impediment and are indicative of a bowel obstruction. Routine films or contrast studies show air-fluid levels, distortion, abscess formation, narrow lumens, mucosal destruction, distention, and deformities at the site of torsion.	Pain, distention, vomiting, obstipation, and constipation.
Strangulating obstruction	"Coffee bean" sign on x-ray film (dilated bowel loop bent on itself, assuming shape of a coffee bean). Gas- and fluid-filled loops may have unchanging locations on multiple projection films. A pseudotumor (a closed loop obstruction filled with water that looks like a tumor) may be present.	Abdominal tenderness, hyperactive bowel sounds, leukocytosis, rebound tenderness, fever.
Gallstones	Air in gallbladder tree, distention of small bowel, and visualization of a stone.	
Hernia		Extraabdominal or intraabdominal hernias may be present: in men, most commonly inguinal; in women, right-sided femoral hernias.
Volvulus		Torsion of mesenteric axis creating digestive disturbances.
Intussusception	"Coiled spring" appearance on contrast x-ray.	

THERAPEUTIC INTERVENTION

IV Ringer's lactate or normal saline   Hospital admission
Antibiotics   Possible surgery
Nasogastric tube

Cholecystitis

Cholecystitis is an inflammation of the gallbladder that may be exacerbated by the presence of gallstones.

SIGNS AND SYMPTOMS

Abdominal pain of sudden onset (especially after ingestion of fried or greasy foods) in
  epigastrium, radiating to upper right quadrant
Low-grade fever (100.4° F [38° C])
Nausea and vomiting
Local and rebound tenderness
Referred pain in right supraclavicular area
Possible slight jaundice
Common in overweight female above age 40

DIAGNOSTIC AIDS

Urinalysis   BUN and creatinine
CBC   Serum glucose
Serum electrolytes   Serum bilirubin

THERAPEUTIC INTERVENTION

Nasogastric tube   Hospital admission
IV Ringer's lactate or normal saline   Possible surgery

Esophageal obstruction

Most of the time an esophageal obstruction is the result of foreign-body ingestion.

SIGNS AND SYMPTOMS

History of foreign-body ingestion (easy to obtain from an adult; much more difficult to
  obtain from a child)
Cervical subcutaneous emphysema (if there is perforation)
Feeling of ''something stuck'' in esophagus

DIAGNOSTIC AIDS

Chest x-ray film (metallic objects will be evident)
Esophagoscopy

THERAPEUTIC INTERVENTION

If object has no sharp edges and can pass into the stomach, it can usually pass through the
  intestines *or*
Retrieval of object through esophagoscopy

Incarcerated hernia

External incarcerated hernia is one of the most common causes of abdominal pain seen in the emergency department. An incarcerated hernia is a protrusion of bowel or other abdominal contents, through the abdominal musculature but not through the skin. There is usually a good blood supply to the hernia unless it is strangulated. Hernias are most commonly found in the inguinal, femoral, and umbilical areas.

SIGNS AND SYMPTOMS

Patient notices the herniation
Pain in abdominal wall after exertion

THERAPEUTIC INTERVENTION

If the hernia is not incarcerated, manual attempt at replacement
Surgery

HEMORRHAGIC CONDITIONS CAUSING ABDOMINAL PAIN
Upper GI bleeding

Several conditions can cause upper GI bleeding (bleeding proximal to Treitz' ligament).

SIGNS AND SYMPTOMS

Hematemesis
Melena (blood and stomach acids mixed with stool)
Possible shock
Possible history of chronic alcohol abuse
Epigastric tenderness
Possible jaundice and enlarged spleen and liver

SPECIFIC AREAS OF UPPER GI BLEEDING
Bleeding peptic ulcer

Two thirds of all cases of upper GI bleeding are caused by bleeding peptic ulcers. It is generally felt that this bleeding is caused by ulcer granulation that erodes into a vessel during the healing process.

Therapeutic intervention

ABCs
IV Ringer's lactate or normal saline
Bed rest
Oxygen
Cardiac monitor and 12-lead ECG
Iced-saline gastric lavage via large (Ewald) tube
MAST application if patient is in shock
Surgery if bleeding is uncontrolled and patient is showing signs of shock
Type and cross-match for possible blood replacement

Bleeding esophageal varices

Patients with liver disease have a high risk of developing esophageal varices. Portal hypertension causes collateral channels of blood to develop between the stomach and the systemic veins of the lower esophagus. Rupture of these channels can cause death rapidly. This is the cause of death in over one third of patients with cirrhosis of the liver.

Signs and symptoms

Massive bleeding in the upper GI tract
History of chronic alcohol abuse or portal hypertension

Therapeutic intervention

ABCs
Balloon tamponade (Sengstaken-Blakemore tube) (Fig. 8-7)
Intraarterial vasopressin infusion
Surgical intervention

Mallory-Weiss syndrome

This syndrome is usually caused by retching and vomiting that is not synchronized with gastric regurgitation. This causes bleeding at the cardioesophageal junction. This syndrome was first described in 1929 by Mallory and Weiss.

Signs and symptoms

History of retching and vomiting with normal gastric content emptying followed by
    hematemesis on subsequent vomiting episodes
Seen on celiac arteriography or via endoscopy if bleeding subsides somewhat

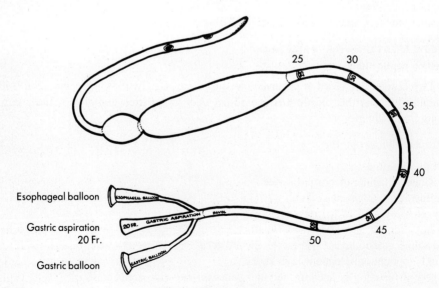

FIG. 8-7 Blakemore tube.

Therapeutic intervention

Whole blood transfusion
Balloon tamponade (Blakemore tube)
Intraarterial vasopressin
Surgical intervention

Borhave's syndrome

Borhave's syndrome is small tears of the esophagus caused by vomiting after a large meal and probably caused by distention of the esophagus.

Signs and symptoms

Bloody expectoration when patient clears vomitus
Possible massive bleeding if tears are severe
Pain in esophageal area

Therapeutic intervention

ABCs
Close observation
Surgical intervention if bleeding is massive

Lower GI bleeding

Bleeding from the large bowel and rectum is usually caused by diverticulitis, ulcerative colitis, carcinoma, cecal ulcers, hemorrhoids, and polyps. The primary sign of lower GI bleeding is bright red blood from the rectum.

THERAPEUTIC INTERVENTION

Depends on cause—control bleeding
Surgical intervention may be required for massive bleeding
Sometimes stops spontaneously

How to insert a nasogastric tube

1. Measure the length of the tube required by measuring from the tip of the patient's earlobe to the tip of his nose and from the tip of his nose to his umbilicus; mark the tube at this point.
2. Explain the procedure to the patient.
3. Lubricate the tube at the tip and a few inches up from the distal end with a water-soluble lubricant.
4. Place the patient in high Fowler's position.
5. Have the patient place his head in a sniffing position.
6. Check the patient for a deviated septum.
7. Insert the tube via the nares, instructing the patient to swallow as the tube is being passed; using a small amount of water and having the patient sip and swallow during this process usually helps (unless water is contraindicated).
8. Continue to pass the tube until it is at the level previously marked; if the patient begins to choke or cough during the procedure, stop and allow him to rest; if coughing

and choking continue, remove the tube and begin again, as the tube may have inadvertently passed into the trachea.

9. Check to be sure the tube is in the stomach; while air is being injected into the tube, auscultate the epigastric region for the sound of air movement or aspirate the tube for the presence of stomach contents.
10. Secure the tube by taping it to the nose and the forehead.
11. Connect the distal end of the tube to intermittent suction if the tube is single lumen and to continuous suction if the tube is double lumen. (Single-lumen tubes are rarely used anymore.)

How to insert a Sengstaken-Blakemore tube

1. Explain the procedure to the patient.
2. Check the tube balloons for patency.
3. The pharynx may be anesthetized.
4. Lubricate the tube with a water-soluble lubricant at the tip and several inches up from the distal end.
5. Insert the tube via the nares for approximately 50 cm.
6. Check to be sure the tube is in the stomach; while air is being injected into the tube, auscultate the epigastric region for the sound of air movement or aspirate the tube for the presence of stomach contents.
7. Fill the gastric balloon with 200 to 250 ml of radiopaque (Hypaque) dye and double-clamp it.
8. Apply gentle traction to check for placement and to wedge the balloon into the cardioesophageal junction.
9. Aspirate the stomach contents to check for continued bleeding; if bleeding is present, inflate the esophageal balloon to a pressure between 25 and 45 mm Hg by attaching the distal end of the balloon to a sphygmomanometer.
10. Double-clamp the tube.
11. Obtain an abdominal x-ray film to verify the tube's position.
12. A small nasogastric tube may be passed to the upper end of the gastric balloon to allow upper esophageal aspiration if required.
13. The esophageal balloon should be deflated every 8 hours to avoid necrosis.
14. Be sure to monitor the patient closely for airway obstruction and keep equipment close by in case the balloons must be deflated rapidly.

Intraarterial vasopressin infusion

Vasopressin is used to control bleeding from lesions such as those caused by erosive gastritis, from Mallory-Weiss syndrome, from esophageal varices, and from peptic ulcers.

Vasopressin is usually infused after the lesion has been identified by angiogram. Vasopressin is infused at a rate of 0.1 to 0.4 units/minute over a 15-minute period. After infusion, the angiogram is repeated. The dose of vasopressin is then adjusted in accordance with angiographic findings.

During the infusion it is important to monitor the patient's heart rate and rhythms and arterial pressure. The infusion should continue for a 24-hour period. The dose is then reduced for the following 24 hours. After medication infusion the patient should be given IV normal saline for the next 24 hours to check for recurring bleeding.

SUGGESTED READINGS

Budassi, S.A., and Barber, J.M.: Emergency nursing: principles and practice, St. Louis, 1981, The C.V. Mosby Co.

Ellis, P.D.: Portal hypertension and bleeding esophageal and gastric varices: a surgical approach to treatment, Heart Lung **6:**791, 1977.

Freitas, J.E., et al: Rapid evaluation of acute abdominal pain by hepatobiliary scanning, JAMA **244:**1585, 1980.

Gammill, S.L., and Nice, C.M.: Air fluid levels: their occurrence in normal patients and their role in the analysis of ileus, Surgery **71:**771, 1972.

Greenberger, N., and Winship, D.: Gastrointestinal disorders: a pathophysiologic approach, Chicago, 1976, Year Book Medical Publishers, Inc.

Kawai, K., and Tanaka, H.: Differential diagnosis of gastric diseases, Chicago, 1974, Year Book Medical Publishers, Inc.

Nase, H.W.: The diagnosis of appendicitis, Am. Surg. **46:**504, 1980.

Philbrick, T.H., et al.: Abdominal ultrasound in patients with acute right upper quadrant pain, Gastrointestinal Radiol. **6:**251, 1981.

Pops, M.A.: Emergency management of gastrointestinal bleeding. Unpublished paper, Los Angeles, 1976, UCLA Postgraduate Institute on Emergency Medicine.

Shahinpour, N.: The adult with bleeding esophageal varices, Nurs. Clin. North Am. **12:**331, 1977.

Smith, G.W., et al.: Oral cholecystography in assessment of acute abdominal pain, Arch. Surg. **115:**642, 1980.

Solomon, A.R.: The value of the amylase/creatinine clearance ratio in the diagnosis of acute pancreatitis, CRC Crit. Rev. Clin. Lab. Sci. **9:**367, 1978.

Wolk, L.A., et al.: Computerized tomography in the diagnosis of abdominal aortic aneurysms, Surg. Gynecol. Obstet. **153:**299, 1981.

CHAPTER 9 Sickle-cell crisis and hemophilia

SICKLE-CELL DISEASE

Sickle-cell disease is an inherited disorder that occurs in 7% of West African and American blacks. It is an autosomal recessive disease with an altered hemoglobin molecule. A person with sickle-cell *trait* has one sickle-cell gene and will have no problems with the disease. In sickle-cell *disease* the individual has two sickle-cell genes and will rarely live past early adulthood.

Sickle-cell crisis

Sickle cells carry a normal amount of hemoglobin, but the cells clump and clog together. When this occurs, oxygen and other products do not reach certain capillaries and ischemic pain occurs; this is sickle-cell crisis. Sickle-cell crisis may be precipitated by exposure to cold, infection, or metabolic or respiratory acidosis. For some reason, sickle-cell crisis occurs more frequently at night. If the ischemia is prolonged, local tissue necrosis occurs.

Common areas for sickle-cell crisis pain in children are the hands, feet, and abdomen (mimicking appendicitis). In adults pain commonly occurs in the long bones, large joints, and spine.

SIGNS AND SYMPTOMS

Pain (a subjective finding; there is no way to assess it)
History of sickle-cell disease
Weakness
Pallor

THERAPEUTIC INTERVENTION

Analgesia (acetaminophen, propoxyphene, meperidine, hydromorphone [Dilaudid], morphine sulfate)
Compassion
Oxygen
Hydration (D5W or dextrose 5% in half-normal saline)
Treatment of infections
Local heat

226

COMPLICATIONS

Recurrent sickle-cell crisis
Hemolytic anemia
Transient aplastic crisis
Cholelithiasis and cholecystitis
Delayed sexual maturation
Priapism
Renal disease
Bone disease (infarction leading to avascular necrosis of femoral heads)
High cardiac output failure
Autosplenectomy
High risk for pneumonia, meningitis, and salmonellosis
Osteomyelitis
Pulmonary emboli
Cor pulmonale
Chronic skin ulcers
High incidence of spontaneous abortion, perinatal mortality, maternal mortality
Hepatomegaly
Hepatic infarctions
Jaundice

HEMOPHILIA

Hemophilia is an inherited, sex-linked disorder that occurs in males and is carried by females. Although all persons with this disorder have abnormal bleeding, the severity is quite variable.

Fig. 9-1 depicts schematically the primary clotting mechanism. Each factor is a protein or glycoprotein that circulates in the plasma. Clotting factors circulate in an inactive form. Initiation of clotting factors first requires factor activation. This occurs

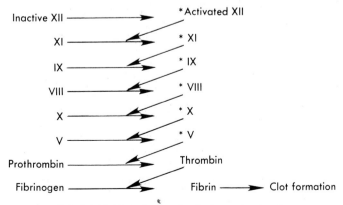

FIG. 9-1 Clotting factors (intrinsic mechanisms).

whenever a cut or bruise is sustained. The subsequent factors are activated in a domino-like fashion; that is, initial activation of factor XII causes activation of factor XI and so on, until fibrinogen becomes fibrin and a clot is formed. Should any one of these factors be removed from the sequence or inactivated, clotting will not take place.

In its simplest expression, hemophilia can be viewed as a bleeding disorder caused by the absence of a clotting factor. However, *hemophilia* is actually a catchall term for a number of different disorders. Most patients with hemophilia have classic, or type A hemophilia, which is a factor VIII disorder. In the majority of patients factor VIII is not missing; it may even be present in excess. However, it either does not function at all or functions at some capacity less than normal. The severity of the bleeding disorder varies with the actual functional activity of the factor in each patient.

Because hemophilia is a genetic disorder, it cannot be treated in a definitive manner. At present health care professionals are only able to offer palliative measures.

A less common form of hemophilia, known as Christmas disease, or type B hemophilia, refers to the absence or functional deficiency of factor IX. For all practical purposes both types of hemophilia have similar presentations.

Usually hemophilia is first manifested in infancy, such as in excessive bleeding on circumcision, bleeding gums, and epistaxis. The possibility of lacerations and major trauma aside, one of the worst features of hemophilia is hemarthrosis, or bleedings into joints. This usually begins in adolescence and primarily involves the knees, ankles, and elbows. Aside from the pain that accompanies the process, improperly managed recurrent hemarthrosis leads to arthritis and ultimate joint destruction. At all ages even minor trauma can produce major bruising, visceral bleeding, and even subdural hematomas.

Because the disorder usually becomes evident in infancy, hemophiliacs who come to the emergency department because of bleeding are usually able to relate the nature of their disorder. Nonetheless it remains a wise policy to take a bleeding history from all patients who have abnormal bleeding and to consider obtaining a screening coagulation panel (prothrombin time and partial thromboplastin time).

It should be remembered that platelet-mediated hemostasis is not dependent on either factor VIII or factor IX. Therefore a bleeding part should be elevated and gentle pressure applied for 5 to 10 minutes.

In a person with type A hemophilia the functional level of factor VIII can be augmented by transfusion with fresh frozen plasma, cryoprecipitate from pooled plasma, or glycine-precipitated antihemophilic factor. The amount of factor VIII in fresh frozen plasma is small. Consequently, volumes that place the patient at risk of circulatory overload are required. Cryoprecipitate is given 1 to 2 units/4 kg of body weight, a much smaller volume, but it carries a high risk of hepatitis. However, it remains the treatment of choice and can actually be used at home by the motivated and educated patient and family.

Episodes of hemarthrosis are usually self-limited by joint capsule distention, which eventually tamponades the bleeding joint. The joint should be immobilized and elevated, ice should be applied, and a light pressure dressing should be applied. After administration of factor VIII has corrected coagulation, the blood in the joint is aspirated. While weight-bearing is limited, range of motion exercises should be recommended along with close hematologic and orthopedic follow-up.

It is fortunate that type B hemophilia is relatively rare, since it presents a greater management problem. Advances are forthcoming, but so far treatment is primarily limited to the less than satisfactory administration of fresh frozen plasma. All other management modalities are the same as those listed for patients with type A hemophilia.

SUGGESTED READING

Saudi, P.: Current concepts: hemophilia, Emerg. Prod. News p. 36, Oct. 1977.

CHAPTER 10 Metabolic emergencies

DIABETES AND DIABETIC KETOACIDOSIS

There are an estimated 4 million diabetics in the United States. The word *diabetes* comes from the Greek word meaning "to run freely through" (i.e., the kidneys). The overall death rate from uncomplicated diabetes is 1% and from complicated diabetes, 10%. Diabetes is caused by an absolute or relative lack of insulin in the body because of either heredity or obesity. A decrease of insulin or an increase of glucose causes the body to use fats instead of glucose for its energy source, as insulin is necessary for cells to be able to use glucose. The breakdown of fats releases ketoacids, which produce a metabolic acidosis. When serum glucose level rises, the serum osmolality increases, and water shifts from the intracellular spaces to the extracellular spaces. This causes a dilutional hyponatremia. The body will try to compensate for this state by producing thirst and causing the body to increase water intake. It will also compensate by eliminating excess glucose from the body (thus glucose levels in urine). Because the body's volume is depleted, both renal blood flow and glomerular filtration rate will drop, and blood urea nitrogen and uric acid levels will increase.

In addition to all this, the body will attempt to compensate for its acidotic state by blowing off CO_2 (an acid) in the form of hyperventilation (Kussmaul's respirations) and by buffering excess acids with bicarbonate and other buffers. Many of these patients will have electrolyte abnormalities because of the sodium and potassium their bodies have lost in the process of osmotic diuresis.

If the acidotic process continues, the body will eventually deplete itself of buffers, and the lungs will no longer be able to compensate. This will result in severe diabetic ketoacidosis and possibly death if the condition goes uncorrected.

Diabetic ketoacidosis may be classified as mild, moderate, or severe. Juvenile diabetes is the total absence of insulin and is treated with insulin injections. Adult-onset diabetes is an insufficient amount of insulin and is treated with diet modifications or oral hypoglycemic (antidiabetic) agents.

SIGNS AND SYMPTOMS

The signs and symptoms of ketoacidosis usually develop slowly.
Ketones and glucose in urine
History of diabetes   Polydipsia (thirst)
Missed dose of insulin   Nausea
Polyuria   Vomiting

Oral hypoglycemic agents

Phenformin HCl (DBI, Meltrol-50)
Chlorpropamide (Diabinese)
Acetohexamide (Dymelor)
Tolbutamide (Orinase)
Tolazamide (Tolinase)

Diarrhea
Abdominal pain
Weakness
Kussmaul's respirations (rapid, deep breathing)
Shortness of breath
Smell of acetone on breath
Dry, warm skin
Rapid, weak pulse
Decreased blood pressure
Chest pain
Fever
Poor skin turgor
Albuminuria
Decreased level of consciousness
Coma
Patient appears very ill

COMMON LABORATORY VALUES IN DIABETIC KETOACIDOSIS

Glycosuria (4+)
Ketonuria (4+)
Serum ketones
Elevated BUN and creatinine
Elevated hematocrit
Serum glucose of 300 to 600 mg/100 ml
Decreased serum sodium
Serum potassium variable/decreased total-body potassium
Elevated serum lipids
Arterial blood gases show acidosis and decreased P_{CO_2}
X-ray films of kidney, ureter, and bladder (KUB) show ileus and gastrectasia

COMPLICATIONS OF DIABETES

Atherosclerosis
Renal failure
Diabetic retinopathy (blindness)

Infection or gangrene
Nerve disorders
Coma

THERAPEUTIC INTERVENTION

Fluid therapy (very critical) IV 0.9% NaCl up to 500 ml/hour

Dextrose 50% IV bolus and naloxone 0.8 mg IV for any unconscious patient in whom the cause of unconsciousness is unknown

Oxygen

Insulin

Bicarbonate if pH is less than 7.1 and blood pressure is decreased or if patient is not responsive to fluid therapy within 2 to 3 minutes; observe the ECG monitor for the presence of U waves that indicate hypokalemia, which often occurs as a result of bicarbonate administration

Insulin dosage in diabetic ketoacidosis

Usually give 10% of the total serum glucose value in units of regular insulin (e.g., if the patient's blood glucose level is 500 mg/100 ml, administer 50 units of regular insulin), giving half via the IV route and half subcutaneously for the first dose. Modify subsequent doses according to serum glucose levels. If ketoacidosis is severe, administer up to 550 units of regular insulin in the first 24 hours IV and subcutaneously or by bolus with 100 units of regular insulin/hour until serum glucose is within normal levels.

OTHER ILLNESSES THAT CAN APPEAR TO BE DIABETIC COMA

Alcohol abuse	Toxic uremia
Smoke inhalation	Myxedema coma
Salicylate overdose	Adrenocortical insufficiency
Barbiturate overdose	Eclampsia
Opiate overdose	Hepatic coma
Bromide overdose	Seizures
Chloral hydrate overdose	Hypoxia
Paraldehyde overdose	Bacterial meningitis
Phenol or fluoride overdose	Systemic infection
Ethylene glycol (antifreeze) overdose	Hypothermia or hyperthermia
Hypernatremia	Tumors
Hypercalcemia	Intracranial catastrophies
Lactic acidosis from any cause	

HYPOGLYCEMIA

Hypoglycemia may be caused by an insulin reaction in which blood glucose level is decreased by too much insulin relative to the patient's dietary intake. Hypoglycemia may also be caused by insulinoma, hepatoma, retroperitoneal sarcoma, anterior pituitary hypofunction, adrenocortical hypofunction, severe liver disease, chronic alcoholism, or severe fasting.

SIGNS AND SYMPTOMS

The signs and symptoms of hypoglycemia develop rapidly.

Cool, moist skin	Tremors or seizures
Diaphoresis	Bounding pulse

TABLE 10-1 Insulins—administration and actions

Type of insulin	Time and route of administration	Time of onset (hours after administration)	Peak action (hours after administration)	Duration of action (hours)
Crystaline zinc* (pH 3-3.5; Zn 0.02-0.04 mg/100 units) (regular)	IV (emergency), subcutaneously 15-20 min. before meals	Rapid, within 1 hour	2-4	6-8
Semilente* (amorphous zinc) pH 7.2; Zn 0.2-0.25 mg/100 units)	½ to ¾ hour before breakfast; deep subcutaneously; never IV	Rapid, within 1 hour	2-4	8-10
Globin zinc (pH 3.4-3.8; Zn 0.25-0.35 mg/ 100 units)	½ to 1 hour before breakfast; subcutaneously	Intermediate, rapidity of onset increases with dose— within 1 to 2 hours	6-8	12-14; also increases with dose
Lente* (combination of 30% Semilente and 70% Ultralente) (pH 7.1-7.4; Zn 0.2-0.25 mg/100 units)	1 hour before breakfast, deep subcutaneously; never IV	Intermediate, within 1 to 2 hours	6-8	14-16
NPH (neutral protamine Hagedorn) (isophane) (pH 7.1-7.4; Zn 0.016-0.04 mg/ 100 units)	1 hour before breakfast; subcutaneously	Intermediate, within 1 to 2 hours	6-8	12-14
Protamine zinc (pH 7.4; Zn 0.2-0.25 mg/ units)	1 hour before breakfast; subcutaneously	Slow-acting, within 4 to 6 hours	16-20	36-72
Ultralente* (pH 4.8-5.7; Zn 0.2-0.25 mg/ 100 units)	1 hour before breakfast; deep subcutaneously; never IV	Slow-acting, within 4 to 6 hours	8-12	24-36

*Contains no modifying protein (protamine or globin).

Decreased or normal respirations   Weakness/syncope
Anxiety   Nausea and vomiting
Normal blood pressure   Decreased temperature
Headache   Confusion
Hunger   Stupor/coma

THERAPEUTIC INTERVENTION

Dextrose 50% and naloxone 0.8 mg IV
IV dextrose 10% *or*
Glucagon (provides glucose to cells by breaking down glycogen) *or*
Glucola if the patient is conscious and able to swallow

HYPEROSMOLAR HYPERGLYCEMIC NONKETOTIC COMA

The mechanisms of hyperosmolar hyperglycemic nonketotic coma (HHNC) are not well understood. Mortality from HHNC is high—up to 60%. HHNC is characterized by severe hyperglycemia, severe dehydration, and severe electrolyte imbalances causing coma. HHNC is often seen in patients who have no obvious history of diabetes or have a history of mild diabetes. The difference between HHNC and diabetic ketoacidosis is that patients with HHNC do not become very acidotic or ketotic. There may be enough insulin in their bodies, but it may not be effective. This could be caused by drugs that decrease the amount of insulin released or available for use (such as thiazides, phenytoins, propranolol, or steroids), or it may be caused by pancreatitis, cerebrovascular accident, dehydration, or extreme glucose overload via parenteral therapy in the burn patient. Although HHNC may take up to 2 weeks to develop, therapeutic intervention must be rapid and aggressive.

SIGNS AND SYMPTOMS

Marked dehydration
Decreased blood pressure
Glycosuria (4+)
Serum glucose greater than 600 mg/100 ml (often greater than 1,000 mg/100 ml)

TABLE 10-2 Clinical laboratory values in ketoacidosis and HHNC*

Value	Ketoacidosis	HHNC
Serum glucose (normal, 65-110 mg/100 ml)	300-1,500 mg/100 ml	600-2,800 mg/100 ml
Serum osmolality (normal, 280-300 mOsm/kg)	Nondefinitive in the presence of ketosis	350-475 mOsm/kg
Serum ketones	Present	Absent
Urinary ketones	Present	Usually absent or slight trace

*From Kolin, M.: J.E.N. **3:**16, January-February, 1977.

No ketonemia
History of recent illness (e.g., renal disease, sepsis, GI bleeding)
Normal or decreased pH
Seizures
Unconsciousness
Usually found in those in their 50s and 60s
Serum sodium greater than 145 mEq/liter
Serum osmolality greater than 320 milliosmoles
Elevated BUN and creatinine
Increased urination (may cause death from severe dehydration)

THERAPEUTIC INTERVENTION

ABCs
IV normal saline and/or plasma protein fraction (human) (Plasmanate) to treat greater than
  25% body-fluid loss; administer 4 to 5 liters in the first 12 hours
Potassium when adequate renal function returns
Insulin 10% of blood glucose value in units of regular insulin; give half IV and half
  subcutaneously

THYROID STORM/THYROID CRISIS

When hyperthyroidism becomes severe the condition is known as thyroid storm or
thyroid crisis. It may be triggered by large-scale infection, sepsis, embolism, diabetes,
surgery, drugs, anxiety, or a decreased intake of thyroid-blocking medications. Thyroid
storm is an extreme medical emergency, and therapeutic intervention must be aggressive
and rapid. There is an associated 20% to 60% mortality.

SIGNS AND SYMPTOMS

Dyspnea
History of hyperthyroidism
Increased pulse (possibly atrial fibrillation or congestive heart failure)
Muscle tremors or weakness
Heat intolerance
Weight loss
Fatigue
Restlessness
Anxiety or agitation
Confusion
Personality changes
Decreased ability to concentrate
Diaphoresis
Diarrhea
Elevated temperature (100° to 104° F [37.8° to 40° C])
Nausea
Vomiting

Decreased blood pressure
Exophthalmos
Vertigo
Stare
Decreasing level of consciousness
Increased appetite
Abdominal pain

Enlarged thyroid gland
Thin hair/hair loss
Warm, velvety skin
Menstrual abnormalities
High serum thyroid
Low serum cholesterol
Elevated T_3 resin uptake

THERAPEUTIC INTERVENTION

IVs
Dextrose 50% and naloxone 0.8 mg IV
Nonaspirin antipyretics
Cooling measures
Increased calories
Increased vitamins
Propylthiouracil 900 to 1,200 mg/day by mouth or nasogastric tube in four divided doses
Hydrocortisone 100 to 300 mg/day IM or IV
Sodium iodide 1 to 2 g/day IV or potassium iodide 30 drops by mouth
Propranolol 1 to 5 mg IV (40 to 80 mg orally twice daily) *or*
Reserpine *or*
Guanethidine
Consider digitalis

MYXEDEMA COMA

Myxedma coma is caused by severe hypothyroidism. It is a major medical emergency with a mortality of 30% to 80%. It is characterized by decreased respirations, an elevated CO_2, a decreased Po_2, a decreased serum sodium level, and a decreased temperature. It will often occur in a patient with untreated hypothyroidism. It is important to note that phenothiazines are not metabolized normally in these patients and may cause severe toxic effects. Myxedema coma may be induced by cold temperatures, infection, trauma, and so on.

SIGNS AND SYMPTOMS

Decreased energy level
Increased stress
Bradycardia
Decreased blood pressure (especially diastolic)
Decreased deep tendon reflexes
Cold tolerance
Decreased temperature without shivering
Decreased perspiration
Personality changes
Constipation
Decreased respirations

Easy weight gain/obesity
Coarse hair
Jaundiced complexion
Fatigue
Inappropriate affect
Psychosis
Paresthesias
Decreased hearing
Ataxia
Anemia
Hyperkeratosis of elbows and knees

Enlarged tongue
Alopecia
Nonpitting edema of periorbital area, hands, and feet
Ascites
Seizures
Menorrhagia
Low-voltage ECG
Hallucinations
Coma
Maybe old surgical scar from thyroidectomy
Decreased serum sodium
History of bleeding, congestive heart failure, cerebrovascular accident, hypoxia, hypercapnia, hypoglycemia, or trauma

THERAPEUTIC INTERVENTION

Oxygen
IV dextrose 5% in normal saline (but be careful not to cause fluid overload)
Thyroid hormone (but may unmask adrenal hypofunction and cause shock)
Steroids; 100 mg hydrocortisone (but too much may produce angina and myocardial infarction)
Sodium
Antibiotics (to treat underlying infection)
Warm slowly with just a blanket to avoid rewarming shock

THYROIDITIS

Thyroiditis is usually characterized by anterior neck pain that comes on gradually or suddenly after an upper respiratory infection. It is most often caused by a bacterium.

SIGNS AND SYMPTOMS

Increased neck pain when the head is turned
Fever
Hoarse voice
Elevated pulse
Increased neck pain on swallowing
Firm or nodular thyroid

THERAPEUTIC INTERVENTION

Aspirin   Propranolol
Bed rest   Glucocorticoids
Antibiotics   Possible surgery

ADRENAL CRISIS

Adrenal crisis is severe hyposecretion by the adrenal gland. It may occur in patients with Addison's disease or hypopituitarism. Adrenal crisis may be caused by an insufficient course of cortisone therapy following adrenalectomy. It produces hyponatremia, hypochloremia, hyperkalemia, and extracellular dehydration. It may also be caused by sepsis, adrenal gland hemorrhage, tumors, trauma to the adrenal gland (from abdominal surgery or abdominal trauma) tuberculosis, or congenital conditions. These patients must be weaned from cortisone. A patient with distress or gastrointestinal upset will require more cortisone than usual.

SIGNS AND SYMPTOMS

History of stress
History of cortisone therapy
Intractable nausea and vomiting
Elevated temperature—103° to 104° F (39.5° to 40° C)—that subsequently drops to 96° to
        97° (35.6° to 36° C)
Abdominal pain
Weakness, lethargy, coma
Hypotension
Irritability
Severe dehydration
Hypovolemic shock
Hyperpigmentation
Weight loss
Anorexia
Salt craving
Moon face
Truncal obesity
Hirsutism
Osteoporosis
Renal calculi

THERAPEUTIC INTERVENTION

Treat the underlying cause
IV dextrose 5% in normal saline to treat dehydration
Corticosteroids (hydrocortisone 100 to 200 mg IV, then 50 mg every 8 hours)
Consider epinephrine (0.1 to 0.3 mg IV)

HYPERCALCEMIA

A serum calcium level of greater than 15 mg/100 ml constitutes hypercalcemia, a medical emergency.

SIGNS AND SYMPTOMS

Lethargy
Thirst
Anorexia

Difficulty swallowing
Dry nose
Nausea and vomiting

Personality changes

Decreased level of consciousness/coma

Elevated BUN

Decreased deep tendon reflexes

Decreased QT interval in ECG

Dysrhythmias

THERAPEUTIC INTERVENTION

General supportive measures

Treat the cause of hypercalcemia

ALCOHOLISM

Acute alcohol intoxication or other alcohol-induced problems may constitute a true medical emergency. Acute intoxication or acute withdrawal from alcohol may be life-threatening. It is essential to assure that there is no other underlying cause of illness or injury than alcohol intoxication, such as head trauma, diabetic ketoacidosis, or overdose.

Assessment

Obtain a good history whenever possible:

When was the patient's last drink?

How much did he drink? (Remember that it is the amount of alcohol and not the type that affects the blood alcohol level.)

How much does he usually drink each day? How much each week?

When was the last time the patient ate?

Is he taking any medications?

Has he taken any medications or drugs? (Specifically ask about disulfiram [Antabuse] and metronidazole [Flagyl].)

Does the patient have any other medical illness?

Acute intoxication

Acute intoxication is caused by consumption of a large amount of alcohol over a short period of time. Acute intoxication can occur at various levels depending on the patient's drinking frequency, the amount of food consumed with the alcohol, and the physiologic tolerance of the drinker (Fig. 10-1).

THERAPEUTIC INTERVENTION

Airway management (aspiration is a major cause of death in the acutely intoxicated)

Oxygen

Draw blood for medical/forensic purposes

Ipecac if necessary, if alcohol was consumed within 1 to 2 hours, especially in children

Gastric lavage if necessary

Control seizures with diazepam (Valium)

IV D5W

Dextrose 50% and thiamin 100 mg (to prevent Wernicke-Korsakoff syndrome)

Other appropriate therapeutic interventions depend on findings

Possible renal dialysis

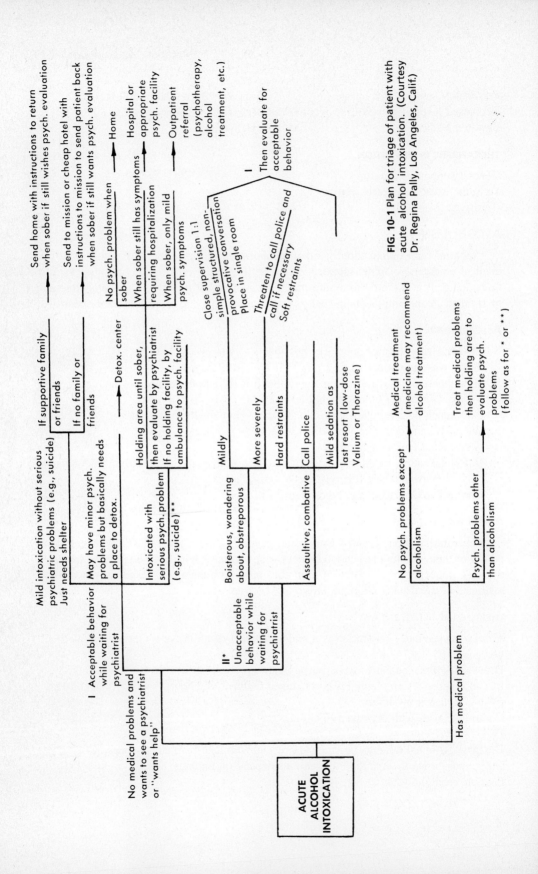

FIG. 10-1 Plan for triage of patient with acute alcohol intoxication. (Courtesy Dr. Regina Pally, Los Angeles, Calif.)

Rum fits

Rum fits are seizures that are concurrent with drinking alcohol. They may be caused by a decreased blood alcohol level, a decreased glucose level, or an electrolyte imbalance.

THERAPEUTIC INTERVENTION

ABCs
Oxygen
Diazepam (Valium)
IV D5W

Alcohol withdrawal

MILD

Signs and symptoms

Hangover
Headache
Shaking
Nausea and vomiting
Mild ataxia

Therapeutic intervention

Rest
Aspirin
Rehydration

SEVERE

Severe alcohol withdrawal occurs in chronic alcoholics who have been without alcohol. It occurs within 24 hours of no alcohol or decreased alcohol consumption.

TABLE 10-3 Alcohol ingestion and equivalent blood alcohol levels

Alcohol (80 proof)	Blood alcohol percentage in 70 kg person	Signs and symptoms
30 ml (2 ounces)	0.05%	Very few
120 ml (4 ounces)	0.10% ("under the influence" in most states)	Giddy; decreased muscle coordination; decreased inhibitions
180 ml (6 ounces)	0.15%	Decreased sensory level; slurred speech; vertigo; ataxia; elevated pulse; diaphoresis
240 ml (8 ounces)	0.20%	Very decreased sensory level; marked decrease in reaction to stimuli; inability to walk; nausea vomiting
480 ml (16 ounces)	0.40%	No response to stimuli; decreased deep tendon reflexes; decreased blood pressure; elevated pulse; cool, clammy, moist skin; seizures
600 ml (20 ounces)	0.50%	Death from primary respiratory arrest

Signs and symptoms

Seizures
Decreased level of consciousness
Nausea and vomiting
Photophobia
Hallucinations (auditory and visual)
Slight lateral nystagmus
Diaphoresis
Ataxia

Therapeutic intervention

ABCs
IV D5W or D10W in half-normal saline
Thiamin 100 mg IM
Vitamins
Dextrose 50%
Diazepam (Valium)

Delirium tremens (DTs)

Delirium tremens occurs after a severe drop in the amount of alcohol consumed by an alcoholic after 72 hours. It may persist for several days. Delirium tremens is an acute medical emergency with a 10% to 15% mortality.

SIGNS AND SYMPTOMS

Gross tremors
Increasing agitation
Hallucinations (auditory and visual)
Seizures
Decreased blood pressure
Elevated pulse
Dysrhythmias

THERAPEUTIC INTERVENTION

Haloperiodol (Haldol)
Chlordiazepoxide
Careful airway management
Protection of head and limbs (padded bedsides)
IV with electrolyte additions

Disulfiram (Antabuse) reactions

Disulfiram (Antabuse) is a drug given to alcoholics in some alcoholic detoxification programs. When combined with alcohol, disulfiram produces some very unpleasant effects. It may react with foods or medications containing alcohol, including cough syrups, fermented vinegar, and so on and perhaps even the odor of rubbing alcohol or after-shave.

SIGNS AND SYMPTOMS

Severe nausea and vomiting (5 to 15 minutes following contact with alcohol) that may
   continue for 6 to 12 days
Flush of face, chest, and neck
Perspiration
Reddened conjunctiva
Headache
Increased pulse
Increased respirations
Decreased blood pressure
Decreased level of consciousness

THERAPEUTIC INTERVENTION

ABCs
Oxygen
IV normal saline
Consider ascorbic acid
Chlorpheniramine (Chlor-Trimeton)
Diphenhydramine (Benadryl)

SUGGESTED READINGS

Addison, T.: On the constitutional and local effects of disease of the suprarenal capsules, London, 1855, Highly.

Ansbaugh, P.: Emergency management of intoxicated patients with head injuries, J.E.N. **3**(3):9, 1977.

Appel, G., et al.: The syndrome of multiple endocrine gland insufficiency, Am. J. Med. **61**:129, 1976.

Beigelman, P.M.: Severe diabetic ketoacidosis (diabetic coma), Diabetes **20**:490, 1971.

Campbell, I.W., et al.: Abdominal pain in metabolic decompensation: clinical significance, JAMA **233**:166, 1975.

Clements, R.S., and Vourganti, B.: Fatal diabetic ketoacidosis: major causes and approaches to their preven-tion, Diabetes Care **1**:314, 1978.

Faber, J., et al.: Subclinical hypothyroidism in Addison's disease, Acta Endocrinol. **91**:674, 1979.

Felig, P.: Combating diabetic ketoacidosis and other hyperglycemic ketoacidotic syndromes, Postgrad. Med. **50**:150, 1976.

Green, W.L.: Guidelines for treatment of myxedema, Med. Clin. North Am. **52**:431, 1968.

Lawson, D. et al.: Massive retroperitoneal adrenal hemorrhage, Surg. Obstet. Gynecol. **128**:989, 1969.

Mackin, J.F., Canary, J.J., and Pittmans, C.S.: Thyroid storm and its management, N. Engl. J. Med. **291**:1396, 1974.

Miller, E.C.: Diabetic emergencies, Am. Fam. Physician **18**:115, 1978.

McCurdy, D.K.: Hyperosmolar hyperglycemic non-ketotic diabetic coma, Med. Clin. North Am. **54**:683, 1970.

Riley, W. et al.: Adrenal autoantibodies and Addison's disease in insulin-dependent diabetes mellitus, J. Pediatr. **97**:191, 1980.

Rosenberg, I.N.: Thyroid storm, N. Engl. J. Med. **238**:1052, 1970.

Sandler, J.A.: Endocrine emergencies. In Warner, C.G., editor: Emergency care: assessment and intervention, ed. 3, St. Louis, 1982, The C.V. Mosby Co.

Steer, M., et al.: Recognition of adrenal insufficiency in the post-operative patient, Am. J. Surg. **139**:443, 1980.

Urbanic, R.C., and Mazzaferri, E.L.: Thyrotoxic crisis and myxedema coma, Heart Lung **7**:435, 1978.

Werner, S.C., and Ingbar, S.H. editors: The thyroid, Hagerstown, Md., 1978, Harper & Row, Publishers, Inc.

CHAPTER 11 Toxicologic emergencies

Toxicology is the science of poisons. The list of substances that can cause poisoning is literally endless. General therapeutic intervention for poisonings includes:

ABCs (consider endotracheal intubation if necessary)

Left lateral swimmer's position with head dependent

Oxygen

IV Ringer's lactate or normal saline solution (for possible fluid challenge)

Naloxone (Narcan) 0.8 mg by IV push

Dextrose 50% 50 ml

Thiamin 50 to 100 mg IV (if possibility of alcohol abuse)

Consider MAST application

Identify the specific poison if possible

Ipecac if indicated and gag reflex is intact

Gastric lavage if indicated and gag reflex is not intact

Activated charcoal to neutralize poison

Magnesium citrate to enhance excretion of poison

The following parameters should be monitored:

ECG

Arterial blood gases

Urinary output

Vital signs

Try to ascertain the type of poison:

What is the nature of the poison?

How is it absorbed?

How is it catabolized?

How is it excreted?

How can it be detected?

In certain cases of poisoning the administration of ipecac is contraindicated. These include:

When caustic or alkaline agents have been ingested

When petroleum distillates have been ingested (very controversial)

When the patient is comatose or has a decreased gag reflex

When the patient is under 1 year of age

When there is not enough poison in the patient's body to be considered dangerous

POISON INFORMATION

Information on poisons can be obtained from a local or regional poison information center or through various resources such as the Poisindex.* The Poisindex is a computer-generated microfiche system that contains specific and detailed protocols for emergency treatment of poisoning. Microfiche product information cards are updated quarterly to include new data and revised management guidelines. The Poisindex can be obtained by subscription. Quarterly updates are mailed automatically to subscribers. Topics included in the management of specific product poisonings are available forms of the poison, pharmacology, clinical effects, range of toxicity, laboratory considerations, treatment regimens, and major references. Entries can be found under trade names, generic names, chemical names, slang terms, or imprint-code designations. Color pictures of poisonous snakes, plants, and mushrooms are also provided to assist in rapid identification.

GASTRIC LAVAGE PROCEDURE

1. Protect the airway.
   a. Endotracheal intubation if the patient is unconscious or has a decreased gag reflex.
   b. Left lateral swimmer's position with head dependent for a patient who has a gag reflex.
   c. Have suction readily available.
2. Select the proper size of tube—preferably 36-gauge French for an adult.
3. Lubricate the tube with a water-soluble lubricant.
4. Check for deviated septum if passing the tube through the patient's nose.
5. If the patient can cooperate, have him sit up and take sips of water while swallowing the tube.
6. Advance the tube.
7. Auscultate with a stethoscope over the gastric area and force some air into the tube to assure proper placement.
8. Secure the tube with tape.
9. Place the patient in left lateral swimmer's position with head dependent if this has not been done already.
10. Administer lavage with warm normal saline solution (50 to 300 ml in an adult, 10 ml/kg in a child).
11. Allow for return by gravity.
12. Repeat lavage until return is clear.
13. Administer activated charcoal solution through the tube.
14. Administer magnesium citrate solution through the tube.
15. Remove the tube.
16. Provide oral hygiene.

---

*The Poisindex is produced by Micromedex, Inc. in association with the Rocky Mountain Regional Poison Center, Denver General Hosital, Denver, Colorado, under the direction of Dr. Barry Rumack.

ACTIVATED CHARCOAL

Activated charcoal is usually given by mouth or nasogastric tube after emesis or lavage. It produces a physical binding effect with any toxic product that may remain in the stomach. It is effective in many types of overdose but does not work effectively in cyanide poisoning. Activated charcoal may be given as a slurry, mixed with water, or in a gelatin mixture topped with chocolate syrup.

PETROLEUM DISTILLATES

Kerosene, charcoal lighter fluid, mineral oil, furniture polish, turpentine, gasoline, and many insecticides have a petroleum-distillate base. A lethal dose is 3 to 4 ounces for an adult and considerably less for a child. Complications usually occur as a result of aspiration or other pulmonary problems. The diagnosis petroleum distillates ingestion is made by:

Vital signs ECG
Arterial blood gases Urinalysis
Chest x-ray examination

THERAPEUTIC INTERVENTION

ABCs (aspiration occurs frequently; intubate if necessary)
Oxygen
Wash surface areas that have been contaminated
Consider ipecac (especially if dose of poison is large)
Consider gastric lavage
Consider catharsis
Consider steroids

ACETAMINOPHEN

Acetaminophen (Datril, Tylenol, etc.), a metabolite of phenacetin, is found in varying quantities in more than 20 miscellaneous remedies for pain, cough, colds, and so on, including the following common agents (and many others):

Bayer Non-Aspirin	Liquiprin	Sinutab
Bromo Quininine	Novahistine	Super Anahist
Bromo Seltzer	Neo-Synephrine Compound	Tempra
Coldene	Nyquil	Trigesic
CoTylenol	Parafon Forte	Vanquish
Darvocet-N	Phenaphen	Wygesic
Excedrin	Romilar	

An overdose of as few as 20 tablets of Tylenol can produce fatal hepatotoxicity. The half-life of acetaminophen is 2 to 4 hours in healthy adults.

Peak plasma levels for tablets are reached within the first hour, slightly sooner for liquid preparations. Peak levels may be delayed if acetaminophen is taken with food or other substances that could retard absorption. Darvocet-N may cause peak blood levels 16 to 18 hours after ingestion. Alcohol accelerates absorption.

Emergency personnel should be alert to signs and symptoms of all three stages of toxicity:

Early (12 to 24 hours)	Intermediate (1 to 3 days)	Late (3 to 5 days)
Anorexia	Symptoms of early phase	Hepatic necrosis
Nausea	continuing in mild form	Renal failure
Vomiting	Pain in right upper quadrant	Myocardiopathy
Pallor	caused by liver tenderness	
Sweating	Decline in renal output	

If acetaminophen ingestion is suspected, *draw blood for measuring the serum acetaminophen level.* Telephone the Rocky Mountain Poison Center (303-893-7771) for information on the location of the nearest laboratory that can provide this analysis. Baseline liver enzyme levels should also be determined.

Specific intervention for the first 24 hours in a patient over 12 years old is as follows: Empty the stomach with lavage via a large-bore tube. Use copious amounts of fluid.

If ingestion is detected within the first 30 minutes, activated charcoal is beneficial. (After 30 minutes charcoal or a cathartic is probably of limited value.) Aspirate the charcoal after 1 hour.

N-Acetylcysteine (Mucomyst) is currently being used in the treatment of acetaminophen poisoning.

Administer 140 mg/kg N-acetylcysteine (20% solution) orally. Carbonated soft drinks and unsweetened grapefruit juice may be used as vehicles to reduce the offensive taste. An alternate method of Mucomyst administration is via a nasogastric tube.

Follow the initial dose with 70 mg/kg every 4 hours for 68 hours. Repeat acetaminophen blood level measurement after this therapy and 24 hours later. Continue to monitor hepatic, renal, and cardiac status for 14 days.

Forced diuresis or hemodialysis is of questionable value.

SALICYLATES

Salicylate (aspirin) overdose is one of the most common and lethal types of overdoses seen in the emergency department. It is a serious overdose that must be treated promptly.

To calculate salicylate levels use one of the following equations (1 Gr = 65 mg):

$$\frac{\text{Number of tablets ingested} \times \text{Grains of salicylate tablet}}{\text{Weight of patient in pounds}} = \text{Dose in grains per pound}$$

or

$$\frac{\text{Number of tablets ingested} \times \text{Milligrams of salicylate}}{\text{Weight of patient in kilograms}} = \text{Dose in milligrams per kilogram}$$

If the dose is greater than 3 Gr/pound or 450 mg/kg or other signs of salicylate intoxication occur, therapeutic intervention is required.

SIGNS AND SYMPTOMS

Hyperpnea	Tinnitus	Confusion	Seizures
Vomiting	Fever	Lethargy	Coma

THERAPEUTIC INTERVENTION

ABCs (consider endotracheal intubation)
Administer oxygen
Induce emesis if gag reflex is intact
  (use ipecac)
Consider gastric lavage when gag reflex
  is not intact
Consider activated charcoal
Consider catharsis

Obtain arterial blood gases
Obtain serum salicylate levels
Tepid sponging for elevated temperature
IV fluids
Treat hemorrhage with vitamin K
Treat seizures with diazepam (Valium)
Consider hemodialysis

DIGITALIS

Digitalis causes increased inotropy (contractility) and a prolonged AV node refractory period and shortens the action potential of Purkinje fibers and ventricular muscle fibers. The overall mechanism of digitalis is to enhance cardiac output and reduce cardiac rate. Most commonly it is used to treat congestive heart failure, arterial fibrillation, atrial flutter, and occasionally paroxysmal atrial tachycardia.

Digitalis is the fourth most commonly prescribed drug. The therapeutic dose is 50% to 60% of the toxic dose. It causes over 50% of adverse drug reactions. Digitalis toxicity should be suspected especially in the elderly when signs and symptoms appear.

SIGNS AND SYMPTOMS

Mild
  Anorexia
  Premature ventricular contractions
  Bradycardia
  Nausea and vomiting
  Headache
  Malaise

Severe
  Blurred vision
  Disorientation
  Diarrhea
  SA or AV block
  Ventricular tachycardia
  Ventricular fibrillation
  Color disturbances (yellow) in vision

THERAPEUTIC INTERVENTION

ABCs
Discontinue digitalis and diuretics

Correct electrolyte imbalances
Correct dysrhythmias

ACUTE IRON INTOXICATION

Overdoses of vitamin tablets containing iron are common among toddlers. The lethal dose is approximately 60 mg/kg.

SIGNS AND SYMPTOMS

Upper GI bleeding
Lower GI bleeding
Severe acidosis
Coagulopathy

Hepatic necrosis
Pyloric stenosis
Shock

THERAPEUTIC INTERVENTION

ABCs
Induce emesis
Gastric lavage with 5% sodium bicarbonate
IV D5W
Arterial blood gases
Deferoxamine 15 mg/kg/hour IV or IM (90 mg/kg every 8 hours)
Consider exchange transfusions

POISONOUS PLANTS

Several poisonous plants may be accidentally or intentionally ingested.

Jimsonweed (Fig. 11-1)

Jimsonweed is a psychedelic agent that produces atropine-like effects, halucinations, and thought-process disturbances. Jimsonweed leaves may be smoked or used to make tea, or the jimsonweed seeds may be chewed and ingested.

SIGNS AND SYMPTOMS

Dry mouth
Intense thirst
Blurred vision
Photophobia
Warm, flushed skin
Difficulty swallowing
Difficulty talking
Difficulty urinating
Fever
Tachycardia
Palpitations

Hyperactivity
Disorientation
CNS depression
Seizures
Coma

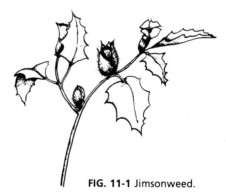

FIG. 11-1 Jimsonweed.

THERAPEUTIC INTERVENTION

ABCs
Low-stimulation environment
Induce emesis if gag reflex if intact
Gastric lavage if gag reflex is not intact
Reduce fever with antipyretics
Administer physostigmine:
    Adult—2 mg diluted to 10 ml IV over 2 minutes; repeat every 5 minutes up to 6 mg maximum dosage (total)
    Child—0.5 mg diluted to 10 ml IV over 2 minutes; repeat every 5 minutes up to 2 mg maximum dosage (total)
Physostigmine may have to be readministered in 30 to 60 minutes because of the short half-life of physostigmine and the long half-life of jimsonweed.

Other poisonous plants are shown and their effects described in Table 11-1.

Text continued on p. 257.

TABLE 11-1 Poisonous plants*

Plant	Toxic parts	Symptoms	Treatment
Bird of paradise (*Poinciana gilliesi*)	Pods and seeds	Vomiting, diarrhea, dizziness, vertigo, drowsiness	Gastric lavage or emesis, symptomatic treatment, demulcents, replace fluids
Dumb cane (*Dieffenbachia seguine*) and philodendron	All parts, especially stem and leaves	Instantaneous swelling of tongue and throat with difficult swallowing, blisters, paralysis of vocal cords	Gastric lavage or emesis (if no blisters present), cold pack to lips and mouth, demulcents, antihistamines, especially epinephrine

Elephant's ear (Colocasia)

Same as dumb cane

Same as dumb cane

Same as dumb cane

English ivy (Hedera helix)

All parts, especially leaves and berries

Skin irritation, nausea, vomiting, severe diarrhea, increased thirst, increased salivation, abdominal pain, difficulty breathing; can lead to coma

Gastric lavage, symptomatically supportive treatment—paraldehyde (2-10 ml) IM, O_2, sometimes artificial respiration

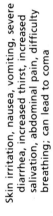

Holly (genus Ilex)

Berries and leaves

Vomiting, diarrhea, stupor, narcosis

Gastric lavage or emesis, symptomatic treatment

TABLE 11-1 Poisonous plants—cont'd

Plant	Toxic parts	Symptoms	Treatment
Jack-in-the-pulpit (*Aris-rema triphyllum*)	Leaves	Irritation of gastrointestinal tract, swelling of tongue, lips, and palate	Gastric lavage, symptomatic treatment, demulcents, cold packs to lips and mouth, antihistamine (epinephrine), aluminum hydroxide (neutralizer)
Jerusalem cherry (*Solanum pseudocapsicum*)	All parts	Stomach pain, low temperature, paralysis, dilated pupils, vomiting, diarrhea, circulation, respiratory depression, loss of sensation, death	Gastric lavage or emesis, support respirations, paraldehyde (2-10 ml) IM

Mistletoe (*Phoradendron serotinum*) 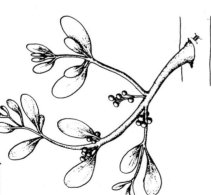	Berries	Stomach and intestinal irritation, diarrhea, bradycardia	Gastric lavage or emesis, supportive potassium, procainamide and quinidine sulfate have been effective (treatment as for digitalis intoxication)
Pencil tree (*Euphorbia tirucalli*)	Spurges, milky sap	Severe irritation of mouth, throat, and stomach	Gastric lavage, symptomatic treatment
Poinsettia (*Euphorbia pulcherima*) 	Milky sap, stem, leaves, flower-bud	Irritation of mouth, throat, stomach, skin, dangerous to eyes	Gastric lavage or emesis, symptomatic treatment

Continued.

TABLE 11-1 Poisonous plants—cont'd

Plant	Toxic parts	Symptoms	Treatment
Star-of-Bethlehem (*Ornithgalum umbellatum*)	All parts—bulbs and leaves (both fresh and dried)	Nausea, intestinal disorders	Gastric lavage or emesis, symptomatic treatment
English yew (*Taxus bacatta*)	All parts, especially leaves and seeds	Diarrhea, vomiting, trembling, pupil dilation, difficulty breathing, muscular weakness, coma, convulsions, dysrhythmias, death	Gastric lavage or emesis, control pain with meperidine, symptomatic treatment

Rhubarb (Rheum rhaponticum)	Leaf blades	Stomach pains, nausea, vomiting, weakness, difficulty breathing, burning of mouth and throat, internal bleeding, coma, death	Gastric lavage or emesis with lime water, chalk, or calcium salts; calcium gluconate, parenterally forced fluids; supportive treatment
Peach	Pits	Breathing difficulty, vocal paralysis, weakness, coma, convulsions	Gastric lavage, emesis
Mushrooms (certain poisonous types) (see also pp. 262-263)	All parts	Respiratory distress, central nervous system disturbances, stomach pains, parasympathomimetic effects, coma, death	Lavage with potassium permanganate, atropine

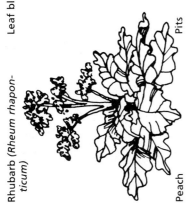

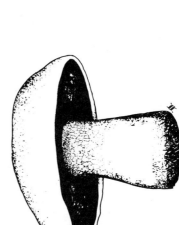

Continued.

TABLE 11-1 Poisonous plants—cont'd

Plant	Toxic parts	Symptoms	Treatment
Cherry	Pits	Shortness of breath, vocal paralysis, convulsions, coma	Gastric lavage or emesis
Lily of the valley	All parts	Gastrointestinal distress, dysrhythmias	Gastric lavage or emesis, potassium, sodium
Castor bean	Leaves, pods (beans)	Gastrointestinal distress, convulsions	Gastric lavage or emesis, sodium bicarbonate

FOOD POISONING

Food poisoning occurs in two forms.

1. Food infection—ingested food substances contain bacteria that produce illness after their multiplication in the intestinal tract.
2. Food intoxication—ingested food substances contain toxins from previous multiplication of bacteria, resulting in poisoning from toxin release into the body system. The causative organism is usually *Staphylococcus aureus*.

Symptoms occur 1 to 5 hours after ingestion of contaminated food. The onset is abrupt, and complaints include nausea, vomiting, diarrhea, and abdominal cramping.

Obtain a history of the patient's food intake and ascertain if other individuals who are the same foods are also affected. Monitor the temperature, which is characteristically subnormal in acute food poisoning. Draw blood samples for electrolyte and osmolarity studies, initiate IV fluids if dehydration is severe or signs of shock are present, and correct electrolyte imbalances if any are present.

Botulism (see also Chapter 26)

Suspect botulism in the presence of any neurologic signs and symptoms that mimic a cerebrovascular occlusive disease, Guillain-Barré syndrome, myasthenia gravis, or arsenic intoxication.

Botulism is a relatively rare condition but occurs typically in a sporadic family or other group outbreak. The usual exotoxins causing poisoning are A, B, and E (E is commonly from fish); rarely toxins C and F are encountered. Botulism is the most serious type of food poisoning, with a mortality of 60% for persons poisoned by botulism spores. (Botulism can also occur following wound contamination with *Clostridium botulinum*.)

The typical cause of botulism is poorly processed or "spoiled" home-canned vegetables, especially nonacid types such as green beans. Bulging cans or lids (resulting from expanding gases as the organisms grow) are often implicated in the history.

Symptoms develop generally 12 to 36 hours after ingestion of contaminated food but may be delayed for as long as 4 days. The presenting symptoms are often vague.

SIGNS AND SYMPTOMS

Lethargy	Eye movement limitations
Constipation	Dilated pupils
Visual disturbances	Decreased tendon reflexes
Dry, sore throat with hoarseness	Impaired speech
Weakness	Headache
Paralysis	

There is no fever in early botulism; in fact, the temperature may be subnormal.

THERAPEUTIC INTERVENTION

ABCs—patient may require tracheostomy and ventilator assistance.

If the patient is asymptomatic or exposure is questionable:

Induce emesis if consumption has been recent.

If several hours have elapsed, administer sodium sulfate (250 mg/kg orally) or magnesium sulfate (250 mg/kg orally) as a cathartic, since the toxin is slowly absorbed.

TABLE 11-2 Food toxins—differential findings

Usual source	Incubation period	Nausea and vomiting	Diarrhea	Neurologic findings	Other common characteristics	Comments
Fish						
Grouper, amberjack, po'ou' (ciguatoxin)	30 min-30 hours	X	X			Fish tastes normal; toxin not inactivated by heat
Puffer (tetrodotoxin)	10 min-4 hours	X	X	Paresthesias, numbness, floating feeling, respiratory paralysis		
Tuna, bonito, dolphin (mahi-mahi) (scombrotoxin)	5 min-2 hours	X	X		Flushing, headache, urticaria, dizziness	
Shellfish (paralytic and neurotoxin poisoning from dinoflagellate)	10 min-1 hour	X	X	Facial paresthesias, ataxia, paralysis, especially respiratory		20% mortality
Uncooked shellfish (Vibrio parahemolyticus)	12-24 hours	X	X			
Heavy metals (beverages)	Minutes to 3-4 hours	X			Metallic taste	
Reheated meats (Clostridium)	8-12 hours	X				
Confections, meat, milk (Staphylococcus)	1-6 hours	X				
Poultry, turtles, human carriers (Salmonella)	8-48 hours	X	X		Fever	
Food, water, human contact (Shigella)	1-7 days	X	X			
Water, fresh vegetables (cholera)	1-5 days	X	X			
Amoeba	Days to weeks	X	X			

Toxin	Onset			Symptoms	Comments
Monosodium glutamate (Chinese food)	5-30 min			Burning sensation of chest, neck, abdomen and extremities; feeling of pressure over face and chest	
Mushrooms—rapid onset Group 1: *Rhodophyllus sinuatus*; *Agaricus arvensis, A. hondensis, A. placemyces*; *Boletus miniatodivaceus, B. luridus, B. satanas*; *Cantharellus floccopus*; *Chlorophyllum molydites*; *Lactarius glaucescens, L. rufus, L. torminosus*; *Naematoloma fasciculare*; *Paxillus involutus*; *Phaeolepiata aurea*; *Russula emetica, Scleroderma aurantium*; *Tricholoma pardinum, T. venenatum*	½-2 hours	X	X		
Group II: *Clitocybe dealbata*; *Inocybe napyses, I. mixtilis, I. griseolilacina, I. lacera, I. decipientoides*; *Omphalotus olearius*	15 min-3 hours	X	X	Seizures; Visual disturbances, sweating, excessive salivation, muscular weakness, tearing, bradycardia, dysrhythmias	Low mortality
Group III: *Amanita muscaria, A. pantherina, A. flavivala, A. cothurrata*	15-30 min	X	X	Hallucinations, intoxication	
Group IV: *Conocybe cyanopus, C. smithii*; *Psilocybe caerulescens, P. mexicana, P. pelliculosa, P. cyanesches, P. baeocystis, P. cubensis*	1-3 hours			Drowsiness, dizziness, ataxia; Muscular weakness, visual and auditory disturbances	

Continued.

TABLE 11-2 Food toxins—differential findings—cont'd

Usual source	Incuba-tion period	Nausea and vomiting	Diarrhea	Neurologic findings	Other common characteristics	Comments
Mushrooms—delayed onset Group 1: *Amanita phalloides, A. virosa, A. bisporigera, A. verna; Galerina marginata, G. autumnalis, G. venenata*	6-24 hours	X	X	Remission after 2-3 days followed by: Paralysis and other variable neurologic disturbances and coma	Abdominal pain, bloody stool, malaise Hematuria, albuminuria, anuria, peripheral vascular collapse, and hepatic failure	30% to 50% mortality
Group II: *Helvella esculenta*	6-12 hours	X	X			Symptoms essentially same as Group I, less severe
Mushrooms—secondary intoxication *Coprinus atramentarius*	12-24 hours until sensitization to alcohol begins	X	X	Vertigo, confusion	Tachycardia, flushing, hyperventilation, palpitations, hypotension, weakness, blurred vision	

Hospitalize the patient if there is evidence of probable exposure, and treat with
antitoxin if symptoms develop.
If the patient has clinical and neurologic symptoms:
Induce emesis if the patient's state of consciousness is unaltered and if there is no
evidence of seizure activity.
Report at once to Centers for Disease Control in Atlanta (404-633-3311 days, 404-
633-2176 nights). Consultation regarding the location of the nearest laboratory for
toxin analysis and antitoxin administration is available 24 hours each day from this
same number.
Obtain 30 ml of venous blood for determination of toxin.
If antitoxin is administered, give a skin test for horse serum sensitivity; if the patient is
sensitive, desensitize him according to the procedure outlined on the package
insert of the antitoxin vial.
Administer antitoxin IM and/or IV as directed.
Admit the patient to the intensive care unit or other area where mechanical respiratory
support is available.
Administer guanidine hydrochloride (15 to 35 mg/kg orally) in divided doses. Its
action is theorized to be a direct blockade of the toxin.
See Chapter 26 for therapeutic intervention for infant botulism.

Traveler's diarrhea (Montezuma's revenge)

The main sign of traveler's diarrhea is watery stool. The causative organism is usually
Escherichia coli. The main therapeutic intervention for traveler's diarrhea consists of
treatment with antibiotics.

Salmonellosis
SIGNS AND SYMPTOMS

Diarrhea   Chills
Nausea and vomiting   Fever

THERAPEUTIC INTERVENTION

Therapeutic intervention for salmonellosis is to treat the symptoms.

Shigellosis
SIGNS AND SYMPTOMS

Bloody diarrhea   Abdominal pain
Severe cramps   Fever

THERAPEUTIC INTERVENTION

Antibiotics should be considered as therapeutic intervention for shigellosis.

Mushroom poisoning

The acute onset of nausea, vomiting, diarrhea, abdominal cramps, and hallucinations—especially in the spring, late summer, and early fall—should alert emergency
personnel to the consideration of mushroom poisoning.

Determine if any "wild" mushrooms were consumed within the last 24 hours and obtain a specimen of the mushroom if possible for mycologic examination.

If sample mushrooms cannot be obtained, elicit where they were harvested, how many were consumed (raw or cooked), and the course of the symptoms. *Psilocybe* and *Amanita muscaria* are often eaten intentionally to produce hallucinatory effects.

THERAPEUTIC INTERVENTION

Induced emesis or gastric lavage is of little value unless the ingestion occurred within the past 1 or 2 hours. It may be useful, however, if the patient has not vomited.

Catharsis may be attempted to hasten passage of the mushrooms through the gastrointestinal tract. *Save the stool specimen* for toxin verification.

Treat fluid and electrolyte imbalances.

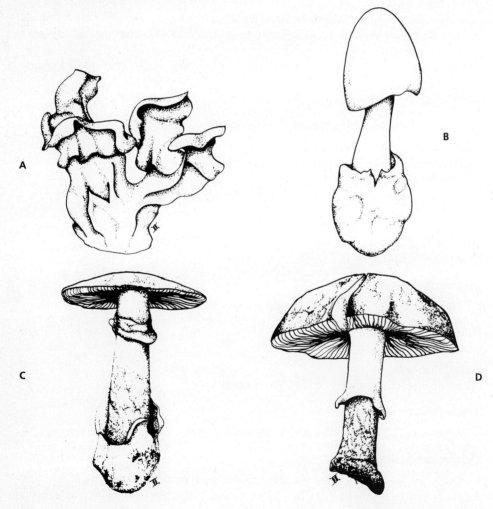

FIG. 11-2 Mushrooms. **A,** *Helvella underwoodii.* **B,** *Amanita phalloides.* **C,** *Amanita verna.* **D,** *Amanita pantherina.*

Administer atropine for muscarinic poisoning symptoms (0.5 to 1.0 mg) subcutaneously every 30 minutes until symptoms cease.

Hallucinogenic and intoxication reactions should be managed with phenothiazine drugs.

Hospitalize the patient for delayed reactions. Hemodialysis is often helpful in managing renal failure.

Thiotic acid is thought to be of some value in coping with hepatocellular damage if it is administered within the first 3 days after poisoning. Thiotic acid is given IV by slow drip (100 to 300 mg/day) concurrently with dextrose in saline for control of resultant hypoglycemia, a side effect of thiotic acid.

Helvella esculanta poisoning can occur by ingestion or inhalation of a volatile toxin (gyromitrin) from certain varieties. (See Table 11-1). Blood transfusion is recommended along with dialysis and a rigorous protocol to monitor and maintain fluid and electrolyte balance. A disulfiram-type reaction can occur as a secondary intoxication response to the mushroom *Coprinus atramentarius* if it is consumed along with alcohol. No specific treatment is necessary. (See Table 11-1 for a comparative description of mushroom poisonings.)

DRUGS OF ABUSE

The following is a list of commonly abused drugs, how they are taken, and their half-lives. For more information, consult your local poison information center or the Poisindex.

Drug	How taken	Half-life
Narcotics		
Heroin	IV, SC, inhaled	2 to 4 hours
Methadone	IV, PO	½ day
Oxycodone (Percodan)	IV, PO	2 hours
Codeine	IV, PO	Variable
Meperidine (Demerol)	IV, SC	Variable
Synthetic narcotics		
Propoxyphene (Darvon)	PO, IV	3 to 8 hours
Pentazocine (Talwin)	IV	Variable
Stimulants		
Amphetamines	IV, PO, inhaled	8 to 30 hours
Cocaine	IV, inhaled, IM, SC	1 hour
Methylphenidate (Ritalin)	IV, PO	1 to 2 hours
Hallucinogens		
Phencyclidine (PCP)	IV, PO, SC, inhaled	1 hour
Marijuana	PO, inhaled	1 hour
Sedatives		
Barbiturates		
Oxazepam (Serax)	PO	8 to 12 hours
Methaqualone (Quaalude)	PO	19 hours
Glutethimide (Doriden)	PO	12 hours or more
Methyprylon (Noludar)	PO	Variable
Ethchlorvynol (Placidyl)	PO	100 hours
Meprobamate	PO	11 hours
Chloral hydrate	PO	8 hours
Bromides	PO	400 hours

CURRENTLY AVAILABLE ANTIDOTES*

Activated charcoal Adsorbant-GI decontamination
> *AD:* 5-10× the est. amt. ingested or 50-100 gm in 2-4 oz water (po or NG tube)
> *PD:* 5-10× est. amt. or 1 gm/kg or 15-30g/60-120 cc water

Adrenalin injection (Epinephrine) 1:1,000 (1 ml-1 mg) Anaphylactic reactions
> *AD:* 0.5 mg IV or SubQ. Dilute 1:1,000 soln in 9 ml of NS before giving it IV
> *PD:* 0.01 ml/kg SubQ or that dose diluted in 5-10 ml NS and given IV

Aminophylline injection (250 mg/10 ml 500 mg/20 ml) To correct drug/chemical bronchospasm
> *Loading dose:* (not prev. on aminophyllin) 5.6 mg/kg IV slowly over 30 min followed
>   by maintenance dose based on age, Hx.

Ammonium chloride Acidification of urine for facilitation of basic cmpds
> *AD:* 1.5 g IV Q6H up to 6 g/day. PO 8-12 g/day
> *PD:* 75 mg/kg dose IV or po up to 2-6 g/day

Amyl nitrite pearls (In Eli Lilly Cyanide Kit) Converts hemoglobin to methemoglobin
> *AD:* Inhalation for 30 seconds of each minute, new ampule Q3min until IV Sod. nitrite
> can be obtained.
> *PD:* Same as AD

Antisnake venom Snake bite with envenomation
> *AD:* 3-20 vials diluted in fluid (i.e. saline) depending on site and severity (not directly
>   into the injured tissue)
> *PD:* Essentially as above, considering size, site, and severity

Atropine sulfate inj Cholinergic poisoning
> *AD:* 2-3 mg/dose IV (0.4 mg/ml soln) q 2-5 min until atropinized, then maintain atro-
>   pinization
> *PD:* 0.05 mg/kg/dose IV (0.4 mg/ml soln) q 2-5 min until atropinized, then maintain
>   atropinization

BAL (Dimercaprol) Heavy metal poisoning
> *AD:* 3 mg/kg/dose q 4-6h for 1st 5 days then q 12h for 5-9 days
> *PD:* 3-4 mg/kg/dose q 4-6h for 1st 5 days, then q 12h for 5-9 days

Calcium chloride injection (1 g 10 ml) 13.6 mEq calcium Hypocalcemia, hyperkalemia
> *AD:* 10 ml IV PRN

Castor oil Oily cathartic where saline cathartics contraindicated but rarely used as such. Also phenol poisoning.
> *AD:* 30-60 ml PO
> *PD:* 15-30 ml PO

Deferoxamine inj 500 mg/5 ml (Desferal) Iron poisoning
> *AD:* 1-2 g IM q6h for severe intox., IV not greater than 15 ml/kg/hr. Not more than 6
>   g/24h.
> *PD:* 90 mg/kg up to 1 g/8h. For severe intox. give IV not greater than 15 mg/kg/hr
>   and not greater than 6 g/24h.

---

*Reprinted with permission by Dr. Mark Thoman, Editor, AACTion. From Vet. Hum. Toxicol. **24**:6, Dec. 1982.

Dexamethasone Cerebral edema
> *AD:* 10 mg IV then 4 mg q6h
> *PD:* 0.4 mg/kg IV then 0.1 mg/kg IV q4-6h

Dextrose injection 50% Comatose pt. or altered mental status, hypoglycemia
> *AD:* 50-100 ml IV

Diazepam inj (Valium 10 mg/2 cc) Seizures, extreme agitated state, drug withdrawal
> *AD:* 5-10 mg slow IV not greater rate than 5 mg/min (Not IM inj. since absorption erratic)
> *PD:* 0.1-0.25 mg/kg slow IV not greater rate than 5 mg/min

Diphenhydramine (Benadryl) Drug induced extrapyramidal reactions, acute allergic reactions
> *AD:* 20-50 mg/kg IV slowly then q6h po × 2 days maintenance
> *PD:* 1-2 mg/kg dose (not over 50 mg) IV slowly then q6h po × 2 days for maintenance

Dopamine Hypotension
> *AD:* 20-2000 μg/min IV
> *PD:* 2-5 μg/kg/min IV infusion and increase to max of 20 μg/kg/min

Edrophonium chloride (Tensilon) Diagnostic aid: Differentiate myasthenia gravis from botulism.
> *AD:* 2 mg (0.2 ml) given rapid IV. If no response 8 mg 1 min later. (CAUTION: These antidotes may aggravate circulatory collapse which occurs during muscular paralysis due to skeletal neuromuscular blocking agents)

Evaporated milk (and opener!) Demulcent

Ethyl alcohol Methanol and ethylene glycol poisoning
> *AD:* Loading: 1.5 ml/kg of 100% ethanol diluted in D5W followed by maintenance of 0.15 ml/kg/h to maintain 100-150 mg% blood level
> *PD:* Same as AD

Glucagon Hypoglycemia, propranolol overdose

Ipecac syrup (Never fluid extract) Induction of vomiting, decrease absorption
> *AD:* 30-45 ml po followed by water, repeat in 20 min if vomiting does not occur
> *PD:* 15-20 ml po and as above

Levophed inj (8 mg/4 ml ampule) Hypotension
> *AD:* Dilute 2 amps (16 mg/8 ml) in IL D5W (therefore 16 μg/ml) use 2-3 ml/min and titrate accordingly

Magnesium sulfate Cathartic to enhance elimination
> *AD:* 30 g diluted in water PO
> *PD:* 250 mg/kg diluted in water PO

Mannitol inj IV Osmotic diuretic, cerebral edema
> *AD:* 25-50 g in 20% soln IV in 30 min period q4-6h. Max: 200 g/day
> *PD:* 1-2 g/kg in 20% soln IV in 30 min period, q4-6h. Max: 100 g/day

Methylene blue inj Reducing agent to convert methemoglobin to hemoglobin
> *AD:* 0.1-0.2 ml/kg of 1% soln (1-2 mg/kg) slow IV inj. May need to be repeated
> *PD:* Same as AD

Methylprednisolone Caustic ingestions to prevent strictures
> *AD:* 0.5-1.5 mg/kg q6h IV
> *PD:* Same as AD

N-acetylcysteine (Mucomyst) Acetaminophen overdosage, also shortens digitalis half-life or prevents digitalis glycoside absorption
> *AD:* Loading dose: 140 mg/kg diluted 1:4 in grapefruit juice, etc. followed by 70 mg/kg for total of 17 doses
> *PD:* Same as AD

Naloxone (Narcan) Opioid antagonist
> *AD:* 2 mg (5 0.4 mg/ml amps) IV push followed as necessary by an infusion of 0.4 mg/h
> *PD:* 0.5-1 mg IV followed by 0.2 mg/h

Nicotinamide Vacor poisoning
> *AD:* 500 mg IV slowly then 200-400 mg q4h for 48h. If symptomatic increase injection frequency to q2h (Max: 36 g/day)
> *PD:* ½ of AD

Nitroprusside Hypertensive crisis
> *AD:* 0.03-0.5 mg via an infusion pump
> *PD:* 1-10 μg/kg/min via an infusion pump

Physostigmine Inhibit esterase responsible for hydrolyzing the parasympathetic effector acetylcholine

Phenobarbital Convulsive seizures
> *AD:* 3-5 mg/kg IV or IM
> *PD:* 2-3 mg/kg IV or IM, if ineffective in 10 min give additional 2-3 mg/kg (Max: 120 mg)

Phenytoin (Diphenylhydantoin, Dilantin) Major motor seizures, status epilepticus
> *AD:* Loading: 10-15 mg/kg or 500-1,000 mg IV not faster than 50 mg/min, undiluted with patient on cardiac monitor
> *PD:* Loading: 8-10 mg/kg IV slowly, not faster than 25 mg/min undiluted with patient on cardiac monitor

Phospho-soda oral Cathartic to enhance elimination to complex iron. (Not recommended for pediatrics)

Procainamide inj (Pronestyl 100 mg/cc) Cardiac arrhythmias
> *AD:* 0.2-1.0 g IV at rates not greater than 25-50 mg/min

Protamine sulfate inj 1% Heparin overdose
> *AD:* 1 mg/100 units heparin. Not more than 50 mg in any 10 min period
> *PD:* 1 mg IV for each 1 mg of heparin in previous 4h

Protopam (2-PAM) Cholinesterase reactivator for use in organophosphate and some carbamate poisonings
> *AD:* 1 gm IV at 0.5 g/min or infuse 250 ml NS or 30 min. In severe poisoning, dose may require increasing or repeating.
> *PD:* 25-50 mg/kg IV

Pyridoxine HCl Isoniazid, ethylene glycol poisoning
> *AD:* 100-200 mg IV (or 1 g per each 1 g Isoniazid ingested)

Sodium bicarbonate inj (50% soln) Acidosis

 AD: 50-100 mEq IV, repeat as necessary

Sodium nitrite inj (0.3 g/10 cc or 3% soln) (Eli Lilly Kit) Cyanide poisoning

 AD: 10-20 cc of 3% soln at 2.5-5 cc/min IV. Repeat once with persistence or recurrence of symptoms

 PD: 0.3 ml/kg of 3% soln at 2.5-5 cc/min IV. Repeat once with persistence or recurrence of symptoms

Sodium sulfate soln (45%) Cathartic to enhance elimination

 AD: 250 mg/dose po

 PD: Same as AD

Sodium thiosulfate inj 12.5 g/cc (Eli Lilly Cyanide Kit) Cyanide poisoning—use after sodium nitrite converts cyanide to thiosulfate

 AD: 50 cc of 25% soln at rate of 2.5-5 cc/min. IV 15 min after sodium nitrite. May be repeated xl.

 PD: 1.65 cc/kg of 25% soln at 2.5-5 cc/min. IV 15 min after sodium nitrite. May be repeated xl.

Thamine HCl Ethylene glycol, Wernicke's alcoholic neuropathy

 AD: 50-200 mg IM or IV. More if encephalopathy is present (500-1,000 mg)

Vitamin K$_1$ (Aquamephyton) Oral anticoagulant overdose

SUGGESTED READINGS

American Academy of Pediatrics: Handbook of common poisonings in children, Washington, D.C., 1976, The Department of Health, Education, and Welfare.

Budassi, S.A., and Barber, J.M.: Emergency nursing: principles and practice, St. Louis, 1981, The C.V. Mosby Co.

Collier, H.: Cellular site of opiate dependence, Nature **283**:625, 1980.

Eastman, J.W.: Hypertensive crisis and death associated with phencyclidine poisoning, JAMA **231**:1270, 1975.

Hill, J.B.: Salicylate intoxication, N. Engl. J. Med. **288**:1110, 1973.

Litten, W.: The most poisonous mushrooms, Sci. Am. **232**:90, 1975.

Mahler, D.A.: Anticholinergic poisoning from jimsonweed, J.A.C.E.P. **5**:440, 1976.

McJunkin, B.: Fatal massive hepatic necrosis following acetaminophen overdose, JAMA **236**:1874, 1976.

Oakley, S.R.: Drugs, society and human behavior, St. Louis, 1978, The C.V. Mosby Co.

Pierce, A.W.: Salicylate intoxication, Postgrad. Med. **48**:243, 1970.

Rumack, B.H., and Matthew, H.: Acetaminophen poisoning and toxicity, Pediatrics **55**:871, 1975.

Turk, S.: Houseplant poisoning in children, unpublished paper, 1978.

Walker, W.F.: Physostigmine: its use and abuse, J.A.C.E.P. **5**:436, 1976.

Wantanabe, A.S., and Conner, C.S., editors: New antidote for acetaminophen poisoning, Rocky Mountain Poison Center Drug Bulletin, 1977.

CHAPTER 12 Environmental emergencies

SNAKEBITES

There are over 3,000 species of snakes; of these 375 from five different families are venomous. These families are:

Crotalidae—copperheads, rattlesnakes, cottonmouths

Elapidae—coral snakes, cobras, mambas

Viperidae (true vipers)—puffer adders

Hydrophidae—sea snakes

Colubridae—boomslangs

There are over 45,000 snakebites each year in the United States. Of these 8,000 are from poisonous snakes. There are, however, fewer than 15 deaths from these bites each year.[1]

Venom is a complex substance that contains enzymes, peptides, glycoproteins, and other substances that can cause tissue destruction. Many venoms contain toxins that are cardiotoxic, neurotoxic, or hemotoxic. Venom is injected by fangs of the snake. The ducts of the fangs are filled with venom, which is manufactured in the salivary glands.

Pit vipers and crotalidae cause most of the serious illnesses and deaths from snakebites. These snakes have two long fangs that originate in the anterior maxilla. They also have teeth than can produce small puncture wounds (Fig. 12-1). Other species of snakes have small, fixed fangs that do not retract into the mouth. Nonpoisonous snakes have fangs that retract into the mouth and rows of several small teeth (Fig. 12-2). When a snake bites, it is usually as a defense mechanism. The most common area for a bite is an extremity that is close to the snake (i.e., an arm or a leg).

SIGNS AND SYMPTOMS

Signs and symptoms of snakebite depend on several factors:

The size and species of the snake

The location of the bite

The depth of the bite

The number of bites inflicted

The amount of venom injected

The age of the patient

The size of the patient

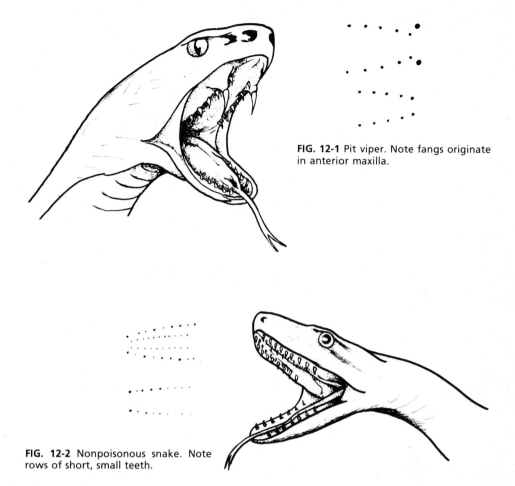

FIG. 12-1 Pit viper. Note fangs originate in anterior maxilla.

FIG. 12-2 Nonpoisonous snake. Note rows of short, small teeth.

The patient's sensitivity to venom

The number of microorganisms in the snake's mouth

Signs and symptoms can be divided into local and systemic reactions:

Local reactions

Fang marks

Teeth marks

Edema (occurs within 1 hour and may extend to 36 hours)

Pain at the site

Petechiae

Ecchymosis

Loss of function of the limb

Necrosis (16 to 36 hours after the bite)

Systemic reactions

Nausea and vomiting

Diaphoresis

Syncope

Metallic or rubber taste in mouth

Constricted pupils

Ptosis

Visual disturbances (mostly diplopia)

Muscle twitching

Paresthesias

Paralysis

Salivation

Difficulty speaking

Seizures

Epistaxis

Hematemesis

Hemoptysis

Hematuria

Melena

Severe systemic reactions

Severe hemorrhage

Renal failure

Hypovolemic shock

THERAPEUTIC INTERVENTIONS

DO NOT USE ICE

DO NOT GIVE ALCOHOL OR SUBSTANCES CONTAINING CAFFEINE TO DRINK

DO NOT ALLOW PATIENT TO SMOKE

Assure ABCs

Keep the patient calm

Immobilize the limb

Keep the limb dependent

Place a loose constriction band 4 inches proximal to the bite

Remove potentially constricting jewelry

Cleanse the wound

Early incision and wound suction (if done immediately, this can remove 25% to 50% of
  the venom)

Analgesia for pain management

IVs (two) with Ringer's lactate or normal saline solution

Place a central venous pressure line or an arterial pressure line

Consider tetanus prophylaxis

Possible surgical intervention

Possible antivenin therapy

Be sure to record the time of the bite and the times of any subsequent therapies

Antivenin

Antivenin administration should be reserved for life-threatening snakebites only, as it carries a high incidence of sensitivity reactions and possible anaphylaxis. It should be administered in the hospital setting only, where the patient can be closely monitored. (Antivenin administration is not a prehospital care procedure!)

Be sure arrest equipment is readily available; be prepared to handle an arrest

Obtain a careful allergy history

Do a conjunctival or skin test to test for sensitivity reaction:

Check for a reaction immediately and after up to 20 minutes

If a reaction does occur (urticaria, wheezing, cyanosis, edema, anaphylaxis), administer 1:1,000 epinephrine (0.2 to 0.5 ml) subcutaneously

Be sure to read the antivenin package insert thoroughly and follow the directions precisely

DOG BITES

Dog bites account for 84% of all bites to humans in the United States. They occur at a rate of 500 bites for a population of 100,000 (1.2 million in the United States each year).[2] Children constitute the population group most frequently bitten. Most bites occur on the extremities. Some of the dogs are provoked and some are not. There is a higher incidence of dog bites in cities as compared to rural areas, probably because of the denser population in the cities.

Dog-bite wounds can range from punctures, to contusions, to severe lacerations, to crush injuries with much tissue damage. The type of injury usually depends on the type and size of the dog. The majority of dog-bite wounds are simple puncture wounds.

If a bite goes untreated, complications such as cellulitis, infection, osteomyelitis, and loss of limb function and usefulness may result.

THERAPEUTIC INTERVENTION

Soak and irrigate puncture wounds
Scrub and irrigate lacerations and other open wounds
Consider debridement
Consider suturing (if wound is very large or on face)
Consider antibiotics
Assure tetanus prophylaxis
Consider rabies prophylaxis
Give thorough aftercare instructions for wound care
Report the bite in cooperation with local health regulations

CAT BITES AND SCRATCHES

Cat bites account for 3% of all bites to humans in the United States.[3] Because cat teeth are sharp and long, the wounds they inflict are usually deep punctures that may involve tendons and joint capsules. The incidence of infection from cat bites is higher than that from dog bites.

Cat scratches usually result in superficial wounds, but the incidence of infection from them is high. This is probably because cat claws may carry saliva, since cats lick their paws while grooming themselves.

THERAPEUTIC INTERVENTION

Scrub and irrigate scratches and lacerations
Soak and irrigate puncture wounds
Assure tetanus prophylaxis
Consider antibiotics
Consider surgical debridement

HUMAN BITES

Because of the high incidence of infection, human bites can be some of the most serious of all bites. The most common sites for these bites are the fingers and hands and the tip of the nose. When a boxer's fracture (first metacarpal fracture) occurs, look for an open wound that may have occurred when the patient's hand impacted with the tooth or teeth of another. Any open wound over the metacarpophalangeal area should be considered and treated as a bite until proved otherwise.

The result of a human bite may be a laceration, soft tissue damage, a crush injury (with structural damage), and possibly amputation of a part.

THERAPEUTIC INTERVENTION

Scrub and irrigate the wound
Explore the wound
Consider debridement
Consider antibiotics
Consider x-ray examinations
Elevate the extremity
Assure tetanus prophylaxis
Suture only if the wound is on the face
Splint if the wound is over a joint

SPIDER (ARACHNID) BITES

All spiders have venom that they inject when they bite. Most spider bites induce itching, swelling, and stinging pain as local complications. Spiders that induce systemic as well as local complications are the black widow spider and the brown recluse spider. There were 65 deaths from spider bites and envenomation in the United States over a 10-year period of time. Black widow spiders were responsible for 63 of these and brown recluse spiders for 2.[4]

Black widow spiders *(Latorodectus mactans)*

Black widow spiders are usually found in damp, cool places, such as under rocks and wood piles. They may be identified by their black bodies and the red hourglass-shaped figure on their abdomens. The venom of the black widow is neurotoxic.

SIGNS AND SYMPTOMS

If aggressive supportive therapy is given, the signs and symptoms of black widow spider bites will usually disappear within 48 hours.

Painful sting at the time of the bite followed by a dull, numb pain
Tiny red marks at the point of entry of the venom
Nausea and vomiting
Hypertension
Elevated temperature
Respiratory distress
Headache

Syncope	Abdominal pain
Weakness	Seizures
Chest pain	Shock

THERAPEUTIC INTERVENTION

Treat the patient symptomatically

Cool the area of the bite with ice packs to slow the action of the neurotoxin

Administer muscle relaxants (methocarbamol [Robaxin] or diazepam [Valium])

Administer calcium gluconate for muscle spasms (use 10 ml of 10% solution mixed in 100 ml of normal saline solution and run it in over 15 minutes)

Consider narcotic analgesics

Consider antivenin; read antivenin literature carefully and thoroughly before administration

Brown recluse spiders (*Loxosceles reclusa*)

Brown recluse spiders are found in the southeastern, south-central, and southwestern states. They inhabit dark areas such as basements, garages, boxes, and closets. These spiders may be identified by their light brown color and the dark brown fiddle-shaped mark on their thoraxes.

SIGNS AND SYMPTOMS

Local reactions

Mild stinging at the time of the bite

Local edema

Bluish ring around the bite

Bleb formation   } Appear within 2 to 8 hours after the bite

Erythema

Local ischemia

Tissue necrosis—appears on third or fourth day

Eschar/open sore—appears in 14 days

Wound healing—appears in 21 days

Systemic reactions

Fever	General malaise
Chills	Arthralgias/joint pain
Nausea and vomiting	Petechiae
Weakness	

Severe systemic reactions (seen in small adults and children)

Seizures

Disseminated intravascular coagulation (DIC)

Renal failure

Hemolysis

Cardiopulmonary arrest

THERAPEUTIC INTERVENTION

Consider antihistamines
Consider antibiotics
Consider systemic or local steroids
Consider local debridement
Consider skin grafting
Rehydration (by mouth or intravenously)
Consider blood transfusions

SCORPION STINGS

Scorpions are found in the warm southwestern states of California, Arizona, and Texas. There seems to be an increased incidence of scorpion stings in the cool evening and night hours. Scorpions usually only sting when provoked or in self-defense—they are not aggressive creatures. Although there are several species of scorpions, only one species injects a lethal venom, *Centuroides sculpturatus*. The tail of the scorpion contains the telson, in which venom is produced and stored, and the stinger, which injects the venom.

SIGNS AND SYMPTOMS

Local pain at the sting site
Edema
Discoloration
Hyperesthesia
Numbness
Agitation or drowsiness
Itching
Speech disturbances
Tachycardia
Hypertension
Tachypnea

Wheezing
Stridor
Profuse salivation
Visual disturbances
Ataxic gait
Incontinence
Jaw muscle spasms
Nausea and vomiting
Dysphagia
Seizures
Anaphylaxis

THERAPEUTIC INTERVENTION

Treat the patient symptomatically
Support ABCs
Assure tetanus prophylaxis
Possible (remote) chance of antivenin therapy*

BEE, WASP, HORNET, AND FIRE ANT (HYMENOPTERA) STINGS

Hymenoptera stings can result in anything from a local reaction to anaphylactic shock. Reactions can occur from almost immediately to 48 hours after the sting. The greater incidence of stings, the greater the possibility of a severe reaction.

---

*In experimental stages at Poisonous Animal Research Lab, Arizona State University, Tempe, Arizona.

SIGNS AND SYMPTOMS
Mild local reactions

Stinging and burning sensation at time of sting
Swelling
Itching

Severe local reaction

Total extremity edema

Systemic reactions

Urticaria   Bronchospasm
Pruritus   Laryngeal edema
Edema (extremities and periorbital region) Hypotension

THERAPEUTIC INTERVENTION
For mild reactions

Remove the stinger with a dull object; do not grasp or pull it, as this contracts the venom
    sac and releases more toxin
Cleanse the sting site
Apply antiseptic cream
Consider oral antihistamines
Consider steroids
Apply ice
Elevate the limb

For severe reactions (see also pp. 147)

Support ABCs   Consider vasopressors ⎫
Epinephrine   Antihistamines   ⎬ Doses will vary
IVs   Consider steroids   ⎪
Application of the MAST   Consider theophylline ⎭

    Fire ants have a painful sting that forms a wheal, which expands into a large vesicle.
The area reddens, and a pustule forms. As the pustule is reabsorbed, crusting and scar
formation follow. This hymenopteran may also cause anaphylaxis. Therapeutic intervention is the same as that for other hymenoptera stings.

PREVENTIVE MEASURES AGAINST HYMENOPTERA STINGS

Avoid areas where hymenoptera are usually present
Wear nonbright colors
Do not wear perfumes outdoors
Wear shoes when walking outdoors

    People who are known to have a sensitivity to hymenoptera venom should carry an
anaphylaxis prevention kit that contains 1:1,000 epinephrine and antihistamines. They
should also be instructed to wear a Medic Alert bracelet or some other type of medical
identification tag. Desensitization is a possibility in some patients; it has been reported as
95% effective.

TICK BITES

Ticks may cause flaccid paralysis when they bite because of the neurotoxins they inject. Initially, the patient will have paresthesias and pain in the lower extremities. Respiratory failure may result from bulbar paralysis.

THERAPEUTIC INTERVENTION

Remove the tick:
    Use gasoline, ether, or a hot match (not burning) on the tick's body
    Paralysis will disappear when the tick is removed

INJURIES CAUSED BY COLD
Chilblains

Chilblains are localized areas of itching, painful redness, and recurrent edema, usually on the earlobes, fingers, and toes. Chilblains usually occur in climates that are cool and damp. They are thought to be a mild form of frostbite. Therapeutic intervention for chilblains is basically to have the patient keep away from cold climates. As there is nothing specific to treat and the symptoms are usually self-limiting, there is no specific treatment.

Immersion foot

Immersion foot usually occurs when there is constant contact of the foot with cold temperatures through moisture inside a boot. It is a common condition in foot soldiers and hunters who spend some time in the water and then later come to dry ground without changing their socks or boots. The foot begins to appear wrinkled and, if the condition is allowed to continue for a prolonged period, may develop gangrene.

THERAPEUTIC INTERVENTION

Dry shoes and socks
Immersion of the affected foot in warm water

Frostbite

Frostbite is a traumatic condition induced when ice crystals form and expand in the extracellular spaces. The enlarging ice crystals compress the cells and this results in cell membrane rupture and the interruption of enzymatic activity and metabolic processes. As histamine is released there is increased capillary permeability with red-cell aggregation and microvascular occlusion similar to that seen in burn patients. This is a condition that is not reversible once it has occurred. It is important, however, to protect the areas surrounding the frostbite to prevent further injury.

Frostbite used to be classified as either first, second, third, or fourth degree. This classification is no longer used, as it is impossible to estimate the true extent of the frostbite until several days after the injury. Frostbite is often accompanied by hypothermia. Depending on the degree of the hypothermia, it may take priority over frostbite for therapeutic intervention.

SUPERFICIAL FROSTBITE

Superficial frostbite usually involves the fingertips, ears, nose or cheeks, and toes.

Signs and symptoms

Burning   Numbness
Tingling   Whitish color

Therapeutic intervention

Apply warm (104° to 110° F [40° to 43.3° C]) soaks
Do *not* apply friction (rubbing)

DEEP FROSTBITE

In deep frostbite the actual temperature of the injured part is lowered. This produces local vascular and tissue changes that can lead to the injury and death of the surrounding cells. There are several things than can affect the possibility of sustaining frostbite:

The ambient temperature
The wind-chill factor (Fig. 12-3)
The amount of time exposed
Whether or not the patient was wet or exposed to direct contact with metal objects
The type and number of layers of clothing worn

There are other factors that may contribute to the predisposition to frostbite:

Darker-skinned people are more prone
Lack of acclimatization (moving abruptly from a warm area to a cold area)
Previous frostbite injury
Poor peripheral vascular status

Cooling Power of Wind on Exposed Flesh Expressed as an Equivalent Temperature (under calm conditions)

Estimated wind speed (in mph)	Actual Thermometer Reading (°F.)										
	50	40	30	20	10	0	−10	−20	−30	−40	−50	−60
	EQUIVALENT CHILL TEMPERATURE (°F)										
calm	50	40	30	20	10	0	−10	−20	−30	−40	−50	−60
5	48	37	27	16	6	−5	−15	−26	−36	−47	−57	−68
10	40	28	16	4	−9	−24	−33	−46	−58	−70	−83	−95
15	36	22	9	−5	−18	−32	−45	−58	−72	−85	−99	−112
20	32	18	4	−10	−25	−39	−53	−67	−82	−96	−110	−124
25	30	16	0	−15	−29	−44	−59	−74	−88	−104	−118	−133
30	28	13	−2	−18	−33	−48	−63	−79	−94	−109	−125	−140
35	27	11	−4	−21	−35	−51	−67	−82	−98	−113	−129	−145
40	26	10	−6	−21	−37	−53	−69	−85	−100	−116	−132	−148

(wind speeds greater than 40 mph have little additional effect)	LITTLE DANGER In < 5 hr with dry skin Maximum danger of false sense of security	Increasing Danger Danger from freezing of exposed flesh within one minute	GREAT DANGER Flesh may freeze within 30 seconds
	Trenchfoot and immersion foot may occur at any point on this chart.		

INSTRUCTIONS
MEASURE local temperature and wind speed if possible, if not, ESTIMATE. Enter table at closest 5°F interval along the top and with appropriate wind speed along left side. Intersection goves approximate equivalent chill temperature. That is, the temperature that would cause the same rate of cooling under calm conditions. Note that regardless of cooling rate, you do not cool below the actual air temperature unless wet.

FIG. 12-3 Wind chill chart.

Anxiety
Exhaustion
Frail body type

Signs and symptoms

Whitish discoloration of the skin, followed by a waxy appearance
Slight burning pain, followed by a feeling of warmth, then numbness
Swelling and burning following numbness
Blisters (usually appear in 1 to 7 days)
Edema of entire extremity
Severe discoloration and gangrene appear later

Therapeutic intervention
Prehospital (or in the wilderness)

Leave the affected part cold unless the temperature of thawing water can be assured and
    maintained and analgesics are available (thawing is extremely painful)
If the extremity is thawed, do not permit the patient to use it
Do not use ice or snow and friction (this causes tissue damage)
Prevent any further heat loss:
    Remove wet clothing
    Cover with dry blanket or sheets
    Give warm liquids if the patient is conscious and has a gag reflex
Protect the injured part from further damage:
    Splinting and soft padding are advisable (avoid pressure)
Attempt to get to a place where there is a heat source and a supply of water that can be
    maintained warm
If in the wilderness, the patient may walk on the frostbitten extremity unless it is thawed
    or begins to thaw; the patient must *not* walk on a thawed extremity

In the emergency department

Immerse the frostbitten part in warm (104° to 110° F [40° to 43.3° C]) water
Administer warm liquids by mouth if the patient is alert and has a gag reflex
Cover the patient with warm blankets; be careful not to place any pressure on the frost-
    bitten part
Administer narcotic analgesics (rewarming is very painful)
After it has thawed, protect the part with bulky sterile dressings
Assure tetanus prophylaxis
Consider antibiotics
Possible escharotomy if there is severe vascular constriction
Amputation is not an emergency procedure; it may have to be done several weeks after the
    injury

Preventive measures against frostbite

Proper dress for climate (layers of loose-fitting clothing)
Diet high in carbohydrates and fats (a heat source)

Avoiding smoking or drinking alcohol or beverages that contain caffeine
Avoiding bare skin contact with metal objects
Keeping dry
Avoiding exhaustion
Protecting previously frostbitten parts from exposure
Having current tetanus prophylaxis

Accidental hypothermia

Hypothermia is generally defined as a condition in which the core temperature of the body is less than 95° F (35° C). Severe hypothermia is defined as a core temperature of 90° F (32.2° C). It is at this temperature that severe physiologic detriments occur. Death usually occurs when core temperature falls below 78° F (25.6° C). Early signs and symptoms of hypothermia are fatigue, a slow gait, muscle incoordination, and apathy.

PATHOPHYSIOLOGY OF HYPOTHERMIA

Many metabolic responses are temperature dependent. When hypothermia occurs, cellular activity drops. As the temperature drops 18° F (10° C), metabolic rate will decrease by two to three times. Renal blood flow decreases, causing a decrease in glomerular filtration rate. As a result of this, water is not reabsorbed and dehydration occurs. In addition, respirations decrease, carbon dioxide is retained, and hypoxia and a resultant acidosis occur. Because of a diminished supply of glucose the patient becomes hypoglycemic.

In addition to the cellular changes, the cells of the heart become more sensitive and prone to dysrhythmias as core temperature begins to fall. Osborne waves develop on ECG (Fig. 12-4). The most common dysrhythmias seen with hypothermia are atrial fibrillation and ventricular fibrillation. The patient is in the greatest danger of ventricular fibrillation when his core temperature falls below 82° F (28° C); at this temperature and below, the heart will not respond to conventional methods of converting ventricular fibrillation (drugs and electric cardioversion). The care giver must be very careful not to cause any sudden

TABLE 12-1 Signs and symptoms of hypothermia

Temperature	Signs and symptoms
96°-99° F (35.6°-37.2° C)	Shivering, loss of manual coordination
91°-95° F (32.8°-35° C)	Violent shivering, slurred speech, amnesia
86°-90° F (30°-32.2° C)	Shivering decreases but is replaced by strong muscular rigidity and cyanosis
Below 86° F (30° C)	Possibility of developing rewarming shock
81°-85° F (27.2°-29.4° C)	Irrational, stuporous; pulse and respirations decrease
78°-80° F (25.6°-26.7° C)	Coma, erratic heartbeat
Below 81° F (27.2° C)	Possibility of ventricular fibrillation
Below 78° F (25.6° C)	Cardiopulmonary arrest

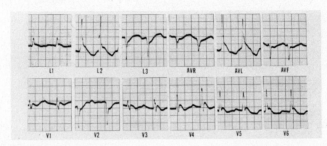

FIG. 12-4 ECG tracing showing characteristic Osborn wave. (From Speich, P.: J.E.N. **3**(2):9, 1977.)

movement of the hypothermia patient, as movement may trigger fibrillation. Precautions against this include driving carefully and avoiding bumps when transporting the patient in a rescue vehicle.

Mild hypothermia, in which the patient is shivering and still alert and oriented, should be treated by placing the patient in a warm (104° to 110° F [40° to 43.3° C]) bath and administering warm fluids that contain glucose or other sugar substances by mouth to provide heat through calories.

THERAPEUTIC INTERVENTION FOR SEVERE HYPOTHERMIA

Core rewarming is essential to prevent rewarming shock. Rewarming shock occurs when the peripheral areas are rewarmed faster than the core. This causes a large amount of lactic acid, which was located in the extremities, to be rapidly shunted back to the heart where fibrillation may occur. There is also the possibility of peripheral vasodilation and hypotension occurring as a result of relative hypovolemia.

Protection of ABCs

> Avoid endotracheal intubation if possible and manage the airway and breathing with a bag-valve-mask device to avoid excess patient stimulation and the possibility of ventricular fibrillation.

Warm humidified oxygen

Core rewarming

> Via peritoneal lavage—two cannulas running warmed normal saline or Ringer's lactate solution into the peritoneal cavity and removing it by suction; this can raise the core temperature 10.8° F (6° C)/hour
>
> Via gastric lavage—not as effective as peritoneal lavage because of smaller surface area of stomach; also, there is a risk of ventricular fibrillation when the lavage tube is placed
>
> Via warmed IV solutions—this will not raise core temperature very much but may prevent further heat loss
>
> Via warm humidified oxygen with IPPB—this also will not raise the core temperature very much but may prevent further heat loss
>
> Via mediastinal lavage—through two chest tubes or through direct contact of warmed fluids on the mediastinum through a thoracotomy incision; this is used only in the event of intractable ventricular fibrillation in which core temperature elevation is the only hope of survival

Via renal dialysis or heart-lung bypass machine—although impractical in most emergency settings, this may be done if the equipment is ready and proper personnel are available to run the equipment

Correct fluid and electrolyte status

Administer IV fluids to compensate for hypovolemic state (avoid use of the MAST, because it may shunt lactic acid and has the potential for tissue destruction)

Consider administration of steroids for adrenal insufficiency

INJURIES CAUSED BY HEAT
Heat cramps

Heat cramps usually occur when a person is doing hard work in hot weather and drinking great volumes of water. This causes the dilution of electrolytes in addition to electrolyte loss from excessive perspiration.

SIGNS AND SYMPTOMS

Cramps (particularly in the shoulders, thighs, and abdominal wall muscles)
Weakness
Nausea
Tachycardia
Pallor
Profuse diaphoresis
Cool, moist skin
History of ingestion of large amounts of hypotonic fluids

THERAPEUTIC INTERVENTION

Sodium chloride by mouth or intravenously (depending on degree of discomfort and clinical status of patient)
Cool environment
Rest

Heat exhaustion

Heat exhaustion occurs when there is a prolonged period of fluid loss (e.g., from perspiration, diarrhea, or the use of diuretics) and exposure to warm ambient temperatures without adequate fluid and electrolyte replacement. It is particularly common in the very young and the very old.

SIGNS AND SYMPTOMS

Thirst
General malaise
Cramps in muscles
Headache
Tachycardia
Orthostatic hypotension
Nausea and vomiting

Anorexia
Anxiety
Syncope
Dehydration
Muscle incoordination
Possible elevated temperature

Rest
Cool environment
Fluids and electrolytes by mouth or intravenously

Heat stroke

Heat stroke can be exercise induced, occurring when a person exercises strenuously in a very hot environment and is unable to dissipate the heat his body produces. It can also be non-exercise induced, occurring in individuals who are vulnerable to high temperatures. Heat stroke can be precipitated by certain medications that affect heat production (thyroid extracts and amphetamines), decrease thirst (haloperidol), and decrease diaphoresis (antihistamines, anticholinergics, phenothiazines, and propranolol). As the body temperature rises to 105.8° F (41° C) there is depressed central nervous system, heart, and cellular function. Death will occur if the body temperature is not lowered, because the body will have lost its ability to dissipate heat.

For every 1.8° F (1° C) rise in temperature, the body's metabolism will increase by 13%.

If body temperature rises to 100.4° F (38° C) metabolism will be increased by 13%.
If body temperature rises to 102.2° F (39° C) metabolism will increase by 26%..
If body temperature rises to 104° F (40° C) metabolism will increase by 39%.
If body temperature rises to 105.8° F (41° C) metabolism will rise by 52%.
If body temperature rises to 107.6° F (42° C) there will not be enough oxygen available to meet the increased needs of the cells.

SIGNS AND SYMPTOMS

The signs and symptoms of heat stroke depend not only on temperature but also on time spent at elevated temperature.

Tachycardia
Tachypnea
Hyperpyrexia of 105.8° F (41° C) or more
Hypotension
Nausea and vomiting
Diarrhea

Decreasing level of consciousness
Decreased urinary output
Hot, dry skin
Seizures
Decerebrate posturing
Dilated, nonresponsive pupils

THERAPEUTIC INTERVENTION

Assure ABCs
Rapid cooling
IVs (for possible fluid challenge)
Other supportive measures:
    Control shivering (will cause temperature to rise)
    Chlorpromazine (Thorazine)
Hospital admission

DIVING EMERGENCIES

In diving a person submits himself to pressures greater than those he is normally exposed to on land. As the gases in the lungs contract as a result of the increased atmospheric pressure, the diver must take in greater quantities of air from the scuba (self-contained underwater breathing apparatus) tank so that his lungs will not collapse. These greater atmospheric pressures bring with them a whole array of medical problems unique to underwater diving and other situations that cause increased atmospheric pressures.

When a person is at sea level, the pressure exerted on his body is 1 atmosphere. At a water depth of 33 feet, the pressure exerted on the diver's body is 2 atmospheres. At a water depth of 66 feet, the pressure is 3 atmospheres.

Water depth (feet)	Pressure (atmospheres)
Sea level	1
33	2
66	3
100	4
133	5
166	6
200	7
300	10
400	13
500	16

Depth of dive and effect on gas volume

As Boyle's law states, the volume of a gas varies inversely with the absolute pressure. In other words, as pressure increases, gas volume decreases. For example, if a normal pair of lungs contains 2,000 cc of air at sea level, the volume of air decreases as the diver descends:

Depth	Air in each lung (cc)
Sea level	1,000
33 feet	500
100 feet	250
233 feet	125

At a depth of 33 feet the total volume of air would be 1,000 cc (half of normal), at 100 feet it would be 500 cc (one fourth of normal), and at 233 feet, it would be 250 cc (one eighth of normal).

A scuba tank is added to the normal lungs at sea level. If the diver forcefully inhales supplemental air from the tank, his lungs will still contain 1,000 cc each:

Depth	Air in each lung (cc)
Sea level	1,000
33 feet	1,000
100 feet	1,000
233 feet	1,000

If the diver ascends but forgets to exhale on the way up, the pressure will decrease as he ascends, and the gas in the lungs will expand:

Depth	Air in each lung (cc)
233 feet	1,000
100 feet	2,000
33 feet	4,000
Sea level	8,000

It is easy to see what will happen; as the gas expands, the lungs expand, to a limit. Then the lungs rupture, a spontaneous pneumothorax results, and air escapes into the circulation, producing an air embolism. The mechanism of injury is breath holding on ascent.

Air embolism
SIGNS AND SYMPTOMS

Tightness of chest
Shortness of breath
Pink frothy sputum from nose and mouth
Vertigo (loss of visual point of reference)
Limb paresthesias or vertical (one-sided) paralysis
Seizures
Loss of consciousness
Other signs and symptoms of pneumothorax (See Chapter 20.)
   This is an extremely serious condition. If the diver does not die before reaching the surface, he must receive extremely prompt therapy.

THERAPEUTIC INTERVENTION

Oxygen under positive pressure
If tension pneumothorax is present, needles inserted into anterior chest wall (See Chapter 20.)
Trendelenburg's position in left lateral decubitus position to avoid cerebral embolization
Prompt recompression

PREVENTIVE MEASURES

The diver should exhale while ascending
Note that pneumothorax can occur in as little as 4 feet of water

Nitrogen narcosis

Nitrogen narcosis is a condition in which, in accordance with Henry's law,* nitrogen (which is 79% of air) is dissolved in solution because the person is breathing nitrogen under greater pressures than normal. Dissolved nitrogen produces effects similar to those of alcohol. The deeper one dives, the greater the narcosis. After 1 hour the effects of nitrogen at various depths are as follows:

---

*At a constant temperature, the solubility of any gas in a liquid is almost directly proportional to the pressure of the liquid.

Depth	Effects
125 to 150 feet	Narcosis begins
150 to 200 feet	Drowsiness, decreased mental functions
200 to 250 feet	Decreased strength, decreased coordination
300 feet	Diver becomes useless
350 to 400 feet	Unconsciousness, death

Therapeutic intervention consists of a gradual ascent to shallower water; symptoms of narcosis should disappear. Nitrogen narcosis can be prevented by avoiding dives to excess depths.

Decompression sickness

If a diver is at a depth long enough for nitrogen to be dissolved and then ascends rapidly, there is not enough time for the nitrogen to reabsorb, and nitrogen bubbles form, producing decompression sickness (the bends, dysbarism, caisson disease, diver's paralysis). Exercise (such as swimming toward the surface) causes a rapid release of nitrogen bubbles, similar to the effect of shaking a bottle of a carbonated beverage, causing gas to be released from solution.

SIGNS AND SYMPTOMS

Itch
Rash
Fatigue
Dizziness
Paresthesias or paralysis
Seizures

Crepitus
Visual loss
Unconsciousness
Joint soreness
Shortness of breath

FACTORS INCREASING SEVERITY OF SIGNS AND SYMPTOMS

Extremes of water temperature
Increasing age
Obesity
Fatigue

Poor physical condition
Alcohol consumption
Peripheral vascular disease
Heavy work while diving

THERAPEUTIC INTERVENTION

Recompression
Oxygen at 10 liters/minute by mask
IV infusion
IV sodium bicarbonate
Transport in left lateral Trendelenburg's position to decrease the possibility of air embolization

SPECIAL NOTES

Any complaint of joint soreness 24 to 48 hours after a dive should be treated by decompression in a decompression chamber.
Bends can occur at depths less than 33 feet (1 atmosphere).

There are several common errors in treating decompression sickness:
    Victim's failure to report his signs and symptoms
    Failure to treat the patient in questionable cases
    Failure to identify severe symptoms as a result of a dive accident

PREVENTION

Do not dive too deeply.
Do not stay down too long.
Follow the U.S. Navy's repetitive dive tables (Tables 12-2 to 12-5) recommendations
    within a safe range for repetitive dives.
Always carry a scuba identification card for at least 48 hours after a dive.

Text continued on p. 291.

TABLE 12-2 U.S. Navy standard air decompression table

Depth (feet)	Bottom time (min)	Time to first stop (min:sec)	Decompression stops (feet)					Total ascent (min:sec)	Repetitive group
			50	40	30	20	10		
40____	200	----------	------	------	------	------	0	0:40	(*)
	210	0:30	------	------	------	------	2	2:40	N
	230	0:30	------	------	------	------	7	7:40	N
	250	0:30	------	------	------	------	11	11:40	O
	270	0:30	------	------	------	------	15	15:40	O
	300	0:30	------	------	------	------	19	19:40	Z
50____	100	----------				------	0	0:50	(*)
	110	0:40	------	------	------	------	3	3:50	L
	120	0:40	------	------	------	------	5	5:50	M
	140	0:40	------	------	------	------	10	10:50	M
	160	0:40	------	------	------	------	21	21:50	N
	180	0:40	------	------	------	------	29	29:50	O
	200	0:40	------	------	------	------	35	35:50	O
	220	0:40	------	------	------	------	40	40:50	Z
	240	0:40	------	------	------	------	47	47:50	Z
60____	60	----------				------	0	1:00	(*)
	70	0:50	------	------	------	------	2	3:00	K
	80	0:50	------	------	------	------	7	8:00	L
	100	0:50	------	------	------	------	14	15:00	M
	120	0:50	------	------	------	------	26	27:00	N
	140	0:50	------	------	------	------	39	40:00	O
	160	0:50	------	------	------	------	48	49:00	Z
	180	0:50	------	------	------	------	56	57:00	Z
	200	0:40	------	------	------	1	69	71:00	Z
70____	50	----------				------	0	1:10	(*)
	60	1:00	------	------	------	------	8	9:10	K
	70	1:00	------	------	------	------	14	15:10	L
	80	1:00	------	------	------	------	18	19:10	M
	90	1:00	------	------	------	------	23	24:10	N
	100	1:00	------	------	------	------	33	34:10	N
	110	0:50	------	------	------	2	41	44:10	O
	120	0:50	------	------	------	4	47	52:10	O
	130	0:50	------	------	------	6	52	59:10	O
	140	0:50	------	------	------	8	56	65:10	Z
	150	0:50	------	------	------	9	61	71:10	Z
	160	0:50	------	------	------	13	72	86:10	Z
	170	0:50	------	------	------	19	79	99:10	Z

*See Table 12-3 for repetitive groups in no-decompression dives.

TABLE 12-2 U.S. Navy standard air decompression table—cont'd

Depth (feet)	Bottom time (min)	Time to first step (min:sec)	Decompression stops (feet) 50	40	30	20	10	Total ascent (min:sec)	Repetitive group
80____	40	----------	------	------	------	------	0	1:20	(*)
	50	1:10	------	------	------	------	10	11:20	K
	60	1:10	------	------	------	------	17	18:20	L
	70	1:10	------	------	------	------	23	24:20	M
	80	1:00	------	------	------	2	31	34:20	N
	90	1:00	------	------	------	7	39	47:20	N
	100	1:00	------	------	------	11	46	58:20	O
	110	1:00	------	------	------	13	53	67:20	O
	120	1:00	------	------	------	17	56	74:20	Z
	130	1:00	------	------	------	19	63	83:20	Z
	140	1:00	------	------	------	26	69	96:20	Z
	150	1:00	------	------	------	32	77	110:20	Z
90____	30	----------	------	------	------	------	0	1:30	(*)
	40	1:20	------	------	------	------	7	8:30	J
	50	1:20	------	------	------	------	18	19:30	L
	60	1:20	------	------	------	------	25	26:30	M
	70	1:10	------	------	------	7	30	38:30	N
	80	1:10	------	------	------	13	40	54:30	N
	90	1:10	------	------	------	18	48	67:30	O
	100	1:10	------	------	------	21	54	76:30	Z
	110	1:10	------	------	------	24	61	86:30	Z
	120	1:10	------	------	------	32	68	101:30	Z
	130	1:00	------	------	5	36	74	116:30	Z
100____	25	----------	------	------	------	------	0	1:40	(*)
	30	1:30	------	------	------	------	3	4:40	I
	40	1:30	------	------	------	------	15	16:40	K
	50	1:20	------	------	------	2	24	27:40	L
	60	1:20	------	------	------	9	28	38:40	N
	70	1:20	------	------	------	17	39	57:40	O
	80	1:20	------	------	------	23	48	72:40	O
	90	1:10	------	------	3	23	57	84:40	Z
	100	1:10	------	------	7	23	66	97:40	Z
	110	1:10	------	------	10	34	72	117:40	Z
	120	1:10	------	------	12	41	78	132:40	Z
110____	20	----------	------	------	------	------	0	1:50	(*)
	25	1:40	------	------	------	------	3	4:50	H
	30	1:40	------	------	------	------	7	8:50	J
	40	1:30	------	------	------	2	21	24:50	L
	50	1:30	------	------	------	8	26	35:50	M
	60	1:30	------	------	------	18	36	55:50	N
	70	1:20	------	------	1	23	48	73:50	O
	80	1:20	------	------	7	23	57	88:50	Z
	90	1:20	------	------	12	30	64	107:50	Z
	100	1:20	------	------	15	37	72	125:50	Z

TABLE 12-2 U.S. Navy standard air decompression table—cont'd

Depth (feet)	Bottom time (min)	Time to first stop (min:sec)	50	40	30	20	10	Total ascent (min:sec)	Repetitive group
120____	15	----------	------	------	------	------	0	2:00	(*)
	20	1:50	------	------	------	------	2	4:00	H
	25	1:50	------	------	------	------	6	8:00	I
	30	1:50	------	------	------	------	14	16:00	J
	40	1:40	------	------	------	5	25	32:00	L
	50	1:40	------	------	------	15	31	48:00	N
	60	1:30	------	------	2	22	45	71:00	O
	70	1:30	------	------	9	23	55	89:00	O
	80	1:30	------	------	15	27	63	107:00	Z
	90	1:30	------	------	19	37	74	132:00	Z
	100	1:30	------	------	23	45	80	150:00	Z
130____	10	----------	------	------	------	------	0	2:10	(*)
	15	2:00	------	------	------	------	1	3:10	F
	20	2:00	------	------	------	------	4	6:10	H
	25	2:00	------	------	------	------	10	12:10	J
	30	1:50	------	------	------	3	18	23:10	M
	40	1:50	------	------	------	10	25	37:10	N
	50	1:40	------	------	3	21	37	63:10	O
	60	1:40	------	------	9	23	52	86:10	Z
	70	1:40	------	------	16	24	61	103:10	Z
	80	1:30	------	3	19	35	72	131:10	Z
	90	1:30	------	8	19	45	80	154:10	Z
140____	10	----------	------	------	------	------	0	2:20	(*)
	15	2:10	------	------	------	------	2	4:20	G
	20	2:10	------	------	------	------	6	8:20	I
	25	2:00	------	------	------	2	14	18:20	J
	30	2:00	------	------	------	5	21	28:20	K
	40	1:50	------	------	2	16	26	46:20	N
	50	1:50	------	------	6	24	44	76:20	O
	60	1:50	------	------	16	23	56	97:20	Z
	70	1:40	------	4	19	32	68	125:20	Z
	80	1:40	------	10	23	41	79	155:20	Z
150____	5	----------	------	------	------	------	0	2:30	C
	10	2:20	------	------	------	------	1	3:30	E
	15	2:20	------	------	------	------	3	5:30	G
	20	2:10	------	------	------	2	7	11:30	H
	25	2:10	------	------	------	4	17	23:30	K
	30	2:10	------	------	------	8	24	34:30	L
	40	2:00	------	------	5	19	33	59:30	N
	50	2:00	------	------	12	23	51	88:30	O
	60	1:50	------	3	19	26	62	112:30	Z
	70	1:50	------	11	19	39	75	146:30	Z
	80	1:40	1	17	19	50	84	173:30	Z

TABLE 12-2 U.S. Navy standard air decompression table—cont'd

Depth (feet)	Bottom time (min)	Time to first stop (min:sec)	Decompression stops (feet)					Total ascent (min:sec)	Repetitive group
			50	40	30	20	10		
160____	5	----------	------	------	------	------	0	2:40	D
	10	2:30	------	------	------	------	1	3:40	F
	15	2:20	------	------	------	1	4	7:40	H
	20	2:20	------	------	------	3	11	16:40	J
	25	2:20	------	------	------	7	20	29:40	K
	30	2:10	------	------	2	11	25	40:40	M
	40	2:10	------	------	7	23	39	71:40	N
	50	2:00	------	2	16	23	55	98:40	Z
	60	2:00	------	9	19	33	69	132:40	Z
	70	1:50	1	17	22	44	80	166:40	Z
170____	5	----------	------	------	------	------	0	2:50	D
	10	2:40	------	------	------	------	2	4:50	F
	15	2:30	------	------	------	2	5	9:50	H
	20	2:30	------	------	------	4	15	21:50	J
	25	2:20	------	------	2	7	23	34:50	L
	30	2:20	------	------	4	13	26	45:50	M
	40	2:10	------	1	10	23	45	81:50	O
	50	2:10	------	5	18	23	61	109:50	Z
	60	2:00	2	15	22	37	74	152:50	Z
	70	2:00	8	17	19	51	86	183:50	Z
180____	5	----------	------	------	------	------	0	3:00	D
	10	2:50	------	------	------	------	3	6:00	F
	15	2:40	------	------	------	3	6	12:00	I
	20	2:30	------	------	1	5	17	26:00	K
	25	2:30	------	------	3	10	24	40:00	L
	30	2:30	------	------	6	17	27	53:00	N
	40	2:20	------	3	14	23	50	93:00	O
	50	2:10	2	9	19	30	65	128:00	Z
	60	2:10	5	16	19	44	81	168:00	Z
190____	5	----------	------	------	------	------	0	3:10	D
	10	2:50	------	------	------	1	3	7:10	G
	15	2:50	------	------	------	4	7	14:10	I
	20	2:40	------	------	2	6	20	31:10	K
	25	2:40	------	------	5	11	25	44:10	M
	30	2:30	------	1	8	19	32	63:10	N
	40	2:30	------	8	14	23	55	103:10	O
	50	2:20	4	13	22	33	72	147:10	Z
	60	2:20	10	17	19	50	84	183:10	Z

THE "NU-WAY" REPETITIVE DIVE TABLES

TABLE 12-4. SURFACE INTERVAL CREDIT TABLE (TIMES IN HR:MIN)

This triangular Surface Interval Credit Table is entered by the beginning repetitive group (A–O) and the elapsed surface interval time; the new repetitive group designation is read at the foot of the column. Readable breakpoint values (times in HR:MIN), by beginning group:

Group	Interval breakpoints (top = 12:00 down to 0:10)
A	12:00 / 2:10 · 2:11 / 0:10
B	12:00 / 2:50 · 2:49 / 1:40 · 1:39 / 0:10
C	12:00 / 3:22 · 3:21 / 2:39 · 2:38 / 1:58 · 1:57 / 1:10 · 1:09 / 0:10
D	12:00 / 3:57 · 3:56 / 3:23 · 3:22 / 2:59 · 2:58 / 2:29 · 2:28 / 1:58 · 1:57 / 1:30 · 1:29 / 1:10 · 1:09 / 0:55 · 0:54 / 0:46 · 0:45 / 0:10
E	12:00 / 4:25 · 4:26 / 3:57 · … · 1:16 / 1:15 · 1:15 / 0:54 · 0:46 / 0:41 · 0:40 / 0:10
F	12:00 / 4:49 · 4:50 / 4:25 · … · 0:45 / 0:41 · 0:40 / 0:37 · 0:36 / 0:10
G	12:00 / 5:40 · 5:41 / 4:49 · … · 0:41 / 0:37 · 0:36 / 0:34 · 0:33 / 0:10
H	12:00 / 5:48 · … · 0:34 / 0:33 · 0:32 / 0:10
J	12:00 / 6:02 · … · 0:31 / 0:28 · 0:27 / 0:10
K	12:00 / 6:18 · … · 0:28 / 0:26 · 0:25 / 0:10
L	12:00 / 6:32 · … · 0:26 / 0:25 · 0:24 / 0:10
M	12:00 / 6:44 · … · 0:25 / 0:24 · 0:23 / 0:10
N	12:00 / 6:56 · … · 0:24 / 0:23 · 0:22 / 0:10
O	12:00 / 10:05 · … · 0:23 / 0:10
Z	0:22 / 0:10

TABLE 12-5. REPETITIVE DIVE TIMETABLE FOR AIR DIVES

NEW REP. GROUP	40'	50'	60'	70'	80'	90'	100'	110'	120'	130'	140'	150'	160'	170'	180'	190'
A	7	6	5	4	4	3	3	3	3	3	2	2	2	2	2	2
B	17	13	11	9	8	7	7	6	6	6	5	5	4	4	4	4
C	25	21	17	15	13	11	10	10	9	8	7	7	6	6	6	6
D	37	29	24	20	18	16	14	13	12	12	11	10	9	9	8	8
E	49	38	30	26	23	20	18	16	15	15	13	13	12	11	10	10
F	61	47	36	31	28	24	22	20	18	17	16	15	14	13	12	11
G	73	56	44	37	32	29	26	24	21	19	18	17	16	15	14	13
H	87	66	52	43	38	33	30	27	25	22	20	19	18	17	15	15
I	101	76	61	50	43	38	34	31	28	25	23	22	20	19	18	17
J	116	87	70	57	48	43	38	34	31	28	26	24	23	22	20	19
K	138	99	79	64	54	47	43	38	35	31	29	28	26	25	22	21
L	161	111	88	72	61	53	48	42	39	35	32	30	28	26	25	24
M	187	124	97	80	68	58	52	47	43	38	35	32	31	29	27	26
N	213	142	107	87	73	64	57	51	46	40	38	35	33	31	29	28
O	241	160	122	96	80	70	62	55	50	44	40	38	36	34	31	30
Z	257	169	122	100	84	73	64	57	52	46	42	40	37	35	32	31
	40'	50'	60'	70'	80'	90'	100'	110'	120'	130'	140'	150'	160'	170'	180'	190'

RESIDUAL NITROGEN TIMES (MINUTES) FOR REPETITIVE DIVE DEPTH BELOW (FT)

TABLE 12-3. "NO DECOMPRESSION" LIMITS AND REPETITIVE GROUP DESIGNATION TABLE FOR "NO DECOMPRESSION" AIR DIVES

DEPTH (FEET)	NO DECOMPRESSION LIMITS	A	B	C	D	E	F	G	H	I	J	K	L	M	N	O
10	-	60	120	210	300											
15	-	35	70	110	160	225	350									
20	-	25	50	75	100	135	180	240	325							
25	-	20	35	55	75	100	125	160	195	245	315					
30	-	15	30	45	60	75	95	120	145	170	205	250	310			
35	310	5	15	25	40	50	60	80	100	120	140	160	190	220	270	310
40	200	5	15	25	30	40	50	70	80	100	110	130	150	170	200	
50	100	10	15	25	30	40	50	60	70	80	90	100				
60	60	10	15	20	25	30	40	50	55	60						
70	50	5	10	15	20	30	35	40	45	50						
80	40	5	10	15	20	25	30	35	40							
90	30	5	10	12	15	20	25	30								
100	25	5	7	10	15	20	22	25								
110	20	-	5	10	13	15	20									
120	15	-	5	10	12	15										
130	10	-	5	8	10											
140	10	-	5	7	10											
150	5	-	5													
160	5	-	-	5												
170	5	-	-	5												
180	5	-	-	5												
190	5	-	-	5												

BOTTOM TIMES FOR AIR DIVES (MINUTES)

COPYRIGHT © 1970 BY RALPH M. MARUSCAK

CAUTION:

THESE "RESIDUAL NITROGEN TIMES" ARE THE TIMES A DIVER MUST ASSUME HE HAS ALREADY SPENT ON THE BOTTOM BEFORE HE STARTS A REPETITIVE DIVE TO A SPECIFIC DEPTH.

—INSTRUCTIONS—

ALL TABULATED BOTTOM TIMES (MINUTES), AND ALL TABULATED DEPTHS (FEET) HAVE BEEN TAKEN FROM THE U.S. NAVY DIVING MANUAL OF MARCH 1970.

1 TO CALCULATE A REPETITIVE DIVE UPON SURFACING FOR DIVES INVOLVING EXPOSURES UP TO AND INCLUDING THE "NO DECOMPRESSION LIMITS": ENTER TABLE 12-3 ON THE EXACT OR NEXT GREATER DEPTH THAN THAT TO WHICH EXPOSED, AND SELECT THE LISTED EXPOSURE TIME EXACT OR NEXT GREATER THAN THE ACTUAL EXPOSURE TIME. THE REPETITIVE GROUP DESIGNATION IS INDICATED BY THE LETTER AT THE HEAD OF THE VERTICAL COLUMN WHERE THE SELECTED EXPOSURE TIME IS LISTED.

2 CONTINUE THE VERTICAL MOTION ALONG THE STRAIGHT LINES JOINING TABLE 12-3 TO TABLE 12-4. ENTER THE TABLE VERTICALLY TO SELECT THE ELAPSED SURFACE INTERVAL TIME. THE NEW REPETITIVE GROUP DESIGNATION FOR THE SURFACE INTERVAL IS TO THE RIGHT OF THE HORIZONTAL COLUMN WHERE THE ELAPSED SURFACE INTERVAL TIME IS LISTED.

3 CONTINUE THE RIGHTHANDED MOTION TO ENTER 12-5 ON THE HORIZONTAL COLUMN TO THE RIGHT OF THE NEW REPETITIVE GROUP DESIGNATION. THE TIME IN EACH VERTICAL COLUMN IS THE RESIDUAL NITROGEN TIME. IT IS A PENALTY TIME; ie, THE TIME A DIVER MUST ASSUME HE HAS ALREADY SPENT ON THE BOTTOM BEFORE HE STARTS A REPETITIVE DIVE TO THE DEPTH SPECIFIED AT THE BOTTOM OF THE COLUMN.

Reprinted courtesy of Ralph M. Maruscak.

USE OF DECOMPRESSION TABLES

Use of decompression tables allows for gradual ascent with delays at certain depths ("decompression stops") to allow nitrogen to be released by the lungs. Decompression tables are used to calculate the rate of nitrogen absorption by the body. Any dive within 12 hours of resurfacing is a repetitive dive, and the repetitive dive table should be used (Tables 12-3 to 12-5).

Other medical problems encountered in diving

THE "SQUEEZE" (Fig. 12-6)

The squeeze results from a compression of air trapped in hollow chambers, producing severe, sharp pain, when outside pressure is greater than inside pressure. It may occur in these areas:

Ears
Sinuses
Lungs and airways
Gastrointestinal tract
Thoracic cavity
Teeth
Added air spaces (face mask or wet suit)

The signs and symptoms are as follows:

Pain
Edema
Capillary dilatation
Rupture
Bleeding

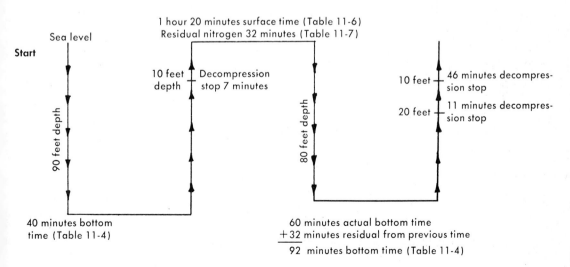

FIG. 12-5 Sample dive plan with use of U.S. Navy repetitive dive tables.

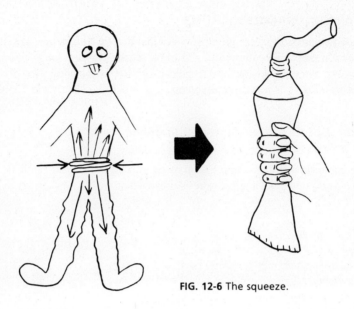

FIG. 12-6 The squeeze.

TABLE 12-6 Gas toxicities in diving

Gas	Signs and symptoms	Therapeutic interventions
Oxygen (from breathing 100% oxygen)	Twitching, nausea, dizziness, tunnel vision, restlessness, paresthesias, seizures, confusion, pulmonary edema, atelectasis, shock lung	ABCs, intubation, controlled ventilation to reduce FIO_2, decompression, PEEP
Carbon dioxide (from inhaling expired air; 8%-10% causes toxicity)	Dizziness, lethargy, heavy labored breathing, unconsciousness	Ascent to surface, ABCs, 100% oxygen
Carbon monoxide (from contaminated tank—filled too close to internal combustion engine)	Dizziness, pink or red lips and mouth, euphoria	Ascent to surface, ABCs (CPR if necessary), 100% oxygen in hyperbaric chamber at 3 atmospheres for 1 hour

The mechanism by which this occurs is breath holding on descent or trapping of air in a hollow cavity.

Therapeutic intervention consists of gradual ascent to shallower depths to decrease the pressure and maintenance of airway, breathing, and circulation.

Ear squeeze or sinus squeeze

The cause of the ear squeeze or sinus squeeze is a blocked eustachian tube or paranasal sinus and an inability to equalize the pressures.

Therapeutic intervention consists of ascent to shallower water.

HYPERPNEA EXHAUSTION SYNDROME

Hyperpnea exhaustion syndrome usually results from diver fatigue. The signs and symptoms are as follows:

Tachypnea

Anxiety

Feeling of impending doom

Difficulty floating

Exhaustion

Therapeutic intervention consists of ascent to the surface and rest aboard a flotation device or boat.

GENERAL SAFETY RULES FOR SCUBA AND SNORKLE DIVERS*

1. Never dive alone.
2. Always wear an inflation vest.
3. Tow a surface float with a diver's flag.
4. Do *not* use ear plugs while diving.
5. Do *not* use nose clips while diving.
6. Do *not* dive with an upper respiratory infection.
7. Check your equipment before diving. Regulators should be overhauled every year, and tanks should be hydrostatically tested every 5 years.
8. In scuba, *always* exhale on ascent.
9. In scuba, do *not* hold your breath.
10. Do not consume alcohol or drugs prior to diving.
11. Observe the "decompression limits" chart.
12. Do not remain at depth when the tank is on reserve.
13. Have an annual physical checkup.
14. Be physically fit; do not dive if you do not feel well.
15. Know the area where you are diving.
16. Avoid dangerous places and poor conditions.
17. Plan your dive.
18. Be ready for emergencies; be certified in lifesaving, first aid, and CPR; have first aid equipment.
19. Carry a diver's identification card for 48 hours after a dive.
20. Seek medical attention if problems occur after a dive.

REASONS FOR NOT DIVING TO GREAT DEPTHS

Water temperature much colder

Visibility poor/darker

Less color/less animation

Less tank time/air used faster

Extra equipment required

Need for "decompression stops"

---

*Adapted from class notes taken at Dworet Dive School in Boston, Mass.

Drug and alcohol effect greater
Emergency ascent difficult

EMERGENCY INFORMATION

The following information should be kept readily available when diving:
Coast Guard telephone number and radio frequency
Police telephone number and radio frequency
Paramedic telephone number and radio frequency
Decompression chamber location and telephone number*
Name and telephone number (24-hour number) of a physician trained in underwater emergencies

*If this information is unavailable, call the U.S. Navy Experimental Diving Unit in Washington, D.C. (202-433-2790, 24 hours a day/7 days a week) and ask for the duty officer, who will give you the name, location, and telephone number of the nearest decompression chamber, or the *Directory of Worldwide Decompression Chambers* is available from the Superintendent of Diving, U.S. Navy, Naval Ships Systems Command, National Center Building #3, Washington, DC 20360.

REFERENCES

1. Russell, F.E.: Snake venom poisoning, Philadelphia, 1980, J.B. Lippincott Co.
2. Bech, A.M.: The public health implications of urban dogs, Am. J. Public Health **65:**1315, 1975.
3. Kizer, K.W.: Epidemiologic and clinical aspects of animal injuries, J.A.C.E.P. **8:**134, 1979.
4. Parrish, H.M.: Analysis of 460 fatalities from venomous animals in the United States, Am. J. Med. Sci. **245:**129, 1963.

SUGGESTED READINGS

Auerbach, P.A., and Geehr, E.C.: Environmental emergencies, New York, 1983, McGraw-Hill Book Co.
Bangs, C.C., et al.: When your patient suffers frostbite, Patient Care **11:**132, 1977.
Barr, S.E.: Insect sting allergy, Cutis **17:**1069, 1976.
Budassi, S.A., and Barber, J.M.: Emergency nursing: principles and practice, St. Louis, 1981, The C.V. Mosby Co.
Burch, G.E., Cade, J.R., and Tintinalli, J.E.: Sorting out the heat syndromes, Patient Care **10:**23, 1976.
Clowes, G.H., and O'Donnel, T.F.: Heat stroke, N. Engl. J. Med. **291:**546, 1974.
Cowan, W.: Summertime—occasion for heat emergencies, Emerg. Prod. News **8:**217, 1976.
Dinep, M.: Cold injury: a review of current theories and their applications to treatment, Conn. Med. **39:**8, 1975.
Duffy, T.P.: Hypothermia and hyperthermia. In Harvey, A.M., et al., editors: The principles and practice of medicine, ed. 19, New York, 1976, Appleton-Century-Crofts.
Ford, A.M.: The management of acute allergic disease, including anaphylaxis, Med. J. Aus. **1:**222, 1977.
Hardy, I.: Depth limits, Naval news, Sept. 1972.
Hildes, J.A.: Accidental hypothermia, Let. Can. Med. Assoc. **112:**420, 1975.
Holm, P.C., and Vanggaarg, L.: Frostbite, Plas. Reconstr. Surg. **54:**544, 1974.
Miles, S.: Underwater Medicine, Philadelphia, 1972, J.B. Lippincott Co.
Mills, W.J.: Out in the cold, Emerg. Med. **8:**134, 1976.
Rich, J.: Case review: hypothermia, J.E.N. **9**(1):8, 1983.
Solar-Mills, A.: Insect sting allergy. In Patterson, R., editor: Allergic diseases, Philadelphia, 1972, J.B. Lippincott Co.
Tintinalli, J.E.: Heat stroke, J.A.C.E.P. **5:**525, 1976.
Wingert, W.A., and Wainschel, J.: A quick handbook on snakebites, Med. Times **105:**68, 1977.
Wingert, W.A., and Wainschel, J.: Diagnosis and management of envenomation by poisonous snakes, South. Med. J. **68:**1015, 1975.
U.S. Navy Diving Manual, vol. 1, Navships 0094-001-9010, Washington, D.C., 1973, U.S. Government Printing Office.

CHAPTER 13 **Genitourinary emergencies**

GENITOURINARY TRAUMA
Renal trauma (see also Chapter 21)

Renal trauma (trauma to the kidneys) should be suspected in any injury that involves blunt or penetrating trauma to the anterior or posterior lower chest, especially those that involve the lower ribs or the abdomen (particularly the flank area). Renal trauma should also be suspected with fractures of the pelvis or in any patient who has sustained a multiple-systems injury.

SIGNS AND SYMPTOMS

History of trauma
Flank pain
Hematoma in flank area
Microscopic or gross hematuria

Possible:
    Abdominal rigidity
    Swelling or mass in flank
    Hypovolemic shock

DIAGNOSTIC AIDS

Check urine for hematuria (with reagent papers specifically designed to check for blood)
Urinalysis
Intravenous pyelogram (IVP)
Renal angiogram

TYPES OF RENAL TRAUMA
Contusion
Signs and symptoms

Ecchymosis
Subcapsular hematoma
Mild hematuria

Therapeutic intervention

Discharge to home
Bed rest
Great volumes of fluids for a few days

295

Laceration

A laceration is an actual disruption of renal tissue:
Through the parenchyma
Through the renal pelvis
Through the capsule

Signs and symptoms

The main symptom of renal laceration is gross hematuria.

Therapeutic intervention

Hospital admission
Observation
Bed rest
Possible surgical repair for partial or total nephrectomy

Vascular disruption

A vascular disruption is a disruption of the renal arteries or veins or both.

Signs and symptoms

Bruits auscultated at the first or second lumbar vertebrae, near the midline
No kidney visualization on IVP

Therapeutic intervention

Therapeutic intervention for vascular disruption is surgical intervention for reanastomosis of artery or vein.

Bladder trauma

The bladder is occasionally injured in blunt abdominal trauma to the pelvis. Bladder trauma should be suspected with a fractured pelvis or direct suprapubic trauma. It is more likely to occur when the bladder is filled with urine. The bladder is also occasionally injured in penetrating trauma in which the bladder is in the path of the penetrating object.

SIGNS AND SYMPTOMS

Suprapubic pain
Urine extravasation
Possible hematuria

Possible shock
Possible anuria

DIAGNOSTIC AID

Cystogram is an aid to the diagnosis of bladder trauma.

THERAPEUTIC INTERVENTION

Therapeutic intervention for bladder trauma is surgical repair.

Penetrating urethral trauma

Penetrating trauma to the urethra is not a common trauma. It usually occurs as a result of a direct penetrating injury.

SIGNS AND SYMPTOMS

Hematuria

Anuria

Flank pain

Urinary fistula

History of trauma

DIAGNOSTIC AID

Intravenous pyelogram is an aid to the diagnosis of penetrating urethral trauma.

THERAPEUTIC INTERVENTION

Therapeutic intervention for penetrating urethral trauma is surgical repair for anastomosis of urethra.

Obstructive urethral trauma

Obstructive urethral trauma may be caused by either a foreign body in the urethral tract or by constricting objects around external urethral structures. These types of injuries are usually seen in young children, senile adults, and those who practice exotic methods of sexual stimulation.

SIGNS AND SYMPTOMS

Bloody discharge

Hematuria

Anuria

Edema

Urethral tears

Possible infection with purulent discharge

Complaint of specific foreign body implantation by patient

Urinary tract infection

Necrosis

Distended bladder

Abdominal pain

Perineal ecchymosis

DIAGNOSTIC AID

Retrograde urethrogram is an aid to diagnosis of obstructive urethral trauma.

THERAPEUTIC INTERVENTION

Analgesia or sedation

Local anesthesia

Removal of foreign body

Suprapubic urine aspiration if the bladder is severely distended

Possible administration of antibiotics

Possible surgical intervention

Fracture of the penile shaft

Fracture of the penile shaft should be suspected in any male with multiple trauma involving the pelvic region. This applies especially when the mechanism of injury was a straddle incident, such as would occur in an accident on a motorcycle or a bicycle with a crossbar.

SIGNS AND SYMPTOMS

May be discovered when attempting to insert a Foley catheter during resuscitation from
multiple trauma
Hematoma
Hemorrhage
Swelling
Discoloration

DIAGNOSTIC AID

Retrograde urethrogram is an aid to diagnosis of fracture of the penile shaft.

THERAPEUTIC INTERVENTION

Splint   Evacuation of hematoma
Ice packs   Placement of indwelling catheter by urologist
Urologic consultation

Soft-tissue zipper injury

Soft-tissue zipper injury, involving the soft tissue of the penis and a metal or plastic zipper, occurs most frequently in preschool boys who are just learning the mechanics of zipping their pants and are beginning to take care of their own elimination needs. It is also seen in the inebriated man who accidentally catches the foreskin of his penis in a zipper.

THERAPEUTIC INTERVENTION

Remove the bottom tab from the zipper this usually involves prying the four sharp metal
teeth) *or*
Cut the distal end of the zipper with strong scissors; the zipper should then easily separate
If the soft tissue is caught in the moving mechanism of the zipper, it may be necessary to
apply regional anesthesia before removal
Control any bleeding
Apply ice packs

NONTRAUMATIC GENITOURINARY EMERGENCIES
Pyelonephritis

Pyelonephritis is an inflammation of the kidneys that involves the tubules, glomeruli, and pelvis of the kidney. It is usually caused by a bacterial infection.

SIGNS AND SYMPTOMS

Severe flank or back pain   Urinary urgency
Fever   Nocturia
Chills   Dysuria
Urinary frequency   Tenderness over the affected flank area

DIAGNOSTIC AIDS

Leukocytosis
Presence of pus in urine
Presence of bacteria in urine
Hematuria

THERAPEUTIC INTERVENTION

Forced fluids
Bed rest
Broad-spectrum antibiotics
Possible hospital admission (especially in cases of abscess, gram-negative septicemia, or
    severe signs and symptoms)

Perinephric abscess

Patients with perinephric abscess usually offer a history of a recent skin infection,
usually within 1 month of the abscess, or a urinary tract infection that has lasted for a
prolonged time.

SIGNS AND SYMPTOMS

High- or low-grade fever
Exquisite tenderness in the flank area
Palpation of a mass in the flank area
Spinal scoliosis (concave on the affected side)

DIAGNOSTIC AIDS

Visualizing an elevated diaphragm on the affected side on x-ray film
Visualizing a decreased psoas shadow on x-ray film

THERAPEUTIC INTERVENTION

Incision and drainage
Antibiotics

Renal carbuncle

A renal carbuncle is an abscess in the periphery of the kidney.

SIGNS AND SYMPTOMS

Severe flank tenderness or pain
Fever
Chills

If these signs and symptoms are present and urinalysis is normal, renal carbuncle is
implicated.

THERAPEUTIC INTERVENTION

Incision and drainage
Antibiotics

Renal colic/renal calculi

Pain from renal colic radiates from the flank to the left or right lower quadrant and occasionally to the leg. This pain results from ureteral distention caused by the passage of a renal stone (calculus) or from blood clots. The size of the stone or clot does not relate to the severity of the pain (Fig. 13-1).

SIGNS AND SYMPTOMS

Restlessness
Severe flank pain that radiates to the right or left lower quadrant (sudden onset)
Urinary urgency and frequency
Diaphoresis
Low-grade fever
Hematuria
Dysuria
Decreased blood pressure

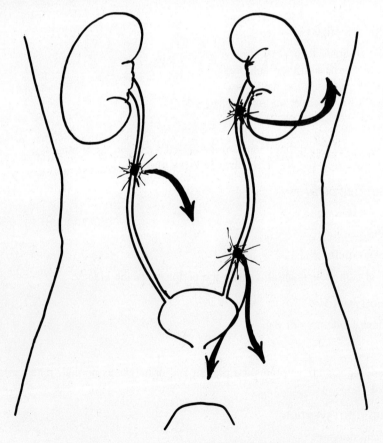

FIG. 13-1 Areas of renal stone lodging and patterns of pain radiation.

DIAGNOSTIC AIDS

Strain urine
Intravenous pyelogram
Urinalysis
X-ray films of kidney, ureter, and bladder (KUB)

THERAPEUTIC INTERVENTION

Analgesics
Do *not* give atropine
Urologic consultation
Antiemetic if there are nausea and vomiting

IV fluids for rehydration
Possible hospital admission
Possible surgical intervention

Urinary retention

Urinary retention is the inability to void. It may be caused by urethral strictures, an enlarged prostate, blood clots, renal stones, a reflex neurogenic bladder (usually associated with a CVA), multiple sclerosis, congenital stenosis, foreign bodies, bladder stones, hysteria, or as a side effect of parasympatholytic and certain other drugs.

SIGNS AND SYMPTOMS

Lower abdominal discomfort

Mass palpated just above symphisis pubis

THERAPEUTIC INTERVENTION

Insertion of an indwelling catheter

Possible urologic consultation

Hematuria

Blood can appear in urine from several causes, including trauma, renal calculi, anticoagulants, blood dyscrasias, prostatectomy, ruptured scrotal varices, and renal or bladder tumor. If bleeding occurs at the beginning of urination, bleeding from the anterior urethral region is suggested. If bleeding occurs at the end of the urinary stream, this indicates bleeding from the posterior urethra or the point at which the bladder connects to the urethra. If bleeding occurs throughout urination it is probably from the upper urinary tract or the bladder itself.

The care giver should be cautious not to assume that all red-colored urine indicates hematuria. Red-colored urine may be caused by food colorings, certain medications, and possibly the ingestion of beets. If bleeding occurs in the female, the care giver should be sure to check if the source of bleeding is the vagina.

DIAGNOSTIC AIDS

History
Urinalysis (if during menstruation, obtain the sample by catheter)
CBC

THERAPEUTIC INTERVENTION

Therapeutic intervention for hematuria will depend on the cause of the bleeding. A careful check of vital signs should be made.

Oliguria/anuria

Oliguria is defined as the excretion of less than 500 ml or urine/day. Anuria is the complete absence of urine. The patient with one of these conditions may complain of inablity to void, yet little or no urine may be obtained on catheterization. Oliguria and anuria may be caused by fluid and electrolyte imbalances, urinary tract obstructions, acute tubular necrosis, tumors, or accidental occlusion during obstetric sterilization surgery.

SIGNS AND SYMPTOMS

Possibly marked dehydration   Weakness
Complaint of inability to void   Uremic frost

THERAPEUTIC INTERVENTION

Urologic consultation
Intravenous pyelogram (IVP) to rule out obstruction
    (there may be a renal condition)
If the cause is severe dehydration, therapeutic intervention is the administration of fluids with electrolyte additives in accordance with serum electrolyte values. If the cause is hypotension from any cause, therapeutic intervention should be aimed toward elevating the blood pressure to a normal level. Whatever the cause, it must be isolated, and therapeutic intervention must be given accordingly. The care giver should consider the possibility of peritoneal or renal dialysis.

Acute cystitis

Cystitis occurs more frequently in females than males. It is an infection of the bladder that occurs as a result of the migration of bacteria from the urethra (also known as "honeymoon cystitis") or acute prostatitis.

SIGNS AND SYMPTOMS

Urinary urgency   Fever in males
Nocturia   No fever in females
Slight hematuria

DIAGNOSTIC AIDS

Females: Males:
    Urinalysis (WBCs and bacteria)   Tender prostate
                                           Urinary retention
                                           Fever

THERAPEUTIC INTERVENTION

Females: Males:
    Nitrofurantoin or sulfonamides   Sulfa combination drugs (Septra)
    Increased fluids   or tetracycline
    Warm baths   Drain abscess if present
                                           Bed rest
                                           Increased fluids

GENITOURINARY PROBLEMS UNIQUE TO MALES
Cryptorchidism

Cryptorchidism is an undescended testis.

DIAGNOSTIC AIDS

History
Mass in inguinal region
Absence of testicle in scrotum

THERAPEUTIC INTERVENTION

Gonadotropins *and/or*
Surgical intervention

Penile/scrotal edema

Penile/scrotal edema is often found in males with congestive heart failure. The main sign of penile/scrotal edema is pitting edema in penile or scrotal skin. The main therapeutic intervention is treatment of the congestive heart failure.

Acute epididymitis

Acute epididymitis is an infection of a portion of the male reproductive system. It may occur as a result of a physical strain. It may also occur after cystoscopic examination, prostate surgery with a history of urethral discharge, or urinary bladder catheterization.

SIGNS AND SYMPTOMS

Swelling/enlargement
Sudden tenderness $\Big\}$ Unilateral, radiating up the spermatic cord
Elevated temperature
Sepsis

THERAPEUTIC INTERVENTION

Antibiotics   Elevation of scrotum
Bed rest   Forced fluids

Hematospermia

Hematospermia is a condition in which blood is present in the semen. This condition usually occurs in middle-aged men. It may be caused by rupture of varicosities. The main sign of hematospermia is blood in the semen.

THERAPEUTIC INTERVENTION

Reassurance
Urologic consultation if the condition recurs

Hydrocele

When fluid collects within the tunica vaginalis the condition is known as hydrocele.

SIGNS AND SYMPTOMS

No pain or tenderness
Presence of a large scrotal mass

THERAPEUTIC INTERVENTION

Surgery is performed for hydrocele only if it is large and uncomfortable.

Acute orchitis

Acute orchitis is an inflammation of the testicle that may result from epidemic parotiditis (mumps) or another viral infection.

SIGNS AND SYMPTOMS

Unilateral testicular swelling
Unilateral tenderness
Elevated temperature

THERAPEUTIC INTERVENTION

Antibiotics
Bed rest
Scrotal support

Peyronie's disease

Peyronie's disease is a syndrome in which a fibrous plaque forms on the corpora cavernosa of the penis. When the patient has an erection there is considerable pain and the penis is curved.

SIGNS AND SYMPTOMS

Curved penis
Difficulty with intercourse

THERAPEUTIC INTERVENTION

There is no specific therapy for Peyronie's disease other than psychologic support and reassurance.

Priapism

Priapism is a prolonged erection that is not relieved by ejaculation. There may or may not be a cause for this condition. Common causes include spinal cord injury, sickle-cell disease, tumors, or hematologic disorders.

SIGNS AND SYMPTOMS

Prolonged erection
Pain (on occasion)

THERAPEUTIC INTERVENTION

Analgesia/sedation
Possible surgical intervention if erection persists

Prostatitis

When prostatitis occurs there is usually an accompanying cystitis (see p. 302). The prostate gland will be very tender on rectal examination.

SIGNS AND SYMPTOMS

Tenderness
Elevated temperature
Possible urinary retention

THERAPEUTIC INTERVENTION

Antibiotics
Bed rest
Forced fluids
Possible incision and drainage if there is abscess

Testicular torsion

When the testicle twists in the tunica vaginalis or the spermatic cord twists, the resultant condition is known as testicular torsion. It occurs most commonly in children and adolescents. When the testicle is elevated there is increased pain (unlike in epididymitis).

SIGNS AND SYMPTOMS

Severe scrotal pain ⎫
Swelling ⎬ Especially during physical activity
Nausea and vomiting ⎭
Elevated temperature
High-riding testicle
Tense scrotal mass (epididymis cannot be palpated)

THERAPEUTIC INTERVENTION

Ice packs
Manual manipulation of torsion
If manual manipulation is unsuccessful, immediate surgical intervention is indicated

Testicular tumor

Testicular tumor is common in the 20- to 30-year age group. The chief complaint will be a scrotal mass with or without pain.

SIGNS AND SYMPTOMS

Swelling
Hard testicular mass with normal epididymitis
Presence or absence of pain

THERAPEUTIC INTERVENTION

Surgical intervention is indicated for testicular tumor.

Nonspecific urethritis

Patients with nonspecific urethritis will frequently come to the emergency department with a chief complaint of urethral discharge.

SIGNS AND SYMPTOMS

Burning on urination and urinary frequency
Dysuria
Urethral discharge
Gram's stain shows no gram-negative intracellular diplococci in cases of nonspecific urethritis.

THERAPEUTIC INTERVENTION

Trimethoprim-sulfonamide combination *or*
Tetracycline

Varicocele

A dilation of the spermatic cord is known as a varicocele. It is caused by poor vascular drainage that results in dilation of the veins.

SIGNS AND SYMPTOMS

Scrotal mass above the testicle
Disappearance of the mass when the patient is supine

THERAPEUTIC INTERVENTION

Surgical intervention may be indicated for varicocele.

VENEREAL DISEASES
Chancroid
SIGNS AND SYMPTOMS

Inguinal adenopathy 3 to 4 days after sexual intercourse
Discharge
Positive skin test

THERAPEUTIC INTERVENTION

Therapeutic intervention for chancroid venereal diseases is treatment with tetracycline.

Gonorrhea

Gonorrhea is a form of urethritis.

SIGNS AND SYMPTOMS

Burning on urination
White, creamy discharge 3 to 7 days after sexual intercourse
Gram-negative diplococci on Gram's stain
Positive gonococcus culture

THERAPEUTIC INTERVENTION

Antibiotics (penicillin or tetracycline)
Follow-up care

Granuloma inguinale

Granuloma inguinale is a chronic venereal infection of the skin and subcutaneous tissue of the genitalia, the perineum, and the inguinal region.

SIGNS AND SYMPTOMS

Swelling
Ulceration
Pain

THERAPEUTIC INTERVENTION

Therapeutic intervention for granuloma inguinale consists of treatment with tetracycline.

Lymphogranuloma venereum

Lymphogranuloma venereum is a venereal disease caused by a virus.

SIGNS AND SYMTOMS

Transient genital lesion ⎫
Lymphadenopathy   ⎬ 1 to 3 weeks after exposure through sexual intercourse
Rectal stricture (in females) ⎭
Painful nodes

THERAPEUTIC INTERVENTION

Therapeutic intervention for lymphogranuloma venereum consists of treatment with tetracycline.

Syphilis

A patient with syphilis may come to the emergency department with a chief complaint of painless ulcerations. The main sign of syphilis is painless ulcerations that appear several weeks after exposure through sexual intercourse. Therapeutic intervention for syphilis consists of treatment with penicillin.

EMERGENCIES IN DIALYSIS PATIENTS

Dialysis patients will often come to the emergency department with a variety of complaints. Some of the more common areas follow.

Shunt clots

There are two common types of shunts used for hemodialysis: the Scribner shunt, which is external, and the Cimino-Brescia fistula, which is an internal arteriovenous fistula. If a shunt is clotted, therapeutic intervention depends on the type of shunt. If a

Scribner shunt is clotted it may be declotted in the emergency department. If a Cimino-Brescia fistula is clotted, surgical intervention is usually indicated.

Shunt infections

If a Scribner shunt is infected (usually with staphylococci), the site should be cultured. Therapeutic intervention is to administer antibiotics. If a Cimino-Brescia fistula is infected, there will usually be signs of systemic infection. Therapeutic intervention is administration of antibiotics and evaluation of blood cultures for more specific therapy.

Cardiovascular problems

Dialysis patients may develop dysrhythmias, hypotension, hypertension, pericardial disease, and cardiac arrest. For the most part, these emergencies are treated as they would be in any other patient. Dysrhythmias usually occur as a result of hyperkalemia. In the typical scenario, the patient will begin to develop dysrhythmias just before a dialysis treatment. This is usually because hyperkalemia has occurred, possibly from an overindulgence of eating. The patient may even develop cardiac arrest because of an intolerably high potassium level. If a dialysis arrest does occur, chances are that it is either caused by hypovolemia, for which fluid replacement is the therapeutic intervention of choice, or hyperkalemia, for which the administration of calcium chloride in large doses and other advanced life support measures are indicated.

SUGGESTED READINGS

Allen, T.D.: Disorders of the male external genitalia. In Kelalis, P.P., and King, L.R., editors: Clinical pediatric urology, Philadelphia, 1976, W.B. Saunders Co.

Banowsky, L.H., Wolfel, D.A., and Lackner, L.H.: Considerations in diagnosis and management of renal trauma, J. Trauma 10:587, 1970.

Bright, T.C., III, and Peters, P.C.: Injuries to the bladder and urethra. In Campbell, M.F., and Harrison, J.H., editors: Urology, ed. 4, Philadelphia, 1978, W.B. Saunders Co.

Bright, T.C., III, and Peters, P.C.: Injuries of the external genitalia. In Campbell, M.F., and Harrison, J.H., editors: Urology, ed. 4, Philadelphia, 1978, W.B. Saunders Co.

Brosman, S.A., and Fay, R.: Diagnosis and management of bladder trauma, J. Trauma 13:687, 1973.

Culp, D.A.: Genital injuries: etiology and initial management, Urol. Clin. North Am. 4:143, 1977.

Holcroft, J.W., et al.: Renal trauma and retroperitoneal hematomas—indications for exploration, J. Trauma 15:1045, 1975.

McAllister, C.J.: Emergencies in dialysis patients, J.A.C.E.P. 7:96, 1978.

Montie, J.: Bladder injuries, Urol. Clin. North Am. 4:59, 1977.

Morehouse, D.D., and McKinnon, J.K.: Posterior urethral injury: etiology, diagnosis, and initial management, Urol. Clin. North Am. 4:69, 1977.

Persky, L.: Urethral injuries, Resident Staff 100:1s, 1975.

Peters, P.C., and Bright, T.C., III: Blunt renal injuries, Urol. Clin. North Am. 4:17, 1977.

Peterson, W.E., and Kirakole, L.U.: Renal trauma: when to operate, Urology 3:537, 1977.

Pontes, J.I.: Urologic injuries, Surg. Clin. North Am. 57:77, 1974.

Pokorny, M.: Urologic injuries associated with pelvic trauma, Urology 121:455, 1979.

Smith, D.R.: Urinary obstruction and stasis. In Smith, D.R., editor: General urology, ed. 8, Los Altos, Calif., 1972, Lange Medical Publications.

Stutzman, R.E.: Ballistics and the management of ureteral injuries from high velocity missiles, J. Urol. 118:947, 1977.

Turner-Warwick, R.: A personal view of the immediate management of pelvis fracture urethral injuries, Urol. Clin. North Am. 4:81, 1977.

Whitaker, R.H.: Benign disorders of the testicle. In Blandy, J., editor: Urology, London, 1976, Blackwell Scientific Publications.

CHAPTER 14 Infectious diseases

Infection is the invasion and multiplication of an agent that causes a response in a host. An infectious disease is caused by the growth of a pathogenic agent. Colonization is the multiplication of an agent without invasion or host reaction. *Contagious* means that the disease can be spread from person to person. A reservoir is the place in which the infectious agent dwells. The mode of transmission is the means by which the infectious agent gains entrance to the new host. The patient must be susceptible to be a host. Many patients come to the emergency department with infectious diseases. Often, therapeutic interventions must be initiated according to pertinent signs and symptoms without the benefit of confirming laboratory tests.

BACTEREMIA (GRAM-NEGATIVE)

Patients often come to the emergency department with hypotensive shock, acute renal failure, lactic acidosis, or disseminated intravascular coagulation caused by gram-negative bacteremia. The most common causative organisms are *Bacteroides, Pseudomonas, Escherichia coli, Klebsiella, Haemophilus, Neisseria, Proteus,* or *Enterobacter.* All of these organisms emit an endotoxin and cause decreased blood-clotting times, fibrinolysis, and a variety of other syndromes. One of the complications is decreased blood flow to the kidneys, liver, lungs, and skin. As perfusion decreases, the brain and heart may be affected. As blood flow decreases, cardiac output decreases. As a result of tissue anoxia, disseminated intravascular coagulation may occur. Lactic acid continues to build up and causes a severe metabolic acidosis. These along with a cascading series of other events eventually produce a shock state in which systolic blood pressure is less than 80 mm Hg. This causes a decrease in renal perfusion and an overall decrease in circulating blood volume. Pulmonary edema will also occur from the passage of fluids and erythrocytes into the lungs.

The severity of bacteremia depends on the previous condition of the patient. The patient may have had an underlying disorder that precipitated the bacteremia, such as a gynecologic infection, a respiratory tract infection, a urinary tract infection, or a burn injury, or his condition may have been compromised by agents such as immunosuppressants or antibiotics. Morbidity and mortality depend on the patient's underlying condition.

SIGNS AND SYMPTOMS

Fever	Shortness of breath
Chills	Tachypnea

Weakness
Syncope
Extremes of underlying condition
Decreased blood pressure

Petechiae
Cool, clammy, moist skin
Cyanosis

THERAPEUTIC INTERVENTION

Prevention (aseptic technique)
Antimicrobial agents
Antibiotics
Oxygen
Decreasing the source of infection
Volume replacement

MAST application
Consider steroids
Consider naloxone (Narcan)
Consider dopamine (Intropin)
Incision and drainage if there is abscess

CELLULITIS (ANAEROBIC)

In cellulitis, connective tisue is infiltrated locally with gas. This may result from an infected injury. The incubation period is generally 3 to 4 days. The care giver must be careful not to confuse cellulitis with gas gangrene.

SIGNS AND SYMPTOMS

Dirty wound
Erythematous area
Foul-smelling exudate
Crepitus

Separation of muscle groups
Minimal pain
Patient appears healthy otherwise

THERAPEUTIC INTERVENTION

Fasciotomy if there is vascular compromise
Incision and drainage
Antibiotics
Consider hyperbaric oxygen therapy

CHANCROIDS

Chancroids are caused by the gram-negative coccobacillus *Haemophilus ducreyi*. They are often seen in conjunction with syphilis and genital herpes. The major complication is reoccurring fistulae in the groin area.

SIGNS AND SYMPTOMS

Females are asymptomatic
One or more nongeometric soft ulcers
Pale gray–colored exudate
Tender unilateral inguinal adenopathy

THERAPEUTIC INTERVENTION

Sulfisoxazole *or*
Tetracycline *or*

Kanamycin *or*
Streptomycin
Possible aspiration of glands

CONDYLOMA ACUMINATA (GENITAL WARTS)

Condyloma acuminatum is a papilloma caused by a papillomavirus. Condyloma acuminata are most common in those aged 15 to 24 years. Occasionally, but rarely, these warts change to malignant tumors.

Condyloma acuminata are papillary or sessile pink growths. They develop around the anus, anal canal, perineal area, glans penis, urethra, vulva, vagina, or cervix.

THERAPEUTIC INTERVENTION

Tincture of benzoin mixed with 10% to 25% podophyllin
Cryotherapy
Curettage

DIPHTHERIA

Diphtheria is caused by the endotoxin *Corynebacterium diphtheriae*. The usual sites of entry are the oropharynx, the nasopharynx, or skin lesions. Significant edema forms and may block the airway. There may also be neurologic and cardiovascular involvement.

SIGNS AND SYMPTOMS

If immunized:
    Low-grade fever and mild sore throat
If not immunized:

Fever	Respiratory stridor
Severe sore throat	Respiratory embarrassment
Cervical edema	Cervical adenopathy
Nonproductive cough	Gray-black diphtheritic membrane

THERAPEUTIC INTERVENTION

ABCs	Consider tracheostomy
Antitoxin	Antibiotics

EPIGLOTTITIS (See also Chapter 26)

Epiglottitis is caused by a bacterial infection, usually *Haemophilus influenzae* type b. In this condition the epiglottis enlarges and causes airway obstruction. Epiglottitis may be a life-threatening condition. It most commonly appears in children aged 2 to 7 years, but it is being seen more and more frequently in adults.

SIGNS AND SYMPTOMS

Sore throat	Muffled voice
Progressive dysphagia	Stridor
Drooling	Difficulty breathing
Low-grade temperature	Cyanosis

THERAPEUTIC INTERVENTION

	IV therapy
Oxygen	Antibiotics
Endotracheal intubation or cricothyrotomy	Consider racemic epinephrine

GAS GANGRENE

Gas gangrene is one form of soft tissue infection. It is caused by the organism *Clostridium perfringens.* It may be found after trauma, infection, or ischemia from causes in which there is an anaerobic environment. *Clostridium* infections are often accompanied by infections with other bacteria, such as *Streptococci* or *Staphylococci.* Many of these organisms produce gases that are secreted into soft tissues. This condition is known as gas gangrene or clostridial myonecrosis, and it is the most lethal of the clostridial infections. Gas gangrene may develop within hours of the bacterial invasion.

SIGNS AND SYMPTOMS

Swelling
Local pain and pain when touched
Oozing serosanguineous material (initially brown or red and sweet smelling, then green or black)
Diaphoresis
Pallor
Low-grade fever
Delirium
Blebs
Inability of muscle to contract

THERAPEUTIC INTERVENTION

Antibiotics
Fasciotomy
Surgical intervention (debridement of necrotic tissue or amputation)
Consider hyperbaric oxygen therapy
Consider polyvalent antitoxin

GONORRHEA ("CLAP," "DRIP")

Gonorrhea is the most commonly seen of all the reportable infectious diseases. It is caused by the organism *Neisseria gonorrhoeae.* It can infect any area of the genitourinary or reproductive system and may also infect the eyes or limb joints. There are approximately 468 cases/100,000 population. The highest incidence is in the 15- to 24-year-old age group. Complications include meningitis, septicemia, endocarditis, epididymitis, pharyngitis, pelvic inflammatory disease, newborn conjunctivitis, sterility, polyarthralgias, skin lesions, and endocarditis.

SIGNS AND SYMPTOMS

Dysuria
Urethritis
Urinary frequency
Purulent discharge from the urethra (especially in females)
Vaginal discharge
Cystitis
Some patients are asymptomatic

Antibiotics
Probenecid
Treat sexual contacts also

GRANULOMA INGUINALE

Granuloma inguinale is caused by the gram-negative coccobacillus *Donovania granulomatis*. It is rarely seen in the United States today, but when it is, it is usually seen in males who live in the southern states. Complications include urethral strictures, engorged pelvic glands, and (rarely) elephantiasis.

The main sign of granuloma inguinale is very red lesions that are granulating and painless. Therapeutic intervention consists of treatment with antibiotics.

HEPATITIS B

Hepatitis B is an inflammatory liver condition caused by the hepatitis B virus, which invades via toxins, drugs, metabolic aberrations, hypersensitivity, or immune mechanisms.* Complications include cirrhosis and death.

SIGNS AND SYMPTOMS

Abdominal pain
Nausea and vomiting
Headache
Fever
Anorexia
Myalgias

Jaundice
Erythema
Urticaria
Arthralgias
Hepatomegaly
Hepatic tenderness

THERAPEUTIC INTERVENTION

Treat symptomatically
Take precautions with stool and needles

HERPES SIMPLEX TYPE 1 (ORAL HERPES, HERPES LABIALIS)

Oral herpes simplex is caused by herpesvirus type 1. Usually it will cause small fluid-filled blisters to form on the facial area, particularly around the mouth and nose.

SIGNS AND SYMPTOMS

Burning
Itching

Low-grade fever
Cervical lymphadenopathy

THERAPEUTIC INTERVENTION

Wash lesions with soap and water to avoid spreading
Consider antibiotics

---

*A vaccine called Heptavax is available from the Merck, Sharpe, and Dohme drug company. It is recommended for health care providers who are at high risk of contracting hepatitis B.

TABLE 14-1 Comparison of hepatitis type A and B

	Type A	Type B
Incubation period	15-45 days	30-100 days
Mode of contact	Fecal-oral transmission; possibly respiratory transmission, blood products and instruments, contaminated food and drinking water, and incompletely cooked mollusks (clams, oysters, etc.)	Physical contact with infected person, maternal-fetal blood mixing, sexual contact, accidents with contaminated articles (e.g., needles), commercial clotting concentrates, and blood transfusion
Incidence	Children and young adults, especially students	Infants and adults with conditions requiring transfusion or dialysis; tattooing or ear piercing; drug users; health care personnel
Communicability	High during prodromal stage but unlikely later, at actual time of diagnosis	3 months after symptom resolution and perhaps longer
Immunity	Lifelong after disease course	Unknown
Mortality	1/1,000	1/100
Prophylaxis	ISG (immune serum globulin): 0.05 ml/kg for nontourist travelers and handlers of nonhuman primates; 0.02 ml/kg for household contacts (usually not given to work-related, hospital, or school contacts). Whenever possible, ascertain if exposure was to antigen-positive or to antigen-negative hepatitis before ISG is administered.	HBIG (high-titer immune globulin preparation for hepatitis B): 1. After exposure to contaminated blood (HB_sAg) by needle or mucous membrane inoculation 2. To sexual partners of acute hepatitis B patient 3. To infants of mothers with type B hepatitis in third trimester of pregnancy or subsequent 2 months. 4. After oral contact, e.g. laboratory accidents such as pipetting accidents, splashing Since HBIG must be administered within 7 days of exposure, demonstrate absence of surface antibodies to hepatitis B antigen in serum of injured person before administering human hepatitis B immune globulin (because of its unusually high cost); Heptavax vaccine to personnel at high risk

HERPES SIMPLEX TYPE 2 (GENITAL HERPES)

Genital herpes simplex is caused by herpesvirus type 2. It is becoming increasingly common and maybe seen in any age group from the very young to the very old. It is especially common in those who are sexually active. Complications include infection of the neonate (if herpesvirus is present in the birth canal at the time of vaginal delivery), kernicterus, and encephalitis.

SIGNS AND SYMPTOMS

Tender vesicles on penile shaft
Vesicles on prepuce or glans penis
Vesicles on scrotum or perineum
Grayish-colored lesions
Vulvar, perineal, vaginal, or cervical lesions
Dyspareunia (painful intercourse)
Erythema
Pain

Lymphadenopathy
Fever
Lethargy
Dysuria
Headache
Recurrent infection
Anorexia

THERAPEUTIC INTERVENTION

At this time there are no known therapeutic interventions for herpes simplex, although many are in experimental stages.

HERPES ZOSTER (SHINGLES)

Herpes zoster is caused by the organism varicella-zoster virus.

SIGNS AND SYMPTOMS

Skin eruptions that follow a cranial or
   spinal nerve tract
Pain along the nerve tract

Fever
Headache
General malaise

THERAPEUTIC INTERVENTION

Topical antipruritics
Analgesics
Bed rest

HISTOPLASMOSIS

Histoplasmosis is caused by the fungal organism *Histoplasma capsulatum*, which is found in the excrement of birds and bats. This disease has an appearance much like that of pulmonary tuberculosis.

SIGNS AND SYMPTOMS

Fever
Nocturnal diaphoresis
Ulcerations on mucosal surfaces
Anorexia

Weight loss
Lymphadenopathy
Hepatomegaly

THERAPEUTIC INTERVENTION

Therapeutic intervention for histoplasmosis consists of treatment with Amphotericin B.

LUNG INFECTIONS

Lung infections and bacterial and nonbacterial pneumonia are reviewed in Chapter 6 as pulmonary emergencies.

LYMPHOGRANULOMA VENEREUM

Lymphogranuloma venereum is caused by the parasite *Chlamydia trachomatis*. It most often occurs in warm tropical regions. It is rarely seen in the United States.

SIGNS AND SYMPTOMS

Genital ulcer that is painless and not indurated
Regional lymphadenopathy

THERAPEUTIC INTERVENTION

Antibiotics
Possible aspiration of glands

MENINGITIS (BACTERIAL)

The causative bacterial organisms of meningitis are *Niesseria meningitiditis*, *Haemophilus influenzae*, and *Diplococcus pneumoniae*. Children under the age of 5 are extremely susceptible to meningitis. Mortality is 10% to 15%. Meningitis is often preceded by a bout of influenza or a urinary tract infection.

SIGNS AND SYMPTOMS

Fever
Lethargy
Headache
Projectile vomiting
Anorexia
Febrile seizures
Restlessness

Respiratory distress
Nuchal rigidity
Positive Kernig's sign
Positive Brudzinski's sign
Papilledema
Petechiae over anterior trunk

THERAPEUTIC INTERVENTION

ABCs
Antibiotics
Anticonvulsants
Antipyretics
Diagnostic lumbar puncture

INFECTIOUS MONONUCLEOSIS

Infectious mononucleosis ("mono") is a mildly contagious disease caused by the Epstein-Barre herpetovirus. It is transmitted by droplet cross-infection. It most often affects young people, but when it affects older people the symptoms are more severe. Once a person is infected, he is immune to further infection.

SIGNS AND SYMPTOMS

Fever
Sore throat

Lymphadenopathy (especially cervical)
Splenomegaly
Hepatomegaly

THERAPEUTIC INTERVENTION

Symptomatic
Rest
Fluids

Analgesics
Warm saline solution gargles

MYCOPLASMA INFECTION

Mycoplasmata are very small bacteria that can cause pneumonia, tracheobronchitis, pharyngitis, or myringitis. Mycoplasma pneumonia usually occurs in children and young adults. Complications include sinusitis, myocarditis, polyneuritis, and Stevens-Johnson syndrome.

SIGNS AND SYMPTOMS

Upper respiratory tract infection
Dry cough
Weakness
Fever

Decreased breath sounds
Inspiratory rales
Pulmonary infiltrates

THERAPEUTIC INTERVENTION

Antibiotics
Rest

Fluids
High-protein diet

NECROTIZING FASCIITIS

Necrotizing fasciitis is a severe infection of subcutaneous tissue and fasciae. This condition may be life threatening. The most common sites of infection are the anterior abdominal wall and the perineal area. *Streptococci* and *Staphylococci* are the most common causative organisms.

SIGNS AND SYMPTOMS

Fever
Hyperesthesia
Decreased blood pressure

Edema
Crepitus
Blebs

THERAPEUTIC INTERVENTION

Surgical intervention
Antibiotics

PAROTIDITIS (MUMPS)

Parotiditis is edema of the parotid glands caused by the virus Paramyxovirus. It usually affects children between 4 and 16 years old. When it occurs in adults it may be critical. It is a seasonal disease, with its highest incidence in late winter and early spring. Complications include orchiditis (usually unilateral with testicular atrophy), arthritis, oophoritis, myocarditis, pancreatitis, nephritis, and mumps meningitis.

SIGNS AND SYMPTOMS

Headache   Painful chewing
Earache   Sore throat
Anorexia   General malaise
Swelling of parotid glands   Fever

THERAPEUTIC INTERVENTION

Airway management   Fluids
Analgesics   Consider IV fluid replacement
Antipyretics   Cool sponging

PEDICULOSIS PUBIS ("CRABS")

Pediculosis pubis is the infestation of the *Pthirus pubis* louse, an insect that is initially gray in color and later turns red or brown when it has filled with blood. Complications are rare but include eczema, impetigo, or furunculosis. Pediculosis pubis can occur in any age group. It is contracted during sexual intercourse or by direct contact with clothing or bedding that is infested with the louse.

SIGNS AND SYMPTOMS

Visualization of lice in pubic, anal, or abdominal hair
Itching
Erythema

THERAPEUTIC INTERVENTION

Therapeutic intervention for pediculosis pubis consists of treatment with 1% lindane and 25% benzyl benzoate lotion (Kwell)

PERTUSSIS (WHOOPING COUGH)

Pertussis is caused by the gram-negative coccobacillus *Bordetella pertussis*. Infants and children up to 4 years old who have not been immunized are most commonly affected. Complications include atelectasis, bronchiectasis, otitis media, seizures, intracranial hemorrhage, epistaxis, dehydration, asphyxia, and hernia.

SIGNS AND SYMPTOMS

Paroxysmal cough with loud end-cough whooping noise
Sneezing
Possible fever
Irritability

Weakness
Vomiting
Anorexia
Large amounts of viscous sputum
Vomiting

THERAPEUTIC INTERVENTION

Oxygen
Suction
Rest
IVs

Adequate diet
Antibiotics
Possible endotracheal intubation

PLAGUE

Plague is transmitted to humans by a bite from a flea that has been contaminated by a rat infested with the bacillus *Yersinia pestis*. There are several types of plague, some of which are described here.

Bubonic plague

Bubonic plague is also known as black death.

SIGNS AND SYMPTOMS

Lymphadenopathy
Fever greater than 106° F (41.1° C)
Tachycardia
Hypotension

Hemorrhage into skin
Delirium
Bubos

THERAPEUTIC INTERVENTION

Antibiotics
Supportive care
Prevention by vaccination

PNEUMONIC PLAGUE

Pneumonic plague has a high mortality. Primary pneumonic plague is defined as bubonic plague with lung involvement. Secondary pneumonic plague is contracted through inhalation of droplets from an infected person.

SEPTICEMIC PLAGUE

Septicemic plague is the development of septicemia with meningitis from bubonic plague. It occurs before bubo formation.

POLIOMYELITIS

Poliomyelitis is caused by the virus poliovirus hominis. It affects more males than females. The most severe complications are respiratory and muscular paralysis.

SIGNS AND SYMPTOMS

Nonparalytic:	Paralytic:
Fever	Fever
Malaise	Malaise
Headache	Headache
Nausea and vomiting	Generalized pain, weakness, and muscle spasms
Abdominal pain	Paralysis of limbs
Neck pain	Paralysis of muscles

THERAPEUTIC INTERVENTION

ABCs	Range of motion exercises
Respiratory support	Prevention by immunization
Rest	

RHEUMATIC FEVER

Rheumatic fever is infestation of the upper respiratory tract with the organism β-hemolytic streptococcus. Rheumatic fever most commonly occurs in young children. It affects the skin, joints, heart, and brain.

SIGNS AND SYMPTOMS

History of sore throat or scarlet fever within 5 weeks
Fever
Abdominal pain
Epistaxis
Nausea and vomiting
Polyarthritis
Carditis (chest pain, palpitations, heart failure)
Syndenham's chorea (akwardness)
Erythema marginatum
Anemia
Leukocytosis

THERAPEUTIC INTERVENTION

Rest	Analgesics
Antibiotics	Fluids

ROCKY MOUNTAIN SPOTTED FEVER

Rocky Mountain Spotted Fever is a tick-borne disease for which the causative agent is *Rickettsia rickettsii*. Complications include renal failure and shock.

SIGNS AND SYMPTOMS

Chills
Fever

Severe headache
Myalgias
Hemorrhagic lesions
Constipation
Abdominal distention
Decreased level of consciousness
Erythema (initially on wrists and ankles, then on extremities, trunk, face, palms, and
    soles of feet)

THERAPEUTIC INTERVENTION

Remove the tick
Antibiotics

RUBELLA (MEASLES, GERMAN MEASLES)

Rubella is a viral illness that is contracted by droplet infection. Once a patient has contracted rubella, he is immunized for life. Rubella is dangerous in the first trimester of pregnancy, because it may cause fetal injuries that lead to deafness, mental retardation, cataracts, and heart defects.

SIGNS AND SYMPTOMS

Fever   Lymphadenopathy
Upper respiratory infection   Arthralgias
Red maculopapular rash

THERAPEUTIC INTERVENTION

Antipyretics
Fluids
Cool compresses

SALPINGITIS AND OOPHORITIS

Salpingitis and oophoritis are bacterial infections of the fallopian tubes and ovaries respectively. Usually these infections are recurrent, and they eventually cause scarring and distortion of the tubes. As the scarring becomes severe and adhesions form, the tubes become filled with exudate and eventually, abscesses form. If rupture occurs, peritonitis will result.

SIGNS AND SYMPTOMS

Fever
Tachycardia
General malaise
Lower-quadrant abdominal pain (bilateral)
Palpated abdominal adnexal masses

THERAPEUTIC INTERVENTION

Cultures
Antibiotics
Possible surgical intervention

SCABIES

Scabies is caused by the mite *Scarcoptes scabiei* when it burrows into the skin in the areas of the ankles, elbows, wrists, fingers, and penis. The mite is transmitted via close body contact, particularly sexual intercourse, and via infested clothing and bedding. Complications include impetigo and pustular eczema.

SIGNS AND SYMPTOMS

Burrows 1 to 10 ml in length
Small red papule at end of burrow
Itching

THERAPEUTIC INTERVENTION

Therapeutic intervention for scabies consists of treatment with 25% benzyl benzoate emulsion and lindane with crotamiton.

SCARLET FEVER (SCARLATINA)

Scarlet fever is caused by group A hemolytic streptococcus.

SIGNS AND SYMPTOMS

Sore throat   Bright red, diffuse rash
Fever   Prostration
Cervical lymphadenopathy

THERAPEUTIC INTERVENTION

Antipyretics   Fluids
Rest   Antibiotics

SYPHILIS

Syphilis is caused by the spirochete *Treponema pallidum*. There are only 10 cases/100,000 population each year. The peak age group in which syphilis is found is 20 to 29 years. Complications include tertiary syphilis, infection of the newborn, and complications of each of these. Syphilis is contracted from an infected partner at intercourse.

SIGNS AND SYMPTOMS

Primary:
    Chancre sore (painless, single or multiple) on genitalia (also may appear in areas other than genitalia)
    Lymphadenopathy

Secondary:
    Lesions of skin and mucous
      membranes

Alopecia
Lymphadenopathy

THERAPEUTIC INTERVENTION

Antibiotics

Treat sexual partner(s) as well

TETANUS (See Chapter 15)

Tetanus is caused by the exotoxin *Clostridium tetani*, an anaerobic bacillus that is found in abundance in soil, human and animal excrement, and household dust. It forms hardy spores that can resist extremes of temperature and strong antiseptic solutions. Under proper conditions, the spores will germinate and infect the injured soft-tissue areas. The bacillus excretes a neurotoxin that is absorbed into the circulation and affects the central nervous system. The incubation period may vary from 3 days to several months, with 3 to 10 days after the invasion of the organism being most common. Cases of tetanus are rare in the United States because of the high immunization rate, but mortality is high.

SIGNS AND SYMPTOMS

History of penetrating injury or burn
General malaise
Muscle rigidity
Low-grade fever
Headache
Trismus (lockjaw)
Inability to swallow

Distortion of facial muscles
Sardonic grin (risus sardonicus)
Opisthotonos
Seizures
Respiratory arrest
Clostridium tetani cultured from wound

THERAPEUTIC INTERVENTION

ABCs
Much supportive care
Dark room with low stimulation
Consider tracheostomy
Diazepam (Valium)
Consider neuromuscular blocking agents
Careful fluid and electrolyte balance
Antibiotics
Tetanus immune globulin (preferably human) *or*
Horse serum antitoxin
Consider sodium nitroprusside for severe hypertension
Consider propranolol for tachydysrhythmias

TRICHOMONIASIS

Trichomoniasis is caused by the protozoan organism *Trichomonas vaginalis*. It is estimated that 5% of all women and 75% of women who practice prostitution have the infection. Trichomoniasis is more prevalent among women than men.

SIGNS AND SYMPTOMS

May be asymptomatic
Erythema of external genitalia
Edema of external genitalia

Vaginal discharge (greenish gray and frothy)
Possible urethritis in males

THERAPEUTIC INTERVENTION

Metronidazole
No alcohol consumption while taking medication
Treatment of sex partners

TUBERCULOSIS

Tuberculosis is caused by the bacteria *Mycobacterium tuberculosis,* which typically locates itself in the lungs and spreads systemically. It is contracted by inhalation of tuberculosis-infested droplets. The infection has the appearance of a form of bacterial pneumonia. The organism may pass into the lymphatic system and the vascular system and then infect the entire body. Common sites for tuberculosis infection besides the lungs are the spine and other bony areas, the meninges, the kidneys, the liver, and the spleen.

SIGNS AND SYMPTOMS

Fever of undetermined origin
Pleuritic chest pain
Tachypnea
Productive cough
Abdominal pain
Nuchal rigidity
Delirium
Positive chest x-ray examination
Positive sputum test
Positive biopsy
Positive tuberculin skin test
Meningeal signs
Other signs and symptoms specific to areas of involvement

THERAPEUTIC INTERVENTION

Antituberculin medications (isoniazid and rifampin)
Antibiotics
Oxygen
Consider steroids

TYPHOID FEVER

Typhoid fever is an infection caused by the bacterium *Salmonella typhi,* which can be found in contaminated food, water, or milk. Typhoid fever has a high mortality. Complications include thrombophlebitis and intestinal hemorrhage.

SIGNS AND SYMPTOMS

Headache   Maculopapular rash on abdomen
Cough   Diarrhea
High fever   Splenomegaly

THERAPEUTIC INTERVENTION

Antibiotics
Antipyretics
Cool sponging
Prevention by vaccination

NONSPECIFIC URETHRITIS

Nonspecific urethritis may be caused by the organisms *Chlamydia trachomatis, Ureaplasma urealyticum, Trichomonas vaginalis, Candida albicans,* herpesvirus, or coliform bacteria. The most common age group affected is from 15 to 24 years. Complications include cervicitis, salpingitis, prostatitis, epididymitis, proctitis, Reiter's syndrome, and ophthalmia neonatorum.

SIGNS AND SYMPTOMS

Urethral discharge
Dysuria
Some males may be asymptomatic

THERAPEUTIC INTERVENTION

Therapeutic intervention for nonspecific urethritis includes treatment with antibiotics.

VAGINITIS (FROM *HAEMOPHILUS VAGINALIS*)

Vaginitis may be caused by the gram-negative organism *Haemophilus vaginalis.* This particular organism is found in up to 96% of women with vaginitis. There are no known complications from this infection.

SIGNS AND SYMPTOMS

May be asymptomatic
Frothy, thin, grayish white vaginal discharge
Vulvar irritation

THERAPEUTIC INTERVENTION

Therapeutic intervention for vaginitis from *Haemophilus vaginalis* consists of treatment with antibiotics.

VARICELLA (CHICKENPOX)

Varicella is caused by the virus varicella zoster. The incidence is highest in young children.

SIGNS AND SYMPTOMS

Purulent vesicular skin eruptions, initially on back and chest, then on head and limbs

Urticaria	Headache
Fever	Anorexia
Lymphadenopathy	General malaise

THERAPEUTIC INTERVENTION

Rest	Immunization:
Antipyretics	Immune serum globulin (ISG)
Topical antipruritics	Zoster immune globulin (ZIG)
Antihistamines	Zoster immune plasma (ZIP)
Topical antibiotic ointment or vesicles	

VARIOLA (SMALLPOX)

Variola is an extremely contagious viral infection caused by the poxvirus variola minor (alastrim) or variola major. It is carried only by humans.

SIGNS AND SYMPTOMS

Fever	Urticaria
Pustular vesicular rash	General malaise

THERAPEUTIC INTERVENTION

Rest
Analgesics
Antipyretics

VULVOVAGINITIS CANDIDIASIS

Vulvovaginitis candidiasis is caused by the gram-positive fungus *Candida albicans*. This organism can be found in approximately 20% of nonpregnant women. There are no known complications from candidiasis infections.

SIGNS AND SYMPTOMS

May be asymptomatic
Erythema of vulva
Edema of vulva
Vaginal discharge (normally whitish and thick, with the appearance of cottage cheese, but may be thin and watery)
Groin lesions
Balanitis found in male sexual partners
Lesions on penis

THERAPEUTIC INTERVENTION

Nystatin vaginal suppositories *or* miconazole vaginal cream

TABLE 14-2 Emergency department isolation techniques*

Type of isolation	Common diseases	Gown	Gloves	Mask	Isolation room	Linen precautions	Eating utensils
Strict	Varicella Herpes zoster	A	A	A	A	A	A
Modified strict	Group A streptococci Staphylococci Streptococcal pneumonia	B	B	A	A	A	A
Respiratory	Tuberculosis Rubella Mumps Pertussis Meningococcemia Meningococcal meningitis	C	C	A	A	C	C
Protective	Leukemia Lymphoma Patient taking immuno- suppressives	B	B	C	A	C	C
Enteric	Viral hepatitis Salmonella Shigella Gastroenteritis	B	B	B	C	A	A
Wound and skin†	Any draining wounds Skin infections Draining ulcers Abscesses	B	B	B	A	A	C

*A = always, B = only with direct contact with patient's secretions, excretions, urine, feces, or blood, C = optional.
†Also, double-bag any waste materials or items that come into contact with drainage.

TABLE 14-3 Incubation periods*

Disease	Duration of incubation
Asiatic cholera	24 hr. to 5 days
Anthrax	2 to 4 days; may be as long as 7 days
Bacillary dysentery (Shigellosis)	1 to 7 days; average of 4 days
Blastomycosis	Unknown
Botulism (food poisoning)	Less than 24 hr.; several days after ingestion of food containing the toxin
Brucellosis (undulant fever)	5 to 30 days
Chickenpox (varicella)	14 to 16 days
Coccidioidomycosis (valley fever)	7 to 21 days
Common cold	1 to 3 days
Diarrhea, viral	3 to 5 days
Diphtheria	2 to 6 days; may be longer
Encephalitis	5 to 15 days; range of 4 to 21 days; varies as to the type
Food infection with *Salmonella*	7 to 72 hr.
Hansen's disease (leprosy, hansenosis)	Short as 5½ mo. or as long as 15 yr.; average about 5 yr.
Hepatitis	
Infectious (epidemic—virus A, catarrhal jaundice)	15 to 50 days
Serum (virus B)	2 to 6 mo.
Herpes simplex (cold sore, fever blister)	2 to 12 days; average of 4 days
Herpes zoster (shingles)	4 to 24 days; average of 4 days
Histoplasmosis (Darling's disease)	5 to 18 days; average of 10 days
Infectious mononucleosis (glandular fever)	Children, less than 14 days; adults, 33 to 49 days; average of 4 to 14 days
Influenza, epidemic	24 to 72 hr.
Malaria	Varies with particular species; 12 to 14 days or as long as 30 days; some strains from 8 to 10 mo.
Measles (rubella, red measles)	9 to 14 days; about 10 days from exposure to onset of fever, and about 14 days to appearance of rash
Meningitis, bacterial	2 to 7 days
Mumps (epidemic parotiditis)	14 to 28 days
Paratyphoid fever	1 to 10 days
Pertussis (whooping cough)	5 to 21 days
Plague *(Pasturella pestis)*	
Bubonic	2 to 6 days
Pneumonic	2 to 4 days

*From McInnes, M.E.: Essentials of communicable disease, ed. 2, St. Louis, 1975, The C.V. Mosby Co.

TABLE 14-3 Incubation periods—cont'd

Disease	Duration of incubation
Pneumococcal pneumonia (bacterial)	1 to 3 days
Poliomyelitis (infantile paralysis)	7 to 14 days
Psittacosis (ornithosis, parrot fever)	4 to 15 days but may vary from 5 to 28 days; the commonest interval after exposure is 10 days
Rabies (hydrophobia)	Dogs, 3 to 8 weeks; man, 10 days to 2 yr. with an average of 2 to 6 weeks
Rocky Mountain spotted fever (tick fever)	2 to 12 days; may be as long as 14 days; average of 7 days
Rubella (German measles)	14 to 21 days; usually 18 days after exposure
Scarlet fever (scarlatina) and septic sore throat	24 hr. to 10 days but first clinical signs generally appear between 2 to 5 days
Smallpox (variola)	7 to 16 days; average of 12 days
Tetanus	3 to 21 days; average of 10 days
Tularemia (rabbit fever)	1 to 10 days; average of 3 days
Typhoid fever	10 to 14 days; may be as short as 7 days or as long as 21 days
Typhus fever	10 to 14 days; variation depending on the size of the dose of the infecting organism
Venereal diseases: syphilis, gonorrhea	10 to 90 days; average of 3 to 4 weeks, short as 2 to 10 days or as long as 21 days; average of 3 to 5 days
Viral pneumonia (atypical pneumonia)	Varies widely, depending on specific virus; may be from a few days to a week or longer
Yellow fever	3 to 6 days

Classification of commonly used antibiotics

Penicillin

Penicillin G
Penicillin G benzathine
Penicillin G procaine
Penicillin V potassium (Pen-Vee K)

Broad-spectrum antibiotics

Amoxacillin
Ampicillin
Carbenicillin (Geopen)

Synthetic antibiotics

Cloxacillin
Dicloxacillin
Methicillin
Nafcillin (Unipen)
Oxacillin (Prostaphlin)

Cephalosporins

Cefazolin (Kefzol, Ancef)
Cephalexin (Keflex)
Cephaloridine
Cephalothin (Keflin)

Macrolides

Clindamycin (Cleocin)
Erythromycin (Ilosone, Erythrocin)
Lincomycin

Aminoglycosides

Amikacin
Gentamicin (Garamycin)
Kanamycin (Kantrex)
Polymixin B (Aerosporin)
Polymixin E (Colistin)
Streptomycin
Tobramycin

Others

Chloramphenicol (Chloromycetin)
Methenamine (Mandelamine)
Naldixic Acid (NegGram)
Nitrofuratoin (Macrodantin, Furadantin)
Sulfonamides
Tetracycline
Vancomycin

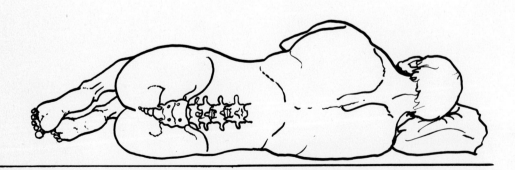

FIG. 14-1 Position of patient for lumbar puncture.

LUMBAR PUNCTURE (SPINAL TAP)

A lumbar puncture is performed to:
Measure cerebrospinal fluid pressures
Remove cerebrospinal fluid:
    To decrease pressure
    For laboratory analysis:
        To detect meningitis
        To detect bleeding
    A lumbar puncture should NOT be done if there is potential for intracranial bleeding, which may lead to brainstem herniation.

PROCEDURE

Explain the procedure to the patient if possible.
Obtain consent for the procedure.
Obtain baseline vital signs.
Empty the patient's bladder.
Position the patient on his side with his neck flexed and his knees drawn up to his
    abdomen.
Prepare the tap site with antiseptic solution.
Drape the site with sterile towels.
Introduce 1% lidocaine into the space between L4 and L5.
Introduce a 20- or 22-gauge spinal needle with a stylet into the subarachnoid space.
Remove the stylet after piercing the dura mater—spinal fluid will drip out at this point.
Rotate the needle to direct the bevel rostrally (to prevent obstruction).
Attach a three-way stopcock with manometer.
Have the patient breathe deeply and straighten his legs and neck.
Open the stopcock and record an opening pressure measurement (lowest level during
    fluctuations).

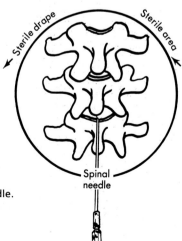

FIG. 14-2 Introduction of spinal needle.

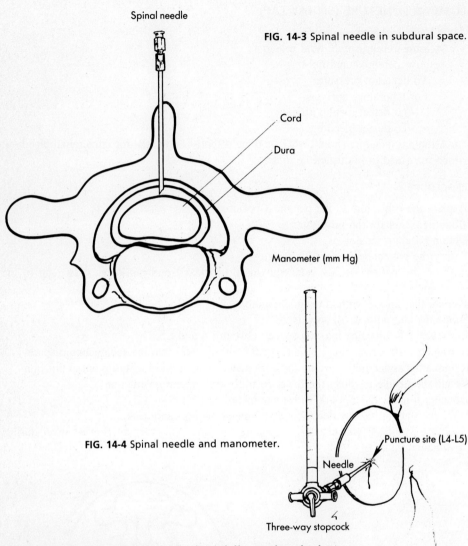

Spinal needle

FIG. 14-3 Spinal needle in subdural space.

Cord

Dura

Manometer (mm Hg)

FIG. 14-4 Spinal needle and manometer.

Puncture site (L4-L5)

Needle

Three-way stopcock

Collect cerebrospinal fluid samples in serially numbered tubes.

Remove the needle and place a sterile dressing over puncture site.

Keep the patient on bed rest for at least 1 hour after the procedure.

SUGGESTED READINGS

Kravitz, T., and Warner, C.G., editors: Emergency Medicine, Rockville, Md., 1983, Aspen Systems Corp.

Sanford, J.P.: Guide to antimicrobial therapy, New York, 1981, Bristol Laboratories. Distributed courtesy of Bristol Laboratories or from J.P. Sanford, P.O. Box 34456, West Bethesda, MD 20034.

U.S. Department of Health and Human Services, Public Health Services, Centers for Disease Control, Bureau of State Services: Sexually transmitted diseases, pub. no. 00-3380, Atlanta, Ga.

Budassi, S.A., and Barber, J.M.: Emergency Nursing: principles and practice, St. Louis, 1981, The C.V. Mosby Co.

TRAUMA EMERGENCIES

CHAPTER 15 Wound management and tetanus

There are two basic principles in the management of wounds:

To decrease the likelihood of infection

To promote optimal wound healing

There are several other important factors to consider in wound management:

What caused the injury?

How did the injury happen?

What were the circumstances surrounding the injury?

On what part of the body is the wound?

In what condition is the tissue surrounding the wound?

Can the edges of the wound be approximated?

What is the patient's age?

What is the patient's occupation?

What is the patient's physical condition?

Is the patient taking any medications or does he have any other pertinent medical history?

What is the condition of the patient's skin?

When did the injury occur?

Was there any care given to the wound before arrival in the emergency department?

Is there movement and sensation distal to the wound?

Is vascular status intact distal to the wound?

THE PROCESS OF WOUND HEALING

When an injury occurs there is immediate vasoconstriction. This causes sludging of blood and then vasodilation, which results in redness and swelling in the subepithelial layer of the skin. Epithelial cells begin to migrate 24 hours after the injury, and fibrin begins to form. This period of wound healing is known as the proliferative phase. During the subsequent days and over the next year, collagen is continually laid down at the areas around the wound that sustain the greatest amount of stress. The tensile strength of a wound will be at its weakest 3 days after the initial injury.

GENERAL PRINCIPLES OF WOUND MANAGEMENT

ABCs

Control bleeding

Treat shock
Check the wound for pain and pallor
Check the area distal to the wound to assess neurovascular status
Splint any possible fractures or dislocations
Determine the mechanism of injury
Notify the police if foul play is suspected
If the wound is from a contaminated object, culture the wound
If the wound is to be prepared for a procedure, anesthetize it first
Scrub the wound with isotonic solution (normal saline)
Scrub the wound for at least 5 minutes (longer for dirty wounds)
Avoid soaking, except for puncture wounds; soak puncture wounds for 10 to 15 minutes
Irrigate the wound
Cleanse both the wound and the surrounding tissue
Remove all foreign materials
If there is much hair around the wound, shave the area proximal to the wound
Never shave eyebrows (they may not grow back)
Debride all devitalized tissue
Suture the wound or pack with iodoform gauze
Dress the wound with antibiotic ointment
Cover the wound with nonadherent dressing

INFECTION

Most wounds contain bacteria. As a general rule, any wound that has remained open for 8 to 12 hours has collected too many bacteria to allow for suturing and proper healing. It is therefore wise to delay closure until the wound can be properly prepared to decrease the bacteria count. The exception to this is wounds to the face, in which there is a large amount of vascularity and in which the incidence of infection is low.

When wound infection does occur it usually does so 2 to 3 days after the incident. Infection appears as a swollen area that is erythematous and painful with red streaks and possibly exudate. The patient's body may respond to this infection by temperature elevation, lymphedema, and lymphangitis.

GENERAL THERAPEUTIC INTERVENTION

Culture the wound to determine the causative organism
Cleanse the wound with saline and antiseptic solution
Soak the wound three times a day
Antibiotics
Remove some sutures (if present) to allow for wound drainage
Close observation through frequent follow-up visits

TYPES OF WOUNDS

There are six basic types of wounds: abrasion, abscess, avulsion, contusion, laceration, and puncture

Abrasion

An abrasion is a wound caused by the rubbing of skin against a hard surface. The friction removes the epithelial layer of the skin, exposing the dermal or epidermal layer. Abrasion is physiologically the same as a second-degree burn.

THERAPEUTIC INTERVENTION

Cleanse the wound by scrubbing and irrigating
Remove any foreign bodies
Apply topical antibiotic ointment
Apply a nonadherent dressing
Change the dressing once each day until formation of an eschar
Instruct the patient to avoid direct sunlight to the area for at least
    6 months

Abscess

An abscess is a localized collection of pus. The care giver should not wait for the abscess to ''come to a head.''

THERAPEUTIC INTERVENTION

Prepare the area
Anesthetize the area
Drain the abscess using a needle and syringe, with the involved part in a dependent
    position
Remove an elliptical area of tissue
Cleanse the wound
Pack the wound loosely to allow for drainage
Cover the wound with a loose dressing
Have the patient return for follow-up care every 2 days until wound is almost completely
    healed
If the patient is febrile, administer antibiotics

Avulsion

An avulsion is a full-thickness skin loss.

THERAPEUTIC INTERVENTION

Cleanse the wound by scrubbing
Irrigate the wound
Debride any devitalized tissue
Repair injured muscles or tendons
Apply a split-thickness graft or flap if necessary
Apply a bulky dressing

Contusion

A contusion is an extravasation of blood into the tissues that usually results from blunt trauma.

THERAPEUTIC INTERVENTION

Apply cold packs
Administer analgesia if necessary
No dressing is usually necessary

Laceration

A laceration is an open wound or cut that may be minor or major. It extends at least into the deep epithelium and varies considerably in length and depth.

THERAPEUTIC INTERVENTION

Control bleeding
Evaluate neurovascular status distal to the wound
Anesthetize the wound
Cleanse the wound by scrubbing and irrigation
Remove any foreign bodies
Excise any necrotic tissue
Approximate the wound edges
Close the wound using sutures or tape strips
Apply antibiotic ointment
Apply a nonadherent dressing
    If a laceration is deep and there is question of damage to underlying structures, the wound should be explored in either the emergency department or the operating suite.

Puncture and penetrating trauma

A puncture wound results from a penetration of tissue by a sharp object. There may be much damage to underlying structures though the wound seems benign. Gross contamination is also a possibility.

THERAPEUTIC INTERVENTION

Therapeutic intervention for puncture wounds depends on the depth of penetration, the amount of underlying damage, and the level of contamination. In general:
Soak the wound twice a day for 2 to 4 days
If the wound is known to be contaminated, soak the wound, anesthetize it, and inspect it
If the foreign body is still in place and it is small enough that removal will not cause further damage, remove it
If there is necrotic tissue, debride it, place a drain, and dress the area
If the foreign body is deep enough that removal may cause further damage, decide whether the object should be removed in surgery or left in place
    In cases of penetrating trauma in which the penetrating object is still in place, *do not remove the object.* The only exception to this rule is if the patient is in shock and the object must be removed to enable MAST placement. If the penetrating object is cumbersome it may be shortened if possible to allow for transport of the victim. Be sure that the penetrating object is secured to the victim so that there is no chance of dislodging it.

GENERAL PRINCIPLES CONCERNING GUNSHOT WOUNDS

The amount of trauma in a gunshot wound depends on the mass, size, and velocity of the bullet.

The position of the victim at the time of injury may be of help in determining the track of the bullet.

Muscle has a high density; damage is usually severe.

Bone may change the direction of the missile.

A small entrance wound with a large, explosive exit wound usually indicates a high-velocity missile fired at close range. The energy dissipated by a high-velocity missile is equal to the difference between the energy present when the missile enters the body and that left when it exits. Usually there is a violent expansion of the missile track, which ruptures arteries, veins, and nerves and fractures bones.

A small entrance wound with no exit wound indicates a low-velocity missile that is retained within the tissue.

FORENSIC CONSIDERATIONS IN MANAGEMENT OF GUNSHOT WOUNDS

1. Report any gunshot wounds to the police, regardless of the circumstances surrounding the incident.
2. Document the exact condition of the patient and the wound on arrival at the emergency department. Prehospital personnel should note the environment of the patient, including his position in relation with objects, doorways, and so on. Document exact information on the record describing the scene (how the patient was positioned on the floor, etc.). Disturb the scene as little as possible, but do not permit this consideration for preserving evidence to interfere with emergency care. Do not touch or move weapons, furniture, or other environmental clues to the incident unless it is absolutely imperative for patient care.
3. Life-saving procedures take precedence over preservation of the chain of evidence. Place the patient on a catch-all sheet, since bullets may dislodge during changes in body position.
4. Cut or tear clothing away from the bullet wound site, preferably along a seam. Do not drop the clothing onto the floor, but hang it up, taking care to handle it as little as possible. Do not shake the clothes. They are to be kept as evidence and should never be given to the family. (All clothing is examined for powder residue, metallic traces, and other foreign material). Later, place all clothing in a brown paper bag (not plastic) and seal it with all patient identification attached. Allow any blood to dry before bagging.
5. Avoid scrubbing powder away from the skin since the area of powder dispersal is a clue to the distance between the patient and the weapon fired. If the skin must be scrubbed before forensic pathologists examine it, careful documentation should be made regarding the appearance of the wound and the surrounding skin. Save any tissue debrided from the wound for forensic pathology.
6. If bullets are removed, gloved fingers or padded forceps should be used, since ordinary surgical clamps or similar devices can mar the bullet and render it useless for evidence.
7. When removed the bullet must be marked on the nose or base with identifying letters

or numbers for later identification by the markings and to facilitate testimony that the particular bullet was indeed removed from the patient's body as described. Place the bullet in a small padded box (e.g., a matchbox) to prevent marring. Do not place bullets in bottles or basins since their rolling causes dulling of the barrel markings. When more than one bullet is removed, they should be placed in separate containers that are sealed and labeled with the physician's name, time, date, exact site of removal, and pertinent patient identification. All bullets should be turned over to the police pathology department at once. If this is not feasible, the bullet must be placed in a locked box. *Always obtain a police receipt* when surrendering any item of evidence. Shotgun wounds may exhibit wadding, pellets, and the inner lining of the cartridge. These may assist in matching the wound to the weapon fired. Place such evidence in a properly marked sealed envelope and retain it for police study.

8. If the patient dies do not clean the body. Leave all invasive tubing and apparatus in the body cavities (endotracheal tubes, catheters, IV lines, etc.). Place brown paper bags over the patient's hands to protect potential sources of evidence, such as fingernail scrapings, foreign hair, blood, and gunpowder. (Do not use plastic bags since condensation destroys evidence.) Do not further probe the wound after the death in an attempt to locate the bullet. Unnecessary probing could create false or misleading forensic reports.

High-pressure paint gun injuries

High-pressure paint gun injuries deserve special mention because a seemingly benign injury may turn out to be devastating. This injury occurs when the patient attempts to clean the tip of the high-pressure paint gun. If the gun releases, a large amount of paint may be injected into the fingertip and perhaps up into the arm and hand. The results will be much tissue swelling, decreased circulation, ischemia, and necrosis.

SIGNS AND SYMPTOMS

Small puncture wound on the tip of the finger
Swelling of the extremity
The extremity appears mottled
Focal tenderness
The extremity is cool to the touch

THERAPEUTIC INTERVENTION

DO NOT soak the wound in warm water ⎫ These measures may increase swelling and
DO NOT inject local anesthesia   ⎬ ischemia and induce vasospasm
                                        ⎭
Obtain an x-ray film to observe the paint,
   which is radiopaque
Tetanus toxoid immunization
Tetanus immune globulin
Antibiotics
Surgical debridement in the operating suite (with possible fasciotomy preceding in the emergency department)

TYPES OF ANESTHESIA FOR WOUND MANAGEMENT

Lidocaine is the most commonly used anesthetic for both local and regional anesthesia in wound management. It may be used with or without epinephrine. It is used with epinephrine when the area to be repaired is a highly vascular and one wishes to control bleeding. Ounce for ounce, lidocaine is more potent than any other anesthetic agent. It is also, however, more toxic than the others. It is not a very irritating agent, and it appears to have a longer effect than other anesthetic agents.

Other agents used for anesthesia include procaine, mepivicaine (Carbocaine), bupivaaine (Marcaine), and tetracaine (Pontocaine).

The care giver may elect to administer regional anesthesia. This is done by injecting an anesthetic agent intravenously distal to the injury. A tourniquet is applied and inflated proximal to the body on the affected extremity.

Another option is application of a local nerve block. This is done by injecting the anesthetic agent along the course of the nerve, abolishing conduction of afferent and efferent impulses for a limited time.

The use of nitrous oxide gas should be considered for procedures that are short but may be painful, such as scrubbing cinders from a wound.

SUTURING

Suturing is the art of stitching wound edges together to promote good healing and minimal scar formation. It is normal for the body to have a certain inflammatory response to suture material, as it constitutes a foreign body. A general rule of thumb is to use the finest (thinnest) suture available that will do the job properly. To prevent large areas of scarring, as small an amount of tissue as possible should be involved in suturing.

Types of suture material

There are two basic categories of suture material, absorbable and nonabsorbable.

Absorbable sutures remove tension from the surface of the wound and close dead space (the space beneath the wound that may become filled with fluid and become a culture medium). Examples of absorbable suture material include:

Catgut
Chromic
Polyglactin 910 (Vicryl)

Nonabsorbable sutures are generally used on the surface layer of the skin. Examples of nonabsorbable suture material include:

Polyglycolic acid (Dexon)	Dacron
Silk	Nylon
Cotton	Steel

When to remove sutures

The location of the wound and the state of wound healing determine when sutures are removed. In general:

Eyelids—2 days	Trunk—7 to 10 days
Face—3 to 5 days	Hands and feet—10 to 14 days

TETANUS AND TETANUS PROPHYLAXIS

Approximately 100 people die from tetanus in the United States each year. Although it is not frequently seen, the process of death is a devastating one that could have been prevented easily with the proper immunizations.

Tetanus is caused by the organism *Clostridium tetani*, a gram-positive, spore-forming, anaerobic bacillus. It is highly resistant to any measures taken against it, including sterilization, because of its tendency to form spores when conditions for its survival are not favorable. The incubation period for tetanus is anywhere from 2 days to 2 weeks or more. The organism is present in soil and garden moss, on farms, and anywhere else where animal and human excreta can be found. It enters the human circulation through an open wound and attaches itself to cells within the central nervous system. Tetanus causes depression of the respiratory center in the medulla and usually progresses to cause death.

SIGNS AND SYMPTOMS

Mild tetanus:
  Local joint stiffness
  Mild trismus (inability to open jaw)
Moderate tetanus:
  Generalized body stiffness   Difficulty swallowing
  Moderate trismus   Decreased vital capacity
Severe tetanus:
  Severe trismus   Tachycardia
  Pain in back   Hypertension
  Pain in penis   Dysrhythmias
  Seizures   Hyperpyrexia
  Opisthotonos   Usually mental alertness until cardiopulmonary arrest

THERAPEUTIC INTERVENTION

ABCs   Antibiotics
Oxygen at high flow rate   Ventilatory support
Hyperalimentation   Much supportive nursing care

Tetanus prophylaxis
INITIAL IMMUNIZATION SERIES

In an infant and young child give diphtheria/tetanus/pertussis (DPT) injections:
0.5 ml at 2 months
0.5 ml at 4 months
0.5 ml at 6 months
0.5 ml at 18 months
0.5 ml at 5 to 6 years
For age 6 years to adult, give tetanus/diphtheria toxoid (TD) absorbed injections:
0.5 ml initially
0.5 ml 4 to 6 weeks later
0.5 ml 6 months to 1 year later
0.5 ml booster every 10 years

TETANUS PROPHYLAXIS FOR INJURIES*

Immunized	Prophylaxis
With booster within 12 months	Meticulous wound care
Within past 10 years	0.5 ml absorbed tetanus toxoid
Booster more than 5 years ago (small clean wound)	0.5 ml absorbed tetanus toxoid
More than 10 years ago (small clean wound)	0.5 ml absorbed tetanus toxoid
Within 10 years (wound severe or more than 24 hours old)	0.5 ml absorbed tetanus toxoid, 250 units tetanus immune globulin (in gluteus maximus), penicillin
More than 10 years ago or no immunization (small clean wounds)	0.5 ml absorbed tetanus toxoid (with instructions for initial immunization series)
More than 10 years ago or no immunization (moderate wounds)	0.5 ml absorbed tetanus toxoid, 250 units tetanus immune globulin (in gluteus maximus) with instructions for initial immunization series
More than 10 years ago or no immunization (severe wounds)	0.5 ml absorbed tetanus toxoid, 500 units tetanus immune globulin (in gluteus maximus) with instructions for initial immunization series

*Recommendations of the Committee on Trauma, American College of Surgeons.[1]

TABLE 15-1 Anaerobic wound infections and complications

Type	Incubation period	Manifestations	Clinical management
Tetanus	6-10 days or longer	Onset of trismus (spasm of masseter muscles); skeletal muscle spasms and seizures may also be apparent.	Assess wound; excise and drain widely. Give large doses of antibiotics. Admit for intensive care giving special consideration to preventing respiratory complications, controlling muscle spasms, and managing seizures.
Gas gangrene (clostridial myonecrosis)	6 hours to 3 days	Contaminated wound appears edematous and necrotic; crepitus from gas production; wound is extremely painful and exudes a sweet, mousy-smelling clear fluid; overlying skin is tense and white to bronze colored.	Debride wound thoroughly and excise as much involved tissue as possible. Give antibiotics, e.g., penicillin and chloramphenicol (Chloromycetin). Transfer to center with hyperbaric chamber facility.

Recommendations of the American College of Surgeons.[1]

HUMAN AND ANIMAL BITES

All bite wounds, whether inflicted by a human, a domestic animal, or a wild animal, must be considered contaminated until proved otherwise.

FACTORS TO CONSIDER

Age of the patient
General physical condition of the patient
Site of the wound
Severity of the wound
    Location
    Size
    Depth
    Amount of contamination
Time between the bite incident and when the patient first sought medical assistance
First aid given at the scene of the incident

COMPLICATIONS

Infection
Abscess
Cellulitis
Septicemia
Osteomyelitis
Tenosynovitis
Pyarthrosis
Rabies
Loss of injured part

AFTERCARE INSTRUCTIONS FOR ALL BITE PATIENTS

Keep the injured part elevated above the heart if possible
Take medications as ordered
Return to your private physician, the clinic, or the emergency department if:
    A fever develops
    Redness appears
    Swelling occurs
    Streaks appear
    The site becomes very hot
    There is increasing pain at the site
    A foul odor develops
    Drainage occurs

Human bites

A human bite may be self-inflicted or inflicted by another person. The many organisms normally present in the human mouth may cause a severe infection and other complications.

The most common location of human bites is on the long or ring finger at the metacarpophalangeal joint, which becomes infected easily. The human mouth contains more than 10^8 bacteria/ml of saliva.[2] Gram-positive organisms are commonly *Staphylococcus aureus* and *Streptococcus;* gram-negative organisms may be *Proteus, Escherichia coli, Pseudomonas, Neisseria,* or *Klebsiella.* More than 3% of these organisms are coagulase-positive, penicillin-resistant *Staphylococcus aureus.*

SIGNS AND SYMPTOMS

History (although the patient may be reluctant to admit to a human bite)
Teeth marks
Lacerations across the knuckles (caused by the first hitting teeth)

THERAPEUTIC INTERVENTION

Apply local anesthesia
Obtain a culture and Gram's stain
Irrigate and scrub the wound thoroughly
Debride devitalized tissue
Do *not* suture the wound (facial wounds are an exception)
Give broad-spectrum antibiotics
Evaluate neurovascular status distal to the wound
Give tetanus prophylaxis
Strict follow-up care is required

ANTIBIOTIC REGIMEN

Initially:
    Cephalexin (Keflex), 50 mg/kg orally over 24 hours in four divided doses for 7 to 10 days
Later:
    Methicillin, 200 mg/kg IV over 24 hours in four divided doses for gram-positive bacilli
    Kanamycin, 15 mg/kg IM over 24 hours in four divided doses for gram-negative bacilli
    Monitor these patients for renal toxicity and ototoxicity of the drugs

COMPLICATIONS

Abscess
Cellulitis
Osteomyelitis
Pyarthrosis

Dog and cat bites

Approximately ½ to 1 million people in the United States are bitten by dogs or cats each year.[3] The organism usually present is *Pasteurella multocida.*[4] The dog's teeth can exert a pressure of up to 400 pounds/square inch.[5] The likelihood of infection increases[6]:

If the patient is younger than 4 years
If the patient is older than 50 years

With an increased time before medical help is sought

With the anatomic location of the wound (e.g., an earlobe is more likely to become infected because of poor vascularity)

If the wound is a puncture wound

SIGNS AND SYMPTOMS

History of a bite	Swelling
Puncture wounds	Inflammation
Infection	Regional lymphadenopathy
Pain	Low-grade fever

THERAPEUTIC INTERVENTION

Obtain a culture and Gram's stain

Irrigate and scrub the wound thoroughly

Debride devitalized tissue

Suture if necessary (many practitioners prefer to leave the wound open)

Give antibiotics (especially penicillin)

Give tetanus prophylaxis

Dressing is optional

Give rabies prophylaxis if necessary

RABIES AND RABIES PROPHYLAXIS

Rabies is caused by a virus that can be found in the saliva of many mammals. The virus is highly neurotoxic. The incubation period for rabies is from 10 days to several months.

SIGNS AND SYMPTOMS

History of bite (type, animal, geographic region, whether animal was provoked)

Malaise for 2 to 4 days

Fever

Headache

Granulomatous lymphadenitis

Photophobia

Muscle spasm

Coma

THERAPEUTIC INTERVENTION

Ensure ABCs

Culture the wound

Irrigate and scrub the wound

Debride devitalized tissue

There is much controversy about suturing the wound or leaving it open

Give antibiotics

Provide tetanus prophylaxis

Report the bite to local health authorities
Follow rabies prophylaxis procedures

Rabies prophylaxis

Give rabies prophylaxis under the following circumstances:
If there is a reason to believe that the biting animal has rabies
If the animal becomes rabid while in 10-day quarantine
If the animal is wild, such as a wolf, fox, bat, skunk, or raccoon
If the animal is not found and rabies vaccination information is not available
There are two types of rabies vaccine in use:
Duck embryo vaccine (DEV)—given in doses of 1 ml subcutaneously for 14 to 21
days, then in boosters 10 to 20 days after the initial series; it is given in the anterior
abdominal wall or the lateral thigh, rotating the site each day
Equine serum (or human serum if available)—when the bite is severe and rabies is highly
suspected; 5 ml directly into the wound site (perimeter) and 40 international
units/kg IM into the buttocks

REFERENCES

1. Committee on Trauma, American College of Surgeons: A guide to prophylaxis against tetanus in wound management, Bull. Am. Coll. Surg. **57:**32, 1972.
2. Henrich, J.J., et al.: Human bites, J.E.N. **2:**21, Jan.-Feb. 1976.
3. Callaham, M.L.: Treatment of common dog bites: infection risk factors, J.A.C.E.P. **7:**11, March 1978.
4. Parks, B., Hawkins, L., and Horner, P.: Bites of the hand, Rocky Mount. Med. J. **71:**85, 1974.
5. Scarcella, J.: Management of bites: early definitive care of bite wounds, Ohio State Med. J. **65:**25, 1969.
6. Thompson, H.G., and Svitek, V.: Small animal bites: the role of primary closure, J. Trauma **13:**20, 1973.

SUGGESTED READINGS

Anast. G.T., Bliss, A., and Warner, C.G.: Emergency treatment of bites and stings, J.E.N. **1:**27, Sept.-Oct. 1975.
Andersen, H.W.: An open wound is a whole patient, Emerg. Med. **9:**127, Nov. 1977.
Boswick, J.A.: Wound care, Postgrad. Med. **55:**171, 1974.
Bryant, W.M.: Wound healing. In Bekiesz, B., ed.: CIBA clinical symposia, Vol. 29, No. 3, Summit, N.J. 1977, CIBA Geigy Corp.
Chenoweth, S.R.: Forensic considerations in gunshot wounds, Unpublished manuscript.
Dushoff, I.M.: A stitch in time, Emerg. Med. **5:**21, Jan. 1973.
Edsall, G., et al.: Excessive use of tetanus toxoid boosters. JAMA **202:**111, 1967.
Frazier, C.A.: Diagnosis and treatment of insect bites, CIBA clinical symposia, Vol. 20, No. 3, Summit, N.J., 1968, CIBA Geigy Corp.
Furste, W.: Four ways to 100% success in tetanus prophylaxis, Am. J. Surg. **128:**616, 1974.
Grabb, W.C., and Smith, J.W., eds.: Plastic surgery, Boston, 1973, Little, Brown & Co.
Graham, W., Calabretta, A., and Miller, S.: Dog bites, Am. Fam. Physician **15:**132 1977.
Harris, D., Imperata, P.J., and Oken, B.: Dog bites—an unrecognized epidemic, Bull. N.Y. Acad. Med. **50:**981, 1974.
Moritz, A.R., and Morris, R.C.: Handbook of legal medicine, ed. 2, St. Louis, 1975. The C.V. Mosby Co.
Peacock, E.E., Jr., and VanWinkle, W., Jr.: Surgery and biology of wound repair, Philadelphia, 1970, W.B. Saunders Co.
Shields, C., et al.: Hand infections, J. Trauma **15:**235, 1975.
Waltz, J.R., and Inbau, F.E.: Medical jurisprudence, New York, 1971, Macmillan Publishing Co., Inc.
Wolcott, M.W., ed.: Ferguson's surgery of the ambulatory patient, Philadelphia, 1974, J.B. Lippincott Co.

CHAPTER 16 **Head trauma**

One half of all trauma deaths in the United States each year are caused by head trauma. Over 4,000 children die from head trauma each year. The brain is a very delicate collection of tissues cushioned by cerebrospinal fluid and protected by the hard, bony skull. Because the brain is enclosed in a rigid space, it cannot increase in size without increasing pressure within this space. To compensate, the brain may be pushed downward through the tentorial notch or the opening in the skull through which the spinal cord passes (the foramen magnum). This is known as brainstem herniation. If it is not corrected immediately, it will produce death, as pressure on the brainstem disrupts the body's vital functions.

In any type of head trauma the care giver should:

Hyperventilate the patient to decrease P_{CO_2} and decrease cerebral edema, *and*

Administer a diuretic agent (furosemide 0.5 to 1.0 mg/kg IV) to decrease cerebral edema, *and possibly*

Administer dextrose 50% and naloxone if hypoglycemia or opiate overdose is a possibility

In head trauma in general, there is usually an initial complaint of headache, a decreasing level of consciousness caused by ischemia at the reticular formation site, and dilation of the ipsilateral pupil (80% of the time). Later symptoms include weakness, decerebrate posturing, bradycardia, and increased respirations. If blood pressure is decreased and pulse is elevated, it is not because of head trauma; enough bleeding into the cranium to produce hypovolemic shock cannot occur, except in small infants, in whom the fontanels will bulge if bleeding occurs. If signs and symptoms of hypovolemic shock appear, look for other causes. A patient may develop hypovolemic shock from a large, bleeding scalp laceration. It is important to also remember than 10% of those with significant head trauma have associated cervical spine trauma. The care giver must pay strict attention to protecting the cervical spine.

PROBLEMS WITH PATIENTS WITH HEAD TRAUMA

The following is a list of frequently encountered problems and appropriate interventions when caring for a patient with head trauma:

Problem	Therapeutic intervention
Scalp laceration and profuse bleeding	Direct pressure on or around wound edges to control bleeding
Airway obstruction	Open the airway, being sure to stabilize the neck in the event of cervical spine injury

Problem	Therapeutic intervention
Emesis or aspiration	Transport the patient on his side whenever possible; be sure to stabilize the cervical spine; insert a nasogastric tube if indicated
Decreased level of consciousness and dilated pupil(s)	Check DERM frequently; record and document accurately; administer oxygen at high flow (hyperventilating the patient) and furosemide IV
Cerebrospinal fluid leak	Apply a loose, dry sterile dressing; check for "target" or "ring" sign; do *not* suction nose or ear
Decreased blood pressure	May be caused by spinal shock or hypovolemia from other causes; apply MAST and administer IV Ringer's lactate or normal saline solution
Seizures	Protect the airway, head, and cervical spine
Pain	Do *not* administer narcotics or sedatives

THE BRIEF NEUROLOGIC EXAMINATION

It is absolutely essential to obtain an initial neurologic evaluation and frequent ones thereafter. Using the DERM mnemonic, the care giver can perform a brief neurologic examination in a consistent, precise manner.

D = Depth of coma

Use a stimulus/response description:

Stimulus	Response
Voice	Appropriate (state how)
Touch	Inappropriate (state how)
Pain	

E = Eyes

Note pupillary response to light and accommodation

If the corpus callosum is intact, there will be simultaneous consensual reaction of the unstimulated pupil on light stimulation

Note that 10% of the population have unequal pupils (anisocoria) with no disease

R = Respirations

Regular or irregular

Pattern

Shallow or deep

M = Motor

Does the patient move extremities? Both?

The Glasgow coma scale may also be used (see p. 351).

DIAGNOSTIC EXAMINATIONS
Cross-table lateral cervical spine x-ray examination

Be sure to visualize all seven cervical vertebrae.

The most common cervical spine fractures are C6 and C7.

Of all patients with significant head trauma, 10% have concurrent cervical spine trauma.

TABLE 16-1 Assessing brainstem function using the DERM mnemonic

The brainstem	Herniation levels	D = Depth of coma	E = Eyes	R = Respirations	M = Motor function	Posturing
	Thalamus	Painful stimulus causes nonpurposeful response	Small; react to light	Eupnea	Hyperactive deep tendon reflexes	Decorticate
				Cheyne-Stokes respirations		
	Midbrain	Painful stimulus causes no response	Midpoint to dilated; fixed; no reaction to light	Central neurogenic breathing	Decreased deep tendon reflexes	Decerebrate
	Pons	Painful stimulus causes no response	Midpoint to dilated; fixed; no reaction to light	Biot's respirations	Flaccid	No tone
	Medulla	Painful stimulus causes no response	Midpoint to dilated; fixed; no reaction to light	Ataxic/apneustic	Flaccid	No tone

Glasgow coma scale*

The Glasgow coma scale has been designed to quantitatively relate consciousness to motor responses, verbal responses, and eye opening. Coma is defined as no response and no eye opening. Scores of 7 or less on the Glasgow scale qualify as "coma"; all scores of 9 or more do not qualify as "coma." The examiner determines the *best* response the patient can make to a set of standardized stimuli. Higher points are assigned to responses that indicate increasing degrees of arousal.

1. **Best motor response.** (Examiner determines the *best* response with *either* arm.)
   a. *6 points.* Obeys simple commands. Raises arm on request or holds up specified number of fingers. Releasing a grip (not grasping, which can be reflexive) is also an appropriate test.
   b. *5 points.* Localizes noxious stimuli. Fails to obey commands but can move either arm toward a noxious cutaneous stimulus and eventually contacts it with the hand. The stimulus should be maximal and applied in various locations, i.e., sternum pressure, or trapezius pinch.
   c. *4 points.* Flexion withdrawal. Responds to noxious stimulus with arm flexion but does not localize it with the hand.
   d. *3 points.* Abnormal flexion. Adducts shoulder, flexes and pronates arm, flexes wrist, and makes a fist in response to a noxious stimulus (decorticate rigidity).
   e. *2 points.* Abnormal extension. Adducts and internally rotates shoulder, extends forearm, flexes wrist, and makes a fist in response to a noxious stimulus (decerebrate rigidity).
   f. *1 point.* No motor response. Exclude reasons for no response; for example, insufficient stimulus or spinal cord injury.
2. **Best verbal response.** (Examiner determines the *best* response after arousal. Noxious stimuli are employed if necessary.) Omit this test if the patient is dysphasic, has oral injuries, or is intubated. Place a check mark after other two test category scores after totaling to indicate omission of the verbal response section.
   a. *5 points.* Oriented patient. Can converse and relate who he is, where he is, and the year and month.
   b. *4 points.* Confused patient. Is not fully oriented or demonstrates confusion.
   c. *3 points.* Verbalizes. Does not engage in sustained conversation, but uses intelligible words in an exclamation (curse) or in a disorganized manner which is nonsensical.
   d. *2 points.* Vocalizes. Makes moaning or goaning sounds that are not recognizable words.
   e. *1 point.* No vocalization. Does not make any sound even in response to noxious stimulus.
3. **Eye opening.** (Examiner determines the minimum stimulus that evokes opening of one or both eyes.) If the patient cannot realistically open the eyes because of bandages or lid edema, write "E" after the total test score to indicate omission of this component.
   a. *4 points.* Eyes open spontaneously.
   b. *3 points.* Eyes open to speech. Patient opens eyes in response to command or on being called by name.
   c. *2 points.* Eyes open to noxious stimuli.
   d. *1 point.* No eye opening in response to noxious stimuli.

*From Teasdale, G., and Jennett, B.: Lancet 2:81, 1974.

Skull x-ray examinations

Treat the patient symptomatically, not by the x-ray film.

Generally speaking, if the patient is neurologically intact, skull films are not required. (This includes findings such as no focal deficits, no complaint of headache, no loss of consciousness, and no nausea and vomiting.)

Computerized axial tomography (CT scan, CAT scan, EMI scan)

CT scan can detect 90% of head trauma accurately.

CT scan should be done quickly if patient has an altered level of consciousness, hemiparesis, or any type of aphasia.

Nuclear magnetic resonance

The atoms of the body broadcast signals from which images may be created. These broadcasts can be tracked through nuclear magnetic resonance (NMR), using ionizing radiation or sound waves as a noninvasive method to obtain a visual image. By using NMR, the care giver can also chemically analyze cellular content by measuring phosphorous emissions.

Doll's eye examination

Do *not* perform the doll's eye examination if cervical spine trauma is suspected.

Normal response—as head is rotated in one direction (Fig. 16-1, *A*) the eyes move in other direction (Fig. 16-1, *B*).

Abnormal response—as head is rotated in one direction, the eyes remain fixed at the midline (Fig. 16-1, *C*).

Ice water caloric

Ice water is squirted into the ear of a patient (check tympanic membrane first).

Normal response—eyes move slowly away from ice water.

Comatose response—eyes move toward ice water.

Brainstem involvement—no response.

Pupillary responses

Normal reactions:
Pupils constrict when exposed directly to light.
Light in one pupil causes the other pupil to constrict also.
Abnormal reactions:
Fixed pinpoint pupils indicate pons involvement or use of opiates.
Ptosis may indicate third cranial nerve involvement.
Dilated fixed pupil (unilateral) indicates third cranial nerve involvement (early).
Dilated fixed pupils (bilateral) indicate third cranial nerve involvement.

Reflexes

Corneal:
Normal reaction—blinks eye
Abnormal reaction—no response

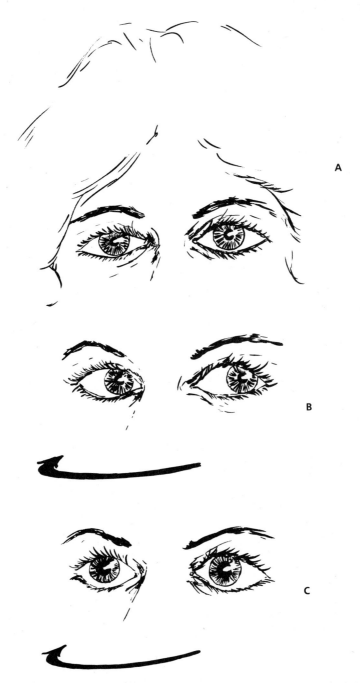

FIG. 16-1 Doll's eye maneuver. **A,** Normal gaze. **B,** Normal reflex. As head is turned to right, eyes rotate to left. **C,** Abnormal or absent reflex. As head is turned to right, eyes stay in midline position.

TABLE 16-2 The cranial nerves

Nerve	Function	Tested by
I Olfactory	Smell	Smell
II Optic	Vision	Vision
III Oculomotor	Pupils; eye movement	Eye movements; pupil reaction to light
IV Trochlear	Eye movement	Eye movements (downward and inward)
V Trigeminal	Facial sensation; jaw movement	Facial sensation; jaw movement
VI Abducent	Outward eye movement	Lateral eye movement
VII Facial	Facial expression; taste in anterior two thirds of tongue	Raised eyebrows; closes eyes tightly to resistance; shows teeth; smiles; frowns; puffs cheeks
VIII Acoustic	Hearing; balance	Hearing; ice water caloric
IX Glossopharyngeal	Taste in posterior two thirds of tongue; sensation in pharynx and nostrils	Gag reflex
X Vagus	Soft palate, pharynx, and larynx muscles; heart; lungs; stomach	Gag reflex
XI Accessory	Sternocleidomastoid and trapezius muscle movement	Shrugs shoulders; turns head against resistance
XII Hypoglossal	Tongue movement	Sticks out tongue

Gag:
  Normal—intact
  Abnormal—loss of gag reflex
Deep tendon:
  Normal reaction—normal reflexes.
  Abnormal reaction—hypoactivity or absence of reaction indicates cerebellar lesions or intricate peripheral nerve or anterior horn cell disease; hyperactivity indicates pyramidal tract lesions and sometimes psychogenic disorders.
Babinski—elicited by cutaneous stimulation of the plantar surface of the foot:
  Normal reaction—great toe will point downward.
  Abnormal (positive) reaction—great toe will point upward toward the head (toward where the problem is).
Posturing—elicited by verbal or painful stimulation:
  Decorticate posturing—arms pull in "toward the core," and legs and feet extend, indicating a lesion above the midbrain (Fig. 16-3).

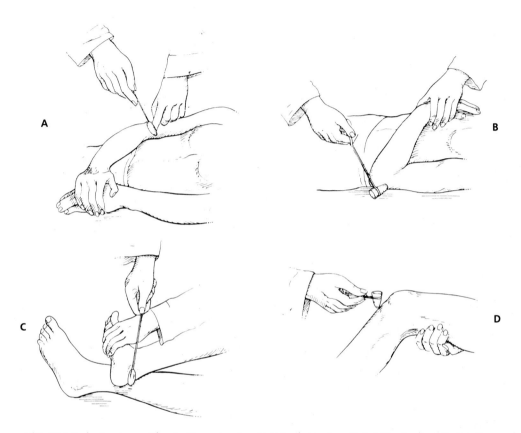

FIG. 16-2 Deep tendon reflex. **A,** Biceps tendon. **B,** Triceps tendon. **C,** Achilles tendon. **D,** Patellar tendon. (From Fowkes, W.C., Jr., and Hunn, V.K.: Clinical assessment for the nurse practitioner, St. Louis, 1973, The C.V. Mosby Co.)

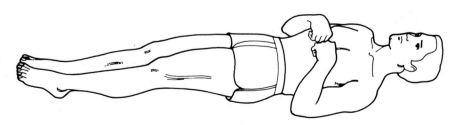

FIG. 16-3 Decorticate position.

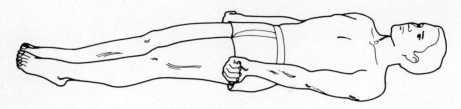

FIG. 16-4 Decerebrate position.

Decerebrate posturing—arms extend, wrists flex, and legs and feet extend, indicating a brainstem compression (Fig. 16-4).

SCALP LACERATIONS

The scalp is a protective covering that contains:
Hair (sometimes)
Subcutaneous tissue
The galea (a tough, fibrous layer)
Loose connective tissue
If there is a laceration of the scalp, it may bleed profusely because of its great vascular supply.

THERAPEUTIC INTERVENTION

Apply direct pressure to control bleeding—the patient may lose a large amount of blood from a large scalp laceration; if hypovolemic shock occurs, treat it
Check the underlying bone with a gloved finger for fracture—a small puncture wound may indicate a penetrating injury to the brain
Protect the cervical spine
Shave a small area around the laceration
Cleanse the area with surgical solution
Suture the wound if indicated
Give aftercare instructions for wound management and head trauma

SKULL FRACTURE

Skull fracture does *not* indicate cerebral injury. The care giver must observe and perform diagnostic tests before making this decision that there has been cerebral injury. There are three types of skull fractures:
Simple
Depressed
Basal

Simple skull fractures (Fig. 16-5)

A simple skull fracture is a linear crack in the surface of the skull. No bone is displaced, and therapeutic intervention involves observation of the patient for other asso-

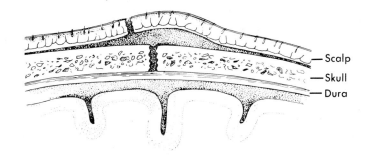

FIG. 16-5 Simple skull fracture. (From Barber, J., Stokes, L., and Billings, D.: Adult and child care, ed. 2, St. Louis, 1977, The C.V. Mosby Co.)

ciated injuries. If there are no other obvious findings and the patient has a good support system (family or friends), he may be discharged to home with head trauma aftercare instructions.

Depressed skull fracture (Figs. 16-6 and 16-7)

A depressed skull fracture is a depression of a part of the bony skull. If the fragment is depressed beneath the table of the adjacent bone by more than 5 mm, surgery must be performed to elevate the depression and decrease the possibility of intracranial infection by ruling out a cerebrospinal fluid leak. If the depression overlies the sinuses (sagittal or lateral) there may be profuse bleeding, underlying brain contusion, or tears of the cerebral tissue. Be sure to examine the cervical spine, the mandible, and the maxilla.

THERAPEUTIC INTERVENTION

Control external bleeding
Hospital admission
Surgical intervention to:
    Elevate the depressed segment
    Remove fragments
    Debride necrotic brain tissue
    Remove hematomas
    Repair lacerations
Consider antibiotics

Basilar skull fracture

A basilar skull fracture is a fracture at the base of the skull. It is more of a clinical finding than a radiographic finding. The danger of a basilar skull fracture is that it may cross the course of the middle meningeal artery. Disruption of this artery may cause:
    Hematoma of the scalp
    Subarachnoid hemorrhage
    Epidural hematoma (disruption causes 90% of epidural hemorrhages)
    Intracerebral hemorrhage

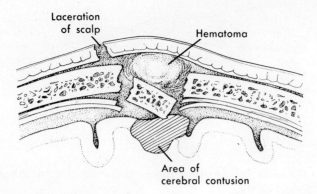

FIG. 16-6 Depressed skull fracture. (From Barber, J., Stokes, L., and Billings, D.: Adult and child care, ed. 2, St. Louis, 1977, The C.V. Mosby Co.)

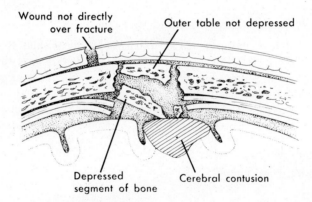

FIG. 16-7 Hidden skull fracture. (From Barber, J., Stokes, L., and Billings, D.: Adult and child care, ed. 2, St. Louis, 1977, The C.V. Mosby Co.)

SIGNS AND SYMPTOMS

There are four cardinal signs of basilar skull fracture:

raccoon eyes—Unilateral or bilateral periorbital ecchymoses that occur as a result of intraorbital bleeding from an intraorbital root fracture.

Battle's sign—Formation of an ecchymosis behind the ears in the mastoid area that usually occurs 12 to 24 hours after the injury.

hemotympanum—Blood behind the eardrum caused by temporal bone fracture near the tympanic membrane.

cerebrospinal fluid leak from nose or ear—Cerebrospinal fluid (CSF) leak caused by a fractured part of the temporal bone that creates an opening between the cranium and the outside of the skull. The absence of otorrhea does not negate the presence of CSF.

The patient may state that he has a sweet taste in his mouth. Blood and CSF will form a "target sign" or "ring sign"—blood and CSF separate to form two distinct rings. If the tympanic membrane is intact, CSF will exit via the eustachian tube, appearing like rhinorrhea.

THERAPEUTIC INTERVENTION

Do not attempt to stop CSF leak
Do a baseline neurologic examination
Obtain an x-ray film (although 25% of basilar skull fractures are not seen on routine skull films)
Initiate antibiotics if a CSF leak is present
Hospital admission and observation
A scar formation from an old basilar skull fracture may dislodge, forming an open fistula into the cranium and a CSF leak.

HEAD TRAUMA WITH NORMAL FINDINGS

Often a patient will give a history of head trauma but there will be no abnormal findings on examination. When this is the case there are usually no complications. It is essential, however, to give careful, explicit aftercare instructions for patients who have incurred head trauma. Pay particular attention to the remote possibility of the formation of a slow, chronic subdural hematoma.

CONCUSSION

A concussion usually occurs as a result of a direct blow to the head or an acceleration/deceleration injury in which the cerebral tissue impacts with the inside of the bony skull. A brief interruption of the reticular activating system may occur, causing a short period of amnesia. This is a transient, limited process that usually requires no therapeutic intervention.

SIGNS AND SYMPTOMS

Nausea and vomiting (especially common in children)
Possible brief loss of sight
Brief loss of consciousness
Brief amnesia
Possible skull fracture
Headache

THERAPEUTIC INTERVENTION

If nausea and vomiting are severe and dehydration results, admit to the hospital for rehydration
If loss of consciousness goes on for more than 2 to 3 minutes, admit to the hospital for observation (if loss of consciousness goes on for more than 6 hours, the injury should be considered a contusion)
If the skull is fractured, admit to the hospital for observation

Administer nonnarcotic analgesics for headache

If there is a reliable family or friends, the patient may be discharged home with good
aftercare instructions

Postconcussion syndrome

Late sequelae of concussion may include:

Headache

Loss of memory

Syncopal episodes

THERAPEUTIC INTERVENTION

Nonnarcotic analgesic for headache

No other therapeutic intervention is necessary

CONTUSION (Fig. 16-8)

A contusion is an actual bruise of the surface of the brain. When this occurs there is
structural alteration of the brain.

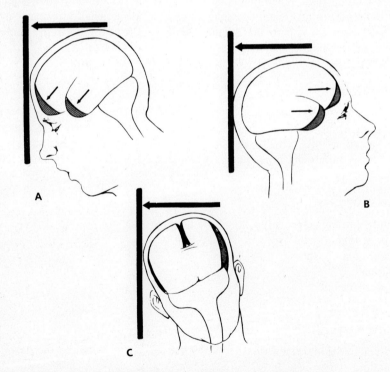

FIG. 16-8 Cortical contusion with relation to direction of head movement. **A,** Forward head
movement. Head strikes object; injury at tips of frontal and temporal lobes. **B,** Back of head
strikes immovable object. Brain is forced forward against front of skull (contrecoup injury); causes
injury in frontal and temporal lobes. **C,** Lateral movement of head against immovable object.
Causes brain to strike opposite side of skull (contrecoup injury). (From Nishioka, H.: In Liechty,
R.D., and Soper, R.T.: Synopsis of surgery, ed. 3, St. Louis, 1976, The C.V. Mosby Co.)

SIGNS AND SYMPTOMS

Altered level of consciousness for more than 6 hours
Nausea and vomiting
Vision disturbances
Neurologic dysfunction (weakness, ataxia, hemiparesis, confusion, speech problems)
Seizures (in 5% of patients)

THERAPEUTIC INTERVENTION

Admit to the hospital for observation
Administer an antiemetic

DECREASED LEVEL OF CONSCIOUSNESS WITHOUT FOCAL NEUROLOGIC DEFICIT

Occasionally a patient will have an altered level of consciousness without focal neuro-logic deficit.

THERAPEUTIC INTERVENTION

Admit to the hospital for close observation
CT scan if level of consciousness decreases or does not improve in a few hours

FOCAL NEUROLOGIC DEFICITS WITHOUT BRAINSTEM COMPRESSION

When there are disturbances in motor movement, speech patterns, or vision the care giver should:
Obtain a CT scan to check for the defect and to determine if the patient requires surgical intervention
Administer oxygen and furosemide to decrease cerebral edema

INTRACRANIAL BLEEDING

The three meningeal layers of the brain are the dura mater, the arachnoid membrane, and the pia mater (Fig. 16-9). Lesions or bleeding sites in the head are named according to their location in respect to these meningeal layers. The body's compensatory mechanism

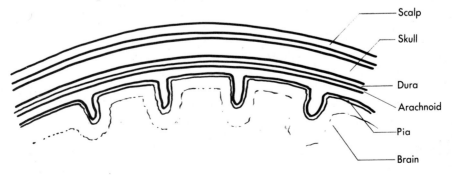

FIG. 16-9 Cross-section of head.

is to shift cerebrospinal fluid into the cerebral sinuses. This can account for up to 75 ml of hemorrhage material. Any material in excess of this amount will cause pressure in the cranial vault to rise (increased intracranial pressure).

Epidural (extradural) hematoma

An epidural hematoma is bleeding between the skull and the dura mater. It usually results from acute, severe head trauma from a direct blow and usually causes a skull fracture and a torn middle meningeal artery. The torn artery causes an arterial hemorrhage and a hematoma that forms rapidly. There is a 50% mortality and a 70% morbidity. Of patients with epidural hematoma, 50% have no evidence of skull fracture.

SIGNS AND SYMPTOMS

Short period of loss of consciousness, followed by a lucid period, followed by another
    loss of consciousness (the initial loss of consciousness is probably caused by a concus-
    sion) *or*
There may be no intial loss of consciousness
Severe headache
Hemiparesis
Ipsilateral dilated pupil
Bradycardia
Decreased pulse
Increased blood pressure
Positive findings on CT scan

THERAPEUTIC INTERVENTION

Hyperventilation with 100% oxygen
Furosemide
Elevation of head at a 15° angle (if not contraindicated)
Surgical intervention

Acute subdural hematoma (Fig. 16-10)

An acute subdural hematoma is bleeding between the dura mater and the arachnoid membrane. It usually results from severe head trauma, usually an acceleration/deceleration incident, in which venous bleeding occurs from a vein lacerated where it crosses the subdural space. There is a 70% mortality and a 90% morbidity associated with this condition. In a child less than 1 year old, subdural hematoma is almost always caused by child abuse. In children from 1 to 18 years old it is usually caused by a cerebral laceration or a bleeding contusion on the surface of the cortex.

SIGNS AND SYMPTOMS

Loss of consciousness
Positive Babinski reflex
Fixed dilated pupil(s)
Hemiparesis
Hyperreflexia (localizing)

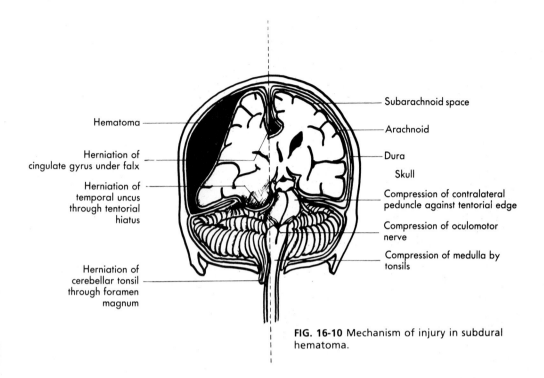

FIG. 16-10 Mechanism of injury in subdural hematoma.

Elevated temperature
Positive findings on CT scan

THERAPEUTIC INTERVENTION

Hyperventilation with 100% oxygen
Furosemide
Antipyretics
Surgical intervention
If the patient is an infant with retinal hemorrhage and decerebrate posturing, performing a
    subdural tap in the emergency department is an option

Chronic subdural hematoma

A chronic subdural hematoma may occur 4 to 8 weeks after head trauma in which the patient had been asymptomatic or level of consciousness improved. It may occur nontraumatically in the elderly or with or without trauma in the chronic alcoholic.

SIGNS AND SYMPTOMS

Headache
Ataxia
Incontinence

Decreased level of consciousness
Increasing dementia
Positive findings on CT scan

THERAPEUTIC INTERVENTION

Surgical intervention is indicated for chronic subdural hematoma.

Subarachnoid hematoma

A subarachnoid hematoma is bleeding between the arachnoid membrane and the pia mater. It is usually caused by the rupture of a congenital intercranial aneurysm known as a berry aneurysm or by hypertension. It can also occur as a result of head trauma.

SIGNS AND SYMPTOMS

Piercing, severe headache
Meningism
Nausea and vomiting
Delirium, obtundation, syncope, coma
Signs of metabolic coma
Respiratory problems (from eupnea to central neurogenic breathing)
Dilated pupil(s)
Papilledema, retinal hemorrhage
Focal motor signs
Grand mal seizures
Positive findings on CT scan

THERAPEUTIC INTERVENTION

Hyperventilation using 100% oxygen
Furosemide
Surgical intervention

BRAINSTEM HERNIATION

When there is an expanding hematoma caused by epidural, subdural, subarachnoid, or intracerebral bleeding (or some other mass), the brainstem will be compressed and forced through the tentorial notch or the foramen magnum. In a caudal transtentorial or uncal herniation the upper portion of the brainstem compresses the midbrain into the tentorial notch. In total herniation the lower portion of the brainstem is compressed into the foramen magnum.

SIGNS AND SYMPTOMS

Dilated pupils (ipsilateral 95% of the time)—caused by third cranial nerve palsy, which is caused by a stretching of the ocular nerve that crosses the tentorial notch because of a shift of the uncus
Decreased level of conciousness—caused by brainstem compression that results in a depression of the reticular activating system

Asymmetric motor movement (weakness in contralateral arm or leg 80% to 85% of time)—caused by compression of the motor movement pathways in the lower brainstem
Positive findings on CT scan

THERAPEUTIC INTERVENTION

When signs of brainstem herniation occur, the care giver must rapidly and carefully apply appropriate therapeutic intervention.

Endotracheal or nasotracheal intubation—if the patient is restless because of increased intracranial pressure, use succinylcholine:

Hyperventilate with 100% oxygen to decrease P_{CO_2} and raise P_{O_2} to decrease cerebral edema

Protect the airway (90% of patients who survive head trauma have aspiration pneumonia)

Diuretics (furosemide may be diuretic of choice):

The use of mannitol is controversial. One school of thought is that mannitol should not be given for head trauma without spinal cord trauma, as it actually increases intracerebral blood flow (the rebound phenomenon) and may increase intracranial pressure

Surgical intervention:

Burr holes are rarely drilled in the emergency department anymore because of the advent of the CT scan and more specific and rapid interpretations and surgical interventions; if burr holes are drilled they are used to decompress hematomas or diagnose bleeding (Fig. 16-11)

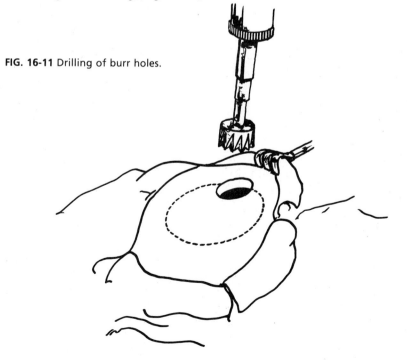

FIG. 16-11 Drilling of burr holes.

Intracranial pressure monitoring

The brain, cerebrospinal fluid, and blood are contained in the skull, which allows very little space for expansion of these substances. When one of these substances increases in volume, the others compensate by decreasing their volume, thereby maintaining a constant intracranial pressure. This compensation can only occur when there is a slight increase in volume. If volume increase is excessive, intracranial pressure will rise.

When intracranial pressure increases beyond mean arterial pressure, the brain cells become anoxic because of inadequate perfusion of brain tissue and eventually suffer irreparable damage. The brain tissue itself begins to shift, compressing the ventricles and forcing brain tissue into the tentorial notch. This compresses the brainstem and the third cranial nerve.

It is therefore necessary to avoid, or at least moderate, those activities that cause an increase in intracranial pressure in those patients who are already at risk of increased pressure.

Signs and symptoms of supratentorial herniation are: coma from impairment of the reticular activating system; changes in pupil size and reaction to light, including the dilated, fixed pupil; decreased motor response, decerebrate posturing if the herniation is at the midbrain level or decorticate posturing if the herniation is at the thalamic level, and flaccidity if the herniation has reached the level of the lower pons; and Cheyne-Stokes, central neurogenic, or ataxic respirations.

Intracranial pressure monitoring may be indicated when there is suspicion of increased intracranial pressure, such as may be found when there has been head trauma resulting in cerebral edema, increased intracranial pressure caused by a tumor or other expanding lesion, and increased intracranial pressure may have occurred as a result of an obstruction in the path of the cerebrospinal fluid.

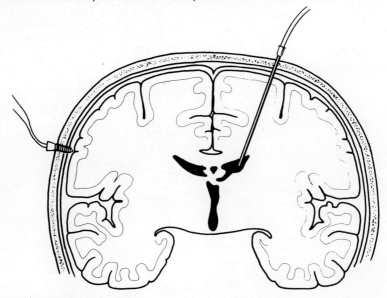

A subarachnoid screw is shown on the left with a catheter in the lateral ventricle.

The most common devices used to monitor intracranial pressure are the subarachnoid screw and a ventricular cannula. The subarachnoid screw is passed through a small threaded drill hole in the skull into the subarachnoid space. The screw is connected to a saline-filled transducer via a stop-cock and pressure tubing, which converts mechanical impulses from the subarachnoid space into electrical impulses that are displayed on a digital readout or as a visible wave form on an oscilloscope. If a catheter is used, it is passed through a burr hole into the lateral ventricle and connected to a saline-filled transducer via a stopcock and pressure tubing. It transmits impulses in the same manner as the subarachnoid screw.

An alternate method, using a sensor implanted in the epidural or subdural space (through a burr hole) provides a constant monitor pattern. This approach to intracranial pressure monitoring is safer in terms of electrical hazards and potential infection, and there is no risk of uncontrolled loss of CSF from ventricles.

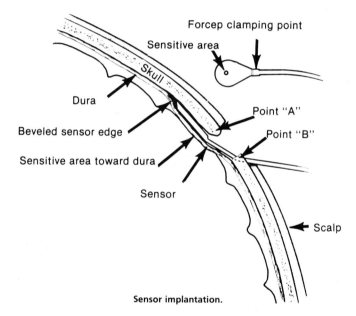

Sensor implantation.

Normal intracranial pressure is 5.8 to 13 mm Hg (70 to 190 mm H_2O). It is quite normal to have brief intracranial pressure elevations of greater than 13 mm Hg with such activities as suctioning, turning, or sneezing. A prolonged intracranial pressure reading of greater than 13 mm Hg, however, is abnormal. If intracranial pressure increases to 50 mm Hg or greater for over 20 minutes, the patient has a very poor prognosis.

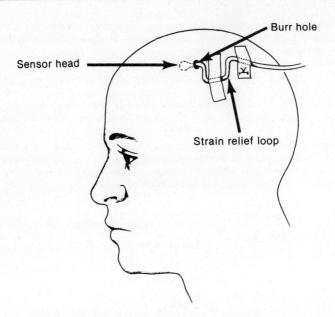

Sensor head

Burr hole

Strain relief loop

A strain relief loop prevents damage if the patient rolls his head.

Cerebral perfusion pressure can be calculated by subtracting intracranial pressure from mean arterial pressure. A result of less than 60 mm H_2O will indicate cerebral ischemia and a cerebral perfusion pressure of less than 30 mm H_2O will result in death.

Administration of osmotic diuretics, such as mannitol or urea, or the use of steroids may increase cerebral perfusion pressure. Fluids can also be decreased by limiting those taken by mouth or by the parenteral route. Cerebrospinal fluid can be removed via ventriculostomy or lumbar puncture. Pressure can be reduced by temporal decompression or by pharmacological measures to increase the mean arterial pressure, and the patient can be hyperventilated to blow off CO_2.

From: Budassi, S.A., J.E.N., May, 1979.

Corticosteroids:
    Rarely used anymore, as they have been found to be ineffective; high doses may
        actually increase the incidence of intracranial infection
Barbiturate coma:
    This is currently being studied but cannot yet be recommended

ALCOHOL INTOXICATION AND HEAD TRAUMA

The care given should be sure to rule out head and cervical spine trauma in the intoxicated patient. The presence of alcohol can interfere with accurate assessment in head trauma. Also, subdural hematoma is a common finding after head trauma (usually from a fall) in the chronic alcohol abuser.

TABLE 16-3 Summary of assessment and management in brain injuries and alcohol intoxication

Assessments	Signs and symptoms		Treatment
	Brain injuries	Intoxication	
Respirations	Underventilation	Slow, stertorous breathing	Oxygen therapy or endotracheal intubation
Arterial blood gases	$P_{CO_2}\uparrow$, $P_{O_2}\downarrow$	Changes at blood levels of 0.30%	Oxygen therapy or endotracheal intubation
Vital signs	Bradycardia Hypothermia Hypertension (late sign)	Tachycardia Hypothermia Hypotension (0.30%)	ECG monitoring Provide extra warmth Treat for shock if necessary
Level of consciousness	Fluctuations worsening	Improvement* (may occur very slowly)	Monitor continually
Pupils	Unequal Unreactive	Dilated Equal	Monitor continually for changes
Motor ability	Nonpurposeful Nonreactive Uncoordinated	Depends on blood alcohol levels	Monitor continually
Reflexes	Absent in fifth cranial nerve damage Absent gag reflex in ninth cranial nerve damage	May be absent if comatose	Provide artificial tears with normal saline Protect airway by proper positioning and suctioning of secretions
Vomiting	Projectile	Occurs normally with nausea at blood levels of 0.20%	Protect airway by positioning and suctioning secretions
Urinary output	Diuresis	Diuresis	Monitor closely, prevent dehydration in diuresis due to diabetes insipidus with proper use of IV fluids

From Anspaugh, P.: J.E.N. **3**:12, June 1977.
*Remember that blood alcohol levels do not peak until 45 minutes following ingestion. You may see worsening symptoms in the intoxicated individual for a short time while blood levels are peaking. A good history on the patient's immediate drinking pattern may explain the worsening symptoms.

SUGGESTED READINGS

Ansbaugh, P.: Emergency management of intoxicated patients with head injuries, J.E.N. **3**(3):9, 1977.

Bouzarth, W.E.: Trauma at the top, Emerg. Med. **7**:71, 1975.

Brock, S.: Injuries of brain and spinal cord and their coverings, ed. 5, New York, 1974, Springer Publishing Co., Inc.

Bruce, D.A., et al.: Resuscitation from coma due to head injury, Crit. Care Med. **6**:254, 1978.

Budassi, S.A.: Trauma notebook #18: intracranial pressure monitoring, J.E.N. **5**(3):45, 1979.

Budassi, S.A., and Barber, J.M.: Emergency nursing: principles and practice, St. Louis, 1981, The C.V. Mosby Co.

Galbraith, S., and Smith, J.: Acute traumatic intracranial hematoma without skull fracture, Lancet **1**:501, 1976.

Kraus, J.F.: Epidemiologic features of head and spinal cord injury, Adv. Neurol. **19**:261, 1978.

Jennett, B., et al.: Severe head injuries in three countries, J. Neurol. Neurosurg. Psychiatry **40**:291, 1977.

Jennett, B., and Teasdale, G.: Management of head injuries, Philadelphia, 1981, F.A. Davis Co.

North, J.B., and Jennett, B.: Abnormal breathing patterns associated with acute brain damage, Arch. Neurol. **31**:338, 1974.

Plum, F., and Posner, J.B.: Diagnosis of Stupor and Coma, ed. 3, Philadelphia, 1980, F.A. Davis Co.

Pohutsky, L.C., and Pohutsky, K.R.: Computerized axial tomography of the brain: a new diagnostic tool, Am. J. Nurs. **75**:1341, 1975.

CHAPTER 17 **Spinal cord trauma**

SPINAL CORD INJURY IN GENERAL

There are two major divisions of the central nervous system:

Central—brain and spinal cord

Peripheral—sensorimotor area and nerves

The spinal cord is an integral part of the central nervous system. The central nervous system controls consciousness, regulates body movement and function, and transmits nerve impulses. It has both voluntary and involuntary functions. The spinal cord carries messages between the brain and the body in the form of electrical impulses.

Anatomy of the spinal cord

The spinal cord is covered by:

The paravertebral muscles

The vertebrae

The dura mater

The arachnoid membrane } The meninges

The pia mater

The spinal cord is enclosed in a canal that extends down through the vertebral column. Spinal nerves extend through openings in the vertebrae. The anterior part of the spinal cord contains motor tracts. The posterior part of the spinal cord contains sensory tracts. A 2 mm compression (the size of a pinpoint pupil) may cause a major motor deficit such as the loss of function of an arm or a leg. If there is an immediate and complete lesion of the spinal cord the prognosis for recovery is poor.

Cervical vertebrae 3, 4, and 5 contain the phrenic nerve. Injury to this area will cause loss of control of the diaphragm (the main muscle of respiration). Survival from such an injury is rare. Any lesion above C3 or C4 usually results in death. There are 7 cervical vertebrae, 12 thoracic vertebrae, 5 lumbar vertebrae, and 1 sacral vertebra. (See Fig. 17-1.)

Innervations at the level of the vertebrae include the following:

C2 to C4—diaphragm, neck muscles

C5, C6—biceps brachii, deltoid, triceps brachii, wrist extensors

C6 to T1—latissimus dorsi

C6 to T1—hand muscles

T2 to T7—intercostal muscles

T6 to L1—abdominal muscles

T12 to L2—quadratus lumborum

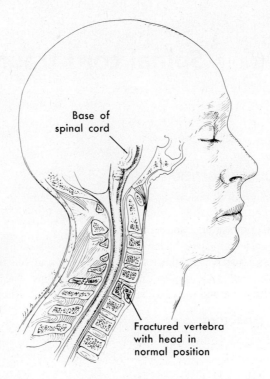

FIG. 17-1 Types of spinal cord injury. (From Barber, J., Stokes, L., and Billings, D.: Adult and child care, ed. 2, St. Louis, 1977, The C.V. Mosby Co.)

L1 to L5—leg muscles
L2 to L3—psoas muscles
L2 to L4—quadriceps
L4 to L5—tibialis anterior
S1—bowel and bladder

Lesions of:	Produce:
C3, C4, or above (quadriplegia)	Usually death
C5, or C6 (quadriplegia)	Reduced respiratory effort; almost total dependence; flaccid paralysis
C7 (quadriplegia)	Reduced respiratory effort; almost total dependence; splints necessary for forearms to function
T1 (paraplegia)	Reduced respiratory effort; partial dependence
T1, T2 (paraplegia)	Reduced respiratory effort; complete independence
T7 (paraplegia)	Complete independence; walking only with long leg braces
L4 (paraplegia)	Walking only with foot braces

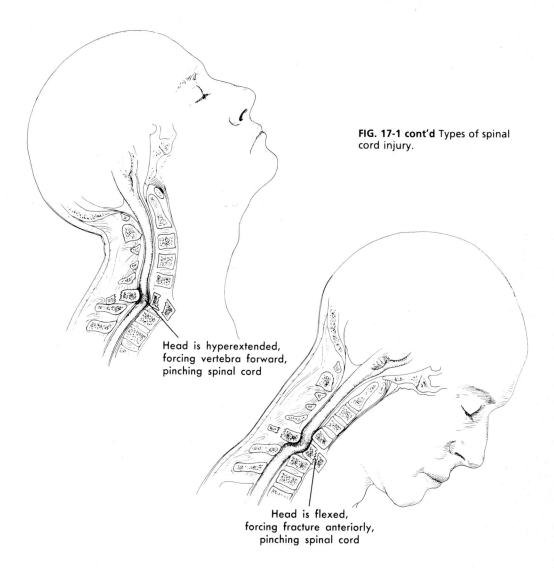

FIG. 17-1 cont'd Types of spinal cord injury.

Head is hyperextended, forcing vertebra forward, pinching spinal cord

Head is flexed, forcing fracture anteriorly, pinching spinal cord

Diagnostic examinations

Bulbocavernosus reflex   Normal findings: Place a finger in the patient's rectum and compress on the glans or clitoris or tug on the Foley catheter—this should cause contraction of the anal sphincter; if this reflex is absent initially and then returns in 24 hours, this is indicative of a total lesion.

Anal contraction ("wink")   Normal findings: The anal sphincter should contract when a pinprick is applied close by.

X-ray examinations   The most common cervical spine fractures/dislocations may be visualized on lateral cervical spine films; all seven cervical vertebrae as well as the first thoracic vertebra must be visualized; also, examine the skull, maxilla, and mandible; check for edema of the airway; the most common fracture/dislocation is at C6-C7.

Check the patient for touch sensation.
Check the patient for paresthesias or paralysis.
Check for the ability to grip with the hands.
Check for the ability to wiggle the toes.
Check total status again after any movement by the patient.

SIGNS AND SYMPTOMS OF SPINAL CORD INJURY

Neck tenderness and pain
Weakness of extremities
Numbness and tingling
Decreased motor activity distal to the injury
Decreased anal sphincter tone
Pain on careful palpation of spine:
    Check for edema
    Check for deformities
    Check for spaces
Decreased blood pressure in spinal shock
Priapism (abnormal erection)

PREVENTIVE MEASURES TO AVOID FURTHER DAMAGE

Have a sufficient number of personnel available so that the patient can be moved by
    log-rolling.
Immobilize the neck in whatever way possible and with whatever means available:
    Sandbags
    Hard cervical collar
    Backboards
    Tape
    Gentle manual traction along lines of axis
If a short spine board or other device is used, use a long board or scoop stretcher also;
    protect the thoracic and lumbar spines as well.
If the patient has a helmet on (motorcycle, football, etc.) leave it in place (if the airway is
    not compromised) until the condition of the cervical spine is confirmed and measures
    can be taken to remove the helmet safely.
Keep the head elevated at a 15° angle if possible.
Have good suction ready and available.
If the patient has a lap seat belt only (without a shoulder harness), suspect a spinal fracture
    until proved otherwise.
Be sure the patient is ventilating well.

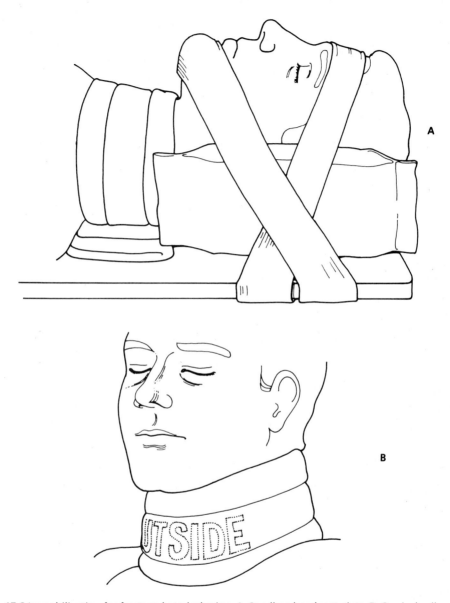

FIG. 17-2 Immobilization for fractured cervical spine. **A,** Sandbag head restraints. **B,** Cervical collar.

THERAPEUTIC INTERVENTION

The goals of therapeutic intervention in spinal cord injury are to:
Protect the neurologic elements
Preserve function
Stabilize the spinal column
Rehabilitate the patient

Specific interventions include:
    Airway management
    Immobilization (in same position if there is pain or paresthesia on movement)
    Gentle traction (in emergency department, possible use of Gardner-Wells tongs) (Fig.
       17-3)
    Assess DERM and level of deficit
    Check for other injuries
    IV
    Nasogastric tube
    MAST (if indicated)
    Foley catheter
    Laboratory tests preparatory to surgery

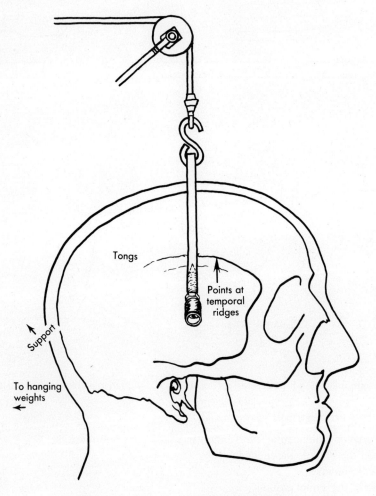

FIG. 17-3 Placement of Gardner-Wells tongs.

Compression fracture:
   Bed rest, then extension exercises
Burst fracture:
   Plaster jacket or bed rest and brace, then surgery for stabilization

Special problems

Bladder—patient should have a Foley catheter; a distended bladder may be fatal in a paraplegic.
Decubitus ulcers—the most common cause of death; use early preventive measures.
Psyche—be realistic with the patient; do not give false hope.

Types of injuries

A spinal cord injury can be either stable or unstable. All spinal cord injuries must be assumed to be unstable until proved otherwise.

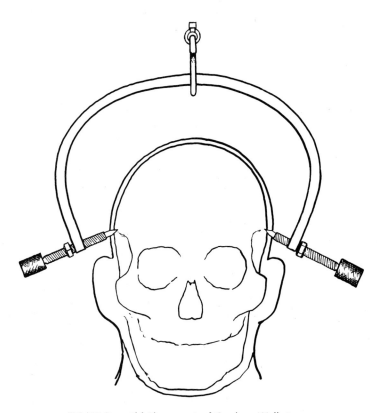

FIG. 17-3 cont'd Placement of Gardner-Wells tongs.

Stable

Further movement will cause no problems

Simple wedge fracture (Fig. 17-4, *A*)

Burst fracture (patient is usually paraplegic or quadriplegic) (Fig. 17-4, *B*)

Extension/hyperflexion injury

Unstable

Further movement may cause further damage

Pure dislocation (very dangerous; may have been dislocated then reduced)

Shear fracture

Rotational disc fracture (patient is often paraplegic)

Extension/hyperflexion injury

In extension or hyperflexion injury, always check the patient's sensory level and always get x-ray films. There may be a tear of the posterior longitudinal ligaments or the anterior longitudinal ligaments.

SPINAL SHOCK

Spinal shock may be caused by spinal cord transection in which there is loss of vessel tone (distributive shock).

Therapeutic intervention for spinal shock includes volume replacement with IVs or MAST placement and administration of alpha-adrenergic agents (Metaraminol [Aramine]) to elevate blood pressure. Note that shock may be caused by other injuries, such as those that would cause hypovolemic shock.

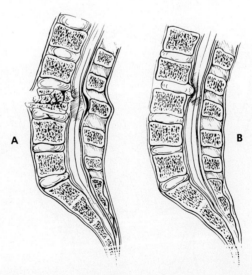

FIG. 17-4 Two causes for spinal cord compression. **A,** Compression fracture of vertebrae. **B,** Herniated nucleus pulposus. (From Barber, J., Stokes, L., and Billings, D.: Adult and child care, ed. 2, St. Louis, 1977, The C.V. Mosby Co.)

SUGGESTED READINGS

Budassi, S.A., and Barber, J.M.: Emergency nursing: principles and practice, St. Louis, 1981, The C.V. Mosby Co.

Dula, D.J.: Trauma to the cervical spine, J.A.C.E.P. **8:**504, 1979.

Gerlock, A.J., et al.: Advanced exercises in diagnostic radiology—the cervical spine in trauma, Philadelphia, 1978, W.B. Saunders Co.

Harris, J.H., Jr.: The radiology of acute cervical spine trauma, Baltimore, 1978, The Williams & Wilkins Co.

Huelke, D.F.: Cervical fractures and fracture dislocations sustained without head impact, J. Trauma **18:**533, 1978.

Weiss, M.H.: Head trauma and spinal cord injuries: diagnostic and therapeutic criteria, Crit. Care Med. **2:**311, 1974.

CHAPTER 18 Facial trauma

Facial trauma is one of the most commonly seen types of trauma in the emergency department. It is far too easy to concentrate on the profuse bleeding of facial trauma, which is caused by the great amount of vascularity to this area, and to overlook a life-threatening but not so obvious problem. ("Never treat the obvious at the expense of the unobvious.") A patient with facial trauma may have other injuries of a more serious nature, such as an airway problem, respiratory distress, shock, a spinal cord injury, or a cranial catastrophy. Always begin assessment of facial trauma with the following:

Airway—avoid the head tilt; use the jaw thrust or oral, nasopharyngeal, or esophageal obturator airway

Breathing—remember: "Noisy breathing is obstructed breathing"

Circulation

Cervical spine—avoid hyperextension of the neck; check for neck injury; check for laryngeal fracture; use a cervical collar; immobilize the neck; obtain a cross-table lateral cervical spine film in the hospital

Control hemorrhage—use direct pressure

Neurologic evaluation—level of consciousness; check for head injury

Evaluate eyes—look at each eye individually; check for loss of vision, diplopia (double vision) in each of four quadrants, hemorrhage, and foreign body penetration.

Also check for the following:

Malocclusion of teeth

Point tenderness

Asymmetry at:

Infraorbital rim

Zygomatic arch

Anterior wall of antrum

Angles of the jaw

Lower borders of the mandible

Cerebrospinal fluid leak (from ears and nose)

Automobile accidents and motorcycle accidents are the major sources of facial trauma in the United States. Facial injuries often involve four of the cranial nerves (Table 18-1).

FACIAL LACERATIONS

Immediate repair of facial lacerations is important. Severe facial lacerations usually do not have associated facial fractures.

380

TABLE 18-1 Cranial nerves involved in facial trauma

Nerve	Name	Activity	Elicits	Test by
Third	Oculomotor	Motor	Eyeball movement; supplies 5 of 7 ocular muscles	Pupil response; ocular movement to four quadrants
Fourth	Trochlear	Motor	Eyeball movement (superior oblique)	Same as above
Fifth	Trigeminal	Motor and sensory	Facial sensation; jaw movement	Assessing pain, touch, hot and cold sensations, bite, opening mouth against resistance
Seventh	Facial	Motor and sensory	Facial expression; taste from anterior two thirds of tongue	Zygomatic branch: have patient close eyes tightly. Temporal branch: have patient elevate brows, wrinkle forehead. Buccal branch: have patient elevate upper lip, wrinkle nose, whistle

Abrasions and contusions:

    Cleanse and debride wounds

    Carefully remove gravel, gunpowder, and other foreign matter, as these will cause "tattooing" at a later time if they are not removed

    Dress with a topical antibiotic

Simple lacerations:

    Cleanse and debride the wound

    Suture the wound (without tension)

    Dress with a topical antibiotic and pressure dressing

Proper cleansing of a facial wound may require a local anesthetic. Usually the anesthetic of choice is 1% lidocaine with epinephrine. Epinephrine causes vasoconstriction and increases the absorption time of lidocaine. It takes approximately 7 minutes to begin to see decreased bleeding as an effect of epinephrine and another 7 minutes for the full effect of the drug. Without epinephrine, lidocaine is absorbed in about 20 to 30 minutes.

Small facial lacerations can be treated under local anesthesia. For larger lacerations a nerve block is indicated.

Facial lacerations can be sutured any time for 8 hours after the accident. If the injury is 8 to 24 hours old, the wound should be sutured and the patient should be given systemic antibiotics. If a wound is more than 24 hours old, saline soaks should be applied until the wound is clear of infection and debris. Once this is accomplished, the wound can be debrided and sutured. The patient should continue taking systemic antibiotics. Lacerations containing glass fragments should have the glass removed before scrubbing and dressing; usually no sutures are required.

Other areas of the face that require special consideration:

    Eyelids—suture as soon as possible before edema sets in

Lips—suture assuring that the vermilion border is intact

Eyebrows—approximate and suture; never shave

Cheeks—check for damage to the parotid gland and Stensen's duct before suturing.

Tongue—sometimes tongue lacerations can be left alone, and sometimes sutures are needed; a child should be sedated ½ hour before suturing

Remember that any patient with a soft tissue injury or open fracture in the facial area should have a current tetanus immunization status or receive tetanus prophylaxis.

AFTERCARE INSTRUCTIONS FOR PATIENTS WITH SOFT TISSUE INJURIES

Keep the wound clean and dry

Cleanse around the area with hydrogen peroxide solution

Apply a topical antibiotic ointment two to three times daily

Observe for infection (heat, redness, and swelling)

Return for suture removal in 4 days

Keep tape strips in place for 10 days following suture removal

FACIAL FRACTURES

In the care of multiple injuries, facial fractures are usually not a priority. The repair of a facial fracture, unlike that of a laceration, can be delayed for up to a week without serious consequences.

Nasal fracture

The most common of all facial fractures is a fracture of the nose. The mechanism of injury is usually blunt trauma to the front or side of the nose. An x-ray film is usually not required to make a diagnosis. Diagnosis may be accomplished clinically by obtaining a good history and observing for swelling, deformity, and crepitus. Also, the care giver may be able to feel the fracture. Nasal fractures will usually bleed externally and internally. If the patient is not seen immediately after the accident, reduction will usually have to be delayed until swelling has gone down. Any fracture of the nose should be treated as an open fracture, and antibiotics should be administered. The care giver should also check for septal hematomas. A septal hematoma that is not excised and packed may become infected. There are three types of nasal fractures:

Nasal bone depression with or without septal dislocation. The mechanism of injury is a blow to the side of the nose.

Fractures of both nasal bones with or without septal dislocation. The mechanism of injury is a hard blow to front or side of nose.

Comminuted fracture with flattening of bridge and fracture of septum. The mechanism of injury is a severe blow, usually from assault with a weapon or a baseball injury.

THERAPEUTIC INTERVENTION

On the scene:

Apply a cold pack

Splint

Control bleeding

In the hospital:
    Administer anesthetic:
        Infraorbital area, anterior nasal spine, and dorsum of nose—inject with 1% lido-
            caine with epinephrine
        Mucosa—pack with cotton pledgets soaked in 5% lidocaine
    Manipulate the impacted bone and cartilage to free them, using fingers and forceps
    Mold the fractured parts with the fingers
    Pack the inside to decrease bleeding; if the septum is fractured, pack both sides
    Splint for 2 weeks

Zygomatic fracture

The most common of zygomatic fractures is the trimaleolar (tripod) fracture in which the zygoma is fractured in three places: at the zygomatic arch, at the posterior half of the infraorbital rim, and at the frontal zygomatic suture. The mechanism of injury is blunt trauma to the side of the face and front of the cheek.

SIGNS AND SYMPTOMS

Palpable infraorbital rim fracture
Limited eye movement in upward gaze
Swelling
The symptoms of the mnemonic TIDES:
    T = Trismus (tonic contractions of the muscles of mastication)
    I = Infraorbital hyperesthesia or anesthesia
    D = Diplopia (double vision)
    E = Epistaxis
    S = Symmetry (appearance of depressed cheek; look down over the forehead to
        observe)

THERAPEUTIC INTERVENTION

Cold
Check for cerebrospinal fluid leak from a fractured cribriform plate
Usually surgical repair

Maxillary fracture

Maxillary fractures are usually caused by tremendous forces such as would be incurred in an automobile accident, a fistfight, or a direct blow to the face with a baseball bat or a club. Maxillary fractures were first categorized by the French pathologist LeFort who struck corpses with clubs to determine the resultant types of fractures:
    LeFort I (Fig. 18-1)—fracture of the transverse alveolar process involving the front
        teeth and a bilateral fracture up to the nose
        Signs and symptoms—malocclusion of the teeth
        Therapeutic intervention—cold and internal fixation
    LeFort II (Fig. 18-2)—fracture of the pyramidal area including the central part of the
        maxilla to the nasal area
        Signs and symptoms—nose moves with dental arch

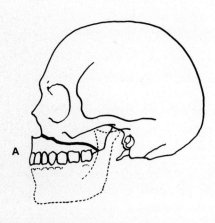

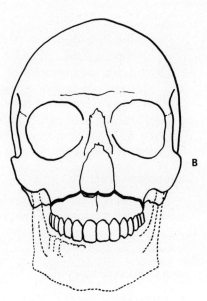

FIG. 18-1 LeFort I facial fracture. **A,** Lateral view. **B,** Frontal view.

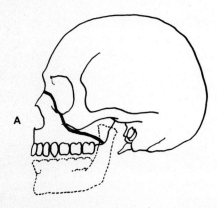

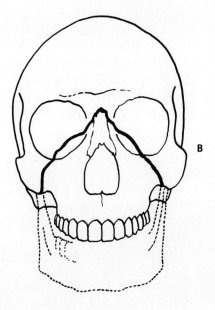

FIG. 18-2 LeFort II facial fracture. **A,** Lateral view. **B,** Frontal view.

Therapeutic intervention—cold, internal fixation, internal stabilization, open reduction

Special note—guard the airway; patient will bleed profusely from the nose and pharynx

LeFort III (Fig. 18-3)—total craniofacial separation including a tripod fracture and craniofacial detachment

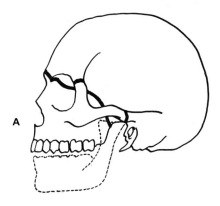
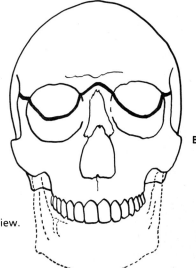

FIG. 18-3 LeFort III facial fracture. **A,** Lateral view. **B,** Frontal view.

Signs and symptoms—nose and dental arch move without frontal bone movement

Therapeutic intervention—cold, internal fixation, antibiotics, and bed rest with the head elevated

Special note—associated fracture of the cribriform plate and resulting cerebrospinal fluid leak are common

Mandibular fracture

Mandible fracture is the second most frequently seen facial fracture. Quite frequently a midline mandibular fracture will be accompanied by other fractures, usually near the condyles. Mandibular fractures are frequently open fractures. The mechanism of injury is usually a severe blunt force to the jaw; it is a common football and basketball injury.

SIGNS AND SYMPTOMS

Malocclusion of the teeth
Pain
Trismus
Bone or fragment displacement
Palpation of fracture

THERAPEUTIC INTERVENTION

Cold
Immobilization
Wiring of an unstable area to a stable area

Orbital blow-out fractures

Orbital blow-out fractures occur when a blunt force directly hits the eyeball, causing an increase in intraocular pressure and a fracture of the orbit floor.

Facial trauma

Where to begin:
Airway
Breathing
Circulation
Protection of cervical spine
Check level of consciousness
Check pupillary reflexes
Control bleeding
Check for malocclusion of teeth
Check for point tenderness

Care of facial lacerations
Abrasions/Contusions:
  Cleanse and debride
  Remove foreign material (as may cause
    "tattooing" later)
  Apply topical antibiotics
Lacerations:
  Cleanse and debride
  Suture without tension
  Apply topical antibiotics
  Apply pressure dressing

Guide to suturing facial lacerations
Laceration less than 8 hours old:
  Suture
  Topical antibiotics
Laceration 8 to 24 hours old:
  Suture
  Topical antibiotics
  Systemic antibiotics
Laceration more than 24 hours old:
  Saline soaks until clean
  Debride
  Suture
  Topical antibiotics
  Systemic antibiotics
Check for asymmetry
  Infraorbital rim
  Zygomatic arch
  Anterior wall of antrum
  Angles of jaw
  Lower borders of mandible
Check for CSF leak (ears and nose)
Check cranial nerves

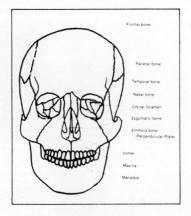

Skull/Anterior view

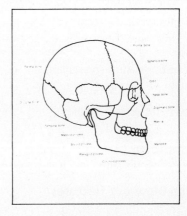

Skull/Lateral view

Cranial nerve check

Nerve	Name	Activity	Causes	How to check
3rd	Oculomotor	Motor	Globe movement; supplies 5 of 7 ocular muscles	Pupillary response; ocular movement to four quadrants
4th	Trochlear	Motor	Superior/oblique globe movement	Pupillary response; ocular movement to four quadrants
5th	Trigeminal	Motor/ sensory	Facial sensation; jaw movement	Response to touch, pain, heat, cold; bite; open mouth against resistance
7th	Facial; three branches	Motor/ sensory	Facial expression; taste (anterior two thirds of tongue)	Zygomatic branch: close eyes tightly Temporal branch: wrinkle forehead; raise eyebrows Buccal branch: raise upper lip; wrinkle nose; whistle

SIGNS AND SYMPTOMS

History of injury
Periorbital hematoma ("black eye")
Subconjunctival hemorrhage

Periorbital edema
Enophthalmos

THERAPEUTIC INTERVENTION

Cold
If displaced, packing of maxillary sinus, reduction of fracture, and checking for intraocular injury
Ophthalmologic consultation

Fractures that do not require treatment

Nondisplaced facial fractures
Fractures of the anterior wall of the maxillary antrum
Fractures of the coronoid process of the mandible
Condylar fractures in children[1]

Facial fractures

Type	Description	Caused by
Nasal (three types)	Nasal bone depression	Blow to side of nose
	Bilateral nasal bones	Blow to side or front of nose
	Comminuted/flattened bridge and septum	Severe blow to front of nose
Zygoma (trimaleolar)	Fracture in three places: Zygomatic arch Infraorbital rim Zygomatic suture	Blunt trauma to side of face and front of skull
Mandible	Fracture of mandible	Serve blunt force to jaw
Orbital blow out	Fracture of orbital floor	Blunt force to eyeball causing increased intraocular pressure
Maxilla LeFort I	Fracture of transverse alveolar process; involves anterior teeth with bilateral fracture up nose	Blunt force to maxilla
LeFort II	Fracture of pyramidal area and central maxilla to nose	Blunt force to maxilla
LeFort III	Total craniofacial separation	Blunt force to maxilla

From Budassi, S.A.: J.E.N. **6**(5):69, 1980.

REFERENCE

1. Leake, D., et al.: Longterm follow-up of fractures of the mandibular condyle in children, Plast. Reconstr. Surg. **47**:127, 1971.

SUGGESTED READINGS

Boles, R., et al.: The face inside and out, Emerg. Med. **10**:27, Feb. 1978.
Kirchner, F.R.: Management of neck and face injuries. In McSwain, N.E.: Traumatic surgery, Flushing, N.Y., 1976, Medical Examination Publishing Co., Inc.

Signs and symptoms	Treatment	Comments
Pain Swelling Epistaxis	Ice pack; splint; control bleeding; anesthetize; manipulate/reduce; mold; interior packing; splint	Most common facial fracture
Palpable fracture; limited upward gaze; swelling; trismus; hypesthesia or anesthesia (infraorbital); diplopia; epistaxis; asymmetry	Ice pack; check for CSF leak; surgery/repair	
Pain; trismus; malocclusion of teeth; palpable fracture	Ice pack; immobilization/wiring	Second most frequent facial fracture; may be seen with other fractures
Periorbital hematoma; periorbital edema; subconjunctival hemorrhage; enophthalmos	Ice pack; pack maxillary sinus; reduce fracture; examine eye	Must have ophthalmology consult
Pain; malocclusion of teeth	Ice pack; internal fixation	
Pain; nose and dental arch move as unit; profuse bleeding from nose and pharynx	Control airway; ice pack; open reduction/internal fixation	
Pain; nose, zygoma, and dental arch move with frontal bone; CSF leak	Control airway; ice pack; bed rest; high Fowler's position; internal fixation; systemic antibiotics	

Kruger, G.: Fractures of the jaws. In Kruger, G., ed.: Textbook of oral and maxillofacial surgery, ed. 6, St. Louis, 1984, The C.V. Mosby Co.

Moore, L.T.: Emergency management of facial injuries. In Warner, C.G., ed.: Emergency care: assessment and intervention, ed. 3, St. Louis, 1983, The C.V. Mosby Co.

Shira, R.: Emergency treatment of patients with facial trauma. In Douglas, B., ed.: Introduction to hospital dentistry, ed. 2, St. Louis, 1970, The C.V. Mosby Co.

Wilson, R.F., and Zamick, P.: Trauma to the face. In Walt, A.J., and Wilson, R.F.: Management of trauma: pitfalls and practice, Philadelphia, 1975, Lea & Febiger.

CHAPTER 19 **Eye, ear, nose, throat, and dental emergencies**

OCULAR EMERGENCIES

There are many occasions when rapid, careful assessment and intervention can prevent permanent or temporary loss of vision.

Basic anatomy of the eye (Figs. 19-1 and 19-2)

bony rim—The bony process that protects the eyeball.

eyelid—The covering that closes to protect the eyeball, distribute tears, and regulate light.

eyelashes—Hairs that minimize the number of dirt particles that enter the eye area.

sclera—The tough protective coating of the eyeball.

cornea—The front section of the eyeball that bulges and through which light passes into the lens.

retina—The inner lining of the posterior eyeball that collects light.

choroid—The middle layer of the eyeball that supplies the retina with blood, oxygen, and other nutrients.

macula—The area of the retina most sensitive to light and color.

lens—The disc through which light passes to the posterior chamber from the cornea and the anterior chamber; light passes through the cornea, the anterior chamber, the lens, and the vitreous humor to the retina.

iris—Diaphragm that controls the amount of light entering the posterior chamber by means of expanding and contracting its opening (the pupil).

oculomotor muscles—The six muscles that control eyeball movement.

lacrimal glands—Glands that secrete fluid (tears) to soothe the eyeball and reduce friction.

tears—Fluid that covers the eyeball; tears are distributed by blinking of the eyelids. They exit the lacrimal gland through the lacrimal puncta into the lacrimal and nasolacrimal ducts.

meibomian glands—Glands that secrete oil that lines the eyelid margins and prevents tears from running out of the conjunctival sac.

visual acuity—central vision; stimuli on macula.

peripheral vision—vision in which stimuli are on an area of the retina other than the macula.

There are certain conditions that should be given priority treatment in the emergency department. These are the following:

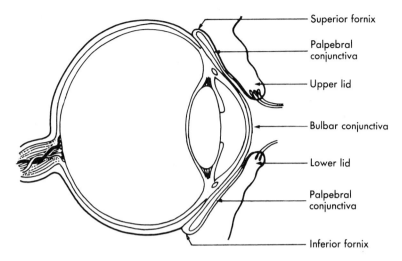

FIG. 19-1 Longitudinal section of eyeball.

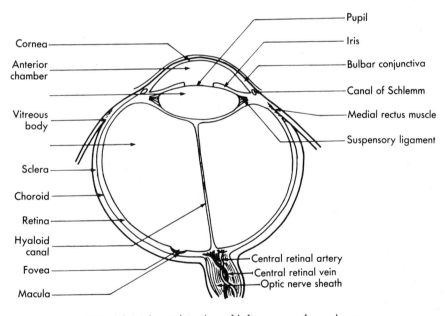

FIG. 19-2 Horizontal section of left eye seen from above.

Loss of vision without pain (may be caused by central artery occlusion or central vein
    occlusion, intraocular hemorrhage, or retinal detachment)
Chemical burns
Foreign bodies
Painful eyes (may be caused by conjunctivitis, iritis, or keratitis)

Examination of the eye

When examining the eye, make sure that there is good lighting. If there is much pain a topical anesthetic agent (such as proparacaine [Ophthaine] or tetracaine) may assist in examination of the eye. Remember to be gentle and explain the procedure to the patient. If an injury or disease process of the eye is identified early and therapeutic intervention is rapid, the care giver may prevent further complications to the eye.

The visual acuity examination (Fig. 19-3)

Whenever possible a visual acuity examination should be performed before examination of the eye.

If the patient wears glasses, examine his vision first with glasses, then without

If the patient's glasses are not available, have him read the chart through a pinhole poked in a piece of cardboard

Check each eye separately and then both eyes together

Follow specific instructions on how to conduct the examination according to the chart to be used:

The Snellen Chart is read at 20 feet

The Rosenbaum Pocket Vision Screener is read 14 inches from the nose

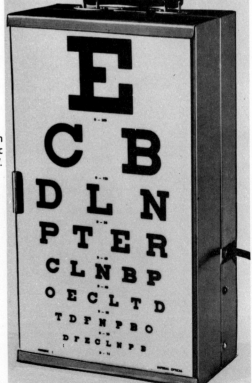

FIG. 19-3 Snellen visual acuity chart. (From Stein, H.A., and Slatt, B.J.: The ophthalmic assistant, ed. 4, St. Louis, 1982, The C.V. Mosby Co.)

If a Snellen or other vision chart is not available, have the patient read newsprint, and record the distance from the eye the paper must be held for the patient to read it

If the patient cannot see newsprint, hold up a specific number of fingers and record the distance at which the patient can see the fingers (and be able to tell how many are being held up)

If the patient cannot see fingers, record the distance at which he can perceive hand motion

If the patient cannot see hand motion, record the distance at which he can perceive light

If the patient cannot perceive light, this should be recorded on his chart

EXAMPLES OF VISUAL ACUITY EXAMINATION SCORES

20/20—when the patient stands 20 feet from the Snellen chart, he can read what the normal eye can read at 20 feet

20/40—when the patient stands 20 feet from the Snellen chart, he can read what the normal eye can read at 40 feet (and, in this example, he has also missed two letters)

20/200—when the patient stands 20 feet from the Snellen chart, he can read what the normal eye can read at 200 feet

10/200—if the patient cannot read any of the letters on the Snellen chart, have him stand half the distance (10 feet) and read what he can; record this as the distance he actually is standing from the chart over the smallest line he can read

CF/3 feet—the patient can count fingers at a maximum distance of 3 feet

HM/4 feet—the patient can see hand motion at a maximum distance of 4 feet

LP/position—the patient can perceive light and determine from which direction it came

LP/no position—the patient can perceive light but cannot determine from which direction it came

NLP—the patient cannot perceive light

When recording information about the eyes, use the following abbreviations:

OD	ocula dexter	right eye
OS	ocula sinister	left eye
OU	oculus uterque	both eyes
gtt	guttae	drops

Eye trauma

Often when there is trauma to the eye, there is associated trauma that may be more life threatening. Also, search for associated eye trauma when there is head or facial trauma.

Never put drops in a traumatized eye before examining it. If there is great pain sometimes it will help to patch both eyes. This minimizes movement and may decrease pain.

If the patient is unconscious, be sure to check for contact lenses and be sure to protect the cornea from drying by instilling ophthalmic ointment and taping the eyelids shut or frequently instilling artificial tears.

The incidence of trauma to the eye is high in industrial areas. Industrial accidents are responsible for half of all blindness to one eye and for one fifth of all blindness to both eyes. Blindness usually results because the worker was not wearing safety glasses.

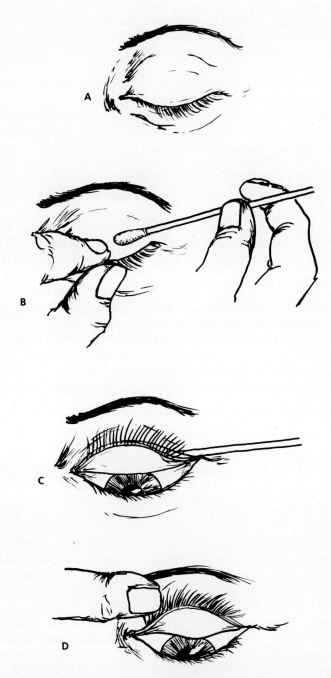

FIG. 19-4 Steps in everting eyelid. **A,** Eyelid. **B,** Placement of cotton swab, pulling eyelashes down and over swab. **C,** Eyelid everted over swab. **D,** Examination of inside of eyelid and eye.

Trauma to the eye is also a leading cause of blindness in children, second only to amblyopia.

When dealing with a patient with eye trauma, it is important to obtain a good history:

What happened?

How did it happen?

Is there something in your eye? What?

Were there chemicals involved? What chemicals?

Where did it happen?

Did anyone see it happen? Who?

Was care given at the scene? By whom?

Were you wearing safety glasses?

Do you have any other medical history? Do you have glaucoma or diabetes? Are you undergoing hormone therapy?

Injuries to the eyelids

Trauma to the eyelid rarely results in infection because of the good blood supply to this area. The care giver will be able to diagnose a lacerated eyelid simply by observing it.

THERAPEUTIC INTERVENTION

Irrigation

Wound approximation and suturing

If a section of tissue is missing, consult a plastic surgeon to reconstruct the section so the cornea will be protected

Check for laceration of the lacrimal duct

Orbital rim trauma

This type of injury may occur as a result of blunt or penetrating injury to the face. The main sign of orbital rim trauma is periorbital ecchymosis.

THERAPEUTIC INTERVENTION

Ice pack

Examination for fracture and eyeball trauma

Include visual acuity examination

If there is a fracture of the prominent supraorbital rim and frontal sinus, check for cerebrospinal fluid leak in the form of CSF rhinorrhea

If there is a visual disturbance, there may be a fracture of the orbital roof resulting in entrapment of the optic nerve

Nonpenetrating blunt trauma to the eye

Blunt trauma to the eye may cause aqueous humor to depress the diaphram of the iris or the ciliary bodies. When this occurs there is a resultant hyphema (a hemorrhage into the anterior chamber of the eye). This condition requires immediate ophthalmologic consultation.

If there is partial hyphema, therapeutic intervention includes the following:

Strict bed rest

Heavy sedation

Bilateral eye patches for a minimum of 5 days
Diuretic to reduce ocular pressure
Steroids
Miotics and/or mydriatics

Massive hemorrhage can occur at any time up to 2 weeks after blunt trauma. It can cause corneal blood staining, secondary glaucoma, loss of vision, and maybe even loss of the eye.

An 8-ball hemorrhage is a condition in which old, clotted blood is found in the anterior chamber. Therapeutic intervention for this condition is to remove the clot surgically.

Retrobulbar hemorrhage may occur as a result of ruptured intraorbital vessels. It can be diagnosed by the presence of a protruding eyeball (exophthalmos) and diplopia (double vision).

A subconjunctival hemorrhage is common after trauma to the eye. It is usually left untreated. It will resolve in about 2 weeks.

Blow-out fracture

Blow-out fracture results from direct blunt trauma to the eyeball, which causes an increased intraocular pressure that fractures the orbit floor. It can be diagnosed by obtaining a history of the event and by observing periorbital hematoma, subconjunctival hemorrhage, periorbital edema, enophthalmos, an upward gaze, and a complaint of diplopia. The diplopia is caused by trapping of the inferior rectus muscle and the inferior oblique muscle in the fracture. A standard facial x-ray film will demonstrate this fracture.

THERAPEUTIC INTERVENTION

Ice packs
Reduction of fracture (if there is bony displacement)
Packing of maxillary sinus
Possible surgery

Foreign bodies

Foreign body in the eye is a common complaint. The particle often is small and feels similar to a corneal abrasion. Occasionally it will be necessary to anesthetize the area so the foreign body can be located. If there is a foreign body in the eye of a child, it may be necessary to induce sleep before the eye can be adequately examined. Always ensure that the lighting is good and that there is a magnification source available for the actual removal of the foreign body. Avoid using sharp needles to remove the body. Occasionally the body can be removed by simple irrigation.

FOREIGN BODIES IN THE CONJUNCTIVA

The foreign body most commonly found in the conjunctiva is an eyelash. Therapeutic intervention includes inverting the eyelid and irrigating it with normal saline, gently removing the foreign body with a moist cotton swab, or *very carefully* removing the foreign body with a 25-gauge needle held at a tangential angle. Local antibiotics should be applied four times a day for 5 days. An eye patch may be applied depending on the nature of the injury and the amount of damage. The patient should return for follow-up care in 1 day.

The main complication of a foreign body to the cornea is a scratched cornea. If this is suspected, the cornea should be stained with fluorescein dye. If there is a scratch, it should be treated as would any other corneal abrasion.

FOREIGN BODIES IN THE CORNEA

The presence of a foreign body in the cornea is a very painful condition. As the eyelid moves up and down over the foreign body, pain is increased.

Therapeutic intervention

Irrigation of eye with normal saline
Removal of foreign body with moistened swab or 25-gauge needle (held *very carefully* at a tangential angle)
Check for more than one foreign body
If the foreign body is metal it will form a rust ring that must be removed, usually by an ophthalmologist

INTRAOCULAR FOREIGN BODIES

Intraocular foreign bodies are easy to overlook, as they are usually caused by a small object moving at a high speed that penetrates the eyeball and comes to rest somewhere within the posterior chamber. Pain may be minimal. The entrance wound may be very small and difficult to locate. Finding the wound requires a high index of suspicion. This condition constitutes an extreme emergency, and therapeutic intervention should take place as soon as possible after the injury. The amount of damage to the eyeball will depend on the size, shape, and composition of the foreign body.

Therapeutic intervention

Usually surgical intervention to prevent further injury
All foreign bodies to the eyeball should be considered contaminated, and the patient should be given a regimen of antibiotics to follow
Assure that tetanus immunization status is current
An x-ray film of the eye should be obtained to inspect for the foreign body

Perforating and penetrating injuries to the eyeball

Penetrating and perforating eye injuries are usually caused by a sharp object. Therapeutic intervention is essential in the early stages of the injury and will decrease the likelihood of further injury.

THERAPEUTIC INTERVENTION

Secure the impaling object
Cover both eyes to decrease eye movement
Reserve detailed examination for an ophthalmologist
Usually surgical intervention
Antibiotics
Tetanus prophylaxis
Steroids

Corneal lacerations

If a corneal laceration is small it is usually not sutured. Therapeutic intervention for small corneal lacerations is a small, light dressing. If the laceration is large it is usually sutured by an ophthalmologist with 8-0 silk or 7-0 chromic suture on a very fine needle.

Corneal abrasions

Corneal abrasion is one of the most commonly seen injuries in the emergency department. It occurs when the epithelium is denuded by a foreign object, such as a contact lens. It is important to obtain a history from the patient as to what caused the injury.

SIGNS AND SYMPTOMS

Tearing
Eyelid spasm
Pain on the surface of the eye
Sensitivity to light

Corneal abrasion can be diagnosed by staining the surface of the eye with fluorescein dye and observing the cornea with a cobalt lamp and magnification.

How to use fluorescein strips to stain the cornea (Fig. 19-5)

Use individually wrapped sterile fluorescein strips (fluorescein is easily contaminated by
  Pseudomonas)
Explain the procedure to the patient
Moisten the end of sterile strip with normal saline
Pull down on the lower eyelid
Touch the strip to the inner edge of the lower eyelid
Ask the patient to blink to distribute the dye
Examine the cornea using a cobalt lamp

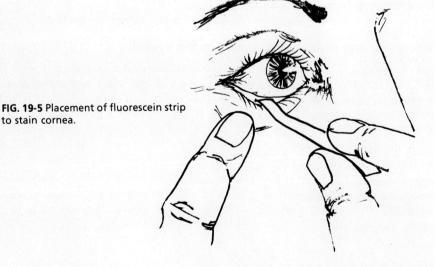

FIG. 19-5 Placement of fluorescein strip to stain cornea.

Local anesthesia during examination
Visual acuity examination
Local antibiotics
Patching of injured eye(s) for 24 hours
Follow-up visit in 1 day
Instruct the patient not to use local anesthetic agents at home, as they will delay healing

Conjunctival lacerations

The most common cause of a conjunctival laceration is a fingernail. The main symptom of conjunctival laceration is swelling and bleeding from the conjunctiva. Therapeutic intervention for small conjunctival lacerations is treatment with local antibiotics, application of an eye patch, and close observation. If the laceration is longer than 5 cm, an ophthalmologic consultation is needed for suturing.

Corneal ulcer

Corneal ulcer is commonly found in the unconscious patient or the patient who has left his contact lenses in place for an inordinately long period.

SIGNS AND SYMPTOMS

The ulcer appears as a whitish spot on the cornea
Pain
Photophobia
Profuse tearing
Vascular congestion
Blue-green cast on fluorescein staining
If *Pseudomonas* are present, the patient may lose the eye within 48 hours

THERAPEUTIC INTERVENTION

Antibiotics
Warm compresses
Eye patch

Optic nerve avulsion

Optic nerve avulsion is not a common injury. It usually results from severe trauma to the eye. The nerve usually avulses at the level at which the optic nerve enters the eyeball. A partial tear will result in partial blindness. A total tear will result in total blindness. An immediate ophthalmologic consultation is indicated for optic nerve avulsion.

Iris injury

Traumatic iridocyclitis is an inflammation of the iris and ciliary body following contusion of the eye. The main sign of iridocyclitis is the presence of uveal pigment and lens tissue in the anterior chamber. Therapeutic intervention for iridocyclitis includes treatment with topical cycloplegics and topical systemic steroids.

Another type of injury to the iris is iris sphincter rupture. It is usually caused by trauma to the eyeball that causes the pupil to dilate and the iris to notch at the edges.

Lens injury

Injuries that can occur to the lens include partial dislocations (subluxations), total dislocations (luxations), and opacifications (cataracts). Surgical intervention is indicated for any of these conditions.

Retina and choroid injury

Trauma to the retina and choroid may produce a white ellipse where the sclera is visible through the rupture. If the macula is injured, there will be a resultant decrease in visual acuity. Surgical intervention is indicated for these injuries.

Problems with contact lenses (Fig. 19-6)

The most common problem experienced by the wearer of contact lenses is the presence of dirt particles or chemical irritants under the lenses causing irritation of the cornea. The second most common problem results when the lenses are worn too long. This causes redness, swelling, and pain. Therapeutic intervention for foreign bodies under the lens is removal of the lens and cleansing of lens and the eye. Therapeutic intervention for prolonged contact lens use is instructing the patient to refrain from wearing the lenses for

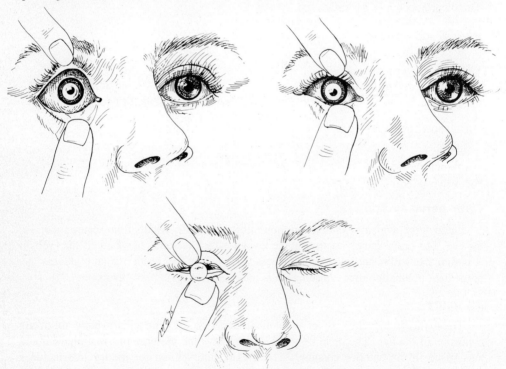

FIG. 19-6 Techniques for removing hard corneal contact lenses from an individual's eye.

24 to 48 hours. If a contact lens is lost in the eye, it is usually in the cul-de-sac of the upper eyelid; the eyelid should be everted and the lens removed. To see if a patient is wearing contact lenses:

Look at the eye tangentially with a flashlight

Check for a Medic Alert bracelet

Check for an identification card

To remove a contact lens:

Corneal hard lens—use a suction tip designed especially for removing contact lenses

Soft lens—locate the lens, grasp it between the thumb and forefinger and lift it off the cornea

Burns of the eye
CHEMICAL BURNS

Chemical burns of the eyes are common both in the home and in the industrial setting. There are three types of chemical burns of the eye:

Nonprogressive, superficial—Usually caused by acids

Progressive—Usually caused by alkalies

Irritant—Usually caused by gases

Therapeutic intervention

Immediate therapeutic intervention for any type of chemical burn to the eye is irrigation with copious amounts of saline solution or water. If the eye is to be examined, the care giver will probably have to apply a local anesthetic agent.

Acid burns

Since tissue denatures form acid and denatured tissue neutralizes acid, therapeutic intervention is limited to irrigation with copious amounts of normal saline solution or water and treatment with topical antibiotics and cycloplegics.

Alkali burns

Alkali burn is a very emergent situation, because alkalies cause much tissue destruction. Initially the burn may appear as white spots in the eye, and severe damage may not be evidenced until 3 to 4 days after the initial injury.

Therapeutic intervention

Irrigation with copious amounts of normal saline solution or water (for 30 minutes, then check pH; if it is not 7.0, continue irrigation)

Antibiotics

Cycloplegics

Steroids

Specific antidotes for chemical burns

Acid burns—sodium bicarbonate 2%

Alkali burns—citric acid or boric acid

Lime burns—ammonium tartrate 5%

Complications of acid and alkali burns

Adhesion of globe to eyelid
Corneal ulceration
Entropion (eyelashes that turn in toward the eyeball)
Iridocyclitis
Glaucoma

THERMAL BURNS

When facial burns are present it is rather common to find associated burns of the eyelids. It is not common, however, to see burns of the eyeballs unless the burning agent was steam, metal, or gasoline. Burns to the eyelids may cause lid contractures.

Therapeutic intervention

Analgesia   Antibiotics
Sedation   Cycloplegics
Eye irrigation   Bilateral eye patches

RADIATION BURNS

There are two types of radiation burns, ultraviolet burns and infrared burns.

Ultraviolet burns

Ultraviolet burns are seen with welder's flash and in snow skiers, ice climbers, people who read on the beach, and people who use sunlamps. The burn is caused when ultraviolet radiation is absorbed by the cornea. Keratitis or conjunctivitis or both result. Symptoms develop 3 to 6 hours after the exposure.

Signs and symptoms

Feeling of a foreign body
Tearing
Excessive blinking
Possible associated facial and eyelid burns

Therapeutic intervention

Topical antibiotics
Analgesics
Cycloplegics
Bilateral eye patches
Signs and symptoms should be relieved in 24 hours after these measures are taken.

Infrared burns

Infrared burn is a much more severe type of burn than ultraviolet burn. It may cause permanent loss of vision, because infrared rays are absorbed by the iris. This results in an increase of the temperature of the lens, which causes cataracts. When the lens is damaged the repair process is very slow. The lens remains much more vulnerable to injury during the healing process.

Common types of infrared burns

Glassblower's cataracts—result from prolonged exposure to intense heat

Focal retinitis—caused by eclipse blindness or exposure to the atomic bomb; the lens condenses heat, causing retinal scarring and blindness

X-ray burns—proportional to the amount of exposure and penetration of the x-rays; grenz rays are soft rays that produce superficial keratoconjunctivitis and dermatitis; gamma rays are hard rays that produce retinal damage and cataracts

Irrigating the eye

Cleanse the external area around the eye and eyelid.

Prepare the equipment.

Have the patient lie down or adjust the treatment chair to this position.

Have the patient turn his head with the affected side down

Pull down on the lower eyelid of the affected side

Run irrigation fluid directly over the globe of the eye and into the cul-de-sac of the lower eyelid from the inner to the outer canthus.

Have the patient blink occasionally to distribute the irrigation solution over the globe.

Irrigate for about 30 minutes (more if pH indicates).

IRRIGATION USING THE MORGAN THERAPEUTIC LENS (Fig. 19-7)

The Morgan Therapeutic Lens is a specially designed lens that is placed on the eye and used to provide continuous ocular lavage or medication. It is a scleral lens made of hard plastic (polymethyl methacrylate). The tubing is made of soft silicone plastic and has a female adapter at the distal end.

1. Explain the procedure to the patient.
2. Instill anesthetic ocular medication.

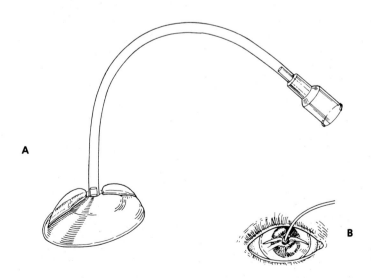

FIG. 19-7 A, Morgan therapeutic lens. **B,** Lens in place for continuous irrigation.

3. Ask the patient to look down.
4. Retract the upper eyelid.
5. Grasp the lens by the tubing and the small finlike projections.
6. Slip the superior border of the lens up under the upper eyelid.
7. Have the patient look up.
8. Retract the lower eyelid and place the lower border of the lens beneath it.
9. Have the patient turn his head toward the affected side and place a folded towel under his head to collect irrigation solution.
10. Attach the female adapter at the end of the lens tubing to:
    a. A syringe filled with the solution of choice, and instill the solution at the desired rate *or*
    b. Intravenous tubing that is connected to the solution of choice in an IV bottle or bag instilled at the selected drip rate
11. To remove the lens, follow steps 3 through 8 in reverse order.
12. Dry the patient's face and eye area with a dry towel.
13. Dispose of the lens.
14. Follow any additional orders for medication instillation and eye dressing.

Medical problems involving the eye
BLEPHARITIS

Blepharitis is an inflammation of the lid margin, usually caused by *Staphyloccus aureus*.

Therapeutic intervention

Cool, moist compresses
Antibiotic ophthalmic ointment

HORDEOLUM

A hordeolum or sty is an infection of the upper or lower eyelid at the accessory gland. It is caused by *Staphylococcus aureus*.

Signs and symptoms

Small external abscess
Pain
Redness
Swelling

Therapeutic intervention

Warm compresses four times a day until the abscess points
Antibiotic ophthalmic ointment
Abscess should be incised by a physician when it points

CHALAZION

A chalazion is a sebaceous cyst that forms on the inside surface of the eyelid. It results from congestion of the meibomian gland.

Signs and symptoms

Small mass beneath the conjunctiva of the lid   Swelling
Redness   Extreme pain

Therapeutic intervention

Antibiotic ophthalmic ointment
Incision and drainage by a physician

KERATITIS (FIG. 19-8)

Keratitis is an inflammation of the cornea.

Signs and symptoms

Light sensitivity
Redness
Pain
Profuse tearing

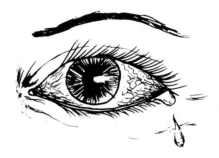

FIG. 19-8 Keratitis

Therapeutic intervention

Culture and sensitivity   Antibiotic ophthalmic ointment
Warm compresses   Topical steroids (except herpetic keratitis)

KERATOCONJUNCTIVITIS

Keratoconjunctivitis is an inflammation of the outer layer of the eye. It can result from an allergic reaction.

Signs and symptoms

Itching   Discharge
Redness   Tearing

Therapeutic intervention

Topical steroids, except for herpetic keratoconjunctivitis
Idoxuridine (Stoxil) or vidarabine (Vira A) for herpetic keratoconjuncitivitis

UVEITIS

Uveitis is a uveal tract inflammation that usually includes the iris, ciliary body, and choroid.

Signs and symptoms

Signs and symptoms of uveitis appear unilaterally.
Photophobia   Pain
Tearing   Blurred vision

Therapeutic intervention

Warm compresses   Topical steroids
Systemic analgesics   Mydriatics to dilate the pupil and prevent
Antibiotic ophthalmic ointment   adhesions of the iris and lens

ACUTE CONJUNCTIVITIS (FIG. 19-9)

Acute conjunctivitis is a bacterial infection of the conjunctiva. It may be caused by *Staphylococcus, Gonococcus, Pneumococcus, Haemophilus,* or *Pseudomonas.* The main symptoms of acute conjunctivitis is eyelids that "stick together" on waking. Therapeutic intervention is application of antibiotic ophthalmic ointment after a culture is obtained.

Acute conjunctivitis is a contagious condition. Careful aftercare instructions should be given to the patient about how to avoid spreading the infection to others.

One specific type of conjunctivitis is caused by *Neisseria gonorrhoeae.* In this condition there is a copious amount of purulent discharge, and the conjunctiva are extremely red and swollen. Therapeutic intervention for this type of infection is treatment with penicillin ophthalmic ointment.

ACUTE IRITIS (FIG. 19-10)

Acute iritis is an inflammatory condition of the iris. It is not an infectious process.

Signs and symptoms

Photophobia
Tenderness of the globe

Therapeutic intervention

Cold compresses   Eye patch
Topical steroids   Dark glasses

CENTRAL RETINAL ARTERY OCCLUSION

Central retinal artery occlusion produces sudden blindness. There is a very poor prognosis for regaining sight.

Therapeutic intervention

Inhalation of amyl nitrate *or*
Sublingual nitroglycerin *or*
Inhalation of alternating carbon dioxide and oxygen in an attempt to dilate the artery and return blood supply to the retina

FIG. 19-9 Conjunctivitis.

FIG. 19-10 Iritis.

CAVERNOUS SINUS THROMBOSIS (Orbital Cellulitis)

Cavernous sinus thrombosis is a pneumococcal, staphylococcal, or streptococcal infection that spreads from an infected sinus to the orbital area.

Signs and symptoms

Facial and globe edema
Vascular congestion in eyelids
Aching pain
Pain in globe
Conjunctival chemosis
Fever
Decreased visual acuity

Decreased pupil reflexes
Papilledema
Paralysis of extraocular muscles

Therapeutic intervention

Antibiotic ophthalmic ointment
Topical antibiotics
Bed rest
Warm compresses

FIG. 19-11 Pterygium.

OTHER MEDICAL AND SURGICAL PROBLEMS

Other medical conditions involving the eye include ptosis, eyelid edema, entropion, ectropion, dacryocystitis, exophthalmos, pterygium (Fig. 19-11), and convergent and divergent strabismus. Refer to a text on ophthalmology for further detail.

Retinal detachment

The normal function of the retina is to perceive light and send an impulse to the optic nerve. When the retina is torn, vitreous humor seeps between it and the choroid. This results in the separation of the retina from the choroid, which decreases blood and oxygen supply to the retina. This decreased blood and oxygen supply renders the retina unable to perceive light.

SIGNS AND SYMPTOMS

Flashes of light
A "veil" or "curtain" effect in the visual field
A dark spot or particles in the visual field

THERAPEUTIC INTERVENTION

Strict bed rest
Bilateral eye patches
Tranquilizers
Possible surgical intervention

Glaucoma (Fig. 19-12)

It is estimated that 1 million Americans have undiagnosed glaucoma. Glaucoma causes 1 out of every 10 cases of blindness in the United States. In the normal eye aqueous

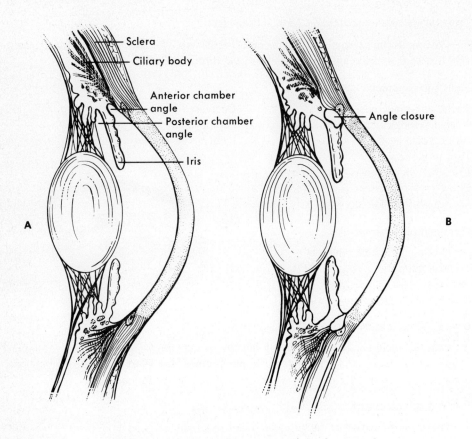

FIG. 19-12 A, Normal eye. **B,** Closed-angle glaucoma.

humor is secreted by the ciliary process epithelium in the posterior chamber of the eye and transported to the anterior chamber of the eye. It leaves the anterior chamber and enters the vascular system via Schlemm's canal at the junction of the iris and the cornea. In glaucoma aqueous humor cannot escape from the anterior chamber. This causes a rise in anterior chamber pressure. This increase in pressure causes a decrease in circulation to the retina and increase in pressure on the optic nerve. Blindness may eventually result.

ACUTE GLAUCOMA (FIG. 19-12, *B*)

Acute (closed-angle) glaucoma results when there is blockage in the anterior chamber angle near the root of the iris. ACUTE GLAUCOMA IS AN EMERGENCY SITUATION! It may cause blindness in just a few hours.

Signs and symptoms

Acute eye pain
Fixed and slightly dilated pupil
Hard globe
Foggy-appearing cornea

Severe headache
Halos around lights
Decreased peripheral vision
Nausea and vomiting

Therapeutic intervention

Therapeutic intervention for acute glaucoma is aimed at decreasing pupil size to allow for aqueous humor drainage.

Frequent (every 15 minutes) instillation of miotic eyedrops (usually 1% or 4% pilocarpine)—the strength of the solution is not so important as frequent instillation

Systemic analgesia (usually morphine sulfate)

Drugs such as acetazolamide (Diamox) in an attempt to decrease intraocular pressure

Possible surgery

CHRONIC GLAUCOMA

Chronic (open-angle or wide-angle) glaucoma comes on gradually and is caused by an obstruction of Schlemm's canal. Because this condition is chronic and comes on very slowly, the patient may be unaware of its presence.

Therapeutic intervention

Instillation of miotic eyedrops

Possible surgery

SECONDARY GLAUCOMA

Secondary glaucoma is an increase in intraocular pressure resulting from surgery, trauma, hemorrhage, inflammation, tumor, or various other conditions that may interfere with aqueous humor drainage. Therapeutic intervention will vary depending on the cause.

HOW TO MEASURE INTRAOCULAR PRESSURE WITH A TONOMETER

Tonometric examination is used to measure intraocular pressure. The Schiøtz tonometer is the most commonly used type. It has a plunger that, when placed on the eye, measures the amount of indentation pressure on the cornea.

To properly use the tonometer, the globe should be anesthetized with an ophthalmic anesthetic agent.

Explain the procedure to the patient

Have the patient lie down

Place a sterile (previously calibrated) tonometer on the globe

Measure intraocular pressure

To read a Schiøtz indentation tonometer:

If intraocular pressure is high—tonometer scale will read low because the plunger cannot indent the globe very much

If intraocular pressure is low—tonometer scale will read high because the plunger will indent the globe more than normal

A normal indentation tonometer reading is 11 to 22 mm Hg. A lower reading indicates increased intraocular pressure and a higher reading indicates decreased intraocular pressure.

Eyedrops and ophthalmic ointments

Eyedrops are used to decrease pain, provide antibiotic therapy, increase or decrease the size of the pupil, decrease allergic reactions of the eye, or cleanse the eye.

PROCEDURE FOR INSTILLING EYEDROPS

Explain the procedure to the patient
Pull the lower eyelid downward
Instill one or two drops of solution into the cul-de-sac (the center of the lower lid)
Have the patient blink to distribute the solution
Instruct the patient not to squeeze his eyelids shut tightly, because this will cause the solution to leak out

PROCEDURE FOR INSTILLING OPHTHALMIC OINTMENT

Explain the procedure to the patient
Pull the lower eyelid downward
Have the patient look up
Apply ointment in a thin line into the inner aspect of the lid from the inner to the outer canthus
Have the patient blink to distribute the ointment
Instruct the patient not to squeeze his eyelids shut tightly, as this will expel the ointment

EAR EMERGENCIES

There are three requirements for proper ear care:
Good illumination
Magnification
Adequate physical control of the patient, including proper positioning and sedation

Simple lacerations

Simple lacerations of the outer ear are probably the most common ear injuries seen in the emergency department.

THERAPEUTIC INTERVENTION

Cleanse the wound (scrub and irrigate)
Debride the wound
Rejoin cartilage edges
Cover the cartilage with skin

Auriculectomy

Auriculectomy (amputation of the outer structures of the ear) usually results from a knife fight. Good results can be obtained if strict attention is paid to detail when reanastomosing the ear.

THERAPEUTIC INTERVENTION

Reanastomose cartilage and skin
Make a prophylactic radial incision in the skin, because arteries repair before veins; this allows for blood release while the veins are mending
Skin grafts are performed after 6 days to protect the cartilage
Give IV antibiotics

Frostbite

For discussion of frostbite see Chapter 12.

Hematoma of pinna

Hematoma of the pinna usually results from a fight or a wrestling injury.

THERAPEUTIC INTERVENTION

Anesthetize the area
Aspirate the hematoma with an 18-gauge or larger needle
Place a drain if necessary
Apply a pressure dressing (cotton soaked in mineral oil or petrolatum gauze)

Bleeding from external ear

Bleeding from the external ear is usually a result of a ruptured eardrum, a foreign body, or a canal laceration. Other sources of bleeding to consider are basal skull fractures and temporal bone fractures. Canal lacerations result from the ear being probed by such items as bobby pins, paper clips, and fingernails. If the temporal bone is fractured there may be cerebrospinal fluid otorrhea, or there may be a ruptured tympanic membrane or a lacerated facial nerve.

THERAPEUTIC INTERVENTION

Cleanse the wound
Apply antibiotic ointment
Otolaryngologic consultation may be indicated

Ruptured tympanic membrane

Ruptured tympanic membrane occurs as a result of positive pressure over the tympanic membrane or a penetrating foreign body. It may be caused by a slap over the ear (pressure from the outside), a diving injury (vacuum from the inside) or an aircraft or altitude injury (expanding air inside).

SIGNS AND SYMPTOMS

Sharp pain
Vertigo
Bleeding
Tinnitus
Slight hearing impairment

THERAPEUTIC INTERVENTION

Leave the area alone (do not probe it); also instruct the patient to leave it alone
Most small perforations will heal spontaneously; large perforations should be repaired by reapproximating the fragments with a suction apparatus; anesthesia is needed
Antibiotics should be given if there is history of seawater or other contaminated water in the ear
Note that diving injuries may cause a permanent loss of hearing and associated infection

Foreign body

Natural foreign bodies within the ear are usually formed from cerumen. Other common foreign bodies include beans, beads, and bugs. Children are especially prone to putting foreign bodies in their ears. Bleeding may occur when the patient attempts to remove the foreign body.

THERAPEUTIC INTERVENTION

If there is no perforation, remove the foreign body (visualize it first)
It may be necessary to administer general anesthetic to a child
Remove round objects with an ear hook or rubber-tipped suction
If the foreign body is an insect, drown it first with mineral oil or some other oily eardrop (do not try to remove it while it is alive; the insect may struggle and cause more damage)
If there is a perforation, make sure that visualization is good and remove the object with suction

Acute external otitis

Acute external otitis, or "swimmer's ear," is an infection of the external ear caused by a bacterium or a fungus. It is a common finding in children.

SIGNS AND SYMPTOMS

Severe pain
Ear tender to touch
Swelling of the canal
Cellulitis of the pinna and other structures

THERAPEUTIC INTERVENTION

Culture
Give analgesics
Drain the abscess
Insert a wick soaked in antibiotic solution or ointment
Apply hot compresses

Acute otitis media

Otitis media is an inflammation of the middle ear lining. As fluid builds up in the middle ear, pain becomes severe.

SIGNS AND SYMPTOMS

Sharp pain
Sensation of fullness in the ear
Difficulty hearing
Bulging of tympanic membrane

Elevated temperature
Nausea and vomiting
History of upper respiratory infection

THERAPEUTIC INTERVENTION

Decongestants
Antibiotics

Analgesics
Myringotomy

COMPLICATIONS

Tympanic membrane rupture
Acute mastoiditis

Acute mastoiditis

Acute mastoiditis is the most common of middle ear infections.

SIGNS AND SYMPTOMS

Pain in the mastoid area
Elevated temperature
Tenderness in the mastoid area
Difficulty hearing

Local swelling
Vertigo
Possible history of acute external or internal
   otitis

THERAPEUTIC INTERVENTION

Heat packs
Analgesia
Antibiotics
Otolaryngologic consultation (in case surgical drainage is required)

NOSE EMERGENCIES
Foreign bodies

Foreign bodies in the nose are common in children and often are discovered only after a purulent discharge is seen to be draining from one of the nostrils.

THERAPEUTIC INTERVENTION

Give decongestant nose drops
Apply a topical anesthetic
Place the patient in Trendelenburg's position
Remove the object with a ring curette or alligator forceps

Trauma

For trauma to the nose see Chapter 15.

Epistaxis (nosebleed)

Epistaxis is seen frequently in all emergency departments. It can be a relatively minor problem or it can turn into a life-threatening emergency. It commonly occurs in the following groups:

Children
Adults 50 to 70 years old
Patients with blood dyscrasias, hypertension, or arteriosclerotic heart disease
Patients on anticoagulant therapy
Alcoholics
Patients with allergies
Patients with hereditary hemorrhagic telangiectasia (Rendu-Osler-
   Weber disease)

ANTERIOR EPISTAXIS

In anterior epistaxis bleeding is common at Kiesselbach's area or in the anterior and inferior turbinates.

Therapeutic intervention

Give much reassurance
Place the neck in slight hyperextension
Suction clots
Check for bleeding site
Soak cotton pledgets in a vasoconstrictor agent (usually 10% cocaine solution)
Insert pledgets into the nostril
Apply pressure for 5 to 10 minutes
Cauterize bleeding sites with silver nitrate
    NOTE: In patients with blood dyscrasias or immunosuppression, use a wedge of salt pork in place of the cotton pledgets; this is much more comfortable and appears to be much more effective.

POSTERIOR EPISTAXIS

Posterior epistaxis is a much more serious problem than anterior epistaxis and is more difficult to control. It usually results from hypertension, arteriosclerotic heart disease, a blood dyscrasia, or a tumor. Bleeding usually occurs from the sphenopalatine artery, the nasopalatine plexus of Woodruff, or the anterior ethmoid artery.

Therapeutic intervention

Check the blood pressure
Give volume replacement if necessary
Ask about the medical history
Anesthetize the nose (10% cocaine)
Check the bleeding site if possible
Pack as described below
If bleeding continues, ligation of the internal maxillary or anterior ethmoid artery may be
    necessary

Packing for posterior nosebleed

Analgesia is usually required during packing for posterior nosebleed. The patient should be given antibiotics and admitted to the hospital for 3 to 5 days.

Equipment

No. 18 or 20 Foley catheter with balloon or nasal balloon catheter or tampon (tonsil or
    vaginal) with three ties or rolled 4 by 4 inch sponge with three ties
Antibiotic ointment
Rubber catheter
Half-inch selvage-edge petrolatum gauze
Bayonette forceps
Gauze pad
Eye pad

Procedure with tampon

1. Pass the rubber catheter through the nostril to the back of the palate (Fig. 19-13).
2. Tie two of the ties of the tampon to the catheter.
3. Pull the catheter out of the nose; the tampon will seat near the choana.
4. With the fingers, push the tampon into place.
5. Bring the other tie, which is dangling in the back of the mouth, forward and secure it to the outside of the face with tape (Fig. 19-14).
6. Pack the nasal cavity bilaterally from the anterior openings through a nasal speculum with bayonette forceps with ½-inch selvage-edged petrolatum gauze, layering front to back. (Be sure to count and record the number of packs used.)
7. Tie the ties from the tampon around a gauze pad outside of the nostril. (Make sure both strings are coming out of the same nostril; never have one string coming out of each nostril as this will cause necrosis.)

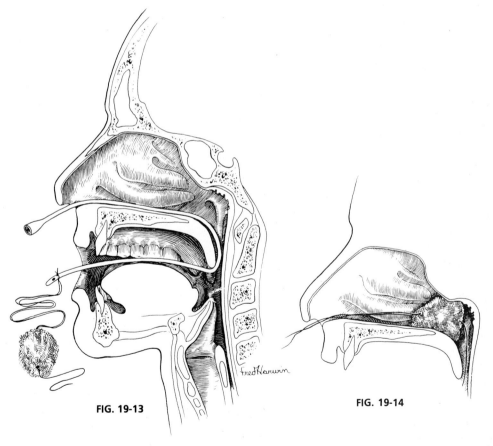

FIG. 19-13

FIG. 19-14

FIG. 19-13 Steps used in passing a postnasal pack. (From DeWeese, D.D., and Saunders, W.H.: Textbook of otolaryngology, ed. 6, St. Louis, 1982, The C.V. Mosby Co.)
FIG. 19-14 Postnasal pack in place. (From DeWeese, D.D., and Saunders, W.H.: Textbook of otolaryngology, ed. 6, St. Louis, 1982, The C.V. Mosby Co.)

Procedure with catheter

1. Pass the Foley catheter into the nostril and to the palate area.
2. Inflate the Foley balloon (with 10 ml of saline).
3. Pull the catheter forward until the balloon seats near the choana.
4. Hold the catheter firmly and pack the anterior chambers with ½-inch selvage-edged petrolatum gauze, layering front to back. (Be sure to count and record the number of packs used.)
5. Place an eye pad or 4 by 4 inch sponge around the Foley catheter.
6. Clamp the Foley catheter distal to the eye pad with an umbilical clamp.

AFTERCARE INSTRUCTIONS FOR PATIENTS WITH EPISTAXIS

If bleeding occurs again:
> Keep your head up and tilted slightly forward
> Do not blow your nose
> Apply steady pressure to both nostrils with your fingers for 5 minutes (by the clock)
> If bleeding does not stop, call your private physician or return to the emergency department
> If you have a medical history of hypertension or you are taking blood thinners, call your private physician or come to the emergency department
> If bleeding results from a nose injury, call your private physician or come to the emergency department

THROAT EMERGENCIES

Foreign bodies of the throat may be penetrating, obstructing, or aspirated. The most common penetrating foreign bodies are chicken bones and fish bones. These frequently lodge in the tonsils.

THERAPEUTIC INTERVENTION

Visualize the foreign body
Remove it with the appropriate instrument
If the foreign body is totally obstructing the airway:
> Give four back slaps
> Give four abdominal thrusts (Heimlich maneuver)
> > (see Chapter 3)
> Attempt to breathe for the victim
> If this is unsuccessful do an emergency cricothyrotomy
> > (see Chapter 3 for procedure)

Fractured larynx

A fractured larynx is usually caused by a direct blow to the neck with a hand or the impact of a steering wheel against the neck. Often the patient comes to the emergency department with multiple injuries, and this injury is missed. A fracture of the larynx produces massive edema and consequently blocks the upper airway. Fracture of the larynx is a surgical emergency.

SIGNS AND SYMPTOMS

Shortness of breath

Vocal changes

Respiratory stridor

History of throat trauma

Respiratory arrest

THERAPEUTIC INTERVENTION

Observe carefully

Palpate the neck

Perform cricothyrotomy or tracheostomy (see Chapter 3)

Give antibiotics

Give steroids

Tracheostomy

See Chapter 3 for the tracheostomy procedure.

INDICATIONS

Mechanical obstruction

    Tumor

    Laryngotracheal injury

    Congenital anomaly

    Maxillofacial injury

Airway obstruction

    Retained secretions

    Ineffective ventilation

Foreign body obstruction

Inflammed larynx, trachea, tongue,

    or pharynx

Bilateral vocal cord injury

EARLY COMPLICATIONS

Hemorrhage

Subcutaneous emphysema

Pneumomediastinum

Pneumothorax

Tracheoesophageal fistula

Laryngeal nerve paralysis

Aspiration of gastrointestinal contents

Malpositioned tube

DELAYED COMPLICATIONS

Hemorrhage

Tracheal stenosis

Tracheoesophageal fistula

Infection

Displaced cannula

Atelectasis

Tracheal granulation

Dysphagia

Neck scar

Aspiration

Upper respiratory tract infection or pharyngitis ("the common cold")

SIGNS AND SYMPTOMS

Sore throat

Difficulty swallowing

Pain referred to the ears

Elevated temperature

Feeling of fullness in the head

Malaise

Foul breath odor

Enlarged tonsils

Enlarged cervical nodes

THERAPEUTIC INTERVENTION

Throat culture
Warm saline gargles
Aspirin or acetaminophen
Antibiotics
Incision and drainage are usually required for symptoms lasting more than 48 hours

DENTAL EMERGENCIES

Patients with dental emergencies usually come to the emergency department complaining of pain or trauma or both. There are, generally speaking, two types of dental pain that bring a patient into the emergency department, especially in the middle of the night or on a holiday when a dentist is not readily available. These two types of pain are maxillofacial pain and dental pain. Maxillofacial pain can be characterized into major and minor neuralgias.

Major neuralgias
TRIGEMINAL NEURALGIA (TIC DOULOUREUX)

Trigeminal neuralgia is a degenerative process or pressure on the trigeminal nerve. It usually occurs in persons over 40 years old. The pain is described as excruciating and paroxysmal and usually radiates (1) along the eye and up into the forehead, (2) from the upper lip, through the nose and cheek, up into the eye, or (3) into the lower lip and on the outside of the tongue. An acute onset of unknown etiology is known as Bell's palsy.

The signs and symptoms are a drooping corner of the mouth, inability to close the eye, difficulty eating, and difficulty swallowing.

Therapeutic intervention is a trigeminal nerve block.

GLOSSOPHARYNGEAL NEURALGIA

Glossopharyngeal neuralgia resembles trigeminal neuralgia but is characterized by severe pain in the middle ear, the back of the throat, and the tonsils, leading to dysfunction or protruding of the tongue.

Therapeutic intervention consists of phenytoin (Dilantin) or carbamazepine (Tegretol).

Minor neuralgias

Minor neuralgias include sphenopalatine neuralgia, occipital neuralgia, and geniculate neuralgia.

Dental pain

The most common cause of dental pain is tooth decay or pulpal disease. Pulpal disease has three phases:
Hyperemic—the vascular system responds to an external stimulus, such as dental caries (cavity) or dental trauma; this is a reversible condition
Pulpitis—the pulp becomes infected
Pulpal necrosis—the pulp dies; fluid and pressure build, causing pain

Therapeutic intervention for these conditions consists of analgesia and referral to a dentist.

OTHER CAUSES OF DENTAL PAIN

Fractured teeth
Periodontal disease (in the gums)
Foreign bodies (such as a toothbrush bristle)
Dry socket
Pressure from a prosthetic device
Mandibular fractures
Vincent's angina, or "trench mouth" (ulcers of the tonsils and pharynx)
Pericoronitis (pain of wisdom teeth erupting)
Causalgia (severe burning pain 2 to 3 weeks following tooth extraction; usually stress related)
Sinusitis
Glossodynia (a burning pain in the tongue usually caused by fungal infection following antibiotic administration)
Fractured styloid process
Hematomas (usually resulting from injections of anesthetic)
Coronary artery disease (referred pain to jaw)
Carcinoma
Unerupted teeth (especially in children)

Toothaches

The most common cause of toothaches is pulpal disease or dental caries. The tooth becomes extremely sensitive to heat and cold. The pain may be reversible if the decay can be removed and the tooth restored. This type of pain is paroxysmal and usually begins with a heat or cold stimulus. Irreversible pain indicates that the tooth will require either a root canal (endodontics) or extraction. This pain usually occurs spontaneously and continues to worsen, especially at night when intracranial pressure increases.

Therapeutic intervention for both pulpal disease and dental caries consists of topical oil of clove or other analgesia and referral to a dentist.

Chipped (broken) teeth

Chipped or broken teeth are the most frequently seen dental emergencies in the emergency department. It is a common injury in children and in participants in contact sports. The four center upper teeth are the teeth most frequently injured.

Check for bleeding from gums and from pulp. Bleeding from pulp requires emergency dental consultation. As these injuries are frequently associated with head injuries, be sure to check the mouth and pharynx area for pieces of teeth and debris that may obstruct the airway.

Avulsed teeth

Avulsed teeth are teeth that have been torn from the mouth by trauma. If found, these teeth may be reimplanted. It is important to place the tooth in a saline solution, irrigate the wound, anesthetize the wound area, and reimplant the tooth as soon as possible following the accident. Once the tooth is reimplanted it should be wired or splinted in place and a referral should be made to a dentist or oral surgeon. The blood supply to the tooth comes via the pulp, so the viability of the tooth depends on the patency of the pulp.

Teeth that have been driven into the gums, especially in children, should be left alone. No attempt should be made to pull the teeth out of the gums. These teeth will usually return to their normal position within 1 month if left alone.

Remember, again, to look for teeth and foreign bodies such as prostheses and bridges in the mouths of trauma patients and remove these objects to avoid airway obstruction. If a head injury is suspected in a patient with dental trauma, the patient should be admitted to the hospital for 24-hour observation.

Dental abscess

Abscesses in the periapical areas usually result from pulpal necrosis, which results from caries or trauma. Periodontal abscesses usually result from bony destruction at the periodontal membrane, which forms a pocket and forms an abscess.

Therapeutic intervention consists of drainage of the abscess, antibiotics, analgesics, hot packs on the area, warm saline rinses every 2 hours, aspirin or other antipyretic for fever above 101° F (38.3° C), and referral to a dentist.

Periodontal emergencies

gingivitis—Inflammation of the gums characterized by redness, swelling, pain, and bleeding.

periodontal disease—Loss of periodontal bone; appears similar to gingivitis; definitive diagnosis is made on x-ray films.

necrotizing ulcerative gingivitis—Painful bleeding, foul-smelling breath, lymphadenopathy, chills, fever, and malaise; therapeutic intervention consists of debridement, antibiotics, warm hydrogen peroxide rinses every 2 hours, soft toothbrush, and a dental consultation.

pericoronitis—Painful eruption of wisdom teeth accompanied by swelling, lymphadenopathy, and trismus; therapeutic intervention is by removal of tissue over the tooth, warm saline rinses, antibiotics, and dental referral for possible tooth extraction.

Postoperative bleeding

Often a patient comes to the emergency department bleeding from the mouth with a history of recent tooth extraction or recent oral surgery. Usually all that is needed is to apply a pressure pack over the area of hemorrhage. If the bleeding persists, a hemostatic dressing such as absorbable gelatin sponge (Gelfoam), oxidized cellulose (Surgicel), or thrombin should be packed into the socket. A home remedy that may also be effective is to place a teabag over the socket. (The tannic acid produces hemostasis.) If the packing is unsuccessful, sutures may be placed or the bleeding vessels may be cauterized. The patient should be cautioned to avoid mouth rinses until the bleeding has completely stopped, to eat a soft diet, and to use intermittent ice packs.

Dry socket (alveoalgia)

Dry socket usually occurs 3 to 5 days after surgery, when a blood clot is lost and bone is exposed. Therapeutic intervention consists of oil of clove packed into the socket, analgesia, and dental referral.

Note about local anesthesia

Both infiltration and regional block techniques may be used when applying dental anesthesia. Strict attention to detail must be paid when injecting the anesthetic. Complications of anesthetic injection include facial paralysis (from injecting into the parotid gland), blurred vision (from injecting into the optic nerve), trismus, and hematoma. Therapeutic intervention is simply to observe the patient until the effects of the anesthetic wear off.

SUGGESTED READINGS

Armstrong, B.W.: Traumatic perforations of the tympanic membrane: observe or repair? Laryngoscope **82:** 1822, 1972.

Ballentyne, J.J.: Diseases of the nose, throat and ear, ed. 12, Philadelphia, 1977, Lea & Febiger.

Budassi, S.A., and Barber, J.M.: Emergency nursing: principles and practice, St. Louis, 1981, The C.V. Mosby Co.

Charles, R., and Corrigan, E.: Epistaxis and hypertension, Postgrad. Med. **55:**260, 1977.

Chee, H.Y.: Emergency ocular care. In Barry, J., editor: Emergency nursing, New York, 1978, McGraw-Hill Book Co.

Coe, R.O., Jr.: Emergency eye care. In Stephenson, H.E., Jr., editor: Immediate care of the acutely ill and injured, St. Louis, 1974, The C.V. Mosby Co.

DeWeese, D.D., and Saunders, W.H.: Textbook of otolaryngology, ed. 6, St. Louis, 1977, The C.V. Mosby Co.

DeWeese, D.D., et al.: Epistaxis: from A to Z nosebleed control, Patient Care, Apr. 30, 1978, pp. 66-83.

Dupont, J.: Eye, ear, nose and throat emergencies. In Giving emergency care competently, Horsham, Pa., 1978, Intermed Communications.

Grant, W.M.: Toxicology of the eye, ed. 2, Springfield, Ill., 1974, Charles C Thomas, Publisher.

Langeman, R.E.: Epistaxis, Am. Fam. Physician **14:**79, 1976.

Lee, K.G.: Essential otolaryngology, Garden City, N.Y., 1977, Examination Publishing Co.

Mechner, F., and Saffiotti, L.J.: Patient assessment: examination of the eye. Part I, Am. J. Nurs. **74**(11):1, 1974.

Mechner, F., and Saffiotti, L.J.: Patient assessment: examination of the eye. Part II, Am. J. Nurs. **75**(1):1, 1975.

Seelenfreund, M.H., and Freilich, D.B.: Rushing the net and retinal detachment, JAMA **235:**25, 1976.

Wood, R.P.: Handbook of emergency ENT care, Denver, 1973, University of Colorado Medical Center Press.

CHAPTER 20 Chest trauma

Chest trauma constitutes one of the most life-threatening conditions that can be sustained in trauma. The chest is, of course, the center of airway, breathing, and circulation. As the numbers of motor vehicle accidents and handgun incidents increase, there is a corresponding increase in the number of chest trauma victims. Of all trauma deaths in this country 25% are caused by chest trauma. Of all patients with serious chest trauma 25% to 50% die. The major causes of blunt trauma to the chest are automobile steering wheels and motorcycle and bicycle handlebars. Gunshot wounds and stab wounds account for the majority of penetrating wounds to the chest, and this number continues to rise epidemically. Many patients with injury to the chest from either blunt or penetrating trauma have severe, life-threatening injuries. The care giver must be able to assess the patient's condition rapidly and apply life-saving therapeutic intervention concurrently.

BASIC ANATOMY AND PHYSIOLOGY OF THE THORACIC CAVITY (Fig. 20-1)

The thoracic cavity extends from the first rib to the diaphragm. It contains the lower airway, the mainstem and right and left bronchi, the lungs, the heart and great vessels, and the esophagus. The thoracic cavity is surrounded by 12 pairs of ribs.

The lungs are elastic in nature and have a natural tendency to collapse. The reason they do not collapse normally is the presence of negative pressure (a vacuum) in the thoracic cavity. When there is inspiratory effort (i.e., when the intercostal muscles pull the ribs upward and the diaphragm drops down), negative pressure increases, and the lungs respond to this negative pressure by stretching and consequently filling with room air. If negative pressure (the vacuum) is lost, the lungs will collapse because of their elastic nature. This condition is known as *pneumothorax*, or air in the thoracic cavity.

The chest wall expands with the help of the accessory muscles of respiration, the diaphragm, the intercostal muscles, the pectoralis major, and the sternocleidomastoid muscles. The diaphragm separates the thoracic cavity from the abdominal cavity. The phrenic nerve runs through the diaphragm. Irritation of the phrenic nerve by bleeding or other sources will cause hiccups. On deep expiration the diaphragm can elevate to as high as nipple level, and on deep inspiration it can descend as low as the tenth rib.

The care giver should be familiar with surface anatomy of the chest to be able to report and record findings accurately.

When assessing the patient with chest trauma, always assume that the injury is serious until it is proved otherwise. Priorities in treatment are maintenance of an adequate airway,

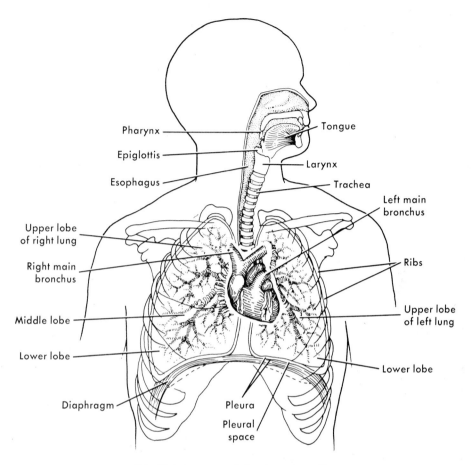

FIG. 20-1 Anatomy of the thoracic cavity.

assurance of good ventilation, assurance of appropriate circulation, protection of the cervical spine, rapid assessment for life-threatening chest injuries, and assessment of level of consciousness.

Immediate assessment in chest injury

ABC[4]

A = airway

B = breathing

C = circulation

C = cervical spine protection

C = chest evaluation for life-threatening trauma (flail chest, tension pneumothorax, pericardial tamponade)

C = consciousness (level of consciousness)

RIB FRACTURES

After the initial assessment, the care giver should go on to assess the chest in further detail. The most common injuries to the chest are rib fractures. They are often seen in athletes involved in contact sports and in elderly people who have a tendency to fall.

SIGNS AND SYMPTOMS

History of trauma to the chest
Pain that increases with inspiration
Crepitus over the fracture site

DIAGNOSTIC AIDS

Palpation
X-ray examination

THERAPEUTIC INTERVENTION

For simple fractures:
    Rest
    Ice for the first 24 hours, then local heat
    Simple analgesia
For displaced fractures or fractures in the elderly:
    Hospital admission recommended
    Local infiltration of anesthetic agent if pain is severe
    Intercostal nerve block if pain is severe

NOTES ABOUT RIB FRACTURES

First rib fracture is often associated with clavicular fracture and sometimes with scapular fracture. It is a serious fracture that carries a mortality of close to 40% because of its proximity to several important structures that may be injured as a result of the fracture. Such injuries include laceration of the subclavian artery or vein or laceration of the tracheobronchial tree. A great deal of force is required to fracture the first rib, as it is not well exposed. Always assume severe injury until it is proved otherwise.

When there are lower rib fractures, consider the possibility of damage to the underlying structures, such as the spleen, the kidneys, or the liver.

If there are more than three ribs fractured the patient should be considered a multiple trauma victim, and a complete examination for other injuries should take place.

Flail chest

When two or more adjacent ribs are fractured in two places or the sternum is detached, this segment becomes a flail segment (Fig. 20-2). This means that the segment has lost continuity with the rest of the chest. It responds to intrathoracic pressure changes, and paradoxic chest wall motion occurs in the areas. If the flail is large enough, respiratory distress will occur. When negative pressure increases (on inhalation) the flail segment is drawn inward (Figs. 20-3). When negative pressure decreases (on exhalation) the segment is pushed outward. It moves in the opposite direction from the rest of the chest wall (Fig. 20-4).

The diagnosis of flail chest is made by thinking about it and looking for it.

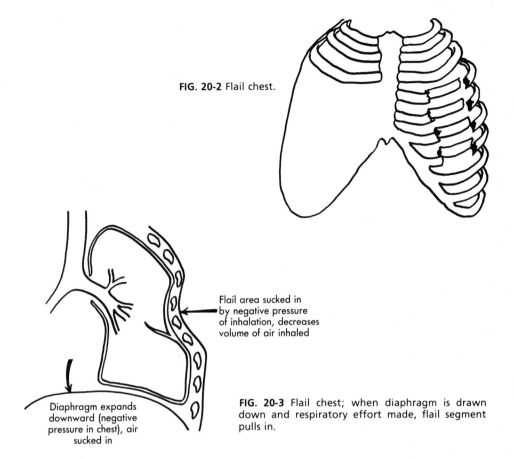

FIG. 20-2 Flail chest.

Flail area sucked in by negative pressure of inhalation, decreases volume of air inhaled

Diaphragm expands downward (negative pressure in chest), air sucked in

FIG. 20-3 Flail chest; when diaphragm is drawn down and respiratory effort made, flail segment pulls in.

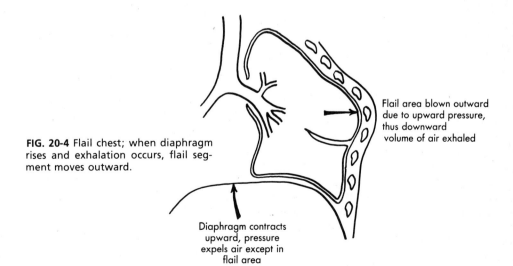

FIG. 20-4 Flail chest; when diaphragm rises and exhalation occurs, flail segment moves outward.

Flail area blown outward due to upward pressure, thus downward volume of air exhaled

Diaphragm contracts upward, pressure expels air except in flail area

SIGNS AND SYMPTOMS

Observed paradoxic motion of the chest wall
Shortness of breath
Difficulty breathing

THERAPEUTIC INTERVENTION

The goal of therapeutic intervention is to stabilize the chest wall.
Place the victim flail side down in semi-Fowler's position
Sandbag the flail segment
Tape the flail segment
Place manual pressure over the flail segment
Attach the center of the flail segment to a towel clip attached to a weighted line that is draped over an IV pole
Administer oxygen under positive pressure via an endotracheal tube
Initiate an IV of Ringer's lactate or normal saline with a large-bore cannula
Monitor the patient for possible underlying myocardial contusion, pulmonary contusion, or tension pneumothorax

Early surgery is now being performed involving the placement of Jorgenson bars across the broken ribs to stabilize them. The patients are now spending far less time being assisted by the ventilator and consequently are developing far fewer complications from long-term ventilation.

Sternal fractures

A fracture of the sternum rarely causes serious complications unless it is totally detached, in which case it becomes a flail segment. Be alert to the fact that sternal fracture may be a clue to an underlying injury, such as a myocardial contusion. A detached sternum is a common finding after cardiac compressions during CPR. If this occurs and the patient survives the arrest the condition should be treated as a typical flail chest.

If the patient was involved in a traffic accident find out if there was an impact with the steering wheel, as this is the most common cause of sternal fracture.

PNEUMOTHORAX
Simple pneumothorax (Fig. 20-5)

A simple pneumothorax is a condition in which air enters the chest cavity, causing a loss of negative pressure (the vacuum) and a partial or total collapse of the lung. Pneumothorax may be caused by a hole in the chest wall or a hole in the lung tissue itself, the bronchus, the trachea, or the alveoli. A spontaneous pneumothorax is the occurrence of a pneumothorax without evidence of trauma. It is thought to be caused by a ruptured bleb or a ruptured cyst in the lung. Spontaneous pneumothorax usually occurs in tall, lanky men between the ages of 20 and 40 while they are performing some type of physical activity.

SIGNS AND SYMPTOMS

History of blunt or penetrating trauma to the chest
Sudden onset of sharp pleuritic chest pain
Decreased breath sounds

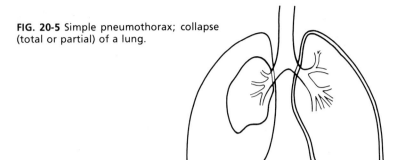

FIG. 20-5 Simple pneumothorax; collapse (total or partial) of a lung.

Hyperresonance on percussion
Shortness of breath
Tachypnea
Observed on x-ray films
Syncope
Hamman's sign (a crunching sound with each heartbeat, caused by mediastinal air accumulation)

THERAPEUTIC INTERVENTION

Observation (only if the pneumothorax is small)
Placement of a large-bore needle through the anterior chest wall if the patient is severely symptomatic
Placement of a chest tube
Oxygen
Semi-Fowler's position

Tension pneumothorax (Fig. 20-6)

When air enters the pleural space during inspiration and is trapped during exhalation, the pressure in the intrathoracic space converts from negative to positive. This causes pressure to build so that not only the injured side but also the uninjured side is affected. This condition is known as a tension pneumothorax. When there is pressure on the uninjured side there will be pressure placed on the heart and great vessels, causing them to be pushed toward the opposite side. This condition is known as mediastinal shift. The trachea will also be pushed to the uninjured side. This shift of the mediastinal contents causes a kink on the great vessels, which results in a backup of blood into the venous system. This backup is demonstrated by distention of the neck veins and a tracheal deviation away from the injured side. THIS IS A LIFE-THREATENING CONDITION!

SIGNS AND SYMPTOMS

Deviated trachea
Difficulty breathing/severe shortness of breath

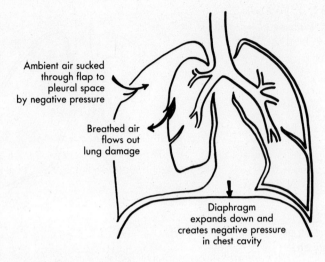

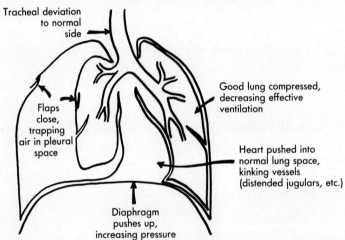

FIG. 20-6 Tension pneumothorax.

Neck vein enlargement
Decreased blood pressure
Increased pulse
Restlessness
Paradoxic movement of the chest

Cyanosis
Distant heart sounds
Hyperresonance on percussion
Can be visualized on chest x-ray film

THERAPEUTIC INTERVENTION

NOTE: If the patient is severely symptomatic, the care giver should not wait for chest x-ray film to provide therapeutic intervention.

ABCs

Oxygen at high flow rate with positive pressure
Needle thoracotomy
Chest tube placement
IV Ringer's lactate or normal saline
Remember that tension pneumothorax is a life-threatening condition and therapeutic intervention should not be delayed.

Needle thoracotomy

The definitive therapy for tension pneumothorax is the placement of a chest tube. If the patient is in the field or it will be a while before a chest tube can be placed, the care giver should consider the placement of a needle into the anterior chest wall to partially relieve the tension until a chest tube can be placed.

Procedure

Rapidly prepare the area in which the needle will be placed: use the second intercostal space at the midclavicular line
Insert the needle (at least a 16-gauge) over the superior portion of the rib (the vein, artery, and nerve are located behind the inferior border) and through the tissue covering the pleural cavity
When the needle has entered the pleural cavity there will be a hissing sound (if desired the needle may be attached to a syringe filled with saline; as air enters the syringe, the saline will bubble)
Leave the needle in place until the chest tube is placed

Sucking chest wound (open pneumothorax) (Fig. 20-7)

A sucking chest wound is a chest wall defect that results in an open pneumothorax. If there is a two-way flap, air will pass into the pleural space and back out again with inspiration and expiration. This causes a simple pneumothorax as negative pressure is lost. If there is a one-way flap, air can enter the pleural space but cannot escape. Air pressure will build with each inspiratory effort, until a tension pneumothorax has formed.

SIGNS AND SYMPTOMS

The sound of sucking
History of trauma to the chest
Dyspnea
Possible signs of tension
    pneumothorax

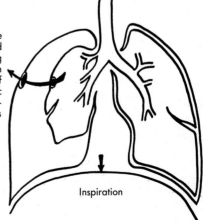

Air exits lung damage and out unobstructed chest wall, preventing full lung expansion because of lack of intrathoracic pressure conditions

Inspiration

FIG. 20-7 Open pneumothorax.

THERAPEUTIC INTERVENTION

ABCs
Cover the wound with an occlusive dressing
Oxygen
Chest tube
If a tension pneumothorax develops:
    Remove the occlusive dressing (this should convert tension pneumothorax to simple
        pneumothorax)
    If this does not relieve the tension pneumothorax follow the steps for therapeutic in-
        tervention for tension pneumothorax

HEMOTHORAX

A hemothorax is a collection of blood in the pleural space. Blood accumulation may
be mild (up to 300 ml), moderate (300 to 1400 ml), or severe (more than 1400 ml). As
hemothorax is essentially a hypovolemic state, carefully observe for signs and symptoms of shock. Hemothorax is often seen in conjunction with simple or tension pneumothorax.

SIGNS AND SYMPTOMS

The signs and symptoms of hemothorax are similar to those of tension pneumothorax
or simple pneumothorax. In addition, the patient will demonstrate signs of shock, including decreased blood pressure, tachycardia, rapid respirations, cool, clammy, and moist
skin, and restlessness, agitation, confusion, or unconsciousness.

THERAPEUTIC INTERVENTION

Therapeutic intervention for hemothorax consists of treating the shock condition and
correcting the chest defect.
    For the shock condition:
        MAST
        IVs
        Oxygen
    For the chest condition:
        Relieve pressure from the pleural cavity by pacing a chest tube to evacuate blood
           and air
        Patient may require surgery if the condition worsens or if chest drainage is greater
           than 200 ml/hour over a 24-hour period

CHEST TUBES AND CHEST DRAINAGE

A chest tube is placed to remove either air or blood from the pleural cavity and thereby
to cause negative pressure to increase. The tube is placed in the second intercostal space at
the midclavicular line for pneumothorax or tension pneumothorax (to remove air) or in the
fifth intercostal space at the midaxillary line for hemothorax (to remove blood or fluid).
    The chest tube should be attached either to a Heimlich valve connected to a collection
chamber, a water-seal drainage system, or one of the newer (waterless) closed-drainage

systems. These will allow air, blood, and fluid to escape from the pleural cavity but will not allow anything to reenter the pleural cavity. Ensure that the system is kept sterile and airtight. The chest tube and connecting tube should be "milked" periodically to evacuate any clots that have formed in the tubing.

Be sure to note the amount of initial drainage and any subsequent drainage. Record this in nurses' notes and directly on the collection chamber.

LUNG INJURIES
Pulmonary contusion

A pulmonary contusion may be small and localized or large and diffuse. This condition is usually associated with other severe injuries. In pulmonary contusion blood extravasates into the parenchyma of the lung because of a lung injury, causing the tissue to become anoxic and changing its permeability. Sometimes this condition may cause tracheal obstruction.

SIGNS AND SYMPTOMS

Diagnosis of pulmonary contusion is usually made by suspecting it and looking for specific signs and symptoms:
Increasing hyperpnea
Dyspnea
Ineffective cough
Agitation and restlessness

THERAPEUTIC INTERVENTION

Oxygen at high flow
Limit fluids during resuscitation (unless there is associated injury causing hypovolemic shock)
Use whole blood, plasma, or salt-poor albumin to replace lost blood
Diuretics
Steroids
If the contusion is severe, endotracheal intubation and positive-pressure ventilation are indicated

Laceration of the parenchyma

Lacerations of the parenchyma are usually caused by penetrating trauma or jagged rib fractures. They are usually self-limiting and rarely require surgical intervention.

Injuries to the tracheobronchial tree

Injuries to the tracheobronchial tree can be caused by either blunt or penetrating trauma. They usually involve the trachea or mainstem bronchus.

SIGNS AND SYMPTOMS

Signs and symptoms of tracheobronchial injury vary greatly but may include:
Airway obstruction
Atelectasis

Hemoptysis (massive)
Mediastinal and subcutaneous emphysema (progressive)
Signs and symptoms of tension pneumothorax

THERAPEUTIC INTERVENTION

Airway maintenance
Breathing
Circulation
Chest tube placement
High-flow oxygen
Semi-Fowler's position
Surgical repair of the tear

DIAPHRAGMATIC INJURIES

Injuries to the diaphragm may be caused by either blunt or penetrating trauma. The care giver should consider the possibility of diaphragmatic injury in injuries below the level of the nipples. DIAPHRAGMATIC RUPTURE IS A LIFE-THREATENING CONDITION.

SIGNS AND SYMPTOMS

Pain referred to the shoulder
Severe shortness of breath
Herniation of bowel contents into the pleural cavity

THERAPEUTIC INTERVENTION

High-flow oxygen under positive pressure
Nasogastric tube
Surgical intervention

CARDIAC INJURIES
Cardiac contusion

Cardiac contusion usually occurs as a result of blunt trauma to the chest. It probably occurs more frequently than it is diagnosed. It may be overlooked because of other, more obvious severe injuries. The care giver should always suspect cardiac contusion in any patient who gives a history of blunt trauma to the chest. It should also always be suspected in any patient who has recently had cardiopulmonary resuscitation.

SIGNS AND SYMPTOMS

Diagnosis of cardiac contusion is usually made by suspecting it. Other signs and symptoms include:

ST-segment and T-wave changes on ECG
Elevated serum enzymes
Shortness of breath
Dyspnea

Chest pain
Tachycardia, hypotension
Dysrhythmias
Shock

THERAPEUTIC INTERVENTION

Therapeutic intervention for cardiac contusion is similar to that for acute myocardial infarction.

Oxygen
Semi-Fowler's position
Analgesia
Treatment of dysrhythmias
Cardiac monitoring
Coronary care unit admission

Penetrating injuries

Penetrating injury to the heart has a high mortality, and the patients usually die rapidly. If the patient survives the prehospital phase and arrives at the emergency department alive, immediate thoracotomy and surgical repair are mandatory.

SIGNS AND SYMPTOMS

Of myocardial rupture:
Severe hypotension
Elevated central venous pressure
Distended neck veins
Decreased ECG voltage
Decreased heart sounds
Of aortic valve or mitral valve rupture:
Sudden onset of severe chest pain
Severe shortness of breath
Dyspnea
Hemoptysis
"Roaring" load murmur
Signs of severe congestive heart failure and pulmonary edema

THERAPEUTIC INTERVENTION

Oxygen
Immediate thoracotomy
Repair of rupture
Replacement of valve (if there is valve rupture)

Cardiac tamponade (see also Chapter 6)

The heart is surrounded by a fibrinous sac called the pericardium. Cardiac tamponade occurs when a relatively minor wound of the heart bleeds into the pericardium. Blood builds up in the sac and causes a rise in pressure. As a result the heart is unable to fill. This interferes with ventricular filling and consequently with cardiac output. The heart attempts to compensate by activating the sympathetic nervous system and becoming tachycardic. As this compensation cannot continue for very long, the heart begins to deteriorate. As the heart rate increases, venous pressure increases, blood pressure falls, and heart sounds diminish.

SIGNS AND SYMPTOMS

Beck's triad or the hallmark of tamponade:
  Increased heart rate
  Decreased blood pressure
  Neck vein distention (caused by venous congestion)
Diminished heart sounds
Dyspnea
Kussmaul's respirations
Paradoxical pulse
Cyanosis

THERAPEUTIC INTERVENTION

MAST (to correct hypovolemic state and distend ventricles)
IVs
Oxygen at high flow
High-Fowler's position
Pericardiocentesis (see Chapter 6 for procedure)

INJURY TO THE GREAT VESSELS

The great vessels are the aorta and the inferior and superior venae cavae. They may be injured as a result of blunt or penetrating trauma. Injury to the great vessels constitutes one of the most severe injuries the human body can sustain. If the victim reaches the hospital alive, immediate thoracotomy and surgical repair are indicated. Of all victims with tears to the great vessels, 10% to 20% survive the event to reach the emergency department alive. This may be because of tamponade by the adventitia, which forms a false aneurysm. (See Chapter 6.)

The most common cause of sudden death from automobile accidents is ruptured aorta. The mechanism of this injury is a rapid acceleration-deceleration force that causes the aorta to shear off at a point of fixation, usually at the ligamentum arteriosum or the aortic root. A transverse tear and exsanguination or massive tamponade result. The patient rarely survives the event.

SIGNS AND SYMPTOMS

Signs of cardiac tamponade
Mediastinal widening
Signs of massive hypovolemic shock
Marked difference in blood pressure from right to left arm
Large murmur heard best in parascapular region

THERAPEUTIC INTERVENTION

IVs
MAST
High-flow oxygen
Thoracotomy
Immediate surgical repair

RUPTURED BRONCHUS

The bronchus most often ruptures near the carina and the right mainstem. Ruptured bronchus is a lethal condition if it is not treated immediately.

SIGNS AND SYMPTOMS

Signs and symptoms of tension pneumothorax
Look specifically for rupture

THERAPEUTIC INTERVENTION

Large-bore IVs
Oxygen
Chest tube placement
Immediate surgical repair

RUPTURED ESOPHAGUS

Ruptured esophagus can occur as a result of either blunt or penetrating trauma to the chest. It can also be caused by a foreign body or iatrogenically at esophagoscopy. Rupture is often at the pharyngoesophageal junction. When the cause is blunt trauma, the rupture often occurs just above the diaphragm. Although ruptured esophagus is rare it is often a fatal event when it occurs. The care giver should consider esophageal rupture whenever there is evidence of first or second rib fracture.

SIGNS AND SYMPTOMS

Sudden onset of severe chest pain or upper abdominal pain
Evidence of trauma to the chest
Pneumothorax signs and symptoms
Pain on swallowing
Mediastinitis
Subcutaneous emphysema
Mediastinal "crunch" sound (Hamman's sign)
Increased respiratory effort
Pleural effusion
Gastric contents or bile in chest tube

THERAPEUTIC INTERVENTION

Oxygen at high flow
Large-bore IVs
Immediate surgical intervention

SUMMARY

The primary focus of therapeutic intervention for chest trauma should be maintenance of airway, breathing, and circulation. All patients with chest trauma should receive supplemental oxygen, and all chest injuries should be considered severe until they are proved otherwise.

Chest tubes

Indications for insertion of chest tube
1. Pneumothorax—an accumulation of air in the pleural cavity.
2. Hemothorax—accumulation of blood in the pleural cavity, usually caused by penetrating injury or blunt trauma to the chest wall.
3. Tension pneumothorax—air accumulation in the pleural cavity accompanied by lung perforation or a bronchial tear causing a valve-like effect in the lung. There is resultant increased intrapleural pressure and eventual mediastinal shift with ensuing shock.

Diagnosis
There is profound hypoxia with agitation, dyspnea, cyanosis, and chest pain.
1. Inspection
   a. Little or no movement on the affected side on inspiration or expiration.
   b. There may be tracheal deviation in the case of a tension pneumothorax.
   c. Subcutaneous emphysema may be present.
2. Auscultation
   Diminished or absent breath sounds on the affected side.
3. Chest X-ray film
   Upright A-P is preferable to illustrate the presence of blood (seen at the bottom of the lung), or air (seen outlining the sides of the lung). However, patients with possible cervical spine injuries should not be placed in an upright position until that is ruled out.

Insertion
1. If there is only air in the pleural cavity, a small chest tube (#28-#32) can be placed in the upper chest. In women, it can be placed laterally in the mid- or anterior axillary line through the fourth to fifth interspace. In men, a tube can be placed in the midclavicular line at the fir.. or second interspace.
2. If blood as well as air is present, a much larger tube (#34-#40) should be used to remove the blood or fluid with less chance of clotting. In this case, the tube should be placed in the seventh or eighth intercostal space at the mid- or anterior axillary line.
3. In the case of a tension pneumothorax, to relieve the increasing intrathoracic pressure, the chest tube may be preceded by the introduction of a needle or cannula in the upper chest in the second intercostal space midclavicular line and later be removed after chest tube insertion.

Procedure
1. Prepare an underwater seal system.
2. Prepare a sterile field with the following:
   a. Povidone-iodine for skin prep
   b. Sterile gloves
   c. Suture material (silk)
   d. Sterile towels
   e. Large chest clamp
   f. Sterile 4 × 4s
   g. Cloth or elastic tape (3 or 4 inch)
   h. Chest tube with trocar
   i. Local anesthetic
   j. Hemostat
3. Attempt to calm patient and explain procedure. Administer pain medication if indicated and ordered.
4. Prep skin with povidone-iodine (Betadine) and apply tincture of benzoin to skin for improved adhesion.
5. After insertion, attach chest tube to underwater seal drainage and securely tape connectors.

Chest tubes—cont'd

Procedure—cont'd

6. Apply sterile dressing and firmly secure tube to chest (without kinks) to prevent any accidental tension on insertion site.
7. Auscultate lungs to assess ventilation.
8. Arrange for postinsertion chest x-ray film to confirm proper placement and lung reexpansion.

The Pleur-evac

Necessary equipment

1. One disposable Pleur-evac
2. One long connective tubing (long enough to reach suction)
3. One suction set-up (continuous)
4. One 500 cc bottle of sterile water
5. One 60 cc piston syringe

Procedure for set-up

1. Unwrap the Pleur-evac carefully and hang it from the gurney by the metal hangers or prop on counter top.
2. To fill the water seal chamber, remove the plastic 5-step connector on the short tube and attach the barrel of the piston syringe.
3. Pour the sterile water using the syringe barrel as a funnel.
4. Fill the water seal chamber to the 2 cm level regardless of what the suctioning level will be (approx 70 cc).
5. If no suction is desired, allow the short tube to remain unclamped for air to escape from the chest cavity.
6. If suction is desired, remove the plastic muffler from the vent at the top of the suction control chamber and again use the syringe barrel as a funnel to pour sterile water into the vent to the 20 cm level or as ordered.
7. Replace the plastic muffler because it reduces the bubbling noise. Be sure nothing occludes the vent.
8. The Pleur-evac is ready to be connected to the patient's chest tube by the long tubing extending from the collection chamber. All connections should be taped securely to prevent air leaks, but should not be completely covered.
9. If suction is ordered, connect the short tube to the suction device with the plastic 5-step adapter. Increase suction slowly until minimal bubbling begins in the suction control chamber. (Suction is generally used if there is a persistent air/fluid leak or if rapid lung re-expansion is desired.)

The Pleur-evac is a durable plastic, self-contained system that uses an underwater seal chamber to collect fluid and/or air from the chest cavity while restoring the normal negative pressure.

From Beninger, L.: J.E.N. **6**(4):35, 1980.   *Continued.*

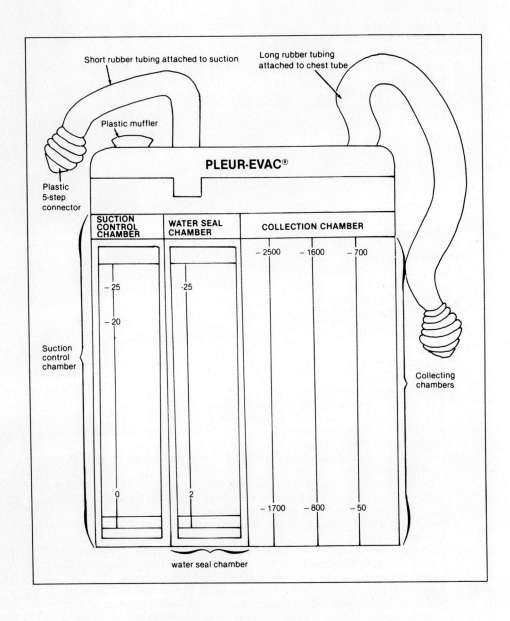

The Pleur-evac—cont'd

Procedure for set-up—cont'd

10. Measure the initial amount of drainage accumulated in the collection chamber and record on the Pleur-evac with date and time. Be sure to measure at eye level.
11. If chest tubes are draining fluid they should be vigorously "milked" every 10-15 minutes initially to assist removal of fluid and to prevent clotting.
12. Clamping the chest tubes during transport is unnecessary as long as the Pleur-evac is attached because of the safety of the water-seal chamber. However, one large chest clamp should always be available in the event of accidental disconnection of the Pleur-evac.
13. Specimens of the drainage may be collected by first clamping the chest tube and then inserting a needle with syringe into the self-sealing rubber grommet at the rear of the collecting chamber. Remove the clamp from the chest tube after the specimen is obtained.

SUGGESTED READINGS

Applebaum, A., Karp, R.B., and Kirklin, J.W.: Surgical treatment for closed thoracic aortic injury, J. Thorac. Cardiovasc. Surg. **77**:458, 1976.

Boeaut, E.P., et al.: Cardiac tamponade following penetrating mediastinal injuries: improved survival with early pericardiocentesis, J. Trauma **19**:46, 1979.

Bricker, D.L., and Mattox, K.L.: About chest tubes, Curr. Concepts Trauma Care, Fall 1979.

Bryant, L.R., et al.: Cardiac valve injury with major chest trauma, Arch. Surg. **107**:279, 1979.

Budassi, S.A.: Chest trauma, Nurs. Clin. North Am. **13**:533, 1978.

Budassi, S.A., and Barber, J.M.: Emergency nursing: principles and practice, St. Louis, 1981, The C.V. Mosby Co.

Chambers, A.A.: Traumatic aortic rupture, JAMA **229**:463, 1974.

Cordell, R.A.: Evaluation of major cardiac and vascular injury to the chest, Emerg. Med. Serv., July-Aug. 1977.

Crawford, W.O.: Pulmonary injury in thoracic and non-thoracic trauma, Radiol. Clin. North Am. **11**:527, 1973.

Davidson, S.J.: Autotransfusion from hemothorax, Curr. Concepts Trauma Care, Fall, 1979.

Defore, W.W., et al.: Surgical management of penetrating injury of the esophagus, Am. J. Surg. **134**:734, 1977.

Doty, D.B., et al.: Cardiac trauma, Ann. Surg. **180**:452, 1974.

Flint, L.N., Jr.: Injuries to major vessels: an overview of current concepts, Heart Lung **5**:301, 1976.

Mandel, A.K., Oparah, S.S.: Penetrating stab wounds of the chest: experience with 200 consecutive cases, J. Trauma **16**:336, 1976.

Moore, E.E., et al.: Post injury thoracotomy in the emergency department: a critical evaluation, Surgery **86**:590, 1979.

Pellegrini, R.V., et al.: Multiple cardiac lesions from blunt trauma, J. Trauma **20**:169, 1980.

Peters, R.M.: Chest trauma. In Warner, C.G., editor: Emergency care: assessment and intervention, ed. 3, St. Louis, 1983, The C.V. Mosby Co.

Symbas, P.N.: Extra-operative autotransfusion from hemothorax, Surgery **84**:722, 1978.

Trinkle, J.K., et al.: Affairs of the wounded heart: penetrating cardiac wounds, J. Trauma **19**:467, 1979.

Wilson, J.M., et al.: Severe chest trauma: morbid implications of first and second rib fractures in 120 patients, Arch. Surg. **113**:846, 1978.

CHAPTER 21 Abdominal trauma

There are two general types of abdominal trauma: blunt and penetrating. Blunt trauma is the result of a force to the abdominal wall that causes energy to diffuse enough to pass through into the abdominal cavity without causing an open injury. Blunt trauma often causes severe trauma to underlying structures. Penetrating trauma is the result of a missile or fragment that pierces the abdominal wall and enters the abdominal cavity. The first question to answer in dealing with a patient with trauma to the abdomen is not so much which organs and structures are injured but whether or not the patient requires surgery.

BLUNT ABDOMINAL TRAUMA (FIG. 21-1)

Traffic accidents account for over 50% of all blunt abdominal trauma. Other causes are home accidents, contact sports accidents, falls, and industrial accidents, just to name a few. Organs injured in blunt trauma to the abdomen are usually the solid organs, that is, the liver, the spleen, the pancreas, and the kidneys. It is difficult to diagnose exact problems in blunt trauma to the abdomen, as there are no entrance or exit wounds and no clues to how the energy may have been dissipated. It is important to remember that trauma to the area between the level of the nipples and the lower costal margin should be considered both an abdominal and a chest injury until one or the other or both are ruled out. One of the most important aspects of care for the patient with blunt trauma to the abdomen is an accurate history. What was the mechanism of injury? How fast was the car going? Where was the impact? Are there any abrasions? Contusions? Ecchymoses? Is Grey Turner's sign (extravasation of blood retroperitoneally, producing an ecchymosis) present? The most important physical finding is the presence of shock, especially shock that does not respond to therapy.

GENERAL SIGNS AND SYMPTOMS

Shock (pale, cool, clammy skin, decreased BP, increased pulse, increased respirations)
Change in bowel sounds
Guaiac-positive specimens from the rectum, bladder, or stomach
Free air under the diaphragm on kidney, ureter, and bladder (KUB) x-ray film
Bruises of the abdominal wall
Tissue separation beneath the skin
Tenderness of the abdomen on palpation
Crepitus   Agitation
Restlessness   Confusion

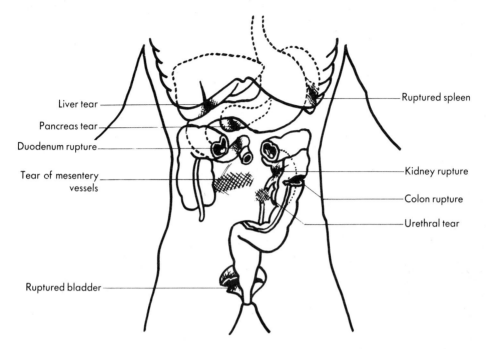

Liver tear

Pancreas tear

Duodenum rupture

Tear of mesentery vessels

Ruptured bladder

Ruptured spleen

Kidney rupture

Colon rupture

Urethral tear

FIG. 21-1 Some possible consequences of blunt abdominal trauma.

DIAGNOSTIC AIDS

Peritoneal lavage—to check for free blood in the peritoneal cavity
Intravenous pyelogram (IVP)—to check for damage to the kidneys, ureters, and bladder
CT scan—to check for intraabdominal bleeding
Retrograde urethrogram—to check for penile fracture

Organs most commonly injured in blunt abdominal trauma

The organ most commonly injured in blunt trauma to the abdomen is the kidney. The incidence of severe injury to the kidney, however, appears to be low. The most common significant injury is to the spleen (Fig. 21-2). The spleen is directly in line with the steering wheel and is often injured on impact with it. The spleen is a dense organ that is encapsulated and easily ruptured. Consider the possibility of splenic injury when the patient has left upper quadrant tenderness or fractures of the eighth through the twelfth ribs or both on the left side.

The liver is commonly injured in blunt trauma to the abdomen because of its physical location, size, and density. It lies anterior to the spleen and is often injured when there are fractures to the eighth through the twelfth ribs on the right side of the chest. There is a relatively unprotected area over the dome of the liver that is easily fractured. Small lacerations to the liver usually heal spontaneously. Stellate lacerations to the liver must be debrided and *large* sutures as well as a drain must be placed. A hepatic lobectomy may have to be

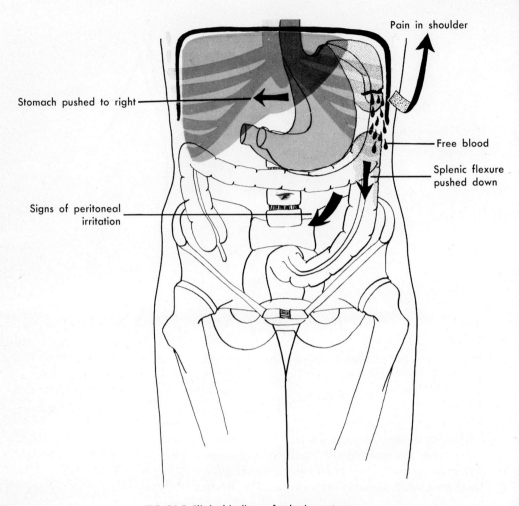

Pain in shoulder

Stomach pushed to right

Free blood

Splenic flexure pushed down

Signs of peritoneal irritation

FIG. 21-2 Clinical indices of splenic rupture.

performed for large lacerations. There is a high incidence of death with extensive lacerations.

A worse injury than liver laceration is laceration of the hepatic vein, which terminates at the inferior vena cava. When this occurs the patient bleeds profusely and usually has to be taken to the operating suite for vascular clamping and repair via a "pathologist's incision," an incision from the sternum to the symphisis pubis.

Other major vessels in the abdominal cavity are the inferior vena cava and the aorta. If these vessels rupture they do not contract sufficiently to control bleeding. Patients with these injuries must be taken to the operating suite immediately for repair of the ruptured vessel. Mortality is high. There may be loss of pulses in aortic injury.

When the diaphragm is ruptured, death may be imminent. An undetected injury may eventually cause evisceration of the abdominal contents into the chest cavity and will

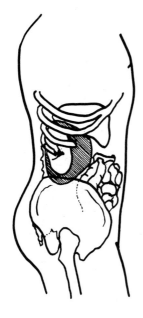

FIG. 21-3 Kidney rupture from rib fracture.

cause severely depressed ventilatory efforts. Normally the diaphragm will rise to the fourth rib on full exhalation and drop to the eleventh rib during full inhalation.

Injuries to the stomach and small intestine are easy to diagnose and usually easy to repair in the operating suite. Injuries to the left side of the colon usually are repaired with a colostomy placed for 3 to 6 months because of the high amount of contamination in that area. Injuries to the right side of the colon act as ileostomies, as the contents of the right colon are very liquid. The bacteria count, however, is usually much lower on the right side of the colon than the left, therefore injuries to the right side of the colon are usually oversewn as opposed to formed into an ileostomy or a colostomy. If there is injury to the transverse colon the surgeon may elect either to oversew or to form a colostomy.

There are three types of injuries to the kidneys (Fig. 21-3):

Contusions—usually self limiting; therapeutic intervention includes bed rest and ingestion of large amounts of fluids.

Fractures/lacerations (Fig. 21-4)—there is a break through the tissue and vessels; this injury usually requires a nephrectomy.

Contusions/fractures—management is highly debatable, especially as to whether surgery should be performed or not; check for urine extravasation and be aware of the possibility of later hypertension caused by scarring of the renal tissue. Exploratory surgery is generally indicated; if there is a pulsatile hematoma the surgeon usually performs a nephrectomy; if the hematoma is nonpulsatile a nephrectomy is generally not done.

Ureteral injuries are almost never seen in blunt trauma to the abdomen.

There are three basic types of injuries to the bladder:

Contusion—most commonly seen with pelvic fracture (Fig. 21-5)

Intraperitoneal fracture and extraperitoneal fracture—usually occur as a result of a full

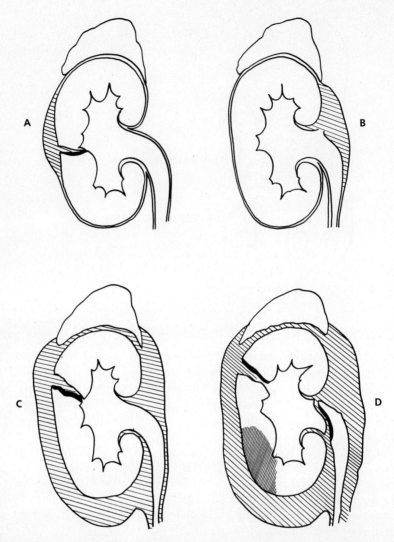

FIG. 21-4 A, Fracture of renal parenchyma; blood extravasates but is contained under capsule. **B,** Tear in renal pelvis causing urine extravasation. **C,** Tear in kidney and capsule causing blood extravasation. **D,** Shattered kidney; much blood and urine extravasation.

bladder and blunt trauma to the abdomen; urine may or may not be present in the peritoneum

Pelvic fracture causes a penetrating injury to the bladder 15% of the time. Contusions of the bladder should be treated with forced fluids. Bladder rupture must be surgically repaired in the operating suite.

Urethral ruptures are more common in males than females. In males the urethra is divided into the anterior and posterior sections. The posterior section is most commonly

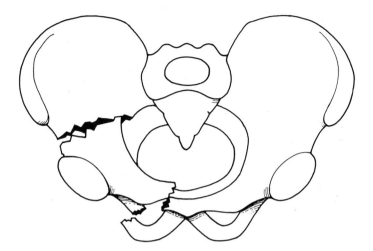

FIG. 21-5 Fracture of pelvis may lead to rupture of bladder.

injured by a pelvic fracture. This injury appears as a partial transection of the urethra with a high-floating prostate gland. Anterior urethral lacerations are rarely seen with blunt trauma to the abdomen; they are most commonly seen as a result of self-instrumentation. As a general rule all patients with blunt trauma to the abdomen should be able to urinate within 1 hour of emergency department admission or further studies should be done to rule out injury to the genitourinary system. When fracture of the penile shaft is suspected the care giver should perform a retrograde urethrogram, in which radiopaque dye is injected into the urethra (via an infant-feeding tube or another small tube) and an x-ray film is taken. If there is no urine extravasation, it is usually safe to attempt to pass a Foley catheter into the urinary bladder. If there is urine extravasation, immediate urologic consultation is indicated.

Massive intraperitoneal bleeding is usually seen with pelvic fracture. The care giver should send blood specimens to the blood bank early for typing and cross-matching of at least 6 units of blood. The patient with pelvic fracture will lose, on the average, 4 to 5 units of blood. It is generally accepted that surgical intervention for pelvic fractures is delayed unless immediate surgery is found to be absolutely necessary. Occasionally, if bleeding is profuse, the care giver may wish to obtain an arteriogram of the hypogastric artery. If it is bleeding, the care giver may wish to use a vasopressor agent IV or a coagulant on the area of the bleeding. If the patient is developing shock from the massive beeding of pelvic fracture, the care giver should apply the MAST to control bleeding by tamponade and supply needed blood to the central circulation. Surgery should not be performed on these patients unless absolutely necessary.

The pancreas may be lacerated though the patient shows no observable signs and symptoms. Peritoneal lavage results may return negative. Amylase, however, may be elevated to 250 ml. There is no good test to rule out pancreatic damage. The best indication is a high index of suspicion. If amylase remains high over a 24-hour period, the care giver should be highly suspicious of pancreatic damage. Up to 70% of the pancreas may be removed without causing any metabolic difficulties. If the entire pancreas must be removed the patient must receive daily doses of insulin, as the pancreas is the body's insulin source.

THERAPEUTIC INTERVENTION FOR ALL BLUNT ABDOMINAL TRAUMA

At least two large-bore cannulas with Ringer's lactate or normal saline
MAST if the systolic blood pressure is less than 80 mm Hg
Oxygen
Backboard support
Nasogastric tube
Foley catheter
Possible surgical intervention

PERITONEAL LAVAGE

Indications for peritoneal lavage include evidence of blunt trauma to the abdomen in which there is ensuing shock but surgery is not inevitable and cases in which the patient is not conscious and cannot tell of abdominal tenderness and signs of abdominal guarding and so on cannot be elicited. Peritoneal lavage is also appropriate as a diagnostic study in patients who are inebriated or have spinal cord injury, from whom it would be almost impossible to elicit signs and symptoms of blunt abdominal trauma. Peritoneal lavage is also useful as a diagnostic tool in children who are unreliable sources of information for evidence of blunt abdominal trauma.

The only absolute contraindication to the procedure is a distended bladder (Fig. 21-6). It is therefore mandatory that the bladder be emptied before peritoneal lavage. Relative contraindications include a gravid uterus, abdominal wall hematoma, and abdominal scars from previous surgery. In all of these instances the location of the incision should be changed, but the procedure may still be performed. If there is evidence of penetrating injury, the wound should be explored surgically.

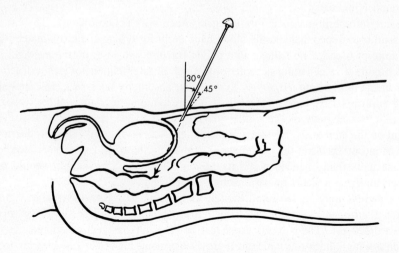

FIG. 21-6 Distended bladder may be perforated by trochar for peritoneal lavage.

EQUIPMENT

Surgical antiseptic solution
Sterile drapes
Sterile gloves
1% lidocaine with epinephrine
No. 11 scalpel
No. 15 peritoneal dialysis catheter (with or without trocar)
Syringe with small-gauge needle
Ringer's lactate (1,000 ml, warmed) and IV tubing
Nasogastric tube
Foley catheter
Skin retractors
4-0 nylon suture and needle
Antibiotic ointment
Small dressing for covering stab wounds

PREPARATION OF PATIENT

Explain the procedure to the conscious patient and instruct him about how to cooperate
   with the procedure
Empty the stomach with a nasogastric tube
Empty the bladder with a Foley catheter

PROCEDURE

1. Prepare the anterior abdominal wall by shaving, cleansing with surgical solution
   (e.g., 1% povidone-iodine [Betadine]), and draping with sterile towels.
2. Inject 5 ml of 1% lidocaine *with epinephrine* in a subcutaneous wheal to 2 to 3 cm
   below the umbilicus.
3. Make a 2 cm incision through the skin and subcutaneous adipose tissue to the linea
   alba with a No. 11 scalpel. Retract the skin and subcutaneous tissue with the skin
   retractor. Provide *absolute* hemostasis. If blood from the incision is allowed to escape
   it can give a false indication to the lavage.
4. Engage the trochar into the linea alba at a 30° to 45° angle. (Instruct the patient to
   tense the abdomen if possible.) Apply rotary motion and pressure until the peritoneum is perforated. Stop all force immediately at that point.
5. Direct the trocar tip toward the pelvis and slide off the catheter 15 to 20 cm into the
   peritoneal cavity.
6. Attach a 20 ml syringe and aspirate the catheter. If aspiration yields 20 ml of blood,
   the tap is considered positive, and the procedure is terminated. If little or no blood is
   obtained, attach the IV line of 1,000 ml Ringer's lactate and infuse over 15 minutes.
   (For a child, use 10 ml Ringer's lactate/kg.) Manually manipulate the abdomen to
   permit the solution to mix with abdominal cavity fluids.
7. Place the IV solution flask on the floor to siphon off the infused fluid.
8. When the majority of the fluid is returned, remove the catheter.
9. Close the skin with a 4-0 nylon suture.
10. Dress stab wounds with antibiotic ointment and a small sterile dressing.

Analysis of findings

NEWSPRINT METHOD

The opacity of the fluid is described by whether or not newsprint can be read when held behind the test tubes.

Opacity	Interpretation
Fluid entirely clear	No chance of significant injury to peritoneal viscera
Fluid appears bloody but newsprint can be read	Further diagnostic study indicated
Newsprint can be seen but not read	90% chance of significant abdominal injury; surgery indicated
Newsprint cannot be seen	98% chance of significant injury

LABORATORY METHOD

The laboratory method requires three samples for analysis. The lavage is considered positive if these results are obtained:

Hematocrit	2% or more
Red blood cell count	100,000/cu mm or more
White blood cell count	500/cu mm or more
Amylase	200 Somogyi units or more
Bile	Any free bile
Culture and Gram's stain	Any significant quantity of bacteria indicates perforation of the intestine

CULDOCENTESIS

A culdocentesis (Fig. 21-7) may be indicated for female patients for the purpose of detecting free intraabdominal blood that may have come from a ruptured ectopic preg-

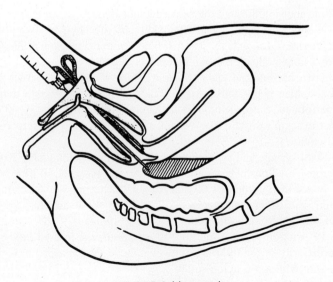

FIG. 21-7 Culdocentesis

nancy or a ruptured ovarian cyst and that gravitates to the cul-de-sac, the most dependent portion of the peritoneal cavity.

EQUIPMENT

Vaginal speculum
Uterine tenaculum
Sponge forceps
18-gauge spinal needle
Glass adapter with rubber tubing
Syringe with aspirating catheter tip
Sterile gloves
Sponges
Antiseptic solution (e.g., benzalkonium [Zephiran])

PROCEDURE

1. Explain the procedure to the patient.
2. Place the patient in the lithotomy position.
3. Introduce the speculum, sponge dry the posterior fornix, and prepare the site with antiseptic solution. (A local anesthetic may also be used.)
4. Insert the spinal needle into the cul-de-sac and, using the syringe, apply suction over 1 minute while withdrawing the needle. (Have extra aspirating sets on hand if the blood aspirated is thought to be from a vein or artery or if it contains feces.)

LABORATORY STUDIES*

Test	Significance
Hemoglobin and hematocrit	Provide baseline data only
	Usually do not reflect recent hemorrhage
	Several hours may elapse before hemodilution will be reflected by the hematocrit
Complete blood count	Provides baseline data
	Splenic injury should be suspected if the leukocyte and platelet counts rise sharply without significant dehydration
Type and cross-match	Preparatory to blood component therapy
Arterial blood gas	Provides baseline data and monitors respiratory status and trends
Electrolytes	Provides baseline data
SGOT	Provides baseline data
Total bilirubin	Provides baseline data
Coagulation studies	Hemostasis must be evaluated before extensive therapy or surgery
BUN and serum creatinine	Provides baseline data
	A rising BUN or serum creatinine level may indicate impaired renal function 24 to 48 hours after trauma, but these are usually not valuable initially
Serum amylase	A high serum amylase level may suggest, but not confirm, pancreatic injury; some patients have no rise in amylase levels despite injury to the pancreas and others have elevations without visceral damage

*From Barber, J.: Nurs. Clin. North Am. **13**:221, June 1978.

RADIOLOGIC STUDIES*

A patient in stable condition may be subjected to various x-ray studies to demonstrate intraabdominal injury. However, these studies should not be done if the delay and manipulation required to accomplish an acceptable study will jeopardize the patient's condition.

Film	Demonstrates
Flat plate of abdomen	Loops of intestine separated by fluid; fractures of lower ribs, pelvis, spine; position of organs and psoas muscle
Upright plate of abdomen	Free air under the diaphragm suggesting hollow viscus rupture†
Lateral decubitus film	Free air above flank†
Upright chest film	Injury or rupture of diaphragm
Flat plate of chest	Intestinal organ herniation into left chest, which may not be visible on upright film
IVP	Renal injury
Abdominal angiography (reserved for poor surgical risks)	Intravisceral hematomas
Excretory urography	Urinary tract integrity or injury before surgically exploring or removing a kidney
Radioisotope scanning	Defects of liver, kidney, or spleen of 2 cm or greater

INDICATIONS FOR LAPAROTOMY

Unexplained hemorrhagic shock
Peritoneal perforation
Increasing abdominal tenderness or rigidity
Evidence of peritonitis
Visualized free air in the abdomen
Positive peritoneal lavage or culdocentesis
Enlarging abdominal mass in the absence of pelvic or vertebral fractures
Progressive drop in hemoglobin and hematocrit in the absence of hypotension, especially in the second 24 hours after injury

OTHER CONSIDERATIONS

If there is a high degree of suspicion of intraabdominal contamination, start IV antibiotics at once so an adequate blood level can be attained before the additional stress of surgery is placed on the defense mechanisms.

FOLLOW-UP

Certain abdominal injuries may progress slowly. Adequate instructions of "warning signs" of impending crisis should be given to families and the patient if the decision is

---

*From Barber, J.: Nurs. Clin. North Am. **13**:221, June 1978.

†The patient must sit upright or lie on his side for 10 minutes before the film to permit air to rise. Absence of air does not rule out hollow viscus rupture, however. Haziness or a "ground glass" appearance caused by accumulated air and fluid is a late sign.

reached to discharge the patient after initial evaluation. The patient should always be referred for follow-up in 3 to 5 days, and this should be documented carefully in the records.

PENETRATING ABDOMINAL TRAUMA

There are a wide variety of presentations of patients with penetrating abdominal trauma. The specific presentations depend on many factors, including the penetrating object, the velocity at which it penetrated, and the angle of projection. There may be merely penetration of the abdominal wall without intraabdominal injury, or there may be extensive intraabdominal injury. One goal in treating the patient with a penetrating injury to the abdomen is to decide if he requires exploratory surgery. Surgical exploration is indicated for a wound produced by a high-velocity missile.

SIGNS AND SYMPTOMS

Signs and symptoms will vary depending on the nature and extent of the injury. Pay particular attention to the signs and symptoms of shock:

Low blood pressure (below 80 mm Hg systolic)	Agitation
Tachycardia	Restlessness
Rapid, shallow respirations	Confusion
Cold, pale, clammy skin	Loss of consciousness

Also:
Look for entrance and exit wounds
Check for evisceration

THERAPEUTIC INTERVENTION

Oxygen
Two large-bore IVs with Ringer's lactate or normal saline
Backboard and cervical collar (missile may cause bone fragments to all parts of the body)
Wet to dry sterile dressing for evisceration
MAST if systolic blood pressure is below 80 mm Hg
Surgery if indicated
Thoracotomy if there is cardiopulmonary arrest (to cross-clamp the aorta and gain control of bleeding)

If there is a penetrating object in place, secure it until it can be removed by the trauma surgeon or emergency physician under controlled circumstances. If there is shock in the presence of a penetrating object, remove the penetrating object if necessary to apply the MAST.

SPECIAL CONSIDERATIONS FOR PREGNANT PATIENTS
WITH ABDOMINAL TRAUMA

If possible, lay the patient on her left side to displace the uterus to the right and thereby avoid vena cava compression
Administer whole blood and packed cells as soon as possible if volume replacement is

required (the mother and the fetus both require the oxygen-carrying capacity of blood as soon as possible)

Shield the uterus as much as possible when obtaining necessary x-ray films

Do not forget to monitor the fetus

If the mother is develoing shock apply *at least* the leg units of the MAST (application of the abdominal section is controversial)

SUGGESTED READINGS

Batalder, D.J., et al.: Value of the G-suit in patients with severe pelvic fractures, Arch. Surg. **109**:326, 1974.

Brownstein, P.W., et al.: Concealed hemorrhage due to pelvic fracture, J. Trauma **4**:832, 1964.

Budassi, S.A., and Barber, J.M.: Emergency nursing: practices and procedures, St. Louis, 1981, The C.V. Mosby Co.

Budassi, S.A.: Peritoneal lavage, J.E.N. **7**(1):27, 1981.

Davidson, I., Miller, E., and Litwin, M.S.: Gunshot wounds of the abdomen, Arch. Surg. **111**:862, 1976.

Davis, J.J., Cohn, I., and Nance, F.C.: Diagnosis and management of blunt abdominal trauma, Ann. Surg. **183**:672, 1976.

Engrav, L.H., et al.: Diagnostic peritoneal lavage in blunt abdominal trauma, J. Trauma **15**:854, 1975.

Generelly, P., Moore, T.A., and LeMay, J.T.: Delayed splenic rupture diagnosed by culdocentesis, J.A.C.E.P. **6**:369, 1977.

Jergens, M.E.: Peritoneal lavage, Am. J. Surg. **133**:365, 1977.

Looser, K.G., and Crombie, H.D.: Pelvic fractures: an anatomic guide to the severity of injury, Am. J. Surg. **132**:638, 1976.

Meads, G.E., et al.: Traumatic rupture of the right hemidiaphragm, J. Trauma **17**:797, 1977.

Nance, F.C., et al.: Surgical judgment in the management of penetrating wounds of the abdomen, Ann. Surg. **179**:639, 1974.

Steele, M., and Lim, R.C.: Advances in the management of splenic injuries, Am. J. Surg. **130**:159, 1975.

Wilson, R., et al.: Shock in the emergency department, J.A.C.E.P. **5**:678, 1976.

CHAPTER 22 Limb trauma

Limb trauma can occur in any age group and at almost any time. It is probably the greatest source of disability in the United States. Prompt, accurate management may not only be life and limb saving but may also prevent later severe disability.

DEFINITIONS

skeleton—Forms the framework of the body; it provides both support and protection.

bone—There are two types of bones: (1) cancellous (spongy) bone, which can be found in the skull, vertebrae, pelvis, and long bone ends, and (2) cortical (dense) bone, which is found in the long bones. Bone has its own blood and nerve supply and is usually capable of healing itself. Bones serve to protect vital organs and serve as levers for movement.

ligament—Fibrous connective tissue that connects bone to bone.

tendon—Fibrous connective tissue that connects muscle to bone.

cartilage—Dense connective tissue found between the ribs; in the nasal septum, ear, larynx, trachea, and bronchi; between vertebrae; and on the articulating surfaces of bones. Cartilage has no neurovascular supply.

joints—Connection of two bones for mobility and stability; may provide flexion and extension, medial and lateral rotation, and abduction and adduction. A joint consists of articulating bone surfaces that are covered with cartilage, a two-layered sac containing synovial membranes (to lubricate), and a capsule that thickens and becomes a ligament. Muscles that overlie joints attach the bone surfaces to one another and provide movement.

EMERGENCY MANAGEMENT

When dealing at the scene with a patient with limb trauma it is important to obtain a brief history and discover the mechanism of injury. Early treatment includes:

ABCs

Quick assessment for other major trauma (head, cervical spine, chest, and abdomen)

Protection of the head and cervical spine

Immobilization of the traumatized limb above and below the trauma site

Evaluation of the vascular status of the limb, before and after immobilization:

Pulses distal to the trauma

Color

Temperature

Capillary refill

453

Evaluation of the neurologic status of the limb before and after immobilization

Reduction of the fracture *only* if the vascular status is compromised

Elevation of the limb if possible

Cold pack application to the area

Transportation to the hospital

Immobilization is accomplished before movement or transport to prevent further damage and to reduce the amount of pain and avoid further pain.

Note must be made of any swelling, discoloration, contusions, abrasion, or obvious deformities. If the trauma is obviously an open fracture:

Irrigate the wound site with normal saline

Apply a dry sterile dressing over the wound

Apply a slight compression dressing

Splint the limb

Do not attempt to reduce the fracture in the field

If a puncture wound is present but no bone is protruding, assume that the wound was made by a jagged bone end or missile, and treat it as an open fracture. To control bleeding:

Apply pressure over the bleeding site or on the edges of the wound

Elevate the extremity if possible

A tourniquet should be used *only as a life-saving measure*. Remember, the limb may have to be amputated if all circulation ceases for an extended period of time.

Once the patient has reached the emergency department, remember to undress him to avoid missing any other injuries that may have occurred. Be sure to examine both the anterior and posterior parts of the body.

SOFT TISSUE INJURIES

Because of the variety of soft tissue injuries, only the most common will be covered in this chapter. See the suggested readings at the end of the chapter for additional references.

Soft tissue injuries can be injuries to the skin and underlying tissues, muscles, tendons, cartilage, ligaments, veins, arteries, or nerves.

Immediate general treatment of soft tissue injuries

Assure ABCs

Control bleeding

Secure any impaling object

Apply a dry sterile dressing

Elevate the injured part if possible

Apply a cold pack

Check the patient's tetanus prophylaxis status

ABRASION

Mechanism of injury	Usually caused by rubbing of skin against a hard surface, scraping the epithelial layer away and exposing the epidermal or dermal layer; similar to a second-degree burn

| Therapeutic intervention | Wound cleansing (scrub and irrigate)
 Removal of foreign bodies
 Topical antibiotic ointments
 Nonadherent dressing
 Dressing change once a day until eschar forms
 Avoidance of sunlight to damaged area for 6 months because of hypopigmentation |

AVULSION

| Mechanism of injury | Full-thickness skin loss; a cutting or gouging injury resulting from penetration of a sharp object or ''pulling away'' of a section of skin |
| Therapeutic intervention | Wound cleansing (scrub and irrigate)
 Debridement
 Restoration of divided deep structures (muscles and tendons)
 Split-thickness graft or flap
 Bulky dressing |

CONTUSION

| Mechanism of injury | Extravasation of blood into tissues where vessels are damaged but skin is not disrupted, usually as a result of blunt trauma |
| Therapeutic intervention | Cold pack
 Analgesia
 No dressing |

LACERATION

Mechanism of injury	Open wound or cut through the dermal layer; may be minor or major, extending to deep epithelium; may vary in length and depth
Therapeutic intervention	Control of bleeding (pressure and elevation) Evaluation of neurovascular status Anesthesia Inspection Cleansing (scrub and irrigate) Removal of foreign bodies Excision of necrotic margins Approximation Closing (Steri-Strip or suture) Dressing
Special notes	If laceration is deep and there is question of underlying structural damage, the patient may require surgery.

PUNCTURE

| Mechanism of injury | Penetration of the skin by a pointed or sharp object; may appear innocent but have damaged underlying structures or be grossly contaminated; rarely bleeds |

Therapeutic intervention	Depends on depth of penetration and amount of contamination
	Generally:
	Soaking in surgical soap solution twice a day for 2 to 4 days
	Removal of foreign bodies (taped to chart)
	If contaminated:
	Soaking
	Anesthesia
	Cleansing (scrub and irrigate)
	Inspection
	Removal of foreign bodies
	Excision of necrotic tissue
	Drain placement
	Packing
Special notes	If the foreign body is deep or if there is a question of vascular or neurologic compromise, the patient should have exploratory surgery and repair.
	If the object is impaling, leave it in place until it can be thoroughly evaluated.

ABSCESS

Mechanism of injury	Localized collection of pus
Therapeutic intervention	Anesthesia
	Drain in dependent position
	Removal of elliptical area
	Loose packing to allow for drainage
	Loose dressing
	Antibiotics if patient is febrile
Special notes	Do not wait until an abscess ''points''; if abscess is suspected, drain with a needle.

HEMATOMA

Mechanism of injury	Escape of blood into subcutaneous space, usually as a result of blunt trauma
Therapeutic intervention	Varies, depending on location

Specific types of soft tissue injuries

WRINGER INJURY

Mechanism of injury	Washing machine wringer causing crush injury
Therapeutic intervention	Wound cleansing
	Sterile bulky dressing

Check of distal pulse
Check of neurologic status
Elevation of part
Tetanus prophylaxis

MISSILE INJURY, GUNSHOT WOUND

Mechanism of injury	Usually bullet or fragments or wadded pieces of clothing (shotguns cause more deaths than any other firearm)
Therapeutic intervention	Wound cleansing Dry dressing Check of distal pulse Assessment of limb if possible Tetanus prophylaxis Further surgical assessment

IMPALING INJURY

Mechanism of injury	Often an industrial accident Fall onto a sharp, immobile object
Therapeutic intervention	Immobilization of extremity Securing of impaling object *(not to be removed if possible)* Check of neurovascular status of limbs distal to injury Transportation to a hospital Tetanus prophylaxis

CRUSH INJURY

Mechanism of injury	Heavy object falls on extremity
Therapeutic intervention	Control of bleeding Dry sterile bulky dressing Check of distal pulses Check of neurologic function Elevation of limb if possible Cold pack Tetanus prophylaxis

KNEE INJURY

Mechanisms of injury	Rotational trauma or extra flexion trauma
Common types	Medial meniscus injury from rotational trauma Collateral ligament injury: medial from valgus stress, lateral from varus stress Anterior and posterior cruciate ligament injury from hyperextension trauma

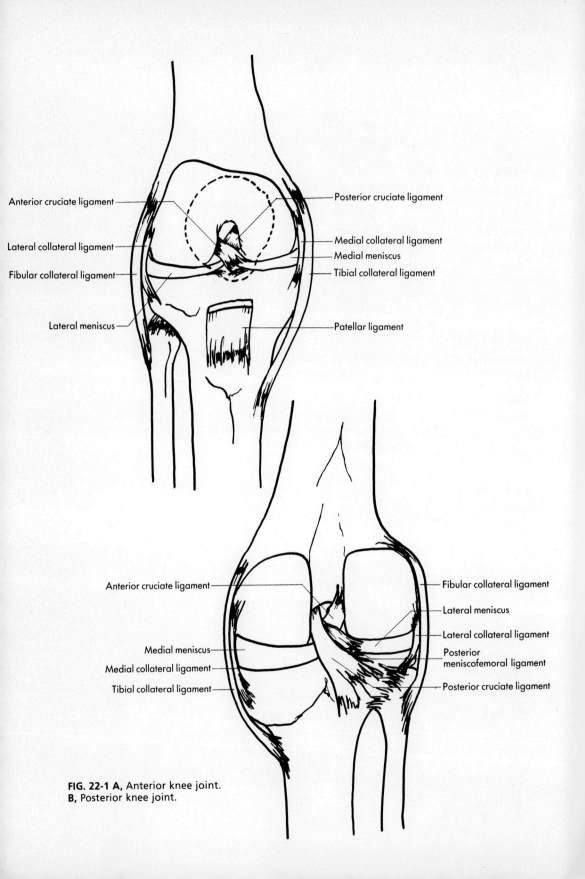

Anterior cruciate ligament

Lateral collateral ligament

Fibular collateral ligament

Lateral meniscus

Posterior cruciate ligament

Medial collateral ligament
Medial meniscus
Tibial collateral ligament

Patellar ligament

Anterior cruciate ligament

Medial meniscus
Medial collateral ligament
Tibial collateral ligament

Fibular collateral ligament

Lateral meniscus

Lateral collateral ligament

Posterior
meniscofemoral ligament

Posterior cruciate ligament

FIG. 22-1 A, Anterior knee joint.
B, Posterior knee joint.

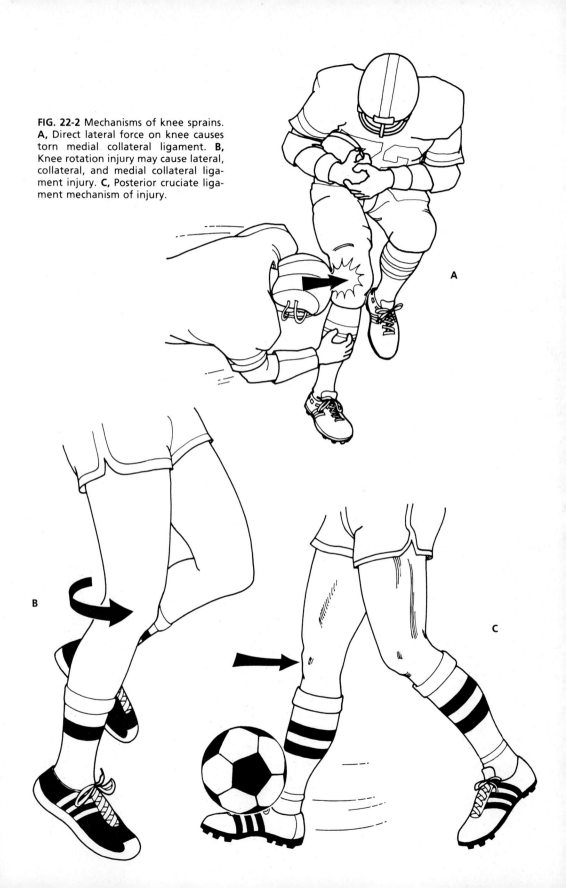

FIG. 22-2 Mechanisms of knee sprains. **A,** Direct lateral force on knee causes torn medial collateral ligament. **B,** Knee rotation injury may cause lateral, collateral, and medial collateral ligament injury. **C,** Posterior cruciate ligament mechanism of injury.

Signs and symptoms	Swelling Ecchymosis Effusion Pain Tenderness
Therapeutic intervention	Compression bandage Elevation Cold pack No weight bearing Ligament tears: surgical repair 24 to 48 hours after injury

FINGERTIP INJURY
High-pressure paint gun injury

Mechanism of injury	Cleaning tip of high-pressure paint gun; gun releases, injecting stream of paint into fingertip and up into the hand, wrist, and arm; appears only as a small pinhole in the tip of finger
Therapeutic intervention	*Immediate* transportation to an emergency facility Keep limb lower than heart level Check for pulses in arm and wrist Check for neurologic status Immediate evaluation by a physician

Crush injury of distal phalanx

Mechanism of injury	Crushing force, heavy object on distal phalanx
Therapeutic intervention	Soft, bulky dressing If hematoma forming under fingernail, nail trephination

Nail trephination

Equipment:
   Nail drill, scalpel, or paper clip
   Antiseptic solution
   Alcohol lamp if paper clip is used
Procedure:
   1. Prepare the nail with antiseptic solution
   2. Penetrate the nail:
      a. With nail drill
      b. With scalpel using rotation motion
      c. With paper clip after it is heated red hot
   3. Release the pressure caused by the hematoma
   4. Dress with an adhesive bandage

STRAINS

Mechanism of injury	A weakening or stretching of a muscle at the tendon area May be the result of anything from stepping off a curb and twisting the ankle or tripping to an automobile accident or an athletic injury

Mild strain

Signs and symptoms	Local pain Point tenderness Spasm
Therapeutic intervention	Compression bandage (Fig. 22-3) Elevation for 12 hours Cold pack for 12 hours Weight bearing

Moderate strain

Signs and symptoms	Point tenderness Local pain Swelling Discoloration Inability to use for a short time
Therapeutic intervention	Compression bandage Elevation for 24 hours Cold pack 24 hours Analgesia Light weight bearing

Severe strain

Signs and symptoms	Point tenderness Local pain Swelling Discoloration Snapping noise at time of injury
Therapeutic intervention	Compression bandage Elevation for 24 to 48 hours Cold pack for 48 hours Analgesia No weight bearing for 48 hours

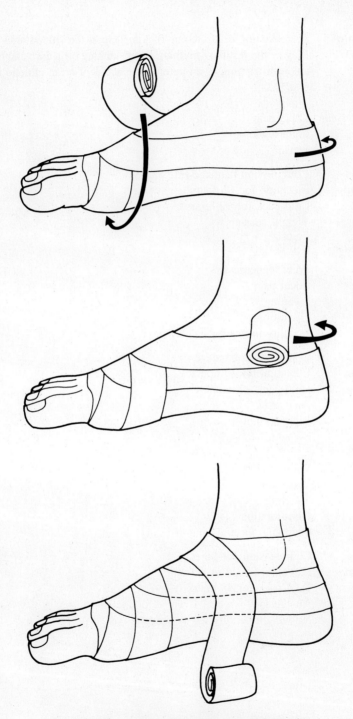

FIG. 22-3 How to wrap and form ankle and foot spica.

SPRAINS

A mild sprain is a ligament that has been stretched. A moderate sprain is a ligament that has been partially torn. A severe sprain is a ligament that has been completely torn.

Mechanism of injury	May be the same as a strain, but usually a much more traumatic force
	Joint motion exceeds its normal limits
	Most common sprains are in the shoulders, knees, and ankles

Mild sprain

Signs and symptoms	Slight pain
	Slight swelling
Therapeutic intervention	Compression bandage
	Elevation for 12 hours
	Cold pack for 12 hours
	Light weight bearing

Moderate sprain

Signs and symptoms	Pain
	Point tenderness
	Swelling
	Inability to use for a short time
Therapeutic intervention	Compression bandage
	Elevation for 24 hours
	Cold pack for 24 hours
	Crutches
	Minimal weight bearing for 3 days

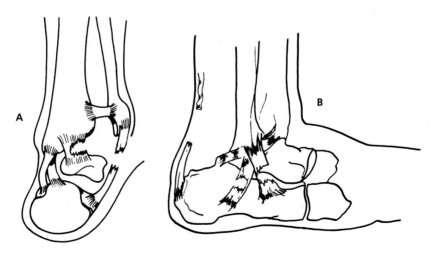

FIG. 22-4 Ankle sprain, torn ligaments in ankle joint. **A,** Posterior view. **B,** Lateral view.

Severe sprain

Signs and symptoms	Pain Point tenderness Swelling Discoloration Inability to use
Therapeutic intervention	Compression bandage or cast Elevation for 48 hours Cold pack for 48 hours Crutches No weight bearing for 3 days

ACHILLES TENDON RUPTURE

Age group	Usually athletes older than 30 years
Mechanism of injury	Usually in stop-and-start sports (such as tennis or racquetball) in which one steps off abruptly on the forefoot with the knee forces in extension[1]
Signs and symptoms	Sharp pain Inability to use foot Deformity Positive Thompson's sign*
Therapeutic intervention	Compression Elevation Cold pack

PERIPHERAL NERVE INJURIES

Peripheral nerve injuries can be caused by trauma (mechanical, chemical, or thermal), toxins, malignancy, metabolic disorders, or collagen disease. In the emergency situation they are usually associated with lacerations, fractures, dislocations, and penetrating wounds.

Accurate assessment requires an understanding of the distribution of nerves, the origin of motor branches, and the muscles they supply.

The clinician should recognize that motor loss tests are accurate only if one can palpate or visualize the tendon or muscle belly under consideration. Diagnostic tests such as electromyography, nerve conduction tests, and electrical stimulation are of little or no value in the emergency evaluation of peripheral nerve injury.

It should be noted that repair of peripheral nerves should not be undertaken as an emergency department surgical intervention.

---

*Positive Thompson's sign: with the leg extended and the foot over the end of a table, squeeze the calf muscle; no heel pull or upward movement will be seen.

TABLE 22-1 Modes for assessing common peripheral nerve injuries

Nerve	Frequently associated injuries	Assessment technique*
Radial	Fracture of humerus, especially middle and distal thirds	Inability to extend thumb in "hitch-hiker's sign"
Ulnar	Fracture of medial humeral epicondyle	Loss of pain perception in tip of little finger
Median	Elbow dislocation or wrist or forearm injury	Loss of pain perception in tip of index finger
Peroneal	Tibia or fibula fracture, dislocation of knee	Inability to extend great toe or foot; may also be associated with sciatic nerve injury
Sciatic and tibial	Infrequent with fractures or dislocations	Loss of pain perception in sole of foot

*Test is invalid if extension tendons are severed or if severe muscle damage is present.

FRACTURES

Fractures are divided into two general categories:
1. Closed (simple)—the skin is not disrupted
2. Open (compound)—the skin is disrupted by:
   a. A bone puncturing from the inside out
   b. An object puncturing from the outside in, with resultant fracture

Types of fractures

Transverse—results from angulation force or direct trauma.

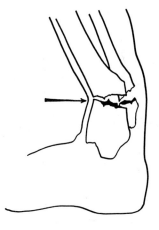

Oblique—results from twisting force.

Spiral—results from twisting force with firmly planted foot.

Comminuted—results from severe direct trauma; has more than two fragments.

Impacted—results from severe trauma causing fracture ends to jam together.

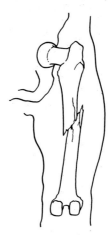

Compressed—results from severe force to top of head or os calcis or acceleration-deceleration injury.

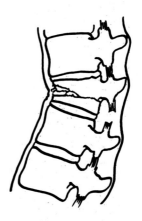

Greenstick—results from compression force; usually occurs in children under 10 years of age and junior or high school athletes.

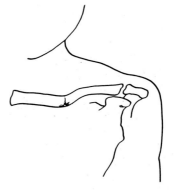

Avulsion—results from muscle mass contracting forcefully, causing bone fragment to tear off at insertion.

Depression—results from blunt trauma to a flat bone; usually involves much soft tissue damage.

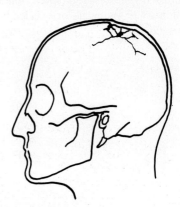

ASSESSMENT

When treating a patient with a suspected limb fracture, always assess for the "five Ps":

Pain and point tenderness

Pulse (distal to the fracture site)

Pallor

Paresthesia (distal to the fracture site)

Paralysis (distal to the fracture site)

The following factors should also be included in assessment:

Deformity

Swelling

Crepitus

Discoloration

Open wounds

Other injuries

Always suspect a fracture in limb trauma until it is proved otherwise. X-ray examination is the most definite way to detect a fracture. The film should include the joints above and below the suspected fracture and should include both anteroposterior and lateral views.

GENERAL THERAPEUTIC INTERVENTION

Assess the patient as just described

Determine the mechanism of injury

Immobilize the limb (above and below the fracture site)

Reassess the neurovascular status

Apply traction if circulatory compromise is present

Elevate the injured limb if possible (to decrease swelling and hemorrhage)

Apply a cold pack (to cause vasoconstriction and decrease swelling, spasm, and pain)

COMPLICATIONS OF FRACTURES

Blood loss causing hypovolemia and shock

Injury to vital organs

Neurologic and/or vascular damage

Infection (in open fractures)

Fat embolism

Delirium tremens

Poor fracture healing may be a result of the following:

Improper immobilization

Poor reduction

Shortened length of immobility

Too much traction

Decreased vascular supply

Decreased neurologic supply

Infection

Fat embolism

Fat embolism may occur 24 to 48 hours after trauma and usually comes from a pelvic, tibial, or femoral fracture, but it may come from any other fracture site. Fat embolism has a high mortality and is a life-threatening situation.

Signs and symptoms

Elevated temperature
Rapid pulse
Decreasing level of consciousness
Inefficient respirations leading to respiratory failure
Cough
Dyspnea
Cyanosis
Pulmonary edema
Petechiae

Therapeutic intervention

Oxygen at high flow
Supportive therapy
Steroids (in some facilities)
Heparin (in some facilities)

Delirium tremens

Patients with multiple fractures are often hospitalized. Many are alcoholics who have fallen or who have been struck by an automobile. If hospitalization is prolonged, these patients may begin to experience delirium tremens. Questions regarding alcohol intake should be included in a history and appropriate attention should be paid to a patient with a history of chronic alcoholism. (See Chapter 10 for additional information.)

Therapeutic intervention

IV alcohol
Diazepam (Valium)
Chlorpromazine (Thorazine)

Specific fractures
CLAVICULAR FRACTURE

Age group	Common in all age groups, but especially in children
Mechanism of injury	A common athletic injury Fall on arm or shoulder Direct trauma to shoulder laterally (contact injury in which athletes run into one another)
Signs and symptoms	Pain in clavicular area Point tenderness Refusal to raise arm

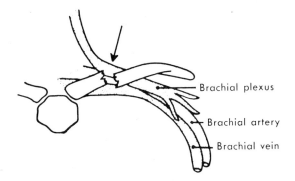

Brachial plexus
Brachial artery
Brachial vein

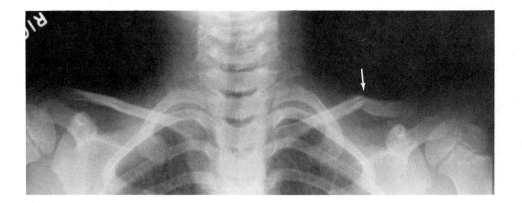

Swelling
Deformity
Crepitus
Head tilted toward side of injury, chin to opposite side[1]

Therapeutic intervention   Assessment of neurovascular status
Support arm
Sling and swath or figure-of-eight bandage
Cold pack

Complications   Rare

Special notes   Pad the axillary area well to avoid damage to the brachial plexus and artery.

SHOULDER FRACTURE (GLENOID, HUMERAL HEAD, OR HUMERAL NECK)

Age group	Common in elderly
Mechanism of injury	Fall on outstretched arm Direct trauma to shoulder
Signs and symptoms	Pain in shoulder area Point tenderness Refusal to move arm Gross swelling Discoloration

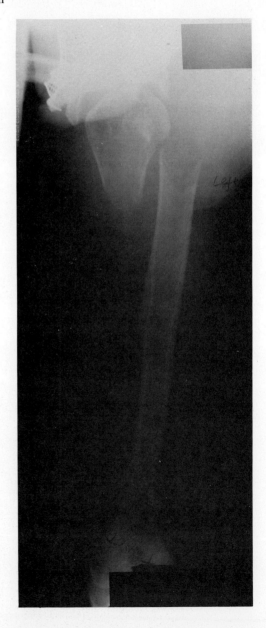

Therapeutic intervention	Assessment of neurovascular status Sling and swath Cold pack
Complications	Humeral neck fracture may cause axillary nerve damage.
Special notes	Shoulder fractures occur in trauma to the shoulder in the elderly because of weaker bone structure; the same mechanisms of injury in a younger person would probably cause shoulder dislocation.

SCAPULAR FRACTURE

Age group	Any
Mechanism of injury	Direct or indirect trauma
Signs and symptoms	Point tenderness Bone displacement Pain on shoulder movement Swelling
Therapeutic intervention	Assessment of neurovascular status Sling and swath Cold pack
Complications	Underlying injury of ribs and viscera

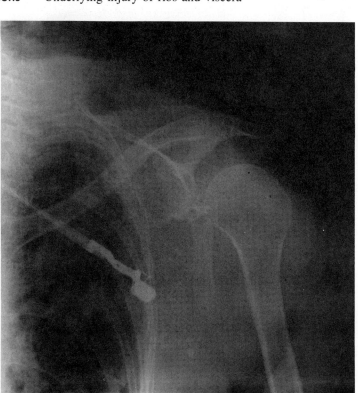

UPPER ARM (HUMERAL SHAFT) FRACTURE

Age group	Common in elderly and children
Mechanism of injury	Fall on arm and direct trauma Dislocation

Signs and symptoms

Pain
Point tenderness
Swelling

Inability or hesitance to move arm
Severe deformity or angulation
Crepitus

Therapeutic intervention

Assessment of neurovascular status
Sling and swath
Traction if there is vascular compromise
Assessment for other injuries, especially to the chest
Cold pack

Complications

Radial nerve damage if fracture occurs in the middle or distal portion of the shaft
Hemorrhage

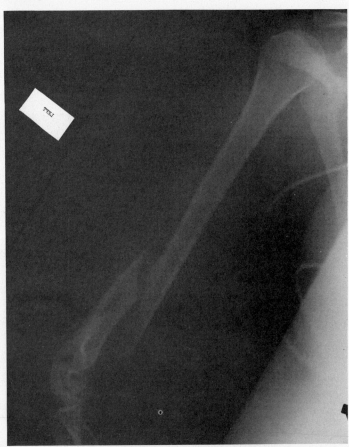

ELBOW FRACTURE

Age group	Children and young athletes	
Mechanism of injury	Fall on extended arm Fall on flexed elbow	
Signs and symptoms	Pain Point tenderness Swelling	Refusal to move elbow Deformity Decreased circulation to hand
Therapeutic intervention	Assessment of neurovascular status Splinting "as it lies," usually with pillow, blanket, or sling and swath Cold pack Flexing of arm to greater degree if there is neurovascular compromise	
Complications	Brachial artery laceration Median and/or radial nerve damage	Volkmann's contracture*
Special note	This type of fracture is seeing an increased incidence with the increasing popularity of skateboards.	

---

*In Volkmann's contracture degeneration and contraction of muscles occur as a result of ischemia caused by decreased arterial blood flow.

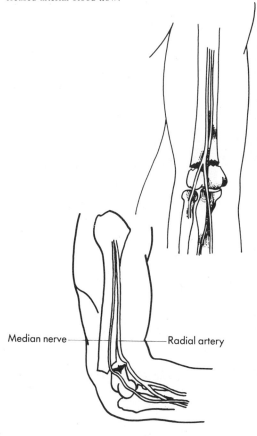

Median nerve — Radial artery

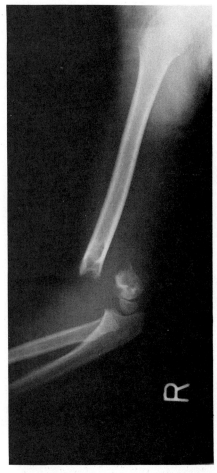

FOREARM (RADIUS OR ULNA) FRACTURE

Age group	Common in children and adults
Mechanism of injury	Fall on extended arm Direct blow
Signs and symptoms	Pain Point tenderness Swelling Deformity or angulation Shortening
Therapeutic intervention	Assessment of neurovascular status Splint Sling Cold pack
Complications	Rare neurovascular compromise Volkmann's contracture

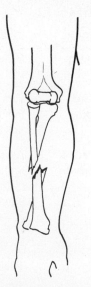

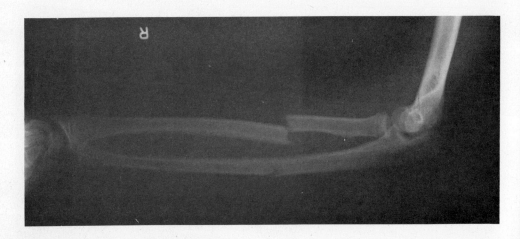

WRIST (DISTAL RADIUS, DISTAL ULNA, CARPAL BONE) FRACTURE

Age group	Common in elderly
Mechanism of injury	Fall on extended arm and open hand
Signs and symptoms	Pain Swelling Deformity

Therapeutic intervention	Assessment of neurovascular status Splint "as it lies" Sling Cold pack Compression
Complication	Rare aseptic necrosis
Special notes	Fracture of the distal radius and ulna is known as a Colles' fracture, or silver fork deformity. Check the mechanism of injury. The patient may have had a fall from a height that originally resulted in a heel (os calcis) fracture, a lumbodorsal compression fracture, and a fall forward into the open hand from the back pain, resulting in a Colles' fracture.

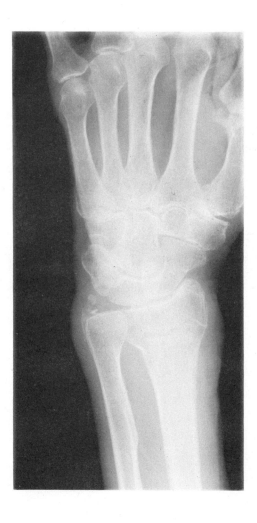

HAND (CARPALS AND METACARPALS) FRACTURE OR
FINGER FRACTURE (PHALANGES)

Age group	Common in athletes (in contact sports)
Mechanism of injury	In fighting, a fracture of the first metacarpal (''boxer's fracture'') In throwing a baseball, a tearing loose of the distal attachment of the extensor tendon, which also breaks off a small piece of bone Industrial crush injury

Signs and symptoms	Pain Severe swelling Deformity	Inability to use hand Often open fracture
Therapeutic intervention	Assessment of neurovascular status Control of bleeding Dry, bulky dressing on open wounds	Splint in functional position Cold pack Pressure

Special note	Should hematoma appear beneath the fingernail, the patient will complain of severe throbbing pain. Therapeutic intervention is nail trephination.

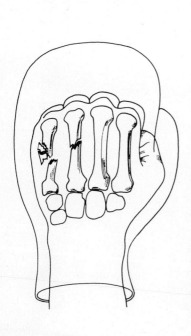

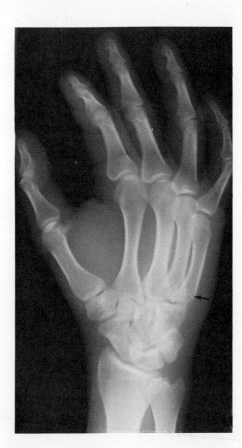

PELVIC FRACTURE

Age group	Commonly occurs in adults and elderly
Mechanism of injury	Crush injury Automobile or motorcycle accident Direct trauma Fall from height Sudden contraction of muscle against resistance
Signs and symptoms	Tenderness over pubis or when iliac wings compressed Paraspinous muscle spasm Sacroiliac joint tenderness Paresis or hemiparesis Pelvic ecchymosis Hematuria

Therapeutic intervention	Immobilization of spine and legs (long board)
	Flexing knees to decrease pain
	Oxygen
	Frequent (every 5 minutes) monitoring of vital signs
	Check for other fractures and injuries (especially internal)
	MAST if indicated
	Rapid transport
	In hospital:
	    Peritoneal lavage
	    Typing and cross-matching for (minimum) 5 units of whole blood

Complications	Internal bleeding (average blood loss, 2 units) Bladder trauma Genital trauma Lumbosacral trauma Ruptured internal organs Shock Death

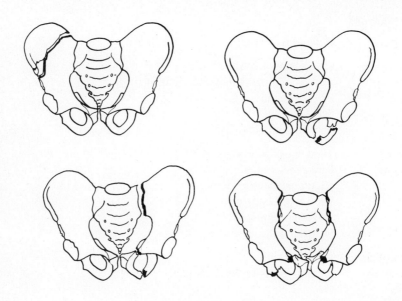

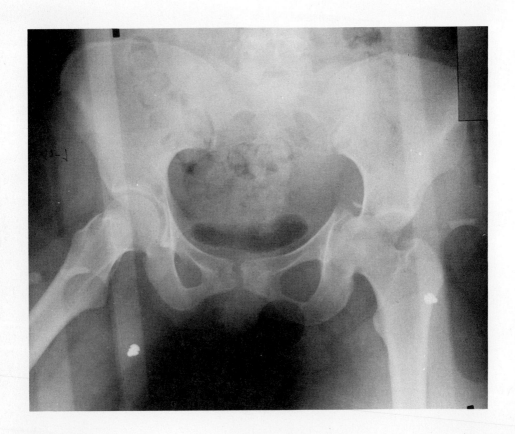

HIP FRACTURE

Age group	Common in elderly
Mechanism of injury	In elderly, usually from a fall or minor trauma In younger people, usually from major trauma

Signs and symptoms	Pain in hip or groin area
	Severe pain with movement
	Inability to bear weight
	External rotation of hip and leg
	Minimal shortening of limb
	If injury is extracapsular and associated with trochanteric fracture:
	    Pain in lateral area of hip
	    Increased shortening
	    Greater external rotation

Therapeutic intervention	Immobilization
	Splint (backboard or one leg to the other)
	Check of pulses distal to injury
	Frequent (every 5 minutes) monitoring of vital signs
	In hospital:
	    Early immobilization
	    Early surgical intervention

Complications	Hypovolemia Shock

 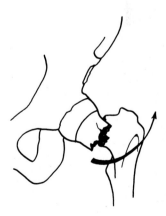

FEMORAL FRACTURE

Age group	All
Mechanism of injury	Usually major trauma
Signs and symptoms	Severe pain Inability to bear weight on leg Swelling Deformity Angulation Shortening of limb and severe muscle spasm Crepitus
Therapeutic intervention	Airway, breathing, and circulation Hare traction or long leg splint (Thomas or other) (Do *not* use long leg air splint and do *not* use other leg as splint.) Two large-bore IV lines Check of distal pulses Check of distal neurologic status Check for other injuries Frequent (every 5 minutes) monitoring of vital signs Cold pack
Complications	Hypovolemia (may lose 2 units of blood for each broken femur) Severe muscle damage Knee trauma (overlooked at time of injury) Shock

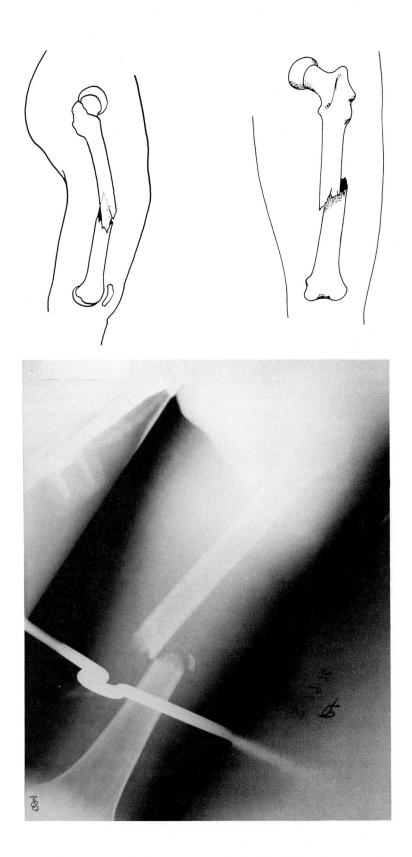

**KNEE FRACTURE (SUPRACONDYLAR FRACTURE OF FEMUR,
INTRAARTICULAR FRACTURE OF FEMUR OR TIBIA)**

Age group	All
Mechanism of injury	Usually automobile, motorcycle, or automobile-pedestrian accident with indirect trauma to the knee area
Signs and symptoms	Knee pain Inability to bend knee or straighten knee Swelling Tenderness
Therapeutic intervention	Long leg splint or one leg splinted to other Check of distal pulses Check of distal neurologic status
Complication	Neurovascular compromise

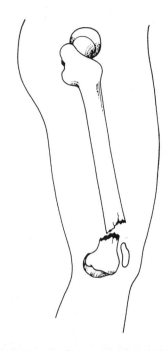

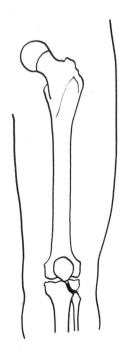

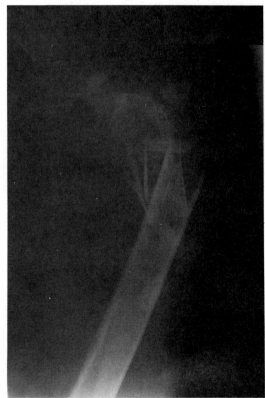

PATELLAR FRACTURE

Age group	All
Mechanism of injury	Usually direct trauma (fall or impact with dashboard) Indirect trauma such as a severe muscle pull
Signs and symptoms	Pain in knee Frequently open fracture
Therapeutic intervention	Long leg splint Cover open wound Cold pack

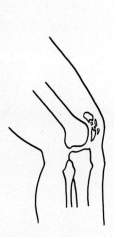

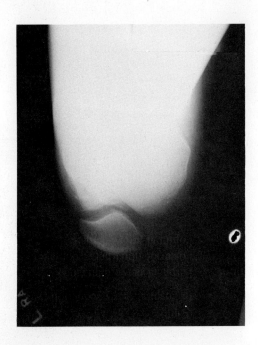

TIBIAL AND/OR FIBULAR FRACTURE

Age group	Common to all age groups
Mechanism of injury	Direct trauma Indirect trauma Twisting injury
Signs and symptoms	Pain Point tenderness Swelling Deformity Crepitus

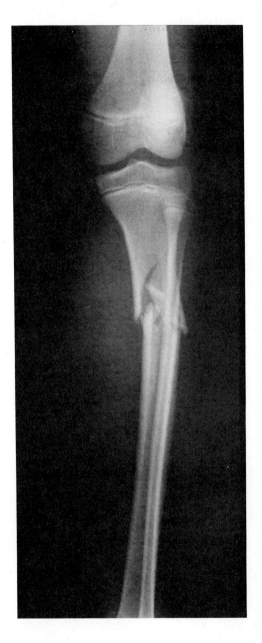

Therapeutic intervention	Splint as found, if no pulse deficit (long leg splint) Check of distal pulses; gentle traction only if there is pulse deficit Sterile dressing over open fracture
Complications	Soft tissue damage Neurovascular compromise

ANKLE FRACTURE

Age group	Common in all
Mechanism of injury	Direct trauma Indirect trauma Torsion
Signs and symptoms	Pain Inability to bear weight Point tenderness Swelling Deformity
Therapeutic intervention	Splint (soft) Check of distal pulses; gentle traction if there is pulse deficit Check of distal neurologic status Elevation Cold pack
Complication	Neurovascular compromise

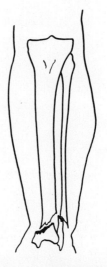

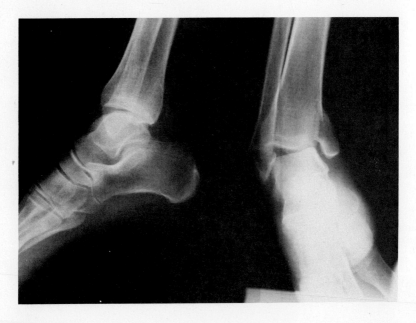

FOOT FRACTURE (METATARSAL FRACTURE)

Age group	Common in all age groups
Mechanism of injury	Automobile accidents Athletic injuries Crush injuries Direct trauma
Signs and symptoms	Pain Hesitancy to bear weight Point tenderness Deformity Swelling
Therapeutic intervention	Compression dressing Soft splint
Complications	Rare

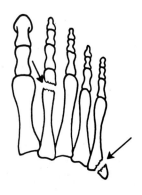

HEEL (OS CALCIS) FRACTURE

Age group	Young adult
Mechanism of injury	Fall from a height
Signs and symptoms	Pain Swelling Point tenderness Dislocation
Therapeutic intervention	Compression dressing Elevation Cold pack
Complications	Often associated with lumbosacral compression fracture

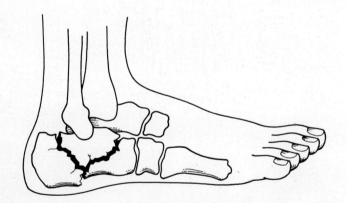

FRACTURE OF TOES (PHALANGES)

Age group	All
Mechanism of injury	Kicking hard object, "stubbing" toe
Signs and symptoms	Pain Swelling Discoloration
Therapeutic intervention	Compression dressing Rigid splint Elevation Cold pack
Complications	Rare

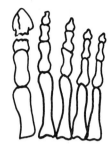

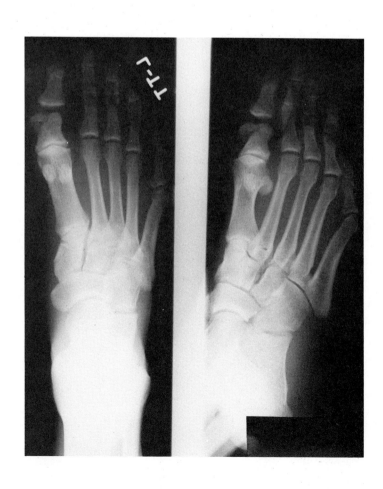

DISLOCATION

Dislocation occurs when a joint exceeds its range of motion and the joint surfaces are no longer intact. With this type of injury come a large amount of soft tissue injury in the joint capsule and surrounding ligaments, much swelling, and possible vein, artery, and nerve damage. When obtaining a brief history, it is important to determine the force that caused the injury to project a diagnosis.

General signs and symptoms of dislocation

Severe pain
Deformity at the joint
Inability to move the joint
Swelling
Point tenderness

General therapeutic intervention

Palpate the joint area carefully
Splint the joint "as it lies"
Do *not* reduce the dislocation in the field
Early reduction with adequate anesthesia is required in the emergency department
Check for fractures
Compare the injured side to the other side

Specific dislocations
ACROMIOCLAVICULAR SEPARATION

Age group	Athletes (young and old)
Mechanism of injury	Common athletic injury produced by a fall or a force on the point of the shoulder
Signs and symptoms	Great pain in joint area Inability to raise arm or bring arm across chest Deformity Point or area tenderness Swelling Hematoma
Therapeutic intervention	Neurovascular assessment Sling and swath Cold pack
Complications	Rare

SHOULDER DISLOCATION

Age group   Usually young adults
Common athletic injury

Mechanism of injury   Anterior dislocation: usually an athletic injury from a fall on an extended arm that is abducted and externally rotated, resulting in head of humerus locating anterior to shoulder joint
Posterior dislocation: a rare form of dislocation, usually found in patient with seizure in which extended arm is abducted and internally rotated

Signs and symptoms   Severe pain in shoulder area
Inability to move arm
Deformity (difficult to see in posterior dislocation)
Recurrent in 55% to 60% of cases

Therapeutic intervention   Support in position found or position of greatest comfort
Cold pack
Relocation of recurrent dislocation *if* it is easy to do
Check of distal pulses
Check of distal neurovascular status

Complications   Much soft tissue damage
Occasional axillary nerve damage
Rare axillary artery damage
Rare brachial plexus damage

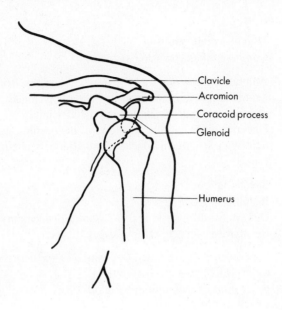

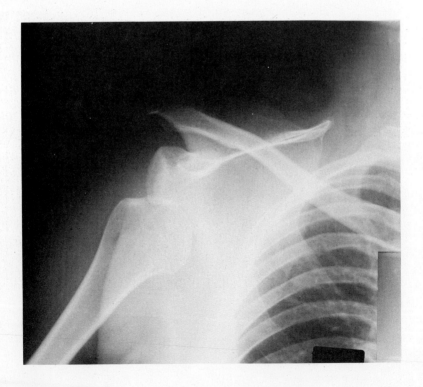

ELBOW DISLOCATION

Age group	Children, teenagers, and young adults Common athletic injury
Mechanism of injury	Fall on an extended arm Jerking or lifting of a child by a single arm, which causes posterior displacement of the ulna (''housemaid's elbow'')
Signs and symptoms	Pain Swelling Deformity or lateral displacement May feel locked Severe pain produced by movement
Therapeutic intervention	Cold pack Immobilization in position of greatest comfort Check of distal pulses Check of distal neurologic status
Complication	Neurovascular compromise

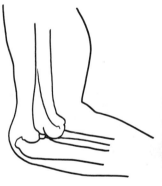
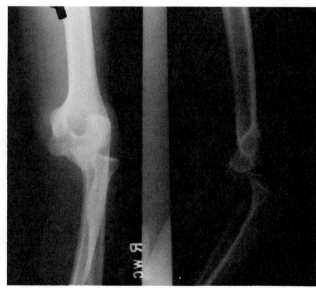

WRIST DISLOCATION

Age group	Usually all
	Common in athletes
Mechanism of injury	Fall on outstretched arm and hand
Signs and symptoms	Pain
	Swelling
	Point tenderness
	Deformity
Therapeutic intervention	Splint
	Sling and swath
	Cold pack
Complication	Median nerve damage

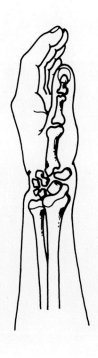 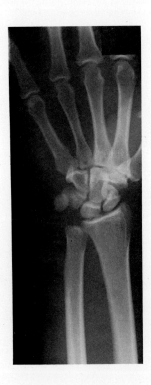

HAND OR FINGER DISLOCATION

Age group	Common in athletes
Mechanism of injury	Fall on outstretched hand or finger Direct trauma or ''jamming'' force on fingertip
Signs and symptoms	Pain Inability to move joint Deformity Swelling
Therapeutic intervention	Splint in position of comfort Cold pack
Complications	Rare

HIP DISLOCATION

Age group	All
Mechanism of injury	Usually a major trauma (with extended leg and foot on brake pedal before impact or with knee hitting dashboard) Falls Crush injuries
Signs and symptoms	Pain in hip area Pain in knee Hip flexed, adducted, and internally rotated (posterior dislocation) Hip slightly flexed, abducted, and externally rotated (anterior dislocation) (a rare injury) Joint feeling locked Inability to move leg

Therapeutic intervention	Splint in position found or in position of comfort
	Check for distal pulses Check for other injuries
	Check for distal neurologic status Cold pack
	In hospital, relocation within 24 hours or necrosis of femoral head may occur
Complications	Sciatic nerve damage Femoral artery and nerve damage

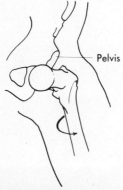

Pelvis

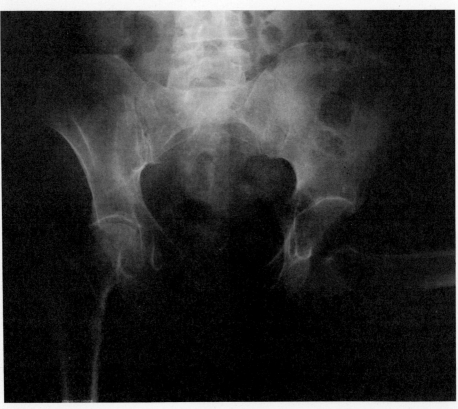

KNEE DISLOCATION

Age group	All
Mechanism of injury	Major trauma
Signs and symptoms	Severe pain Much swelling Deformity Inability to move joint
Therapeutic intervention	Splint in position of comfort Check of distal pulses Check of distal neurologic status Cold pack In hospital, early reduction (within 24 hours) to avoid arterial damage
Complications	Peroneal nerve damage Posterior tibial nerve damage Popliteal artery damage

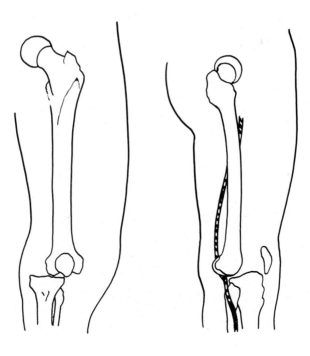

PATELLAR DISLOCATION

Age group	All Common in athletes
Mechanism of injury	Direct trauma Rotation injury on planted foot
Signs and symptoms	Pain Knee usually in flexed position with inability to function Tenderness Swelling
Therapeutic intervention	Splint in position found Cold pack
Complication	Bleeding into knee joint (hemarthrosis)

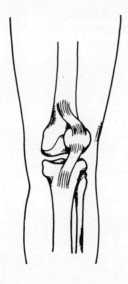

ANKLE DISLOCATION

Age group	Usually an athletic injury
Mechanism of injury	Usually associated with a fracture
Signs and symptoms	Pain Swelling Deformity Inability to move joint
Therapeutic intervention	Splint in position of comfort Check of distal pulses Check of distal neurologic status Cold pack
Complications	Neurovascular compromise

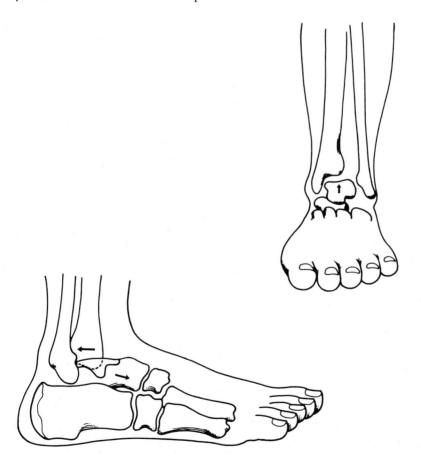

FOOT DISLOCATION

Age group	All
Mechanism of injury	A rare injury Usually automobile or motorcycle accident Usually associated with open wound
Signs and symptoms	Pain Tenderness Swelling Deformity Inability to use foot
Therapeutic intervention	Sterile dressing on open wound Soft splint Check of distal pulses Check of distal neurologic status Cold pack
Complication	Neurovascular compromise

PEDIATRIC LIMB TRAUMA

Special attention should be paid to pediatric limb trauma in which fractures occur at the epiphysis, or growth center. A fracture at the epiphysis may cause an early closure of the plate, which results in a short extremity as the child grows. If the fracture is only a partial fracture, an angular deformity may result. A child with such a fracture should be followed up by an orthopedic surgeon for several months, as it is difficult to predict the outcome at the time of injury.

TRAUMATIC AMPUTATIONS

Traumatic amputations are common to farm workers, factory workers, and motorcyclists; they occur under many different circumstances (Fig. 22-5). Common types of traumatic amputations are as follows:

Digits (fingers and toes)	Hand
Transmetatarsal	Forearm
Tarsometatarsal	Arm
Below knee	Ears
Through knee	Nose
Above knee	Penis

THERAPEUTIC INTERVENTION

Assure airway, breathing, and circulation
Control bleeding
Support the limb in functional position in a partial amputation
Start two large-bore IV lines

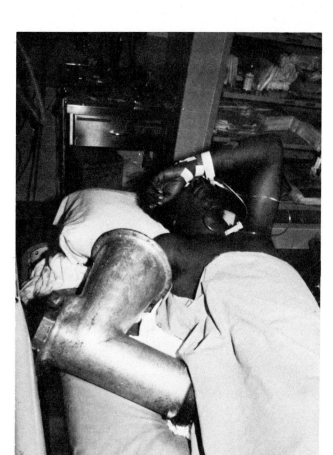

FIG. 22-5 Traumatic amputation of right arm by meat grinder. (Courtesy *Paramedics International.*)

Give oxygen
Transport the patient to the hospital

PRESERVATION OF AMPUTATED PART

Use hypothermia (usually with cooled saline solution); do not freeze the part
Soak or dress the part in sterile normal saline or Ringer's lactate solution
Maintain the correct anatomic position of the severed limb

LIMITING FACTORS IN REIMPLANTATION

Availability of a reimplantation team
Severity of damage to the amputated part *(including preservation technique)*

Amount of time since the accident

Physical status of the patient

Upper extremity reimplantations have been more successful than lower extremity reimplantations.

Fingertip amputations have recently been treated conservatively by Farrell[2] without reimplantations and have been found to grow back within 1 year.

SPLINTING

Splinting is done to prevent further damage to soft tissues; prevent damage to nerves, arteries, and veins; and decrease pain.

Always splint above and below the injury site; for example, if the ankle is injured, also splint the foot and knee. If the knee is injured, also splint the lower leg and the trunk on the injured side.

Splints are divided into four basic types:

Soft splint—soft, not rigid, such as a pillow

Hard splint—firm surface; rigid, such as a board

Air splint—inflatable; provides rigidity without being hard

Traction splint—provides support, decreased angulation, traction (Fig. 22-6)

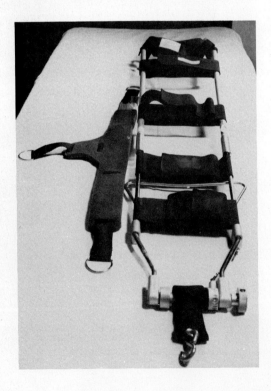

A

FIG. 22-6 A, Hare traction splint. Application: **B,** Remove cover. Twist collet sleeves to unlock. Place splint parallel to injured leg. Adjust splint to desired length, approximately 8 to 10 inches past foot. Twist collet sleeves to lock (excessive pressure not required). Fold down heel stand until it locks into place. Slide heel stand up splint about 5 inches. Position Velcro support straps (two above knee and two below knee) and open. **C,** Remove tri-ring ankle strap from cover and place under patient's heel with padded side against foot. Place bottom edge of heel even with lower edge of sponge. **D,** Crisscross top straps over instep, keeping straps high up on instep. **E,** Grasp all three rings, bottom ring first, and exert manual traction to align leg using slow firm pull. Steady foot by placing one hand under heel. When establishing manual alignment, be sure to support lower portion of involved extremity just below point of fracture.

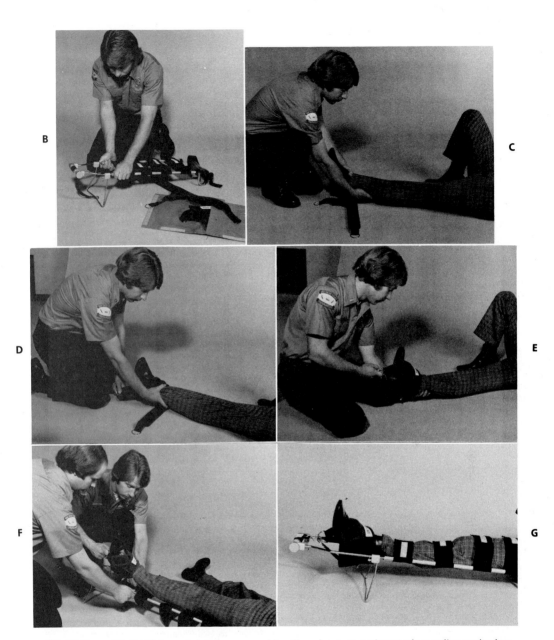

FIG. 22-6, cont'd. F, While maintaining manual traction, have an assistant place splint under leg with half-ring placed just below the buttock. Secure half-ring strap. Once alignment is started, continue to maintain constant manual traction until alignment has been secured by splint. **G,** Insert the S hook into three D rings, heel ring first. Twist knurled knob to apply traction. Tighten until strap is snug. Injured leg is now in traction. Fasten the Velcro straps, which may also be used to apply pressure over an open wound. Position strap so it will close over bleeding area, apply gauze pad, and secure strap. The patient may now be moved. You should adjust location of heel stand after patient has been placed on cot so that solid contact is established with cot. (Manufactured exclusively by Dyna Med, Inc., 6200 Yarrow Drive, Carlsbad, CA 92008.)

Management of the severed part

Causes of traumatic amputations:

Although most frequently seen with people who work with machines, such as farm workers, industrial workers, and mechanics, a substantial number of traumatic amputations are caused by automobile and motorcycle accidents, as well as home accidents caused by lawnmowers or saws. Emergency personnel must take steps to enhance the viability of the severed part so that it can be replanted, if the physician decides on that course of action.

Common types of amputations are:

Digits	Transmetatarsal	Above knee
Hands	Tarsometatarsal	Nose
Forearms	Below knee	Penis
Ears	Through knee	

Intervention in the field:

1. Find the severed part (with small digits this is not always easy).
2. Using sterile gloves, debride the part of any gross foreign matter.
3. Wrap the part in a sterile gauze (for digit, ear, etc.) or towel or clean sheet (for larger limbs).
4. Wet the wrapping with sterile normal saline or Ringer's lactate.
5. Place the part in a suitably sized bag or container and seal shut. (Do *not* immerse part in a solution bath!)
6. Place bag or container inside another container that is filled with ice, if available, or cold water.
7. Transport as soon as the patient's condition is stabilized.
8. A reminder, do not compromise patient care. Life-saving procedures *always* take priority over management of the severed part.

In the emergency department:

Assuming the part arrives as outlined above, all that remains to be done is to maintain the temperature of the part at 39° F (4° C). This is easily accomplished by using an ice packing in the outer bag. A hypothermic thermometer will be necessary to monitor the temperature. If the amputated part arrives without prior management, follow the steps previously outlined.

What NOT to do:

Do not: place part in tap, distilled, or sterile water
place in soapy water, formalin, or antiseptic solution
apply a tourniquet
freeze the part
make a judgment as to the viability of the part; this is the physician's decision
immerse part completely in solution bath (this would cause the part to become water-logged)

Survival time:

The quality of the preservation of the amputated part will greatly influence its survival time. A well-preserved part without a large amount of muscle tissue (which necroses quickly) can be replanted up to 24 hours after the trauma. However, a nonpreserved part can remain viable for six hours at the most.

From Wohlstadter, T.: J.E.N. **5**(4):35, 1979.

1. Wrap the part completely in gauze or towel and wet wrapping.

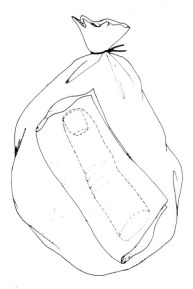

2. Place in a plastic bag and seal shut.

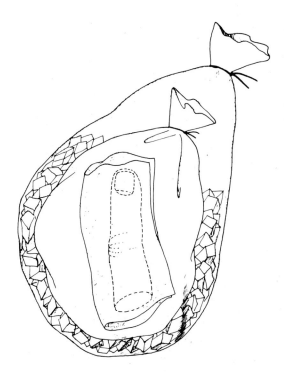

3. Place bag inside outer bag filled with ice and seal.

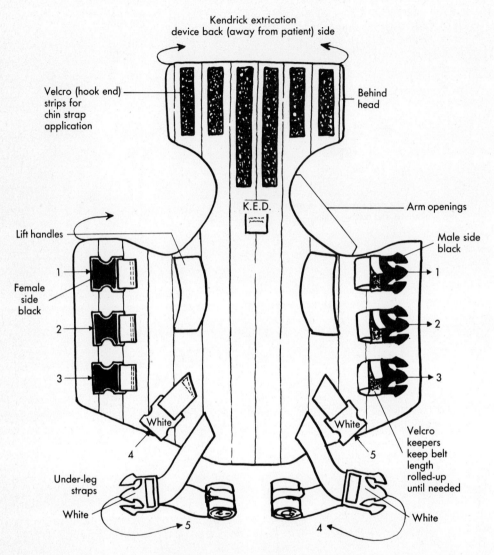

FIG. 22-7 Kendrick extrication device.

There are many varieties of splint materials and uses, for example:

Thomas ⎫ For femoral shaft fractures or fractures of the upper third of the tibia;
⎬ these should *not* be used on fractures of the hip, lower tibia, fibula, or
Hare ⎭ ankle.

Backboard
    Shortboard (or Kendrick extrication device)
    Longboard
Aluminum long leg

FIG. 22-8 Cervical arm sling.

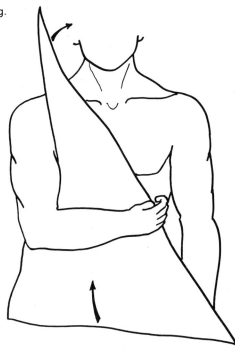

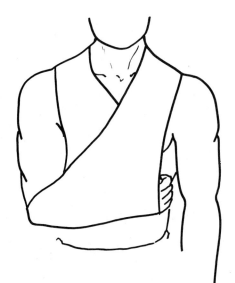

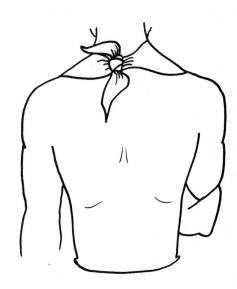

Cardboard
Ladder
Padded board
Air

Vacuum
Improvised
Sling (Fig. 22-8)

GENERAL PRINCIPLES OF SPLINT APPLICATION

Immobilize the injured part proximal and distal to the injury
Correct severe angulation only if it is impossible to splint or if vascular compromise is
   present
Have a second rescuer place the padding and splint
Secure the injured part to the splint (do *not* use an elastic bandage)

APPLICATION OF AIR SPLINT (OPEN ON BOTH ENDS*)

Slip the splint over the rescuer's arm backward
Grasp the distal portion of the injured limb with the arm that has the air splint in place
Slide the splint onto the injured limb
Inflate the splint

PLASTER CASTS

Refer to a textbook for orthopedic assistants for a complete description of techniques
and types of casts.

APPLICATION

Ready the plaster-impregnated gauze
Place the Stockinette over the casting area and pad where necessary
Soak the plaster gauze in warm water
Apply the cast
Warn the patient about the "heat" of the casting material
Allow the cast to dry for 24 to 48 hours

SIGNS AND SYMPTOMS OF PRESSURE SORE

Elevated temperature
Pain over bony prominences beyond initial few days after injury
Disturbed sleep

AFTERCARE INSTRUCTIONS FOR PATIENTS WITH CASTS

Return to the emergency department, the orthopedic clinic, or your private physician in 24
   hours for follow-up care.
Keep the cast dry.
Keep the limb elevated above the level of the heart for 24 hours after the injury.
If any of these abnormalities is present, return to the follow-up clinic immediately:
   Check the temperature of the digits; it is abnormal if they are very cold or very hot.
   Check the color of the digits; it is abnormal if they are blue.
   Check if there is feeling in the digits; it is abnormal if there is no feeling.
Wiggle the digits at least once each hour.
If a foreign object is dropped into the cast, return to the follow-up care facility immedi-
   ately.
Return to the follow-up clinic if swelling recurs or if a foul odor is present.

---

*Note: With a closed-end air splint it is impossible to assess the distal pulses and neurovascular status once the
splint is in place.

CRUTCH AND CANE FITTING

In fitting crutches, measure with the shoe the patient will be wearing, preferably a low-heeled, tie shoe.

AXILLARY CRUTCHES (FIG. 22-9, A)

Length:
Arm piece should be 2 inches from axilla (no weight on axilla)
Tips should be 6 to 8 inches to side and front of foot at 25° angle.
Hand piece:
Elbow should be at 30° angle of flexion

LOFTSTRAND CRUTCHES (FIG. 22-9, B)

Length:
Tips should be 6 inches to side and front of foot at 25° angle
Hand piece:
Elbow should be at 30° angle of flexion

CANE (FIG. 22-9, C)

For assisting balance; offers minimal support; offers assistance in hip injury.
Elbow should be at 30° angle of flexion with cane next to heel.

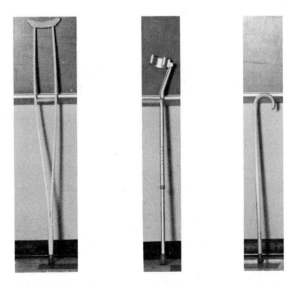

FIG. 22-9 A, Axillary crutches. The underarm crutch illustrated is not adjustable but is lighter in weight than the adjustable crutch. This type of crutch is available in either wood or metal. **B,** Loftstrand crutches. **C,** Cane with half-circle handle is available in wood or metal. (From Larson, C., and Gould, M.: Orthopedic nursing, ed. 9, St. Louis, 1978, The C.V. Mosby Co.)

GAIT TRAINING

Have the patient stand and balance

Have the patient hold the crutches 4 inches to the side of the foot and 4 inches in front of the foot

All weight is carried on the hands by straightening the elbows. Instruct the patient *not to place any weight* on the axillae, even while resting.

In the emergency department, a three-point gait is usually taught, as this type of gait is used when little or no weight bearing is desired (Figs. 22-10 to 22-12).

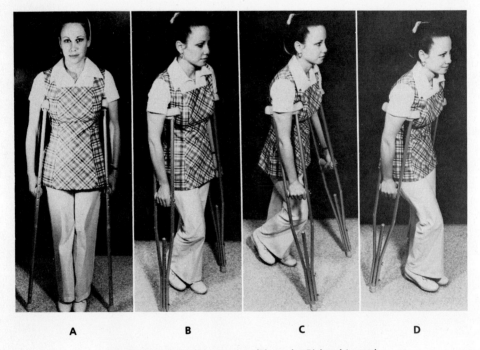

A   B   C   D

FIG. 22-10 Gait training series. (Photo by Richard Lazar.)

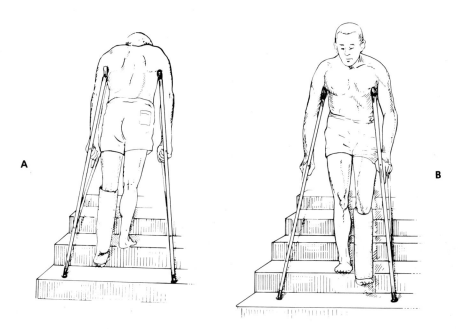

FIG. 22-11 Going upstairs, **A**, and downstairs, **B**, with crutches. (From Barber, J., Stokes, L., and Billings, D.: Adult and child care, ed. 2, St. Louis, 1977, The C.V. Mosby Co.)

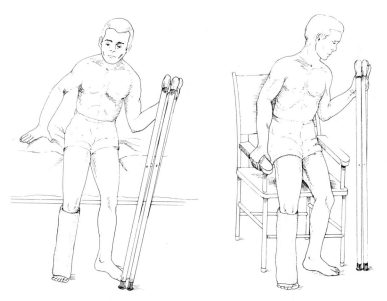

FIG. 22-12 Transferring from sitting to standing with crutches. (From Barber, J., Stokes, L., and Billings, D.: Adult and child care, ed. 2, St. Louis, 1977, The C.V. Mosby Co.)

REFERENCES

1. Klafs, C.E., and Arnheim, D.D.: Modern principles of athletic training, ed. 5, St. Louis, 1979, The C.V. Mosby Co.
2. Farrell, R.G.: Conservative management of fingertip amputations, J.A.C.E.P. **6:**6, June 1977.

SUGGESTED READINGS

American Academy of Orthopedic Surgeons: Emergency care and transportation of athletic injuries, Chicago, 1970, The Academy.

American Academy of Orthopedic Surgeons: Symposium on sports medicine, St. Louis, 1969, The C.V. Mosby Co.

Badger, V.M., et al.: Fractures of the lower extremities. In Ballinger, W.F., Rutherford, R.B., and Zuidema, G.D., editors: The management of trauma, ed. 2, Philadelphia, 1973, W.B. Saunders Co.

Berg, E.W.: Fractures and dislocations: recognition and treatment. In McSwain, N.E., ed.: Traumatic surgery, Flushing, N.Y., 1976, Medical Examination Publishing Co.

Cole, J.M., et al.: Injuries of bones, joints, and related soft-tissue structures. In Cosgriff, J.H., and Anderson, D.L., editors: The practice of emergency nursing, Philadelphia, 1975, J.B. Lippincott Co.

Collins, H.R.: Acromioclavicular dislocations: mechanisms and treatments, J. Sports Med. **2:**11, Jan.-Feb. 1974.

Committee on Trauma, American College of Surgeons: Emergency care of the injured patient, Philadelphia, 1972, W.B. Saunders Co.

Corbitt, R.W.: Female athletes, JAMA **228:**1266, 1974.

DePalma, A.F.: The management of fractures and dislocations, 2 vols., Philadelphia, 1970, W.B. Saunders Co.

DePalma, A.F., and Flannery, G.F.: Acute anterior dislocations of the shoulder, J. Sports Med. **1:**2, Jan.-Feb. 1973.

DiStephano, V.J., and Nixon, J.E.: Rupture of the Achilles tendon, J. Sports Med. **1:**4, Jan.-Feb. 1973.

Hirato, I., Jr.: The doctor and the athlete, Philadelphia, 1968, J.B. Lippincott Co.

Hoopes, J.E., and Jabaly, M.E.: Soft tissue of the extremities. In Ballinger, W.F., Rutherford, R.B., and Zuidema, G.D., editors: The management of trauma, Philadelphia, 1973, W.B. Saunders Co.

Hughes, J.L.: Initial management of fractures and joint injuries: thoracic and lumbar spine, pelvis and hip. In Ballinger, W.F., Rutherford, R.B., and Zuidema, G.D., editors: The management of trauma, Philadelphia, 1973, W.B. Saunders Co.

Larson, R.R.: Fractures about the shoulder, J. Sports Med. **2:**48, Jan.-Feb. 1974.

Miller, R.H.: Textbook of basic emergency medicine, ed. 2, St. Louis, 1980, The C.V. Mosby Co.

Nicholas, J.A.: Ankle injuries in athletes, Orthop. Clin. North Am. **5:**153, 1974.

Paradies, L.H., and Gregory, C.F.: Specific fractures and dislocations. In Shires, G.T., editor: Care of the trauma patient, New York, 1966, McGraw-Hill Book Co.

Ralston, E.L.: Handbook of fractures, St. Louis, 1967, The C.V. Mosby Co.

Rang, M.: Children's fractures, Philadelphia, 1974, J.B. Lippincott Co.

Reid, D.C.: Ankle injuries in sports, J. Sports Med. **1:**3, March-April 1973.

Rockwood, C.A., Jr.: Posterior dislocations of the shoulder, J. Sports Med. **2:**47, Jan.-Feb. 1974.

Rockwood, C.A., Jr., and Green, D., editors: Fractures, Philadelphia, 1975, J.B. Lippincott Co.

Rodi, M.F.: Emergency orthopedics. In Warner, C.G., editor: Emergency care: assessment and intervention, ed. 3, St. Louis, 1983, The C.V. Mosby Co.

Ryan, J.: Musculoskeletal trauma. In Walt, A.J., and Wilson, R.F., editors: Management of trauma: pitfalls and practice, Philadelphia, 1978, Lea & Febiger.

Schmeisser, G., and Freidman, M.: Initial management of fractures and joint injuries: upper limbs. In Ballinger, W.F., Rutherford, R.B., and Zuidema, G.D., editors: The management of trauma, Philadelphia, 1973, W.B. Saunders Co.

Stephenson, H.E., Jr.: Immediate care of the acutely ill and injured, ed. 2, St. Louis, 1978, The C.V. Mosby Co.

Stewart, J.D.M.: Traction and orthopedic appliances, Edinburgh, 1975, Churchill Livingstone.

CHAPTER 23 **Multiple trauma: an overview**

MULTIPLE TRAUMA: THE NEGLECTED EPIDEMIC

Multiple trauma has come to be known as the neglected epidemic or the disease of the 80s. There were more than 164,000 deaths from trauma in the United States in 1980.[1] It has been stated that more than half of these deaths could have been prevented with increased safety measures, improved prehospital care programs, and easier accessibility to major trauma centers. Over 15 people die from trauma every hour. Trauma kills more people between the ages of 15 and 24 than all other causes combined. Half of all deaths of those under the age of 15 are from trauma. After sudden infant death syndrome (SIDS), the top six causes of pediatric deaths are traumatic in nature. In those between the ages of 15 and 24 there were 106 deaths/100,000 population in 1960 and 120/100,000 population in 1978—a 13% increase.[2] The overall death rate from trauma for teenagers in the United States is 50% greater than that for their counterparts in Great Britain, Japan, and Sweden. Trauma is the leading cause of death for all groups up to the age of 38. In the 17-year-old group, 1 in 3 males and 1 in 5 females sustain an injury that requires the attention of a physician each year. Trauma is the fourth leading cause of death overall in the United States, following cancer, heart disease, and stroke. One death in every 10 in the United States is from a traumatic cause.

The total number of murders in this country has increased from 8,464 in 1960 to 24,800 in 1980[3]—a 293% increase. There are over 28,000 deaths each year from gunshot wounds (and this number is rising).

The cost to U.S. industry in terms of productivity lost to trauma is greater than $75 million each day. An estimated 0.4% of this amount is spent on trauma prevention. In addition to deaths, over 1,200 people are disabled by trauma each hour, and over 10.6 million each year (5% of the population). Accidents account for one third of all hospital admissions—over 2 million each year. There are more than 22 million hospital bed days used to care for victims of trauma. To put these figures into perspective, 43,000 American soldiers were lost during the war in Vietnam. During those same 11 years, 25 times that number of people died from trauma, and over 10 times that number died from traffic accidents alone.

Of all motor vehicle injuries, 5% involve multiple or critical injuries. It is interesting to note that twice as many males are involved in fatal motor vehicle accidents as females. Blunt trauma is the most frequent mechanism of multiple trauma. The major points of impact are the head, chest, abdomen, and long bones. Patients with blunt trauma are the most difficult to manage at every point along the way.

The more alcohol a person has consumed, the greater his chance of getting into an accident. The use of alcohol is directly implicated in half of all motor vehicle accidents. A blood alcohol level of 50 to 100 mg/100 ml is evidence of intoxication in most states. In the average 150-pound male, 5 ounces of 80-proof alcohol taken with a meal will produce a blood alcohol level of 50 mg%. Concentrations of 100 to 250 mg% are the most commonly found blood alcohol levels in drinking or drunk drivers who have been involved in automobile accidents. Alcohol use has been implicated in one third of all motor vehicle accidents fatal to pedestrians. Of all adults who die in nonhighway accidents, 42% have "legally intoxicated" blood alcohol levels.

Accidents in the home account for 50% of trauma deaths in females and 20% of trauma deaths in males. One third of all accidents occur in the home because of problems with such items as kitchen appliances, home furnishings, and housewares.

In motor vehicle accidents that cause injury, the following organ systems are commonly injured:

Head—80% of the time

Legs—40% of the time

Chest—25% of the time

Abdomen—15% of the time

Conditions ranked in terms of severity are:

1. Chest injuries
2. Hypovolemia from any cause
3. Head trauma with decreasing level of consciousness
4. Abdominal injuries
5. Multiple fractures

The ranking of management problems in terms of severity is:

Airway

Dysrhythmias

Shock caused by hemorrhage

Cervical spine fractures/dislocations

Long-bone and pelvic fractures

On autopsy of patients who died from trauma the following injuries have been noted:

40% to 70% had head trauma

35% had chest and abdominal trauma

It is unknown how many had airway obstructions

There are two excuses that are commonly heard when a trauma death is described:

1. "By the time we got there, the patient was already so far gone that nothing we could have done would have saved him." (It is interesting to note that of all patients who die of trauma only 8% die in the first hour and 24% in the first 2 hours.)
2. "The patient's injuries were so bad that there was no way we could have saved him." (It is interesting to note that only 29% of patients who die from trauma have multiple-system injuries.)

The most important factor in the survival of the multiple-trauma victim is team leadership by a physician who understands the priorities and is able to apply therapeutic interventions rapidly and effectively. This person should work well with a trauma team and be able to take charge of the patient's care.

When establishing a response to trauma in a community it is important to know the capabilities and limitations of the trauma care system. Know the available resources and know how to make contact with them when they are needed. The key to a successful trauma program is an effective communications system (see Chapter 2).

The scene of the trauma must be secured so that it is safe not only for the victim(s) but for rescuers and bystanders as well. After securing the area, the care giver must be concerned with extrication of the victim(s) if necessary. Extrication requires teamwork on the part of the extricators (often fire department personnel) and the rescuers and understanding on the part of the emergency department team. In addition to this, the care giver must appreciate the difficulties of street rescue with poor lighting, crowds, freeway traffic, grieving families and friends, and all sorts of other obstacles.

Once the scene is secured and the victim has been extricated (or before extrication if possible) the care giver should begin a rapid assessment and a just-as-rapid intervention. It is important to note that assessment and therapeutic interventions may take place simultaneously in the patient with multiple trauma.

The 2-minute survey (ABC⁴)

The 2-minute survey is also known as the primary survey. It has been designed to assess rapidly conditions that are of immediate threat to a patient's life. In this assessment the care giver must use the senses of sight, hearing, touch, and smell. The 2-minute survey consists of:

A = Airway
B = Breathing   } If not present, begin CPR immediately
C^1 = Circulation
C^2 = Cervical spine
C^3 = Chest (tension pneumothorax, flail chest)
C^4 = Consciousness (assessment of level of consciousness)

A = AIRWAY

Airway management should be a reflex action with anyone involved in emergency care. The care giver should first assure that the tongue (the most frequent cause of airway obstruction) is pulled forward out of the posterior pharyngeal area. A good suction source should always be readily available. The usual early airway management technique is the modified jaw-thrust maneuver (see Chapter 3 for other airway management techniques) or the use of airway adjuncts.

Airway management should be based on findings and be in accordance with the patient's needs so as not to cause any further harm. Always assume that a patient with multiple trauma has sustained a cervical spine fracture until it is ruled out by x-ray examination.

B = BREATHING

All multiple-trauma patients should receive supplemental oxygen. If the patient is breathing on his own, administer oxygen at 6 liters/minute via nasal cannula. If respirations are shallow or slow, assist ventilations with supplemental oxygen via a bag-valve-mask device. If the patient is apneic, administer 100% oxygen under positive pressure via an esophageal obturator airway, an endotracheal tube, or a cricothyrotomy. Under any circumstances, assure adequate oxygenation (that is, oxygen from the outside reaching the alveoli inside).

When to do a cricothyrotomy:

When there is laryngeal fracture with upper airway obstruction

When there is a suspected cervical spine fracture, the patient is apneic, and it has not been possible to control the airway with other airway adjuncts

When the patient is apneic and it has not been possible to control the airway with other airway adjuncts

Always auscultate the lungs to assure adequate air movement through both lungs. Obstruction or lack of air passage can also be detected by auscultation. Always assure that good suction is available when dealing with the multiple-trauma victim.

C¹ = CIRCULATION

When assessing circulatory status in the multiple-trauma victim, assess both the carotid and femoral pulses. Then:

Check for massive external bleeding

Check vital signs

Include skin vital signs (color, temperature, and moistness)

Note that 10% of blood volume must be lost before there is resultant tachycardia and a drop in postural blood pressure. Less blood volume may be lost in the elderly patient when vital signs changes occur. There must be a 30% blood loss before a significant change in supine blood pressure is seen. The relation of blood volume to hypovolemic shock is as follows:

The average 70 kg person has 11 pints of blood

A 30% blood loss (more than 3 pints) will cause shock

What is shock?

Shock is a condition in which there is inadequate tissue perfusion. Shock causes inadequate delivery of oxygen and other nutrients to the cells, which results in a buildup of carbon dioxide and cellular metabolites.

It is important to remember that blood pressure and pulse are not reliable indicators of shock in a young person, because there may be a great compensatory mechanism response.

It is important to estimate blood loss in the multiple-trauma patient whenever possible.

Mild blood loss—10% to 20%

Moderate blood loss—20% to 40%

Severe blood loss—greater than 40%

A 10% to 20% blood loss in elderly people may cause severe shock because of their inability to activate compensatory mechanisms.

If the distal extremities are cool and clammy, assume that the patient is in shock until it is proved otherwise. The following occur as signs of hypovolemic shock:

The patient becomes restless and anxious

Pulse becomes rapid and weak

Respirations become shallow

Skin becomes cold and clammy

Blood pressure decreases

Pupils dilate

The body's compensatory mechanisms in shock include sympathetic activation, renin-angiotensin mechanism activation, and antidiuretic hormone (ADH) release.

Sympathetic activation:

Sympathetic nervous system is activated

Small vessels contract

Blood is diverted from the splanchnic bed to the peripheral circulation

Renin-angiotensin mechanism activation:

Renin is released from the kidneys

Angiotensin is released

Aldosterone is released

Sodium reabsorption from the renal tubules is increased

Intravascular volume is increased

Antidiuretic hormone (ADH) release:

Causes increased water resorption in the kidneys

Causes increased intravascular volume

Causes increased mean systemic pressure

When there is shock, check the neck veins. They will give a clue as to the origin of the shock:

If the cause is cardiogenic in nature the neck veins will be distended

If the cause is hypovolemic in nature the neck veins will be flat

Shock intervention

Oxygen

Application of MAST

IV fluids—vascular access is critical

Position

Intravenous solutions in shock

For shock the care giver should initiate two large-bore IV lines (14-gauge or larger if possible), using a crystalloid solution for volume replacement. If the MAST is being used and a lower-limb IV site is required, be sure to use a pressure cuff on the IV solution bag and inflate the cuff to a pressure above that of the MAST.

The antecubital fossa is usually the IV site of choice in prehospital care and early emergency department care, because it is large and readily accessible. The care giver should consider central-line placement if peripheral veins are not accessible. If there are enough skilled personnel available the care giver may consider a venous cutdown, usually into the saphenous vein.

Use of the MAST

The MAST can autotransfuse 750 to 1,000 ml of blood from the legs and the abdomen to the chest and the head, where it is needed most during shock.

Mechanisms of action of the MAST:

Increases arterial resistance

Increases venous return to the right side of the heart

Tamponades arterial bleeding

Immobilizes fractures

The MAST should be used when the patient's systolic blood pressure drops below 90 mm Hg. It should be used for any hypotensive state secondary to hypovolemia. It should only be deflated when the patient's systolic blood pressure is stable above 100 mm Hg or when the patient is on the operating table and the surgical procedure is imminent.

C^2 = CERVICAL SPINE PROTECTION

Assume that all multiple-trauma victims have cervical spine injury until it is proved otherwise by x-ray examination. The care giver must be very cautious. A cervical collar, sandbags, a backboard, or a specially designed extrication device should be used to protect the cervical spine. The care giver must secure the patient so that, in the event that he must vomit, he can be turned without disrupting the integrity of the cervical spine.

C^3 = CHEST EXAMINATION

The care giver should perform a very rapid chest examination, checking for tension pneumothorax or flail chest. Both of these conditions are potentially lethal if they go unnoticed and untreated. If the patient has a severe tension pneumothorax, the tension must be relieved either by placing a needle in the anterior chest (needle thoracotomy) or by placing a chest tube (tube thoracostomy). If the patient has a flail chest, either place him on the affected side with sandbags over the affected area or use other methods of flail chest management (see Chapter 20). Also, give oxygen under positive pressure.

C^4 = CONSCIOUSNESS

The care giver should perform a brief neurologic check. The easiest way is to use the DERM mnemonic:

D = Depth of coma:
Use stimulus/response

E = Eyes:
Check pupillary response

R = Respirations:
Describe rate, rhythm, and depth of respirations

M = Motor:
Check motor movement; if it is present, describe whether it is unilateral or bilateral

Conditions requiring immediate therapeutic intervention

Upper or lower airway obstruction

Laryngeal fracture

Tension pneumothorax

Flail chest

Severe head trauma with altered level of consciousness

Ruptured great vessel(s)

Trauma-induced cardiopulmonary arrest

Cases in which field time should be limited include:

Severe chest injuries

Hypovolemic shock from any cause

Head trauma with decreasing level of consciousness

It is important to keep the patient who is in shock warm. As temperature decreases there will be decreased acid and potassium metabolism. This causes a shift of the oxy-hemoglobin curve to the left and a resultant decrease in oxygen delivery to the tissues.

The secondary survey

Auscultate the lungs

Check skin vital signs

Recheck vital signs

Initiate IVs if not already done

Reevaluate airway

Check for bleeding

Splint fractures

Transport (may vary, depending on patient and system)

In the emergency department

Triage

Undress the patient

Check the patient's back as well as front

Do a rapid systemic evaluation of:

Head and neck:

Check for lacerations, fractures, or deformities

Hyperventilate head-trauma patients to lower P_{CO_2} to 20 to 25 mm Hg

Mannitol and osmotic diuretics such as urea or furosemide (Lasix)

Computerized axial tomography (CT scan) to detect fractures, clots, underlying conditions; use of Nuclear magnetic resonance (NMR) seeing increased popularity

Remember that scalp avulsions can bleed heavily

Ears, nose, and throat:

Check airway

Check for fractured larynx

Check for cerebrospinal fluid leak

Check for penetrating objects

Eyes:

Check pupillary responses

Check for trauma

Chest:

Check for wounds

Check heart sounds

Check lung sounds

Check for symmetry

The steering wheel is the leading cause of blunt trauma to the chest

Any injury between the nipple line and the tenth rib should be considered both chest and abdominal trauma until one or the other is ruled out

Obtain arterial blood gases if possible

Obtain a 12-lead ECG

Check for:

  Chest:

    Rib fractures

    Sucking chest wounds

    Flail chest

    Simple pneumothorax

    Tension pneumothorax

    Pericardial tamponade

  Neck:

    Wounds

    Pulses

    Deformity

    Pain

  Abdomen:

    Rigidity

    Pain

    Tenderness

    Wounds

  Spine:

    Deformities

    Pain

  Pelvis/hips:

    Fractures

    Deformities

    Pulses

  Extremities:

    Pulses

    Neurologic status distal to injury

    Fractures/dislocations

  Perineum:

    Bleeding

    Urine extravasation

  Buttocks:

    Wounds

Cover open wounds

Remember to:

  Recheck ABCs

  Monitor ECG

  Get an early cross-table lateral cervical spine film

Trauma flow sheet

Administrative data

Patient's name _____ Age _____ Sex _____ Weight _____ Date _____

Hospital no. _____ Emergency Department no. _____

Time of accident _____ Time ED notified _____ ED arrival time _____

Type of accident (brief statement) _____

_____

_____

_____

Injuries (prehospital report) _____

_____

_____

_____

Field treatment: ☐ O₂ per _____ at _____ L/min

☐ IVs (r) # _____ ga. with R/L N/S Other

(l) # _____ ga. with R/L N/S Other

☐ C-collar/backboard

☐ MAST   ☐ Legs inflated   ☐ Abdominal section inflated

☐ Other _____

Prehospital care team: Unit _____ Rescuers _____

ED physician _____ ED nurse(s) _____

General/trauma surgeon _____ Notified _____ Arrival time _____

Other physicians _____ Notified _____ Arrival time _____

_____ Notified _____ Arrival time _____

Operating room: Time notified _____ Time will be ready _____

Blood bank: Time notified _____ T&C# _____ units; Time sent _____ Time will

be ready _____

Other bloods to lab: Time _____ Type _____; Time _____ Type _____

Family notified: Time _____; By whom _____; Time will be here _____;

Located _____; Physician spoken with them   ☐ yes   ☐ no

Religious needs: ☐ yes   ☐ no; Who contacted _____; Time will be here _____

Continued.

Time	Airway type: O-P EOA ET Other	O₂ at L/min	T	B/P	Pulse	Resp.	Pupils: R/L ● pinpoint ○ midpoint ● dilated r = react s = slow to react n = non-reactive	Depth of coma: Stimulus: v = verbal p = painful Response: p = purposeful n = nonpurpose o = no response	Motor movement: R/L	Skin: Color: n = normal p = pale c = cyanotic Temperature: w = warm c = cool Moistness: d = dry w = wet c = clammy
							R / L	S: R:	R / L	C = T = M =
							R / L	S: R:	R / L	C = T = M =
							R / L	S: R:	R / L	C = T = M =
							R / L	S: R:	R / L	C = T = M =
							R / L	S: R:	R / L	C = T = M =
							R / L	S: R:	R / L	C = T = M =
							R / L	S: R:	R / L	C = T = M =
							R / L	S: R:	R / L	C = T = M =
							R / L	S: R:	R / L	C = T = M =
							R / L	S: R:	R / L	C = T = M =
							R / L	S: R:	R / L	C = T = M =
							R / L	S: R:	R / L	C = T = M =

MAST: Legs/ Abdomen: ↑ = up ↓ = down include pressure	IVs: Type/amount Time infused		Tube #1 _____ (type) Time/ amt.	Tube #2 _____ (type) Time/ amt.	Tube #3 _____ (type) Time/ amt.	Lab Values ABGs:				Other diagnostic studies
						pH	PO₂	PCO₂	Other	
L / A										
L / A										
L / A										
L / A										
L / A										
L / A										
L / A										
L / A										
L / A										
L / A										
L / A										
L / A										

Continued.

Procedures, notes, ECG strips, etc.

From: Budassi, S.A.: J.E.N. **9(1)**:61.

SUGGESTED READINGS

American Academy of Orthopaedic Surgeons: Emergency care and transportation of the sick and injured, ed. 2, Chicago, 1977, George Bonta Co.

American College of Surgeons, Committee on Trauma: Early care of the injured patient, ed. 2, Philadelphia, 1976, W.B. Saunders Co.

Ayella, R.J.: Radiology and the massive trauma victim, Am. Surg. **45**:126, 1979.

Budassi, S.A.: The multiple trauma patient. Lecture given at the American College of Emergency Physicians annual scientific assembly, San Francisco, September, 1982.

Budassi, S.A., and Barber, J.M.: Emergency Nursing: principles and practice, St. Louis, 1982, The C.V. Mosby Co.

Civetta, J.M., and Nussenfeld, S.R.: Prehospital use of the military anti-shock trousers (MAST), J.A.C.E.P. **5**:581, 1969.

Cloutier, C.T., Lowery, B.D., and Carey, L.C.: The effects of hemodilutional resuscitation on serum protein levels in human beings in hemorrhagic shock, J. Trauma **9**:514, 1969.

Cohn, J.N.: Blood pressure measurement in shock: mechanisms of inaccuracy in auscultatory and palpatory methods, JAMA **199**:972, 1967.

Coram, A.G., et al.: The effects of crystalloid resuscitation in hemorrhagic shock on acid base balance: a comparison between normal saline and Ringer's lactate solutions, Surgery **69**:874, 1971.

Fischer, R.P., et al.: Diagnostic peritoneal lavage: 14 years and 2586 patients later, Am. J. Surg. **136**:1701, 1978.

Fischer, R.P., et al.: Direct transfer to operating room improves care of trauma patients, JAMA **240**:1731, 1978.

Gill, W., and Long, W.: Shock trauma manual, Baltimore, 1979, The Williams & Wilkins Co.

Hardaway, R.M.: Syndromes of disseminated intravascular coagulation: with special reference to shock and hemorrhages, Springfield, Ill., 1966, Charles C Thomas, Publisher.

Hartong, J.M., and Dixon, R.S.: Monitoring resuscitation of the injured patient, JAMA **237**:242, 1977.

McSwain, N.E.: Pneumatic trousers and the management of shock, J. Trauma **17**:719, 1977.

Sohmer, P.R., et al.: Transfusion therapy in trauma: a review of the principles and techniques used in the MIEMS program, Am. J. Surg. **45**:109, 1979.

Trunkey, D.D.: Overview of trauma, Surg. Clin. North Am. **62**:3, 1982.

CHAPTER 24 **Burn trauma**

Burns are injuries to the tissues caused by intense heat or flame (thermal burns), acids or alkalies (chemical burns), electrical current (electrical burns), overexposure to sun or x-rays (radiation burns), or friction (friction burns). The severity of the burn is determined by the amount of body surface area (BSA) involved, the degree (depth) of the burn, and other factors, such as the patient's age, previous medical or surgical conditions, current underlying trauma, and complications from the original burn injury.

First-degree burns are burns through the epithelial layer of skin. They appear as areas of erythema. Second-degree burns are burns that include a partial thickness of the dermal layer of the skin. These appear as erythematous areas with blisters. Third-degree burns are full-thickness burns of the dermal layer of the skin. These appear white and leathery and have no blisters. Sometimes thrombosed vessels can be visualized beneath these burns. Fourth-degree burns are burns that extend to muscle and bone. These have a charred appearance.

Burns are categorized as major, moderate, or severe.

MAJOR BURNS

A major burn may be a second-degree burn over more than 25% of BSA or a third-degree burn over more than 10% of BSA in an adult; or a second-degree burn over more than 20% of BSA in a child. Other burns that may be classified as major include:

Burns involving the hands, face, eyes, ears, feet, or perineum

All inhalation burns

All electrical burns

Burns with associated major trauma

Burns in any poor-risk patient

When conditions are ideal, patients with major burns should be stabilized in the field and transported to a facility with a burn unit. When this is not possible, these patients should be transported to the closest possible facility that is able to provide appropriate resuscitative care and stabilization. Communication links between prehospital care providers and primary and secondary receiving facilities are essential. Pay particular attention to the fact that many of the patients in this category may be victims of multiple trauma as well. Sometimes problems associated with multiple trauma are more urgent than those associated with the burn injury and may have to be tended to first.

	Depth of burn		Pain and pinprick sensitivity	Appearance	Healing time	End result of healing	Treatment
		Detailed classification					
1°	Partial skin loss	Erythema only, no loss of epidermis	Hyperalgesia	Erythema		Normal skin	Allow to heal by natural processes Protect from further injury and infection
2°	Partial skin loss	Superficial, no loss of dermis	Hyperalgesia or normal		6-10 days		
		Intermediate, healing from hair follicles	Normal to hypo-algesia	Erythema to opaque, white blisters are characteristic	7-14 days	Normal to slightly pitted and/or poorly pigmented	
		Deep, healing from sweat glands	Hypoalgesia to analgesia		14-21 days	Hairless and depigmented Texture normal to pitted or flat and shiny	
3°	Whole skin loss	Deep dermal, occasionally heal from scattered epithelium	Analgesia	White opaque to charred, coagulated; subcutaneous veins may be visible	More than 21 days	Poor texture Hypertrophic Scar frequent	Elective skin grafting may save time and give better end result
		Whole skin loss, healing from edges only			Never if area is large	Hypertrophic scar and chronic granulations unless grafted	
4°	Deep tissue loss	Deep structure loss	May be some algesia				Skin grafting mandatory

FIG. 24-1 Classification of burns according to depth of burn. (From Frank, H.A., and Wachtel, T.L.: In Warner, C.G., ed.: Emergency care, ed. 3, St. Louis, 1983, The C.V. Mosby Co.)

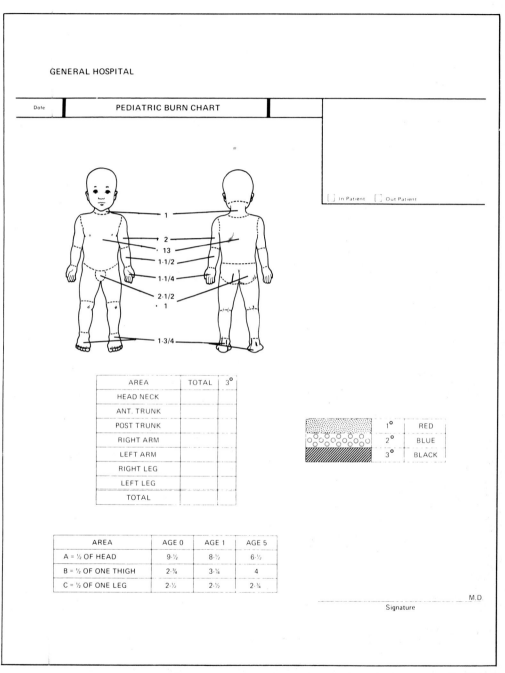

FIG. 24-2 A, Pediatric burn chart.

Continued.

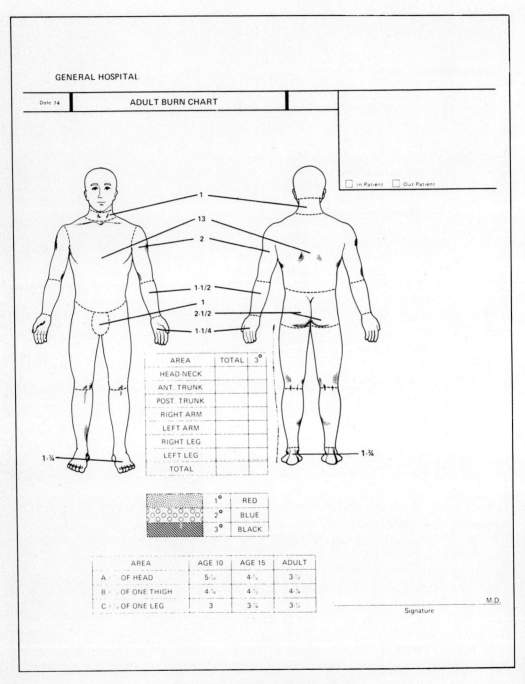

FIG. 24-2, cont'd. B, Adult burn chart.

MODERATE BURNS

A moderate burn may be a second-degree burn over 15% to 25% of BSA in an adult; or a second-degree burn over 10% to 20% of BSA in a child. Burns of this nature that involve the eyes, ears, face, hands, feet, or perineum are considered major burns.

MINOR BURNS

A minor burn may be a second-degree burn over less than 15% of BSA or a third-degree burn over less than 2% of BSA in an adult; or a second-degree burn over less than 10% of BSA or a third-degree burn over less than 2% of BSA in a child.

Hospital admission is recommended for patients with the following:

Second- or third-degree burns over greater than 10% of BSA

Burns of hands, feet, and perineum

Circumferential burns

Electrical or chemical burns

Burns associated with multiple or significant trauma

Burns associated with suspected child abuse

BURN CARE

Burn care should be initiated by the first person to arrive at the scene of the incident. Remember that the safety of the rescuers is the first priority. They should be physically protected, and they should not rush into a situation without first assuring their own safety.

Of first priority in care of the patient are maintenance of airway, breathing, and circulation. Always check for a patent airway, especially where there is evidence or suspicion of smoke inhalation. Signs and symptoms of smoke inhalation include:

Fire in an enclosed space

Soot in the nostrils

Carbonaceous sputum

Hoarse voice

Stridor

Cough

Burns around mouth

Therapeutic intervention for smoke inhalation is oxygen at high flow by mask or nasopharyngeal or endotracheal tube.

At the scene, after or concurrent with assuring ABCs and doing a rapid (2-minute) survey for multiple trauma, perform the following interventions:

Remove burning clothing

Apply cool water or saline solution to burned areas (being careful to avoid hypothermia)

If burned areas are small, wash with soap and water

Cover with clean dressings or sheets

Initiate IV therapy with two large-bore cannulas, running Ringer's lactate or normal saline solution

Remove constricting jewelry

Keep the patient warm by using a Space Blanket or Burn Pac

Once in the emergency department:
  Reassess ABCs
  Continue oxygen therapy (endotracheally intubate if Po_2 is less than 50 mm Hg)
Obtain arterial blood gases
Remove all clothing
Assess the patient systematically (head to toe)—be sure to check the patient's back as
    well as his front
Pay particular attention to signs and symptoms of trauma
Obtain a history:
  About current injuries and the incident
  About details of the incident
  About past medical history
Administer tetanus prophylaxis is required
  Consider tetanus immune globulin (see Chapter 15)
Administer antibiotics
Place a nasogastric tube
Place a Foley catheter:
  Send a urine specimen to the laboratory to check for myoglobulinemia
Obtain a chest x-ray film
Have patient cough and breathe deeply every 20 minutes
Monitor the cardiac rhythm
Obtain a 12-lead ECG
Obtain the patient's weight
Administer analgesics in accordance with policy

Airway management

If there is a burn injury in the facial area, edema usually develops rapidly. Nausea and
vomiting are also common early findings in burn injuries. The risk of aspiration is high.
Consider early placement of a nasogastric tube to prevent this from occurring.

Because of the potential for massive edema, it is important to establish a patent
airway. It may be necessary to initiate a nasopharyngeal or endotracheal tube (see Chapter 3). If there is airway obstruction, it may be necessary to perform emergency cricothyrotomy (see Chapter 3). Tracheostomy is usually performed as an elective or semielective
procedure in the operating suite. If the patient has been intubated remember to deflate the
cuff on the endotracheal tube periodically. If there has been considerable damage to the
tracheobronchial tree it may be necessary to keep the tube cuff inflated and provide not
only positive pressure but positive-end-expiratory pressure (PEEP) (see Chapter 6) to prevent the alveoli from collapsing.

Sometimes pulmonary damage is not evident in the early prehospital and emergency
department phases. Always anticipate pulmonary complications and have equipment
standing by so that intervention can take place readily and rapidly.

When a patient gives a history of exposure to smoke or other toxic products of
combustion, assume and anticipate pulmonary complications and pulmonary damage until
it is proved otherwise. Obtain a carboxyhemoglobin level; this may help to predict
pulmonary complications and allow for preventive therapeutic interventions early in the

course of the injury and the period immediately after. It has also been recommended that a course of steroids be given by IV bolus to reduce the occurrence of pulmonary edema.

Pain management

Often simply cooling the area of the burn will provide an analgesic effect. It is important to remember *not* to cool the entire burn area all at once if there is extensive surface area burned, as doing so may cause severe hypothermia. If an analgesic is to be given, it should be administered via the IV route to assure uniform, timely distribution throughout the body. The most common analgesic agent administered is morphine sulfate, given in 2 to 4 mg increments slowly and titrated to achieve the desired analgesic effect. Pay close attention to respiratory status, because morphine sulfate may cause respiratory depression. If this does occur, naloxone (Narcan), a narcotic antagonist, may be given (see p. 652).

An alternative to morphine sulfate administration is the administration of nitrous oxide gas (see Chapter 3), which can be self-administered by the patient.

IV fluid replacement

In major burn injuries there is deterioration of the patient's circulatory systems. Problems with fluid and electrolyte balances are directly proportional to the extent of the burn injury. When a burn occurs there is a breakdown of capillary integrity. All kinds of substances may then pass freely through the capillary membrane. Approximately 18 to 36 hours after the burn injury, this capillary permeability state reverses, allowing the body to retain colloids in the vascular system. In the second 24-hour period after the injury, plasma volume is maintained by colloids and colloidal pressure. The care giver should place a Swan-Ganz catheter to measure pulmonary capillary wedge pressure and give an early indication of changes. The care giver should also place a Foley catheter and carefully measure hourly urine output. Fluid replacement is calculated, however, in accordance with the extent of the burn using one of the major burn formulas, two of which are described here.

THE BAXTER FORMULA

1 to 24 hours—give 4 ml Ringer's lactate/kg multiplied by the percentage of burned BSA:
> Give half the calculated dose in the first 8 hours
> Give the remaining half over next 16 hours

24 to 48 hours—give D5W to maintain serum sodium at less than 140 mEq/liter with potassium chloride supplement

Also give plasma or plasma substitute to return plasma volume to normal

THE PARKLAND FORMULA

Only isotonic crystalloid solution is given in the first 24 hours (use Ringer's lactate solution); calculate fluid requirements for the first 24 hours using the following:
> 2 ml solution/kg multiplied by the percentage of burned body surface area (BSA)
>> Give 50% of the calculated amount in the first 8 hours
>> Give 25% of the calculated amount in the second 8 hours
>> Give 25% of the calculated amount in the third 8 hours

In the fourth 8 hours (24 to 32 hours after the injury) give plasma 0.5 ml/kg multiplied by
the percentage of burned BSA

No matter which fluid-replacement formula is used, half of the calculated daily fluid-
replacement volume is usually given in the first 8 hours after the injury. Blood and blood
products are not given in the initial phases of the burn injury unless the patient is
hypovolemic from associated trauma.

Burn wound care

Small burns of the trunk or extremities:
Cleanse
Shave hair
Dry sterile dressing
Change dressing in 5 days
Face or perineum:
Usually requires hospital admission for at least 48 hours
Cleanse
Shave (if perineum)
Irrigate eyes every 8 hours and instill ointment to avoid the formation of purulent
conjunctivitis (see Chapter 19)
Cleanse the mouth
Apply topical burn ointment to affected skin areas
Large burns:
Cleanse
Shave hairy areas
Debride necrotic epithelium
Evacuate blisters and bullae
Apply topical burn ointment
Cover with dry sterile dressing or leave open to air
Change dressing in 5 to 7 days (unless hospital admission, then more frequently)
Massive burns:
Exposure to air
Debridement of necrotic epithelium (usually in hydrotherapy tank)
Topical burn ointment
Determination of extent of burn
Early wound grafting
Escharotomy for circumferential burns
Anticipate:
The need for collection of laboratory specimens (have appropriate tubes ready)
The need for documentation (have appropriate forms available)

Burn management

Types of burns

Thermal—from scalds or flames; treated as described for minor, moderate and major burns

Chemical—caused by strong acids or alkalies; treatment depends on type of chemical causing burn

Electrical—wound may be small, but internal damage may be great; common complication may be ventricular fibrillation; treatment is mainly in support of ABCs

Degrees of burn

Appearance	Depth
First degree—erythema	Epidermal layer
Second degree—erythema; blisters	Partial thickness of dermal layer
Third degree—white; leathery; no blisters; thrombosed vessels seen beneath	Full thickness of dermal layer
Fourth degree—charred	Extends to muscle and bone

Severity of burn

Determined by:
    Amount body surface area involved
    Depth of burn
    Age of victim
    Location of burn
    Complicating medical history

Categories of burns

Major

Any of the following:
    Second degree—greater than 25% body surface area on an adult (greater than 20% of body surface area on a child)
    Third degree—greater than 10% of body surface area
    Face, eyelids, ears, perineum, genitalia, or circumferential burns of hands or feet
    Inhalation injury
    Electrical burn
    Burns associated with trauma
    Burns where victim has other serious illness

Moderate

Any of the following:
    Second degree—greater than 15 to 25% body surface area on an adult (greater than 10% body surface area on a child)
    Third degree—less than 10%

Minor

    Second degree—less than 15% body surface area on an adult (less than 10% body surface area on a child)

From Budassi, S.A.: J.E.N. 6(1):45, 1980.   Continued.

Lund and Browder chart

Area	Age—years					% 2°	% 3°	% Total
	0-1	1-4	5-9	10-15	Adult			
Head	19	17	13	10	7			
Neck	2	2	2	2	2			
Ant. Trunk	13	17	13	13	13			
Post. Trunk	13	13	13	13	13			
R. Buttock	2½	2½	2½	2½	2½			
L. Buttock	2½	2½	2½	2½	2½			
Genitalia	1	1	1	1	1			
R.U. Arm	4	4	4	4	4			
L.U. Arm	4	4	4	4	4			
R.L. Arm	3	3	3	3	3			
L.L. Arm	3	3	3	3	3			
R. Hand	2½	2½	2½	2½	2½			
L. Hand	2½	2½	2½	2½	2½			
R. Thigh	5½	6½	8½	8½	9½			
L. Thigh	5½	6½	8½	8½	9½			
R. Leg	5	5	5½	6	7			
L. Leg	5	5	5½	6	7			
R. Foot	3½	3½	3½	3½	3½			
L. Foot	3½	3½	3½	3½	3½			
Total								

Care of minor to moderate burns

Remove smoldering material
Remove restrictive clothing and jewelry
Assess extent of burn
Apply cool compresses or soak burned area in cool tap water
Soak in mild antiseptic soap solution
Shave hair surrounding wound, but do not shave eyebrows
Debride devitalized tissue
Leave blisters intact
Cover wound with antimicrobial agent and bulky dressing
Check for tetanus prophylaxis
Consider antibiotics
Provide after-care instructions
    Keep dressing clean and dry
    Elevate burned extremity for 24 hours
    Give prescriptions or instructions for analgesia
    Provide follow-up care; check wound in two days

Care of moderate to major burns

Prehospital:
    Rescuer should protect self against flames, noxious gases, smoke, explosions, falling
        debris, etc.
    Cool thermal burns with water, flush chemicals from the surface, or remove victim
        from electrical source
    ABCs (especially in those with facial and neck burns)
    Check for signs of smoke inhalation (flames in a closed space, carbonaceous sputum,
        facial and neck burns, hoarse voice, coughing)

Check for other injuries (especially victims involved in explosions, motor vehicle accidents or jumping from a burning building)

Remove smoldering clothing (if nonadherent to skin)

Control bleeding

Remove restrictive clothing and jewelry

Brief neurologic exam (include level of consciousness, pupils, motor and sensory function)

Splint fractures

Initiate an intravenous line of Ringer's lactate (if the burn is less than 30% of body surface area, run at rate of 3 to 4 ml/pound/hr; if burn is greater than 30% body surface area, run at rate of 6 to 8 ml/pound/hr)

Later, use Baxter's formula

Control pain (if burn is not associated with trauma, administer morphine sulfate or meperidine hydrochloride intravenously)

Estimate extent of burn

Cover burned area with clean, dry sterile (if possible) sheet. Do not wrap large burns in saline soaked dressings, as cool dressings will reduce body temperature, unless you can maintain body warmth with Space Blanket or Burn Pac

Check vital signs (do not avoid taking a blood pressure because the limb is burned)

Administer humidified oxygen at 100% concentration

Pay strict attention to airway and suctioning

In the emergency department:

Repeat vital signs every 15 minutes

Obtain arterial blood gases

Endotracheal intubation if PO_2 is less than 50 mm Hg

Use nasogastric tube to decompress stomach; avoid possible aspiration of gastric contents

Have the patient assume a comfortable position

Obtain chest x-ray film

Have patient cough, turn, and deep breathe every 20 minutes

Start central venous pressure line and additional IV lines

Insert Foley catheter; send urine to lab to check for myoglobulinuria and/or hemoglobinuria

Initiate hourly urine measurements

Start arterial line if blood pressures difficult to obtain

Lab: complete blood count, electrolytes, calcium, magnesium, blood urea nitrogen, creatinine, glucose, bilirubin, phosphorus, alkaline phosphatase, total protein, carboxyhemoglobin, and toxicology screen, if indicated

Get type and crossmatch if indicated

Use cardiac monitor

Take 12-lead ECG

Weigh

Consider analgesia

Burn unit admission

Baxter formula

First 24 hours:

4 ml Ringer's lactate/kg; give half of calculated dose in first 8 hours; give remaining half over remaining 16 hours

Second 24 hours:

D5W to maintain serum sodium at less than 140 mEq/liter; with potassium chloride supplement; also give plasma or plasma substitute to return plasma volume to normal

Laboratory specimens

Venous blood specimens should be sent to the laboratory for the following:
Complete blood count

Electrolytes	Phosphorus
Calcium	Alkaline phosphatase
Magnesium	Total protein
BUN	Carboxyhemoglobin
Creatinine	Toxicology screen (if indicated)
Glucose	Blood alcohol (if indicated)
Bilirubin	

Escharotomy

Escharotomy is performed if circumferential burns are causing constriction of arteries and venous structures and impairing circulation. The most common sites for escharotomies are:

Fingers
Hands
Arms
Chest
Legs
Toes

These may be performed in the early phases of emergency department care if there is a threat to life or limb from the impairment. Escharotomy is done by simply cutting through all the layers of the skin with a sterile scalpel and blade allowing for separation of the tissue and for circulation to be reestablished. Incisions are made in the areas shown in Fig. 24-3.

Special management of specific burns

CHEMICAL BURNS

All chemical burns, no matter what the causative agent, should be flushed with copious amounts of water or normal saline solution. The only exception to this rule is when powdered chemicals are present and addition of water or normal saline solution will cause them to activate. Powdered chemicals should be brushed from the skin.

If there are chemical burns of the eyes (see also Chapter 19) the eyes should be irrigated with copious amounts of normal saline solution or water for 20 to 30 minutes. Immediately after irrigation but before fluoroscein staining and slit-lamp examination, visual acuity examination results should be obtained (see Chapter 19). Chemical burns of the eyes usually require ophthalmologic consultation.

ELECTRICAL BURNS

Sometimes an electrical burn may appear very minor because of the low visibility of electrical burn damage. Entrance and exit sites may be small, but there may be extensive destruction of underlying tissue. This destruction is caused by the intense heat that results from the passage of electrical current through the tissues.

One of the most common complications of electrical burn injury is ventricular fibrilla-

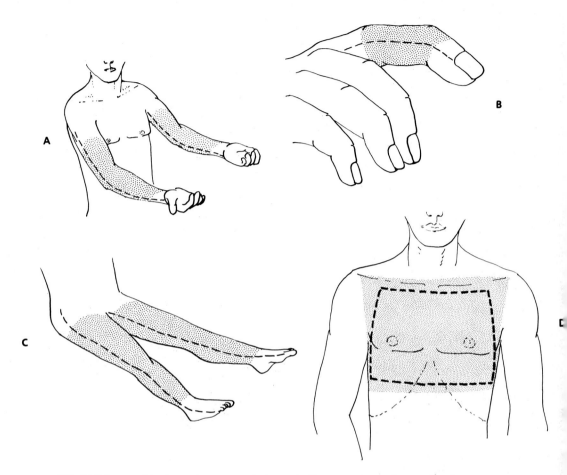

FIG. 24-3 Proper sites for escharotomy. **A,** Arms. **B,** Fingers. **C,** Legs. **D,** Anterior thorax.

tion caused by the passage of electrical current through the myocardium. If ventricular fibrillation is present cardiopulmonary resuscitation should be initiated immediately. This is one instance where prolonged resuscitation efforts are often successful. If ventricular fibrillation is seen, the definitive therapeutic intervention is electrical defibrillation (see Chapter 3).

Another complication that can result from high-voltage electrical burns is renal failure. This results from damaged muscle cells that release myoglobin, which causes acidosis and disrupts normal renal tubular function.

Types of electrical burns

Type I—tissue damage occurs along the conduction pathway; complications include venous and arterial damage and thrombosis

Type II—these result from arcing or flashes from a high-tension source; there is usually a small entrance wound and a very large exit wound caused by the explosive force of the current; this type of injury may result in massive edema, skin discoloration or actual charring of tissue, and deformity caused by fractures from trauma

Type III—this type of burn includes types I and II with a concurrent ignition of the patient's clothing causing additional surface burn trauma

Other important considerations in management of electrical-burn victims include:

Remove the victim (carefully) from the source of the current:

Avoid direct contact with the victim

Use a nonconductive object to remove the source of the electrical current *or*

Turn off the electrical current

Initiate ABCs immediately if patient has no pulse and is not breathing

Check for concurrent trauma and apply appropriate life-saving therapeutic intervention

Notify the receiving hospital as soon as possible, as they may have to make arrangements for:

a burn-unit bed *or*

transfer of a patient to a burn center once stabilization is assured

Hospital admission is essential for electrical-burn victims who have demonstrated:

Major burn injury

Loss of consciousness

Cardiac dysrhythmias

THERMAL BURNS

With thermal burns it is important to remember to remove the source of the burn. One frequent causative agent is hot tar. If this is the case:

Cool the hot tar

Remove the tar:

By using cold water compresses and peeling it off *or*

By loosening it with mineral oil

RADIATION BURNS

Radiation burns are usually caused by overexposure to the sun. Sunburn cases are typically first and sometimes second-degree burns. The most comforting measure for this patient is the application of cool, moist compresses. If fever and chills are present, administer antipyretic agents such as aspirin or acetaminophen.

FRICTION BURNS

Friction burns are also known as "brush burns," "floor burns," and "road burns." This type of burn is caused by heat produced by friction. Friction burn is frequently seen in athletes who fall on gymnasium floors, tennis courts, or artificial-surface football fields or running tracks. The care giver should:

Remove foreign bodies or debris (cinders, dirt particles, etc.)—this often requires a topical local anesthetic or the administration of nitrous oxide gas (Chapter 3)

Scrub the wound with a surgical soap solution and a soft brush

Assure that all particles are removed to avoid permanent scarring known as tattooing

SUGGESTED READINGS

Allyn, P.: Inhalation injuries, Crit. Care Q. 1(3):37, 1978.

Artz, C.P., Moncrief, J.A., and Pruitt, B.A.: Burns: a team approach, Philadelphia, 1979, W.B. Saunders Co.

Baxter, C.R.: Pathophysiology and treatment of burns and cold injury. In Hardy, J.D., editor: Rhoads textbook of surgery: principles and practice, ed. 5, Philadelphia, 1977, J.B. Lippincott Co.

Braen, G.R.: Emergency management of major thermal burns, Kansas city, Mo., 1977, Marion Laboratories.

Budassi, S.A., and Barber, J.M.: Emergency nursing: principles and practice, St. Louis, 1981, The C. V. Mosby Co.

Edlich, R.F.: Emergency department management: triage and transfer protocols for the burn patient, J.A.C.E.P. 7:152, 1978.

Fischer, J.C.: Immediate care of the burn victim, Emerg. Prod. News 9:58, 1977.

Fitzgerald, R.T.: Pre-hospital care of the burned patient, Crit. Care Q. 1(3):13, 1978.

Gursel, E., and Tintinalli, J.E.: Emergency burn management, J.A.C.E.P. 7:209, 1978.

Harding, J., and Walraven, G.: Pre-hospital management of burn injuries: a case study, Emerg. Prod. News 6:34, 1977.

Hersperger, J.E., and Dahl, L.M.: Electrical and thermal injuries, Crit. Care Q. 1(3):43, 1978.

Lloyd, J.A.: Thermal trauma: therapeutic achievements and investigative horizons, Surg. Clin. North Am. 57:121, 1977.

Lund, C.C., and Browder, N.C.: The estimation of areas of burns, Surg. Obstet. Gynecol. 79:352, 1944.

Marvin, J.: Acute care for the burn patient, Crit. Care Q. 1(3):25, 1978.

Moncrief, J.A.: Burns: initial treatment, JAMA 242:179, 1979.

Moylan, J.A., and Chan, C.K.: Inhalation injury: an increasing problem, Ann. Surg. 188:34, 1978.

Stein, J.M., and Stein, E.D.: Safe transfer of civilian burn casualties, JAMA 238:489, 1977.

OBSTETRIC AND GYNECOLOGIC EMERGENCIES AND PEDIATRICS

CHAPTER 25 **Obstetric and gynecologic emergencies**

Obstetric and gynecologic emergencies are frequently seen problems in the emergency department. In this chapter, many of the more common obstetric and gynecologic emergencies will be discussed.

CHILDBIRTH

The birth of a healthy child in the emergency department is the delight of everyone involved, including the mother, the medical staff, and the ancillary staff. The most important thing to do during an emergency childbirth is remain calm.

DEFINITIONS

labor—Process by which the fetus, placenta, and membranes are expelled from the uterus; normally occurs 280 days after the last menstrual period.
gravida—Number of pregnancies (present included).
para—Number of pregnancies that have gone to 20 weeks of gestation (including stillborns).
primigravida—Woman who is pregnant for the first time.
nullipara—Woman who has never delivered a child.
primipara—Woman who has delivered one child.
multipara—Woman who has delivered more than one child.

EXAMPLES

Gravida II, Para I—Woman in her second pregnancy; she has delivered one live child.
Gravida IV, Para 0—Woman in her fourth pregnancy; she has delivered no live children.
Gravida II, Para II—Woman in her second pregnancy; she has delivered two live children (twins).

Stages of labor

Stage I—Dilation stage: From the first uterine contraction until complete cervical dilation occurs.
Uterine contractions occur; verify fetal heart tones between contractions.
Membranes rupture (naturally or surgically).
Averages 12.5 hours in a primipara and 7 hours in a multipara.

Stage II—Expulsion stage: From the time of complete dilation until the fetus is expelled. Mother begins to "bear down." Averages 80 minutes in a primipara and 30 minutes in a multipara.

Stage III—Placental stage: From the time the fetus is expelled until the placenta is delivered; 5 to 15 minutes.

Questions to ask a woman in labor

The answers to these questions will assist in setting priorities in the management of a woman in labor:

When is your due date?

When did the contractions begin?

How long do they last?

How far apart (or close together) are they?

Did you rupture your membranes (break your bag of water)?

Are you having any bleeding?

Are you having any other difficulties?

How many other pregnancies have you had?

Emergency delivery

SIGNS AND SYMPTOMS OF IMPENDING DELIVERY

If the following signs and symptoms are present, prepare for immediate delivery, readying the necessary equipment first if time permits. When delivering an infant, attempt to maintain sterile technique if possible. If delivery is imminent, do not delay at the risk of endangering both the mother and the infant.

Heavy bloody show

Frequently occurring contractions

Desire to "bear down" by the mother

The mother stating that she is going to defecate

Bulging membranes from the vulva

Crowning of the fetal head

EQUIPMENT

Basin for placenta

Scissors (sterile) to cut cord

2 Kelly clamps

1 cord clamp

1 bulb syringe

Sterile towels

Receiving blanket

Sterile gloves

Infant resuscitation equipment

Heated Isolette

Identification bands for mother and infant

PROCEDURE (FIG. 25-1)

1. Be calm.
2. Prepare the mother by placing her in a dorsal position, with her knees bent and hands grasping her knees.
3. Take vital signs (including fetal heart tones) if time permits.
4. Offer much verbal support; explain to the mother everything that is going on.
5. Put on sterile gloves.
6. Drape the perineal area if time permits.
7. Have the mother pant with each contraction.
8. Place gentle pressure on the head when it crowns to avoid rapid expulsion of the fetus.
9. Support the head with both hands, but allow it to rotate naturally.
10. Check for the cord around the infant's neck.
    a. If it is there, attempt to slip it over the infant's head.
    b. If it is too tight, immediately clamp the cord in two places and cut the cord between the clamps.

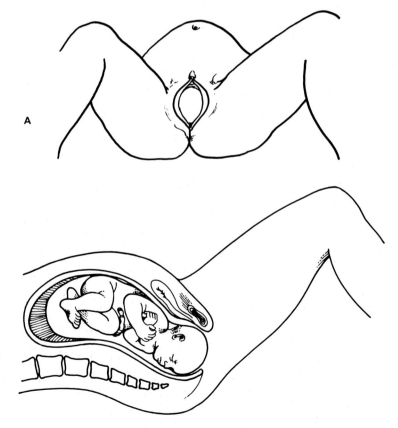

FIG. 25-1 Childbirth sequence. **A,** Crowning. **B,** Cross-section view of crowning.

Continued.

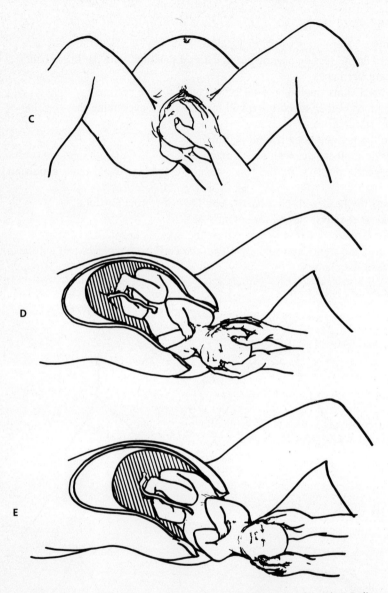

Fig. 25-1, cont'd C, Delivery of head. **D,** Cross-section view of delivery of head. **E,** Delivery of rest of body.

11. Suction the infant, first the nose and then the mouth. (Remember that newborns are obligate nose breathers.)
12. Deliver the shoulders by guiding the head downward to deliver the anterior shoulder and then upward to deliver the posterior shoulder.
13. The remaining parts of the infant will deliver quickly.
14. Note the time of birth.

TABLE 25-1 Apgar score chart

	0	1	2
Heart rate	0	Less than 100	More than 100
Muscle tone	Limp	Some flexion	Well flexed
Reflexes (catheter in nose)	No response	Grimace	Cough or sneeze
Color	Blue, pale	Pink body, blue extremities	Pink

15. If the membranes are still intact, quickly cut them at the nape of the neck and immediately peel them away from the face.
16. Hold the infant along the length of your arm with the head down and suction the nose and mouth once again.
17. The infant should make a first effort to breathe by crying spontaneously.
    a. If this does not occur, apply a mild noxious stimulus to the soles of the feet or the back.
    b. If spontaneous breathing still does not occur, initiate cardiopulmonary resuscitation. (See Chapter 3.)
18. After the cord stops pulsating, clamp it in two places—10 inches from the infant and 2 inches distal to the first clamp.
19. Cut the cord between the two clamps with sterile scissors.
20. Apply the umbilical clamp approximately 3 to 4 inches from the infant's body.
21. Determine an Apgar score at 1 minute and again at 5 minutes (Table 25-1).
22. Keep the infant warm by wrapping in a blanket and/or placing in a heated Isolette. If an Isolette is not available, allow the mother to hold the infant.

Delivery of the placenta
SIGNS AND SYMPTOMS OF IMPENDING PLACENTA DELIVERY

Umbilical cord advances 2 to 3 inches farther out of the vagina
Fundus rises upward in the abdomen
Uterus becomes firm and globular
Large gush of blood comes from the vagina

PROCEDURE

Instruct the mother to "bear down"
Apply *gentle* traction on the cord; do *not* pull on the cord
Once the placenta is delivered, inspect it for missing sections
Save the placenta in a basin to be sent to the laboratory later

Care of the mother

Wipe the perineal area with a clean dry towel
Place a sanitary napkin or towel in the perineal area
Have the mother hold her legs together

Massage the fundus

Initiate IV therapy (usually Ringer's lactate or Ringer's lactate with 5% dextrose) at approximately 150 ml/hour (faster if there is excessive bleeding)

Administer oxytoxic agents in accordance with the facility policy or in accordance with physician's orders

Keep the mother warm

Observe closely; monitor the vital signs frequently until they are stable

Put an identification band on the mother's wrist

While someone is caring for the mother, another person should be caring for the infant.

Care of the infant

Maintain the airway by placing the infant on its side and in slight Trendelenburg's position

Apply penicillin or silver nitrate eye prophylaxis (in accordance with the facility policy)

Administer phytonadione (Aquamephyton) for hypoprothrombinemia prophylaxis (in accordance with the facility policy)

Observe the cord for bleeding

Put an identification band on both the wrist and ankle

COMPLICATIONS OF DELIVERY
Fetal distress
SIGNS AND SYMPTOMS

Decreased fetal heart tones

Meconium in amniotic fluid

THERAPEUTIC INTERVENTION

Have the mother "pant like a dog"

Instruct the mother not to push until the head is visible

Administer oxygen at 8 liters/minute by nasal cannula

Place the mother on her left side

Check for a prolapsed cord

Initiate IV therapy with Ringer's lactate

Follow the steps for a normal vaginal delivery

Prepare to administer basic and advanced life support to the infant

Breech position of fetus

In 3% of all births the fetus presents in the breech position with either the buttocks first or a foot first (known as a footling breech). Breech position is believed to occur either because there is too little room for the fetus to turn or too much room such as in a premature birth, in which the fetus is small. These positions are dangerous for the fetus because of the increased likelihood of a prolapsed cord and the increased likelihood of amniotic fluid aspiration. Delivery of the fetus in these states is best accomplished by cesarean section. However, if delivery is imminent, the care giver must apply the following therapeutic intervention.

THERAPEUTIC INTERVENTION

1. Support the leg(s) or buttocks of the fetus
2. When the abdomen appears rigid, begin to pull on the protruding part
3. Then bring the arms out, with the fetus' back (posterior side) up
4. Deliver the head by:
   a. Placing a finger in the fetus' mouth to flex the head
   b. Gently pulling on the shoulders
5. If the head is not delivered in 2 minutes, apply firmer traction with a second person applying suprapubic pressure

Prolapsed cord (vasa previa)

A prolapsed cord is a state in which the cord precedes the infant. This is not a common condition but it is a very serious one.

SIGNS AND SYMPTOMS

Visible cord
Fetal distress

THERAPEUTIC INTERVENTION

Elevate the mother's hips
Administer oxygen at 8 liters/minute by nasal cannula
Keep the mother warm
Place a gloved hand into the canal and elevate the fetus' head slightly to relieve pressure on the cord; once this has been accomplished, leave the hand in place
Leave the cord as it is; do not attempt to place it back in the vagina
Feel the cord for pulsations
Initiate IV therapy with Ringer's lactate
Transport the patient to a facility where an immediate cesarean section can be performed

Postpartum hemorrhage

Normal bleeding after delivery is 250 to 300 ml. More than this amount is excessive bleeding. Hemorrhage is considered to be 750 ml or more.

SIGNS AND SYMPTOMS

Decreasing blood pressure
Increasing pulse
Much visible blood
Tears in the perineal area
Possible retained placenta

THERAPEUTIC INTERVENTION

Give oxygen at 8 liters/minute by nasal cannula
Place the mother in Trendelenburg's position
Begin IV therapy with Ringer's lactate with oxytocin (Pitocin, Syntocinon)
Apply manual pressure to tears

Massage the uterus
Apply the MAST (see Chapter 5)
Place a fist in the vagina and massage the uterus

COMPLICATIONS OF PREGNANCY
Placenta previa

Placenta previa accounts for 85% of cases of hemorrhage in the last trimester of pregnancy. This occurs when part or all of the placenta covers the cervical os.

SIGNS AND SYMPTOMS

Sudden painless bleeding (usually after 7 months of gestation)
Bright red blood from the vaginal area
Shock (decreased blood pressure and elevated pulse)

THERAPEUTIC INTERVENTION

Place the patient in Trendelenburg's position
Begin IV therapy with Ringer's lactate
If there is mild bleeding and a mature fetus, rupture the membrane, initiate a drip of
    oxytocin, and deliver the fetus; if this is ineffective, cesarean section is indicated
If there is heavy bleeding, cesarean section is indicated

Abruptio placentae

Abruptio placentae is one of the major causes of bleeding in the last trimester of pregnancy. The placenta separates from the uterine wall before the delivery of the fetus. This usually occurs after 20 weeks of gestation. The fetus usually dies from the absence of circulation.

SIGNS AND SYMPTOMS

Painful bleeding
Sudden colicky pain
Decreased blood pressure
Increased pulse
Diaphoresis
Cold clammy skin
Uterine rigidity
No fetal heart tones if placenta is greater than 50% separated

THERAPEUTIC INTERVENTION

Administer oxygen at 8 liters/minute by nasal cannula
Begin IV therapy with Ringer's lactate
Mark the level of the uterus on the abdomen
Transport the patient rapidly to a facility where an immediate cesarean section can be
    performed

Preeclampsia

Preeclampsia is a toxemia of pregnancy.

SIGNS AND SYMPTOMS

Elevated blood pressure (systolic pressure of 140 to 200 mm Hg)
Albuminuria
Oliguria
Edema (dependent), usually of limbs
Increased weight gain
Visual changes
Facial puffiness
Headaches
Nausea
Temperature above 103° F (39.4° C)

THERAPEUTIC INTERVENTION

Give supportive care
Monitor the growth of the fetus

Eclampsia

Eclampsia is a toxemia of pregnancy that is more severe than preeclampsia. It is a dangerous state characterized by seizures; status epilepticus (see Chapter 7) is a possibility. It may cause both maternal and fetal anoxia.

SIGNS AND SYMPTOMS

Elevated blood pressure (greater than 140 mm Hg systolic)

Albuminuria	Headache
Dependent edema (especially in the legs)	Nausea and vomiting
Facial puffiness	Elevated temperature
Increased weight gain	Decreased fetal heart tones
Visual changes	Seizures

THERAPEUTIC INTERVENTION

Maintain the airway
Give oxygen at 8 liters/minute by nasal cannula
Give magnesium sulfate (2 to 5 gm) by *slow* IV push
Provide supportive care

Trophoblastic disease

Trophoblastic disease may be experienced by a patient any time during pregnancy. The image on a sonogram appears like snow. The patient usually has a history of episodes of heavy bleeding. She will also have a hydatidiform mole. (One must differentiate between a mole and a choriocarcinoma, as choriocarcinomas are susceptible to chemotherapy.)

THERAPEUTIC INTERVENTION

Suction and curettage
Observe the patient for preeclampsia and eclampsia

Ectopic pregnancy

An ectopic pregnancy follows implantation of a fertilized egg outside of the endometrial cavity. It occurs in 0.6% to 2.5% of pregnancies and accounts for 2% to 3% of maternal deaths. Ectopic pregnancy reoccurs in 10% of women. Of all ectopic pregnancies 98% are tubal, with cervical, abdominal, and ovarian implantations accounting for the remaining 2%. Ectopic pregnancy may appear in many ways, such as:

Vaginal spotting with regular menses and irregular unilateral pain usually means an "unruptured" ectopic pregnancy.

Patients with a small uterus, irregular vaginal bleeding, and negative pregnancy tests may still have an ectopic pregnancy and should have a sonogram.

Tubal pregnancies may escape the tube and become uterine pregnancies.

SIGNS AND SYMPTOMS

Nausea and vomiting
Severe sudden onset of lower abdominal pain (which may be caused by distention of a hollow viscus)
Amenorrhea
Vaginal bleeding
Suspected pregnancy
History of IUD use
If ruptured:
Elevated temperature
Decreasing blood pressure
Elevated pulse
Decreasing level of consciousness
Cold, clammy skin

THERAPEUTIC INTERVENTION

Administer oxygen at 8 liters/minute by nasal cannula
Initiate IV therapy with Ringer's lactate
Administer antibiotics
Apply the MAST if indicated (see Chapter 5)
Surgery may be necessary for salpingectomy or salpingostomy
Give $Rh_o(D)$ immune globulin (RhoGAM) if indicated

Ruptured ovarian cyst

There are three types of ruptured ovarian cysts: dermoid, mucinous, and hemorrhagic corpus luteum. A ruptured ovarian cyst may be confused with an ectopic pregnancy.

SIGNS AND SYMPTOMS

Lower abdominal pain
Nausea and vomiting

Peritoneal irritation
Irregular menstrual cycle
History of previous strenuous exercise
Low-grade temperature
Hemoperitoneum

THERAPEUTIC INTERVENTION

Administer oxygen at 8 liters/minute by nasal cannula
Initiate IV therapy with Ringer's lactate
Place the patient in Trendelenburg's position
Apply the MAST if indicated (see Chapter 5)
Give antibiotics
Surgery is required for removal of the cyst

ABORTION

Abortion is a termination of pregnancy before 26 weeks of gestation (or before the fetus weighs 500 g), counting from the first day of the last menstrual period. It is estimated that 15% of known pregnancies terminate in abortion. Many abortions are caused by abnormal development of the germ cell, chromosomal abnormalities, infections (bacterial or viral), teratogens, abnormalities of the reproductive tract, or trauma. The mortality for mothers is 1.8/100,000 pregnancies.

Types of abortions

Threatened abortion—A threatened abortion is said to occur in cases of episodic painless uterine bleeding and mild cramping. The cervical os is closed, the uterus is enlarged and soft, and the pregnancy test is positive. Therapeutic intervention consists of bed rest and sedation.

Inevitable abortion—Bleeding becomes moderate, cramping becomes moderate, and the cervical os is open. Therapeutic intervention consists of bed rest and sedation.

Incomplete abortion—In an incomplete abortion, bleeding is heavy, cramping is severe, and the cervical os is open. The uterus is enlarged and the pregnancy test is positive. Some tissue has been passed but some products of conception have been retained. Therapeutic intervention is as follows:
Oxygen at 8 liters/minute by nasal cannula
IV therapy with Ringer's lactate
Oxytoxic agents
Surgery
RhoGAM if indicated

Complete abortion—In complete abortion there is a small amount of bleeding, cramping is mild, all tissue has been passed, and the cervical os is closed.

Missed abortion—A missed abortion is one in which it has been 12 weeks since the last menstrual period, the uterus is 6 weeks' size, there is no pain or bleeding, and the os is closed. Therapeutic intervention consists of dilation and curettage.

Infected (septic) abortion—A septic abortion is one complicated by infection of the uterus and the products of conception. There is usually evidence of threatened or incomplete abortion and sepsis (temperature approximately 100.3° F [37.9° C]). The pregnancy test is usually negative. Therapeutic intervention is as follows:

IV therapy
Antibiotics
Oxytocic agents
Surgery
Prophylactic measures to avoid gram-negative septic shock (see Chapter 5).

Induced abortion—Induced abortion is termination of a pregnancy by a physician at the discretion of the pregnant woman for medical or personal reasons.

Postabortion problems

Sometimes bleeding persists after abortion. Light bleeding is normal for 7 to 10 days. If bleeding persists, a pelvic examination should be performed to identify the source of bleeding. If the uterus is boggy, this is indicative of retained products of conception. If there is an elevated temperature, sepsis may be impending. Therapeutic intervention may include the following:

IV therapy
Antibiotics
Surgery

Another complication of abortion is *Clostridium* infection. It can be a devastating process that leads to gas gangrene and sloughing and necrosis of uterine tissue. If this does occur, the woman must have a hysterectomy, as the disease process may be fatal. Other therapeutic intervention includes penicillin, tetracycline, and clostridial antitoxin.

VAGINAL BLEEDING

One of the more common chief complaints heard in the emergency department is vaginal bleeding. To establish a firm diagnosis, it is important to obtain a good history from the patient. Important questions to answer are:

Are the vital signs stable? Is the hematocrit stable? If not, initiate IV therapy with Ringer's lactate and have the MAST standing by.

Is the patient pregnant? Do a 2-minute and 2-hour pregnancy test. Perform a vaginal examination.

If the patient is pregnant, is she aborting? Do not do a vaginal examination if the patient is in the third trimester of pregnancy.

Is the cervical os open or closed? If it is closed, abortion may be threatening.

If the patient is not pregnant yet is showing signs of aborting, she may be experiencing dysfunctional uterine bleeding. It is characterized by noncyclic bleeding. She may pass large clots and show signs of shock. Dysfunctional uterine bleeding may occur postpartum or after abortion. Therapeutic intervention consists of combinations of birth control pills, estrogen, and progesterone for 5 days. The endometrium will reimplant in the uterus, bleeding will stop, and in about 1 week the patient will have a painful period with heavy bleeding.

Dysfunctional uterine bleeding may be caused by trauma, such as perforations into the abdomen and the uterus. It may also be a result of cervical lesions, tumors, or polyps. Cancer is not an emergency department emergency, but it is an emotional emergency to the patient. Any woman with postmenopausal bleeding should be encouraged to seek medical help.

GYNECOLOGIC INFECTIONS
Pelvic inflammatory disease

Pelvic inflammatory disease (PID) occurs as a result of upward migration of bacteria into the fallopian tubes and may extend to the ovaries and the peritoneum. It usually follows acute salpingitis with an exacerbation of chronic PID, hydrosalpinx, pelvic pain, and adhesions.

SIGNS AND SYMPTOMS

High fever (102.2° F [39° C])
Malaise and chills
Increased heart rate
Anorexia
Nausea and vomiting
Abdominal pain
Abdominal tenderness
Rebound tenderness

Irregular bleeding
Vaginal discharge
Dysuria or urinary frequency
Adnexal mass(es) larger than 6 cm (probably not
  an ectopic pregnancy, which would have
  ruptured by this point)
Fixed pelvic organs
Cervicitis

THERAPEUTIC INTERVENTION

Bed rest
Analgesia
Douches
Fluids
Local heat
Antibiotics
Low-dose heparin (occasionally)
Possible surgery

Infections of external genitalia

Recognition and diagnosis of external genitalia infections are made through visual observation. Some of the more common ones are:

Infection	Therapeutic intervention
Scabies	Kwell lotion or shampoo
Vulvar abscess	Incision and drainage
	Antibiotics
	Sitz baths
Simple cyst	Sitz baths
Bartholin's cyst (infected)	Antibiotics
	Sitz baths
	Later, incision and drainage
	Urination via Foley catheter
	Check for gonorrhea

Vaginal infection

If the ecology of the vagina is disturbed vaginal infection may occur. Vaginal infection is not usually an emergency situation, but it is seen quite frequently in the emergency department, as it is an annoyance to the patient. The four most common types of vaginal infection are described in Table 25-2.

VENEREAL DISEASE

Venereal disease is transferred from one person to another during sexual intercourse. Gonorrhea and syphilis are the two most common venereal diseases in the United States.

Syphilis

Syphilis is a venereal disease caused by the spirochete *Treponema pallidum*. After an incubation period of 2 to 3 weeks a painless chancre will appear at the inoculation site. Other associated findings are lymphadenopathy and a positive VDRL.

THERAPEUTIC INTERVENTION

Give penicillin G procaine, or penicillin G benzathine

Extensive counseling of the patient is needed

If the patient is pregnant, give 2.4 million units of penicillin G benzathine (Bicillin) every other day for 10 treatments (because of the risk of the fetus developing congenital syphilis)

TABLE 25-2 Common vaginal infections

Type	Diagnosed by	Therapeutic intervention
Trichomonas (16% of all vaginal infections)	Yellowish gray discharge; fishy odor; creamy, bubbly consistency; wet mount	Metronidazole (Flagyl), 250 mg 3 times/day for 7 days by mouth; as infection may be harbored by male, he should also be treated with same drug at same dosage. If female is pregnant, treat with Tricofuron.
Candida albicans (causes monilial vaginitis; 26% of all vaginal infections)	White, cheesy discharge; odorless; heavy flow; pseudohyphae from KOH wet mount	Nystatin (Mycostatin) vaginal tablets, 1 to 2 times/day for 7 to 14 days, or clotrimazole (Gyne-Lotrimin) vaginal tablet once daily for 7 days
Haemophilus vaginalis (most common; 31% of all vaginal infections)	Whitish gray; watery discharge; foul odor; wet mount	Sultrin, 1 applicator twice daily for 4 to 6 days
Bacterial (nonspecific; 27% of all vaginal infections)	Yellow discharge; foul odor; culture and Gram's stain	If culture is positive, antibiotics such as penicillin or tetracycline

Gynecologic emergencies

Differential diagnosis of common vaginal infections

Organism	Occurrence	Color	Odor	Consistency	Other	Lab test(s)	Therapeutic intervention
Hemophilus vaginalis	31% of all vaginal infections	Whitish-gray	Foul	Watery		Wet mount Culture and Gram's stain to exclude other organisms	Sultrin, 1 applicatorful 2 times a day for 4-6 days
Bacterial (nonspecific) vaginitis	27% of all vaginal infections	Yellow	Foul	Watery/creamy	May be caused by retained foreign body	Wet mount Culture and Gram's stain to exclude other organisms	Antibiotics (type specific); Remove foreign body
Candida albicans	26% of all vaginal infections	White	Odorless	Cheesy; heavy flow	Causes Monilial vaginitis	Pseudohyphae from KOH wet mount	Nystatin (Mycostatin) vaginal tablets one to two times daily for 7-14 days or clotrimazole (Gyne-Lotrimin) vaginal tablets once a day for 7 days
Trichomonas vaginalis	16% of all vaginal infections	Yellowish-gray	Fishy	Creamy; bubbly	Frequently, erythema around cervical os	Wet mount shows motile protozoa	Metronidazole (Flagyl) 250 mg po 3 times daily for 7 days. Male partner must also be treated with same drug and dosage. If woman is pregnant, substitute Tricofuron

From Budassi, S.A.: J.E.N. **6**(3):35, 1980.
Other causes of vaginal discharge include: (1) cancer of cervix or uterus, (2) IUD, (3) pelvic inflammatory disease, (4) rectal or bladder fistula, and (5) senile vaginitis.

Continued.

Gynecologic emergencies—cont'd

External genitalia infections

Complaint	Therapeutic intervention
Scabies	Kwell lotion/shampoo
Simple cyst	Sitz baths
Bartholin's cyst (abscess)	Sitz baths
	Antibiotics (controversial)
	Incision and drainage when appropriate
	Check for sexually transmitted diseases
Vulvar abscess	Sitz baths
	Antibiotics
	Incision and drainage when appropriate

Pelvic inflammatory disease (PID)

Caused by the upward migration of bacteria into the fallopian tubes and sometimes into the ovaries and peritoneum.

Signs and symptoms:
Fever (> 39° C)
Chills
Abdominal pain (lower, bilateral)
Abdominal tenderness (lower, bilateral)
Rebound tenderness (lower, bilateral)
Vaginal discharge
Adnexal mass(es)
Tachycardia
Irregular vaginal bleeding
Frequent urination
Malaise
Fixed pelvic organs

Cervicitis
Nausea and vomiting
Anorexia

Therapeutic intervention:
Bed rest
Local heat
Analgesia
Forced fluids
Antibiotics

Consider:
Low-dose heparin
Surgery

Contraceptive emergencies

Type	Problem	Therapeutic intervention
Diaphragm	Unable to remove	Remove with ring forceps
IUD	Lost string	X-ray or ultrasound to determine position; may be removed with IUD hook
	Partial expulsion	Remove; consider alternate form of contraception
	Migration to abdominal cavity	X-ray or ultrasound to determine position; may require exploratory laparotomy
Oral contraceptives	Thrombophlebitis	Bed rest; local heat; anticoagulation
	Pulmonary embolus	ABCs; oxygen, IV, analgesia, bronchodilators, heparin, reassurance
	Cerebrovascular accident	ABCs; oxygen, IV

Herpes genitalis type II

Herpes genitalis is discussed in Chapter 14.

Lymphogranuloma venereum

Lymphogranuloma venereum is caused by a viral agent and is contacted through sexual intercourse or by contact with an infectious discharge.

SIGNS AND SYMPTOMS

Reddened contact area
Usually not painful
Transitory genital lesion

Inguinal lymphadenopathy
Perineal lymphadenopathy

THERAPEUTIC INTERVENTION

Give tetracycline
Give sulfonamides

CONTRACEPTIVE EMERGENCIES

Type	Therapeutic intervention
Intrauterine device	
"Coming out"	Remove and consider alternative contraceptive device
Lost string	X-ray or ultrasound to assure placement in uterus; may have to be removed with IUD hook
Burrowing into abdominal cavity	X-ray or ultrasound to assure position; may require exploratory laparotomy
Birth control pills	
Thrombophlebitis	Bed rest, local heat, and anticoagulant therapy
Pulmonary embolus	See Chapter 6
Cerebrovascular accident	See Chapter 7
Diaphragm: unable to remove	Remove with ring forceps

SEXUAL ASSAULT

Forcible rape introduces a major disruption into a person's life. It is one of the four major violent crimes in the United States. Nearly one third of all rapes are committed by a neighbor or a friend. During the assault the woman fears death and has a desire to survive. After the rape the woman will experience a sense of disbelief and shock. She may feel guilty, have self-blame, be fearful, and feel very vulnerable. She may also experience a feeling of helplessness, personal violation, shame, and embarrassment. She may find herself crying for no apparent reason.

A few days after the rape she may say that she wants to forget about it and return to work or school or her everyday pattern of life. Later she will become depressed and angry and will have a need to verbalize her feelings.

General guidelines

When a rape victim comes to the emergency department it is important to remove her to a place away from the typical noise of the waiting room. She should not be left alone at this time.

It would be ideal to have all emergency department nursing and medical personnel trained as rape counselors, but this is not always possible. The person who is taking an initial history from the patient should make every attempt to remain with the patient throughout her emergency department visit.

Informed consent is required to treat the rape victim. If she comes to the emergency department without the police, the police must be called. The victim does not, however, have to speak with them, or she may talk with the police but choose to have a medical examination only and refuse to have specimens collected for evidence. Encourage the victim to speak with the police. Let her know that the police need information to apprehend the rapist and that her information may help someone else. Usually the hospital bill is paid by a community resource (such as state compensation for victims of violent crimes).

It is not a medical role to decide if a woman was raped. The role of the medical team is to assure physical well-being, collect specimens, and provide for psychologic well-being. If the victim merely wants medical treatment, a regular emergency department consent form will be adequate. If evidence is collected, a specific form for release of evidence to law enforcement officers should be obtained.

Before the patient leaves the emergency department, establish if she has a family member or friend with whom she can stay the night. Also, immediately place her in contact with a rape crisis center or a rape hotline person and arrange for her to obtain immediate counseling.

History

Explain to the patient that some of the questions you will be asking may be somewhat embarrassing but that she should make every attempt to answer your questions as accurately as possible. Allow her to talk openly.

It is essential to collect specific details such as the date, time, place, event, type of penetration, number of assailants, identifying information about the assailant(s), and possible use of a condom. Ask the victim if physical force was used. Ask her about her menstrual history. When was the last time she had intercourse before the rape? What did she do after the rape? Did she shower or douche? Did she suffer any physical harm? Was she under the influence of drugs or alcohol at the time of the rape? Does she have any allergies? Does she have any history of gynecologic conditions? Has she ever been pregnant? Is she now pregnant?

Physical examination

Inspect the entire body for bruises, cuts, and other injuries
Inspect the external genitalia, perineum, cervix, and vaginal wall
Collect specimens for wet mount, dry smear, fixed smear, and culture (do not use a lubricant)
Collect an oropharyngeal culture specimen if indicated
Send urine for a pregnancy test (to see if the woman was pregnant at the time of the rape)
Note any negative findings on the chart also
Arrange for a psychiatric examination or a psychologic follow-up
Check for alcohol or drugs

Therapeutic intervention

Treatment for physical trauma

Protection against pregnancy and/or venereal disease:

Ovral, two tablets in emergency department, two tablets 12 hours later

Penicillin 4.8 million units IM and probenecid (Benemid) 1 gm orally

Emotional assessment and counseling: psychiatric or rape counselor follow-up in 24 hours, 48 hours, then weekly

Legal evidence:

Fingernail scrapings

Pubic hairs (combed or clipped)

Vaginal slides

SUGGESTED READINGS

Brownmiller, S.: Against our will: men, women, and rape, New York, 1975, Simon & Schuster, Inc.

Burgess, A.W., and Holstrom, L.L.: Rape! Victim of crisis, Englewood Cliffs, N.J., 1974, Prentice-Hall, Inc.

Burgess, A.W., and Holstrom, L.L.: Rape trauma syndrome, Am. J. Psychiatry 131:981, 1974.

Burgess, A.W., and Holstrom, L.L.: The rape victim in the emergency ward, Am. J. Nurs. 73:1741, 1973.

Connell, N., and Wilson, O.: Rape: the first sourcebook for women, New York, 1974, New American Library.

Garland, G.W., Quitley, J.M.E., and Cameron, M.D.: Obstetrics and gynaecology for nurses, ed. 3, London, 1976, Hodder & Stoughton, Ltd.

Gordon, R.T.: Emergencies in obstetrics and gynecology. In Warner, C.G., ed.: Emergency care: assessment and intervention, ed. 3, St. Louis, 1983, The C.V. Mosby Co.

Green, T.H.: Gynecology: essentials of clinical practice, Boston, 1977, Little, Brown & Co.

Hyde, M.D.: Hotline, New York, 1976, McGraw-Hill Book Co.

Hyde, M.D.: Speak out on rape, New York, 1976, McGraw-Hill Book Co.

Netter, F.H.: Reproductive system. In Oppenheimer, E., ed.: CIBA collection of medical illustrations, vol. 2, New York, 1974, CIBA-Geigy Corp.

Paulsen, K., and Kuhn, R.A.: Women's almanac, Philadelphia, 1976, J.B. Lippincott Co.

Pritchard, J., and MacDonald, P.: William's obstetrics, ed. 15, New York, 1976, Appleton-Century-Crofts.

Sexually transmitted diseases, U.S. Department of Health, Education and Welfare Bull. No. 97-796, Washington, D.C., 1974, U.S. Government Printing Office.

CHAPTER 26 **Pediatric emergencies**

This chapter presents a broad overview of pediatric problems commonly seen in the emergency department. As there is not enough space to detail every possible emergency condition, the reader is referred to the list of suggested readings at the end of the chapter.

THE GENERAL APPROACH TO THE PEDIATRIC PATIENT

As most health care personnel are not used to working with large numbers of sick children on a daily basis, it is normal to feel a bit anxious when a pediatric patient arrives in the emergency department, especially a very sick child. It is important to remain calm and to have self-confidence. There are a few basic rules to follow when dealing with a sick child:

Be gentle but firm

Use common sense

Speak directly to the child

Be honest with the child—if something is going to hurt, say that it is going to hurt

Tell the child what is about to be done

Tell the child what is being done while it is being done

Remember that parents may be very anxious, too:

    Allow the parents to be with the child whenever possible

    If for some reason the parents cannot be with the child, be sure that someone is available to stay with them or at least to keep them informed periodically about the child's condition

    Some procedures are more easily accomplished if the parent holds the child (e.g., examination of a child's ear)

    Between examinations allow the child to sit in the parent's lap if possible

Hypoxia is not an uncommon finding in children. Children have higher metabolic rates than adults. Oxygen consumption is 50% greater in a child than in an adult. With each degree of temperature increase there is an associated oxygen consumption increase of 7%. Pay close attention to this and to the patency of the child's airway.

MEDICATION ADMINISTRATION

Pediatric dosages of medications are given in accordance with the child's weight (Table 26-1). Total pediatric dosage should never exceed adult dosage. It is important to be able to quickly and accurately estimate a child's weight (a parent is not always

TABLE 26-1 Estimated weight of a child by age

Age	Kilograms	Pounds
Newborn	3-5	6-11
1 year	10	22
3 years	15	33
5 years	20	44
8 years	25	55
10 years	30	66
15 years	50	110

From Melker, R.: Crit. Care Q. 1(1):50, 1978.

available or always a reliable source for this information) and to be able to rapidly calculate the correct dosage for the child. Keep medication dosage charts for pediatric patients readily available in case of an emergency.

INTRAVENOUS LINES

Establishment of an IV line in an infant or small child may sometimes be a difficult task. Be sure to secure the site chosen for IV placement before attempting to cannulate the vein. Usually the best site for IV cannulation in an infant is a scalp vein. The care giver can assist with venous distention by placing an elastic band around the infant's head at the level of the forehead. Use a small (21- or 23-gauge) scalp vein needle. Once the IV is established, protect the cannulation site carefully (usually a paper cup or medicine cup is taped over the site). In a small child, the best sites for initiating an IV line are the dorsa of the hands and the feet. Other sites for emergency IV administration in a small child are the external jugular vein and the femoral vein.

Occasionally the physician may choose to initiate an intravenous cutdown. (See Chapter 4 for procedure.) The site chosen for this procedure is usually the saphenous vein.

AIRWAY OBSTRUCTION

The most common cause of respiratory distress in children is airway obstruction. The four main areas of airway obstruction are the nasopharynx, the oropharynx, the larynx and upper trachea, and the lower airway. If the child is in respiratory distress but is moving some air, try to identify the cause of the obstruction. Do a rapid assessment for:

Level of consciousness
Signs of hypoxia
Breath odor
Lung sounds
Midline trachea
Distended neck veins
Tracheal in-drawing
Use of accessory muscles of respiration
Tidal volume
Vital signs (be sure to include temperature)
Skin vital signs (color, temperature, moistness)
Dehydration

Text continued on p. 572.

Intravenous therapy in pediatric trauma

The most **difficult** aspects of starting an IV on an infant or child are finding a vein, controlling the patient during puncture, and anchoring the needle to prevent infiltration and mechanical irritation to the vessel. The most **significant** aspect is supporting the patient and the parents emotionally and performing so efficiently that little pain is caused. The most **underrated** aspect is fear and discomfort of the clinician in performing the task of establishing an IV on a tiny child, particularly when the clinician has not used the skill frequently enough to be precise and efficient.

Young children tend to have deep veins well covered with subcutaneous tissue, and in the presence of volume depletion may not evidence peripheral veins even with a tourniquet applied. Application of a pediatric MAST may provide enough volume to cause venous distention in the upper extremities; however, if the volume is severely depleted and the child is thus compromised, do not attempt peripheral extremity lines. Such cases are emergencies of the highest magnitude; to avoid a time delay, central lines or a cutdown by an experienced clinician would be best.

In cases where time is not of the essence, scalp veins or veins on the dorsum of the hand or foot may be used to place either a 19-gauge butterfly (scalp) needle, or a 22-gauge over-the needle catheter.

Sites to avoid are:
Antecubital fossa (clinical lab technicians will need access to these areas)
Veins over joints
Veins that might need to be used for cutdown (femoral, saphenous)
Bruised, fractured or burnt areas
Large veins should be selected when:
Large quantities of fluid must be administered
Administering blood products
The solution is hypertonic
Equipment needed for peripheral vein IV:
19-gauge butterfly or 22-gauge over-the-needle catheter (with syringe attached)
Alcohol or iodinated solution (CAUTION: may obscure vein in poor light)
IV extension tubing attached to a 100 ml volume control chamber, connected to an IV
   solution and properly flushed
Armboard
Tourniquet
Nylon tape, cut in strips
NOTE: Prepare all equipment before inserting the needle. Many nurses elect to attach the butterfly needle to the infusion set before the vein is punctured. The IV bottle can then be positioned at a level lower than the patient. When the clamp is opened the lower position creates a slight negative pressure in the system causing a backflow of blood when the vein is entered.

Technique for inserting an over-the-needle catheter into a peripheral vein

Explain the procedure to the child and parents.
Select a vein and restrain all extremities before beginning. You will probably need assistance especially with an infant or toddler.
All preliminary actions are the same as above, with the exception of attaching the infusion set to the needle before puncture.
The puncture is made with the bevel away from the vein and the point toward the vein; the indirect method is preferred (entering from the side and at a slight angle to the vein) when using an over-the-needle catheter to avoid flattening the vein or piercing the posterior wall.

From Simoneau, J.K.: J.E.N. **5**(5):37, 1979.

Intravenous therapy in pediatric trauma—cont'd

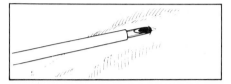

To insert an over-the-needle catheter the needle should be properly aligned with the bevel up

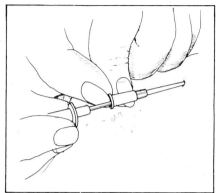

Withdraw the needle before advancing the catheter

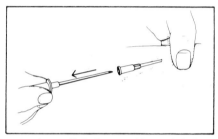

Remove the needle before attaching an infusion set

Once the skin and vein are entered, realign the needle and advance slightly. Blood will generally appear in the hub. If a small syringe is attached before puncture, slight negative pressure can be applied to the plunger to elicit a flashback of blood.

On flashback of blood, stop advancing the needle. Stabilize with one hand while the thumb and forefinger of the other disengage the catheter from the needle and advance it into the vein as far as possible.

Release the tourniquet, remove the needle, and begin the flow of IV fluid.

Tape the catheter to the skin with a crossed tape around the hub and one or two strips of tape across the hub over a sterile pad. Tape in such a manner that the puncture site can be cleansed daily.

Tape the IV tubing securely, since children often pull at tubing.

Technique for inserting a butterfly needle into a peripheral vein

Tell the child and parents what you are going to do and give reassurance.

Restrain the child properly to avoid unexpected movement.

Get into a comfortable position with adequate lighting for the site.

Place a tourniquet proximal to the site and allow time for the vein to fill.

Palpate gently to identify vein pathways; gravity may help distend the vessels.

Clean and prepare the site thoroughly; do not touch cleansed vein before puncture (always take adequate time to identify the site you are most likely to puncture effectively the first time before cleansing the site).

Continued.

Intravenous therapy in pediatric trauma—cont'd

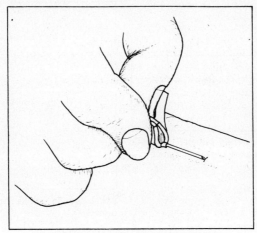

Position for scalp vein puncture

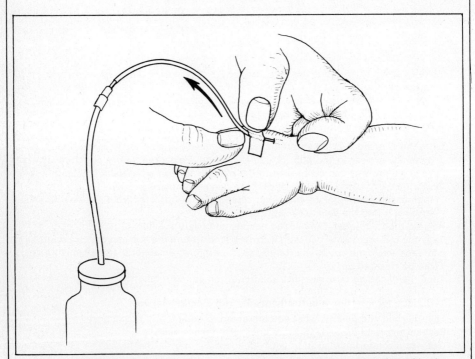

When an IV bottle is placed slightly lower than the patient, the negative pressure forces blood to flow into the butterfly tubing

Intravenous therapy in pediatric trauma—cont'd

Grasp the hand or foot and place your thumb below the insertion site to increase skin tension and stabilize the vein.

Pinching the wings together, position the needle either **beside** the vein with the bevel away and the point toward the vein, or directly **above** the vein with bevel up.

Puncture the skin and enter the vein swiftly.

When blood flows back into the butterfly tubing, release the tourniquet and open the clamp to begin solution flow; adjust to proper rate.

Tape each wing individually, then secure the needle. Curl tubing and tape.

Technique for inserting a butterfly needle into a scalp vein

The veins of the scalp are small in infants and will not accommodate an over-the-needle catheter; therefore, these veins are not often used in the traumatized infant.

A rubber band is placed around the infant's head to distend the veins distal to it.

The site is shaved and cleansed.

A butterfly is inserted using the same technique as in an extremity; anchor the vessel and direct the needle at an angle nearly parallel with the skin.

A small drip rate may help "float" the needle into the vein. These veins are so tiny it may be difficult to know just where the needle is initially. Always use a gentle and light touch. Positioning the IV bottle lower than the patient and using the slight negative pressure may be a big help when inserting a needle into a scalp vein.

A small medicine cup may protect the site from being disturbed by the patient's movement.

Technique for venous cutdown

Obtain correct equipment including venous cutdown tray, local anesthetic, sterile gloves and sterile catheter or polyethylene tube.

Select the insertion site.

Clean and prepare the skin aseptically.

Sterile gloves must be worn by all persons working at the site.

After the skin is infiltrated at the site, a 2 to 2.5 cm horizontal incision is made either above the medial malleolus or below the inguinal ligament, depending on the site selected.

Tissue is bluntly dissected away from the vein either with a hemostat or a blunt end of the blunt/sharp scissors, and the vein is "lifted" out of the wound by placing a hemostat under it and anchoring the instrument on the skin.

Two silk ligatures are placed under the vein; the distal is tied and the proximal tie is drawn up and toward the head to aid in stabilizing the vein during incision and cannulation.

A small incision is made into the vein with a pair of iris scissors or a sharp #11 blade on a handle.

A sterile IV catheter is threaded into the vein and tied by the proximal ligature; when blood returns through the catheter the infusion may then be started.

A single suture is placed loosely through the skin and tied around the catheter to prevent disruption.

The wound is closed with interrupted sutures and dressed and bandaged.

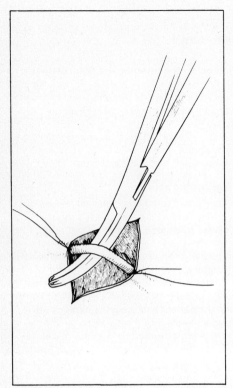

A "V" is about to be cut in the vein with iris scissors

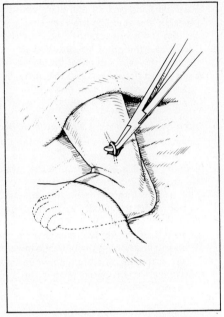

In a venous cutdown the vein can be listed from the wound by hemostat

Anchoring IVs

Small pads may be used to support the butterfly needle and help to maintain the flow.
A tiny paper cup placed over the needle and anchored to the skin may help prevent dislodging of the needle by the child's movement.
Use of soft restraints may prevent manipulation of the needle by tiny fingers.
A padded tongue blade may be an effective "armboard."

References

Dube, S., and Pierog, S.: Immediate care of the sick and injured child. St. Louis, 1978, The C.V. Mosby Co., pp. 257-258.
Venipuncture—catheters and scalp vein needles, Trainex Corp, 1973.

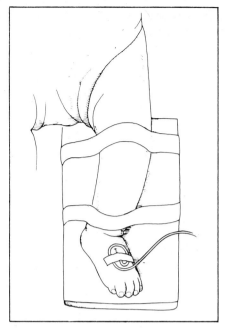

The infant's leg can be immobilized by taping it to a legboard

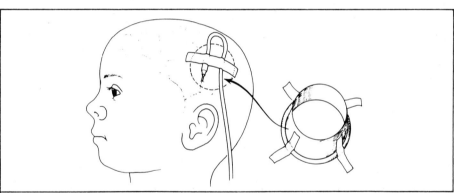

Part of a paper cup can be taped over a scalp venipuncture to protect the site

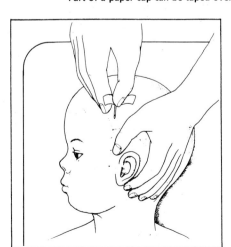

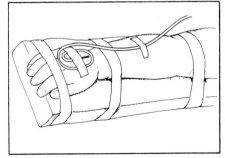

The patient's arm should be restrained when the hand is the infusion site

The wings of the butterfly are grasped between the thumb and forefinger and the needle is pointed in the direction of venous flow.

Nasopharynx obstruction

Nasopharynx obstruction may occur as a result of foreign bodies, edematous adenoids, edema from trauma, or carcinomas.

SIGNS AND SYMPTOMS

Mouth breathing (remember that very small infants are obligate nose breathers; a nasal obstruction in an infant may be life threatening)
Cyanosis

THERAPEUTIC INTERVENTION

Turn the child on his side
Insert an oropharyngeal airway
Administer oxygen

Oropharynx obstruction

Obstruction of the oropharynx may be caused by facial trauma with swelling of the tongue or by foreign body aspiration.

SIGNS AND SYMPTOMS

Noisy breathing (gargling or snoring sounds) or absence of breath sounds
Neck extended "like a turtle"
Insistence on sitting up
Cyanosis
Difficulty speaking
Difficulty swallowing

THERAPEUTIC INTERVENTION

Insert an oropharyngeal or nasoharyngeal airway if epiglottitis has been ruled out
Administer oxygen therapy
If the patient is moving air, *do not attempt to remove the foreign body* and *do not change the patient's position*
If there is no air movement, use gravity to advantage; turn the child upside down and give four back blows; if this is not sufficient to dislodge the foreign body, turn the child upright and attempt a Heimlich maneuver
Once again, attempt to ventilate the child

INFECTIOUS OBSTRUCTIONS OF THE OROPHARYNX

Tonsil enlargement or peritonsilar abscess
Signs and symptoms

Sore throat   Elevated temperature
Difficulty swallowing   Exudate on tonsils

THERAPEUTIC INTERVENTION

Insert an oropharyngeal airway
Administer oxygen
Give antibiotics

Epiglottitis

Epiglottitis is a medical emergency. The diagnosis is made by "thinking of it"—the child "looks sick."

Signs and symptoms

Massive swelling of epiglottis (usually from a bacterial infection)
Commonly seen in 2- to 5-year-olds (but may be seen even in adults)
Elevated temperature (above 103.1° F [39.5° C])
Tachycardia
Respiratory difficulty
Muffled voice
Patient refusal to change to other than a sitting position (*Never* place the child on his back.*)
Neck extended "like a turtle"
Profuse salivation
Dysphagia
No cough
Hypoventilation
History of infection, ingestion of a hot beverage, or steam inhalation

Therapeutic intervention

Do not attempt to look into the child's mouth as doing so may cause respiratory arrest*
Give oxygen therapy (this usually requires intubation; do *not* intubate in the field, as this may further close the airway and reduce any chance of later intubation; the exception to this is respiratory arrest)
Rapidly transport the child to an emergency facility
Consider an emergency cricothyrotomy
Administer steroids
Give antibiotics
Give nebulized racemic epinephrine (2% solution—nebulize 0.5 ml of racemic epinephrine in 3 ml of saline to be given over 5 to 15 minutes)

Larynx and upper trachea obstruction
GENERAL SIGNS AND SYMPTOMS

Inspiratory stridor
Increased inspiratory/expiratory ratio
Difficulty breathing
Possibly no sounds on auscultation
Agitation
Cyanosis

CROUP

Croup is a viral or bacterial infection of the trachea, larynx, and bronchi that causes edema and inflammation of the lining of the trachea and larynx.

---

*Inserting a tongue blade into the mouth or having the child lie down may induce respiratory arrest.

Signs and symptoms

Child usually 3 months to 3 years of age
History of increasing nocturnal distress for several days resulting from an upper respiratory infection
Low-grade fever
"Barking" cough
Hoarse voice
Inspiratory stridor
Sternal retraction
Tachypnea
Tachycardia
Cyanosis

Therapeutic intervention

Administer humidified oxygen
Administer humidified cool air

FOREIGN BODIES

Foreign bodies in the larynx and upper trachea are common findings in children. Foreign body airway obstruction is the cause of more than 2,000 deaths in the United States each year. The most commonly aspirated foreign bodies in children are peanuts, nuts, beans, and seeds, which cause an inflammatory response.

Signs and symptoms

Inspiratory stridor (but there may be no sounds if the airway is completely blocked)
Agitation

Therapeutic intervention

Administer oxygen therapy
Use four back blows, four abdominal thrusts, finger sweep of the back of the throat, and ventilation (do this only if the airway is completely obstructed; *do not do this if the airway is only partially obstructed and the child is still able to move some air*)
Perform emergency cricothyrotomy for complete obstruction not corrected by these procedures

LARYNGOSPASM

Laryngospasm is not common, but when it occurs, it can be a life-threatening situation. It is difficult to distinguish from a foreign body airway obstruction. It may be caused by anaphylaxis.

Signs and symptoms

Vomiting   Bronchospasm
Urticaria   Hypotension
Periorbital edema   Absence of breath sounds

Therapeutic intervention

Assure airway management
Give oxygen therapy
Perform emergency circothyrotomy if the airway cannot be opened
Give epinephrine
Give antihistamines
Give bronchodilators
Give steroids

TRAUMA

Trauma to the airway may be a life-threatening situation; it usually involves trauma about the head and neck.

Therapeutic intervention

Ensure airway maintenance
Administer oxygen therapy
Apply a therapeutic intervention appropriate to the specific type of trauma

Lower airway obstructions
ASTHMA

Asthma is the most common cause of lower airway obstruction. It is caused by bronchial constriction and mucous plugs. It can be easily confused with bronchiolitis and foreign body aspiration.

Signs and symptoms

Expiratory wheezes (sometimes inspiratory also)
Decreased inspiratory/expiratory ratio (it takes longer to exhale)
Possibly no expiratory sounds if there is no air movement

Therapeutic intervention

Give epinephrine 1:1,000 solution subcutaneously
Administer oxygen therapy
Place the patient in high-Fowler's position
Give aminophylline
Give antibiotics
Give steroids

Status asthmaticus

Status asthmaticus is asthma that does not respond to two to three doses of epinephrine 20 minutes apart. It will soon lead to respiratory failure if therapeutic intervention is not applied.

Therapeutic intervention

Establish an IV line
Give aminophylline

Give isoproterenol
Treat fluid and electrolyte imbalances according to laboratory values
Administer oxygen therapy according to arterial blood gas values
Be prepared to handle respiratory arrest

BRONCHIOLITIS

Bronchiolitis is a viral infection of the bronchioles that usually occurs in children less than 1 year old.

Signs and symptoms

History of mild upper respiratory infection
Respiratory difficulty
Wheezing, dyspnea, and cyanosis, as in asthma
Infant who "appears ill"
No response to epinephrine
Frequent coughing
Forced expirations
Dehydration

Therapeutic intervention

Therapeutic intervention for bronchiolitis consists of administering humidified oxygen.

FOREIGN BODIES

Foreign bodies are a common cause of lower airway obstruction in children.

Signs and symptoms

Wheezing (unilateral)
Air trapping
Mediastinal shift
Rare tension pneumothorax

Therapeutic intervention

Administer oxygen
Place a needle for tension pneumothorax
Perform a criocothyrotomy if maneuvers for obstructed airway are not successful

PNEUMONIA

Also see Chapter 6.

Signs and symptoms

History of upper respiratory infection for several days
History of otitis media or conjunctivitis
Elevated temperature (103° F to 104° F [39.4° to 40° C])
Cyanosis

Nausea and vomiting
Seizures
Tachycardia
Tachypnea

Cough
Meningism
Abdominal pain
Shock

Therapeutic intervention

Administer oxygen therapy
Hospitalize young children
Give antibiotics

FEVERS

An elevated temperature is probably the single most common cause for which a parent brings a child to the emergency department. Approximately 10% of children from 1 to 6 years old are susceptible to febrile seizures in the first 12 to 24 hours of a fever.

ASSOCIATED SIGNS AND SYMPTOMS

Rapid pulse
Tachypnea
Diaphoresis

Flushed look
Agitation

THERAPEUTIC INTERVENTION

Force fluids (clear liquids, at least 4 quarts a day)
Undress the child
Sponge with tepid water (no ice water or alcohol)
Give antipyretic medication:
    Aspirin, 10 to 20 mg/kg every 6 hours or 1 g/year of age
    Acetaminophen (Tylenol), 5 to 10 mg/kg every 6 hours
Treat the cause of the fever
Give instructions to the parents on how to take a temperature and how to perform "cooling measures" if necessary

SEIZURES

Seizures are common problems in pediatric medicine. Benign febrile seizures are a common type and are usually the result of an upper respiratory infection. Fever can appear rapidly and rise to 105.1° F (40.6° C). It is usually the result of a bacterial infection. Other causes of seizures are central nervous system infections, poisoning, epilepsy, and head injury. Of children who have febrile seizures, 75% will not have another. If a child's temperature is less than 103.3° F (39.6° C), consider that the cause of the seizure may not be the fever.

SIGNS AND SYMPTOMS

Seizures are of short duration (less than 5 minutes)
Seizures are generalized (grand mal or tonic-clonic)
A focal seizure may indicate meningitis, cerebral abscess, or epilepsy
There is no postictal state

THERAPEUTIC INTERVENTION

Ensure ABCs

Give oxygen therapy

Put the child in the left lateral decubitus position

Protect the child from bodily harm

Induce hypothermia (by loosening clothing, tepid sponging, and antipyretic medications)

Give IV fluids, but be careful not to overhydrate

Obtain a good drug history

Give anticonvulsant medications only during active seizures

Recheck the vital signs

Give diazepam (Valium) (half-life of 4 to 8 hours) 2 to 10 mg IV *slowly,* monitoring respirations, until the seizure ends

Give phenobarbital (for a longer effect), 5 mg/kg IV or IM not to exceed 300 mg

Give paraldehyde 1 ml/year of age by rectum

Repeat the phenobarbital in 30 minutes if the seizure recurs

Then give 3 mg/kg phenobarbital IM every 60 minutes

If all of these medications are unsuccessful, call for general anesthesia

See Chapter 7 for the neurologic evaluation

DEHYDRATION

Approximately 80% of the body weight of a child is fluid, 40% of which is extracellular and thus unstable. This fact and the child's high metabolic rate (with a high fluid turnover) and kidneys that are inefficient (producing a large amount of dilute urine) predispose the child to dangerous dehydration when large amounts of fluid are lost rapidly through fever, vomiting, or diarrhea. Signs and symptoms include the following:

Weight loss

Sunken fontanels

Ashen or mottled skin with poor turgor

Listlessness

Unresponsiveness

Therapeutic intervention consists of planning infant hydration of 180 to 200 ml of fluid/kg/day to meet the basic requirements and additional fluids to compensate for deficits.

NEAR-DROWNING

Drowning and near-drowning account for 10% of all accidental deaths each year. Half of these deaths occur in children under 5 years of age. It is the second most common cause of death in children over 1 year of age. Most of the drownings and near-drownings occur in fresh water such as backyard swimming pools and bathtubs. (See also Chapter 6.)

THERAPEUTIC INTERVENTION

Establish and maintain the airway

Breathing—initiate ventilation while the victim is still in the water

Maintain circulation (if present, it will usually appear on an ECG as a supraventricular rhythm)

Correct acidosis in accordance with arterial blood gas values

Initiate an IV infusion of Ringer's lactate

Use drugs of resuscitation (See Chapter 3.)

In the field rapid transportation to an emergency facility is required

If the stomach is distended, turn the patient to one side and press firmly on the abdomen; be careful to avoid aspiration

All near-drowning victims must be admitted to the hospital for a period of 24 to 48 hours following the incident *(even if they look well)*

POISONING*

Pediatric poisoning can be difficult to diagnose in the field and the emergency department. It is important, on the telephone as well as in person, to obtain a good history from the child's parents, relatives, friends, or neighbors:

What drug or product did the child take?

How much did he take?

Is he having any symptoms at present?

Is he having difficulty breathing?

What medications does he take routinely?

Has he ever done this before?

Ask the parents or other to bring in the product and the product container, including empty containers. Tell them to give the child milk and to transport the child to the nearest emergency department for evaluation and therapeutic intervention if needed. Instruct them to save all emesis.

WHAT IS POISONING?

Poisoning is the ingestion, inhalation, absorption, or injection of a toxic substance that requires therapeutic intervention and that may demonstrate specific signs and symptoms. Poisoning is the most common pediatric emergency. More than 2 million poisonings occur in the United States each year; more than 5,000 of these result in death, with more than 500 of the deaths in children under 5 years of age. Unfortunately, the source of the poisoning is usually a common household product. Of all pediatric poisonings, 50% occur in the kitchen, 20% in the bathroom, and 10% in the bedroom.

In a child of less than 1 year poisoning is usually from an unintentional overdose by the parents or physician. In a child of 2 to 3 years poisoning is usually from older siblings "sharing" their find. Children of 3 to 4 years are usually poisoned as a result of the child's own curiosity and experimentation. In the preadolescents, poisoning is usually from

---

*This section is not designed to be a comprehensive guide to poisons but rather offers a broad overview. For more detailed information the reader is referred to Arena, J.M.: Poisoning: toxicology, symptoms, treatment, ed. 4, Springfield, Ill., 1976, Charles C Thomas, Publisher; Done, A.K.: The toxic emergency, Emerg. Med. **6:**289, 1974; the Poisindex (Rocky Mountain Poisoning Center, Denver); and local poison control centers. (See Directory of poison centers, Superintendent of Documents, Stch. No. 1712-0129, U.S. Government Printing Office, Washington, D.C. 20402.)

Drug cart for poisoning/overdose treatment room

Activated charcoal	Ipecac syrup
N-Acetylcysteine (Mucomyst)	Isoproterenol (Isuprel)
Ammonium chloride	Kayexalate
Amyl nitrate	Levarterenol (Levophed)
Apomorphine	Magnesium sulfate
Ascorbic acid	Mannitol
Atropine	Metaraminol (Aramine)
BAL	Methylene blue
Diphenhydramine (Benadryl)	Nalorphine (Nalline)
Deferoxamine	Naloxone (Narcan)
Dexamethasone (Decadron)	Pralidoxime (2-PAM, Protopam)
D-Penicillamine	Physostigmine (Eserine, Antilirium)
EDTA	Sodium sulfate
Ethanol	

"playing with drugs." In adolescents, poisoning may be the result of a suicide attempt.

Most substances are absorbed in 2 to 4 hours, and signs and symptoms of intoxication will be evident during absorption or shortly thereafter. It is therefore necessary to act promptly and knowledgeably. Therapeutic intervention should be performed in the following sequence.

THERAPEUTIC INTERVENTION

1. Airway
   a. The airway is always the first priority.
   b. Remember "Noisy breathing is obstructed breathing."
   c. Intubate the patient if necessary.
2. Breathing
   a. Assess the respiratory rate, depth, and symmetry; the lung sounds; and use of accessory muscles.
   b. Be prepared to perform mouth-to-mouth breathing or bag-valve-mask breathing.
   c. Check the odor of the breath (Table 26-2).
3. Circulation
   a. Check the pulses, perfusion and blood pressure.
   b. Be prepared to perform chest compression.
   c. Check the skin temperature, moisture, and color (Table 26-3).
   d. If the blood pressure is very low, use pediatric MAST.
4. Initiate IV D5W TKO wherever a vein can be found; the saphenous vein may be the best. Check for track marks.
5. Evaluate the neurologic status: level of consciousness and pupils (Table 26-4). Treat seizures with diazepam (Valium) IV.
6. Administer dextrose 50% and observe and document the result.
7. Administer naloxone (Narcan) and observe and document the result.

TABLE 26-2 Breath odors produced by poisons

Odor	Source
Acetone	Aspirin (salicylates), methanol, isopropyl alcohol
Alcohol	Alcohol, whiskey, wine, beer
Almonds (bitter)	Cyanide
Camphor	Camphor (mothballs)
Coal gas	Carbon monoxide
Ether	Ether
Garlic	Parathion, arsenic, phosphorus, thallium
Paraldehyde	Paraldehyde
Pears	Chloral hydrate
Pungent odor	Ethchlorvynol (Placidyl)
Shoe polish	Nitrobenzene
Sweet smell	Chloroform
Tobacco	Nicotine, marijuana, phencyclidine
Violets	Turpentine
Wintergreen	Methyl salicylate

TABLE 26-3 Skin stains caused by poisons

Skin stain	Cause
Black	Iodine
Blue-black	Silver nitrate
Brown	Bromides, methemoglobinemia
Gray	Mercuric chloride
Pink	Carbon monoxide
Red	Boric acid
White	Phenols
Yellow	Aniline, arsenic, arsine, benzene, carbon tetrachloride, chromates, fava beans, mushrooms, nitric acid, nitrobenzene, phenothiazines, phosphorus, picric acid, quinine, thiazide

TABLE 26-4 Causes of miosis and mitosis

Causes of miosis (constricted pupils)	Causes of mitosis (dilated pupils)
Barbiturates	Alcohol
Caffeine	Amphetamines
Chloral hydrate	Antihistamines
Ergot (and other sympatholytics)	Atropine (and other parasympatholytics)
Ipecac	Barium
Muscarine	Camphor (mothballs)
Nicotine	Carbon dioxide
Opiates	Carbon monoxide
Organophosphates	Cerebral anoxia
Parasympathomimetics	Chloroform
Pilocarpine	Cocaine
Physostigmine	Cyanide
Propoxyphene	Ether
	Glutethimide (Doriden)
	Isoproterenol (and other sympathomimetics)
	LSD
	Meperidine (Demerol)
	Papaverine
	Scopolamine
	Thallium
	Tricyclic antidepressants

8. Decontaminate the skin—check for skin color, skin burns, and stains. Remove insecticides, which are absorbed through the skin.
9. Prevent absorption by chemical or mechanical means.
10. Promote excretion by chemical means.
11. Treat cerebral edema with prophylactic dexamethasone (Decadron) and hypertonic solutions (urea, mannitol).
13. Check the temperature and correct metabolic abnormalities.
14. Evaluate the renal function and urinary output.
15. Control infection, especially aspiration pneumonia. Always transport the patient in the left lateral decubitus (swimmer's) and slight Trendelenburg's position to avoid aspiration of gastric contents and to delay gastric emptying.
16. Evaluate the blood, nasogastric aspirate, and urine for the presence of toxic substances.
17. Check the mouth for salivation, dryness, and lead lines.

Methods to prevent further absorption

CHEMICAL REMOVAL

Syrup of ipecac

Ipecac *extract* is 14 times stronger than the syrup; *do not use it*

Give 15 to 30 ml of *syrup* of ipecac (Not to children under 1 year of age)

Give 6 to 8 ounces or more of water (no milk or carbonated beverages)

Keep the child active

Observe closely

Emesis should occur within 15 minutes

Do not give ipecac in cases of hydrocarbon, corrosive material, or strychnine ingestion

Do not give ipecac to patients with
seizures or to unconscious patients
or patients with no gag reflex

} 3 Cs (when *not* to give ipecac): caustics,
convulsions, coma

NOTE: If the patient does not vomit, ipecac should be removed by gastric lavage (ipecac is cardiotoxic)

Apomorphine

Apomorphine may be used instead of ipecac

Give water before apomorphine

Give 0.1 mg/kg subcutaneously (6 mg tablet with 3 ml diluent equals 2 mg/ml)

Give naloxone 0.01 mg/kg IV when adequate emesis has occurred

Emesis should occur in 2 to 15 minutes

Do not induce emesis in cases of hydrocarbon, corrosive material, or strychnine ingestion

Do not induce emesis in patients having seizures, unconscious patients, or patients with no gag reflex

Do not use a discolored solution

Activated charcoal

There are no known contraindications or side effects

Give 15 to 30 g mixed with water

It may be taken orally or given through an Ewald tube

The following compounds are absorbed by activated charcoal*:

Alcohol	Ipecac	Phenolphthalein
Amphetamines	Malathion	Phenothiazine
Antimony	Mercuric chloride	Phosphorus
Antipyrine	Methylene blue	Potassium permanganate
Arsenic	Morphine	Quinidine
Barbiturates	Muscarine	Salicylates
Camphor	Nicotine	Selenium
Cantharides	Opium	Silver
Cocaine	Oxalates	Stramonium
Digitalis	Parathion	Strychnine
Glutethemide	Penicillin	Sulfonamides
Iodine	Phenol	

*Courtesy B. Rumack, Rocky Mountain Poison Center, Denver, Colo.

MECHANICAL REMOVAL

Lavage is used if the patient is unable to vomit, should not vomit, has no gag reflex, or is unconscious.

Do not lavage in cases of hydrocarbon (controversial), corrosive material, or strychnine ingestion.

In lavaging a child, always protect the airway.

The patient is intubated by an anesthesiologist or pediatrician skilled in pediatric intubation. First give 10 to 30 mg succinylcholine to induce paralysis if the patient is alert.

Place the patient in a left lateral decubitus and slight Trendelenburg's position; this allows for secretions to drain and decreases absorption by moving the gastric contents away from the pylorus.

Use a No. 28 to 36 French Ewald tube with large openings at the distal end. Place the tube through the mouth.

Use normal saline for lavage. Do not use water, which causes dilutional hyponatremia. Do not use oil-based lavage solutions, which increase the incidence of aspiration.

The solution should be slightly warmed.

Use 10 ml/kg for each lavage "round" (more may force ingested poison through the pylorus) until the fluid returned is clear, a total of 2 to 10 liters.

The initial returned fluid should be sent for toxicologic study.

CATHARTICS

Do not use magnesium-containing cathartics in renal failure. Do not use oil-based cathartics in pesticide poisonings.

Magnesium sulfate

Give 250 mg/kg orally
In adults give 50 ml of a 10% solution (5 g)

Antidotes
LOCAL ANTIDOTES

Acids
Alkalies
Iron

SYSTEMIC ANTIDOTES

Antidote	Given for
Activated charcoal	Many types of oral overdoses
Nalorphine	Narcotics
Naloxone	Narcotics
Atropine	Insecticides
BAL	Arsenic, cobalt, copper, lead
Nitrate thiosulfate	Cyanide
Deferoxamine	Iron
Physostigmine	Tricyclic antidepressants, antihistamines, poisonous plants
Oxygen	Carbon monoxide

Antidote	Given for
N-Acetylcysteine (Mucomyst)	Acetaminophen (Tylenol)
Atropine 0.5 to 1.0 mg initially then 2-PAM	Organophosphorus insecticides (parathion and malathion)
	Cyanide
Amyl nitrite	
Sodium nitrite*	
Sodium thiosulfate	Nitrites and nitrates
Methylene blue 0.2 mg/kg of 1% solution in water IV over 5 minutes	

OTHER METHODS OF EVACUATING POISONS

Hemodialysis
Peritoneal dialysis
Exchange transfusion, forced diuresis

AN APPROACH TO HYDROCARBON INGESTION†

1. If the patient has taken 1 ml/kg of hydrocarbon or less of a chlorinated or metal containing solvent, CNS or respiratory depression may occur. If depression has occurred do not induce vomiting, intubate with a cuffed endotracheal tube and perform gastric lavage, administer a cathartic, and provide other supportive measures.
2. If the patient has taken a possibly toxic amount and has a good gag reflex, has no CNS depression and is breathing normally, ipecac-induced emesis should be used. The time to remove a potentially lethal amount of material from the stomach is before CNS, respiratory, or cardiac depression occurs.
3. If the patient has clearly had less than 1 or 2 ml/kg of nonchlorinated or nonmetal-containing hydrocarbon, then catharsis with magnesium or sodium sulfate should be adequate.
4. Mineral oil or other oil-based cathartics should not be used as there is an increased risk of lipoid pneumonia. It has been clearly demonstrated that oils previously used to "thicken" ingested hydrocarbons do not work and provide some risk.
5. In any event, if there is any question as to aspiration, a chest x-ray film should be taken. It used to be thought that aspiration pneumonia occurred as a result of emesis because initial x-ray films showed a clear chest and after emesis a pneumonia. It is now obvious that this is not true and most aspirations occur on the way down, not up. X-ray films should be done at the first sign of aspiration and if negative should be repeated if the patient is symptomatic at 6 to 8 hours.
6. If the patient arrives coughing, then aspiration is almost a certainty. It may not be evident on chest x-ray films for 6 to 8 hours.
7. Steroids provide no assistance in treatment of aspiration and may cause harm.
8. Epinephrine is *contraindicated* as it may produce ventricular dysrhythmias.
9. Antibiotics provide no prophylactic benefit and should not be used unless infection is documented.

---

*Use caution with the dosage—for hemoglobin of 12 gm/100 ml, give 10 mg/kg immediately and 5 mg/kg in 30 minutes if needed.
†Courtesy B. Rumack, Rocky Mountain Poison Control Center.

SKIN DECONTAMINANTS

For pesticides, cyanides, caustics, acids, alkalies, and hydrocarbons on the skin, a combination of tincture green soap and lots of water is used for skin decontamination. If these substances get in the eyes, irrigation for 20 minutes (at home under the faucet or in the emergency department) is needed.

Aftercare instructions for parents

Discuss:
>   Follow-up care
>   Use of poison center for follow-up calls
>   Syrup of ipecac at home (do not use ipecac if the poison is caustic, there are convulsions, or there is coma)
>   Prevention:
>>   Keep all drugs, chemicals, cleaning fluids, pesticides, and so on out of reach of children and *locked up*
>>   Do not use food containers to store poisons
>>   Do not tell children that medicine is candy!
>>   Buy items with safety caps

INFANT BOTULISM

Infant botulism is a clinical condition caused by *Clostridium botulinum* toxin in the small intestine from ingestion of foods contaminated with the toxin (especially home-canned products).

SIGNS AND SYMPTOMS

Constipation (initial symptom)
Poor feeding
Severe vomiting
Decreased activity, hypotonia, and generalized weakness
Ophthalmoplegia
Respiratory paralysis (in severe cases)

THERAPEUTIC INTERVENTION

Differentiate from failure to thrive, Guillain-Barré syndrome, myasthenia gravis, or CNS disease
Obtain stool sample for toxin studies
Admit for stabilization of fluid and nutritional status and further study in neonatal intensive care setting
Administer botulism antitoxin: AB Bivalent* or polyvalent†

---

*Lederle Laboratories, Pearl River, N.Y.
†Available from the Center for Disease Control, Bacterial Disease Section, Atlanta. Telephone (404) 633-3111 (days), (404) 634-2561 (nights).

MEASLES

Measles has a 10- to 12-day incubation period. It is usually contracted from respiratory droplets. Measles is contagious from the fifth day of incubation through the first few days of the rash. Children with measles usually appear sick. They most commonly have an elevated temperature (102.2° F [39° to 40° C]) and have red spots with small white centers (Koplik's spots) that appear initially in the mouth on the buccal mucosa. The rash extends from the face to the feet and lasts a week to 10 days. This is often preceded by a fever, cough, and conjunctivitis.

Therapeutic intervention consists of antipyretic agents such as aspirin or acetaminophen and plenty of oral fluids.

VARICELLA (CHICKENPOX)

Varicella is caused by the same organism that causes herpes zoster. There is a 14- to 16-day incubation period. Varicella is contagious from 1 day before the appearance of the rash to 5 to 6 days after. Children with varicella appear to be mildly sick. The level of illness seems to parallel the amount of rash involved. The rash, which consists of macules, papules, and vesicles, occurs primarily on the trunk and extremities, although it is not uncommon to find some amount of rash on the face. Children with varicella usually develop a rash as the first sign of the disease. Occasionally they will have a slight fever for 1 or 2 days before the appearance of the rash. If a child is immunosuppressed there is great danger of severe illness. Hospital admission is required.

Therapeutic intervention includes administration of antipyretics and lots of oral fluids as well as other supportive therapy. The care giver should be sure that the child's fingernails are short to avoid bacterial infection when the child scratches the lesions. Calamine lotion may be applied to reduce itching.

EPIDEMIC PAROTIDITIS (MUMPS)

Mumps is contracted from the saliva of an infected person. The incubation period is from 14 to 21 days. Mumps is contagious up to 7 days before and 9 days after the parotid swelling is evident. It is seen as a generalized infection with parotiditis.

There is no specific therapeutic intervention except supportive measures until the swelling has gone down. In the postpubertal male mumps could possibly cause orchiditis.

TRAUMA

Trauma is the leading cause of death in children. Therapeutic intervention is the same as for an adult (see Chapters 15 through 24):

Assure ABCs

Protect the cervical spine

Control bleeding

Check neurologic status

Splint fractures

Hypovolemia is treated with Ringer's lactate IV (20 ml/kg in 5 to 10 minutes) and pediatric MAST

Pay special attention to head trauma. Children, especially infants, have an increased incidence of brain injury because of a less protective skull. In an infant head trauma may cause hypovolemic shock because the infant has a large distendable head and small blood volume.

Child abuse

Child abuse was not recognized as a common cause of trauma in children for many years. It is estimated that there are 50,000 to 70,000 cases of child abuse each year in the United States. Of the known cases, 49% are reported by hospitals and physicians, 23% by police, 12% by schools, and 16% by others (sometimes the parents themselves). Child abuse is restricted to no certain social class or ethnic group.

Child abuse takes many forms and may consist of physical abuse, physical neglect, emotional abuse, emotional neglect, verbal assault, sexual assault, or any combination of these. These following are common clinical findings in abused children:

Suspicious fractures in children less than 3 years old
Frequent multiple injuries
Bites
Cigarette burns (especially on the buttocks and bottoms of the feet)
Rope marks (strangling)
Genital and perineal injuries
Burns
Subdural hematoma
Intraabdominal injuries
Abrasions
Ecchymoses (Fig. 26-1)
Bruises
Lacerations
"Failure to thrive"
Retinal detachment
Suffocation
Starvation

The following are common findings in parents of abused children:

Contradictory stories regarding child's injury
Evasive answers to questions
No volunteering of information regarding the injury
Anger directed at child for being injured
Little concern for the child with decreased touching and looking at the child
Inappropriate response to the child crying
Bringing child to the emergency department frequently for nonspecific problems
Use of different emergency departments to prevent discovery of the abuse pattern

THERAPEUTIC INTERVENTION

Report *suspected* child abuse to the appropriate agency
The child should be placed in custody if child abuse is suspected
Undress the child

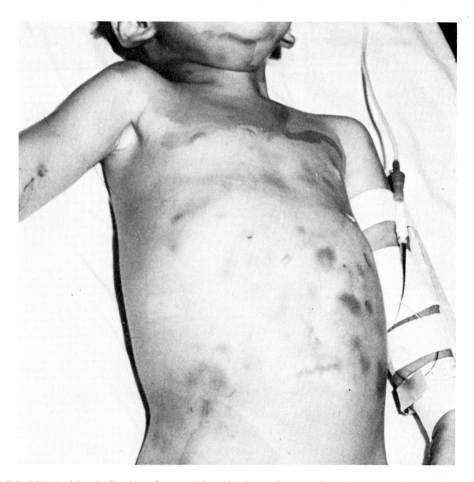

FIG. 26-1 Bruising indicative of nonaccidental injury; also note burn in upper chest and neck region. (Courtesy Dr. Gabriel Rosenburg, Methodist Hospital of Indiana; from Weller, C.M.R.: J.E.N. 3[2]:17, 1977.)

Perform a skeletal survey
Perform a hematologic survey
Perform an eye examination
Perform a neurologic examination
Perform an abdominal examination
Perform a chest examination
Perform a developmental evaluation

HELPFUL INFORMATION IN REPORTING CHILD ABUSE*

Name of victim:
Address and phone:

---

*Courtesy Sgt. Carol Walker Brown, Child Abuse Unit, Los Angeles County Sheriff's Department, Los Angeles, Calif.

Birthdate of victim:
Describe suspected abuse injury:
Cause of injury:
Extent of injury:
Circumstances surrounding incident:
Location of incident with date and time:
Name of suspect:
Suspect's address (home and work):
Suspect's phone (home and work):
Name of informant, address, and phone:
Description of child:
Various names used by child:
Names of parties living at home:
Day and time incident reported and to whom:
Children removed to and by whom:
Remember you are reporting a suspected child abuse case, and police staff are available
for ad hoc consultation.

INDICES OF SUSPICION OF CHILD MALTREATMENT*

A. History
1. An unexplained injury in a young child; especially a fracture in a child under two years of age.
2. An accident history that does not adequately account for the child's injury.
3. An accident history inconsistent with the development age of the child.
4. History of a previous accident, easy bruising, or frequent falling in a young child.
5. X-ray evidence of unsuspected skeletal trauma.

B. Observations
1. Failure to thrive (height and/or weight in less than third percentile).
2. Developmental retardation.
3. Evidence of disturbed parent-child interaction; lack of attachment of child to mother and inappropriate maternal empathy.

C. Physical examination
1. Skin and subcutaneous tissues—(a) cradle cap, diaper rash, uncleanliness, and other evidence of unconcern or unawareness of infant needs; (b) cigarette burns, bite marks, belt lashes; (c) ecchymoses, hematomas, abrasions, and lacerations unusual for the child's developmental age; (d) injury of external genitalia; (e) marks on neck from strangling by hands or rope; (f) external ears traumatized by pinching, twisting, and pulling; (g) unusual skin rashes that defy dermatologic diagnosis; (h) burns, particularly of the soles of the feet and buttocks.
2. Skeletal system—(a) tenderness, swelling, and limitation of motion of an extremity; (b) periosteal thickening; (c) deformities of long bones.
3. Head—(a) cephalhematomas; (b) biparietal bruising suggesting subdural hematomas; (c) irregularities of contour resulting from skull fractures; (d) signs of intracranial trauma.
4. Eyes—(a) subconjunctival hemorrhages; (b) traumatic cataracts; (c) retinal hemorrhage; (d) papilledema.

---

*Courtesy Sgt. Carol Walker Brown, Child Abuse Unit, Los Angeles County Sheriff's Department, Los Angeles, Calif.

5. Ears—ruptured ear drums from blows to the head.
6. Face—(a) periorbital ecchymoses; (b) displaced nasal cartilages; (c) bleeding from nasal septum; (d) fractures of the mandible.
7. Mouth—(a) lacerated frenulum of upper lip; (b) loosened or missing teeth; (c) burns of lips and tongue.
8. Chest—(a) deformity of chest and limitation of motion by fractured ribs; (b) subcutaneous emphysema; (c) hemothorax.

THE SEXUALLY ABUSED CHILD

Sexual abuse of children, although not rare, is very often not reported. It has been estimated that one third of all children have experienced some form of sexual abuse (during childhood or adolescence). The incident is most likely to be reported if it was a single incident performed by a stranger. The better the child knows the person committing the assault, the less likely he is to tell anyone that it happened. It has also been estimated that 50% to 80% of assaults are performed by persons who are familiar to the child.

Parents of sexually assaulted children often have feelings of disbelief, shock, alarm, confusion, embarrassment, anger, fear, and guilt. The child can have very confusing reactions, as he may confuse his feelings with what others are feeling. The initial interview in the emergency department can set the tone for the entire process of dealing with the incident. The primary goals of therapeutic intervention are to care for the immediate medical needs of the child, to prevent further harm from coming to the child, and to help the child and the family to deal with this crisis.

The parents and the child should be interviewed separately. This allows for the parents to become emotional without fear of transmitting their emotions to the child. Interview techniques will vary with a child in accordance with age. Avoid questions that deal with the actual sexual assault initially. Attempt to make the child feel comfortable. It is better to have a single interviewer rather than many. When questioning the child about the sexual assault, use a direct approach. It is frequently helpful to have a doll in the room so that the child can point to anatomic areas in his conversation. Occasionally when the child is reluctant to talk play therapy may be indicated, perhaps reversing roles and having the child play the doctor or nurse trying to find out why the child (now played by the doctor or nurse) came to the hospital and what happened.

Unless the child is very young, it is usually preferable to perform the physical examination in private. Allow the child to remain dressed until just before the examination. Proceed with the normal examination for a rape patient, paying particular attention to the fact that the child is not an adult, using smaller instruments, and explaining procedures in terms that the child will understand.

In the male child pay particular attention to the penis, as damage to the urethra is common. Also, in both males and females, examine the rectum and anal region carefully for evidence of trauma.

After the physical examination the examiner should take the time to answer specific questions the child may have. The parents should then be allowed to know the findings of the physical examination. It is important at this time to stress that follow-up care is very beneficial for both the child and the family. Of course the family will probably be concerned as to whether the assault will have a deep psychologic effect on the child.

Encourage them to seek follow-up care—even make the appointments for them and call them in subsequent days to see how they and the child are doing.

Cases of sexual assault of children must be reported to law-enforcement agencies. It is up to the parents as to whether or not they wish to speak with the police or have their child speak with the police.

SUDDEN INFANT DEATH SYNDROME

Sudden infant death syndrome (SIDS), or crib death, is the sudden, unexpected death of an apparently healthy baby. It usually occurs in infants between the ages of 1 to 24 months, with peak incidence being at 2 to 3 months. There are several theories as to why SIDS occurs. The most prominent, though unproved, of these are that SIDS is caused by:

A disorder (apnea) of sleep

Nasal congestion (infants are obligate nose breathers)

Laryngeal spasms

On postmortem examination of SIDS victims some of the more common findings are:

Frothy sputum in the mouth and nose

Emesis

Small height and weight for age

Empty bladder and rectum

Petechiae on lungs

Pulmonary congestion

Dilated right heart

THERAPEUTIC INTERVENTION

As there is usually nothing that can be done to save the infant despite rigorous resuscitation efforts, most therapeutic intervention will be directed toward the grieving parents. The most common reaction by parents of a child who dies of SIDS is complete devastation. There are many guilty feelings and much self-blame or blame of the other parent, especially if one parent is away at the time of the infant's death. There is a very high incidence of divorce among parents with infants who have died from SIDS.

It is important, after some preparatory counseling, to state that the baby is dead and has died from SIDS. Let the parents know that SIDS is a common cause of death in infancy and that there was nothing they could have done to prevent it. It is important to let them know that it is not a hereditary disease and that their other children have no greater chance of it.

It is important to arrange for an autopsy and to inform the parents that they will be notified of the cause of death within 48 hours. SIDS is now accepted as a cause of death, and the death certificate of the child should state so. Usually once the parents receive notification of the official cause of death it is wise to schedule another counseling session with them. If this is beyond the capabilities of the hospital staff, the family may be referred to the National Foundation for Sudden Infant Death Syndrome at telephone number (312) 663-0650. The number of a local SIDS parent group can be obtained from the national group, or refer to the list provided for addresses and numbers of regional organizations.

**REGIONAL CENTERS FOR SUDDEN INFANT DEATH SYNDROME (SIDS)—
INFORMATION AND COUNSELING (JULY 1, 1977)***

Alabama

SIDS Information and Counseling Project
248 Cox Street
Mobile, Alabama 36604
Telephone: (205) 431-1631, x32
Project Director: George Newburn, MD
Project Administrator: John R. Williamson, MPH
Director of Public Health Nurses: Joy Rolison, RN
Area Served: eight counties in SW Alabama, including Mobile
Sponsored by: Mobile County Board of Health

Arkansas

Arkansas SIDS Project
Arkansas Department of Health
4815 West Markham
Little Rock, Arkansas 72201
Telephone: (501) 661-2242
Project Director: J.B. Norton, MD
Project Coordinator: Glenda Donaldson, RN
Area Served: State of Arkansas
Sponsored by: Arkansas Department of Health

California

SIDS Information and Counseling Project
2151 Berkeley Way
Berkeley, California 94704
Telephone: (415) 843-7900, x367
Project Director: Warren Hawes, MD
Nursing Consultant: Carol Cook, RN
Area Served State of California
Sponsored by: California State Department of Health

Colorado

SIDS Center
4210 E. 11 Avenue
Denver, Colorado 80220
Telephone: (303) 861-8888, x2381
Project Director: Susan Williams, RN
Program Coordinator: Susan Perron
Area Served: State of Colorado
Sponsored by: Colorado Department of Health

---

*From Beckwith, J.B.: The sudden infant death syndrome, DHEW Publication No. (HSA) 75-5137, 1975.

Connecticut
Management Program for SIDS
79 Elm Street
Hartford, Connecticut 06115
Telephone: (203) 566-3286
Project Director: Carol A. Christoffers, RN
Area Served: State of Connecticut
Sponsored by: Connecticut State Department of Health

Florida
SIDS Information and Counseling Project
1323 Winewood Boulevard
Tallahassee, Florida 32301
Telephone: (904) 488-2834
Project Director: Emily Gates, MD
Project Coordinator: J. Robert Griffin
Area Served: State of Florida
Sponsored by: State Department of Health and Rehabilitation Services

Illinois
SIDS Regional Center
2160 South 1st Avenue
Maywood, Illinois 60153
Telephone: (312) 531-3374
Project Director: Louis E. Gibson, MD
Counseling Director: Milda Dargis
Area Served: Chicago, Illinois (Cook County)
Sponsored by: Loyola University, Stritch School of Medicine

SIDS Information and Counseling Project
535 West Jefferson Street
Springfield, Illinois 62761
Telephone: (217) 782-2736
Project Director: Joseph Kihn, MSW
Health Educator: Nancy Reining
Area Served: State of Illinois excluding Chicago (Cook county)
Sponsored by: Illinois Department of Public Health

Iowa
SIDS Information and Counseling Project
Lucas State Office Building
Des Moines, Iowa 50310
Telephone (515) 281-3732
Project Director: Roger Chapman
Public Health Educator: Monica Eischen
Area Served: State of Iowa
Sponsored by: Iowa State Department of Health

Maryland
Central Maryland SIDS Center
645 West Redwood Street
Baltimore, Maryland 21201
Telephone: (301) 528-5062
Project Director: Sanford B. Friedman, MD
Project Administrator: Stanley Weinstein, MSW
Counseling Director: Denise Thornton
Area served: Baltimore and 12 surrounding counties (90% of State's population)
Sponsored by: University of Maryland

Massachusetts
Regional Center for SIDS
Boston City Hospital
818 Harrison Avenue
Boston, Massachusetts 02118
Telephone: (617) 424-5742
Project Directors: Frederick Mondell, M.D., and Robert M. Reece, M.D.
Nursing Coordinator: Jill McAnulty, RN
Area Served: State of Massachusetts
Sponsored by: Trustees of Health and Hospitals of the City of Boston

Michigan
SIDS Information and Counseling Project
Michigan Medical-Legal Research and Educational Association, Inc.
400 East Lafayette Street
Detroit, Michigan 48226
Telephone (313) 963-1528
Project Director: Werner Spitz, MD
Project Coordinator: Zoë Smialek, RN
Area Served: Wayne County (with services being extended)
Sponsored by: Michigan Medical-Legal Research and Educational Association, Inc.

Minnesota
SIDS Information and Counseling Project
2525 Chicago Avenue South
Minneapolis, Minnesota 55404
Telephone: (612) 874-6285
Project Director: Ralph Franciosi, MD
Project Coordinator: Kathleen Fernback
Area Served: State of Minnesota
Sponsored by: Children's Health Center

Missouri
St. Louis SIDS Project
525 University Club Building
607 North Grand Boulevard
St. Louis, Missouri 63103
Telephone: (314) 531-4100
Project Directors: Laura Hillman, MD, and George Gantner, MD
Service Coordinator: Marjory J. Mathews
Area Served: St. Louis City and County; Franklin County; Jefferson County; St. Charles County
Sponsored by: St. Louis Regional Maternal and Child Health Council

New Hampshire
New Hampshire SIDS Management Project
61 South Spring Street
Concord, New Hampshire 03301
Telephone: (603) 271-2492
Project Director: Samuel W. Dooley, MD
Project Coordinator: Denis G. Demers
Area Served: State of New Hampshire
Sponsored by: State Health Department, Bureau of Maternal and Child Health

New Jersey
New Jersey SIDS Program
P.O. Box 1540
Trenton, New Jersey 08625
Telephone: (609) 292-5617
Project Director: Margaret Gregory, MD
Project Coordinator: Patricia Dorsa, MSW
Area Served: State of New Jersey
Sponsored by: New Jersey Department of Health

New Mexico
SIDS Information and Counseling Project
University of New Mexico
School of Medicine
Albuquerque, New Mexico 87131
Telephone: (505) 277-2861
Project Director: James T. Weston, MD
Project Coordinator: Beverly White
Area Served: State of New Mexico
Sponsored by: University of New Mexico School of Medicine

New York

Information and Counseling in Cases of SIDS in New York City
Office of Chief Medical Examiner
40 Worth Street
New York, New York 10013
Telephone: (212) 684-1600
Project Director: Dominic DiMao, MD
                Jean Pakter, MD
Program Coordinator: Joan Hagen
Area Served: New York City
Sponsored by: Medical and Health Research Association of New York, Inc.

Genesee Region SIDS Program
601 Elmwood Avenue
Rochester, New York 14642
Telephone: (716) 263-6015
Project Directors: Margaret Colgan, MD, and Robert Hoekelman, MD
Project Coordinator: Jeannie Healy
Area Served: 8 counties surrounding Rochester, New York (Genesee Health Service
    Area)
Sponsored by: University of Rochester School of Medicine

SIDS Information and Counseling Project
Health Sciences Center
State University of New York
Stonybrook, New York 11794
Telephone: (516) 444-2080
Project Director: Marvin Kuschner, MD
Project Coordinator: Sandi Boshak
Area Served: Suffolk and Nassau Counties
Sponsored by: Research Foundation, State University of New York

North Carolina

SIDS Information and Counseling Project
Division of Health Services
P.O. Box 2488
Chapel Hill, North Carolina 27514
Telephone: (919) 966-2253
Project Director: Page Hudson, MD
Project Coordinator: Ruth Ann Yauger, RN
Area Served: State of North Carolina
Sponsored by: State of North Carolina
    Office of the Chief Medical Examiner

Ohio

A Program for SIDS in Ohio
408 E. Town Street
Columbus, Ohio 43216
Telephone: (614) 466-2253
Project Director: John H. Ackerman, MD
Project Administrator: Robert M. Mai, MPH
Area Served: State of Ohio
Sponsored by: Ohio Department of Health

Pennsylvania
Delaware Valley SIDS Community Resource Center
One Children's Center
Philadelphia, Pennsylvania 19104
Telephone: (215) 387-6000, x240
Project Director: George Peckham, MD
Program Coordinator: Leo Lefebrve
Area Served: Philadelphia and Chester, Montgomery, Delaware, and Bucks Counties
Sponsored by: Children's Hospital of Philadelphia

Rhode Island
SIDS Information and Counseling Project
Rhode Island Department of Health
75 Davis Street, Room 302
Providence, Rhode Island 02908
Telephone: (401) 277-2231
Project Director: J.E. Cannon, MD
Project Coordinator: Neil Young
Area Served: State of Rhode Island
Sponsored by: Rhode Island Department of Health

Texas
SIDS Information and Counseling Project
2370 Rice Boulevard
P.O. Box 25249
Houston, Texas 77005
Telephone: (713) 526-1841
Project Director: Francine Jensen, MD
Project Coordinator: Ceretha S. Cartwright
Area Served: Houston County and surrounding areas
Sponsored by: Harris County Health Department

Utah
SIDS Information and Counseling Project
44 Medical Drive
Salt Lake City, Utah 84113
Telephone: (801) 328-6111
Project Director: Willis C. Sutliff, MD
Project Nurse: Roberta Mahin, RN
Area Served: State of Utah
Sponsored by: State of Utah Department of Health

Vermont
Information and Counseling for SIDS
115 Colchester Avenue
Burlington, Vermont 05401
Telephone: (802) 862-5701, x311
Project Director: Roberta R. Coffin, MD
Project Nurse: Cheryl Cyr, RN
Area Served: State of Vermont
Sponsored by: Vermont Department of Health

Washington
SIDS Northwest Regional Center
4800 Sand Point Way, NE
Seattle, Washington 98105
Telephone: (206) 634-5323
Project Director: Nora E. Davis, MD
Area Served: 22 western counties of Washington State
Sponsored by: Children's Orthopedic Hospital and Medical Center

Inland Empire Regional Centers SIDS
  Information and Counseling
West 1115 Mallon Avenue
Spokane, Washington 99201
Telephone: (509) 456-3630
Project Director: F. Lee Mellish
Project Coordinator: Merilyn Lloyd, PHN
Area Served: 17 counties of eastern Washington; 10 counties of northern Idaho; and 8
  counties of western Montana
Sponsored by: Spokane County Health District

SUGGESTED READINGS

Budassi, S.A., and Barber, J.M.: Emergency nursing: principles and practice, St. Louis, 1981, The C.V. Mosby
  Co.
Dube, S.K. and Pierog, S.H., editors: Immediate care of the sick and injured child, St. Louis, 1978, The C.V.
  Mosby Co.
Gaffney, K.: The pre-schooler in the emergency department, J.E.N. **2**(6):15, 1976.
Gorman, R.J.: Febrile seizures, Am. Fam. Physician **19:**101, 1979.
Hansen, M.: Accident or child abuse? challenge to the emergency department nurse, J.E.N. **2**(1):13 1976.
Melker, R.: CPR in infants and children. In Auerbach, P.A., and Budassi, S.A., editors: Cardiac arrest and
  CPR, ed. 2, Rockville, Md., 1983, Aspen Systems Corp.
Miles, M.S.: SIDS: parents are the patients, J.E.N. **3:**29, 1977.
Pascoe, D., and Grossman, M.: Quick reference to pediatric emergencies, Philadelphia, 1973, J.B. Lippincott
  Co.
Resnick, R., and Hergenroeder, E.: Children and the emergency room, Nurs. Dig. **4**(6):37, 1976.
Rosman, N.P.: Pediatric head injuries, Pediatr. Ann. **7:**55, 1978.
Schwartz, G.R., et al., editors: Principles and practice of emergency medicine, 2 vols., Philadelphia, 1978,
  W.B. Saunders Co.
Singer, H.S., et al.: Head trauma for the pediatrician, Pediatrics **62:**819, 1978.
Smith, C.A.: The critically ill child: diagnosis and management, ed. 2, Philadelphia, 1977, W.B. Saunders Co.
Toloukian, R.J., editor: Pediatric trauma, New York, 1978, John Wiley & Sons, Inc.
Weller, C.M.R.: Assessing the non-accidental injury, J.E.N. **3**(2):17, 1977.

PSYCHIATRIC EMERGENCIES

CHAPTER 27

Psychiatric emergencies

The goal of emergency care of the mentally incapacitated patient is to describe that patient in accordance with his perceived or real behavior and to intervene in terms of short-term management or referral. The care giver should also determine whether the problem is organic in nature or is a functional impairment. Organic problems are usually caused by metabolic or neurologic problems. The patient with an organic illness may be disoriented or confused and have a decreased sensorium, a recent, very sudden memory loss, and visual disturbances.

GENERAL MANAGEMENT TECHNIQUES

The care giver must first identify the nature and severity of the patient's presenting problem. Often the care giver must rely on the patient's family or friends for this information. There are certain key questions that should be answered:

What were the events that led up to this condition?

Was there some thing or event that triggered it?

Why is this person coming for help now?

Who brought the patient in?

What does the patient expect from this visit?

In the interview of the patient:

Appear calm and collected

Set firm limits on the patient

Do not allow the patient to ramble

Be sure that help is nearby should be patient become physically dangerous to himself or others

Try to decrease the patient's anxiety

Accept the patient's behavior as fact; do not agree or disagree with him

Be clear in your explanations to the patient as to what is happening

Be honest with the patient about your therapeutic plan

MENTAL STATUS EXAMINATION

Patients who come to the emergency department with a chief complaint that may represent a psychiatric problem should have a mental status examination performed. A mental status examination should include the following parameters:

TABLE 27-1 The mental status examination

Examination	Anxiety	Depression	Schizophrenia	Manic	Depression	Organic brain syndrome
General and orientation	Active Diaphoretic Oriented	Slow Oriented	Unkempt Detached; odd Oriented	Hyperactive Funny ? Oriented	Inactive Morbid ? Oriented	Variable Level Disoriented
Mood	Anxious Uptight Afraid	Depressed	Odd Anxious or depressed	Manic	Depressed	Variable
Affect	Moderately increased	Moderately decreased	Flat	Greatly increased	Greatly decreased	Variable
Associations	OK Rapid	OK Slowed	Loose	Fast Loose	Slow	Labile
Intelligence	OK	OK	May be decreased	Seems increased	Decreased	Impaired
Memory: Recent Remote	OK Dissociated	OK	OK	? OK	? OK	Loss OK
Thought process	Rapid	Slow	Increased or decreased Hallucinations Delusions	Speedy Hallucinations Delusions	Slow	Increased or decreased Hallucinations Delusions
Thought content	Preoccupied Uptight	Preoccupied Sad; blue	Bizarre	Wild Funny	Morbid Awful Suicidal	Variable Fear
Abstract thinking	OK	OK	Concrete	Fair	Poor	Poor
Insight	Varies	Varies	None	Poor	Poor	Poor
Judgment	OK	OK	Impaired	Bad	Awful	Poor

Used with permission of Gerald C. Crarey, MD, Associate Director, Department of Emergency Medicine, Los Angeles County/University of Southern California Medical Center, Los Angeles, Calif.

General:
  Level of consciousness
  Motor behavior
  Age
  Sex
  Marital status
  Relationship to others
  Orientation to time, place, person, reason for being there
Mood:
  What is the predominant emotion the patient is displaying?
Affect:
  Does the patient have a flat, normal, or increased affect?
Associations:
  Does the patient have normal progression of ideas? Are ideas and thoughts loose
      or illogical?
Intellect:
  Is the patient slow? Normal? Bright?
Memory:
  Is the patient's memory poor? Good?
Thought processes:
  Are thought processes normal? Is the patient having hallucinations or delusions? Is
      he confused?
Content of thoughts:
  Does the patient have phobias? Is the patient constantly repeating himself? Is the
      patient obsessive? Compulsive? Suicidal? Preoccupied?
Abstract thinking:
  Can the patient interpret proverbs correctly?
Insight and judgment:
  Can the patient answer questions of judgment rationally?

STRESS

Stress is a state that is always present but is intensified when there is a change or threat
with which the individual must cope. The effects of stress have both personal and environmental implications. Using stress as a motivating force can help both the patient and
the health care provider. Unchanneled, stress can be inhibiting and debilitating. In the
emergency care setting a patient and his significant others may anticipate or actually feel
pain, injury, disability, disfigurement, or death. There is a fear of the unknown, the
known, the unpredictable, the predictable, and the suddenness of the illness or injury, all
of which add a great deal to the level of stress.

A concept of stress can be formed by considering certain assumptions, for example,
that stress is:
A universal human experience
Essential for life and growth
Always present to some degree, since every individual is continually adapting to
    internal and external environmental changes

A response to living

Subject to individual response and stimulus specificity

A human state that produces specific signs and symptoms of structure and function

Measurable qualitatively and quantitatively

Growth promoting or growth impeding

Considered psychologic when it focuses on the meaning of a stimulus and its *antici-pated* capacity to produce harm

Considered physiologic when it focuses on the harm or disturbance to tissue structure or function that has *already* occurred

A stressor is a factor or agent that is perceived as a threat to existence or life-style and thereby causes an increase in the stress state. Assumptions regarding stressors include that they are:

A source of motivation for change

Categorized by origin: social, psychologic, or physical

Uniquely perceived by each individual

The product of perception and not the cause of it

A condition that imposes a demand on the individual for adjustment

Some generalized sources of stressors can be identified:

Sense of helplessness

Sense of hopelessness

Diminished ability to meet expectations of self or others

Diminished ability to function

Sense of isolation or alienation

Threat to identity through altered body image (real or imagined)

Loss of control (real or imagined)

Pain (emotional or physical)

Change in status (real or imagined)

Loss of someone or something important (a person, pet, home, job, or health)

Factors that influence stress response include:

Cognitive activity

Personality traits

Past experiences

Cultural learning

Present level of energy

Genetic influences

Past coping patterns

Situational factors

Environmental factors

Biologic variables

Classes of response to stressors include:

Affective

Motor-behavioral

Alteration of cognitive functioning

Physiologic changes

All responses to stressors (mental, emotional, cognitive, and somatic) consume energy. There is no correlation between the intensity of the stressor and the coping behavior used by an individual.

Assessment of stress level

Assessment of an individual's stress state is done by observation, interactional data, and clinical data. People respond to stress in a holistic manner, but the central nervous system and endocrine system create the most specific physiologic indices. Baseline information about blood pressure, pulse rate, and respiratory rate provide parameters for assessment of stress level, but an ongoing comparison of these parameters is needed since none of them shows an absolute increase or decrease during periods of increased stress.

LABORATORY INDICES

Increase in 17-ketosteroid level (obtained by 24-hour urine sampling)
Shift in potassium/sodium ratio
Decrease in eosinophils
Increase in epinephrine in short-term stress period
Increase in norepinephrine in depressed person (longer term stress)

OBSERVATIONAL AND INTERACTIONAL INDICES

Identification of stressors:
    Origin
    Number
    Duration
Assessment of patient:
    Degree of perceived threat
    Past experience with comparable stressors
    Physical and psychologic energy reserve
    Resources, capabilities, and potential
    Personality variables
    Level of anxiety (Table 27-2)
    Appearance and physical history
Evaluation of environment:
    Situational constraints   Social controls
    Cultural restraints   Support systems available

ANXIETY

Anxiety is a diffuse response that alerts an individual to an impending threat, real or imagined. Fear is a natural psychologic and physiologic response to an actual threat. Fear is object focused, but anxiety is "faceless fear"—no identifiable object can be isolated.

The cause of anxiety is any perceived threat to the security of an individual. The origin may be because of:
    Biologic factors:
        Alteration in homeostasis
        Lack of food, water, shelter, clothing
        Fear of illness, injury, surgery, old age, pain

Psychologic factors:
　　Decreased self-esteem
　　Death or loss of a loved one or thing
　　Pain
　　Real or imagined rejection or abandonment
Sociologic factors:
　　Inability to meet expectations of role, status, values
　　Inability to maintain sense of belonging

THERAPEUTIC INTERVENTION FOR ANXIETY

The goal of intervention with the patient who is experiencing an anxiety reaction is to promote an environment in which the patient can achieve an adequate degree of self-control.

To decrease anxiety:
　　Provide general support
　　Have the patient talk
　　Keep calm and appear calm
　　Direct the patient toward reality
　　Assist the patient in setting priorities
　　Help the patient identify the source of his anxiety
　　Let the patient have some control of the situation
　　Use consultations and referrals when necessary

LEVELS OF ANXIETY

mild—Usually a productive state; use this situation as an information-sharing relationship.

moderate—May be productive but expands more energy than is necessary; use this as a directive-supportive relationship.

serious—Usually nonproductive and even counterproductive; the care giver must take control of the situation. Give direct commands in short, simple sentences, and focus on intellectual functioning.

severe—Crippling to witness and experience, and rapidly becomes contagious. Isolate the individual from others (use physical restraints if needed). Do not leave the patient alone. Be supportive but firm.

terror—A "do-or-die" situation; assume total responsibility for the patient. Take over total care.

MANAGEMENT STRATEGIES TO USE WITH THE ANGRY BELLIGERENT PATIENT*

I. Why do people get angry?

　　A. *The helpless child:* Under stress (such as pain or illness), many people feel helpless like a child. They then become angry with "parental" figures (e.g., physicians and nurses) who they see as not taking care of them.
　　　Strategy: Decrease the stress by telling the patient that you are interested in taking care of him.

　　B. *The temper tantrum:* Many people have learned that anger will get them what they

---

*Courtesy Dr. Regina Pally, Los Angeles.

TABLE 27-2 Assessment guide for level of anxiety

Level of anxiety	Auditory and visual perception	Spatial and temporal perception	Power of concentration	Cognitive processes	Objectively observable processes
Normal: mild anxiety, productive	Hearing keener, vision keener	Aware of surroundings; past, present, and future balanced	Alert, focus on reality, relationships connected with ease	Rational, logical, critical, problem-solving intact	Mildly tense, in control of environment, fine and gross motor movement coordinated, affect congruent and spontaneous
Anxiety: Moderate anxiety, productive but decreased return for energy used	Normal hearing decreased, limited focusing ability, peripheral vision decreased, distant vision lost	Environmental field normal, past and present oriented	Single topic focus, selective inattention, relationships connected with difficulty	Single thought slower and scattered, needs guidance in use of logic, minimal problem-solving ability	Blood pressure and pulse increased, respiration decreased, dry mouth, constricted pupils, tense and concerned, takes longer to complete tasks, accelerated speech, hyperactivity affect congruent but forced, diarrhea or indigestion
Anguish: Serious anxiety, counter productive	Limited hearing, focus on one detail or scattered	Environmental field greatly reduced, past oriented	Focus on minor details, relationships minimal	Fragmented thought process, illogical, nondiscriminating	Respiration rate increased, respiration depth decreased, marginal control, motor activity useless and purposeless, dilated pupils, affect inappropriate or rigid, nausea, vomiting or diarrhea
Panic: Severe anxiety, exhausting, debilitating	Rapid observation (scanning) or limited to one distorted detail	Gross distortion of environment, no perception of details, present oriented	Loss of reality, attention to one distorted detail	Confluent thought processes blocked, lack of memory power	Inability to make decisions, obvious bewilderment, lack of control of self, and environment, cool, clammy skin, startled facial expression
Terror: Death producing	Vision gone, hearing acutely increased or diminished	Incapable of response, "frozen with fear"	All human powers and behavioral patterns absent, unable to attend to self or environment		Sitting or lying in one position, state of fugue, whole-body tremors, twisted, contorted expression

want. For example, a child throws a temper tantrum to get ice cream and his mother gives it to him just to stop the screaming. The child learns he will get his ice cream if he yells loud enough. (You can see how this might apply to the patient demanding pain medication.)

Strategy: Point out to the patient that his anger will not get him what he wants but will in fact make it more difficult for those trying to help him.

C. *Scapegoating:* Sometimes when you are feeling angry with one person, you end up taking it out on another. Patients do the same thing.

Strategy: If the patient's anger seems out of proportion to the situation, *you might* ask who he is really angry at.

D. *Inadvertent provocative behavior:* Sometimes without realizing it, you may be talking in such a way as to provoke someone's anger toward you (especially with nonverbal gestures, facial expressions, or tone of voice).

Strategy: Be aware of both verbal and nonverbal communication.

II. Additional tools

A. *Bullfight technique:* Agree with the *reality* aspects of the patient's anger. ("Yes, you really have a point there, you have been waiting for the doctor for a long time.")

B. *Engage the patient as an ally in his own treatment.* ("Given the realistic limitations we are under, how do you think we can best help your situation?") Ask the patient for suggestions.

C. *"Show your jugular."* ("I'm just as upset by this impersonal emergency room as you are.")

D. *Make yourself a person, not an impersonal target.* ("It really upsets me when you get angry like this, and makes it harder for me to help you.")

E. *Suggestion box technique.* ("Could you write down your complaints?")

F. *Set firm limits and expectations of behavior.* Point out clearly the consequences to the patient of not keeping within those limits. ("You know, if you keep acting like this, we will have to call the security guards.")

G. *Time-out:* Give the person a private place to get angry and hostile and tell him to come back when he has cooled off.

PSYCHIATRIC AND PSYCHOLOGIC EMERGENCIES

Psychiatric problems come under emergency management when an individual's anxiety has increased beyond self-management levels. The health team's most important function is to establish in the patient and those family members or friends who come with him the feeling that capable assistance to establish self-control is available. Patients come to the emergency department with problems in living, feelings of inadequacy, marital discord, and other interpersonal dysfunctions. Some individuals are obviously both out of self-control and out of contact with reality. The primary concern of the emergency department nonmedical personnel is not to specify an etiology or give a label to the presenting syndrome but to facilitate an evaluation of the degree of dysfunction and amount of contact with reality so that immediate treatment is made or referral to another resource for more extensive treatment is accomplished.

The management procedures outlined are not physician oriented and can be carried out by various levels of technically trained emergency personnel.

General approach to the patient who is mentally disturbed

Remember that illness has three components:

Physical

Psychologic

Sociologic

In dealing with the patient with mental illness:

Establish good rapport

Establish eye contact

Appear relaxed

Let the patient know he is really cared about as a patient

Listen well, but establish parameters to questions; do not project thoughts

Establish a chief complaint

What is the patient asking for?

Why is he asking for it at this time?

What precipitated this visit?

What usually precipitates it?

What has helped in the past?

Use questions carefully and intentionally

Observe and record critically

Speak so the patient can understand

Recognize regression—regression causes increased suggestibility; be careful about what is said and do not allow lengthy regressions

Be honest

Expect proper behavior

Anticipate the emotional component

Explain each thing that is done for the patient

Take the patient seriously

Do not cut corners; be thorough

Validate behaviors

Do not be afraid to ask for help

Do not be afraid to admit to not knowing something

Include the family whenever possible

Nonpsychotic situations
ACUTE ANXIETY ATTACK

An attack typically lasts from a few minutes to several hours. The individual does not have loss of contact with reality, but judgment and insight are impaired. The major management focus is on preventive aspects through teaching self-management.

Signs and symptoms

Hyperactivity

Dry mouth

Fidgety movement of hands

Precordial discomfort (sense of pressure in chest)

Choking sensation
Dysphagia or inability to swallow
Feelings of "impending danger"
Literal attempts to escape
Hyperventilation: breathlessness, paresthesias, and acute restlessness
Sweaty palms
Tachycardia
Tremors
Profuse sweating
Urinary frequency

Therapeutic intervention

Rule out:
> Hyperventilation syndrome (also see Chapter 6):
>> Have the patient rebreathe his own CO_2 by use of a paper bag
>> Teach the patient that symptoms are under self-control; demonstrate the cycle of anxiety: rapid breathing, hyperventilation, air hunger, fear of suffocating, and increased anxiety
>> Have the patient talk (it is difficult to hyperventilate while talking)
> After a thorough physical examination with attention to the cardiopulmonary systems, if no physical cause is found, emphasize to the patient the importance of seeking mental health treatment on a nonemergency basis to work on the underlying cause of the anxiety
> Avoid false or excessive reassurance; give supportive, reassuring attention during the attack

ACUTE BRAIN SYNDROME

An acute brain syndrome is caused by intoxication with or withdrawal from alcohol or other drugs, metabolic toxins, or direct trauma to the brain, which produces changes in the cerebral chemistry or tissue.

Signs and symptoms

Clouded sensorium, ranging from confusion to disorientation
Memory deficit
Loss of judgment
Ataxia
Inability to attend to the environment
Slurred speech
Visual or auditory hallucinations
Deviant vital signs

Therapeutic intervention

Observe the patient carefully
Monitor and record vital signs frequently

ACUTE DELIRIUM
Causes

Biochemical disturbances, for example, electrolyte imbalance, hypoglycemia, uremia, porphyria, or hepatitis
Metastatic neoplasm
Systemic infection
Cerebral hypoxia
Drug withdrawal
Heavy metal toxicity

Signs and symptoms

Delusions
Illusions
Disorientation
Frightening dreams
Outbursts of rage
Difficulty in retention and recall
Hyperventilation
Tachycardia
Tremors
Restlessness

Therapeutic intervention

Identify and remove any toxic substance
Orient the patient to reality by making simple repetitive statements
Simplify the environment
Maintain normal lighting (keep lights on at night)
Have a responsible person stay with the patient
Avoid physical restraints, which only increase confusion, disorientation, and general agitation

ACUTE GRIEF

Acute grief is caused by loss of a significant object or person within a recent time.

Signs and symptoms

Dazed, confused state
Emotional lability with overt tears or moaning
Diminished and slowed speech
Inability to concentrate
Narrowed intellectual functioning
Thought content focused on "lost object"
Feelings of helplessness
Vital signs within normal limits
Anorexia or change in appetite
Weight change

Therapeutic intervention

Accept the individual's behavior and provide supportive dialogue
Encourage expression of feelings, especially sadness and loss
Provide privacy in a room with normal lighting but decreased environmental stimuli
Teach the importance of proper nutrition and fluid intake even if the desire to eat is diminished
Encourage the individual to seek out a close friend or family member to discuss feelings of grief

DEPRESSION

Depression is generally perceived by health professionals as anger turned inward. It is considered dysfunctional after an actual loss if it extends beyond a 4- to 6-week period or renders the individual incapable of normal coping behavior. Feelings of sadness accompanied by feelings of guilt without reason may be present. Psychotic depression generally includes an inability to reality test with delusions or hallucinations as evidence of disorder.

Signs and symptoms

Feelings of worthlessness, loneliness, helplessness, and sadness
Need for self-punishment and self-blame
Lack of impulse control
Diminished interest
Physical fatigue, especially in the morning
Psychomotor retardation or agitation
History of sleep disturbance
Indecisiveness
Auditory hallucinations
Weight change, loss of appetite, and easy fatigability
Reduced facial animation
Abnormal electrolyte values (sodium and potassium)
Possible diuretic, antidepressant drug, and minor tranquilizer side effects
Wringing of hands
Suicidal ideation
Decreased libido
Constipation
Pacing

Therapeutic intervention

Do not isolate the patient
Avoid excessive environmental stimuli or forced decision making
Provide safety and psychologic security
Reality test while encouraging the expression of feelings, especially underlying anger
Help the patient express grief at loss of a loved one; point out that this is normal
Explore sources of emotional support
Antidepressant medications

Involve family members and social network for continued support
Assess the risk of suicide

SUICIDE

Suicide is the tenth leading cause of death in the United States. It is the third leading cause of death in young adults. There are over 30,000 successful suicides a year, or 80 each day. In addition to successful suicides, there are over ½ million unsuccessful attempts each year, or 1,300 each day, or 1 each minute.

Assessing suicide potential

Sex

Males are more serious suicide risks than females
Females attempt suicide three times more often than males
Males are three times more successful at suicide than females
There are 6/100,000 female suicides
There are 18/100,000 male suicides
Females tend to use drugs
Males tend to use firearms

Age

Suicide potential increases with age
Younger people try more often
Older people are more often successful on the first attempt

Race/ ethnic groups/ minorities

Suicide rate in United States is higher in foreign-born people
High rate of suicide among homosexuals
Moslems have the lowest suicide rate of any religious group, followed by Catholics, Jews, and Protestants

Marital status

Married people have the lowest rate
Risk is high in the widowed or divorced group
Singles commit twice as many suicides as married people

Family history

If high, there is increased risk of suicide
Risk is high if there have been previous attempts (70% to 80% of people who are successful at suicide have made previous attempts)

Seasonal

More in spring and fall
More on Wednesdays and Saturdays; fewest on Sundays

Other

Substance abuse (alcohol, drugs) greatly increases risk
Risk is more serious if the plan is well thought out or the patient has a weapon
Do not be afraid to ask if the patient is planning a suicide
Mental illness increases the risk
Debilitating physical illness increases the risk
History of serious emotional loss increases the risk (at the time of the loss or on an anniversary of the loss)

SIGNS AND SYMPTOMS

Feelings of worthlessness, hopelessness, helplessness, confusion
Restlessness
Agitation
Irritability
GI complaints
Insomnia
Fatigue
Indifference
Decreased physical activity
Actual suicide attempt that was unsuccessful

APPROACH TO THE SUICIDE PATIENT

The approach to the suicide patient has as its goal the psychologically and physically protective environment. It is important to establish an empathetic rapport with suicidal patients.

Problem solving

Suicidal thoughts are attempts by the patient to solve problems. Try to find out what the patient thinks his problem is. This must be done after intervention for the crisis, such as care for the patient after overdose or wrist slashing. Common areas for problems include:

Love life
Job situation
Work problems
Financial problems
Family problems
Interpersonal problems
Illness (mental and physical)
Alcohol abuse
Drug abuse

Evaluate with the patient

Look for alternatives for the patient. If the patient is unsure of his alternatives or has no alternatives, hospitalization is mandatory. If there are alternatives, be specific about them. Try to involve the family or friends whenever possible in the decision making and/or planning. When in doubt, obtain a psychiatric consultation. If this is not available, admit the patient to the hospital for observation. The patient may require sedation.

HOMICIDAL AND ASSAULTIVE BEHAVIOR

Homicidal and assaultive behavior is experienced in acute intoxication, paranoia, or mania or is seen in sociopathic individuals. Extreme caution should be used to protect oneself and others in the environment, especially any individual who is the focus of the patient's distorted thinking.

THERAPEUTIC INTERVENTION

Approach the individual with an obvious show of force (group of people)

Confiscate all real or potentially harmful objects

Physically restrain and establish psychologic and physical controls on behalf of the individual

Establish one person as a liaison who assumes a calm, authoritative, and unhurried manner

Speak in simple, directive sentences

Separate the individual from his family and/or the intended victim; if the victim is not present, emergency personnel are responsible for making sure that the person is warned of the patient's ideations

Observe for suicidal as well as homicidal attempts since suicide may follow homicidal attempts because of generally impaired judgment

HOMOSEXUAL PANIC

Homosexual panic is a behavior seen in those who have a reaction to latent homosexuality (usually males). The individual has misperceived a recent male- or female-centered association that may have provided visual stimulation of homoerotic fantasies, for example, movies, singles bars, or body-contact sports.

Signs and symptoms

Obsessive thinking focused on sexual activity

Inability to isolate fact from fantasy

Therapeutic intervention

Provide an opportunity for the patient to express his or her fears in a nonjudgmental environment

Avoid physical contact

Avoid physical techniques such as injections of medicine and rectal examinations

Offer referral for follow-up counseling

ORGANIC BRAIN SYNDROME

Organic brain syndrome is diffuse disruption and impairment of the functioning capacity of brain tissue from a variety of causes.

SIGNS AND SYMPTOMS

Decreased orientation

Decreased memory

Decreased judgment

Decreased ability to calculate and figure

Shallow affect

Acute organic brain syndrome is usually rapid in onset, temporary in nature, and very reversible.

Chronic organic brain syndrome is very slow in progression and is usually nonreversible. Signs and symptoms of chronic organic brain syndrome include:

Dementia

Delirium

Stupor, coma, or death

Whenever a care giver comes into contact with a patient who has organic brain syndome, he or she should ask about the possibility of a medication-induced syndrome (many medications may cause this).

ACUTE PSYCHOTIC REACTIONS

A psychosis is the deterioration of a person's thought process, affective response, and ability to be in touch with reality, communicate, and relate with others. Deterioration continues to the point at which the patient cannot deal with the processes of daily living. In acute psychotic reactions the patient has a disorder of mood or thinking to the degree that he loses contact with reality. It is important to remember that health care personnel should not agree with reality distortion, but should avoid arguing in their approach to guiding the individual in reality testing. This patient should be treated in a quiet, sparsely decorated room. Some of these patients may be a danger to themselves and others. If the patient is extremely violent or has the potential to become so, restraints or a locked room may be considered. Undress the patient and place him in a hospital gown (remove clothing or other objects that may conceal weapons).

Schizophrenic reactions
SIGNS AND SYMPTOMS

Delusions

Auditory hallucinations

Difficulty with associations

Disordered thought with clear sensorium

Combative or assaultive behavior

Withdrawn or catatonic behavior

Bizarre gesturing

THERAPEUTIC INTERVENTIONS

Establish a history of previous hospitalization and/or use of major tranquilizers that the patient voluntarily stopped or was requested to stop taking

Use simple, concrete expressions and brief sentences

Avoid figures of speech that are subject to misinterpretation

Use an authoritative manner to help assure the patient of your ability to control yourself and the environment

Listen as the patient talks of delusions to gain clues about his thinking disorder

If the patient is paranoid, avoid closed doors or blocked doorways; allow the patient to feel "uncornered"

If phenothiazines are given, observe for postural hypotension and pseudoparkinsonism side effects

Consider hospital admission

Paranoia

Paranoia is a syndrome within the schizophrenic classification. A paranoid person demonstrates his loss of reality contact through a delusional system, generally of persecution or excessive religious statements. The patient's false beliefs are generally based on certain factual aspects of his life that have been distorted and personalized to the point of gross exaggeration. The paranoid patient can be dangerous because of his feelings that either specific people or unnamed forces are out to get him.

SIGNS AND SYMPTOMS

Delusions of a projective nature
Feelings of uniqueness going toward grandiosity
Auditory hallucinations
Difficulty with association
Illogical thought process
Obsessive thinking
Combative or assaultive behavior
Restlessness
Agitation

THERAPEUTIC INTERVENTION

The key to management is to avoid psychologic and physical threats or challenges while
   providing limits and reality testing
Use simple, concrete expressions
Remain calm and authoritative
Move slowly and quietly to avoid appearing intrusive
Sit or stand on the same level with the patient to avoid a "power" position
Allow the patient to be close to the slightly ajar door
Allow the patient to verbalize distorted or illogical thinking
If the patient threatens violence or aggression against a particular person or group, notify
   them
Avoid trying to convince the patient that his delusions are erroneous and avoid adding
   validity to his false belief

Hypomania/manic psychosis

Hypomania or manic psychosis patients usually have recurrent episodes of either mood elevation or depression. The first question that should be asked is if the person has a history of this type of behavior and if he is taking lithium carbonate. If so, ask about the most recent serum lithium level. A serum lithium level shoud be measured immediately. A knowledgeable family member can help establish if the individual is in a hypomanic exacerbation or in an acute episode.

SIGNS AND SYMPTOMS

Elation or increased mental excitement that is unstable
Irritability, sometimes irrational anger
Pressured speech (delivered rapidly through tight lips)
Increased motor activity (talks easily and endlessly)

Demanding or euphoric manner
Grandiose ideas
Loud voice
Sexual acting out or content focused on sex
Loud-colored clothing, bright-colored makeup (overdone)

THERAPEUTIC INTERVENTION

Assume an authoritative, nonthreatening manner
Guard the patient, care givers, and environment against physical harm
Decrease environmental stimulation
Provide an unencumbered, safe, and private room to allow pacing or ritualistic motor
    activity
Do *not* encourage the patient to talk; ask succinct questions
Respond in an unhurried, simple speech pattern
Avoid mechanical restraints if possible

DRUG-RELATED PSYCHIATRIC EMERGENCIES

The function of emergency personnel in an acute drug-induced crisis is one of critical observation and supportive therapeutic communication. The presenting clinical signs and symptoms are a combination of the physiologic responses to the abused substance, the number of times the drug has been used in combination with other types of abused drugs, the physical and mental health of the user, and the premorbid personality. Friends are often the best source of information. The following guidelines apply to all suspected drug-abuse situations. (See Chapter 11 for medical management of overdose.)

SIGNS AND SYMPTOMS

Airway obstruction
Increased temperature, pulse, and respirations and decreased BP
Increased or decreased pupil size
Decreased muscle tone
Tremors
Gastrointestinal symptoms
Decreased level of consciousness
Distortion of mood/thought pattern

QUESTIONS TO ASK

What type of drug was taken?
What has happened since the drug was taken?
What other drugs have been used (drug history)?
At what time was the last dose of the drug taken?
At what time did the patient start abusing the drug?
How was the drug taken (orally, subcutaneously, by injection, by inhalation)?
How much of the drug was taken?

Belladonna alkaloids

Over-the-counter hypnotic drugs such as Nytol and Sominex contain scopolamine. Taken in large amounts, they produce an atropine-like psychosis. Phenothiazines, tricyclic antidepressants, and antihistamines are potent anticholinergic drugs. Some plants contain belladonna alkaloids and when ingested cause an atropine-like psychosis. The classical description of belladonna effects is ''blind as a bat, dry as a bone, red as a beet, and mad as a hatter.''

SIGNS AND SYMPTOMS

Delirium
Mental confusion
Intense thirst and dry mouth
Dysphagia
Restlessness
Talkativeness
Thought blockade
Dilated pupils
Inability to visually accommodate
Flushed, hot, and dry skin
Rapid and weak pulse
Hoarse, raspy voice
Urinary retention or slow, painful urinary stream

THERAPEUTIC INTERVENTION

Give frequent sips of water
Use a saline flush to moisten the eyes
Urinary bladder catherization if needed
Provide a calm environment in subdued lighting
Serve as a calm, nonjudgmental listener, but *do not* encourage talking

Opiates and related compounds

Included in the opiate group are heroin, morphine, hydromorphone (Dilaudid), pentazocine (Talwin), methadone (Dolophine), and propoxyphene (Darvon). The list is in order of intensity of euphoria and diminished sensorium.

SIGNS AND SYMPTOMS

State of sluggishness
State of euphoria
Somnolence
Track marks (popliteal fossa, ankles, forearm veins, sublingual)
Constricted pupils
Decreased blood pressure
Decreased heart rate
Decreased body temperature

THERAPEUTIC INTERVENTION

Observe for withdrawal syndrome: coryza, yawning, lacrimation, increased pulse and respiratory rate, perspiration, and tremors (these start 6 to 12 hours after the last dose)

Observe in addition for insomnia, severe abdominal cramps, vomiting and diarrhea, tachycardia, and hypertension (these start 12 to 48 hours after the last dose)

Observe for respiratory depression and impending heroin pulmonary edema if that drug is suspected

If naloxone (Narcan) has been given, be alert for agitation and aggressive behavior as the patient responds

Hallucinogens

Hallucinogens are psychedelic drugs such as LSD and DMT (acid), peyote, mescaline, STP, psilocybin, and phencyclidine (PCP, angel dust). Individuals on a "bad trip" are especially sensitive to the environment and suspicious of people. Subjective symptoms wax and wane.

SIGNS AND SYMPTOMS

Grossly impaired judgment
Intense visual or auditory hallucinations
Unusual changes in self-perception
Rapid mood swings
Flight of ideas
Lack of coordination
Loss of control that comes in waves
Panic state
Increased blood pressure and pulse rate
Pupil dilation
Chills and shivering
Increased muscle tension
Tremors
Nausea (especially with mescaline)
Convulsions

THERAPEUTIC INTERVENTION

1. Provide a constant vigil by a supportive person (a trusted, responsible friend or one particular staff person).
   a. Give simple, repetitive statements.
   b. *Do not* challenge the patient's values, beliefs, life-style, or distorted thinking.
2. Use "talk down" techniques. (do *not* use "talk down" with PCP)
   a. Establish verbal contact to allay fears.
   b. Encourage the patient to talk.
   c. Encourage expressions of perceptions and feelings.
3. Reality test on a continuous basis.
   a. Focus on physical characteristics of the room.
   b. Repeatedly identify person(s) in the room.

    c. Have the patient focus on inanimate, stationary objects in the room as a center of orientation

    d. Encourage the patient to keep his eyes open.

4. Provide a protective, quiet, and nonthreatening room.

    a. Normal lighting.

    b. Decreased visual and auditory stimuli.

5. Guard yourself against spontaneous aggressive behavior.

6. Be alert for suicidal behavior.

Phencyclidine (angel dust)

Phencyclidine (PCP) is the number three drug of abuse in large cities. It is easy to obtain as it is made with over-the-counter chemicals. It is classified as an analgesic and a hallucinogenic agent. It can be taken by inhalation, ingestion, or intravenously.

SIGNS AND SYMPTOMS

Severe anxiety, agitation, drowsiness, or coma

Psychosis (acute onset)

Constricted pupils

Increased then decreased respirations, followed by respiratory arrest

Elevated then decreased blood pressure

Vertical nystagmus

Ataxia

Euphoria

Increased then decreased deep tendon reflexes

Nausea and vomiting

Clonus

Increased then decreased urinary output

Tremors followed by seizures

Amnesia

Opisthotonos

Distorted images and thought processes

Depersonalization

Hallucinations

Dysrhythmias

THERAPEUTIC INTERVENTION

Reduce external stimuli (quiet, dim room)

Decrease the number of people present

Restraints and total observation

Do not attempt to talk the patient down

Haloperidol (Haldol) IV (but remember that haloperidol has a shorter half-life than PCP)

    or

Diazepam (Valium)

Consider hospital admission

Central nervous system stimulants

All psychostimulants produce excitation of the central nervous system. Tolerance develops rapidly and is sometimes accompanied by psychologic dependence. A physical withdrawal syndrome is unlikely, but a real let-down feeling accompanies discontinuation of the drug.

AMPHETAMINES
Signs and symptoms

Increased rate of speech
Extraordinary hyperactivity
Rapid flight of ideas
Mood swings
Irritability and hostility
Aggressiveness
Unexplained fear and jitteriness
Talkativeness
Hallucinations (auditory or visual)
Clear sensorium and memory
Delusions of persecution
Increased blood pressure, pulse rate, and temperature
Dilated pupils
Insomnia
Twitching muscles
Nausea or vomiting
Severe abdominal pain
Grand mal seizures

COCAINE
Signs and symptoms

Euphoria and feeling of mental agility
Formication (sense of insects crawling under skin)
Loose association
Paranoid delusions
Perforated nasal septum
Elevated body temperature
Dilated pupils
Skin pallor

Therapeutic intervention

Place the patient in a quiet, secure, large room
Reduce environmental stimuli
Allow the patient to move about
Observe vital signs, especially temperature
Allow the patient to "talk down"
Be alert to violent or aggressive tendencies and protect care givers and the environment

Be aware of repetitious compulsive behavior and chart it

A period of "crash" is followed by marked depression, which can lead to suicidal behavior; therefore use precautions to prevent suicide

Central nervous system depressants

Of all abused drugs, the depressants are the most dangerous in terms of acute overdose and withdrawal morbidity. Withdrawal represents a medical emergency of the first order. Tolerance develops rapidly; the shorter the half-life, the more physiologically addicting the drug. Alcohol and barbiturate intoxication are similar in signs and symptoms.

ACUTE ALCOHOL INTOXICATION

Signs and symptoms

Slowed thinking

Impairment of memory and judgment

Labile emotions

Uninhibited behavior

Inattention and distractibility

Euphoria or depression

Slurred speech

Agitation or extreme compliance

Unsteady gait

Smell of alcohol on the breath

Nausea and vomiting

Tremors

Flushed or pale face

Systolic hypertension

Tachycardia

Muscle weakness

Therapeutic intervention

Observe the patient carefully

Monitor the vital signs, especially the blood pressure and heart rate

Place the patient in a quiet, protected area

Guard against aspiration and physical injury

Speak in a calm, authoritative manner

If a sedative or barbiturate drug is given, be alert to respiratory depression

If a major tranquilizer is given, be alert to hypotension

Obtain an ingestion history including alcohol in combination with other drugs

See Chapter 10 for measurement of alcohol withdrawal symptoms, as the patient who stops drinking may precipitate a withdrawal crisis in increasingly serious stages

See Chapter 10 for medical management

BARBITURATES

The main danger of overdose is stupor and cardiorespiratory collapse. Because of their ability to depress CNS functioning, there is an extremely high incidence of barbiturate use for intended or gestured suicide.

Signs and symptoms

Muscular incoordination	Postural hypotension
Slurred speech	Hypothermia
Paranoid ideation	Depressed respiration
Restlessness	Nausea
Clouded sensorium progressing to coma	Convulsions
Wide-based ataxic gait	Tremors
Irritability	Hyperreflexia
Dilated pupils	Muscular weakness

Therapeutic intervention

Management generally includes withdrawal of the abused drug under inpatient conditions for close monitoring of misuse of drugs

Provide a quiet, secure room

Carefully observe and record signs and symptoms

Be especially alert for convulsions, which can progress to status epilepticus, and respiratory distress

Avoid physical restaints

A withdrawal syndrome appears within 10 to 15 hours: apprehension, muscle weakness, hypotension, seizures, and psychosis may occur

BROMIDES

Bromides are more likely to produce chronic poisoning than an acute overdose.

Signs and symptoms

Gradual increase in drowsiness without release by sleep

Depression

Confusion

Hallucinations (visual)

Delusions of a paranoid nature

Hypomanic state

Acneform skin eruptions (especially on the face and around the hair roots)

Serum drug level above 75 mg/100 ml

Heavily fixed tongue

Foul breath

Therapeutic intervention

Provide a quiet, secure room

Ascertain the source of bromide intake; many patients are unaware of the poisonlike effect of over-the-counter sleep agents

Reality test regarding delusions and hallucinations

MARIJUANA

Marijuana is the number two substance abused in the United States, following alcohol. The most common complication is that the user experiences an anxiety attack.

Signs and symptoms

Elevated blood pressure   Apprehension
Tachycardia   Restlessness
Tachypnea   Feeling of doom

Therapeutic intervention

Psychologic support
Reassurance
Diazepam by mouth if the reaction is severe

PHENOTHIAZINE DYSTONIC REACTIONS

Phenothiazine dystonic reactions may be caused by prochlorperazine (Compazine), trifluoperazine (Stelazine), chlorpromazine (Thorazine), fluphenazine (Prolixin), and haloperidol, all of which are phenothiazines. Signs and symptoms of phenothiazine dystonic reactions are often mistaken for hypocalcemia, seizure disorders, and tetany. Be sure to ask about a medication history when a patient comes to the emergency department with the signs and symptoms listed here.

Signs and symptoms

Signs and symptoms of phenothiazine dystonic reactions usually appear 4 to 5 days after ingestion.
Oculogyric crisis
Protruding tongue
Torticollis
Facial grimaces
Opisthotonos
Tortipelvic crisis

Therapeutic intervention

Diphenhydramine (Benadryl) IV *or*
Benztropine (Cogentin) *or*
Trihexyphenidyl (Artane)

ADVERSE CENTRAL NERVOUS SYSTEM REACTIONS TO ANTIPSYCHOTIC DRUGS

Sometimes the drug of choice in treating a psychiatric condition produces more stress than relief for the patient. One such instance is the severe extrapyramidal side effects of some major tranquilizers. These reactions are more likely to occur during the *initial* phase of psychotropic drug therapy. The appearance of undesirable side effects can be anxiety provoking for the patient and his family. The potential hazard and the sudden onset of symptoms can cause him to refuse to take any type of prescribed medicine that could be effective in decreasing his psychotic symptoms. Emergency personnel can do much to help the individual realize that use of antipsychotic drugs requires patience in obtaining a satisfactory therapeutic response.

Medical management to counteract adverse reactions is quickly achieved in most instances by anticholinergic drugs such as diphenhydramine (Benadryl) or antiparkinsonian drugs such as benztropine mesylate (Cogentin) or trihexyphenidyl (Artane).

Parkinsonism usually develops within 20 days of the initial drug therapy. Symptoms include muscular rigidity, resting tremors, a masklike face, and drooling.

Dystonia usually develops within 1 hour to 5 days.

Therapeutic intervention

Educate the patient to the fact that untoward symptoms will disappear rapidly with proper medication, usually go away even if untreated, and usually are completely reversible

Provide a quiet, darkened room for the patient to lie down until the antagonist drug takes effect

Have a nonthreatening person stay with the patient until the undesirable symptoms have subsided (generally within 1 hour after administration of an antagonist drug IM)

DISPOSITION OF THE PATIENT

The major question that arises with the therapeutic intervention of the psychiatric patient is whether or not he should be hospitalized. One important factor is the presence or absence of a solid support system in terms of family or friends and their willingness to observe or supervise the patient.

When to hospitalize the patient involuntarily:

If the patient is a physical threat to himself (suicidal)

If the patient is a physical threat to others (homicidal)

(Involuntary hold criteria differ in each state, but most states have included these two criteria.)

If the patient is addicted to alcohol or drugs

The hold is usually placed by a psychiatrist or psychiatric consultant. These holds are usually for a limited time (72 hours in most states).

SUMMARY

By definition, a psychiatric emergency occurs when a person's adaptive capacity is ineffective in coping with life's stressors. Psychiatric emergencies require careful listening and a great deal of common sense. It is not easy to remain calm, appear authoritative, and thereby be therapeutic when the entire situation is anxiety provoking. Self-sufficiency and self-control should be the goal of any intervention. The most powerful strategy in helping the individual establish a sense of self-control (power) is to show an attitude of decisive action (authority) and compassion (care).

In psychiatric emergencies the signs and symptoms of the health problem are sometimes so obvious in the individual's bizarre behavior or thinking that it is often easier to evaluate what is wrong than to assess what is right. The strengths to build on are as important as isolating the impairments causing the dysfunction. The total evaluation of the patient includes the healthy as well as the unhealthy parts of him. The treatment process is based on the individual's strengths that have been identified and validated through the assessment process. Emergency personnel need to develop an understanding of people and their coping behaviors. This basic knowledge of human behavior synthesized with medical and surgical knowledge should provide the needed tools of sensitivity and knowledge to meet the patient's immediate needs.

SUGGESTED READINGS

American Psychiatric Association: Diagnosis and statistics manual of mental disorders, ed. 2, Washington, D.C., The Association, 1968.

Anderson, W.H., and Kuchnle, J.C.: Diagnosis and early management of acute psychosis, N. Engl. J. Med. **305:**1128, 1981.

Crarey, G.C.: Psychiatric problems in the emergency department. Lecture given at Emergency Nursing Conference, Santa Monica, Calif., July 15, 1980.

DiSclafani, A., II, Hall, R.C.W., and Gardner, E.R.: Drug induced psychosis: emergency department diagnosis and management, Psychosomatics **22:**845, 1981.

Freedman, A.M., and Haplan, H.I., editors: Comprehensive textbook of psychiatry, Baltimore, 1978, The Williams & Wilkins Co.

Gerson, S., and Bassul, E.: Psychiatric emergencies: an overview, Am. J. Psychiatry **137:**1, 1980.

Lee, A.: Drug induced dystonic reactions, J.A.C.E.P. **6:**351, 1977.

Pisarcik, G.: Psychiatric emergencies. In Budassi, S.A., and Barber, J.M., editors: Emergency nursing: principles and practice, St. Louis, 1981, The C.V. Mosby Co.

Pisarcik, G.: The violent patient, Nurs. '81, **11**(9):63, 1981.

Rada, R.: The violent patient: rapid assessment and management, Psychosomatics **22:**101, 1981.

Rivera-Camlin, L.: The pharmacology and therapeutic application of phenothiazines, Ration. Drug Therapy **11:**4, 1977.

Medications appendix

Drug dosages and uses listed are those currently accepted at the time of this writing *for emergency use*. Be sure to read the product information provided with most medications, the *Physician's Desk Reference* (PDR), or *U.S. Pharmacopeia* or consult the hospital pharmacist for updates or further medication information.

GUIDELINES FOR ADMINISTERING MEDICATIONS

Check the patient's current drug history and document it
Check for previous side effects and allergies or anaphylactic reactions
Reconfirm all verbal medication orders
Do not give medications that are unfamiliar
Document medications given:
    Name of medication
    Time given
    Amount given
    Rate given
    Route given
    Site of administration
    Any noted response or lack of response
Question any order that is out of the ordinary and verify it
Do not administer any medication that appears to be dangerous to the patient

Aminophylline (formerly called theophylline ethylenediamine)

Category
Bronchodilator

Emergency uses
Asthma with bronchospasm
Pulmonary edema
Emphysema
Chronic bronchitis
Propranolol overdose

Actions
Relaxes smooth muscles
Increases cardiac output
Increases urinary output
Increases sodium excretion
Peripheral vasodilation
Decreases pulmonary artery pressure

Special notes
Has a cumulative effect
Administer slowly (rapidly may produce ventricular fibrillation)
Do not administer with another xanthine derivative or sympathomimetic agent
Be especially cautious with children

Side effects

Anxiety	Restlessness
Seizures	Hypotension
Syncope	Cardiac dysrhythmias
Headache	
Nausea and vomiting	

Dosage
Adult—250 to 500 mg in 20 to 30 ml D5W over 30 minutes followed by IV drip 0.5 to 0.7 mg/kg/hr
Pediatric—4 mg/kg via IV drip may be repeated in 8 hours

Ampicillin sodium (Polycillin-N, Principen/N, Amcill-S, SK Ampicillin-N, Omnipen-N, Pen A/N, Penbritin-S, Totacillin-N)

Category
Antibiotic

Emergency uses
For gram-positive and gram-negative organisms

Actions
A broad-spectrum antibiotic effective against gram-positive and gram-negative organisms

Special notes
Do not give if patient has a history of penicillin allergy
Must be used within 1 hour of reconstitution
Do not give with erythromycin, kanamycin, tetracline, chloramphenicol, or any other drug in the IV line
Potential increases with concurrent administration of probenecid (Benemid)
Do not administer in pregnancy

Side effects
Urticaria
Rash
Anemia
Anaphylaxis

Dosage
Adult—150 to 200 mg/kg/24 hours IV diluted
Pediatric—50 mg/kg/24 hours IV diluted in four divided doses

Antihemophilic factor (Factorate, Humafac, Koate, Profilate, Hemofil)

Category
Antihemophilic agent

Emergency uses
To control hemorrhage in a hemophiliac

Actions
Acts in clotting mechanism

Special notes
Must be documented factor VIII deficiency hemophiliac
Must be used within 3 hours of reconstitution
Check prothrombin time before use

Side effects
Fever
Erythema
Back pain
Hepatitis

Dosage
Adult—10 to 40 units/kg
Pediatric—10 to 40 units/kg

Atropine sulfate

Category
Anticholinergic/parasympatholytic agent

Emergency uses
Asystole
High-degree AV block with slow ventricular rate
Bradydysrhythmias with hypotension or ventricular ectopy
As antidote in organophosphate poisoning
Biliary or ureteral colic

Actions
Blocks vagal tone

Special notes
Do not give less than 0.3 mg in an adult as this may cause a paradoxical slowing of the heart rate
Potentiated by antidepressants, antihistamines, isoniazid (INH), phenothiazides, and MAO inhibitors

Side effects
Blurred vision   Fever
Pupil dilation   Rash
Dry mouth   Decreased level of conscious-
Delirium   ness
Hypertension   Tachycardia
Hypotension   Decreased respirations
Urinary retention   Coma
                          Death

Dosage
Adult—1 to 2 mg by IV push in asystole;
    0.5 to 1.0 mg IV over 2 minutes for dysrhythmias (may be repeated in 5 minutes to a total dose of 2 mg)
Pediatric—0.01 to 0.03 mg/kg IV over 2 minutes

Benztropine mesylate (Cogentin)

Category
Anticholinergic, antihistaminic agent

Emergency uses
Psychosis
Parkinson's disease
Acute drug reactions

Actions
Decreases drooling and dysphagia
Decreases tremors and muscle rigidity
Decreases ataxia

Special notes
Usually given IV or IM
Potentiated by barbiturates, tricyclic antidepressants,
and phenothiazines

Side effects

Rash	Overdose: Dilated pupils
Blurred vision	Flushed skin
Syncope	Fever
Dry mouth	Glaucoma
Nausea and	Paralytic ileus
vomiting	Respiratory
Numb fingers	depression
Constipation	Anhydrosis
Depression	Coma
	Death

Dosage
Adult—0.5 to 2 mg IM or PO (IV in psychotic patients); may increase to 4 to 6 mg in 24 hours
Pediatric—Do *not* use in children

Bretylium tosylate (Bretylol)

Category
Antidysrhythmic agent/chemical defibrillant

Emergency uses
Ventricular fibrillation
Ventricular tachycardia

Actions
Increases fibrillation threshold
Decreases ventricular dysrhythmias and aberrancies
Increases refractory period
Increases inotropy

Special notes
May be considered a first-line antidysrhythmic agent
  in ventricular fibrillation
Monitor vital signs and rhythm regularly
Potentiates catecholamines
Use with extreme caution with digitalis users
Correct hypotensive states concurrently

Side effects

Angina	Ventricular premature
Bradycardia	beats
Syncope	Syncope
Hypotension or hyper-	Vertigo
tension	

Dosage
Adult—Ventricular fibrillation: 5 mg/kg diluted by
  rapid IV push; increase to 10 mg/kg in second dose;
  do not exceed 30 mg/kg total dose; Ventricular
  tachycardia: 5 to 10 mg/kg diluted in 50 ml normal
  saline over 10 minutes; repeat in 1 to 2 hours
Pediatric—Unknown; use only in life-threatening
  situations

Calcium chloride

Category
Myocardial irritant

Emergency uses
Hyperkalemic arrest situations (common in renal dialysis patients)
To convert fine ventricular fibrillation to coarse
Electromechanical dissociation
Antidote for magnesium sulfate poisoning

Actions
Increases myocardial contractility
Prolongs systole
Enhances ventricular automaticity

Special notes
Do not use with patients taking digitalis
Precipitates with sodium bicarbonate to form calcium carbonate (chalk)
Three times more potent than calcium gluconate
May be given IV or intracardiac

Side effects
Bradycardia
Hypotension

Dosage
Adult—5 to 10 ml of a 10% solution IV over 5 to 10 minutes; may be repeated in 5 to 10 minutes
Pediatric—1 to 2 ml of 1% solution IV over 5 to 10 minutes; may be repeated in 5 to 10 minutes

Calcium gluconate (Kalcinate)

Category
Myocardial irritant

Emergency uses
Cardiac arrest (electromechanical dissociation, asystole, fine ventricular fibrillation)
Antidote for magnesium sulfate

Actions
Increases myocardial contractility
Prolongs systole
Enhances ventricular automaticity

Special notes
One third the potency of calcium chloride
May be given IV only
Use with caution with patients taking digitalis

Side effects
Bradycardia
Hypotension

Dosage
Adult—10 ml/24 hours (up to 60 ml) IV
Pediatric—2 to 5 ml/24 hours IV

Carbenicillin (Geopen, Pyopen)

Category
Broad-spectrum antibiotic

Emergency uses
Urinary tract infection
Septicemia

Actions
Broad-spectrum antibiotic for *Pseudomonas, Proteus, Haemophilus influenzae, and Escherichia coli*

Special notes
Must be administered within 24 hours of reconstitution
Probenecid given concurrently to enhance effects
Possibility of anaphylactic reaction

Side effects

Anaphylaxis	Itching
Seizures	Nausea
Fever	Urticaria

Dosage
Adult—1 to 10 g every 4 hours IV
Pediatric—50 to 500 mg/kg over 24 hours in 4 to 6 divided doses IV

Cefazolin sodium (Ancef, Kefzol)

Category
Antibiotic

Emergency uses
Serious infections of unknown cause
Potential of serious infection (e.g., multiple trauma) as a prophylactic measure

Actions
Broad-spectrum antibiotic

Special notes
May induce allergic reaction
Do not give with procainamide (Pronestyl), quinidine, promethazine (Phenergan), diuretics, and aminoglycosides
May be given with probenecid (Benemid) to enhance potency
Do not give to infants under 1 month of age

Side effects
Anaphylaxis
Nausea and vomiting

Dosage
Adult—250 mg to 1 g every 6 to 8 hours IV; do not exceed 6 g/24 hours
Pediatric—25 to 50 mg/kg over 24 hours in 4 divided doses IV; may give up to 100 mg/kg for severe infection

Cephalothin sodium (Keflin)

Category
Antibiotic

Emergency uses
Severe infections
Potential of severe infections (e.g., in multiple
   trauma)

Actions
Broad-spectrum cephalosporin antibiotic
Effective against gram-positive and gram-negative
   organisms

Special notes
May cause anaphylaxis
Pseudomonas is resistant
Administer via large vein
Incompatible with many medications

Side effects
Anaphylaxis
Nausea and vomiting
Urticaria

Dosage
Adult—1 to 2 g every 4 to 6 hours IV; may give up to
   12 g for severe infection
Pediatric—40 to 80 mg/kg in divided doses over 24
   hours IV

Chloramphenicol sodium succinate (Chloromycetin, Mychel-S)

Category
Antibiotic

Emergency uses
Salmonella typhi infection
Meningitis
Rocky Mountain spotted fever
Bacteremia

Actions
Inhibits protein synthesis

Special notes
Do not give with oral anticoagulants
Do not give with oral hypoglycemic agents
May cause bone marrow depression
May be given IV only
A potentially *lethal* medication; use with much cau-
   tion

Side effects

Anaphylaxis	Nausea
Bone marrow depression	Vomiting
Diarrhea	
Fever	

Dosage
Adult—50 mg/kg/24 hours IV in 4 divided doses
Pediatric 25 mg/kg/24 hours IV in 4 divided doses

Chlordiazepoxide hydrochloride (Librium)

Category
CNS depressant/tranquilizer

Emergency uses
Severe anxiety
Severe agitation
Acute alcohol withdrawal
Tremors

Actions
Depresses CNS
Relaxes smooth muscle

Special notes
May be given IV or IM
Potential of habituation
Increased potential with concurrent use of narcotics, barbiturates, phenothiazines, and alcohol
Use with caution with patients using oral anticoagulants, as this may potentiate them
Give reduced dose for elderly patients

Side effects

Hypotension	Urticaria
Hiccups	Urinary retention
Nausea and vomiting	Overdose: Hypotension
Tachycardia	Bradycardia
Syncope	Coma

Dosage
Adult—50 to 100 mg (preferably PO); may be repeated 25 to 100 mg in 2 to 4 hours
Pediatric—Not recommended for emergency use in children

Chlorothiazide sodium (Diuril)

Category
Diuretic

Emergency uses
Preeclampsia
Edema

Actions
Enhances excretion of sodium, potassium, water, and chlorides at the renal tubule level

Special notes
Should not be given concurrently with blood products
Usually given PO
May be given IV
Frequent laboratory analysis of fluid and electrolyte status during use
Close monitoring of vital signs
If used concurrently with alcohol or narcotics, causes a hypotensive effect

Side effects

Syncope	Overdose:
Muscle cramping	Anaphylaxis
Nausea and vomiting	Dehydration
Paresthesias	Severe hypotension
Rash	Hypokalemia
Urticaria	Hematuria
Vertigo	Metabolic acidosis
	Embolism

Dosage
Adult—0.5 to 1 g once or twice daily PO or IV
Pediatric—Do not use in children

Chlorpromazine hydrochloride (Thorazine, Clorazine)

Category
Tranquilizer/Sympatholytic agent

Emergency uses
Acute restlessness
Severe nausea and vomiting
Severe hiccups
Antidote for hypertension caused by methylergonovine (Methergine)
Antidote for amphetamine overdose and LSD trip

Actions
Acts on CNS, autonomic nervous system, and peripheral nervous system to reduce anxiety and tension

Special notes
May be given IV or PO
Decomposes in light
Causes hypotension because of alpha blockade
Potentiates other CNS depressants, antihistamines, and anticholinergics
Do not give concurrently with epinephrine, thiazides, quinidine, and dipyrone

Side effects
Hypotension
Anaphylaxis
Fever
Tachycardia

Dosage
Adult—2 mg given at 2-minute intervals, IV titrated to effect
Pediatric—1 mg given at 2-minute intervals, IV titrated to effect, but not commonly used in children

Deferoxamine mesylate (Desferal)

Category
Iron chelating agent

Emergency uses
Acute iron intoxication

Actions
Combines with iron to form ferrioxamine

Special notes
Should be used in conjunction with other procedures commonly employed in acute poisoning, such as inducing emesis with ipecac and gastric lavage
May be given IV or IM
Pay strict attention to airway maintenance

Side effects
Abdominal pain (usually occurs with rapid administration)
Anaphylaxis
Diarrhea
Blurred vision
Hypotension fever
Tachycardia
Urticaria

Dosage
Adult—1 gm IM initially, followed by 0.5 gm every 4 hours in two doses, then 0.5 gm every 4 to 12 hours; total dosage not to exceed 6 gm in 24 hours. If patient is in shock, give by slow infusion at not more than 15 mg/kg/hour, using same amounts as in IM administration
Pediatric—Not specifically stated

Dexamethasone sodium phosphate (Decadron, Decadrol, Betamethasone, Decaject, Delladec, Dexasone, Dezone, Hexadrol, Savacort, Solurex)

Category
Steroid (adrenocortical)

Emergency uses
Shock
Severe allergic reactions
Head trauma
Cerebral edema
Thyroid crisis

Actions
Antiinflammatory agent

Special notes
May mask indications of infection
Contraindicated in pregnancy
Contraindicated in diabetes, renal insufficiency, acute
   psychosis
Decreased potential with concurrent use of phenytoins
May cause central nervous system excitement

Side effects

Hypertension	Headache
Hyperglycemia	Euphoria
Anaphylaxis	Weakness
Electrolyte imbalances	Paresthesias

Dosage
Adult—Usual dose in head trauma is 10 mg IV; Other
   doses will vary; check product literature
Pediatric—Variable; check product literature

Dextrose 50% (glucose 50%)

Category
Hyperglycemic agent

Emergency uses
Unconsciousness of unknown cause
Hypoglycemia

Actions
Provides glucose for metabolism
Counterbalances excessive insulin states or hypo-
   glycemic states

Special notes
Draw serum glucose before administration
Should be given in conjunction with thiamin 100 mg
   IV if chronic alcoholism is suspected to prevent
   Wernicke-Korsakoff syndrome
May cause sloughing; administer in a large vein
Monitor serum glucose levels closely after administra-
   tion

Side effects
Rare
Hyperglycemia
Hypoglycemia (following infusion in patient with hy-
   poglycemia)
Hypokalemia (May precipitate Wernicke-Korsakoff
   syndrome

Dosage
Adult—50 ml of 50% solution IV
Pediatric—1 mg/kg of 50% solution IV

Diazepam (Valium)

Category
Nervous system depressant

Emergency uses
Status epilepticus
Acute alcohol withdrawal
Psychoneurotic states
Before cardioversion or joint dislocation relocation
Acute stress reactions

Actions
Depresses central, peripheral, and autonomic nervous
systems
Decreases amount of patient recall

Special notes
Do not give in IV line with any other medication
Contraindicated in pregnancy
Administer slowly, as rapid administration may cause
respiratory depression
Have crash cart standing by

Side effects

Ataxia	Drowsiness
Blurred vision	Headache
Bradycardia	Syncope
Respiratory depression	Apnea
Confusion	Cardiovascular collapse
Dyspnea	Arrest

Dosage
Adult—2 to 10 mg by slow IV push, titrated to effect
Pediatric—Not recommended for use in children

Diazoxide (Hyperstat)

Category
Rapid-acting antihypertensive agent

Emergency uses
Malignant hypertension

Actions
Produces vasodilation by relaxing smooth muscles at
the arteriolar level

Special notes
Acts in 1 to 5 minutes
Patient should be in supine position during adminis-
tration
Frequent blood pressure checks before, during, and
after administration

Side effects

Cerebral ischemia	Myocardial ischemia
Seizures	Nausea and vomiting
Hypotension	Diaphoresis
Hyperglycemia	Tachycardia
Syncope	

Dosage
Adult—30 mg by rapid IV push; may be repeated in
30 minutes
Pediatric—5 mg/kg by IV push

Digoxin (Lanoxin)

Category
Cardiac glycoside

Emergency uses
Congestive heart failure
Atrial fibrillation or flutter
Cardiogenic shock
Paroxysmal tachycardia
Shock not responsive to fluid therapy

Actions
Increases strength of myocardial contraction
Enhances cardiac output
Increases AV conduction time
Increases sensitivity of carotid bodies

Special notes
Do not administer concurrently with calcium chloride
Special caution with patients taking phenytoin (Dilantin) reserpine (Serpasil), or epinephrine
Do not give if the patient is hypokalemic or hyperkalemic
Do not give in Mobitz type I or II block

Side effects
Prolonged PR interval   Confusion
Any dysrhythmia   Yellow vision
Abdominal pain   Headache
Blurred vision   Nausea and vomiting
Diarrhea   Syncope

Dosage
Adult—0.5 to 1 mg for initial digitalization IV or PO; 0.25 to 0.5 mg for maintenance IV or PO
Pediatric—Consult product literature

Diphenhydramine hydrochloride (Benadryl)

Category
Antihistamine

Emergency uses
Allergic reactions
Anaphylaxis
Antidote for phenothiazine reactions
Severe nausea and vomiting

Actions
A potent antihistamine
Antispasmodic with antiemetic and sedative effects

Special notes
Do not give in pregnancy
Do not give if patient has hypertension, glaucoma, or asthma
Should only be given IV in emergency situations
Enhances epinephrine effects in anaphylaxis

Side effects
Drowsiness   Headache
Blurred vision   Dry mouth and nose
Diarrhea   Hypotension
Confusion   Urticaria
Diplopia   Vertigo
Rash   Nausea and vomiting
Difficulty urinating   Anaphylaxis

Dosage
Adult—10 to 50 mg IV or PO over 1 to 4 minutes
Pediatric—2 mg/kg IV over 1 to 4 minutes

Dobutamine (Dobutrex)

Category
Synthetic catecholamine

Emergency uses
Cardiac decompensation caused by depressed contractility

Actions
Acts directly on beta-adrenergic receptors in the myocardium to increase inotropic effect and chronotropic effect, causing an increase in cardiac output and a decrease in left ventricular diastolic pressure and pulmonary capillary wedge pressure

Special notes
Primary hypovolemia should be corrected before administration
Used in conjunction with digitalis preparations
May be reduced in capability if used in conjunction with propranolol (Inderal)
Careful administration in myocardial infarction

Side effects

Chest pain	Hypertension, tachycardia
Angina	Increased ectopy
Headache	
Shortness of breath	

Dosage
Adult—2.5 to 10 μg/kg/minute IV, then titrated
Pediatric—Not recommended for use in children

Dopamine hydrochloride (Intropin)

Category
Alpha- and beta-stimulating agent

Emergency uses
Hypotension resulting from myocardial infarction, septic conditions, renal failure, and congestive heart failure

Actions
Alpha and beta stimulator depending on dosage
Increases cardiac output without increasing myocardial oxygen use
Dilates renal and mesenteric blood vessels at certain dosage rate
Increases blood pressure without significantly increasing heart rate at certain dosage rate

Special notes
Hypovolemic states should be corrected before use
Monitor vital signs carefully
Should not be given with alkaline solution
Monitor urinary output
Potentiated by tricyclic antidepressant medications

Side effects
Chest pain
Bradycardia
Shortness of breath
Ectopy
Nausea and vomiting
Palpitations
Tachycardia

Dosage
See dosage chart on p. 644

Intropin®
(dopamine HCl)
Dosage Chart

The chart at the right is intended for quick reference. It is based on the concentration of 1600 mcg dopamine HCl/ml obtained when *FOUR* 5 ml ampuls (200 mg dopamine HCl/ampul) of Intropin are added to 500 ml of a compatible IV solution or *TWO* 5 ml ampuls are added to 250 ml of a compatible IV solution.

Because fluid management is often a concern in shock patients, a different and higher concentration might be necessary for long-term therapy in order to restrict fluid intake while maintaining the therapeutic dose of the drug. An *Intropin Flow Rate Converter* is available for calculating dosage and flow rate for other concentrations. Always titrate to patient response since individual dosage requirements may differ widely.

FOR A CONCENTRATION OF 1600 mcg DOPAMINE HCl/ml (4-5 ml AMPULS INTROPIN/500 ml OR 2-5 ml AMPULS INTROPIN/250 ml)

Body Wt lbs	77	88	99	110	121	132	143	154	165	176	187	198	209	220	231	242
kgs	35	40	45	50	55	60	65	70	75	80	85	90	95	100	105	110
5	3.8	3.4	2.9	2.6	2.4	2.2	2.0	1.9	1.8	1.6	1.55	1.5	1.4	1.3	1.25	1.2
10	7.6	6.7	5.9	5.3	4.9	4.5	4.1	3.8	3.6	3.3	3.1	3.0	2.8	2.7	2.5	2.4
15	11	10	8.9	8.0	7.3	6.6	6.1	5.7	5.3	5.0	4.7	4.4	4.2	4.0	3.8	3.6
20	15	13	12	11	9.7	8.9	8.2	7.6	7.1	6.7	6.3	5.9	5.6	5.3	5.1	4.9
25	19	17	15	13	12	11	10	9.5	8.9	8.4	7.8	7.4	7.0	6.6	6.3	6.0
30	23	20	18	16	15	13	12	11	11	10	9.4	8.9	8.4	8.0	7.6	7.3
35	27	23	21	19	17	16	14	13	12	12	11	10	9.8	9.3	8.9	8.5
40	31	27	24	21	19	18	16	15	14	13	13	12	11	11	10	9.7
45	34	30	27	24	22	20	18	17	16	15	14	13	13	12	11	11
50	38	33	30	27	24	22	21	19	18	17	16	15	14	13	13	12
55	42	37	33	29	27	24	23	21	20	18	17	16	15	15	14	13
60	46	40	36	32	29	27	25	23	21	20	19	18	17	16	15	15
70	53	47	42	37	34	31	29	27	25	23	22	21	20	19	18	17
80	61	53	47	43	39	36	33	31	28	27	25	24	23	21	20	19
90	69	60	53	48	44	40	37	34	32	30	28	27	25	24	23	22
100	76	67	59	53	49	45	41	38	36	33	31	30	28	27	25	24

FLOW RATE IN DROPS* PER MINUTE

DOSAGE = mcg DOPAMINE HCl/kg/min

*Based on a microdrip calibration of 60 drops equal to 1.0 milliliter.   Note: All dosages of 10 mcg/kg/min and above have been rounded off to the nearest mcg/kg/min.

Intropin®
(dopamine HCl)
Dosage Phenomena

The Effects of Intropin at Three Dose Ranges:	2-5 mcg/kg/min	5-20 mcg/kg/min	over 20 mcg/kg/min
Cardiac Output	no change	increase	increase
Stroke Volume	no change	increase	increase
Heart Rate	no change	there is an initial increase followed by a decrease toward normal rates as infusion continues	
Myocardial Contractility	no change	increase	increase
Potential for Excessive Myocardial Oxygen Demands	low* coronary blood flow increased	low* coronary blood flow increased	data unavailable
Potential for Tachyarrhythmias	low*	low*	moderate
Total Systemic Vascular Resistance	slight decrease to no change	no change to slight increase	increase
Renal Blood Flow	increase	increase	decrease
Urine Output	increase	increase	decrease

*Low but needs monitoring.

See reverse for full prescribing information.

Courtesy Arnar-Stone Laboratories, Inc., McGraw Park, Ill.

Edrophonium chloride (Tensilon)

Category
Anticholinesterase

Emergency uses
Paroxysmal atrial tachycardia
Myasthenia crisis
Antagonist to curare

Actions
Inhibits cholinesterase and restores transmission of
nerve impulses

Special notes
Have atropine standing by
Use with caution in patients with asthma or hypoten-
sion
Do not use in pregnancy

Side effects

Abdominal cramps	Cool skin
Anxiety	Constricted pupils
Seizures	Diarrhea
Laryngospasm	Syncope
Respiratory arrest	Salivation
Nausea and vomiting	Insomnia
Bradycardia	Diaphoresis
Dysrhythmias	Incontinence

Dosage
Adult—1 to 10 mg by IV push over 2 to 4 minutes or
by continuous drip
Pediatric—0.05 mg/kg up to 5 mg by IV push over 2
to 4 minutes or by continuous drip

Epinephrine (Adrenalin)

Category
Sympathomimetic agent

Emergency uses
Cardiac arrest (asystole, ventricular fibrillation)
Anaphylaxis
Bronchial asthma
Stokes-Adams syndrome

Actions
Vasoconstriction
Cardiac stimulation/strengthens myocardial contrac-
tions
Increases cardiac output via beta stimulation
Relaxes smooth muscles and bronchioles
Elevates systolic blood pressure via alpha stimulation

Special notes
May be given IV, IM, subcutaneously, endotrache-
ally, or intracardially
Comes in two solutions: 1:1,000 and 1:10,000

Side effects

Anxiety	Severe headache
Tachycardia	Pulmonary edema
Dyspnea	Ventricular fibrillation
Palpitations	Cardiac arrest
Hypertension	

Dosage
Adult—In arrest: 5 to 10 ml of 1:10,000 solution IV,
endotracheally or intracardiac; may be repeated
every 5 minutes if necessary
In anaphylaxis: 1 ml of 1:10,000 solution IV or endotracheally; may be repeated every 5 minutes if
necessary
In asthma: 0.3 to 0.5 ml of 1:1,000 solution subcutaneously
Pediatric—In arrest: 0.1 mg/kg of 1:10,000 solution
IV or endotracheally; may be repeated every 5 minutes if necessary
In anaphylaxis: 0.03 ml of 1:10,000 solution IV or
endotracheally
In asthma: 0.1 to 0.5 ml of 1:1,000 solution subcutaneously

Furosemide (Lasix)

Category
Diuretic

Emergency uses
Pulmonary edema/congestive heart failure
Intracranial pressure

Actions
Affects the proximal and distal renal tubules to enhance excretion of sodium, potassium, chlorides,
and water

Special notes
Do not administer in pregnancy
Closely monitor fluid and electrolyte levels and BUN
and CO_2
Potentiates antihypertensive medications
Potentiates muscle relaxants

Side effects

Blurred vision	Urinary frequency
Tinnitus	Urticaria
Deafness (temporary)	Nausea and vomiting
Hypokalemia	Syncope
Mental confusion	Anaphylaxis
Limb cramps	Metabolic acidosis
Paresthesias	Cardiac arrest
Hypotension	

Dosage
Adult—20 to 80 mg by IV push over 2 to 4 minutes
Pediatric—1 mg/kg by IV push over 2 to 4 minutes

Glucagon hydrochloride

Category
Hyperglycemic agent/pancreatic extract

Emergency uses
Hypoglycemia
To reverse effects of propranolol (Inderal)

Actions
Activates phosphorylase and converts liver glycogen
to glucose

Special notes
May produce severe vomiting episode
Protect airway
Potentiates oral anticoagulant agents
May be given by family of a diabetic with a known
hypoglycemic reaction

Side effects
Emesis
Hyperglycemia
Anaphylaxis
Nausea and vomiting
Hypotension

Dosage
Adult—5 to 10 mg IV, IM, or subcutaneously; may
be repeated in 20 minutes
Pediatric 50 μg/kg IV, IM, or subcutaneoulsy; may
be given every 4 hours up to 1 mg

Heparin (Panheprin, Liquaemin, Lipo-Heprin)

Category
Anticoagulant

Emergency uses
Preparation of blood gas syringes
Autotransfusion
Disseminated intravascular coagulation (DIC)
Prophylactically in cerebrovascular accident
Atrial fibrillation with embolization

Actions
Inhibits prothrombin conversion to thrombin and fibrinogen conversion to fibrin
Does not dissolve old clots but prevents the formation of and may decompose new clots

Special notes
Do not administer with salicylates
Prothrombin time and partial thromboplastin time should be measured before administration and repeated throughout the course of therapy
Potentiates oral anticoagulant agents, thyroxine, and phenytoin (Dilantin)

Side effects
Epistaxis
Hematuria
Excessive coagulation times
Hematochezia
Bruising

Dosage
Adult—Blood gas syringe preparation: 0.5 ml; discard excess after coating syringe and needle
Other: 5,000 to 10,000 units rapid IV followed by IV drip of 500 to 1,500 units/hour
Pediatric—Check product literature

Hydralazine hydrochloride (Apresoline)

Category
Antihypertensive agent

Emergency uses
Hypertensive crisis
Eclampsia

Actions
Relaxes vascular smooth muscle
Increases cardiac rate and cardiac output
Increases renal blood flow

Special notes
Monitor blood pressure frequently during administration
Do not give concurrently with tricyclics
Inhibits epinephrine and norepinephrine (Levophed)

Side effects
Anxiety	Chest pain
Dry mouth	Coronary insufficiency
Headache	Fever
Nausea and vomiting	Delirium
Palpitations	Myocardial infarction
Postural hypotension	Toxic psychosis
Paresthesias	
Tachycardia	

Dosage
Adult—10 to 40 mg IV over 1 to 4 minutes; may be repeated
Pediatric—1.7 to 3.5 mg/kg/24 hours IM or IV in 4 to 6 divided doses

Syrup of ipecac

Category
Emetic agent

Emergency uses
Poisoning or overdose
Accidental ingestion

Actions
Acts on brainstem and gastric mucosa to induce
vomiting

Special notes
Contraindicated in patients with loss of gag reflex or
decreased level of consciousness
Contraindicated in children under 1 year of age
Protect airway
Should not be given after ingestion of caustic sub-
stances
Should be followed by several glasses of water
Induced emesis usually followed by activated charcoal
and magnesium citrate PO

Side effects
Myocardial irritability if absorbed in large amounts

Dosage
Adult—30 ml PO with 4 to 5 glasses of water; may be
repeated once if ineffective the first time; gastric
lavage if second attempt is unsuccessful
Pediatric—15 ml PO with 2 glasses of water; may be
repeated once; gastric lavage if second is unsuccessful

Isoproterenol hydrochloride (Isuprel)

Category
Sympathomimetic amine

Emergency uses
AV block unresponsive to atropine
Sinus bradycardia unresponsive to atropine
Bronchospasm
Asystole
Idioventricular rhythms

Actions
Cardiac stimulation (chronotropic and inotropic)
Increases coronary and renal blood flow
Improves AV conduction
Relaxes bronchial smooth muscle
Increases systolic blood pressure

Special notes
Contraindicated in hypokalemic states
Contraindicated in hypovolemic states
Contraindicated in patients taking digitalis
Contraindicated in diabetes
May cause dysrhythmias

Side effects

Palpitations	Ventricular tachycardia
Anginal pain	Cardiac arrest
Headache	

Dosage
Adult—For cardiac conditions: 1 to 2 mg in 500 ml
D5W titrated for effect IV; may also be given 0.02
mg intracardiac
Pediatric—1 mg in 500 ml D5W titrated for effect IV

Lidocaine hydrochloride (Xylocaine)

Category
Local anesthetic agent/antidysrhythmic agent

Emergency uses
Ventricular dysrhythmias (PVCs or ventricular tachycardia)
Prophylactically in the setting of myocardial infarction

Actions
Decreases ventricular irritability

Special notes
Must be administered by IV bolus followed by IV drip or another bolus
Reduce dosage if history of liver disease
Contraindicated in idioventricular rhythms
Contraindicated in AV blocks

Side effects

Seizures	Anaphylaxis
Blurred vision	Bradycardia
Syncope	Hypotension
Light-headedness	Respiratory depression
Paresthesias	

Dosage
Adult—50 to 100 mg by IV bolus (over 2 minutes) followed by IV infusion at 1 to 4 mg/minute or followed by 50 mg bolus 5 minutes after first, then additional 50 mg boluses every 10 minutes up to 325 mg
Pediatric—0.5 mg/kg over 3 minutes followed by IV infusion at 0.02 to 0.03 mg/kg/minute

Magnesium sulfate

Category
CNS depressant

Emergency uses
Seizures in eclampsia
Severe hypomagnesemia

Actions
Depresses CNS and smooth, skeletal, and cardiac muscle

Special notes
Works almost immediately
Discontinue when desired effect obtained
If in third trimester pregnancy, consider inducing labor with oxytocin (Pitocin) or consider cesarean section

Side effects
Hypotension
Diaphoresis
Respiratory depression
Cardiac arrest

Dosage
Adult—1 to 2 g of 10% solution for seizures IV 5 g in 1,000 ml D5W titrated IV
Pediatric—See product literature

Mannitol (Osmitrol)

Category
Osmotic diuretic

Emergency uses
Increased intracranial or spinal cord pressure
Sedative overdose

Actions
An osmotic diuretic
Promotes excretion of toxic substances caused by
  sedative overdose

Special notes
Contraindicated in pregnancy
Contraindicated in congestive heart failure
Place Foley catheter and record hourly urine output
May have short rebound effect and actually increase
  cerebral blood flow to the head for a short time
Check serum electrolytes frequently
May cause hypovolemia

Side effects

Seizures	Chills
Backache	Electrolyte imbalances
Blurred vision	Syncope
Dehydration	Dry mouth
Hypertension/hypotension	Fever
Pulmonary edema	Headache
Tachycardia	Nausea
Chest pain	Thirst

Dosage
Adult—50 to 200 g of 20% solution over 20 to 60
  minutes IV or 1.5 to 4.5 g/kg by slow IV bolus
Pediatric—2 to 3 g/kg of 20% solution over 20 to 60
  minutes

Meperidine hydrochloride (Demerol)

Category
Narcotic analgesic

Emergency uses
Relief of pain (moderate to severe)

Actions
A synthetic narcotic analgesic agent that depresses the
  CNS

Special notes
May cause habituation
Administer slowly
Not as potent as morphine sulfate
May induce emesis

Side effects

Syncope	Seizures
Nausea and vomiting	Allergic reactions
Hypotension (postural)	Apnea
Rash	Respiratory depression
Diaphoresis	Cardiac arrest
May mask signs and	Important for diag-
symptoms	nosis

Dosage
Adult—10 to 100 mg IV or IM
Pediatric—Not recommended for children

Morphine sulfate (MS)

Category
Narcotic analgesic agent

Emergency uses
Pain from myocardial infarction
Pain from biliary or renal colic
Any severe pain
Pulmonary edema
Pain from severe burn injuries without concurrent
  trauma

Actions
Alters pain perception
Elevates pain threshold
Causes peripheral vasodilation to pool blood in
  pulmonary edema

Special notes
May cause respiratory depression
Contraindicated in patients with pain from trauma
  until cause of pain is isolated and therapeutic inter-
  vention decision has been reached
Always have crash cart standing by
May be reversed with naloxone (Narcan) 0.4 to 0.8
  mg IV
More potent than meperidine hydrochloride (Dem-
  erol)
May cause habituation

Side effects

Hypothermia	Anaphylaxis
Increased intracranial pressure	Coma
Nausea and vomiting	Constricted pupils
Respiratory depression	

Dosage
Adult—2 to 15 mg IV slowly titrated to effect
Pediatric—0.1 to 0.2 mg/kg IV slowly titrated to ef-
  fect

Nalbuphine hydrochloride (Nubain)

Category
Synthetic narcotic agent

Emergency uses
Relief of moderate to severe pain

Actions
Relieves pain in 2 to 3 minutes in potency equivalent
  to morphine sulfate

Special notes
May cause habituation
May cause respiratory depression
Have crash cart standing by

Side effects

Blurred vision	Headache
Anaphylaxis	Nausea and vomiting
Bradycardia	Hypertension/hypotension
Cool moist skin	Tachycardia
Dry mouth	Sedation
Syncope	

Dosage
Adult—10 to 20 mg IV; may be repeated every 3 to 6
  hours
Pediatric—See product literature

Naloxone hydrochloride (Narcan)

Category
Narcotic antagonist

Emergency uses
To reverse narcotic depressant effects
To diagnose acute opiate overdose or propoxyphene (Darvon) overdose
To reverse propoxyphene (Darvon) overdose effects
Septic shock

Actions
Reverses narcotic-induced respiratory depression and other narcotic overdose problems
Reverses propoxyphene overdose problems
Review literature for effects in septic shock

Special notes
If narcotic overdose is certain, the care giver may wish to manage airway and respirations with a bag-valve-mask device until naloxone is given, as naloxone reverses respiratory depression and this avoids the possibility of the patient pulling out an esophageal obturator airway or endotracheal tube as his sensorium lightens
The care giver may wish to restrain the patient, as naloxone will cause a narcotic withdrawal

Side effects
Elevated partial thromboplastin time

Dosage
Adult—0.4 to 0.8 (or more in propoxyphene overdose) mg IV, endotracheally or injected sublingually
Pediatric—0.01 mg/kg IV, endotracheally or injected sublingually

Nitroglycerin (NTG) (formerly called glyceryl trinitrate)

Category
Vasodilator

Emergency uses
Angina
As differential diagnosis tool in angina vs. myocardial infarction
Pulmonary edema
Acute glaucoma

Actions
Vasodilator; pools venous blood and decreases myocardial work load and myocardial oxygen consumption
Relaxes smooth muscle
Redistributes coronary blood flow

Special notes
Headache and flushing are common
Drug may lose potency with time or if exposed to light

Side effects
Headache
Flushing
Syncope
Hypotension

Dosage
Adult—1/150 Gr. (0.4 mg) sublingually if systolic BP is above 100 mm Hg; may be repeated once in 5 minutes
In pulmonary edema: 0.8 to 1.6 mg (1/150 Gr. tablets; repeat four times) sublingually if systolic BP is above 100 mg Hg
Pediatric—Dose not established

Norepinephrine (Levophed) (formerly called levarterenol bitartrate)

Category
Sympathomimetic agent

Emergency uses
Hypotensive states

Actions
Peripherally vasoconstricts and provides blood flow to brain, heart, liver, and kidneys without increasing cardiac work load
Dilates coronary arteries

Special notes
Blood pressure should be checked frequently
Replace fluids in hypovolemic state
May cause severe tissue necrosis
Infuse sloughing areas with phentolamine (Regitine)
May precipitate ventricular fibrillation

Side effects
Bradycardia
Chest pain
Tissue ischemia and necrosis at IV site

Dosage
Adult—4 to 8 mg in 500 ml D5W IV titrated for effect
Pediatric—2 to 4 mg in 500 ml D5W infused at 0.1 to 1.0 μg/kg/minute, titrated for effect

Oxytocin (Pitocin, Syntocinon)

Category
Synthetic posterior pituitary derivative

Emergency uses
Postpartum hemorrhage

Actions
Contracts uterine muscles
Constricts uterine blood vessels

Special notes
Labor should not be induced in the emergency department

Side effects

Anaphylaxis	Tachycardia
Cardiac dysrhythmias	Fluid retention
Subarachnoid hemorrhage	Vomiting
Hypotension	

Dosage
Adult—10 to 20 units in 100 ml D5W or dextrose 5% in half-normal saline IV infused at 0.5 to 1 ml/minute
Pediatric—Dose not established

Pentazocine lactate (Talwin)

Category
Narcotic antagonist and potent analgesic

Emergency uses
Moderate to severe pain

Actions
Depresses CNS
Less effective than meperidine or morphine

Special notes
May cause respiratory depression and increased intracranial pressure
Naloxone is the antidote
Have crash cart standing by
Low habituation factor
May not work well in patients who are heavy smokers

Side effects

Blurred vision	Flushing
Syncope	Hallucinations
Confusion	Headache
Depression	Hypertension
Diarrhea	Nystagmus
Dry mouth	Tachycardia
Shortness of breath	

Dosage
Adult—30 to 60 mg IV every 3 to 4 hours by slow IV bolus; may also be given IM
Pediatric—Dose not established

Phenobarbital sodium (Luminal, Eskabarb)

Category
Barbiturate/anticonvulsant/hypnotic agent

Emergency uses
Status epilepticus

Actions
CNS depression

Special notes
Used primarily for seizure prevention
Given after diazepam (Valium) administration
Record frequent vital signs
Treat underlying cause of seizures

Side effects

Bronchospasm	Nausea and vomiting
Fever	Coma
Headache	Pulmonary edema
Hypotension	

Dosage
Adult—30 to 130 mg by IV bolus over 5 to 10 minutes until seizure is controlled
Pediatric—3 to 5 mg/kg/dose IV bolus over 5 to 10 minutes until seizure is controlled

Phenytoin (Dilantin) (formerly called diphenylhydantoin)

Category
Anticonvulsant

Emergency uses
Status epilepticus
Neurologic trauma with seizures
Cardiac dysrhythmias (PVCs, PAT with block, nodal, or ventricular tachycardia)

Actions
Stabilizes seizure threshold and depresses seizure activity at cerebral cortex
Myocardial depression (elevates irritability threshold)

Special notes
Contraindicated in bradycardia, complete heart block, and second-degree heart block
Inhibited by alcohol, antihistamines, and barbiturates

Side effects
Ataxia
Heart blocks
Bradycardia
Hypotension
Respiratory arrest
Ventricular fibrillation
Tonic seizures

Dosage
Adult—Anticonvulsant: 150 to 250 mg IV over 5 minutes
Antidysrhythmic: 100 to 300 mg IV over 24 hours (divided doses)
Pediatric—1 to 2 mg/kg IV over 5 minutes

Physostigmine (Antilirium)

Category
Parasympathomimetic agent

Emergency uses
Atropine-like drug overdose
Anticholinergic findings (hypertension, hallucinations, seizures, coma, dysrhythmias)

Actions
Cholinesterase inhibitor
Exaggerates acetylcholine response

Special notes
Rapid administration may induce seizures or bradycardia
Do not administer in asthmatics, diabetics, or those with cardiovascular disease, intestinal obstructions, or gangrene

Side effects

Cholinergic overdose	Salivation
Emesis	Diaphoresis
Defecation	Urination
Nausea	Hypertension

Dosage
Adult—0.5 to 2 mg IV over 2 minutes; may also be given IM; may be repeated
Pediatric—0.5 mg IV over 2 minutes; may be repeated

Potassium chloride

Category
Electrolyte

Emergency uses
Hypokalemia from diuretic therapy, diabetic ketoacidosis, digitalis toxicity, or other conditions

Actions
Maintains osmotic pressure
Increases cell resting membrane potential
Decreases cell membrane permeability

Special notes
Do not give in second-degree block
Do not give if patient has oliguria, dehydration, or
acidosis
Assure normal kidney function
Check electrolyte balance

Side effects
Bradycardia
Ventricular fibrillation
AV block
Asystole

Dosage
Adult—20 to 40 mEq in 1,000 ml D5W at 10 mEq/
hour or less
Pediatric—Should not exceed 3 mEq/kg/day

Procainamide (Pronestyl)

Category
Antidysrhythmic agent

Emergency uses
Supraventricular dysrhythmias
Ventricular dysrhythmias
Paroxysmal atrial tachycardia
Atrial fibrillation
Premature ventricular contractions

Actions
Slows heart rate
Slows conduction
Reduces myocardial irritability
Prolongs refractory period

Special notes
Contraindicated in heart block
Rapid administration may cause heart block

Side effects
Anorexia   Hypotension
Fever   Increased PR interval
Chills   Widened QRS
Hallucinations   Prolonged QT interval
Confusion   Ventricular dysrhythmias
Nausea and vomiting
Syncope

Dosage
Adult—IV bolus: 100 mg slowly over 2 minutes re-
peated every 5 minutes up to 1 g maximum
Drip: 1 g in 500 ml D5W at 1 to 3 ml/minute IV
Pediatric—IV bolus: 2 mg/kg/dose given over 2 to 4
minutes
Drip: 10 to 100 mg in 500 ml D5W titrated

Propranolol (Inderal)

Category
Beta-adrenergic blocking agent

Emergency uses
Tachydysrhythmias associated with digitalis toxicity
Severe angina
Acute myocardial infarction after first hour with heart rate above 100 and normal or elevated blood pressure
Atrial extrasystoles that are not responsive to other medications

Actions
Inhibits cardiac response to sympathetic nervous system
Inhibits AV conduction

Special notes
Use concurrently with digitalis agents
Contraindicated in asthma, sinus bradycardia, and second- and third-degree heart block
May produce bronchospasm
May precipitate congestive heart failure
May induce hypoglycemia

Side effects
Bradycardia
Hypotension
AV block
AV dissociation
Cardiac arrest

Dosage
Dosage varies widely; consult product literature

Quinidine gluconate

Category
Antidysrhythmic agent

Emergency uses
Atrial fibrillation or atrial flutter
Paroxysmal atrial tachycardia
Ventricular tachycardia
Premature systoles

Actions
Slows heart rate
Slows conduction
Reduces myocardial contractility
Prolongs refractory period

Special notes
Keep patient supine during administration
Use cautiously with procainamide, propranolol, and digitalis
May increase prothrombin time

Side effects

Hypotension	Ventricular fibrillation
Tachycardia	Fever
Blurred vision	Headache
Idioventricular rhythms	

Dosage
Adult—800 mg (10 ml) in 40 ml D5W; administer 1 ml/minute
Pediatric—30 mg/kg/24 hours given in 5 divided doses diluted 5:1 in D5W; administer not faster than 1 ml/minute

Sodium bicarbonate

Category
Alkaline agent

Emergency uses
Cardiac arrest
Acidosis
Hyperkalemia

Actions
Combats acidosis

Special notes
Incompatible with calcium chloride
Best to administer in accordance with arterial pH values
Contains much sodium chloride (consider hypernatremia)
Be cautious not to overadminister and produce metabolic alkalosis, which may take days or weeks to correct

Side effects
Restlessness
Tetany

Dosage
Adult—1 to 2 ampules (44.8 mEq) by IV bolus initially then 1 ampule IV every 10 minutes while patient is pulseless and nonbreathing or administer in accordance with arterial pH
Pediatric—1 mEq/kg IV every 5 to 10 minutes or in accordance with arterial pH

Sodium nitroprusside (Nipride)

Category
Hypotensive agent

Emergency uses
Pulmonary edema with hypertensive response
Chronic refractory heart failure and myocardial infarction
Dissecting aneurysms
Hypertensive emergencies

Actions
Directly dilates arterioles and veins
Improves left ventricular function
Increases cardiac output

Special notes
Solution is light sensitive and must be covered during administration
Do not give with any other medication
Monitor the patient constantly

Side effects
Nausea
Vomiting
Headache
Diaphoresis
Restlessness
Chest pain

Dosage
Adult—50 mg in 250 ml D5W infused at a rate of 0.5 to 10 μg/kg/minute (average dose is 3 μg/kg/minute)
Pediatric—same as adult dosage

Verapamil (Isoptin)

Category
Calcium channel blocker

Emergency uses
Paroxysmal supraventricular tachycardia

Actions
Inhibits calcium ion influx through slow channels
Slows AV conduction
Prolongs refractory period

Special notes
May worsen underlying congestive heart failure
Does not alter serum calcium levels
Do not give if patient is severely hypotensive
Do not give in second- or third-degree block
Do not give in patients receiving beta-adrenergic
   drugs (e.g., propranolol)

Side effects
May cause transient reduction in arterial pressure
   seizures
Hypotension
Bradycardia
Asystole

Dosage
Adult—5 to 10 mg by slow IV bolus over 2 minutes;
   may be repeated at 0.15 mg/kg 30 minutes after
   initial dose
Pediatric—See product literature; generally, 0.1 to
   0.2 mg/kg IV slowly over 2 minutes

SUGGESTED READINGS

Gahart, B.L.: Intravenous medications, ed. 3, St. Louis, 1981, The C.V. Mosby Co.
Goodman, L.S., and Gilman, A., editors: The pharmacological basis of therapeutics, ed. 6, New York, 1982, MacMillan Publishing Co., Inc.
Physician's desk reference, ed. 37, Oradell, N.J., 1983, Medical Economics Co.
Trissel, L.A.: Handbook on injectable drugs, ed. 2, Bethesda, Md., 1980, American Society of Hospital Pharmacists, Inc.

Index